ANTI-RACIST WORK WITH YOUNG PEOPLE: EUROPEAN EXPERIENCES AND APPROACHES

D0130176

Edited by

Anna Aluffi-Pentini and Walter Lorenz

Russell House Publishing Ltd

First published in 1996 by

Russell House Publishing Limited
38 Silver Street
Lyme Regis
Dorset
DT7 3HS

British Library Cataloguing-in-Publication Data:
A catalogue record for this book is available from the British Library.

ISBN: 1-898924-01-5

Typeset by: Ed Skelly

Printed by: Bourne Press,
Bournemouth.

Anti-racist Work with Young People

Edited by Anna Aluffi-Pentini and Walter Lorenz

Contents

Biographical notes

Anna Aluffi-Pentini is a post-doctoral research assistant at the pedagogical faculty of the Third University, Rome. She is involved in several national and international projects dealing with migration, citizenship and inter-cultural educational approaches and serves as consultant to multi-ethnic school and pre-school projects.

Karen Chouhan, born in Pakistan, came to the UK as a child. She worked as a youth and community worker in Leicester and did research on the history of racism and the rise of the New Right at the University of Bradford. She is a lecturer at De Montfort University, Leicester and gives training workshops and consultancies on anti-racism in various parts of Europe.

Ummi Esmail was born and brought up in Britain. She joined the Asian Action Group as a young member in 1983 and worked for the group as a volunteer in various capacities. She is now qualified as a medical doctor.

Edwin Hoffman is of 'Indo-European' background and a native of Bandung on the island of Java (Indonesia). He works as a trainer on inter-cultural communication and the 'management of diversity' at the Department of Social and Community Work of the Hogeschool Eindhoven, Netherlands, and as consultant to multi-ethnic youth and training projects.

Joe Joseph arrived in Britain from Kenya in 1971. A graduate of Birmingham University he worked for nine years as a youth and community development worker. Since taking up the post of lecturer at De Montfort University, Leicester, in 1989, he has paid particular attention to the development of anti-racist and inter-cultural approaches in youth and community work training.

Bärbel Kampmann is a qualified teacher, psychologist and Gestalt therapist and director of a local authority youth department specialising in giving support to children from a migrant background. She is a member of the action group 'Schwarze Deutsche' (Black Germans) and has initiated numerous anti-racism projects and campaigns in her region of Germany.

Walter Lorenz holds the Jean Monnet Chair (Social Europe) at University College Cork, Ireland. He was born in Germany and trained and practised as a social worker in the UK. His fields of interest include comparative aspects of practice and training in social work and social pedagogy in Europe, particularly in relation to ethnic and cultural diversity.

Rubén Maduro was born on Aruba in the Dutch Caribbean and has been working for 25 years in the Netherlands, most recently as trainer and counsellor to projects by 'allochthonous' communities. His work with minority groups specialises in inter-cultural communication, organisational development and skills management.

Kurian Mathai arrived in the UK from Kenya in 1974 to undertake further studies. He is a founder member of the Asian Action Group and was employed with the group as a youth and community development worker for several years. He now acts as a consultant to inter-cultural youth projects.

Jeff Modayil was born in Kenya and came to Britain in 1971. A founder member of the Asian Action Group he served as chair from 1982 to 1985. He since worked as a youth worker for several Black youth projects.

Concetta Sirna, Associate Professor of Educational Science at the University of Messina, Italy, has devoted much of her research and publications to problems of communication and language in the school context and to inter-cultural educational methods.

Gita Steiner-Khamsi took up a position as Associate Professor of Comparative and International Education at the Teachers' College of Columbia University, New York, USA in 1995. A Swiss citizen of Iranian descent she previously established and directed the multi-cultural education sector at the Ministry of Education in Zurich, Switzerland. She has published and taught widely on multi-cultural education from a comparative perspective.

Carol Anne Spreen is a Research Assistant at the National Center for Restructuring Education, Schools and Teaching

(NCREST), New York, and researches educational methods, school restructuring initiatives and multi-ethnic peer group relations in multi-ethnic school settings. An American citizen of European and Native American descent she is currently working on a dissertation in comparative education at the Teachers' College Columbia University, New York, USA.

Introduction

The contributions in this volume are inter-cultural in every sense: they reflect the work experience of practitioners from different European countries, they bring together applied and theoretical perspectives, and they aim at expanding the discourse on anti-racist pedagogical approaches beyond national confines. They have their origin in a European project commissioned by the PETRA Youth for Europe project and carried out by the European Centre for Community Education (ECCE). We had been asked to design a training module to promote anti-racist competences in young people who want to engage in European youth exchanges. The idea seemed intriguing and straight forward: we could use encounters across national boundaries to facilitate young people from different ethnic backgrounds in sharing their experiences; they could learn from each other how to cope with the constant challenges of racism and to understand the origins and mechanisms of this insidious phenomenon.

ECCE through its extensive European contacts brought together a group of highly experienced youth workers and youth work educators from five European countries who began to draw up plans for such exchanges. But at the first meeting of this group we soon realised that we used very different concepts and terms to describe our experiences and to articulate our concerns over the growing menace of racism. Despite the fact that the majority of the members of the group belong to a minority ethnic group in their countries of residence, their experiences, their struggles, their resistance, their hopes and aspirations differed not only individually but also in patterns which were influenced by the 'dominant culture' of their country. Where the participants from Britain seemed to have no difficulties in using the term 'race' in a positive way this seemed completely unthinkable to the German members of the group. For them racism was inexorably linked with fascism (old and new) and evoked instant associations with anti-semitism. Racism for them concerns the arbitrary association of physical and personal/social characteristics; it 'invents' and constructs differences where they may not necessarily be marked by the colour of skin. This view was also shared by the Irish participants though against a very different background of history and personal experience of 'being at the receiving end' of racism.

Equally the term 'anti-racism' did not find favour with all participants. To the Dutch, for instance, it seemed unacceptable to give even minimal credibility to the category of race by focusing one's opposition on the term. Whiteness and Blackness to some French and Italian participants sometimes seemed to be more a matter of cultural belonging and therefore of individual choice. This implied that any intervention which was merely 'anti' restricted such choices which pedagogical work seeks to enhance. In addition, according to the French colleagues, the acceptance of the dominant culture holds the promise of emancipation from oppression which is centred on difference constituted by physical attributes.

It became clear that we were all steeped in the discourses prevailing in our countries. We could only express our principles and convictions (on which much of the solidarity among minority ethnic groups within our own country was based), in concepts which were threatening to become barriers to a meaningful inter-cultural encounter. And yet, once the terminological arguments had been temporarily suspended and we shared our personal experiences and above all accounts of our youth work practice, communication became much easier. At that practical level we did have so much in common, we did share a very differentiated and quite compatible approach to politics, culture, socialisation and education, and we did pursue converging practice aims. For instance, we agreed that we were dealing with so much more than 'prejudice', that multi-cultural festivals were niceties which often concealed and legitimated fundamental divisions, that we had to lay bare the structural origins of inequality and discrimination. But we also knew that the realisation of political aims did not preclude work on prejudice, psychological support in the search for personal identities, the necessity to deal with shame and guilt. We celebrated this discovery in the formulation of our module and were eager to implement it. Overall, we realised how much more we could learn from the practice of colleagues in other countries precisely because it seemed strange, provocative and forced us to go right back to some fundamental questions about our own practice.

It was in this spirit of optimistic provocation that we launched our first collection of contributions for an Italian publication. We wanted to give Italian youth and social workers who, like workers in all countries, were locked into a national framework of debate, the opportunity of sharing some of the liberating strangeness we had encountered when we examined our taken-for-granted terminology together with workers from very different traditions. By focusing on anti-racism we sought to disturb the 'cosiness' into which the pedagogical debate had settled in that country and invite people to stand back from the assumptions which guided their practice. A sign of that cosiness was that psychological strategies of prejudice reduction prevailed over political analysis and that racism could be seen as a problem only for those working in areas with high concentrations of immigrants. Instead we wanted to emphasise that racism was a challenge to educators in all parts of the country, that all pedagogical interventions had to be embedded in a clear political analysis, that cultural differences reflected power differentials. This seemed necessary in the educational debate in order to prevent the curious perversion of cause and effect which blames ethnic minorities indirectly or directly for being the cause of racism.

In preparing our contributions for an English-speaking readership we would have liked to be able to report on progress with international youth exchanges and to give further encouragement for such conceptual and physical border-crossings. Unfortunately, all but one of the planned projects got stymied by material difficulties and constraints, and by the time it takes to build up trust in multi-ethnic youth groups. Even the one successful project (reported in the Dutch contribution) did not progress to its international phase. Compared to this lack of practical progress we realised at the conceptual level that the anti-racist debate had indeed advanced very quickly. The critique of race awareness training on the one hand and of political correctness on the other had led to the development of a set of clear and determined political strategies in anti-racist youth and social work. We are concerned, however, that this consensus could overlook the need to pay attention to micro-processes of ambivalence and conflict in personal relationships and in personal identity formation. It seems useful to follow the political analysis through into the sphere of 'the personal' and 'the cultural' in order to keep up with the changing manifestations of racism.

To us the constant inter-section of different perspectives and the questioning it implies is the central advantage of approaching anti-racist work from an international perspective. Concepts and methods need to be kept on the move, to be critically examined and transformed in constantly changing historical conditions. Political conscientisation is made up of so many subtle processes which have to be traced very sensitively back to early childhood development, to various contexts of socialisation and to personal relationships. It is for this reason that we sought to explore the complementarity of inter-cultural and anti-racist pedagogical approaches in this volume. We reject the polarised alternative between paying attention to the psychological implications of growing up in a multi-cultural society and addressing the structural issues and political mechanisms of discrimination. The practice and the personal experience of the contributors amounts to the realisation that young people need to develop competences at both levels and above all that they need to be given opportunities of relating one level to the other. We seek to demonstrate this partly in the form of case studies and practice suggestions, partly in the form of conceptual clarifications.

The first chapter examines the role which education and social services came to play in stabilising the nation states of Europe. These modern political creations on the one hand hold the promise of emancipation, self-determination and liberation, and on the other hand brought with them nationalism, oppression and racism of the most insidious kind. Social service agents are often not aware how their work is part of the nation state project, how they can be made to define and maintain internal borders between those who 'belong' to the nation and those who are excluded on account of their culture, their behaviour, their origins. As European integration begins to follow in many ways the pathway of the nation states and draws once more on the assistance of educators and social workers we need to guard against building racism into the very fabric of a European civil society.

The next chapter looks at how debates on educational methods in multi-cultural societies disseminate across different countries. It makes the point that this dissemination needs to be accompanied by the transformation rather than the preservation of key concepts. The authors ask some very uncomfortable questions concerning the value of programs which focus explicitly on 'race' and let physical characteristic determine social relations. While remaining committed to the principles of anti-racism they stress the need to develop the pedagogical means whereby young people can learn to handle conflictual situations and define their own identities. To this end, new methods of peer-directed conflict resolution in schools in the USA are being evaluated. They appear to offer adolescents opportunities for locating inter-group conflicts within a wider political context, and for developing more differentiated definitions of their identity, than an emphasis on racial and ethnic identity as an end in itself would allow.

The third chapter, based on work with pre-school migrant children in Italy, further demonstrates the complementarity of inter-group methods and political analysis. At a political level, Italy's illusion of being a non-racist society is wearing thin and young people can only make sense of their many daily experiences and observations if racism is being named for what it is. But these analytical tools alone do not equip young people to express their identity positively, to critically analyse their cultural traditions or to become competent in the kind of daily personal interactions characteristic of a diverse, multi-cultural society. The chapter reaffirms 'traditional' educational principles of dignity and autonomy. However, these can only be realised in a multi-cultural complex society if diversity and common group identities are addressed simultaneously and the structural conditions for their realisation are secured.

The fourth chapter highlights the function of language in promoting racism in ever more subtle ways. Most of us remain hardly aware of the potential for discrimination and exclusion contained in ordinary phrases. The author by no means advocates 'political correctness' as a solution – racism is constantly 'on the move' and out of reach of such blunt measures. But the chapter's analysis points at the political momentum that a more conscious use of language can generate. It stresses the need to regain control over the use of language starting with small communities like schools where learning about structural issues is contained in the awareness of linguistic differences.

The three subsequent chapters represent case studies of anti-racist youth work in Britain, Germany and the Netherlands. Although written from very different perspectives they share one central characteristic: young people must be facilitated in developing their own coping strategies and above all their own versions of identity. Validating their experiences, working on first hand encounters with conflicts, building up a repertoire of social skills immediately relevant to their situation are some of the pedagogical measures that these case examples highlight. Beyond that, being 'Black' or belonging to an ethnic minority in the UK, in Germany or in the Netherlands means something very different, and yet the mechanisms by which differences get constructed and social exclusion is achieved are strikingly similar. Strategic progress comes not just from new concepts and theories but also from giving young people the opportunity to define their own realities.

The final two chapters are an attempt at systematising the basic principles that inform the practice described in earlier chapters and at giving practical examples of games and activities which put these principles into practice. The pedagogical strategy follows and addresses the processes of identity formation not merely from a developmental point of view but also from a social and political perspective. While focusing on the threat of racism this approach refuses to let racism dictate the pedagogical agenda. Instead it seeks to treat the multi-cultural reality of European societies as an educational opportunity and a fundamental challenge against which the validity of all educational approaches need to be tested.

Youth work and social work, pre-school education and inter-cultural pedagogy by themselves cannot eliminate racism, but their contribution is nevertheless vital to the creation of societies in which all citizens participate in the negotiation of equality on the one hand and diversity on the other. Racism threatens this emanicpatory process from many unexpected sides and international cooperation in the social professions can be a vital means of staying one step ahead of this threat.

Anna Aluffi-Pentini
Walter Lorenz
Florence May 1996

1. The education of the nation: racism and the nation state

Walter Lorenz

The role of workers in social and youth work in combating racism in Europe needs to be developed out of an historical context. Only the historical reflection can highlight the intricate connections between the growth of the European nation state and the development of the various functions of all social services, and it is in this connection that the particular vulnerability of social services for nationalist and racist exploitation becomes apparent. This perspective takes an understanding of racism beyond the psychology of prejudice which has a validity in as much as prejudice and intolerance are the material from which racist ideologies are constructed. Racist ideologies play in particular upon the ambivalences and anxieties over collective identities which are the hallmark of modern societies and seek to replace them with plausible 'simple truths'. Because of this inherent ambivalence and the instability of modern nation states, social and educational services came to assume an important stabilising role in modern societies. Workers in those services need to examine very critically, therefore, the images of identity which guide their interventions as to their implicit or explicit racist character. In refusing to yield to the 'simple truths' proposed by racist beliefs, in generating a better understanding of the connection between psychological, cultural and political processes in the production of these beliefs, and in developing strategies that are critical of assumed homogeneous national identities, youth and social workers can make their contribution to breaking the power of racism.

The nation as a reference point for identity has become questionable worldwide, but especially so in Europe, despite the simultaneous rise in nationalism. On the one hand it has a legacy of nationalism and imperialism, of inter-nation rivalries which twice this century erupted in world wars, and of intolerance, racism and oppression resulting in the holocaust and in 'ethnic cleansing'. On the other hand, the idea of a nation carries with it notions of democratic self-determination, citizenship and social protection which have been an important source of inspiration and emancipation in many liberation and human rights movements. The decision about which direction 'national policies' will take (at both a national and increasingly a European level) is not simply a matter of party politics. It is also influenced by the patterns and processes of collective identity formation at neighbourhood and community level, especially among young people. This is where political awareness and anti-discriminatory strategies by grass roots workers matter. Their work, as the case illustrations in this volume demonstrate, takes place at the inter-section of global political and intricate personal processes of identity formation, of inclusion and exclusion, of domination and empowerment. A comprehensive set of reference points is, therefore, required.

The uncertainties over collective identities in the modern world manifest themselves in a fundamental paradox (Giddens 1991). On the one hand, the traditional barriers between classes, cultures and countries break down and give way to global connections and influences. The 'global village' shares the same fashions, the same tastes in music and visual entertainment, and communicates via satellites and the internet instantaneously. It also shares common ecological concerns as the intricate links that exist between all parts of the life system become apparent. On the other hand, lifestyles begin to differentiate themselves ever more strongly with a high degree of exclusivity as regions, countries, ethnic groupings, sub-cultures and individuals define their identities in a self-referential manner.

Globalisation, therefore, has the effect of both relativising and, to some extent, suspending the nation as a meaningful reference point. The experience of the Second World War provided the impetus for the formation of supra-national organisations such as the United Nations, the Council of Europe and the European Common Market. Political leaders of the post-war era were determined to prevent the evil of nationalism and national rivalry plunging the world yet again into the abyss of war. Despite this, the strategies of the military alliances of the Cold War era still utilised the basic principles of competition and 'superiority' characteristic of nation states.

Economic interests within the capitalist and the communist blocks relativised national borders still further. This created an interdependence upon specialised production sites which former communist states today find hard to disentangle themselves from, whilst capitalist market forces created their own global economic structures (Wallerstein 1991). In terms of consumer goods, eating habits and entertainment, the diversity available in every European country has a global dimension. National reference points are reduced to a matter of convenience: pizzas are marketed as 'Italian' and sports teams as 'national', when, in fact, their relationship to 'the national' has often become spurious.

One of the more unsettling effects of globalisation is the 'intensification of consciousness' (Robertson 1992: 8) caused by media technology. This allows for instant and close participation in world events in the privacy of every living room equipped with a TV screen. This 'virtual participation' in events such as wars, natural disasters and political dramas in other parts of the world, appeals to the conscience of the viewer in such a way that solidarity, at least momentarily, extends far beyond national and cultural boundaries. The surge of help for African famine victims induced by 'Band-Aid' and the spontaneous relief actions for Romanian or Chinese orphans are examples of this. Suddenly, distant events and distant lives can no longer be externalised emotionally along the reliable dividing line between 'them' and 'us'.

Globalisation is accompanied by a weakening and re-structuring of the traditional bonds of solidarity within nation states. Beck's contemporary diagnosis of an "unleashed process of modernization [which is] overrunning and overcoming its own coordinate system" paints a picture of the 'detraditionalization' of a class-based culture and consciousness, of gender and of family roles (Beck 1992: 87). People no longer have stable expectations of the paths their lives and careers will take. Instead, they share in a range of experiences (unemployment, luxury commodities, travel etc.) which seem more randomly allocated across class divisions in a 'lottery of life' in which individuals must calculate their own stakes. Family obligations, gender roles, formats of social contacts no longer follow a clearly discernible pattern, individuals must now make their own choices. This promotes narcissistic tendencies which are further exploited by commercial interests in all spheres of life, but particularly with regard to leisure activities. The result is greater social inequality which is aggravated by the fact that traditional 'defensive solidarities' in terms of social class or of labour organisations are losing their relevance and influence.

Overwhelmed by the necessity to make constant choices individuals may take refuge in certainties that present themselves as 'factual' (e.g. the biology of sex differences, the physiology of ethnicity); or in forms of community that seek to revive nostalgic enclaves in the bleak and impersonal industrial social landscape and which allow one to derive one's identity from 'common roots' like tribes and nations (Taguieff 1990). The renewed rise in nationalism and the growing importance of ethnicity as a reference point in political discourse are indications of this fundamental ambivalence and the seeming attractiveness of such reactive solutions.

These observations point to an important connection between personal and political processes and are ultimately the reason why professions such as youth and social work cannot ignore the broader political framework within which their interventions take place. There appears to be a parallel between the uncertainties confronting individuals in search of their personal identities and those that are being acted out in the political arena when defining the limits of our collective responsibilities at both a national and an international level. With the dismantling of the welfare state, (not just in Britain), there goes the dismantling of a welfare consensus forged in the experience of the last world war (Mishra 1990, Squires 1990). It can no longer be taken for granted that the well being of all people living in a state is ultimately the responsibility of that state. Solidarity is being fragmented beyond the limits that have so far been politically acceptable as a tolerable degree of inequality within a welfare system. The state not only withdraws its responsibility for providing a minimum of public support to asylum seekers and other categories of non-nationals, it also seeks to privatise solidarity in all aspects of social policy by referring issues back to the obligations of families and communities (Culpitt 1992).

Where do the specific boundaries of national solidarity and responsibility lie and according to what principles can they be legitimated? These questions take us back to the historical roots of the European nation state and the assumptions which guided its development. We will argue that the fundamental flaws of these assumptions, which constructed the nation states on a nationalism infused with racism, are now contributing to the fragmentation of a type of solidarity which does not value the cultural and ethnic diversity that is, and has always been, a fundamental aspect of every modern society.

In an intriguing parallel to this question of the internal cohesion of nation states lies the dilemma over the geographical and political definition of the boundaries of Europe. Since the Iron Curtain no longer provides a ready-made limit to Europe's eastern geography, the European Union must search for criteria and reasons for excluding and including countries eager to join its privileged 'club'. Economic criteria alone will not suffice to decide on the membership of, for instance, Hungary or Turkey; of crucial importance are cultural considerations of how 'western' these countries want to be and whether it can be justified 'expanding' Europe towards 'the Orient' and possibly Northern Africa. The sensibilities associated with such an expansion (on both sides) will become all the more acute as the EU moves towards political integration and the formation of a *de facto* 'European nation state'. The ambivalence of 'Project Europe' and its effect on the sovereignty of the nation state adds to this general uncertainty, and not only in Eurosceptic Britain (Delanty 1995). The shaping of solidarity among the nations of Europe through joint social policies is still a side issue of the unification drive but could set important criteria for the re-working of national solidarities. This is because the European level simply cannot avoid taking account of the existing cultural diversity of nations (Leibfried and Pierson 1994). What is at stake (and awaits, therefore, the active participation of those working at the grass roots of inter-cultural social issues) is whether the social policies of the European Union will ultimately reproduce the nationalist principles characteristic of national welfare, or whether they can draw on the lessons of the national experience, and safeguard the rights of all European citizens without preconditions.

At both the personal and the political level two strategies of defining the boundaries of solidarity and identity are currently competing, but each has its own problems. One is the more pragmatic attempt of acknowledging that the boundaries of any collective identity are to some extent arbitrary. If people or societies have chosen to contract a form of mutual solidarity then substantive differences between the contracting partners should not present barriers. This position accepts that all boundaries are historically contingent and arbitrary and treats identity and obligations as a matter of pragmatism and convenience. This liberal solution appears to suit a modern mind set that values freedom from traditional bonds. However, seen in the light of the instability of such freely contracted bonds, such as the break up of the Soviet Union and the conflicts of former Yugoslavia, but also demonstrated by the slowing of the European unification process, this solution does not promise permanence. It seems incapable of accommodating a psychological need for continuity, for the 'reality' behind symbols and cultural norms essential for their legitimacy and relevance for identity. The other, 'essentialist' solution to establishing a common identity concentrates on the definition of a 'common core' and searches, not for negotiated outer perimeters, but for a 'centre' to which a common identity might be anchored.

Correspondence with this core of essential characteristics or ideas decides then over membership to the whole. For instance, the question then becomes, not 'Is Turkey willing to contract into the conditions of the EU?', but 'Is Turkey a European nation?' (and therefore entitled to negotiate in the first place). This approach has a popular appeal, but on closer examination all such 'essentials' turn out to be fictions, in other words myths, that have been constructed for political ends and which belie their appearance of stability and continuity. They are as much a source of instability as the pragmatic criteria outlined above and are just as arbitrary.

As we will show, both strategies have been applied in the development of European nation states. The 'essentialist' strategy in particular has been used more frequently and more forcefully, often with the assistance of education and social services. Hroch (1985) argues that the concept of the nation contains within itself a fundamental and fateful ambivalence between both these approaches to a collective identity. There is always a danger that a racist solution will be found to resolve this ambivalence. The cultural bond between citizens of a nation has never grown automatically out of their formal membership of a political unit. If European citizenship is to become a reality, it will not be because all European citizens carry the same passports, but because a new kind of citizenship (Meehan 1993) that has overcome the split between individualism and collectivism, particularism and universalism, liberalism and essentialism, has been created.

In tracing the history of the European nation states, Hobsbawm (1990) distinguishes between a 'revolutionary-democratic' version of the nation (associated with the French Revolution) and which emphasises the contract between citizens as the basis of their rights, and a 'nationalist' version which derives solidarity from a 'common cultural heritage' as in the Italian or German tradition. The revolutionary construction of the nation was by no means the product of cultural homogeneity or purity. For example, at the time of the French Revolution, only 50% of the population spoke French (Balibar 1985) and the 'social contract' negotiated between citizens affirmed the right 'to be different' as the basis of legal equality. Thus, what united them was, not so much a common past, but a common task: the ending of traditional privileges. Nevertheless, heterogeneity soon became a problem for the French revolutionaries because citizenship is far more than a pure formality. It soon became conditional upon a knowledge of the French language and an ability to participate in the 'official French culture'; a criterion of 'cultural and civic collectivism' (Greenfeld 1992) that still has enormous integrative power in France to this day (Brubaker 1990).

In the fundamental re-ordering of the political map of continental Europe which followed the Napoleonic wars, a curious mixture of ideological-mythical and rational-economic criteria gained prominence when determining the territorial outlines of the new political entities of Belgium, the Netherlands, Norway, Sweden, Denmark, Greece, Spain and Portugal. Nation states had to be big enough to be economically viable, according to the famous pragmatics of Mazzini (Hobsbawm 1990: 31). This meant that not every wish for national independence, formed by nationalist movements in the wake of the anti-Napoleonic resistance, came to be satisfied. However, in every case, national identities were informed by two overriding principles: the difference to a neighbouring culture (Swedish/Norwegian, Spanish/ Portuguese, Danish/German, French/Dutch etc.), and the claim for the 'antiquity' of one's own culture.

In the course of the nineteenth century European societies became increasingly concerned with nationalism (Balibar 1991). "Nationalism played the role of the hinge fastening together state and society" (Bauman 1992: 683). The 'nationalist' version of the nation state, choosing as its unifying principles a common essence and a common past, established itself as the dominant model in Europe. This culminated in the national projects of the unification of the states of Italy and of Germany. In both those countries the internal amalgamation of diverse kingdoms, each with their very different histories, traditions and language-versions, into one nation state required considerable intellectual and educational efforts. So much so that Massimo d'Azeglio, one of the chief ideological architects of a united Italy, could say at the opening of the first Italian parliament, "We have made Italy, now we have to make Italians" (Hobsbawm 1990: 44). Similar 'formative efforts' applied in all new nation states. The Austro-Hungarian monarchy and the Russian empire were perhaps the only large continental European entities which managed to resist the emerging identification of nation and state: Austria until the end of the First World War, and Russia, one could argue, until the 1990s. National independence movements, inspired by romantic intellectual movements searching for 'cultural roots' and spurred by new political élites sensing ripe opportunities for power, spelled troubled times ahead for these multi-cultural and multi-ethnic colossi.

Contrary to the impression nurtured by the new nation states, that their modern form was the manifestation of a historical destiny and a realisation of ancient dreams just waiting for their moment in history, the European nation state is neither the product of a cultural nor ethnic unity and purity. Instead, "it is the state that makes the nation and not the nation the state" as the Polish 'liberator' Józef Pilsudski remarked (quoted in Horsman and Marshall 1994: xviii). Many national languages, from modern Greek and Italian to Czech, Flemish and Romanian have either been 're-worked' or refined and elevated from the status of dialects to that of official languages through the efforts of academics and philologists. Towards the end of the nineteenth century, nationalism became a means of consolidating and securing the new political entities whose boundaries were notoriously difficult to justify on 'historical grounds'. The crucial ally and the driving force behind this national project, in the opinion of many historians, was industrial capitalism, which derived its conquering power from the concept of 'national economies' competing with each other (Wallerstein 1991). The liberal notion of the state gave free enterprise the support and protection it required, by means of education and social control, which secured the 'loyalty of the masses'. This left business free to transcend the boundaries of traditions and territories whenever and wherever it suited its interests.

As nationalism began to dominate the political agenda of the nation state, the 'emancipatory component' of the idea which had inspired and which continued to inspire many national liberation movements, the fight against "the arbitrary rule of princes and small aristocratic elites" (Mommsen 1990: 215) gave way to new forms of power being exercised through the hegemony – or leadership – of a 'national culture'. National culture became not just an external ideological symbol of superiority over 'rival cultures' but also an instrument of internal domination over a country's own ethnic and cultural minorities (Mommsen, *ibid*). The means of legitimating and of bolstering this assumed superiority soon reached beyond cultural arguments and the creation of a common language, to incorporate new methods of affinity and exclusion. It is within this context that the uniformity of a nation through the 'second-degree fiction' of a common race (Balibar 1991: 99) became activated. As a consequence, grounding the 'togetherness' of a nation, not primarily in solidarity (which requires an act of will by the individuals), but in 'blood and soil' i.e. something that we are born into, removes belonging from the sphere of choice (Bauman 1992). Collective identity becomes destiny, secured with references to the findings of modern science. Darwinism and the first scientific speculations of genetics were utilised to assemble a pervasive ideology of racism which conveniently filled the gaps left by scientific evidence. Ideology became disguised as science. And, when the superiority of the white race over black races cannot be based on biological evidence, the cultural argument takes over with the claim of the greatness of one's own 'civilization', having proven itself through its rise to imperialist world domination. Indeed, racism of this kind, tried and tested within the colonial context, served the power élites within Europe itself, to class themselves as superior over for instance, those of the Jewish, the Gypsy and the Irish peoples, as well as over the sub-stratum of a 'residuum' defined by their 'deviant' behaviour. The 'substance' that is assumed to constitute a European nation changes from political to cultural and eventually to ethnic and racist criteria (Miles 1989). This produced a particularly lethal bonding of nation and race in the case of German nationalism and Nazism.

The European nation state depended for its stability on the creation of homogeneity, or 'oneness', and in the production of this cultural conformity it employed the ideological assistance of nationalism. The dynamics of this nationalism expanded the nation state project globally. Its aggressive energies, in the form of colonialism, spilled over the edges of Europe to reach for the furthest corners of the world. The political agenda of colonialism exceeded the 'economic necessity' generated by the expansive tendencies of capitalism, in its ideological pursuit of wanting to civilize the world (Fryer 1984). Colonial rule became a paradigm for new forms of internal social control which allowed the exercise of power to be advertised as being 'in the best interest of the ruled'. Cultural hegemony on a world stage further legitimated the hegemony of the dominant culture 'back home', whether this manifested itself through the education system, the civil service, or indeed the testing and perfecting of methods of community development. European culture was 'destined' to rule the world: such is the logic of 'progress'.

It is within this logic of progress and superiority that racism found its niche, and the aggressive forms of nationalism provided it with rich nurture. This belief in progress, however, had its limits when the incorporation of 'natives' and their traditions into Western belief systems either did not work (because of their 'stubborn resistance') or could turn into a threat to White superiority (on account of their 'cleverness in learning'). Colonial rule came to 'ring-fence' certain aspects of other cultures it dominated where this helped to maintain clear boundaries and set up separated political and administrative structures (for instance with 'tribal chiefs' in Africa), thus paving the way for elaborate systems of apartheid (Miles 1989). Colonialism structured the encounter with the 'dark continent' and 'primitive societies' to create the Black person as the archetypical 'other' precisely in order to underline a fundamental distance between superior and inferior populations generally. In the process it united the disparate characteristics of 'whiteness' into a coherent whole (Said 1994). Racism sought to eliminate the cultural basis of the construction of this difference and superiority and to replace the lingering doubts and uncertainties with 'facts' backed by science. It became a means of avoiding discourse and debate and became a way of continuing (and thereby totally subverting and corrupting) the educational project of cultural unification of the nation state with the means of oppression.

Henceforth education and socialisation which are centred on taken-for-granted notions of 'the national' are at core racist.

The emerging nation states were potentially as heterogeneous as their colonies. In addition to the early democratic measures which gave at least some of the citizens a stake in 'their country' they also relied on social and cultural efforts to secure their stability. Gellner argues that these universal nationwide cultures which became the hallmarks of nations were an essential requirement of industrialisation itself. "A modern industrial state can only function with a mobile, literate, culturally standardized, inter-changeable population" (Gellner 1983: 46).

But this standardization exercise was by no means confined to the establishment of a compulsory education system. The whole project of creating a national heritage as the foundation of a national culture became the criterion by which it could be decided who was to belong properly to the nation. Parallel with the school system, the social agencies of both the public and the private sphere drew on patriotism for their inspiration and legitimation. Sport, for example, became the means by which not only the physical health of the (male) nation could be improved in functional readiness for war, it also became a forum for the dissemination of national fervour and a means of incorporating the young population which has always been regarded as a potential source of instability and disaffection. As 'Vater Jahn', the chief ideologue of German national sports during the nineteenth century, expressed it: "The rights of citizens are dependent upon the activity of such citizens. That citizen loses his rights who deserts his flag, besmirches his Fatherland in foreign countries, or loses his reason" (quoted in Greenfeld 1992: 369f).

Philanthropy through countless charitable organisations unfolded an unprecedented crusade against destitution in what amounted to a national effort at rescuing people from the margins of society, and bringing aboard those who had been left stranded despite the rising tide of national progress. The bourgeois element of the women's movement during the nineteenth century derived much of its energies from patriotism. It gave expression to women's desire to have a publicly acclaimed part to play in the affairs of the nation, equivalent to the part that men were called upon to play through military service (and which itself formed an essential plank of the nation-forming exercise).

Incorporating the masses into the nation state was by no means unconditional. It operated with the blunt and brutal instrument of distinguishing the 'deserving' from the 'undeserving'. This moral category of old, designed to set limits on solidarity and moral obligations, was revived in its 'modern' form as a curious mixture of functional and ethical criteria. The moral institutions of the state, the schools, workhouses and prisons, were themselves 'setting examples' of where the line between acceptable and unacceptable behaviour should be drawn. That boundary became questionable when it permitted the 'wrong kind of people' to be punished or excluded or indeed when 'the wrong kind of people' came to enjoy the protection of society. The rescue efforts of the blossoming welfare societies of the Victorian age, in Britain as well as in those parts of Europe that followed Britain's industrial lead, had both a practical and a vital symbolic significance for the consolidation of the nation state. They demonstrated that the boundaries of the nation state ran through every community and every individual and that membership of society and citizenship depended upon the willingness to conform and become worthy members of that entity.

Under modern conditions in industrial societies welfare and education services ultimately redraw the boundaries of solidarity where traditional community and family bonds and allegiances have become suspended in a massive upheaval of social and geographical mobility. The nation constitutes its identity through these educational efforts, through not leaving the socialisation of its young to chance, through setting up and enforcing internal boundaries of acceptable behaviour and by standardising those criteria. "Let us simply say that schooling is the principal institution which produces ethnicity as linguistic community" (Balibar 1992: 98).

It is in this way that workers in the emerging educational and social services became unavoidably hitched to the national bandwagon whether they were employed in the public or in the private/voluntary sphere. What obscured the realisation of this national agenda for most of them, to this day, is that they sought to deliver their service from a perspective of professional autonomy and 'neutrality' rather than from an overtly political position. Professionalisation became vital to the legitimation of their functions since the state, as a modern state, was keen to advertise its 'attractiveness' and its conditions of solidarity through the principle of rationality rather than through coercion and arbitrary authority. Participation in the national project, and choosing to behave properly, were ultimately to be seen as functions of reason. Those failing to exercise rational choice were considered to be impaired in their mental functions (in which case they needed treatment) or lacking in insight (in which case they needed education). Rationality came to inform the methods and principles applied by professionals operating the educational and therapeutic services in a fundamental way; only the use of such methods, developed in a process of systematic and scientific reflection, could lend their action legitimacy.

For the social professions, the reliance on rational principles of intervention was an ambiguous tool. On the one hand it helped to overcome the vestiges of moralism which had marred the pioneer phase of social services where volunteers set out in a patronising way to teach the poor how to manage their affairs better. The individualism implicit in rationalism, the method of diagnosing each case according to its particular circumstances, also acted as a restraint against the wholesale stereotyping and condemning of categories of 'problem populations' as inferior. On the other hand it operated with principles and values of 'normality' derived largely from positivist notions of mental health and social adjustment which allowed for little engagement in a cultural discourse on the subjective meanings of 'differences'. Even marxist models of revolutionary social intervention, of which there were sporadic 'experiments' in youth work and residential care in many parts of Europe earlier this century (Lorenz 1994: 58), were constructed around a fixed model of a desired state of society which seemed oblivious to perspectives of gender and ethnicity.

Social services developed quite rapidly in all countries of Europe in the 1920s and 1930s with increasing direct support by the state. As social service staff came more directly under state control the position of value neutrality demonstrated its blindness to political misuse most catastrophically in Hitler's Germany. That regime had elevated nationalism to the status of a central political device not just of its foreign but also of its social policy programme. Most western European countries (and the USA) had sympathised with the technical and rational solutions to social problems suggested by the fledgling science of genetics, as promoted by the 'eugenic societies', which advocated programmes of sterilisation for a broad spectrum of medical conditions considered hereditary (Proctor 1988). Despite the extremely tenuous scientific evidence, a sweeping range of mental illnesses and disabilities, usually including alcoholism and epilepsy, were assumed to have a genetic basis and the case was made that if science could not cure these diseases in the present generation it could at least prevent them from burdening future generations. Nazism seized avidly on these ideas and as soon as it came to power in 1933 it enacted, as one of its first pieces of legislation, a law permitting and promoting the involuntary sterilisation of people with conditions deemed hereditary, 'where necessary' (Klee 1985).

The urgency and speed with which this law was passed underlines its central ideological function within fascist social policy which is the complete segregation of those worthy to belong to the nationalist state and the unworthy rest (Lorenz 1994: 64f). Nazism did not stop at symbolic, partial, and temporary physical segregation. Disguising its ideology as science, it swept aside the 'sentimentality of half-measures' constrained by 'moral scruples' and proceeded to constantly and consistently select and segregate in all its policies with the sterilisation, with the incarceration in concentration camps, and with the extermination of 'unworthy life' as its infamous 'final solution'. The racism of Nazi social policies against 'weak members of society' runs parallel to and becomes at times indistinguishable from the racism perpetrated against the Jewish, Roma and Sinti and other minority populations. The 'ethnic cleansing' culminating in the Holocaust engulfed not only the millions of people classed as racially inferior but additional thousands of children, women and men diagnosed as 'inferior forms of life' on account of their disabilities, their homosexuality or perhaps their social condition as vagrants or delinquents (Aly *et al* 1985). This was not an evil afterthought of a regime losing its sanity in the desperation of a war it had unleashed; it was the deliberate, calculated and well-prepared implementation of an overall policy design with nationalism as its pinnacle.

This machinery of segregation and extermination was operated not only by people who would commit the final atrocities but also by those experts who would assist in 'drawing the line' by virtue of their diagnostic skills. In this insidious way a whole range of professionals became implicated in the system:

doctors, social workers, health visitors, care staff, teachers and many others, were providing evidence for the courts so that in a charade of legality they could issue orders denying marriage certificates to people 'posing a threat to the health of the nation', for compulsory sterilisation, or for admission to institutions. The system relied upon all welfare personnel filing case reports in which they listed the family histories of epilepsy or alcoholism, assessed the chances of rehabilitation of offenders, or of children with learning difficulties. Sticking to their professional task with the air of value neutrality and scientific detachment (especially after the 'non-conforming', 'politically active' workers had been sacked or imprisoned) they did not feel responsible for the consequences of their assessments and may indeed not have been conscious of the full implications their work had in 'the national context' (Otto and Sünker 1989). This diagnostic service was not only provided by statutory services. The main voluntary welfare organisations of Germany, with the exception of the socialist one, continued to operate under Nazism, on the condition that they 'support the national cause'. Whilst some individuals and organisations offered resistance at enormous personal risk, all institutions within German civil society, including the churches and their welfare services, de facto supported national policies. They were de-sensitised by the fact that, seen from a functional perspective, this system appeared 'only' to continue and perfect the incorporation of welfare into the national interest.

After the defeat of Fascism the programmes at 'democratic re-construction' instigated by the United Nations, the United States and Britain, targeted very explicitly the welfare services and their personnel for re-training in 'democratic' approaches. However, they ignored the element of 'scientific value neutrality' as a fatal chain of Nazi dis-welfare. Values were confined to appeals to self-determination in case work (which became the dominant social work paradigm), and in group work where 'democratic', self-directed styles did away with hierarchical notions of group leadership (Lorenz 1994: 76). These efforts were not accompanied by a fundamental critique of positivism and its function in diagnostic categorisation. The evil of a fascist approach to welfare had not emanated primarily from its collectivism and from the imposition of ideologically determined forms of practice (which social workers usually knew how to get round). Rather, it emanated from the disjuncture of the political from the professional discourse that prevented 'ordinary welfare workers' from realising the consequences of their actions. The individualist consensus of a 'social pathology' discourse (Mills 1943), which prevailed in the social sciences of the 1950s and 1960s, left social and youth workers inadequately equipped to face up to a radical critique of welfare agendas which continued to be nationally oriented.

This became evident above all in the area of education and youth and community work in those European countries confronted once more with cultural diversity in a manner reminiscent of the nation-founding period. The massive population displacement of the war, combined with labour shortages, had made many countries of Europe recipients of migration and thereby locations of a new cultural and ethnic diversity. Whereas in earlier periods, emigration was often treated as a kind of cleansing process to reduce diversity by sending convicts to penal colonies and by forcing those to leave the country who potentially constituted 'social problems', diversity now appeared on Europe's own doorstep. The welfare consensus after the Second World War had been built on the myth that new social policies had eliminated structural poverty. Those individuals and families still not able to cope were cast in the light of people who had 'problems of adjustment', and who required treatment or education in order to be able to fully participate in society. In analogy, those members of recently arrived migrant groups (e.g. from the British New Commonwealth, from former French colonies or from Mediterranean countries as *Gastarbeiter* in Germany) who came to the attention of educational and welfare services were also regarded as being in need of help with their adjustment. Indeed, 'integration' and 'assimilation' became the initial chief objectives of 'remedial responses' in all European countries (Miles 1993). Spurred often by the wishes of immigrant families themselves who wanted their children to adopt the language of the host country as quickly as possible, these early strategies aimed at 'levelling differences' by 'bringing newcomers up to standards'. In all this the normality of the national standards remained unquestioned or, as can be recognised from the historical perspective outlined above, became affirmed ever more strongly.

Integration and assimilation as methods of dealing with cultural diversity were a first line pedagogical – educational – response in virtually all European countries. However, it did not fulfill the declared objective of establishing 'racial harmony' (Mullard 1982). But it contributed to the interest ethnic minority groups took in affirming their own separate identities. A second phase of responses which can be classed as the 'multi-cultural approaches' recognised this autonomy and the value of plurality. These initiatives tended to celebrate cultural diversity and suggested that many of the 'foreign' cultures contained an exotic promise or a truth lost to the 'indigenous' culture and that, as such, they represented a source of renewal. However, these responses failed to deal with the actual process of defining cultural and ethnic boundaries, and with the power acted out in the conflicts not so much over cultural contents but over their hierarachical differences (Todd 1991). Children carrying out projects at school on village life in Turkey or Bangladesh felt only too well that such accounts served merely to endorse the image of their culture as 'backward' and that the invitation to show difference by no means bestowed the right to be different.

Rights reappeared on the political agenda in the last three decades of the twentieth century at the instigation of social and civil rights movements. This serves as an interesting historical parallel to the role such movements played in the latter part of the nineteenth century. Since the 1970s, social movements such as the peace movement, the women's liberation movement, and the ecology movement, highlight yet again the importance of 'civil society' as the site of political action. Their significance for the political process was firstly, that all these movements cut right across the concerns of national politics to forge very strong and immediate international allegiances; and secondly, that they had their issues defined by the participants in the political process themselves. Before any experts could tell a group of women or a group of black young people 'what was good for them' they had sought to define their own agenda for change and in this process had come to identify and challenge the structures of discrimination which had deliberately kept them out of the political process.

The methodological implications for youth and social work of this radically changed agenda will be discussed in the following chapters. What is important to highlight in this historical overview is the fact that the significance of this change towards a rights discourse, and the key to overcoming the serious limitations of previous programmes, lies not in designing new anti-racist methods, but in the closer and more consistent analysis of the political context in which education, social work, and the struggle against racism take place (Macey 1995). In other words, it is only through re-examining their relationship with national agendas that youth, welfare, and educational workers can start their search for appropriate methods. An anti-racist approach *per se* that does not conceptualise this wider political agenda, no matter how radical it presents itself, can easily end up playing right into the hands of a national agenda of exclusion and discrimination.

This national agenda, in the context of the contradictory trends outlined at the start of this chapter, is now at a crossroads. Its influence and power is being weakened by European unification, by international treaties and conventions; and by an international human rights awareness which begins to set common standards across nation states. Many improvements in the position of oppressed groups in European countries came about as a direct result of European or international standards being brought to bear on national legislation through treaties or rulings of international courts. At the same time, new forms of exclusion are becoming apparent at both national and international levels. The treatment of migrants and asylum seekers by the EU itself has become much more selective and restrictive as 'fortress Europe' erects perimeter controls around its territory in a sinister symmetry to the functions of the former Iron Curtain (Miles 1993). These types of consolidation and protection policies mirror ominously the strategies of exclusion and of racism by which the nation states shaped themselves. "Unification for Europe", in the words of Lyotard (1993: 159), may yet also come to mean "unification of its hatreds".

Whilst a 'European nationalism' being established at the level of the European Union itself is perhaps too remote a possibility, the power of 'national nationalism' has become once again a pronounced item on the political agenda, and not just in the programmes of explicit right wing and neo-fascist parties which have seen a frightening resurgence in Europe. In the insecurities caused by globalisation for personal and collective identities, nationalism advertises itself as a safe solution which takes recourse to sensible, popular certainties. National sentiments are once more presented as 'natural feelings', not necessarily genetically determined, but certainly as the guarantee of a sense of belonging. Norman Tebbit's 'cricket test', which expects black youngsters to cheer for the

English team as a 'condition' of their British citizenship, plays on exactly that substitution. National belonging as a sentiment centred on a set of taken-for-granted contents appears to offer stability and continuity where identities are threatened with fragmentation and discontinuity.

But these contents of what it means to be British, Dutch, French, German, Italian etc. are invariably highly complex, contradictory, and ambivalent creations of historical processes in which any 'dominant traits' became established, not as a result of quasi-biological 'natural selection', but by the power of one elite over all other contenders. This type of nationalism, which maintains the principle of 'one state, one culture', deliberately obscures the multiplicity and diversity of characteristics and reifies instead the ideological assumptions on which they are built. In this regard it shows its affinity to racism, which can become the cutting edge of this nationalist construction, and which can enforce the idea of national purity and superiority by systematic exclusion and discrimination. The underlying principles of this version of nationalism and of racism are identical in that they reduce socially created characteristics into fixed hierarchical 'facts' whose meanings are not negotiable.

Seen in this historical context, the crisis of national identity in Europe is not a product of migration and 'imposed diversity'. It is, rather, a crisis of collective solidarity stemming from the inherent instability of the nationalist construction of the nation state which manifests itself in relation to migration in a particularly forceful manner. Signs of this crisis of solidarity are as much the fragmentation of the welfare consensus when certain groups of citizens like the young unemployed, pensioners, or homeless people can no longer rely automatically on a minimum level of support guaranteed by the state; as in the numerous political conflicts where regions within nation states and, indeed, small communities, make claims for cultural and often also political autonomy (Wieviorka 1994: 180). These conflicts have become exacerbated by the ending of the Cold War, which re-focused political concerns from an East-West to a national agenda, and thereby upon all the ambiguities of nation state solidarity. In the attempts at rescuing the nationalist agenda, migration and the 'threat of cultural alienation' have become political instruments that divert attention away from both the need for negotiating diversity (which has always existed in every nation state), and from the need to extend the boundaries of solidarity beyond the borders of the nation state and beyond assumed, and imagined, 'natural communities' (Anderson 1983). Racism and xenophobia have become negative substitutes for an inability to face up to changing, developing, and multiple collective identities.

This also highlights the necessity of the anti-racist and black identity discourse to go beyond a taken-for-granted notion of 'Blackness', which has led at times to oppressive forms of homogenisation (Gilroy 1992). Whilst the strategy of turning the label 'Black' from a racist ascription into an emancipatory self-referent may have been an important step in the struggle of oppressed people to re-claim the right to self-definition, it also brings with it the danger of 'essentialising' Blackness within a dichotomised agenda still dictated by existing power interests. In this regard international dialogue within the anti-racist debate has been most fruitful in recent years in promoting a "de-centring and de-essentialisation of 'race' and 'ethnicity'" (Rattansi 1994: 58; see also Steiner-Khamsi and Spreen in this volume).

This critique is not to deny minority groups the right to define their own identities and to have those identities more visibly represented in schools, services, community centres, and political parties. But in all such 'representations', the danger of culture becoming an instrument of exclusion and oppression, needs to be monitored against the historical background of Europe's experience with nationalism in constant affinity with racism. In the search for non-exclusive, non-repressive forms of representation and identification, it may help us to return to the as yet under-utilised emancipatory version of the idea of the nation and its unrealised potential. This version of the nation implies sets of citizenship rights which constitute mutual obligations precisely on the basis of differences. The need for negotiation, for putting into practice the human right to equality of all members of a community, which is ultimately a political rather than a biological postulate, arises only once diversity has been fully recognised. The ensuing political and legal arrangements, once they have secured such equality, are in turn the basis upon which cultural, ideological, and indeed biological differences, can be recognised and evaluated and given a negotiated social significance.

The main argument put forward in the contributions in this

volume is that youth, educational, and social services need to foster the critical emancipatory potential contained within the concept of the nation in all their educational, therapeutic, and empowering efforts. The building of reliable political structures of solidarity and a sense of belonging based on such trust is indeed an educational process or rather a pedagogical one in the terminology of continental European traditions. It concerns the formation of the social abilities of human beings as a two-way process, and not the imposition of social norms which are simply 'given', but the fostering of active participation of all members of a society in the articulation of reliable norms. Pedagogy is the art of facilitating the competences necessary for such negotiations. These competences must, therefore, incorporate psychological as well as political considerations.

But this programme also needs to go begond the 'empty' postulates of a liberal construction of the nation and of citizenship. It is not a matter of emphasising only the development of and adherence to abstract political principles of equality. This may leave a dangerous vacuum for young people who need to be able to acknowledge that they have been born into definite social and cultural relations, to identify with concrete social groups and their norms and ideals, and who must not be made to feel guilty or defensive about showing preferences in lifestyle and collective identity. Nor is it a matter of concentrating only upon the nurturing of group identities, no matter how 'tolerant' they might be, and to see the pedagogical mandate exhausted in the harmonious differentiation of multi-cultural identities. This alone will not enable groups to engage in discourses over the limits of that identity and over those universal values that may legitimately cut across cultural differences.

It becomes necessary to strengthen the critical political function of pedagogy in recognition of these lessons from the history of the European nation state and the crucial crossroads which its development appears to have reached. The development of anti-racist approaches map out the broad agenda of this complex but urgent task and in this sense the authors of this volume subscribe to them; not as a new set of methods, but as a re-affirmation of the fundamental principles of 'good pedagogy and social work'. Anti-racism has come to signify the resistance that all youth and social work has to offer to the pressure of becoming subsumed, unwittingly or deliberately, under a nationalist political agenda. But the anti-racist agenda goes well beyond the strengthening of this resistance. It searches for the positive contents of collective, inter-cultural, non exclusive identities and their realisation within negotiated rights of citizenship.

Bibliography

Aly, G., Ebbinghaus, A., Hamann, M., Pfäfflin, F., and Preissler, G. (1985), Aussonderung und Tod. Die klinische Hinrichtung der Unbrauchbaren, Berlin: Rotbuch Verlag

Anderson, B. (1983), Imagined Communities, London: Verso

Balibar, R. (1985), L'Institution du français: essai sur le co-linguisme des Carolingiens à la République, Paris

Balibar, E. (1991), The nation form: History and ideology, in E. Balibar and I. Wallerstein, Race, nation, class: ambiguous identities, London: Verso

Bauman, Z. (1992), Soil, blood and identity, The Sociological Review 40.4: 675-701

Beck, U. (1992) Risk Society, London: Sage

Brubaker, W. R. (1990), Immigration, citizenship, and the nation-state in France and Germany: a comparative historical analysis, International Sociology 5,4: 379-407

Culpitt, I. (1992), Welfare and citizenship: Beyond the crisis of the welfare state? London: Sage

Delanty, G. (1995), Inventing Europe. Idea, identity, reality, London: Macmillan

Fryer, P. (1984), Staying Power: The History of Black People in Britain, London: Pluto Press

Gellner, E. (1983), Nations and Nationalism, Oxford: Blackwell

Giddens, A. (1991), Modernity and Self-Identity, Cambridge: Polity Press

Gilroy, P. (1992), The end of anti-racism, in J. Donald and A. Rattansi (eds.), 'Race', Culture and Difference, London: Sage

Greenfeld, L. (1992), Nationalism. Five roads to modernity, Cambridge: Harvard University Press

Hroch, M. (1985), Social preconditions of national revival in Europe, Cambridge: Cambridge University Press

Hobsbawm, E. J. (1990), Nations and nationalism since 1780: programme, myth and reality, Cambridge: Cambridge University Press

Horsman, M. and Marshall, A. (1994), After the nation-state; citizens, tribalism and the New World Order, London: Harper Collins

Klee, E. (1985), 'Euthanasie' im NS-Staat. Die 'Vernichtung lebensunwerten Lebens', Frankfurt: Fischer

Leibfried, S. and Pierson, P. (1994), The prospects for social Europe, in A. de Swaan (ed.), Social policy beyond borders. The social question in transnational perspective, Amsterdam: Amsterdam University Press

Lorenz, W. (1994), Social work in a changing Europe, London: Routledge

Lyotard, J.-F. (1993), Europe, the Jews, and the Book, in Political Writings, London: UCL Press

Macey, M. (1995), Towards racial justice? A re-evaluation of anti-racism, Critical Social Policy 44/45, vol. 15; 2/3: 126-146

Meehan, E. (1993), Citizenship and the European Community, London: Sage

Miles, R. (1989), Racism, London: Routledge

Miles, R. (1993), Racism after 'race relations', London: Routledge

Mills, C. W. (1943), The professional ideology of social pathologists, American Journal of Sociology 49: 165-180

Mishra, R. (1990), The welfare state in capitalist society. Policies of retrenchment and maintenance in Europe, North America and Australia, London: Harvester Wheatsheaf

Mommsen, W. J. (1990), The varieties of the nation state in modern history: liberal, imperialist, Fascist and contemporary notions of nation and nationality, in M. Mann (ed.), The rise and decline of the nation state, Oxford: Blackwell

Mullard, C. (1982), Multi-racial education in Britain: from assimilation to cultural pluralism, in J. Tierney (ed.), Race, Immigration and Schooling, London: Holt Educational

Otto, H.-U., Sünker, H. (1989), Nationalsozialismus, Volksgemeinschaftsideologie und soziale Arbeit, In H.-U. Otto, H. Sünker (Hrsg.) Soziale Arbeit und Faschismus, Frankfurt: Suhrkamp

Proctor, R. N. (1988), Racial hygiene: Medicine under the Nazis, Cambridge/Ma.: Harvard University Press

Rattansi, A. (1994), 'Western' racisms, ethnicities and identities in a 'postmodern' frame, in A. Rattansi, S. Westwood (eds.), Racism, modernity and identity, Cambridge: Polity Press

Robertson, R. (1992), Globalization: Social theory and global culture, London: Sage

Said, E. W. (1994), Culture and imperialism, London: Vintage

Squires, P. (1990), Anti-social policy: welfare, ideology and the disciplinary state, London: Harvester Wheatsheaf

Taguieff, P.-A. (1990), The new cultural racism in France, Telos 83: 109-122

Todd, R. (1991), Education in a multicultural society, London: Cassell

Wallerstein, I. (1991), The construction of peoplehood: Racism, nationalism, ethnicity, in E. Balibar and I. Wallerstein, Race, nation, class: ambiguous identities, London: Verso

Wieviorka, M. (1994), Racism in Europe: unity and diversity, in A. Rattansi, S. Westwood (eds.), Racism, modernity and identity, Cambridge: Polity Press

2. Oppositional and relational identity: a comparative perspective

Gita Steiner-Khamsi and Carol Anne Spreen

In the last few years both multicultural education and anti-racist youth work have been criticized for promoting polarization. Their proponents have been attacked for perpetuating a dichotomic perspective on intergroup relations by artificially dividing individuals into Whites and Blacks, majority and ethnic minorities, natives and immigrants, and, on a broader level, distinguishing between periphery and core, between sending and receiving countries of immigration, or as Stuart Hall has put it so astutely, between the 'West' and the 'rest' (Hall 1992).

Today, the research and practice of multicultural education in the United States and anti-racist youth work in Europe are facing major challenges. The research must now take into account the recent debates in the social sciences and in philosophy that are relevant to the field. In light of the debates on universalism and particularism, essentialism and difference, researchers of multicultural and anti-racist education need to come out against the criticism of having pursued an essentialist notion of race and ethnicity. Practitioners, in turn, need to prove that they truly moved beyond traditional approaches that amounted to nothing more than celebrating diversity and promoting a 'harmonious empty pluralism' (Mohanty 1994: 146).

Writing for a readership that is alarmed by rising levels of racism, anti-semitism and neo-fascism in Europe, particularly among youth, and addressing readers that are committed to improving intergroup relations, this study aims at drawing attention to a new anti-essentialist, multiperspective and anti-moralistic perspective in anti-racist youth work. The perspective is based on the following observations:

First, contrary to commonly held beliefs among anti-racist youth workers, there is not too little, but rather too much awareness among youth with regard to cultural diversity, 'race' and ethnic relations.

Second, anti-racist youth work that focuses merely on minorities is prey to neglecting the relational nature of identity formations, and hence is oblivious to inclusionary and exclusionary processes that account for ethnic and racial intergroup tensions.

Finally, there are serious constraints upon adults teaching adolescents ethical and social issues, and it seems indicated that we find innovative strategies which facilitate adolescents in learning from each other on how to improve their intergroup relations.

This chapter has two parts. The first deals with the critique of anti-racism from a comparative perspective. We compare critical reviews of multicultural and anti-racist education published in Great Britain, Germany, and the United States. In this part we explore in more depth John Ogbu's work on oppositional identity and reflect upon its conceptual and practical significance to intergroup youth work. The second part presents one practical approach in which interpersonal conflicts are dealt with in ways that transcend essentialist notions of anti-racist youth work. To illustrate our argument we will refer to peer-mediation and conflict resolution programs, which are moderated by adolescents for adolescents. These programs have been increasingly implemented in inner city public schools in New York City and throughout the United States.

Transnational flow of discourses

This study presents the preliminary findings of a large research project which compares relevant debates (on issues such as difference, alterity, essentialism, and universalism) in the field of multicultural and anti-racist education from a cross-national perspective. Other scholars researching comparative education also focus on comparisons of academic discourses. Paulston (1993) used the method of cartography to illustrate conceptual proximity and distance of comparative educational texts.

The carthographic method allowed Paulston to produce

insightful conceptual maps depicting the inter-relation of relevant theories in the field. In contrast to his pioneering research, our research project targets the transnational flow of discourses, and is, therefore, interested in texts that are cited outside their original context. The purpose of our study is to understand the specificity of (national) contexts by tracing the transnational borrowing process of discourses, and more precisely by examining adaptations and modifications, i.e. additions and omissions that have occurred in the course of a transnational transfer.

Scholars in comparative education research are used to keeping a close eye on developments and debates in different parts of the world. It is striking, however, how many concepts in multicultural and anti-racist education refer to debates that emerged in other countries. For instance, the demand to move away from cultural enrichment concepts and turn to educational concepts that combat structural discrimination emerged first in England in the early 1980s. A similar demand then surfaced in Canada and Australia in the late 1980s and on mainland Europe in the early 1990s (Steiner-Khamsi 1990, 1992). Identifying the process of 'borrowing', in this case the adoption of anti-racist education concepts by education researchers and practition, is meaningful for three reasons:

Firstly, it allows us to specify the geographic origin of a debate, and then to map the direction of the transnational flow of one specific debate, from its geographic source to other national contexts. Almost all debates in educational theory and practice emerge either in Europe and flow to North America, or the other way round. The transnational discourse on postmodern theory, for instance, moved from Europe to the United States, and from there, the politicized version of postmodernism moved back again to Europe (Huyssen 1990). Another example of this heavy transatlantic traffic is the transnational flow of the decentralization and privatization movement in formal education. These movements, emanating from debates regarding 'choice' and 'excellency in education' (Clune and Witte 1990), emerged in the United States during the Reagan administration and were subsequently borrowed by policy makers in England during the Thatcher administration (Flude and Hammer 1990). They are being discussed at length in continental Europe in the mid 1990s, at a time when European states have chosen to drastically cut down on public expenditures. To our knowledge, the only discourse in education which did not originate in Europe or North America, has been Freirean pedagogy. It would greatly contribute to comparative studies on educational discourse to examine exactly how and why Paulo Freire's work, developed in Latin America and Africa, has found fertile grounds in North America and Europe.

There are several conditions that account for the inequity of research production and dissemination. Sociologists of education oriented towards Dependency Theory and World-Systems Theory have discussed at length the reasons for the accumulation and control of knowledge in highly industrialized nations of the western hemisphere (see Featherstone 1990). Bourdieu (1979), for instance, uses the concept of cultural capital to explain how one body of knowledge, based on specific middle-class values, becomes framed as general knowledge or 'official knowledge' (Apple 1993), i.e. knowledge about everything and for everyone, will subsequently gain prevalence and global dissemination. More importantly for our international framework of study, we need to acknowledge that cultural capital is embedded in an economy of cultures and languages. As a result native speakers of certain languages (English, French) have easier access to publishing companies than others, and hence, are more likely to contribute to the production of what is generally viewed as cultural capital.

Secondly, it is meaningful to map the transnational flow of debates and discourses in order to obtain a clearer picture of where exactly an educational concept, or an idea, is circulating. Verbalizing intergroup and interpersonal tensions in terms of inter-ethnic and racial conflicts is such an idea that has circulated widely. It was meant to replace traditional multi-cultural education concepts which were criticized for emphasizing commonalities and mutual cultural enrichment. In contrast, not verbalizing racial and inter-ethnic conflicts directly, but working instead with underlying images and symbols of racism and anti-semitism is another (fascinating) idea that Cohen has developed and adopted for educational practice (1991, 1992, see also Cohen and Bains 1988). Again, this second idea has found considerable resonance in continental Europe. On closer examination, we can see that new ideas and educational concepts draw concentric circles around the North American, European, and Australian continents. It is only when these ideas become out-dated and are dismissed in these highly industrialized parts of the world that they are usually handed over to the rest of the world. It is not surprising that the speed with which new debates in any one particular field are emerging, circulating and then fading away is constantly accelerating. Wallerstein views this preference for 'newness' as a consequence of capitalism's requirement for movement and change (1990: 36ff). He relates his observation to the 'conditio sine qua non' of capitalism: capitalism's urge to believe in inevitable progress. Being innovative in capitalism means being powerful. Conversely, cultural hegemony in the modern world-system is based on the ability to constantly innovate.

The third purpose of mapping transnational discourses is to understand the diversity of national settings by examining how changes that have occurred in the course of a borrowing process have become crystallized in ideas and concepts. When educational researchers, youth workers, or practitioners, adopt or borrow ideas that were developed elsewhere, they drop certain aspects or add their own conceptions and ideas according to the context in which they are operating. The concept of anti-racist education has changed drastically over time and it has taken on different meanings in different geographical locations. Hence, it is very informative to trace this modification process in order to understand what is going on in any one specific context. To make matters more complex it needs to be said that every idea and concept is contested, and that there is within each national context a multitude of contending concepts. Having highlighted the fact that there is always a pool of ideas and concepts, it becomes crucial to identify which ones have found resonance, and which ones went unnoticed outside their original national context.

Strategies of multicultural and anti-racist youth work

In this preliminary study, we focus on the literature produced in Great Britain, Germany and the United States. Hamburger names three educational strategies that have been applied by practitioners of multicultural education in Germany (1995: 33ff.). One is to highlight difference and to adopt education programs that promote tolerance of difference. The second is to highlight commonalities and to create a general sense of belonging. The third strategy is to promote an ethic of justice, equality, and equivalence without emphasizing either difference or commonality. The third strategy, which he favours, and to which we also adhere, differs considerably from the first two strategies. The third strategy addresses young people as individuals and not as representatives of a specific nationality, ethnicity, or 'race'.

Our assessment of various anti-racist education and training programs in different countries leads us to suggest that anti-racist youth work has mainly adopted the first and second strategies. However, they still differ substantially from former multi-cultural concepts that were based on a harmonious model of cultural enrichment and mutual understanding. Instead of enforcing inter-ethnic and inter-racial harmony, anti-racist training programs now centre on notions of conflict, power, exploitation, structural discrimination (Gaine 1988) and, in some more psychologically oriented programs also on 'white' guilt (see Sivanandan 1985, Steiner-Khamsi 1992).

On a broader level, however, there are striking similarities between the two concepts. The prevailing critique of anti-racist education concepts uses arguments which were formerly levelled at traditional multicultural education projects. However, the most serious charge to which neither the proponents of multicultural education nor of anti-racist education have been capable of responding satisfactorily is the charge of being essentialist. It is argued that both multicultural and anti-racist education perpetuate the myth that ethnicity and 'race' are fixed categories and that this tends to reduce the multiple self-representations and identities of individuals to manifestations of ethnicity and 'race'. Rather than dismantling ethnicity and 'race' as constructs that are, more often than not, used to legitimize inequality and exclusion, multiculturalists and anti-racists view these social and political constructions as essential and biological categorizations. This supposedly determines the social position of individuals, often in a very simplified binary way: either exploiter or exploited, oppressor or oppressed, majority or minority, native or ethnic, black or white.

This charge of essentialism has been expressed in the relevant literature of the three countries we have been scrutinizing. In Germany, Radtke (1992), Bommes (Bommes and Radtke 1993) and Bukow and Llaroya (1988) were among the first to analyze inequity and segregational programs in schools that resulted from insisting upon cultural difference and ethnic identity. In Germany, an extensive process of critical self-reflection among multiculturalists resulted in the demand to depart from essentialism (Steiner-Khamsi 1992).

Similarly, advocates of multiculturalist and anti-racist education in Britain have been engaged for quite a while in critical self-reflection. Proponents of a non-essentialist perspective include scholars at the University of Warwick (e.g., Troyna, Rex), at the University of London's Institute of Education (Centre for Multicultural Education, Gundara, Cohen), and internationally renowned scholars in cultural studies (e.g., Hall). The volume "Race', Culture and Difference', edited by Donald and Rattansi (1992), compiles several contributions by authors based in Britain that deal with multicultural and anti-racist education from a non-essentialist perspective.

In contrast to Germany and Britain, multicultural education research in the United States has only started to combat essentialist notions of multicultural education in the 1990s. Originally, this departure from essentialist notions of intergroup relations was mainly informed by academic debates on essentialism, universalism/particularism, and difference in the humanities and feminist theory. It emerged to a much lesser extent from critical self-reflection within the education research community. Lately, however, an increasing number of American scholars in multicultural education have chosen to pursue a non-essentialist perspective on multicultural education. The volumes edited by McCarthy and Crichlow (1993), Heath and McLaughlin (1993), and Hawley and Jackson (1995), contain contributions reflecting a non-essentialist perspective on multicultural education.

In this preliminary study we do not analyze the common sources for the paradigm shift in multicultural and anti-racist education. Other publications analyze the process of critical self-reflection and scrutinize the impulses that the field received from ongoing debates in other academic disciplines (Steiner-Khamsi 1995, 1996). Instead, we would like to use our literature review to trace the transnational flow of three critical issues that seem to hold the key for a more thorough understanding of anti-racist youth work: firstly, 'othering' and racialization; secondly, difference and identity; thirdly, relational and oppositional identity.

'Othering' and racialization

Does the emphasis on ethnicity and 'race' in anti-racist youth work help adolescents to formulate a counter-discourse to the racist discourse in society? Or, on the contrary, does it support racialization processes which we can observe in the United States (Omi and Winant 1986), Britain (Miles 1990) and in Germany (Dittrich and Radtke 1990, Radtke 1995)? More importantly, does such an emphasis merely reinforce the division between 'them' and 'us' along lines of ethnicity and 'race'?

Some authors prefer to use the term 'alterity' (French: *alterité*, Italian: *alterità*, German: *Alterität*) instead of 'otherness'. However, authors in these different countries use a similar analysis to depict the process of 'othering'. In describing the process of 'othering' many authors have argued in a manner similar to Memmi (1992) who outlines the tripartite construction of racism as follows. First, (cultural and racial) differences between individuals of two different ethnic or racial groups are emphasized and highlighted (e.g., educated – non educated, urban – rural). These differences are then semantically framed in a hierarchical structure (educated, urban, etc. means 'civilized', 'modern', whereas non-educated, rural, etc. means 'uncivilized', 'barbarian'). In a third step these value judgements are used to essentialize ('they have always been like this'), to generalize ('they all look the same'), and ultimately to legitimate unequal distributions of power.

Difference and identity

It is important to recognize the basic assumption that identity is always based on the perception of individual difference, and, moreover, to recognize findings in developmental psychology that suggest that the search for sexual, professional, and political identities, are key themes during the phase of adolescence. However, the question anti-racist youth workers really need to come to terms with is the following: Do we want to offer, or reinforce, cultural and racial categories for the identity-formation process during adolescence?

There is a striking inconsistency in the way adults react to identity choices of adolescents. Adults tend to take the slightest manifestations of ethnic and racial identity among youth very seriously and expect them to last for the entire life span. Other manifestations of identity choices, such as professional and policical preferences, are generally viewed as transitory. At stake is the question, For what purposes do adults see ethnic and racial self-representations of adolescents as immutable?

At this poont, we cannot present different kinds of explanations and answers to this question in a conclusive manner. One plausible answer, however, relates to ethnic and race relations as a societal concern. It is a commonly held belief that ethnic and racial identity contribute more than any other form of self-representation to social cohesion or social disruption in society. It is interesting to note here that sociologists and educators in Germany have only turned their attention to white or German identity after German unification, at a time when Germany was hit by an outburst of increased racism, neo-fascism, and anti-semitism. In the early 1990s, several authors suggested that this outburst of racism should be viewed within the context of an overall national identity crisis in Germany. According to these authors (Heitmeyer 1992, Heitmeyer *et al* 1992, Krafeld *et al* 1993, Eisenberg and Gronemeyer 1993, see also criticism by Leiprecht 1993), adolescents from former East Germany were bound to be afflicted by a major identity crisis as they experienced the economic and social disadvantages of unification more acutely than other German groups. They perceived themselves as second-class Germans, losing out in the process of modernization (German: *Modernitätsverlierer*) and losing their jobs as a result of unification. Their racism towards immigrants and asylum-seekers was interpreted as a demonstration of newly-awakened Germanness, i.e., as an attempt to cut non-Germans off from rights and resources in order to demonstrate that everything on the unified German territory belonged rightfully and exclusively to Germans only. These studies suggest that this act of exclusion by male German adolescents, often very brutal and violent, is closely linked to their urge to reconstitute a sense of ethnic identity as Germans. Being racist and acting in an exclusive manner allowed them to regain a sense of collective identity and helped them to constitute a functional in-group with common values (machismo, German supremacy, etc.). We find these studies worth considering since they draw on a relational concept of identity formation in which acts of exclusion are viewed as a means to generate a sense of social identity, belonging, or inclusion.

From a comparative perspective, however, this body of research, which treats the cohesion and identity creating effects of exclusion as a basis for explaining racism (German: *identitätsstiftende Wirkung von Ausgrenzung*), is fundamentally flawed. It disregards the structural racial features of Germany and those of other countries where ethnicity, nationality and 'race' permeate every social interaction. In addition, they neglect the fact that ethnicity, nationality and 'race' had already been in place as lines of division before unification and hence could be readily activated as markers for both exclusion and inclusion.

Oppositional and relational identities

Ogbu presents a series of interesting comparative and ethnographic studies (Ogbu 1987, 1991, 1995) in which he introduces the concept of 'oppositional identity'. He uses this concept to explain why academic achievements of one ethnic group vary considerably depending upon the national setting. He shows that minorities are performing academically better in countries where they have the status of an immigrant minority than in countries where they are involuntary minorities. Ogbu refers to the fact that West Indian children are the least successful in Britain, where they are seen as citizens of a former colony, whereas they are academically most successful in the United States where they are one immigrant group among others. In Canada, where they are identified as part of the Commonwealth, they score in the middle ranges.

Ogbu identified a series of survival strategies that children of involuntary minorities develop to resist assimilation of values that are associated with whites. To survive socially among their peers they choose to develop an oppositional cultural frame of reference and identity which can become detrimental in a school setting and other learning contexts. Referring to his ethnographic study in Stockton, California, (Ogbu 1991: 27) he writes: "It follows that involuntary minority students who adopt attitudes conducive to school success are often accused by their peers of acting like their enemy, i.e. like their 'oppressors'. Among U.S. blacks, such students may be accused of acting white or acting like Uncle Toms. They are accused of being disloyal to the group and to the cause of the group, and they risk being isolated from their peers."

For several reasons, Ogbu's work seems relevant for

intergroup youth work. First of all, he studies in depth how adolescents actively reproduce a cultural frame of reference and an identity that helps them to survive in a racialized society. Secondly, his research perspective reflects the relational nature of identity formation processes. He shows that in a racialized society, adolescents constantly use ethnicity and 'race' as identity markers. Thirdly, he demonstrates the severe limitation of adult interventions, a potential cause for reinforcing oppositional identity, and points out, instead, the strength of peer influence.

Ogbu's work, and the studies of other authors reviewed so far, suggests that anti-racist and intergroup youth workers should de-emphasize and de-essentialize ethnic and race relations, and instead develop innovative ways that allow adolescents to drop ethnicity and 'race' as the main cultural frame of reference. This approach differs fundamentally from both a 'colour-blind' perspective and from other apolitical approaches, since it acknowledges the fact that ethnicity, nationality and 'race' are powerful markers that are used to legitimate inequity. We doubt, however, that anti-racist education practices which adopt and perpetuate existing racialization patterns will allow adolescents to develop empowering cultural frames of reference that can reach beyond existing distinctions of ethnicity, nationality, and 'race'.

From intergroup to interpersonal conflicts

Having so far outlined the three major challenges to traditional anti-racist youth work, we now turn our attention to the key question that addresses every form of intergroup approach: What makes us believe that framing a conflict in terms of an ethnic and racial intergroup conflict is more efficient than dealing with these conflicts as interpersonal conflicts?

Evaluation and research studies dealing with intergroup conflict resolution programs suggest that the long-term outcomes and the efficacy of programs that focus specifically and exclusively on ethnicity and 'race' are indeed minimal. We would like to confine ourselves here to a study that has been carried out by Casparis (*Eidgenössische Jugendkommission* 1992). Casparis evaluated the short-term and long-term effects of a program that aimed at improving intergroup relations by explicitly addressing ethnic and racial tensions. The group on which he focused his study consisted of white and black Swiss adolescents, young immigrants, and two white Swiss adolescents who identified themselves as 'Skins' (skinheads). The two 'Skins' had been previously accused of trespassing on a Brazilian party and of engaging in acts of racism, violence, and vandalism. The organizers of the event withdrew their charges on the condition that the two 'Skins' participate in a multi-ethnic and multi-racial group that discusses ethnic and racial conflicts. Two researchers took part in these sessions as participant observers. They documented how the two 'Skins' actively engaged, shared their views and experiences on race relations, and seemed to come to grips seriously with their past racist actions. Moreover, in the course of the ten sessions, the two 'Skins' developed close friendships with other members of the group across lines of ethnicity and 'race'. However, the program did not succeed in having any long-term or generalized effects whatsoever. Already during the program, the 'Skins' began to frame the immigrants and blacks of the group they were beginning to form friendships with, as 'special cases' and as 'atypical' of immigrants and blacks in general.

Conflict resolution and peer mediation programs

In this second part we present a new approach that aims at improving intergroup relations without focusing explicitly on 'race', nationality, or ethnicity.

Since the early 1990s, a new approach to learning social responsibility, conflict resolution, and conflict mediation has been developed and implemented in numerous inner city high schools in the United States. One such program is Project SMART. Project SMART, which has been adopted in many New York City high schools, is a peer mediation program designed to help students, staff and families resolve disputes and disagreements through mediation. The project is usually staffed by an adult coordinator and 25 trained high school students. In Project SMART mediators help individuals involved in disputes to identify, discuss, and resolve their differences through negotiation and compromise. Programs such as SMART assist students in developing conflict resolution and other mediation skills which are critical in communities with diverse needs and perspectives.

In the past, conflict resolution programs were introduced into schools when relationships between students reached the point of violence. Gradually, these programs moved away from a reductionist approach that focused on violence. Instead, they began to emphasize negotiation and mediation skills in order to prevent conflicts from heating up and the need to have more long-term effects on peer relations. This violence prevention, or crisis management approach, was combined with training that focused upon the constructive aspects of conflicts by teaching long-term positive resolution methods and problem-solving strategies in a non-labeling and non-moralizing way. Thus, peer mediation programs such as Project SMART, that emphasize conflict resolution, negotiation, and mediation, have enabled students to negotiate intergroup and inter-racial conflicts and to develop meaningful long-term relationships across lines of ethnicity and 'race'. The executive director of the National Association for Mediation in Education (NAME) estimates that 5,000 schools in the United States now have peer mediation and/or conflict resolution programs (Raider 1994).

Whilst violence prevention training teaches students to identify and disengage from potentially life-threatening situations and to deal productively with anger, negotiation and mediation skills training goes further because it empowers students to know that they can handle conflict through positive means. According to Raider, Training Director of the International Center for Cooperation and Conflict Resolution at Teachers College, Columbia University (ICCCR), "conflict resolution and peer mediation training teaches students how to discuss feelings, communicate openly with each other, and make practical group decisions. They learn how to compromise, apologize, mete out fair punishment, and forgive each other" (Raider 1994: 6).

Pedagogical practices for conflict resolution and peer mediation

Peer mediation and conflict resolution training aims to develop social skills, e.g. communicating, perspective-taking, social problem-solving, finding common ground, and sharing through student-directed learning situations. An emerging body of research is beginning to identify those practices and conditions in schools that enable all students to succeed (Lee, Bryk and Smith 1993, Darling-Hammond, Ancess and Falk 1995, Lucas, Henze and Donato 1990, Meier 1995, Newman, Marks and Gamoran 1995). These studies concur that personalised, caring, learner-centre schools that provide challenging and authentic curricula and multiple opportunities to learn in diverse ways, increases the students' chances of achieving higher performance standards. As Fine (1991) has illustrated, teachers in inner city public schools in the United States are reluctant to discuss issues such as racism, sexism, heterosexism, and class domination because they fear they will create more intergroup tension among students. In contrast to more traditional approaches, where teachers structure discussions and address racial and ethnic issues directly, often in a very moralizing way, these new programs have chosen a new approach. Central to this new approach is the notion that conflict resolution is most efficient when it is moderated by peers and not by adult facilitators. These peer-directed strategies provide a structure and opportunity for adolescents to engage in meaningful discussions with each other in a non-moralistic and non-threatening way.

Whilst there is an emphasis on violence prevention and the process of negotiation, these programs also address 'group process skills' and working together effectively in cooperation learning situations. Role play, group activities and discussion groups are utilized as practical applications of negotiation skills to the students' lives at home, and in school, community and work settings.

Students have the opportunity to practice mediation skills by facilitating constructive conflict resolution. By helping others they can reinforce their desire to apply these newly acquired skills to their own conflicts. These skills lead to an improvement of those social skills which facilitate positive intergroup relations. According to Deutsch (1993: 3) "the increased positiveness of the student's social environment toward him/her would, in turn, lead to greater self-esteem as well as more frequent positive mental states (e.g., 'cheerfulness', 'life is interesting') and less frequent negative mental states (e.g., 'upset', 'tense', 'depressed')." As the students' self-esteem increases and their social environment becomes more positive, students gain a greater sense of control over what happens to them.

Methods for teaching conflict resolution

Conflict resolution training methods range along a continuum from those using lectures and discussions to more experimental types. Methods include role play, simulation exercises, cooperative reading, discussions, practice dyads, controlled space, 'fishbowl' (where an inner circle of participants are observed by an outer circle), negotiations with trainer feedback, questionnaires, readings, lectures, demonstrations, performance of what has been learned, journal writing, and video/audio tape recording of role plays.

Mediation training for students consists of 10-15 hours of initial concept and skills training with subsequent follow-up supervision as they begin to mediate. For instance, ICCCR's training teaches students the steps of mediation including: setting the ground rules, hearing each disputant's perspective, helping disputants walk in each other's shoes (perspective-taking), brainstorming solutions, and writing the resolution contract. While an adult coordinator is always within reach, the students conduct mediations themselves, either singly or in pairs.

Learning objectives of peer mediation programs

Peer mediation programs emphasize the following learning objectives: knowledge, skills, and attitudes. Knowledge objectives are designed to give students new information about the components of negotiation and conflict resolution. These may include: the ability to identify the difference between cooperative and competitive negotiations, identify the difference between needs and positions, identify five conflict resolution behavioural styles, or discuss how culture can impact upon the negotiation process. Skills include: active listening, asking open-ended questions to probe for underlying needs, reframing conflicting interests into a joint problem to be solved, diffusing anger. Attitude examples might include: valuing cooperation, appreciating and respecting cultural difference in conflict resolution styles, attention to tendencies toward bias, misperceptions, misjudgments, and stereotypical thinking commonly occurring during heated conflicts.

Integrating conflict resolution into the curriculum

Some schools and districts have brought conflict resolution into the curriculum either as a stand-alone course or as units within existing programs. The International Center for Cooperation and Conflict Resolution, Children's Creative Response to Conflict, Educators for Social Responsibility, The Community Board, and Johnson and Johnson Inc., to name only a few, have developed curriculum and training programs which have been widely implemented in public schools in New York City and across the United States.

These curricula provide lessons and activities grouped under such themes as: understanding conflict, communications, dealing with anger, cooperation, affirmation, bias awareness, cultural diversity, conflict resolution, and peacemaking. Besides offering an innovative contribution to improving intergroup relations among youth, peer mediation and conflict resolution programs have applications in broader aspects of school change. In fact, it is imperative that these fundamental changes in students' abilities to handle conflict and reduce the risk of violence go hand in hand with efforts towards change in the culture of schools. The literature on school improvement in the United States provides plenty of evidence of the difficulty in changing school culture to meet the needs of its increasingly diverse populations. One of the major obstacles inhibiting successful school reform is interpersonal and intergroup conflict (Lieberman 1991). Such restructuring efforts will not have the intended impact on fundamental system changes without specific training in cooperative conflict resolution and problem solving.

Significance for anti-racist youth work

Because of its relative newness, little research had been conducted on the long-term effects of training in peer mediation or conflict resolution, although initial studies indicate that there are positive effects on students (Johnson and Johnson 1989, Deutsch 1993, Lam 1989). These data show that as students improved in managing their conflicts, they experienced increased social support and less victimization from others.

Social skills can be seen as learned behaviour that individuals use in interpersonal situations to find common ground. By focusing on interpersonal or social skills, adolescents learn to situate intergroup conflicts within a wider context. These programs help to support adolescents to develop identities that are not exclusively based on a process of in-group and out-group distinctions along racial, national, and ethnic lines.

Moreover, through peer mediation, adolescents are exposed to situations where they come to realize that their ethnic, national, or racial self-representations and alliances within the peer-group vary, depending upon situation and context. In contrast to traditional anti-racist youth work, peer mediation and conflict resolution programs do not force adolescents into taking sides because they de-emphasize polarization, essentialism, and labeling. Instead, these programs allow adolescents to experience how their identity is, in fact, a product of relationships and therefore always relational and situative. Furthermore, the renunciation of a moralistic and value-driven setting imposed by adults empowers adolescents to engage in forms of self-representation that are not reactive or oppositional.

Thus, peer mediation and conflict resolution programs can prove to be a viable alternative to traditional anti-racist youth work. These strategies transcend the critical issues of anti-racist youth work that were discussed earlier in 'Othering' and Racialization, Difference and Identity, and Relational and Oppositional Identity.

References

Apple, M. (1993), Official Knowledge. New York: Routledge

Bommes, M. and Radtke, F.-O. (1993), Institutionalisierte Diskriminierung von Migrantenkindern. Zeitschrift für Pädagogik, 39/5, 483-497

Bourdieu, P. (1979), Outline of a Theory of Practice. Cambridge: Cambridge University Press

Brice Heath, S. and McLaughlin, M. W. (ed.) (1993), Identity and Inner-City Youth: Beyond Ethnicity and Gender. New York: Teachers College Press

Bukow, W.-D. and Llaroya, R. (1988), Mitbürger aus der Fremde. Opladen: Westdeutscher Verlag

Clune, W. H. and Witte, J. F. (eds.) (1990), Choice and Control in American Education. Volumes 1 and 2. London, New York, Philadelphia: Falmer Press

Cohen, P. (1991), Monstrous Images, Perverse Reasons. London: University of London Institute of Education, Centre for Multicultural Education

Cohen, P. (1992), 'It's racism what dunnit': hidden narratives in theories of racism. In: J. Donald and A. Rattansi (ed.): 'Race', Culture and Difference. London: Sage and The Open University, 62-103

Cohen, P. and Bains, H. S. (eds.) (1988), Multi-racist Britain. London: Macmillan

Darling-Hammond, L., Ancess, J. and Falk, B. (1995), Authentic Assessment in Action: studies of schools and students at work. New York: Teachers College Press

Deutsch, M. (1993), Conflict Resolution and Cooperative Learning in an Alternative High School. Cooperative Learning, 13/4, 2-5

Deutsch, M. (1973), The Revolution of Conflict: Constructive and Destructive Processes. New Haven: Yale University Press

Dittrich, E. J. and Radtke, F.-O. (1990), Der Beitrag der Wissenschaften zur Konstruktion ethnischer Minderheiten. In: E. J. Dittrich and F.-O. Radtke (Hrsg.): Ethnizität. Wissenschaft und Minderheiten. Opladen: Westdeutscher Verlag, 11-40

Donald, J. and Rattansi, A. (eds.) (1992), 'Race', Culture and Difference. London: Sage and The Open University

Eidgenössische Jugendkommission (1992), Bericht der eidgenössischen Jugendkommission. Auszug Kapitel 2.5.: Erklärungsversuch für rassistisches Verhalten Jugendlicher. Bern: EDMZ, 39-52

Eisenberg, G. and Gronemeyer, R. (1993), Jugend und Gewalt. Der neue Generationenkonflikt oder Der Zerfall der zivilien Gesellschaft. Reinbek bei Hamburg: Rowohlt

Featherstone, M. (ed.) (1990), Global Culture. Nationalism, Globalization and Modernity. London, Newbury Park, New Delhi: Sage

Fine, M. (1991), Framing Dropouts: Notes on the politics of an urban public high school. Albany: State University of New York Press

Flude, M. and Hammer, M. (1990), The Education Reform Act 1988. Its Origins and Implications. London, New York, Philadelphia: Falmer Press

Gaine, C. (1988), No Problem Here. A practical approach to education and 'race' in white schools. London: Hutchinson (first print 1987)

Hall, S. (1992), The West and the rest. In: S. Hall and B. Gieben (eds.): Formations of Modernity. Cambridge: Polity, 275-331

Hamburger, F. (1995), Pädagogik der Einwanderungsgesellschaft. Frankfurt: Cooperative

Hawley, W. D. and Jackson, A. W. (eds.) (1995), Toward a Common Destiny. Improving Race and Ethnic Relations in America. San Francisco: Jossey-Bass

Heitmeyer, W. (1992), Desintegration und Gewalt. Deutsche Jugend, 3, 109-122

Heitmeyer, W. et al. (1992), Die Bielefelder Rechtsextremismus-Studie – Erste Langzeituntersuchung zur politischen Sozialisation männlicher Jugendlicher. Weinheim/München: Juventus

Huyssen, A. (1990), Mapping the Postmodern. In: L. J. Nicholson (ed.): Feminism/Postmodernism. New York: Routledge, 234-277

Johnson, D. W. and Johnson, R. T. (1989), Cooperation and Competition: Theory and Research. Edina, MN: Interaction Book Company

Krafeld, F. J., Lutzebäck, E., Schaar, G., Storm, C., Welp, W. (1993), Akzeptierende Jugendarbeit mit rechtsextremen Jugendlichen. In: H. Heil, M. Perik and P.-U. Wendt (Hrsg.): Jugend und Gewalt. Ueber den Umgang mit gewaltbereiten Jugendlichen. Marburg: Schüren, 91-100

Lam, J. A. (1989), The Impact of Conflict Resolution Programs on Schools. A Review and Synthesis of the Evidence. Amherst: The University of Massachusetts (reprint)

Lee, V., Bryk A. S., and Smith, J. B. (1993), The organization of effective secondary schools. In Linda Darling-Hammond (ed.): Review of Research in Education, Volume 19. Washington, DC: AERA, 171-268

Leiprecht, R. (1993), Das Modell unmittelbare und/oder direkte Konkurrenz: Erklärung von Rechtsextremismus oder Rechtfertigungsangebot? Informationsdienst zur Ausländerarbeit, 1/2, 115-120

Lieberman, A., Darling-Hammond, L. and Zuckerman, D. (1991), Early Lessons in Restructuring Schools. New York: NCREST.

Lucas, T., Henze, R., and Donato, R. (1990), Promoting the success of Latino language-minority students: An exploratory study of six high schools. Harverd Educational Review, 60, 3, 315-340

McCarthy, C. and Crichlow, W. (eds.) (1993), Race, Identity and Representation in Education. New York: Routledge

Meier, D. (1995), The power of their ideas: lessons for America from a small school in Harlem. Boston: Beacon Press

Miles, R. (1990), Racism. London: Routledge

Memmi, A. (1992), The Colonizer and the Colonized. Boston: Beacon (reprint)

Mohanty, C. T. (1994), On Race and Voice: Challenges for Liberal Education in the 1990s. In: H. A. Giroux and P. McLaren (eds.): Between Borders, Pedagogy and the Politics of Cultural Studies. New York: Routledge, 145-166

Ogbu, J. (1987), Variability in Minority School Performance: A Problem in Search of an Explanation. Anthropology and Education Quarterly, 18, 312-334

Ogbu, J. (1991), Immigrant and Involuntary Minorities in Comparative Perspectives. In: M. Gibson and J. Ogbu (eds.): Minority Status and Schooling. New York: Garland, 3-33

Ogbu, J. (1995), Understanding Cultural Diversity and Learning. In: J. A. Banks and C. A. McGee Banks (eds.): Handbook of Multicultural Education. New York: Macmillan, 582-593

Omi, M. and Winant, H.; (1986), Racial Formation in the United States: From the 1960s to the 1980s. New York: Routledge

Paulston, R. G. (1993), Mapping Discourse in Comparative Education Text. Compare, 23/2, 101-114

Radtke, F.-O. (1992), Multikulturalismus und Erziehung: Ein erziehungswissenschaftlicher Versuch über die Behauptung: 'Wir leben in einer multikulturellen Gesellschaft'. In: R. Baehler and P. Dudek (Hrsg.): Fremde – Heimat. Frankfurt/M: Verlag für interkulturelle Kommunikation, 185-208

Radtke, F.-O. (1995), Demokratische Diskriminierung. Exklusion als Bedürfnis oder nach Bedarf. Mittelweg, 36/1, 32-48

Raider, E. (1994), Conflict Resolution Training in Schools: The Challenge and the Promise. In: B. Bunker and J. Rubin (eds.): Conflict, Cooperation and Justice. New York: Jossey-Bass

Sivanandan, A. (1985), RAT and the Degradation of Black Struggle. Race and Class, 26/4, 1-34.

Steiner-Khamsi, G. (1990), Community Languages and Anti-racist Education: the open battlefield. Educational Studies, 16/1, 33-47

Steiner-Khamsi, G. (1992), Bildungspolitik in der Postmoderne. Opladen: Leske and Budrich

Steiner-Khamsi, G. (1995), Attraversamento delle frontiere nel lavoro antirazzista con i giovani. In: A. Aluffi Pentini and W. Lorenz (a cura di): Per una pedagogia antirazzista. Teorie e strumenti in prospettiva europea. Bergamo: Edizioni Junior, 123-146

Steiner-Khamsi, G. (1996), Transnationalität und kulturelle Staatsbürgerschaft. In: G. Auernheimer and P. Gstettner (Hrsg.): Jahrbuch Pädagogik. Frankfurt: Cooperative Verlag, forthcoming

Wallerstein, I. (1990), Culture as the Ideological Battleground of the Modern World-System. In: M. Featherstone (ed.): Global Culture. Nationalism, Globalization and Modernity. London, Newbury Park, New Delhi: Sage, 31-55

3. The specific and complementary nature of inter-cultural and anti-racist pedagogical approaches

Anna Aluffi-Pentini

This chapter has two basic aims. The first is to demonstrate the necessity of viewing the approaches of 'inter-cultural education' and 'anti-racist education' [1] as being complementary to one another. The second aim is to argue that both these approaches are a means of putting into practice fundamental pedagogical principles in the conditions of modern multi-cultural societies. These principles have always been based on universal values such as respect for fellow human beings, and the dignity and uniqueness of the individual throughout life.

In Italy, the concept of 'inter-cultural education' (Demetrio 1990; Demetrio and Favaro 1992; Durino and Allegra 1993; Poletti 1992) is used in preference to the concept of 'anti-racist education' (Giustinelli 1991). This reflects the belief amongst educators that to know and to value another culture is quite sufficient as a means of preventing intolerance and discrimination amongst school pupils. Although the interests of teachers for inter-cultural themes and their readiness to deal with other cultures in the classroom favour the integration of a child from a foreign background into the Italian education system, this alone does not necessarily prevent the development and spread of racist attitudes. When I wrote on this topic in an Italian publication (Aluffi-Pentini 1995) and placed the emphasis on anti-racist education as a distinct and necessary measure complementary to the inter-cultural

approach it was considered quite provocative. It had indeed
been my intention to challenge a prevailing consensus which
refuses to look at the stark political reality that surrounds
education. In the present context I intend however to re-affirm
the importance of inter-cultural education and to emphasise
the complementary and circular nature of the relationship
between anti-racist and inter-cultural approaches. In doing so,
I am assuming that this is being read in contexts where anti-
racist principles are considered to be more 'advanced' than,
and therefore superior to, inter-cultural education; so much so
that the concept of the latter may appear to be obsolete. The
analysis of the Italian experience as an example of where the
complementary nature of the two approaches has proved
useful (despite their uncoordinated introduction) will add new
dimensions to the debate.

Inter-cultural education in Italy

It is worth remembering that Italy has only recently become a
destination of immigrants. It has traditionally been a country
of emigration and of internal migration from the south to the
north. In those countries with a far older tradition and
experience of immigration, the educational debate has passed
through several phases: from integration programmes to multi-
cultural, inter-cultural and eventually anti-racist approaches,
with each phase building on the functional inadequacy and the
political critique of the previous one (Todd 1991). Pedagogues
in Italy have only recently started to face the issue of the
enrolment of children with a foreign background within the
Italian school system. The tasks arising from this are being
discussed under the heading of 'inter-cultural education', with
conscious reference to similar concepts that have been
developed in other countries. But in reality, the Italian inter-
cultural school programmes are often technically less well-
developed than their foreign counterparts such as, for
example, the German *Ausländerpädagogik* ('pedagogy for
foreign children') of the 1960s and 70s which had amounted to
a very comprehensive and systematic programme
(Auernheimer 1990). In Italy, there are still no special
language courses for non-Italian pupils and neither can they
continue learning their mother tongue at school. On the other
hand, children from a foreign background are immediately
placed in the age-appropriate school class. This means, at least
superficially, that there is no segregation. Within two or three
months they generally show good comprehension of the Italian

language and have learned to express themselves fairly well. Schools offer a first and unconditional welcome and pupils are automatically admitted to the year following the one which they had last attended in their country of origin regardless of their knowledge of the Italian language. This practice proves positive in the sense that a child makes good social contacts within a short period of time, but it is too early to assess its long term impact on the young person's growth and development [2].

In terms of daily contacts between non-Italian children and their parents with the school much depends on the good will of the teachers and on the natural communicative ability of fellow pupils. Individual teachers are given scope to develop their own initiatives. It is in this spontaneous way that the concept of inter-cultural education began to spread and to sensitize many of them to the needs of pupils from abroad. This has had paradoxical consequences. Well-meaning gestures have resulted in highly inappropriate practices which have yet to be publicly exposed. At the same time, it has also led to successful experiences of integration in multi-cultural classroom settings and to good educational results. The copious documentation produced by the Ministry of Education in recent years (*Ministero della Pubblica Istruzione* 1992; Annali *MPI* 1995) reflects this and demonstrates that amidst the numerous contradictions there are undoubted improvements.

Italy and anti-racist education

When the topic of racism is discussed in Italian schools it usually refers only to the world of adults. The struggle against racism is not generally introduced at the level of everyday classroom realities and of peer relations, where everything is seen as a matter of cultural differences. The history of every country produces its own particular forms of intolerance. Until about 20 years ago Italians, within the context of their European neighbours, saw themselves as victims of discrimination, (for instance as *Gastarbeiter* in Germany or in the treatment of them by tourists), rather than as perpetrators. This collective memory remains alive in the thoughts and sentiments of ordinary people, particularly in the south of Italy. During the same years people in the north of Italy discriminated against migrant labourers from the south, subjecting them to similar stereotypical prejudices and discriminatory work practices as Italians experienced abroad.

Today, the majority of southern Italians living in the north are perfectly well-integrated in the workplace and have no intention of returning to the south. However, they share the same prejudices against the south although they continue to maintain contacts with the regions from where they came. This means that the phenomenon of 'localism' and 'regionalism' and indeed of the *Lega*, (the political parties advocating regional separation and politics of self-interests in Italy), are relatively popular politically. However, this does not actually correspond to the lived multiple identities of a whole section of the population of the north (Pileri, Schmidke and Ruzza 1993).

In the context of this historical experience Italians, until a few years ago, did not consider themselves as racist or, at least if they were, they did not talk about it openly (Balbo and Manconi 1990; Balbo 1995). After the recent electoral successes of the political rightwing the taboo covering all talk of racism has been shattered. The memories of emigration, of war, of nazism and of the extermination camps had contributed to this taboo and for many years public discourse on racial hatred and contempt was utterly impossible. Those who held racist beliefs had either to hide them or express them in very restricted circles. In the early 1990s a deep crisis occurred in Italian political life which can be attributed partly to the scandals and collapse of the Christian Democrats as the leading party of the post-war era and partly to the confusion within the disoriented political Left. This crisis paved the way for personalities and ideas which had previously and clearly been fascist and marginal to come into the political limelight, to re-constitute their political identity, and to legitimate themselves in the name of the moderate Right. In addition, the extreme Right in parliament has split away from the majority of the party of the Right. This has endorsed the reformed 'moderate' image of the majority part.

With these political shifts, and the opportunist nature of current politics, the question of immigration in Italy is not an issue on which politicians want to commit themselves. Consequently, the initiatives that have been put forward do not spell out a precise and comprehensive political programme. In this ambivalent situation intolerance against foreign people may find fertile ground and, in some cases, may even be given open and serious consideration as one of several possible options. These attitudes of rejection may also be seen as a reaction to the general climate of acceptance and of solidarity fostered, amongst others, by voluntary organisations and by the churches. The voluntary sector has come to play an ever more important role in giving practical assistance and in advocating the rights to dignity of immigrants in a situation where there are few official guidelines and responses to the pressing issues posed by immigration in Italy in the last decade.

It is, therefore, conceivable that incidents of scandalous protests against immigrant camps – shown often on television and during which 'ordinary citizens' shout slogans and utter racist threats – might attract popular support and suddenly become portrayed as culturally acceptable reactions. Changes at the cultural level in Italy are happening on a parallel with political changes. Racist incidents on a bus or in the street occur more frequently whilst the general public appear to acquiesce and be less prepared to intervene in defence of the victims of racism. Newspapers and journals pick up on these acts and report them as racist incidents. At the same time they maintain the overall belief that Italians are not racist. In the absence of serious and comprehensive political responses, the issue of immigration is treated mainly on an emotive level on both sides.

It is against this background that suggestions for anti-racist education are being resisted and perceived as an unhelpful exaggeration. I will give two brief examples. Firstly, I was asked to give an in-service seminar for teachers in a series of sessions on inter-cultural issues. When I suggested giving my contribution the title 'anti-racist education' I was reminded by the organisers that this was an inappropriate choice; if I wanted to deal with the issue I should at least call it something different so as not to alienate the participating teachers. Secondly, a dictionary on racism is in preparation. Despite being edited by experts in the field of immigration, the terms 'anti-racist pedagogy' and 'anti-racist education' will not be included. My insistence on the importance of introducing these terms was accepted provided that they were items subsumed under the heading of 'multi-cultural education'. This rejection was based on the assumption that the 'natural' forms of racism which we all carry in us in the form of a fear of what is different and 'external' can be driven out, merely by fostering an awareness of 'the other' framed in terms of cultural differences. This explains the success and persistence of the concept of inter-cultural education as an approach which, it is hoped, will bring about the transformation of society into a multi-cultural entity. Only occasionally is the issue of anti-racism raised within the discourse of multi-cultural education (Annali *MPI* 1995), but it lacks a focus on the specific merits of one or other approach.

Nevertheless, many critical observations have been made in Italy of an interpretation of inter-cultural education as compensatory education. In this context, compensatory education means an approach which is directed at individuals who are supposed to present specific deficits in relation to an assumed baseline of normality. In this sense 'special education' for children with learning difficulties is a form of compensatory education. This is similar to the concept of *Ausländerpädagogik* in Germany – an educational method designed to deal specifically with the 'difficulties' foreign children have at school. Indeed, the early educational programmes in Italy that sought to integrate immigrant children into the education system were, in effect, adaptations of the ideas that had been generated in the field of the education of children with learning difficulties. From the perspective of this logic, foreign children who do not speak Italian are presented as handicapped in relation to the other children, and require a whole branch of educational science dealing with their specific needs.

The differentiation of pedagogical disciplines like inter-cultural pedagogy and special pedagogy has undoubted benefits in as much as it creates a forum in which educational principles and programmes for specific situations may be developed. But this specialisation of fields runs the risk of implicitly reinforcing the uncritical concept of normality which in turn becomes the undisputed basis for 'ordinary' education. To put it provocatively: inter-cultural pedagogy is indeed compensatory, but compensatory only in relation to the shortcomings of a general pedagogy. This latter fails to realise its objectives when facing up to new challenges such as the presence of children from different cultural backgrounds in the same classroom. Compensatory strategies should not address 'deficits' in non-Italian children but those of the chosen educational methodology. The validity of any educational approach in my opinion should be measured against its capacity to deal appropriately with diversity; and wherever educational skills engage constructively in situations where diversity manifests itself, the benefits created will also accrue for pupils considered to be 'standard'.

I was able to confirm this latter point during my work in a multi-cultural pre-school in Rome where we observed children regularly over three years. We followed some of those children into primary school and it became evident that the multi-cultural orientation of the pre-school centre was of great benefit to all pupils and infinitely superior to the preparation given by the average Roman pre-school (Aluffi-Pentini and Talamo 1996).

In the light of these inadequacies, the whole field of 'general educational sciences' in Europe reveals itself implicitly as a mono-cultural, nation-state oriented project, taking the model of a 'Western Culture' for granted seeking merely to hand it on 'intact' to future generations of white, western and 'normal' children. As these underlying assumptions begin to crumble in European societies, the implications for general educational discourses are far-reaching. We have to start from a completely different set of principles. Inter-cultural pedagogy will inevitably assume a central role and we must ensure that it influences the thinking of all educators.

The return to fundamental educational objectives and their application in a multi-cultural reality

Having pointed out the limitations of a pragmatic approach to the challenges posed to education by a multi-cultural social reality, it becomes imperative to return to the question: What are the fundamental objectives of all education? There is a general consensus among educational scientists that the educational process is aimed at enabling learners to fully realise their potential. Education needs to take account of the particular requirements of each individual and strive to contribute to the physical and psychological well-being that is appropriate to their social environment. The educator must, therefore, accompany and sustain a process of identity formation in the learner that acknowledges both the special qualities and dignity of the individual and the equal value of each person in the face of all differences. This, in turn, will emphasise the importance of mutual respect.

The starting point of the educational process is, therefore, the postulate that the equal dignity of all individuals is the key criterion of the validity of any chosen method. Such high-

minded principles of the equal rights of each person are easy
enough to state, but the actual pedagogical task lies precisely in
the translation of this principle into practice. This can only
happen in conjunction with an examination of the wider social
task of education (see Lorenz in this volume). Education
cannot be expected to adhere to and to realise such goals,
when the prevailing economic and political conditions in
society militate against their realisation. It then also becomes
the task of pedagogical reflection to expose the factors which
impede education from doing its job properly, to make the
political agendas more transparent which impinge on
education, and to involve learners in the processes of change
that are needed to bring about an emancipatory process of
education.

This gives education a mandate to become involved in political
demands and struggles. A pedagogical starting point here
would be the task of providing an analysis of the extent and
operations of injustice. Or, it could mean critically sifting
through the types of information and knowledge spread by
governments, the media, and other powerful interest groups,
which violate the principle of the equal dignity of all people. In
this case, the educational task would be documenting and
demonstrating the relativity and subjectivity of the sources of
such information. School projects could analyze the language
used in official reports that deal with migrant workers, collect
newspaper articles on crime reporting, respond to distorting
surveys carried out on employment or housing and to point out
questions that have deliberately not been asked, etc.

In practical terms, recovering this fundamental educational
mandate requires efforts at two complementary levels. On the
one hand, learners must become aware of cultural and
individual differences in everyday situations and learn how to
cope with them more effectively. In this regard, inter-cultural
pedagogy has a distinct contribution to make. On the other
hand, these differences are linked to and influenced by major
issues of social inequality and of social conflict. Young people
need to gain access to these wider political processes,
understand the origins and the social construction of prejudice,
the nature of inequality and of power and how they impinge on
cultural differences, as they experience them daily. This task is
more explicitly developed within the anti-racist discourse.
Both levels are, however, intricately connected in the question
of identity formation: the central concern of education.

Identity may be conceptualised as the process of a gradual, never completed differentiation of the individual, during which various reference points condense around a personal nucleus. Pedagogy may correspondingly be seen as the facilitation of this process. Education creates the space in which individuals can reflect on their own place in society, in continual personal and social transformations which constitute growth. This process of 'continuity and change' may also be interpreted as a balancing of general human needs and personal, unique identity (Demtrio 1990). Whilst such general needs are common to all, and have to be addressed in general education as well as in inter-cultural education, it is nevertheless vital that there are spaces left within our complex societies, so that different identities may be explored in the encounter with 'others' who pose questions of identity from very different positions. It does not then matter whether 'the others' are strangers, or simply people who represent 'otherness' in a more general sense [3], because the encounter with 'difference' is vital for the formation of identity.

Seen from this angle, visible differences (such as skin colour or other physical characteristics) as well as other differences which emerge when personal experiences are openly exchanged amongst learners, become important elements in learning how to accept and value the specific characteristics of each person. The necessity of dealing with such differences may, therefore, become an indispensible basis for the educational process in its wider sense. This does not mean that diversity as such will automatically benefit the 'standard' participants or that having a member of a group who is visibly different will by itself enhance the learning of the group. A pedagogical approach must demonstrate its usefulness through the ability to deal with diversity, but particularly through those approaches aimed at fostering the development of non-exclusive forms of identity which take into account the actual complex and multi-dimensional nature of personal and collective identity (Marramao and Meghnagi 1993).

This means that one of the most important educational conditions in schools and in other learning contexts (youth work, adult education, community action, etc.,) is that a place should be provided for a dialogue with and between young people on questions of identity and of values. Diversity always points to the question of equality, and not only in those specific learning contexts where anti-racist and inter-cultural education apply. Any new variable in a group implicitly or explicitly questions the norms of that group and may, therefore, trigger changes. If the potential for such changes is given attention, other factors that differentiate a group can become significant. This provides an opportunity to involve every member of a group in questioning and re-grouping their values and in defining their identity in a new light. This is the essence of the educational process (Dewey 1916).

If we conceive of education as the fostering of the development of identity, it becomes apparent that in practice it must be promoted through a parallel approach. This is where the complementary nature of inter-cultural and anti-racist approaches matter. Inter-cultural education is a constant reminder of the infinite forms that identity takes, whilst anti-racist education raises issues of inequality and warns against the arbitrary and discriminatory attribution of identity that results from the unjust distribution of power in society. It follows, therefore, that the 'normal' process of identity formation itself gives rise to discrimination. Because differentiation from others and identification with the in-group are the central elements of these processes, it can easily happen that they become instruments for intolerance and discrimination (Hogg 1988). This infringes the rights of every individual to develop their particular potential, and the development of identity must therefore be grounded in and safeguard these rights.

It has been demonstrated that the majority of people in any country or region are inclined to hold central characteristics of their identity in common with each other. This may be termed the 'ethnic' element of identity. Common features become stabilised when they are surrounded by a system of values which guide the members of the group in central aspects of their behaviour to the extent that all other characteristics become secondary (Weinrich 1986). The wish for identification may outweigh that for differentiation, but it can also happen that differences are attributed exclusively to 'the others' and not to members of the in-group, especially when the degree and range of differentiations are further narrowed. At times of a crisis of identity, triggered perhaps by war or by an unexpected and extensive encounter with other ethnic groups, this tendency will become pronounced (Weinrich 1986: 301).

The issue of identity is, therefore, an intricate part of all educational action. In looking now at the two types of pedagogy in question, one of their more immediate dangers might be that they reduce the process of identity formation to cultural and ethnic criteria of diversity alone. The issue of identity is posed primarily by the uniqueness of each individual and this allows for a reciprocity in discovering differences. Anti-racist education will help to make differences visible, but in doing so it must remain within the general educational discourse and not prioritize 'ethnic' differences. Nor should the clarification of differences become simply a matter of defending the group with the greatest needs; it must be integrated into the general objective of facilitating a wider range of social abilities and valuing and understanding the qualities of each individual.

Education must always pioneer new approaches for specific tasks and situations, and inter-cultural and anti-racist approaches are, therefore, a source of stimulation and a corrective that brings education back to its central objectives. The history of education and of educational policies has shown, time and again, that at the moment when the pedagogical objective of facilitating identity formation constructively is thwarted, it becomes inclined to take recourse to antiquated and defensive methods, to traditional and often nationalist curriculum contents, and to promote fictitious and artificial forms of identity [4].

To put it provocatively: many of the tasks that anti-racist and inter-cultural education seek to tackle stem from the weaknesses and failures of general concepts of education that would become redundant as specific approaches as soon as the educational project returned to its proper objectives.

The need for a more critical discourse on identity in education arises not primarily from the weakness of its traditional discourse. Complex social transformations occurring in Europe at this moment necessitate an astute monitoring of political developments and their impact upon education. Intolerance and racism (which at certain times becomes more evident) are always a latent threat to the integrity of communities. An explicit pedagogical response is required. However, inter-cultural and anti-racist education are, by necessity, an integral part of education in a multicultural society; to give them specialist status would separate educational methods in the same way that groups of people are segregated and marginalised in society. The identity formation of all young people has become infinitely more complex because so many more variables are involved. Hence inter-cultural and anti-racist methods of education are of value even in those contexts considered to be 'mono-cultural' – the question of identity still requires equal attention.

It is now possible to summarise the observations made so far. Inter-cultural and anti-racist approaches have two principles in common which in turn relate back to general pedagogical principles: the task of fostering the process of identity formation and the task of creating a space in which learners may reflect upon their position in society in the context of constant personal and social changes. In relation to the general educational debate they are a reminder that both society and individual identity should no longer be thought of as (and have in reality never been) monolithic entities.

The particular contribution of inter-cultural aspects challenges us to take account of the fact that society requires people that are skilled in being members of diverse groups and life spheres. The differences most visibly present in a group can function as a stimulus for the recognition of other differences which might otherwise escape attention.

The anti-racist dimension analyzes and highlights the existence of power interests in all aspects of education. Power manifests itself by nurturing prejudice, trivialising and simplifying differences, or declaring differences as absolute, natural and irreconcilable. All this for the purpose of turning differences into an advantage for one group to the detriment of another.

The specific contributions that the inter-cultural dimension makes is concerned more with the conceptualisation of individual and cultural diversity, the recognition of the specific qualities of each person, and the ability to express and represent an autonomous personal identity. The anti-racist dimension is concerned more with the acquisition of skills that identify and dismantle the mechanisms where these differences become tools for exploitation and oppression.

This debate on education in a multi-ethnic, unequal society, and which has just started in Italy, recognises the criticism levelled at earlier concepts of inter-cultural education for being centred upon an apolitical understanding of multi-culturalism.

Radtke (1992), for instance, sharply rejects multi-culturalism as a concept which seeks the solution to all social conflicts in the educational field, and which sees diversity only from the perspective of the culinary advances it brings or of a widening of everybody's cultural horizon. In the USA and the UK in particular, but also in other parts of Europe, the critique of inter-cultural, multi-cultural, or multi-racist education, has been conducted systematically. "Multi-racial education in Britain has become more of an instrument of control and of stability than an instrument of change, of oppression more than of liberation of Blacks in schools and in society" (Mullard 1982: 131). This view is shared by many critics who have pointed out and documented the contradictions contained in these multi-cultural approaches (Essed 1991; Troyna and Hatcher 1992; Banks 1995).

Nevertheless, following Banks' (1995) historical overview, it seems possible and appropriate to salvage essential elements from each of these approaches for our current debate, as well as for the idea that there may be a progression from one approach to the other without invalidating the critique. Banks differentiates between the following dimensions of multi-cultural education: a) integration of contents; b) construction of knowledge; c) prejudice reduction; d) education for equality; e) empowering school culture. He argues that all are necessary elements for an educational discourse within a multi-cultural society. In a similar vein, Auernheimer (1990) reconstructs the various phases of educational methods dealing with cultural diversity in Germany. Starting with a critique of the notion of assimilation in *Ausländerpädagogik* he identifies four areas that inter-cultural education should address:

(i)   the promotion of social skills such as empathy, tolerance, solidarity and the ability to handle conflicts;

(ii)   the enhancement of political understanding and awareness through fostering the ability to perceive issues from a variety of positions;

(iii)   the identification and the challenging of racism;

(iv)   constructive engagement in the search for identities by children of minority groups.

This overview indicates that a critical and comprehensive

application of the principles of inter-cultural education will unavoidably lead to the inclusion of an anti-racist dimension. The programmes proposed by both Banks and Auernheimer contain the main themes that need to be addressed by both educationalists and wider society within a multi-cultural context. What is particularly attractive about Banks' analysis and pedagogical suggestions is that he recognises that any modification of the curriculum must correspond with the process of social transformation towards a multi-ethnic society and that this can be a gradual process.

For instance, at the first level, the pedagogical aim is to facilitate closer encounters between cultural traditions through information on the heroes, traditions, and festivals of other peoples. At the second level, this is followed up with additional curriculum elements which do not require a change in the overall structure of the curriculum. At the third level, the curriculum is transformed so that it reflects different cultural viewpoints. The fourth level of this 'action approach' aims at discussions on important social and political issues, and at facilitating students to make decisions and find positions appropriate to their specific circumstances. The gradual nature of such an approach appears to stand a better chance of convincing teachers of the benefits of training and re-training, and encourages the development of new didactic instruments for the classroom. It also broadens the range of people who would want to become directly involved in work on these issues. The discovery that there are so many inter-related aspects to be covered deepens our understanding of cultural and ethnic diversity and the issues at stake for everybody. It facilitates access to the daunting complexity of these issues and increases the likelihood that people who begin to change their approach will continue to change in the future.

An historical overview of the development of these methods provides further evidence that there is no one definitive remedy to the problems posed by cultural and structural differences in society, and that the identification of the concrete practical aims of anti-racism depend substantially upon an analysis of the ever-changing forms in which racism presents itself (Gallissot 1992). Far from being discouraging, this realization can lead to a pragmatic step-by-step perseverance, an experimenting with what seems useful in the struggle against prejudice and discrimination, and a new integration of diverse elements. A study of the methods and proposals which have been debated internationally are a source of encouragement and new ideas. They must then be modified to the specific work context according to the situation and interests of the participants in other countries (see the chapter by Steiner-Khamsi and Spreen in this volume).

The sense of defeatism that pervades inter-cultural education often stems from the fear that, by concentrating on cultural issues, education may become isolated from wider social concerns, political action and changes. It may, therefore, be useful to refer to the distinctions Hamburger (1991) makes in relation to the term culture. He distinguishes between: a 'private' culture, which represents a unique and individually validated combination of elements; an 'operational' culture, based on one's private culture but modified to operate in interactions and social situations; a 'generalised' culture, which consists of the standardised intersections of norms within particular networks of interaction; and a 'public' culture, which is based on an implicit or explicit consensus on generalised cultural standards. When talking about inter-cultural issues, it therefore becomes important to be specific to which level the term culture refers. For example, educational activities with very small children will invariably relate to the level of 'private' culture, whilst the other levels will gain in importance and interact with each other to different degrees and in constantly changing ways at later educational stages.

We have found indications of this in our research at a multi-cultural pre-school in Rome [5]. Our findings suggest that one decisive variable in the effectiveness of didactic methods is whether teachers start from the premise that differences exist between all children. This would allow them to recognise that all children's basic needs are substantially the same. Teachers may subsequently widen their understanding of those differences in their contacts with the families of the children concerned and, as such, would give them access to stories and accounts that are indicative of cultural patterns. In this way different cultural traditions (of Italian or immigrant children) may be accessed and shared and the children would not be distanced from one another because they had found common ground in their personal stories. For instance, it proved useful to avoid using the abstract term 'Egypt' and to talk instead of the Egyptian grandfather of a member of the class and that child's encounter with him during holidays. In an atmosphere of trust and of mutuality which had been carefully nurtured in the class, it became possible for the child to volunteer such stories. Talking about an Egyptian grandfather was the same as talking about a grandfather from Naples.

Paying attention to personal diversity does not preclude but, on the contrary, fosters the progressive growth of a common group identity. Through the sharing of memories (whilst avoiding a fixation on memories) children come to share and accept new memories. This allows them to form new identities related to the present, as well as identities that may become fully realised in the future. The differentiated use of the concept of 'culture' also cautions us against projecting cultural identities onto the past in the sense of an 'exclusive re-structuring of memories', where collective identities become fixed entities with sometimes oppressive effects (Hamburger 1991: 102).

This is the point where the introduction of anti-racist pedagogical elements may help to realise the full potential of multi-cultural school situations. An anti-racist perspective does not focus on differences of skin colour or of customs as such but rather on the arbitrary significance of superiority and inferiority which these characteristics have assumed in historical and political contexts. Nevertheless, it also has a personal and inter-personal dimension because it considers the impact of structural inequalities on individuals. Whilst anti-racism at the political level aims at changing the unequal distribution of power between groups and nations it helps at the educational level to clarify personal experience in terms of those structures.

Whilst I am convinced that anti-racist competences are essential for all those engaged in educational work, I remain convinced that not every multi-cultural group needs to deal with the issue of anti-racism from the outset. Facing up to the topic of racism without having had the opportunity of a positive encounter with 'diversity', and without being given the space to meet 'others' in a relaxed and reassuring way, is risky. Indeed, it may prove ineffectual and risky in the same way as the playing down of all differences, or emphasising only the exotic aspects of cultural differences. In such a situation, an inter-cultural approach may promote personal encounters in a relaxed atmosphere: at the beginning it avoids questions which may otherwise elicit feelings of guilt and resentment, even though these may have to be confronted eventually.

Anti-racist education sets itself more specific political goals than inter-cultural education. It accepts that conflicts over differences are unavoidable, that they do not necessarily point at psychological or inter-personal problems, but reflect structural conflicts within society. This link may not always be immediately accessible to the individual or group and a central task of anti-racist education is to clarify the nature and origin of such conflicts, and to develop comprehensive strategies of conflict resolution that are applicable at both the personal and the wider political level. It is useful, however, to bear in mind that there are inter-cultural situations which may not necessarily be conflictual and that, in an open atmosphere in which differences may be acknowledged, racially constructed differences may not necessarily be wholly related to issues of power. As such, they need not necessarily be given priority over other differences. An openness to both inter-cultural and anti-racist approaches may increase the educational potential of every teaching situation.

Practice implications

Personal dignity and equality between people are fundamental assumptions in education. However, without the practical impetus which anti-racism gives to the treatment of these issues they can easily become trivialised or treated in a tokenistic fashion. This complementary perspective should allow educators to motivate a group to address and realise these fundamental values in a constructive manner [6].

The issue of equality becomes trivialised when the diversity between members of a group, their different habits and backgrounds etc., are ignored. This might happen, for example, in a group which, because it considers itself to be homogeneous, takes equality for granted. The fact that some differences between people are very pronounced presents an educational opportunity to examine the conditions under which equality might be established. By thematising existing diversity, anti-racist education can move beyond the concept of equality, and facilitate individuals to discover their own particular value in each concrete group or community context. In its complementary way, inter-cultural education, by dwelling on cultural diversity, can make room for dreams of a society where no social tensions exist and all members of that society enjoy substantial equality. This ideal situation does not exist of course and the knowledge derived from this construct can, therefore, be only one element in an overall programme. By itself it can never do justice to the total complexity and vastness of the educational task.

Although the reality in schools and classrooms is a far cry from this ideal situation, the school or class can nevertheless take on the model character for a community between people of different backgrounds where the level of conflict and tension has been reduced to a minimum. Teachers might even facilitate the parents of those pupils participating in this conflict-free learning situation. By reducing the emotional and psychological impact of racism through information and group exercises, the empathic skills of young people would be enhanced. This would allow them to analyze the consequences of discrimination and injustice in the relative safety of the school community [7].

These steps and measures do not 'close' the proposed educational circle, but neither does it mean that anti-racist and inter-cultural education are, in themselves, sufficient to bring about change. Outside of the classroom, differences are hierarchically structured around the socio-economic and cultural prejudices that lead to discrimination and the negation of basic rights. These in turn perpetuate difference and prejudice. For example, the parents of an immigrant child who is well-integrated into the classroom may be involved in illegal work and be discriminated against on the housing market. This will lead to conflicts of which the child will be aware. In order to help the child in dealing with this it is necessary to turn to anti-racist educational methods to explain the nature of this injustice, and the dynamics which arise and perpetuate racism.

The ultimate aim of anti-racism is to achieve equality recognised in law. The struggle for this political goal may overlook the importance for negotiating the actual substance of identities, as legal protection does not automatically bestow an identity. The negotiation of rights and the negotiation of identities are closely related processes. Both require the active participation of members of minority groups. If not, the framing of the law and the allocation of collective identities will continue to come 'from above' and it will remain the prerogative of the 'indigenous population' at the 'centre' of society to give or deny access to equality. It is therefore important to examine the issue of equality law within the context of cultural and personal differentiations of identity. These considerations become thematic within the inter-cultural discourse which explores the relationship and tension between identity and equality.

In reality, the circle between the different approaches to education cannot become closed because racism manifests itself in continually changing forms. A young person who has had a positive experience in a multi-cultural class may still become a victim or a perpetrator of discrimination in another class or school. This is because social pressures of a racist kind will increase as young people grow older. Adolescence, for example, may reactivate anxieties related to 'being different' and may provide a new impetus in the search for identity. Schools and other organisations involved in education must constantly be aware of opportunities to thematize diversity. This should not be by way of reacting to crises but by ensuring that the themes of diversity and inequality become an integral part of the general educational process.

The educational concepts that have developed to deal with the social and inter-active implications of diversity demonstrate that the solutions themselves suffer from the continuous tension within society: between the personal and the social; the emotional and the rational; the promotion of assimilation or segregation; and between tolerance and intolerance. All educational methods relate to the inter-personal dimension. However, at a certain point, racism will be encountered because it is a pervasive structural phenomenon that is maintained by both political and economic interests. Instead of denying the relevance of psychological and cultural aspects of other educational approaches, anti-racist education must integrate these into a perspective of power relations on both a national and an international level. It is not enough to take note of the 'tactical errors' committed by education programmes in other countries and to think that such knowledge will automatically immunise against a repetition of such errors. This is because a confrontation with 'diversity' will always be specific to a particular country. Nevertheless, reflection upon the experience of other countries may help to identify the positive features of the tensions and the contradictions encountered.

If the various forms of racism that exist in society are not made explicit there is little point in having a broad multi-cultural approach to education – the integration of differences would not be achievable. It is a fact that immigrants from outside the EU have a social and economic position which on the whole is worse than that of Italians. Any Italian child will see that the vendors on the beaches, and the window cleaners at the traffic lights, are almost exclusively black. At the same time these children and their parents very rarely have any contact with the neighbourhoods and areas where black people live. Through such daily experiences the notions of being black, and of being economically and socially inferior, become synonymous and children become used to a social difference that appears unbridgeable. "To teach race relations purely from the perspective of different cultural groups which live in perfect equality would mean ignoring the reality of cultural domination" (Kringas and Stewart 1992: 21). It is, therefore, important to analyze the historical roots of immigration. At the same time, children require personal tools appropriate to their circumstances and with which they can make sense of their daily encounters with diversity. The language they learn and the statements and opinions they hear, become part of the repertoire of 'gut reactions' that they reproduce as soon as they lack confidence and feel anxious in an encounter with others who are visibly different. To deal with these feelings, to take them apart and integrate them in a different way is, in methods appropriate to the age and the situation of a group, the key task of anti-racist education. This work must be tackled at all different levels; it cannot be rigidly prescribed within one theoretical framework, although it must relate back to a consistent theory and social analysis. This step-by-step approach examines the contradictions within society and, at the same time, pays attention to their effect on our personal socialisation. We may not be able to resolve them all, but in recognising these limitations we at least become more aware of what is happening to us (Kringas and Stewart 1992: 21).

Our discussions above confirm that the specific aim of both inter-cultural and anti-racist education is to constantly bring the learning process back to the negotiation of identities and to establish reliable coordinates with which learners may gradually define their actual and desired position within society. The understanding this brings may help to prevent the rejection of oneself and of others. It will also hinder the development of irrational behaviour, and above all retain an element of rationality within the discovery of irrational attitudes. This can be attained more easily from a negotiated position of identity rather than from a feeling of emptiness and powerlessness.

I would like to summarise the following advantages of treating inter-cultural and anti-racist educational approaches as being complementary to one another:

1.   It allows for a greater variety of positions to become thematic within the education process. There is no longer a reliance upon one fixed method, and it counteracts the belief that there can only be one method that will eliminate racism and intolerance. Pedagogical action must constantly re-calibrate itself according to the specific circumstances of the learners and their learning situation.

2.   It opens up the issue of 'difference' and its pedagogical value to a greater number of teachers and learners because 'difference' is no longer defined from the perspective of one set of political convictions.

3.   It balances the awareness of personal identity with group identification in a gradual process that takes into account personal and collective aspects of the conflicts and issues concerned.

4.   It fosters the growth of personal and group identity in such a way that this identity does not in turn become a moment of oppression for other individuals or groups.

5.   It provides a greater variety of levels at which identities may be negotiated.

6.   It becomes possible to approach the issue of diversity from the point of view of either the majority or the minority community.

7.   It facilitates personal access to a 'collective memory' [8]. The stories of injustice and oppression that exist within all cultures will assume both personal meaning and relevance within the present social context. Similarly, it allows individuals and groups to trace their negative self-image back to their wider social and historical conditions.

8.   It provides a space within schools and other educational settings where aspects of identity, (including, for instance, the family background of immigrant children), may be incorporated into the educational process. New forms of identity may be explored and new educational models developed taking into account the multi-cultural reality of any particular society.

The actual educational work on the ground covers a spectrum between two polarised styles of work. The pole of inter-cultural education is geared towards analyzing and describing the many facets of diversity. The pole of anti-racist education puts issues and problems firmly in a social and historical context and aims at direct political changes.

References:

Ajello, A. M., Aluffi-Pentini, A. and Talamo, A. (1996), *Multiculturalità e Continuità*, Florence: NIS

Aluffi-Pentini A. (1995), *Potenzialità dell'azione pedagogica in una società* in *trasformazione: complementarità e specificità di educazione interculturale ed educazione antirazzista*, in A. Aluffi-Pentini and W. Lorenz (eds.), *Per una pedagogia antirazzista, Teorie e strumenti in prospettiva europea*, Bergamo: *Edizioni Junior*

Aluffi-Pentini A. and Talamo, A. (1996), *Integrazione e continuità dei bambini immigrati nella scuola*, to be published in Conference Proceedings *"Minori a rischio a Roma e nel Lazio"*, Rome 30/11 – 1/12/1995

Annali *MPI* (1995), *L'educazione interculturale e l'integrazione degli alunni stranieri*, Florence: *Le Monnier*

Auernheimer G. (1990), *Einführung in die interkulturelle Erziehung*, Darmstadt: *Wissenschaftliche Buchgesellschaft*

Balbo, L. (1995), *Une societié pas trop raciste*, in C. Neveu (ed.), *Nation, Frontières et immigration en Europe*, Paris: *L'harmattan*, pp.35-48

Balbo L. and Manconi, L., (1990). *I razzismi possibili*, Milan: *Feltrinelli*

Banks, J. A. (1995), Multicultural education: historical development, dimensions and practice, in Banks J. A. (ed.) Handbook of research on intercultural education, New York: Macmillan, pp.3-20

Demetrio, D. (1990), *Dalla pedagogia alla didattica interculturale; rendere quotidiano il rapporto educativo con le nuove etnie*, in G. Favaro (ed.), *I colori dell'infanzia, Bambini stranieri nei servizi educativi*, Milan: *Guerini e ass.*

Demitrio, D. and Favaro, G. (1992), *Immigrazione e pedagogia interculturale. Bambini, adulti e comunità nel percorso di integrazione*, Florence: *Na Nuova Italia*

Dewey, J. (1915), Democracy and education, New York: Macmillan

Essed, P. (1991), Understanding everyday racism: An interdisciplinary theory, London: Sage

Gabe, J. (1994), 'Race'-education policy as social control? The Sociological Review 42; 1 pp.26-61

Gallissot, R. (1985), *Mishre de l'antiracisme*, Paris: Ed. *de l'Arcanthre*

Giustinelli, F. (1991), *Razzismo scuola società. Le origini dell'intolleranza e del pregiudizio*, Florence: *La Nuova Italia*

Hamburger, F. (1991), *Interkulturelle Erziehung*, in D. Kiesel and R. Wolf-Almanasreh (eds.), *Die multikulturelle Versuchung: ethnische Minderheiten in der deutschen Gesellschaft*, Frankfurt: *Haag und Herchen*, pp.91-106

Hamburger, F. (1995), *Pädagogik der Einwanderungsgesellschaft*. Frankfurt: *Cooperative*

Hogg, M. A. (1988), Social identifications: a social psychology of intergroup relations and group processes, London: Routledge

Kringas, P. and Stewart, I. (1992), Class, Race and Education. An Australian Case Study, Discourse, 13;1, pp.20-35

Kristeva, J. (1991), Strangers to ourselves, Hemel Hempstead: Harvester Wheatsheaf

Marramao, G. and Meghnagi, D. (1993), *Per una cultura del confronto*, in *Lettera internazionale*, 38 (Oct./Dec.), pp.25-30

Ministero della Pubblica Istruzione, (1992), *Educazione interculturale: Esperienze e prospettive*, Rome: *MPI, Direzione scambi culturali*

Mosse, G. . (1992), *Il razzismo in Europa. Dalle origini all'olocausto*. Bari: *Laterza*

Mullard, C. (1982), Multiracial Education in Britain: from assimilation to cultural pluralism, in Tierney J., Race, migration and schooling. London: Holt, Rinehart and Wiston, pp.120-133

Pileri, S., Schmidke, O. and Ruzza, C. (1993), The League and the crisis of Italian politics, Telos 96, pp.86-102

Poletti, F. (1992), *L'educazione interculturale*, Florence: *La Nuova Italia*

Radtke, F. O. (1992), *Die Konstruktion des Fremden im Diskurs des Multikulturalismus. Die Programmatik des Multikulturalismus*, in *"Informationen zur Politischen Bildung"*, n.3, pp.71-78

Short, G. (1991), Prejudice, power and racism: some reflections on the anti-racist critique of multi-cultural education, Journal of Philosophy of Education 25; 1, pp.5-15

Todd, R. (1991), Education in a multicultural society, London: Cassell Educational

Todorov, T. (1989), *Nous et les autres. La reflexion française sur la diversité humaine, Seuil*

Troyna, B. (1986), Racism, education and the state: the racialisation of education policy, Dover: Croom Helm

Troyna, B. and Hatcher, R. (1992), Racism in children's lives: a study of mainly-white primary schools, London: Routledge

Weinrich, P. (1986), Operationalisation of identity theory in racial and ethnic relations, in J. Rex and D. Mason, Theories of race and ethnic relations, Cambridge: Cambridge University Press

NOTES

1.   I am deliberately not dealing here with the concept of black empowerment which could be called the 'third pillar' of the educational discourse in multi-cultural societies. This concept has not so far played any role in Italy and is referred to in the chapter reporting on youth work approaches in the UK.

2.   Another open question is the situation of illegal immigrants. A ministerial circular to schools in 1995 invites heads to accept those children who had not been issued with a residence permit. A school retains the right to fully ratify the enrolment once a residence permit has been presented, although it knows full well that in many cases this is unlikely to happen. Real difficulties occur when educational certificates have to be issued but cannot be awarded to somebody who 'officially' does not exist in Italy. This situation is about to change through a new decree regulating the status of illegal immigrants.

3.   For a fundamental discussion of the concepts of 'alterity' and 'externality' see Kristeva (1991) and Todorov (1989). See also Steiner-Khamsi and Spreen on 'othering' in this volume.

4.   For a discussion of the role of mythology as a source of racial identification, and of 'folk and land' for racist stereotypes, see Mosse (1992).

5.   Ajello, A. et al. (1996); the findings are based on direct classroom observations and intensive interviews with teachers.

6.   For examples of didactic suggestions see Walter Lorenz's chapter on 'Pedagogical principles and methods'.

7.   The Department of Education at the University of Bologna has, for instance, developed a video, 'The Class Divided', on ways of bringing about greater empathy in relation to racist discrimination.

8.   I should like to clarify this aspect as it is of special importance to me. In Italy, and probably in other European countries, some anti-racism approaches have a tendency to use historical events as a warning example. This is especially true in relation to the mass murder of Jewish people this century, it builds on the assumption that information about such an event,

and providing evidence for it having actually happened, acts as an antidote to racism. I would maintain that merely confronting young people with such information does not result in effective learning. It is only when the information is linked to an element of personal experience that it communicates and initiates change, for instance, in the personal encounter with survivors or relatives of victims. If the reactions of a group are not analysed carefully from an educational point of view, such encounters with history may lead to more stereotyping, guilt feelings, the identification of scapegoats, and the wish for revenge. Within this context particularly, a combination of both inter-cultural and anti-racist considerations can play a vital role in the pedagogical treatment of historical conflicts.

4. The significance of language in socio-cultural marginalisation

Cettina Sirna

Language is one of the most complex and highly developed instruments that humanity has, in the course of its development, produced. Its forms, its use, and its relations, express and reflect the conditions and the problems of the people that use it.

All languages are equally functional in relation to the requirements of any particular language community, but not all enjoy equal status. In fact, in relation to global distribution and the economic, political and cultural status of the populations that speak a particular language, these differences are pronounced, and the same differences become attached to the users. Language therefore conveys information quite independently from the intentions of the speakers, and creates frames of reference which can structure social distance. This can have a substantial effect on personal development.

If it is true that language is only one of the factors that affects the personal and social actualisation of a person, it is also true that the ability to speak a prestigious language is a passport which facilitates access to the cultural world of dominant elites. In the reverse, being a member of a small language community with low prestige will almost invariably represent an obstacle to social self-realisation, as it brings with it marginalisation and restricted developmental and existential opportunities. Indeed, people speaking such languages find themselves at a disadvantage as soon as they go beyond the limited territorial and cultural context to which they are tied, because of the instrumental properties of the language and the concepts that they use.

Language is, therefore, the card with which everybody presents their proper credentials so that they may be admitted.

To speak the same language, to use the same style and vocabulary, means being able to belong to a 'we', and to overcome any barriers in confidence that strangeness inevitably evokes. In contrast, to hear a strange language or one's own language spoken with an accent, rhythm or intonation that is different or non-standard, puts one on the defensive; the fear of not being understood and not understanding the behaviour, the values, and the rules which the other represents is triggered (Weinrich 1989). The anxiety of not being able to control these types of situations and relationships may provoke a sense of alienation and of insecurity that is potentially hostile.

The communication between people of a different social, cultural, ethnic or national background is often influenced by the stereotypes and preconceptions prevalent in one's own reference group, and within whose ideological frame of reference we interpret the communicative signals of the other. This may lead to a point where attitudes and forms of behaviour that do not readily correspond to one's own expectations can assume a hostile and aggressive meaning.

Those who find themselves in a linguistically privileged position on account of their command of a language with higher status tend not to make the extra effort required to understand speakers of a different language or accent. Instead, they may be tempted to point out the errors of the other speaker, and to deduce negative connotations from linguistic shortcomings to personality traits, long before the person's abilities in other respects are known.

These processes apply equally to a person belonging to a disadvantaged social class as it may to someone, for instance, from the Italian south who moves to the north, or to non-European immigrants, particularly if they are of dark complexion. Prejudices spring rarely from direct intentions, but on a broad-front they are rooted in the preconceptions of those who belong to a high status language community. This bias regards the other as 'incapable' or 'inferior', unless the other makes the effort to prove otherwise (Sirna 1992). It is in this way that, in Italy, all those who speak dialect, who are from the south, immigrants from outside Europe, and those who use a low status language or who 'make mistakes', become labelled 'poor and ignorant'. They are perceived as needing to be 'corrected' and 'normalised' as a kind of linguistic cleansing for their original sin of having a different language. In general, dialects have the effect of excluding their users from the 'actual' language community, and their 'improper' use of language is taken as a signal for other negative traits (Haugen 1972).

Mono-linguism, in the forms of linguistic purism and of intolerance against linguistic errors, is a widespread attitude amongst socially and culturally dominant groups. It often reveals an ideologically elitist mentality that is not prepared to engage in exchanges on the basis of equality. Not paying attention to the actual contents of a conversation and dwelling instead upon its formal contours, becomes a means of belittling an opinion and of rejecting it, on the grounds that it implies the cultural poverty of the speaker. To seize upon a linguistic error is, for instance, a favourite technique of politicians, of teachers, or of anybody trying to assert authority. Power is implicit in the mastery of the stronger language – the language that carries the dominant values and that signals privileges. One cannot share in this power unless one appropriates the language, makes it one's own, and learns to use it to one's own ends.

Language as a vehicle of mono-culturalism, ethnocentrism and intolerance

For these reasons, the politics of integration, directed at those people considered to be at the margins of society, generally converge on a programme of linguistic and cultural assimilation. This represents a mono-cultural approach. The process of becoming literate often serves as a kind of 'lay baptism' that is considered necessary to purify and initiate the ignorant into the 'normal' world as the only basis of a social existence. (Through learning the official vocabulary of everyday life, it is hoped that the 'other' will be relieved of its troublesome burden and exorcized of its subversive potential. These are perceived as constant dangers for the internal social cohesion and world view of the dominant community).

It is important not to disregard the value of competence in an official common language as an indispensable instrument of full participation in social life. But the emphasis upon alphabetisation and on the cultivation of pure forms of language, may sometimes conceal quite different motives. In fact, an excessive insistence on linguistic competence, regarded as a didactic objective without any value implications, is typical of many educational initiatives that appear to be democratic but which are substantially incapable of bringing about communicative equality. Having participated in a literacy programme or having received remedial education may easily become the criteria by which learners are excluded from further educational and indeed from employment opportunities.

In this regard it becomes important to analyze the methodology adopted by literacy programmes, particularly in educational situations of an inter-cultural nature. In work with children of migrants, for example, their value ultimately depends on whether they foster educational processes of self-actualisation or whether they operate from a perspective of selection. In the first instance, the actual experiences and existing linguistic competences of the student are the starting point from which the structure and function of different languages may be compared, competences re-evaluated, and themes of direct relevance identified. In the second instance, existing competences are ignored or, worse, they are portrayed as the reason for the student's lack of success in learning the standard language (Cummins and Swain 1987). Dialects, or the speaking of a foreign language, become the scapegoat for the school problems of young people from a socially and culturally disadvantaged background. They are often perceived as the cause of a 'contaminated' form of language and of deficits in the use of the official formal language which are regarded as unitary and unchangeable. This approach confirms these mono-cultural attitudes that ultimately do not recognise 'diversity' and which tolerates differences only momentarily until they have been neutralised and can no longer pose searching and provocative questions. It puts forward bureaucratic answers and formal and expressive correctness as the answer to all problems of inequality. By focusing only upon the formal aspects of communication, on a lack of 'neatness', or on the grammatically incorrect way in which questions and statements are formulated, it is easy to ridicule and discredit their contents.

In this way, situations of intolerance and processes of marginalisation are created, to which we are all daily witnesses and, at times, inadvertent perpetrators. We find them in the interactions between people of different social class background, or in the way public agencies function and, above all, in the whole educational experience both inside and outside the school. To give an example; a teacher may ridicule a hyperactive child by making cynical remarks about that child's linguistic errors. This approach humiliates rather than addresses the reasons for the hyperactivity, and the underlying needs that it expresses. This sets up a cycle of aggressiveness where ultimately the blame is attributed to the child. The latter's communicative deficit is transformed into an objective lack of power: the child is unable to talk about and negotiate a different connotation to the incident. The linguistic competence of the adult, instead of being utilised to decode the poorly articulated needs of the child, is used instead to confirm the power and control of the linguistically stronger party and to bring about a further process of marginalisation.

The same dynamics are set in motion in the context of the work of official departments when employees or management decide to apply the criterion of formal linguistic competence in order to create difficulties of access for service users and to confirm their inferiority. The role of a civil servant as 'servant to the public' is turned into that of a 'gate-keeper of handouts' to powerless subjects, through the underlining of any linguistic imprecisions. This happens more frequently when the claimant is less literate and cannot master the official language of the bureaucratic system. The correct use of this official language thus becomes a condition for access to services and benefits when in reality they are an entitlement. The impersonal criteria governing the work of bureaucracies in all countries, (although it is quite pronounced here in Italy), tends to treat all non-standard forms of communication as 'dys-functional', and therefore incompatible with the aims of bureaucracy.

A case has been documented, for instance, where refugees from Eritrea were unable to take up the offer of a house from a special housing allocation list because the officials processing the application had completely mishandled and in fact invalidated it on account of the poor language abilities of the applicants. It had been a matter of not filling in the application form properly, as became clear when a legal advisor took on the case and managed to restore their original entitlement.

With this system of control, bureaucracies frequently manage to block the application of laws that are potentially innovatory through the creation of impediments, delays, ambiguities, and obstacles, and thus hindering claimants from getting their rights. By taking command of the language, the system acquires a power of veto and of absolute decision-making and renders bureaucracies incapable of political and institutional changes.

From verbal intolerance to racism

Language represents an ideal vehicle for all forms of intolerance and the various types of prejudice concerning class, ethnicity and culture. Language plays a central role when it comes to highlighting differences, enlarging distance, and sanctioning inequality, through the creation of invisible and yet real and profound barriers. It confirms a Sicilian proverb which (in a reversal of its English version of "sticks and stones can break my bones but words can never hurt me") goes, "language has no bones but can break bones". This expresses figuratively just how difficult it is to curtail its power of sanction.

Intolerance feeds into various processes of marginalisation against people, communities and institutions. Intolerance may start out with a statement that appears merely as a stronger emphasis on a social, ideological or racial difference. Only the tone of voice or the context betrays its actual disparaging quality. Linguistic intolerance may also mix with a subtle racism which avoids giving itself a blaring and vulgar appearance; preferring instead to use indirect references which are difficult to challenge but equally effective in bringing about marginalisation. It is the diffusion of this subtle form of racism across all social strata, and whose damaging effects are hardly recognised, that lends overt and aggressive forms of racism a semblance of credibility.

Within the same dynamics, all those parlances of our everyday language which refer to strangeness, to strangers, and to the out-group, also make a reappearance and bear out the durability of many negative language stereotypes and prejudices. This gives a permanent boost to the growth of attitudes of intolerance and racism. Much of this finds expression in sexist phrases ('he cries like a girl', 'take it like a man'), or in the use of a physical or social attribute in the form of an insult ('spastic', 'peasant'). To this have to be added the numerous nationalist or racist jokes playing on the assumed typical attributes of a people in order to demonstrate the superior quality of one's own. Then there are all the emblematic references to a person's shortcomings with nationalist labels. In Italy we use 'Scottish' or 'from Genoa' for a miserly person; 'Italian' or 'Neapolitan' for a rogue, a careless worker or an idler; 'German' for a hard or rigid person; and 'Sicilian' as a synonym for a mafioso. In fact, our ordinary language is so permeated with these types of expressions that we often use them purely as semantic conventions without reflecting on the negative charge they carry. Italian expressions include: 'to act like an Indian' (i.e. to turn a deaf ear); 'this is Arabic to me' (equivalent to the English 'this is Greek to me'); 'he smokes like a Turk'; 'don't be a Zulu' (i.e. a lout), etc.

Seemingly neutral phrases may also be infused with hidden fears, anxieties, and attitudes of disguised hostility, such as the use of the image 'waves of immigration' (Ongini 1991). This image contains associations of the dangers a wave can bring to those on firm dry land and of the natural necessity that, after the flow, there will be an ebb taking back with it all that has been perceived as alien. In the same way, we have to consider the habit of giving strangers a more or less offensive collective name, especially when they belong to a different racial group or to categories of people who are easily identifiable on the grounds of physiognomy ('Uncle Tom', 'Paki', 'Paddy' etc.).

The same influence that stereotypes play applies also to the alternating use of two languages among bilingual communities where speakers may still feel the lived emotional connotations of a language beyond its mere functional character (Amati-Mehler, Argenieri and Canestri 1990). Wanting to cancel the memory of a painful past experience may for instance accelerate the forgetting of the mother tongue. Or bi-lingual speakers restrict their use of each language consistently to specific situations such as reprimanding, cognitive analysis, positive connotations, etc. This widens the affective gap between both sets of languages and values. All these stereotypes disseminate by means of their emotive qualities, only to influence cognitive processes in unexpected and unnoticed ways. They do not allow for differentiation and provide the soil on which a latent racism may flourish – particularly when a favourable combination of factors, such as widespread public consent to those prejudices, an inability to challenge them through the legal process, and their explicit use and endorsement by political leaders, arises.

In post-modern societies such as ours, where the degree of complexity and diffuseness has grown immensely, and where everything is difficult to identify, define, represent, and difficult to manage, the forms in which intolerance and racism present themselves have also changed and become less open and visible. They take shape and conceal themselves in new cultural expressions, new symbols, and new metaphors, which articulate old forms of hatred and prejudice and other barriers to solidarity between classes, cultures and racial groups (Balbo and Manconi 1993). Perhaps this has gathered a momentum because we thought of ourselves as somehow immune to racism or as having developed antibodies against particular ideological infections whose dangers history has so amply demonstrated. We may even observe that democratic and anti-racist slogans themselves have been turned into a means of concealing power structures that have grown up behind the façade of such mottoes.

In reality, the formulas and phrases that are meant to reveal new aspects of marginalisation, sooner or later turn out to be simplifications themselves and are, therefore, prone to being manipulated and instrumentalised. In the name of democracy, those who do not readily subscribe to certain words or forms of argument, may come to be labelled 'anti-democratic'. The word 'racist' itself may become a deceiving label when it is attributed to those who engage polemically with people from different racial backgrounds even when their motives are justified and valid.

Certain charged and emblematic metaphors, even when they are superficially positive (such as the use of Black athletes in advertising as symbols of virility), may be utilised to induce in people an immediate visceral acceptance or rejection of certain topics, and to thwart the possibility of more differentiated perceptions. Some issues are surrounded by such a taboo that prevents their articulation or expresses them only in a misleading form (e.g. 'incest', 'coloured'). This means that the phenomena they refer to cannot be analyzed and reflected upon critically and objectively for as long as they are cloaked by such vague or ambivalent terms. These are precisely the conditions under which prejudiced attitudes spread and which muddy social and political life. All of us are exposed to these dynamics and the instrumentalisation it implies. This requires even more astute attention to the influence of the written and spoken word. We witness an enormous increase in the manipulative use of language through the mass media and its capacity to generate categorisations, labels, and intolerance: how quickly does someone become a 'monster', 'hero', or a 'genius'? A rhetoric that tends to demonise or exaggerate is not seriously striving to understand the issues with which it deals.

It is not often that we become aware of the extent to which manifestations of verbal intolerance help to spread negative social behaviour, such as racism. A case can clearly be made for a direct connection between those verbal pronouncements, invectives and insults that are at first mimicked, but which then turn into hostile behaviour through changing the contents of the insults into a reality and in finding a justification for them. A recognition of this may lead to a more cautious and reflected use of everyday language (Bolognari and Sirna 1995).

New processes of racialisation

Numerous studies have demonstrated that the school is one institution where language functions as a key instrument in effecting selective marginalisation (Renzi and Cortellazzo 1977, De Mauro 1977). Language mediates not only the positive tensions in the interactions of teachers, pupils and the organisation as a whole, but also probable prejudices.

Even though the process of marginalisation is not confined to language, it is nevertheless important to pay attention to the use of language within the school context as a kind of litmus test for the degrees of equal opportunity that exist. The use of language can be either a means of emancipation and of cultural and human growth, or it can precipitate a slide into selective, discriminatory, and racist attitudes which are reflected in both official pronouncements and everyday speech (Bongiorno, Ruggeri and Sirna 1994).

By underlining these processes, we wish to take up, amongst other things, the arguments and suggestions emanating from anti-racist education which have been developed recently and, at the same time, avoid ideological and simplistic interpretations. New fields of research, in which the analysis of linguistic aspects has played an important part, have revealed the complexity of factors and connections that are involved in the dynamics of marginalisation. They operate particularly within educational institutions and block the possibility of emancipation and equal chances of development.

In these findings, racism does not appear as an homogeneous phenomenon. Rather, it presents itself in constantly changing forms which makes it difficult to pin down. Socio-economic difference becomes superimposed upon ethnic or racial divisions. This leads to further fragmentation and the consequent effect that disadvantage, derision, and racism do not necessarily affect all the members of a community equally. The famous Black footballer, or the top fashion model who is Black, is not subjected to the same level of racism as, for instance, a Black unemployed immigrant. It is more appropriate therefore to replace a static notion of racism with a dynamic one that incorporates this process of racialisation (Troyna 1993). This approach requires us to be specific and to trace the complex historical pathways through which the dynamics of inequality transmit themselves in different contexts. It is not race as such that produces discriminatory behaviour and racist marginalisation, but the various intersections between race, competition, exploitation, and cultural selectivity. This should not be regarded as a mechanical cumulative process of marginalisation so that, for instance, Black women are always and automatically doubly disadvantaged – as the example of Black models or actresses demonstrate.

The newer forms of racism could be called 'implicit racism' (De Mauro 1993), and they are to be found in educational and social practices as well as in political documents. This type of racism expresses itself in subtle, sophisticated, indirect forms which appeal to inertia and indifference; refer to the unequal distribution of services; or hide in general, ambiguous, indirect statements or well-targeted omissions. Difficulties in decoding the connotations and intentions of this new form of racism may sometimes cause its victims to become its unwitting mouthpieces and champions.

Rizvi (1993), for instance, points this out in his critique of those educational proposals that appear democratic but which are in reality so vague and unimaginative that they serve to conceal the problems of racism within their rhetorical affirmation of equality. For the purposes of eliminating discrimination, it is simply not enough to insist on a better and more sympathetic understanding of other cultures, or on the insertion into the curriculum of elements of the history and the cultural experiences of minority groups. Nor is the solution to concentrate on and 'reform' the core of violent racists and identify them as the 'bad apples' of society and thus making them responsible for all racism (Berardi 1993).

A perspective which insists that racism is merely a form of social pathology restricted to a few ignorant individuals, overlooks those forms of hidden racism that are far more diffuse and widespread, and which operate undisturbed in institutions, relationships, and in the beliefs of the majority of people including the 'well educated' (Jesi 1979). The latter group are the makers and disseminators of public opinion and their behaviour, elegant and formally correct, can have a more damaging effect than particular incidents of hooliganism, precisely because it provides an alibi and a justification for the discriminatory attitudes and behaviour of others. The theoretical justifications of intellectuals becomes all the more dangerous the more it camouflages itself in apparently progressive statements; in self-definitions of the type 'I am anti-racist myself but...'; or when they play on the appeal of superior style and class, and on profound sources of knowledge that allegedly confirm the inevitability of certain forms of discrimination. Unless racist behaviour is analysed in detail and tackled in specific educational projects instead of being demonised, the spread of racism will continue unabated.

For the development of effective egalitarian and anti-discriminatory attitudes and skills, it is not sufficient to reduce the opportunities for social conflict. Silence and conflict avoidance are forms of collusion or subordination that are achieved via the manipulation of information. It may even contribute to a better concealment of racism which can thereby remain substantially intact. Also, when parts of the Black community reject their marginalised status, this logic does not allow for a reduction in inequality and a fostering of self-confidence, but rather serves to heighten the social conflict (Troyna 1993).

As Troyna (1993) points out in his detailed and balanced account of the various anti-racism approaches, it is useful to underline the danger of certain naive and simplistic forms of anti-racism, in order not to let such errors undermine the credibility of the whole project of a fully developed anti-racist pedagogy. In this context, it becomes urgent to expose the ambiguities that hide in certain apparently democratic and anti-racist discourses and which, through dressing up in a rhetorical language that holds out irredeemable promises, ends up justifying the status quo. Troyna criticises the danger of 'deracialised discourses', that appear to be democratic, but which in essence maintain fixed boundaries and inequalities. To this deliberate use of ambivalence may be added all those condensed symbols used in official documents ('pluralist society', 'fairness', 'equality', 'collective memory', 'identity') which may carry contradictory meanings (Gentiloni 1992). In given political contexts, the purpose of these kinds of expressions is to assure those who find themselves on the margins that their interests have been taken into consideration – when in fact the realisation of the promises contained in the statements is further delayed.

Equal attention must also be given to the process of 'discursive racialisation', which is the explicit use of racial categories and values. This instrument also has an ambivalent effect: it can be put to racist uses when it distinguishes and groups people on the basis of race for the purpose of labelling and penalising them and making them feel guilty. But when it enhances the awareness of racial inequality and indignation against racial injustice by making discrimination visible so that it may be fought more effectively, it has anti-racist uses.

In reality, all processes of racialisation, like those of discrimination, are diverse and complex. They can only be discovered and analyzed in the specific context in which they occur by tracking down the processes which generate and sustain them. These everyday situations can be identified in the media (e.g. in the reporting of racial incidents); in schools (e.g. in the attitudes, expectations and verbal behaviour of teachers); in the way race is portrayed to children; in institutional reforms, etc. In all these situations, initiatives may be developed which either heighten the awareness on all parts and bring about a commitment to action towards the realisation of equal opportunities, or which, on the contrary, further the aims of racism.

Not even research projects on racism and inter-cultural issues are exempt from ambivalence in the messages they implicitly carry in the selection of research objects and the choice of methodology. Some of the interpretations of data, the connections between factors established, and the validity of the findings for practice, are all directly influenced by the methodology adopted and may be far from neutral. Research techniques that use racist and ethnicist categories, force interviewed subjects to give stereotypical answers. Oversimplified results which do not represent the situation of those interviewed at all are consequently produced. In many instances, data on racial incidents is not collected or, if it is, it is in a distorted form; or the data gives undue attention to particular aspects or only to indirectly obtained or emotively conditioned testimonies; or the tenuous correlation between attitudes and behaviour is not made clear, and so on.

On the other hand, there is the argument that white people could not possibly undertake research on such topics because they have no access to the lived experience of racism. There is a tendency in such research to focus on contentious issues such as identity crises, the construction of negative self-images, inter-generational conflict, unrealistic expectations, cultural conflicts, etc. These are issues which implicitly support the assumption that the Black community has pathological attributes whilst paying little attention to the racism of the white community.

Anti-racism from an inter-cultural perspective

As has been shown, racism today presents itself less in the form of explicit direct aggression and ever more at the level of language and the information it explicitly or implicitly conveys. Even if one were to banish certain explicitly racist expressions there are still enough culturally acceptable phrases that carry the same prejudices. In order to stop the spread of discriminatory thoughts and attitudes it is not enough to ban and declare racial insults illegal. It would be much better to analyze the combination of factors which trigger and consolidate such belief systems.

The interpretation which anti-racist pedagogy gives to the processes of racialisation suggests that it is vitally important to analyze the language which is used in the educational and school context. This could become the prime instrument for identifying implicit forms of racism within education and prepare more precisely targeted interventions aimed at giving real equality of opportunity to all.

Whilst we cannot afford to pay less attention to explicit and violent racism, we have to become more sensitised to the new forms of racism which are often submerged in de-racialised discourses, in new malicious forms of discursive racialisation, and in communicative racism (Bastenier and Dassetto 1990, Vedovelli 1993). We must not be afraid of conflicts which need to be brought to people's attention so that they may be confronted consciously and openly. We must find out: how and when spoken language and behaviour move in tandem and in separate directions; when we are dealing with really new contents and when the newness is only a new wrapper; when the scientific language makes ideological claims and when it promotes a clearer view of reality. We must utilise: linguistic analysis in order to discover and overcome the unilateralism of ideological positions as well as of those claiming to be free of ideology; and those of the ahistorical stance of a 'neutral' pedagogy, as well as those of a politicised pedagogy soured by polemicism.

It is time to have these replaced with a pedagogy that pays attention to the historical and situational context in which learning takes place and which at the same time opens up imaginative ideas for change. A pedagogy which does not, as Troyna says, put new wine in old vessels, but one which "moves from a language of critique to a language of possibilities". Within the context of educational institutions, this may mean implementing the principle of the acceptance of the other and respect for diversity; analyzing the implicit direction of normative educational values; uncovering the use, by educators, of racist and discriminatory forms of 'logic'; and confronting forms of hostility which may be present within the organisational structure of a school. These are the actual obstacles to an egalitarian, democratic, and inter-cultural version of education (Filtzinger 1993) which offers equal opportunities to all. To this programme belong those activities which Balbo and Manconi (1993) call 'acts of non-racism': initiatives which aim at creating spaces and key situations so that mutual learning may take place.

Such action requires institutional recognition, the necessary financial resources, and the appropriate publicity, so that they may become models and reference points for good everyday practice. There are positions which must be applied time and again so that indifference, excuses for inaction, and disorientation, (none of which are, in themselves racist acts, but which can pave the way for racism through the inertia they create), may be combatted.

The times of ideological enthusiasm and of technological myopia are long gone. It is time that education realised that its ability to promote self-actualisation and emancipation must be based on an improved ability to 'read the signs of our times': the signs of its multiple languages and of its requirements and its resources. And where intercultural education cannot flourish because a racist ideology prevails with racist legislation permitting racist conduct, it becomes necessary to promote change in all these areas throughout the educational programme. These are the weapons with which racism – in all its forms – must be fought.

We must become more aware of negative metaphors, ambiguity, implications, omissions, disparaging talk, offensive name-calling, insulting graffiti, restrictions on language diversity, codes which conceal forms of discriminatory behaviour, rhetorical and ritualistic opposition to racism, etc. All this is not the sole object of egalitarian education, but it certainly is a means of laying down positive markers in the fight against racism and discrimination.

Bibliography

Amati-Mahler, L., Argentieri, S. and Canestri, J. (1990), *La babele dell'inconscio. Lingua madre e lingue straniere nella dimensione psicoanalitica*, Milano: *Raffaello Cortina*

Balbo, L. and Manconi, L. (1993), *Razzismi. Un vocabolario*, Milano: *Feltrinelli*

Bastenier, A. and Dassetto, F. (1990), *Nodi conflittuali conseguenti all'insediamento definitivo delle popolazioni immigrate nei Paesi europei*, in *Fondazione Agnelli* pp.3-64

Banfi, E., (ed.) (1993), *L'altra Europa linguistica. Varietà di apprendimento e interlingue nell'Europa contemporanea*, Florence: *La Nuova Italia*

Berardi, F. (1993), *Come si cura il nazi*, Roma: *Castelvecchi*

Berruto, G. (1987), *Sociolinguistica dell'italiano contemporaneo*, Florence: *La Nuova Italia*

Bocca, G. (1988), *Gli italiani sono razzisti?*, Milano *Garzanti*

Bolognari, V. and Sirna, C. (eds.) (1995), *Razzismo e frantumazione etnica. Politiche sociali e interventi educativi*, Roma: *Herder*

Bongiorno, F., Ruggeri, F. and Sirna, C. (1994), *Quale lingua a scuola*, Messina: *Edas*

Chistolini, S. (1994), *L'antirazzismo in Italia e in Gran Bretagna. Uno studio di educazione comparata*, Milano: *F. Angeli*

Corson, D. (1990), Language Policy across the Curriculum, Clevedon: Multilingual Matters Ltd.

Cummins, J. and Swain, M. (1987), Bilingualism in education: Aspects of theory, research and practice, London: Longman

De Mauro, T. (1993), *"Nel duemila parleremo così"* in *La Repubblica*, 3 August 1993

Ferrarotti, F. (1988), *Oltre il razzismo*, Roma: *Armando*

Ferrarotti, F. (1994), The temptation to forget: Racism, Anti-Semitism, Neo-Nazism, London: Greenwood

Filtzinger, O. (1993), *'Costruire l'interculturalità'*, in Filtzinger, O. and Sirna, C. (eds.), *Migrazione e società multiculturali. Una sfida per l'educazione*, Bergamo: *Junior*

Franchini, R. and Giudi, D. (1991), *Premesso che non sono razzista. L'opinione di mille modenesi sull'immigrazione extracomunitaria*, Roma: *Editori Riuniti*

Giustinelli, P. (1991), *Razzismo, scuola, società. Le origini dell'intolleranze e del pregiudizio*, Florence: *La Nuova Italia*

Haugen, D. (1992), Dialect, language, nation, in J. Pride and J. Holmes (eds.), Sociolinguistics, Harmondsworth: Penguin

Kristeva, J. (1991), Strangers to ourselves, Hemel Hempstead: Harvester Wheatsheaf

Ongini, V. (1991), *La biblioteca multietnica*, Roma: Ed. *Bibliografica*

Palomba, D., Bertin, N. (1993), *Insegnare in Europa. Comparazione dei sistemi formativi e pedagogia degli scambi culturali*, Milano: *F. Angeli*

Rizvi, F. (1993), Critical Introduction: Researching Racism and Education, in B. Troyna, Racism and Education. Rearch Perspectives, Milton Keynes: Open University Press pp.1-17

Sirna, C. (1992), *Lingua e apprendimento in prospettiva interculturale*, Messina: *Edas*

Troyna, B. (1993), Racism and Education. Rearch Perspectives, Milton Keynes: Open University Press

Troyna, B. and Hatcher, R. (1992), Racism in children's lives: a study of mainly-white primary schools, London: Routledge

Vedovelli, M. (1993), *Note per una sociolinguistica dei movimenti migratori europei*, in E. Banfi (ed.), *L'altra Europa linguistica*, Florence: *La Nuova Italia*, pp.1-34

Weinrich, H. (1989), *Vie della cultura linguistica*, Bologna: *Il Mulino*

Wieviorka, M. (1993), *Lo spazio del razzismo*, Milano: *Il Saggiatore*

5. Anti-racism and Black empowerment in Britain: principles and case studies

Karen Chouhan, Ummi Esmail, Joe Joseph, Kurian Mathai and Jeff Modayil

For the purpose of developing anti-racist and Black empowerment [1] strategies, we have found analysis to be central to all areas of our activity – as lecturers working within formal education on youth and community work (YCW) programmes, as community workers working with concepts of informal education [2], and as Black [3] activists. This does not mean getting stuck in 'classroom' debates to the detriment of practical activity, but the case studies in this chapter will illustrate how our personal experiences, shared and reflected upon with others, have informed our educational practice in a way that no amount of theory alone would have done, although reading and study often promoted further action.

One of our shared early experiences in different parts of the country was the activity of the National Front (NF). In London in 1979, the NF marched through Southall, and Blair Peach, a peaceful anti-Nazi campaigner and teacher, was killed by Special Patrol Group police. The NF Headquarters was based in Leicester in those days, and in 1979 they marched through Leicester with massive police protection. The irony was not lost on the thousands of Black people who had been pleading for more police protection from racial attacks, and the community took to the streets. But whilst Black resistance eventually led to the downfall of the NF (Sivanadan 1982), there was at that time no coordinated strategy from the youth services or community workers in response to this crisis. How could you practice YCW if you were not involved in the life of the community and in the issues that affected them every day? In the light of those experiences it became paramount to ensure that YCW did not stay on the periphery of anti-racism. This is not to suggest that anti-racist work only occurs when dealing with extremists, but YCW has to be embedded in actions creating social change for equal rights and justice. Otherwise it becomes a means of social control and self-gratification for workers who want to 'help people'.

Pedagogically speaking, one of our first tasks was to generate an understanding that anti-oppressive practice is the root of youth and community work and not an optional area for specialists. To be fair, most students accept this very quickly or have already come to this understanding. More difficult is the acceptance of this basic principle by local authorities and government departments responsible for youth work. In the late 1980s, the government initiated a series of ministerial conferences to map out the purposes and curricula of the youth service. At the second such conference, over 200 youth workers agreed the statement of purpose for the youth service as follows:

> "To address all forms of inequality to ensure equality of opportunity for all young people to fulfill their potential as empowered individuals and members of groups and communities and to support young people during their transition to adulthood. Youth work offers young people opportunities which are: educative... designed to promote equality of opportunity... participative... empowering" (NYA 1991).

The government minister responsible replied:

> "The relationship of the youth service to politics does, I believe, need the most careful consideration. I do not want the role of the youth service to become a matter of political controversy. The youth service needs to be strongly positioned to play its vital part alongside the formal education system..." (NYB 1991: 18).

The Statement of Purpose was in our view absolutely correct. We felt that YCW needed to incorporate all four basic principles – equality, development, empowerment and education – as they were especially relevant with regard to actions by Black young people. But how does the youth service realise them? From our experience there are few statutory or voluntary youth services that have developed consistent anti-racist strategies. The majority of efforts have resulted in limited policy statements or one-off workshops.

A more comprehensive strategy needs to take account of the history of racism and its political analysis: we will attempt this in the pages that follow, before presenting our personal experiences as case studies.

Central to strategic anti-racism in Britain is an understanding of the nature of the strategy it is trying to fight. For Black people, the goal is Black empowerment. We must therefore understand the disempowering structural, ideological, and practical blocks of racism. To be one step ahead of the beast (racism) we need to know in which direction it will turn next. Our contention is that to do this we must understand racism's roots, its paths of development, and the elements of its virulent nature.

Husband (1986) writes about the particular continuity of the concept of 'race'. He suggests that there is a highly emotive body of ideas that are interwoven, matrix-like, and which makes it extremely difficult to challenge 'race' thinking. This 'body of ideas' sustains racism by forming an ideology which is gathering, rather than losing, momentum. We wish to take a brief look at six of the main ideas that fused by the end of the nineteenth century and which still echo in today's forms of racism. They are:

1. The needs of capitalism.
2. The belief in White superiority.
3. Scientific theories concerning biological origins of social differences.
4. Colour imagery associated with Black and White.
5. Christian religious beliefs.
6. Theories of sexuality.

1.   The history of colonialism and slavery are vile testament to the link between capitalism and racism. Britain contributed not only to the underdevelopment of colonised countries (Chouhan 1991), but had perverted their economies by draining them of their wealth and leaving "them at independence with a large labour force and no capital with which to make that labour productive. And it is to these vast and cheap resources of labour that Britain turned in the 1950s" (Sivanandan 1982: 102).

In 1949, a Royal Commission report identified the problem of labour shortages that faced certain sections of the British economy, and where the conditions of employment were unattractive to the White British population. The Commission calculated that there would have to be approximately 140,000 people migrating annually into Britain to meet the shortage (Chouhan 1991). It stated:

"Immigration on a large scale into a fully established society like ours would only be welcomed without reserve if the immigrants were of good stock and were not prevented by their religion or race from intermarrying with the host population and becoming merged in it." (Cited in Miles and Phizacklea, 1984, p.24)

2.   The quotation above clearly betrays the underlying notion of English superiority. This is a second element of racism. Colonialism and slavery had fuelled and exemplified this idea. Frameworks of 'otherness' and 'inferiority' helped to reinforce the 'us' of empire and superiority. Once started down this path, there was no turning back, save to face up to the inhumanity, bigotry, and totally unjust nature of Britain's actions in the world.

3.   The phrase 'good stock' is of particular note because it derives from, and draws attention to, the 'scientific' component of race, some of which lead to claims that biological differences are the basis of superiority and inferiority of the races (particularly along a White/Black division).

In 1950 a UNESCO conference of experts identified race as not so much a biological phenomenon as a social myth (Miles 1993). But, despite the scientific basis of 'race' having been challenged again and again, some biologists, geneticists and psychologists reasserted the validity and social significance of the concept 'race' in the form of sociobiology.

"Sociobiology then offers a highly sophisticated account of racism. It turns all the localised worries people have about immigrants – from worries over housing and jobs to trivial worries about the smell of curry – into xenophobia: an evolutionary trait bred into us over millions of years because of its genetic advantage. In short it naturalizes racism. To me, there is no doubt that it offers the most dangerous theorisation of racism currently available" (Barker 1981: 100).

4. Colour imagery has had a particular impact on race. By the time Englishmen were setting out on their worldwide adventures, the term 'Black' already had a loaded meaning.

"No other colour except White conveyed so much emotional impact... the meaning of Black before the sixteenth century included: 'Deeply stained with dirt; soiled, dirty, foul... Having dark or deadly purposes, malignant; pertaining to or involving death, deadly; baneful, disastrous, sinister... foul, iniquitous, atrocious, horrible, wicked... indicating disgrace, censure, liability to punishment etc.' Black was an emotionally partisan colour, the handmaid and symbol of baseness and evil, a sign of danger and repulsion." (Jordan 1974: 6)

5. Christianity was also loaded with colour symbolism: white angels stood for purity, devils were black, original sin was cast as a black spot on the soul, etc. Some writers also gave the negativity of Blackness a biblical source. In Genesis IX, Noah was supposed to have cursed his son Canaan, who had looked upon his father's nakedness as he lay drunk. This curse was turned by writers of the sixteenth and seventeenth centuries into a curse of Blackness. Jordan (1974) suggests that this was probably because of ancient associations with heat and sensuality and the fact that some sub-Saharan Africans had been enslaved by Europeans since ancient times. Whatever the explanation, the tale persisted. It appealed because of its relation to scripture and therefore the 'rightness' of the White man's superiority.

6. A further dimension concerns sexuality. The logic went: if Black people were less (human) than White people, they were closer to animals (in the natural evolutionary order), and therefore instinctual and emotional. And as sex was more instinctive, Black people were regarded as more libidinous. This demanded a great distance between Black men (in particular) and White women – though not necessarily between White men and Black women for whom slavery frequently meant also rape (Hoch 1979).

These images consolidated a dualistic system of race thinking where opposites are used in theoretical conjunction to bolster the position of the people wanting to hold on to status or power (Hodge *et al.* 1975):

- Mind and Body symbolised White and Black people.
- Control and Instinct symbolised White and Black people.
- Rationality and Emotion symbolised White and Black people.
- Good and Evil symbolised White and Black people.
- Christian and Heathan symbolised White and Black people.
- Civilized and Barbaric/Savage symbolised White and Black people.

"Christianity too contributed greatly to dualism and racism. It refused to confront slavery, inequalities and its own contradictions until the 'Abolitionists' movement was well under way, and even then it has not ever come out strongly, in a way it could because of its power, to undermine racism" (Chouhan 1986).

Race and immigration policies in Britain

From the 1905 immigration legislation to the Immigration Acts of 1988 and the Asylum and Immigration Act of 1993, controls including deportations were justified if they were 'conducive to the public good'. Balanced against this careful restriction of persons who could enter Britain were always the needs of capital. This led to the active recruitment of Black commonwealth citizens in the immediate aftermath of the Second World War, and 'numbers' became a political issue in a similar manner to the preoccupation with 'good stock'. In 1955, Eden's government had drafted a bill which would have effectively banned Black immigration into Britain. However, they backed down after the Colonial Secretary, Alan Lennox-Boyd, argued against it fearing that such legislation would damage Britain's position in the Commonwealth. By 1955, Gwilym Lloyd George, Home Secretary, reported that immigration from the West Indies and the Indian sub-continent was running at 20,000 and 7,000 a year, respectively. A cabinet memo written in 1955 by Alec Douglas-Home, the Secretary for Commonwealth Relations stated:

"The problem faces us with a dilemma. On the one hand, it would presumably be politically impossible to legislate for a colour bar and legislation would have to be non-

discriminatory in form. On the other hand, we do not wish
to keep out immigrants of good type from the old
dominions." (cited in *The Guardian*, 2.2.86)

However, by 1962 the Macmillan government legislated to
curb coloured immigration and this was swiftly followed by the
1968 Immigration Act passed by a Labour government, and
the Race Relations Act of the same year.

For Black people this was a disillusioning and bewildering
time. The British had come to their countries, plundered them,
exploited materials and people for profit. Now, in some
'recompense', they were made British subjects and encouraged
to work and live in the 'mother' country, only to be given the
worst jobs and housing conditions, to face open racism on the
streets, in pubs and clubs and in employment, only finally to be
legislated against and bounded like some disease (some
mother!).

British dualistic thinking emerged in new and subtle terms. On
the one hand, British capitalism needed labour and, as it
happened, cheap labour was available. The main problem was
that this cheap labour was Black and not entirely desirable. So
limitations had to be made, especially when employment
expansion slowed down. But Britain prided itself on 'fair play'
and 'tolerance', so arguments about discriminatory
immigration policy were played down in favour of a debate on
numbers: in the name of good race relations the number of
Blacks must be small. In 1965, Roy Jenkins laid out Labour's
view:

"First, we have a community made up of a preponderant
indigenous majority and a small, but nevertheless
substantial, minority of different ethnic origins with family
ties in Africa, Asia and the Caribbean. This part of our
community is now developing into a second generation.
Secondly, the British people occupy a largely urban, densely
populated, industrialised island of limited size, possessed
still of great natural and human resources but also with real
economic and social problems and limitations. Our imperial
history, combined with the maladministration of wealth and
prosperity in the world has traditionally produced strong
pressures to migrate to this country. These are basic facts.
They necessitate both a strict limit on the amount and rate of
inward immigration for settlement and an acceptance of

certain well-defined obligations to those we have already accepted here and are settled" (quoted in Barker 1981: 19).

The debate on race, racism, and justice, was turning into one of cultural difference that was tolerable only to a certain extent. This was epitomised by Margaret Thatcher's famous speech of 1978:

"If we went on as we are, then by the end of the century there would be four million people of the New Commonwealth or Pakistan here. Now that is an awful lot and I think it means that people are really rather afraid that this country might be swamped by people with a different culture. And, you know, the British character has done so much for democracy, for law, and done so much throughout the world, that there is a fear that it might be swamped, people are going to react and be rather hostile to those coming in" (*Daily Mail*, 31 January 1978).

This speech marked the onset of what has been termed 'The New Racism' (Barker 1981). This argues: (i) that it is in our human nature to be wary of strangers; (ii) that it is only natural that we should wish to protect those closest to us; (iii) it is, therefore, not racist to dislike strangers or alien cultures, but is, instead, both common sense and natural. This appeal to people's 'genuine fears' links with the sociobiological argument mentioned earlier in a form reminiscent of the philosophy of David Hume. As Barker (1981) has shown, the New Right makes explicit references to Hume's idea that the role of government is to direct the limited, kinship oriented altruism we are 'naturally' equipped with, towards the good of the state. The New Right uses 'instinct' and common sense as central to its thesis of a natural order, but at the same time insists that the state has a role to play in controlling these instincts (the necessity of rationality of white men), and it uses dualistic thinking to its advantage.

Continued and renewed restrictions on immigrants and asylum seekers exploit this combination of 'genuine fears' and 'common sense'. As the 1990 Trust states (1990 Trust 1995: 2): "Since 1968 with the introduction of increasingly harsh immigration legislation, Black communities have seen a massive rise in racial attacks, Black unemployment has increased dramatically and Black people now make up a large percentage of the prison population ... there is no evidence to suggest that strict immigration controls lessen the degree of racism existent within the country at large, in fact all evidence points to the contrary. Stricter immigration measures lead to an increase in racism in society".

Against this backdrop, debates on political correctness deny the existence of racism as a structural reality, whilst accepting that there are different races and alien cultures in Britain.

"It is ironic that in the 1980s in Britain, whilst the belief in the objective existence of race remains consensual in everyday speech and in considered opinion, there is considerable unwillingness to examine the ramifications of racism throughout British life. The irony lies in the fact that race is not a real entity, whilst racism as a range of personal and institutional practices is very real in its existence and impact" (Husband 1986: 3).

The six elements of racism we considered earlier are central to the new racism, but it now contributes to a new strategy that defines 'racism' out of existence. By whipping-up feelings against 'political correctness' it also dismisses the structural nature of racism, reducing it to a matter of personal opinion and even pillories anti-racism in social work education as illiberalism (like Melanie Phillips in her invective in the *Observer* 1.8.92).

Most Black people we know deplore the notion of 'political correctness'. At the same time, it is impossible to deny the structural basis of racism, given what we know about its roots, development, and current direction. Indeed, there needs to be debate and argument as to how we tackle racism and empower Black communities. It is no secret that some racism awareness training has been ineffectual; perhaps badly set-up with poor trainers and unclear goals, and against which there has been enormous implicit or explicit resistance from participants. But this is not a justification for avoiding anti-racist teaching/training/work altogether. In fact, we believe the opposite: now, more than ever, anti-racist teaching and learning strategies must be revised to engender a far wider range of strategic approaches. We must not get sucked into back-pedalling and spending inordinate amounts of time debating terminology. We require more positive and assertive strategies and action that are Black-led.

In the case studies that follow, the development of two groups which started as Asian youth groups in the late 1970s, are outlined. To the authors, they illustrate developments in the history of colonialism, where Black young people, disillusioned and angered by unfulfilled promises and hostile and discriminatory treatment, take a route of self-determination and self-organisation not only for themselves, but also on behalf of a wider anti-racist struggle and for Black empowerment.

Black self-determination (and self-determination is also a term colonised by Tory party philosophy with its individualist interpretation) has historically been concerned with methods and courses of action aimed at the liberation of whole groups of Black people, by people from within those groups. The ANC said the "liberation of each is dependent on the liberation of all". Black self-determination has been necessitated by the lack of real response to the injustices faced by people of colour in the history of slavery and colonialism. Experience has shown that if Black people wait for justice to be done it is a very long time in coming. If there had been no slave rebellions, how long would it have been before abolition? If there was no resistance movements in India, how long would it have been before independence? If there had been no Black Panther movement in the 60s or strikes by Asian workers (women in particular) at Grunwick, Imperial and Chix in the 70s and later in Burnsall in the Midlands, where would we as Black people be? Most of the great Black leaders have advocated self-determination, not primarily because they want Black people to be separate, but because Black people have been separated by white racism; and the only way to achieve rights and justice is to organise away from the various guises of white racism.

One of these guises has been the liberal softly-softly approach of multicultural education, equal opportunity policies, and anti-racist training. Whilst these may be necessary, they are never sufficient and are usually bounded by whoever is commissioning them into what will be acceptable within a racist structure. They very rarely pose a real challenge to this structure and are therefore artifices with limited impact. In order to survive and move beyond survival, in order to start to challenge the sources and infrastructure of racism, it has been necessary for many Black groups to organise for themselves. Again, this is not done just for their own benefit. It is not worthy of us as human beings to merely survive, clinging to lifelines thrown to us by others. For human life to be worth anything we must participate in the world – and it is this participation which is so often unequal and 'racially' blocked by greater powers.

Case Studies

In presenting our studies of Black organisations which we were involved in and which impacted on our pedagogical practice, we are well aware that they were not the first organisations of Black people in Britain. Countless others have been formed since the times of slavery and colonialism (Sivanandan 1982, Fryer 1984). By way of example:

1757 – one of the first known political leaders of Britain's Black community was Oluadah Equaino who arrived here from eastern Nigeria at the age of 12.

1892 – Raja Rammohan Roy was the first Asian to be elected to the House of Commons as a liberal MP for Central Finsbury.

1917 – the first African Students' Union was founded.

1931 – the League of Coloured Peoples was founded.

1945 – the Pan African Congress meeting in Manchester decided to fight for "the absolute and complete independence" of the colonies: if needs be by Gandhian methods of passive resistance (Sivanandan 1982: 3).

1974 – Workers at the Imperial Typewriter factory in Leicester, with mainly Asian women on the front lines, went on strike over racism and exploitation. The strike was won but shortly afterwards the factory was closed down.

(Sources: Fryer 1984, Sivanandan 1982.)

We would also like to acknowledge that if it had not been for the struggles of our mothers, fathers and ancestors our action groups would not have happened at all.

The two organisations below developed entirely separately without knowledge of each other's existence until we came to share our experiences in teaching and in other Black self-organisations.

The Belgrave Baheno Women's Organisation, Leicester

Belgrave Baheno (which started off as Belgrave Girls' Youth Movement, BGYM) was founded in 1979. This was a highly significant time as many of the ideas expressed above were impacting on second generation children of Asian 'immigrants' who were now in their twenties, and in their most politically active period. It was the period just after the passing of the Race Relations Act 1976 and at the time of widespread NF activities. Margaret Thatcher had recently come to power and had just made her infamous 'swamping speech' referred to above. Racial attacks increased, skinheads went 'Paki bashing' and countless Black people were assaulted. A greater awareness of the impact of structural racism created first, disillusionment, then anger, in Black communities – after all the efforts of our parents to integrate and to contribute to this country, our colour was singling us out for the most unhost-like treatment.

A group of young women including Rita Patel, Nayna Bhikha and Karen Chouhan founded the Belgrave Girls' Youth Movement. We were motivated by our own anger and a dawning realisation of the pervasiveness of racism, and also inspired by the Mangrove 9 defence campaign [4] in London and the Bradford Asian Youth Movement which had led to the Bradford 12 defence case [5]. If we were not to be offered state protection but, rather, state attack (e.g. through discriminatory immigration legislation and Thatcher's speeches), we knew we had to organise our own facilities and community supports.

As a radical Asian young women group BGYM was unique in Leicester. Initial scepticism from some of the men in our communities soon turned to support following prejudiced and sexist expectations of one white male development officer who told us that until we got the sexism sorted out in our communities there was no point in providing facilities for us!

We saw ourselves as a movement. We were not dependent upon structures or funding, but driven by purpose, with its pace determined by its constituents, embracing diversity and

difference. It was vital in every sense of the word. It was
inclusive, progressive and extrovert, not afraid to speak up for
its causes, welcoming women and girls from any religion and
any colour provided it was clearly understood that our aim was
to meet the needs of Asian women.

Structural and funding matters were helped by the experience
in banking by two of the founder members. Others contributed
their experiences in the arts, and in running a Raas-Garbe
(Gujarati folk dance) group and giving Gujarati lessons.

It is also extremely important to us to document the support of
our parents. Instead of experiencing a generation gap we
benefited from inter-generational inspiration. We took
guidance from their own struggles in India whilst waiting for
Indian independence; in surviving the violence against Asians
in East Africa; and in starting a life all over again in the alien
environment in Britain.

Our parents' stories need more time and respect, for example:
not having money for a bus fare and having to walk to work;
living off one slice of bread when there was nothing left until
pay day; and not being able to find places to live because of
open colour bars from landlords (they remember the notices in
London saying "no coloureds, no Irish, no dogs"). These
stories made our hearts burst with anger and sorrow and we
knew that our struggle was conducted in luxury by comparison:
we know the system, we know the language, we have many
more choices about education than they did, and we have
access to more money than they had, etc.

BGYM started with very basic concerns. Many of the young
women in our communities had no place to meet. At first we
revelled in the opportunity to play sport together and listen to
music and we were able to get some small grants for meeting
room space in the local neighbourhood centre. We shared
personal griefs and heartaches, dealt with domestic violence
and betrayals, racial violence on the streets or in schools, cried
together and laughed together, and then kicked arse together
where we needed to!

However, it became increasingly difficult to meet at the local
neighbourhood centre because of the unwarranted attention of
young lads and White 'Status Quo' look-alike youth workers

who felt it was cool to be working with Asian women. Looking back, although we used to get pretty fed up with the Asian lads, we really loved them in a sisterly way because they tried to protect us as well. It was hard for them because they were expected to be tough by everyone; so they had to learn to be – very fast. They could not tell their parents because they were afraid of being told-off for fighting or because they would also want to protect them. They were fighting hard battles on the streets and in the schools with White youths. One secondary school in the area was notorious because coming out of school meant you had to cross a bridge and every day the White kids would wait to beat the Asians up. So the authorities let the Asian kids out of school earlier than the White kids! It didn't stop the fighting because there were always the mornings and break times. So we had to organise ourselves to ensure we moved in large groups and we learned to fight and strategise.

In BGYM we learned our politics on the street, In the uprisings of 1980 and 1981 many young women were on the front lines or organising support services. We set up training courses for ourselves and worked with African and Asian youth groups across the city. We invited councillors, police, trade unions, chief officers of local authorities, and government ministers to come and speak. Surprisingly many of them did! These sessions were great because we opened a dialogue and made contacts with people we had always believed to be inaccessible. Equally, the speakers realised that we weren't going to bite their heads off, but really wanted to talk and learn. After that we went to council meetings, lobbied councillors, ran campaigns, and sometimes even helped the authority, for example, in organising demonstrations against ratecapping. But, under the weight of government pressure, our relationship with the local authority changed. They became more bureaucratic than ever and distanced themselves from local radical activity. This even applied to individuals from the ranks, who one day were with us on the streets and the next they were councillors who had forgotten how they got there.

After the uprisings of 1981, we applied for and received Inner City Programme funding for a women and girls' centre. This was the first women's centre of any description in Leicester. This was not an easy task because the authority's first priority was keeping young men occupied. The money available for inner city programmes and Michael Heseltine's 'task forces' were intended for three projects that aimed at containment. However, without addressing the causes and roots of dissatisfaction, these projects could not hope to provide containment – only temporary diversions. Even after the Scarman report (1982), which identified unemployment and policing strategies as crucial factors, the government's emphasis remained on projects, with limited resources and unable to deal with structures and systems at the root of the problems. Today, these problems are as manifest as in 1980, and cuts in public spending have hit Black projects very hard.

By 1983, BGYM became Belgrave Baheno (Sisters) because we wanted to include in our name women of all ages. On the first day of opening a refurbished terraced house in Belgrave, 300 people came to see the centre, 100 women joined up immediately, and annual membership grew to 1,000. Belgrave Baheno helped in the development of other organisations in Leicester, e.g. the Leicester Asian Youth Project. It set up projects on employment and domestic violence as well as for a range of social, educational, and issue-based activities. Now we have another house and are completing a feasibility study for a purpose-built centre which will act as a state-of-the-art conference and training facility for women and girls. We firmly believe that Asian women are leaders and have a potential which has not yet been appreciated. It is our wish that, by the beginning of the next millennium, Asian women will be in leading positions in economic and social fields at both national and international levels.

Belgrave Baheno were also founder members of the National Black Caucus which is an alliance of Asian and African people with national networks. This reflects a guiding principle throughout our development: if we recognise the keen sense of colour on which racism is focused then it is our duty to fight alongside those who also suffer from it. We know that the use of the term Black to cover Asian and African people is contentious among many Asians and Africans. However, for us, the term is important because we use it in an inclusive and radical way. Inclusively, because in an age of multiple identities, using the 'identity' Black does not mean you have to relinquish other identities. Radically, because it is obvious that Black is not descriptive; it does not literally relate to anyone's true skin colour and was an exaggeration first used by White men. Therefore, when it is used by Black people now, it is a challenge, it is a rebellion, it is radical, and it symbolises the fight for change. We would not argue that it is an automatically unifying term because, as Sivanandan says (1982), Black communities are more a mosaic of unities. True unity comes through accepting that there will never be uniformity, in the sense of everyone thinking or doing the same, but that it will be achieved by working for each other. Black, then, is a rallying call for radical action for those people who wish to stand behind it and who recognise its loaded history and meaning.

Belgrave Baheno also initiated the 1990 Trust which is a national Black charity that aims to influence and develop social policy in relation to Black people. It has received a substantial sum of money from the lotteries board to develop an information technology network for Black communities.

The strength of our organisation is not celebrated by those who feel threatened by it, as many councillors do on account of it being a women's group, mainly Asian, and a voluntary organisation. All three factors together are supposed to spell 'quiet and marginal'. Putting together the facts: nearly 5,000 have joined us since we opened; many of us are active politically; we are never afraid to speak out; we have a track record of squeaky-clean financial management; we have just produced feasibility plans for a £5m new centre. All this has been achieved despite having had our local authority grant cut over the last five years. It is apparent, therefore, that Belgrave Baheno cannot be marginal or tranquil: we have become a local and national symbol of empowerment.

Asian Action Group Ltd (AAG)

Asian Action Group Ltd (AAG) is a youth and community action group which was founded in 1978 to represent the needs and aspirations of Asians living in the London Borough of Haringey.

The Census for Haringey of 1981 showed that out of a total population of 200,247 people, there were 59,632 people from the New Commonwealth countries and Pakistan (29.8%, compared to the national total of just under 4%). The Asian population from the Indian sub-continent of Haringey had reached 10,090, forming approximately 17% of the total ethnic minority population, with the rest being made up of people from the Caribbean (22,005 or 37%) and from Cyprus, Greece, Turkey, etc. (CRE 1981).

Our personal path in becoming active in AAG was typical of many Black and Asian young people. Coming from an Asian Kenyan background, we had brought with us an image of England that clashed with out actual experiences of discrimination and harrassment. We only gradually gave up blaming ourselves for 'educational failures', and for 'not trying hard enough to adjust', and began to understand the nature of structural racism.

By the time we had joined AAG in 1980, the group had already been in existence for two years. It operated from a Youth Centre in Tottenham which was made available by the local authority for four hours every Sunday. The main functions of the group were to provide leisure and sporting activities. This played an important role in bringing together young Asian people into a safe and comfortable environment.

However, the group had a small number of politically committed members who became involved in campaigns that addressed racism and immigration issues. These campaigns were not attended by all the members of the group but they served to raise awareness of broader issues that affected the Asian communities.

Although racial discrimination in both its direct and indirect forms was acknowledged in the 1976 Race Relations Act, our understanding of racism was very much located within our own experiences of schooling, housing, employment, and our social lives. The persistence and pervasiveness of racist ideology, set within a 'democratic' political framework, and which distinguished and graded you on the basis of race, colour, or culture, proved difficult to rationalise and come to terms with. The NF continued its provocative confrontational marches, which often proved violent, through areas with large immigrant populations. The lack of protection from these attacks led to a loss of confidence in the police and a recognition of the need for Black and Asian communities to defend themselves.

AAG members became actively involved in national campaigns to protest against the racist attacks on our communities, the lack of police action against the perpetrators, and the deportations of immigrants who had settled in Britain. One major campaign in which the group became involved was the Bradford 12 Defence Campaign [6]. Marches were organised in towns and cities where racist attacks were at their highest, and this brought together similar organisations from all over the country in a united effort to free the 12 charged. This engaged us in frequent campaign meetings, inviting speakers and community activists to give talks to members, and attending protest marches. This campaign ended successfully with all the charges being dropped.

Although these campaigns gave members of the AAG confidence and a belief in our ability to take actions against injustices, the demands of organising such involvements through voluntary effort, and with little finance, led to severe strains being placed on just a few members. This forced a fairly radical evaluation of our strategies and objectives.

An internal reflective evaluation during the early 1980s led to an agreement that we needed to focus more systematically on local issues that concerned young Asians in Haringey than we had done in the past, and to establish a full-time operational base in Haringey. This required skills in accessing finance and other resources and recruiting new members. National events provided an acute context and eventually some financial basis for our work.

In 1981, 13 young Black people died in a fire in a house in Deptford, south London; one of many attacks on the Black community that the police discounted as racially motivated. However, members of the community were convinced that the fire and attacks had been started by fascists. The police in response launched their campaign "Swamp 81"; a London-wide exercise designed to quell the protest marches that followed the Deptford fire. In 6 days, 943 people were stopped in the street and 118 arrested.

Soon after, in Brixton, south London, Black people took to the streets in protest. Three months later, after an attack by fascists from outside the area on an Asian woman in Southall, west London, people once again took direct action. A major uprising in the Toxteth district of Liverpool followed where both Black and White young people fought the police and burned down 150 buildings. Within a few days, this uprising had spread to: Manchester, Birmingham, Leeds, Bolton, Luton, Leicester, Nottingham, Birkenhead, Hackney (London), Haringey (London), Walthamstow (London), Hull, Southampton, Halifax, Bedford, Gloucester, Sheffield,

Coventry, Portsmouth, Bristol, Edinburgh, Reading,
Huddersfield, Blackburn, Preston, Chester, Stoke,
Shrewsbury, Wolverhampton, Newcastle, Derby, Stockport,
and numerous other places (Fryer, 1984).

As a response to these uprisings, the government set up an
Urban Aid Grant scheme specifically targeting deprived inner
city areas. In the same year, the Greater London Council
(GLC), an elected body that managed London's services,
became Labour controlled. They set up an Ethnic Minorities
Unit whose brief was to provide financial resources and
support to anti-racist efforts. The new initiatives of the GLC
culminated in the anti-racist year of 1984/5 during which a very
successful public campaign against racism was run.

In spite of not having had training in how to fundraise and
lobby, we were fortunate to receive considerable support and
encouragement from individuals both in Labour controlled
Haringey and the GLC. For the first time, we felt we had
access to people with power who were truly concerned for the
needs of groups such as ours. Walking through the corridors of
power, and lobbying council officers and politicians was a
daunting, and at times, overwhelming experience. Making
public presentations and arguing our position were new and
difficult skills to acquire. We learned on our feet.

Following a number of attempts, we succeeded in securing
substantial grants to set up our base in Haringey in 1983. The
hard core group of members who had worked on this felt
inspired and this in turn attracted new members to the group.
There were those that disagreed with the new strategy because
they felt that relying on grants would create dependency and
compromise our political beliefs. The majority, however,
believed that some money was better than no money.

As our awareness of race and racism grew we began better to
analyze our experiences. By networking with other Black and
Asian organisations, the group came to accept racism as a
system of domination, either directly or indirectly, by one
racial group over another on the basis of an assumed
superiority. Racism was often reduced to the formula:
prejudice-plus-power-equals-racism. Whilst this was a gross
over-simplification of the issue, it nevertheless served to open
up a dialogue with those in the group who were less political or
academic.

The new membership of AAG expanded to non-Asian friends or partners who took part in the activities of the group and now wished to become active members, including taking up positions on the management committee. After many heated debates it was resolved that the leadership of the group would remain Asian, but that the membership criteria would be widened to include non-Asians, allowing a limited number of them to take up positions on the management committee.

Anti-racism for us became a struggle led by Asian people but which included trusted and committed anti-racist members irrespective of their racial origin. This position stood us apart from other 'Black' organisations in Britain that insist that their membership should strictly be confined to 'Black' people [7].

Growing awareness within the group spurred dialogue across a variety of fronts. Sexism, sexuality, disability, class, caste, age, and a whole host of other issues, were opened up for debate and actions. Compulsory representation on the management committee for women and young people was written into the constitution. The women of the group established their own centre in another part of Haringey. Some members organised leisure activities for disabled people. Cultural events were held to celebrate and learn about the diversity within the Asian community.

The 1987 general election saw the return of the Thatcher government for the third time. All was not lost though because Haringey saw its first Black Labour MP Bernie Grant elected to parliament. This reflected local peoples' discontent with the changes affecting them.

Between 1981 and 1989, the gap between the rich and the poor widened: income in the top bracket increased nearly twice as much as for those in the bottom bracket (CSO 1991). Unemployment, the relative decline in the youth wage, worsening housing supply, and the impact of policies such as 'community care', led to a major increase in youth homelessness (Thornton 1990). The loss of income support for those aged 16-18 meant that the majority of young people remained dependent on their parents for longer. These policies had a disproportionate impact on Black and Asian communities, particularly in terms of unemployment and poverty (OPCS 1985), but also in their ability to respond effectively to issues of concern to them.

AAG became increasingly popular as a meeting place for young Asians and their friends. In 1987 the group elected its first woman chair. Structured and unstructured activities of the group provided opportunities for members to share ideas and experiences. The 'home from home' atmosphere allowed members to break their alienation from their own cultural groups as well as from society at large.

Tensions between the elderly people in the Asian community and the youth surfaced from time to time. The inter-generational conflict between a yesterday that sought to resist changes to cultural traditions and norms clashed with the emerging values of the new generation seeking to affirm new ideas and values. AAG provided an important setting for those young people who were unable to explore their feelings and new identities with their parents or other elders in the family.

During this period, three successive generations of young people passed through the group. A few of the older members and some of the newer members have remained consistently involved, but the constitutional three year term for committee members failed to stem the rapid turnover on the management committee. As a consequence, the workload became shouldered by a committed few.

A new and young committee in 1989, found itself caught between the growing social needs of its members on the one hand and addressing financial shortages on the other. These had arisen as a result of the cuts in public expenditure and the abolition of the Inner London Education Authority and the Greater London Council, as well as by the rate capping measures imposed on local authorities. Voluntary organisations were coerced into undertaking work for the local authority. "Increasingly they are having to bid against one another" (Smith 1991). AAG became one of only two voluntary youth organisations serving the ethnic minority communities in Haringey. The group prioritised the need to secure future funds through a borough-wide campaign, and run over a period of several years. Lobbying and campaign work consumed a large portion of workers' and management committee's efforts. Normal activities of the group suffered and this reduced opportunities for networking and learning through sharing experiences.

From 1992 onwards, new arrivals of refugees and Bangldeshi

families from East London into Haringey have given rise to a new youth membership. Their needs have been unique and different to those young people born and brought up in this country. Workers at AAG became engaged in case work to assist young people with seeking employment and housing. Increasingly though, we have had to refer young people to other services because we were unable to cope with the demands of the new membership.

The cuts in its funding may force the group to re-examine its entire relationship with, and the dangers of depending upon, the local authority. Although the local authority has clear responsibilities to fund such work, the group now has to find alternative ways of raising income through grant aid from a variety of government and non-government programmes, as well as through the development of community businesses.

Despite these financial cut-backs, the group has firmly held on to its belief that the needs of its membership should be central to its work. This has allowed AAG to develop even in times when securing future finances has been a priority. However, to focus too heavily on individuals in trouble can lead all too easily to a situation where their difficulties are seen as personal rather than political. The group has more recently been developing and improving ways in which it fosters learning and development. It is as crucial now as it has always been to engage members in a dialogue that allows them to formulate their own personal and political opinions in order to take collective actions to address the causes, rather than the symptoms, of their oppression.

Activities of the European far-Right, including that of the British National Party, have led to an increase in the number of attacks on Black and Asian people. "Banding together in prosperous nation states, Fortress Europe is hostile not just to non-white people but to poor whites from Eastern Europe as well" (New Internationalist 1994). The recent European recession has seen politicians blaming immigrants and refugees, pitting poor people against each other, when the economy, and not race, is the real problem. The European Union does not appear to offer greater security for Black and Asian people. On the contrary, our lives appear to be more threatened. For the membership of AAG these developments are a major concern.

The group has now been in existence for close-on 16 years. It will not be long before the offspring of the older members become part of the group! The group needs to provide a sense of history, of change and stability, of continuity and development for all its members past, present and future. The liberation struggle has always been an historical one unifying generations of people across time. The group has been the creative expression of our community's struggle in Britain.

Conclusions and implications for YCW

Though written separately, these case studies show significant similarities, and illustrate the continued relevance of the core elements of racism identified above. In the histories of their parents and through their own experiences, both groups of young people had witnessed the effects of a capitalism which used race for its own ends: firstly, by exploiting the reserves of other countries, and then inviting a contingent labour force after the war and rejecting them when they were no longer needed. At the same time, social needs were ignored, and attacks on these communities were condoned by the utterances of MPs such as Enoch Powell and Margaret Thatcher, and by racist immigration laws. Young people growing up in English schools experienced attacks and insecure prospects. From this early realisation anger grew and, whilst a minority of people expressed this in riots, most turned to self-organisation and self-help in community projects and businesses [8]. As young people, we were surrounded by the ideology of the inferiority of Blackness in opposition to the superiority of Whiteness. This was reinforced by erroneous explanations of the position of Black people: they could not get a good job because they could not get qualifications (they were less intelligent) and sponged off social security. Paradoxically, they were also held responsible for: taking all the jobs and worsening the unemployment situation; they lived all crowded together in squalor in the slum areas (Black equalled dirty); they smelled different, talked a funny language and practised strange religions; they had lots of children and many African women were single mothers; and what about all the Black rapists – so their sexual desires had to be different. We were truly alien.

We claimed at the beginning that more emphasis on analysis and strategy in Black-led action is required. The case studies demonstrate that many groups are already doing this and are thinking ahead. From this experience the notion of Black empowerment has become crucial. Black empowerment is the process by which self-organised Black groups engage in self-directed learning aimed at taking collective actions to address their own oppression. This does not exclude White people. On the contrary, it is vital that White people understand and work alongside Black people in a supportive and strategic role. But there is a difference: a White person can always choose to step out of the struggle and return to a life without Black people or racism. Black people cannot.

This is, in part, why we feel it is a mistake for youth and community workers or workplace and community groups to invest the greater part of their anti-racist strategy in anti-racist training for White workers, particularly if there is no opportunity to work with what has been learned. At least an equal amount of time should be invested in Black communities and groups on empowerment strategies. One successful Black group can be the spur for so many more, as we have seen in the case of Belgrave Baheno whose foundation led to the National Black Caucus and the 1990 Trust, as well as support for many other groups in Leicester. Both case studies demonstrated the national effect that the Bradford 12 Defence Case and the Mangrove 9 had in inspiring people to fight back and organise for their own rights.

We will now return to the implications for the pedagogy of anti-racism. We work with White and Black students and we have found that some White students in particular find these arguments hard to understand. It is not our role as teachers to give them this analysis and command them to digest or accept it, but neither is it our role to be so liberal and non-committal that they are left with no reference points at all. We all have to seek to engage in critical dialogue starting from our very different positions and experiences. This is mirrored throughout the history of race relations. Once the dialogue is severed, relationships break down and this leads to increased misunderstandings. On the other hand, we see it as our duty to tell about the White people who have courageously worked alongside Black people and fought racism in South Africa, America, Germany etc.

In terms of our teaching on racism and anti-racism within the context of youth and community work courses, it has been important for us to bring our experiences as Black activists to bear. This has been for several reasons:

1. We expect students to use their experiences but they sometimes need help to recognise and transform them into an analytical process. It helps if tutors can share their own developmental practical and theoretical paths and demonstrate how to make analytical links.

2. Giving real examples of where practice worked or did not work gives a sense of connection with practice and enables students to use tutors as resources.

3. Only few of the textbooks document Black youth and community work development from the perspective of Black authors (e.g. John 1981, Ohri et al. 1982, Dadzie 1993).

4. Being able to give facts as well as telling true life 'stories', makes for a good combination of teaching methods: it places these facts of racism within an everyday context. Incidentally, this is a method that the ancient civilisations of India, China and Africa used, as well as many western and eastern philosophers.

5. It empowers students to take some action themselves by demonstrating how a small group of people can indeed organise and get results.

6. It provides role models for students by demonstrating the need to be active as well as academic. This enables Black students to feel 'validated' because they frequently question themselves and are in turn questioned by White students and tutors. They are often beginning to face up to the fact that racism is not just a personal thing, at a time when some White students and tutors will unwittingly and completely deny Black students their experience.

7. Through talking about our personal development paths, we can show that we were not born into activism or anti-racism. All our own efforts to be accepted led to the realisation of how impossible this is beyond the micro-level of family and friends. Typically a personal path can go something like this (and much of this has been illustrated in our case studies):

a. Attempts to be accepted (for example by talking like

'they' do, trying desperately to wear fashion clothes, avoiding entering the kitchen at home because you did not want to smell of 'wog' food as they call it).

b. Personal anger and hurt at rejection and discrimination despite all attempts to integrate.

c. Realisation of the extent and structural nature of racism. Once you understand racism for yourself you can then see more clearly where it is happening to others. For some Black people there is a tendency to deny discrimination. This is because they do not want to deal with either the repercussions of that fact for themselves or the harshness of the dehumanisation it implies, or the action they may feel they have to take.

d. Sense of powerlessness. Once you know more about racism the possibility of getting redress seems even more removed; the talk of a multi-racial society or the occasional equal opportunities policy is just a rosy façade. The need to share this frustration becomes urgent.

e. Everyday contacts with others who feel the same powerlessness and keep struggling can bring a cathartic and empowering sense of release. This is often the start of alliances and networks of people with similar interests.

f. Building of organisations and movements. With the knowledge of other people's experiences, support, and determination, voluntary and community organisations can be developed.

g. Developing strength through education (sometimes self-directed). Training and continuous education for as many as possible are essential.

h. Developing analyses and strategies. With gathering experience and knowledge comes the ability to assess events around you – why they are happening, who is behind them, what is the purpose, how to take appropriate action.

i Wider networking nationally and internationally.

> Eventually groups see the need to take the struggle
> further afield and build bigger alliances.

The above development path, which is set out in a
chronological order, is, in reality, more likely to be a spiral. In
the movement forwards, previous stages are often revisited
within a different sphere of action. Analysis and strategy are
developmental and ongoing by their very nature and they
therefore need to draw on the past to prepare for the future.

Our main pedagogical concern is to help students understand
Black empowerment and the importance of anti-racist
movements that work according to the agendas of Black
people. There is a need for YCW workers to critically appraise
the work they are doing and to see what kind of model it is
following so as to determine whether it facilitates meaningful
engagement with young Black people. The history of racism
and of the anti-racist struggle shows that the phenomena are
complex and that racism changes its forms continuously.
Therefore, anti-racist strategies have to be continuously re-
evaluated and adapted. Above all, our strategies and
movements will need to be multi-faceted and operate across
political, ideological, structural, cultural, and personal
domains. One central challenge remains: to destroy the
mythical ideology of White superiority that has underpinned
western racism and which has been used to justify so much
injustice.

Bibliography

1990 Trust (1995), Briefing Paper on the Asylum and
Immigration Bill 1995/6, London: 1990 Trust

Banton, M. and Harwood, J. (1975), The Race Concept,
Newton Abbot: David and Charles

Barker, M. (1981), The New Racism, London: Junction Books

Central Statistical Office (1991), Social Trends 21, London:
HMSO

Chouhan, J. (1991), The Communication Environment of the
Gujarati Community in Leicester, unpublished Ph.d. thesis:
University of Bradford

Chouhan, K. (1986), The Paranoia of the New Right, unpublished M.Sc. thesis: University of Bradford

Chouhan, K. (1984), Western Dualism and Racism, unpublished report

Chouhan, V. (1992), Beyond Steel Bands 'n' Samosas, Leicester: National Youth Agency

CRE, (1985), Ethnic Minority: statistical information on the pattern of settlement in Britain, London

Dadzie, S. (1993), Racetracks, London: Greenwich County Council

Fryer, P. (1984), Staying Power: The History of Black people in Britain, London: Pluto Press

Hoch, P. (1979), White Hero, Black Beast: racism, sexism and the mask of masculinity, London: Pluto Press

Hodge, J. L., Struckman, D. K., Dorland Trust, L. (1975), Cultural Bases of Racism and Group Oppression, Berkeley, California: Two Riders Press

Husband, C. (1987), 'Race' in Britain – continuity and change, London: Hutchinson (2nd ed.)

Husband, C. (1986), Racism, Prejudice and Social Policy; in Coombe, V. and Little, A., Race and Social Work, London: Routledge

Jeffs, T. and Smith, M. (1990), Using Informal Education, London: Macmillan

John, G. (1981), In the service of Black youth: A study of the political culture of youth and community work with Black people in English cities, London: National Association of Youth Clubs

Jordan, W. D. (1974), The White Man's Burden, Oxford: Oxford University Press

Layton-Henry, Z. (1992), The Politics of Immigration, Oxford: Blackwell.

Miles, R. and Phizacklea, A. (1984), White man's country –
Racism in British Politics, London: Pluto Press

Miles, R. (1993), Racism after 'race relations', London:
Routledge

New Internationalist (1994), Race: Unlocking Prejudice, No
260

NYA (1991), Consultation Seminars – towards the Third
Ministerial Conference, Leicester: National Youth Agency

NYB (1991), Towards a core curriculum – the next step.
Report of the Second Ministerial Conference, Leicester:
National Youth Bureau

Ohri, A., Manning, B. and Curno, P. (1982), Community
work and racism, London: Routledge

OPCS, (1985), Labour Force Survey, London: HMSO

OPCS, (1991), Office of Public Census Statistics: Census:
Great Britain 1991, London: HMSO

Scarman, L. G. (1982), The Scarman Report: The Brixton
disorders 10-12 April 1981, Harmondsworth: Penguin

Sivanandan, A. (1982), A Different Hunger: Writings on
Black resistance, London: Pluto Press

Smith, M. (1991), The Challenge for Voluntary Youth Work
Organisations, YMCA National College, London

Thornton, R. (1990), The New Homeless. The crisis of youth
homelessness and the response of the local housing authorities,
London: SHAC

Notes

1.   Anti-racism is work against racism which is directed at all
people; Black empowerment is work primarily focused on
Black people in anti-racist struggles. It is work which is geared
to ensuring that the investment in ourselves gives us enough
power to take more control of what is happening to us.

2.   Informal education denotes the recognised practice of good YCW workers who concentrate on working from where people are and in using dialogue and engagement as primary methods for work. See Jeffs and Smith (1990).

3.   Black refers to all people of Asian and African descent, whilst the terms Asian and African are used when specifically relating to one group only. For a discussion of the usage of the term see case study 'Belgrave Baheno'.

4.   The Mangrove restaurant in Notting Hill, a meeting place for Black people, became the target for police harassment. Things came to a head when they tried to close the restaurant down and nine Black people were arrested. The community took on the judicial system and won (see Sivanandan 1982, and the Institute of Race Relations (1979) 'Police Against Black People'). Several of the people involved at this time later became active in the National Black Caucus, which is discussed in the BGYM case study.

5.   This was a case where 12 young Asian men from Bradford had been arrested for taking direct action to defend their communities without relying on the police. Their slogan "Self Defence is No Offence" became the rallying cry for many campaigns.

6.   See note 5.

7.   The group did not, at this stage, make the distinction between anti-racism and Black empowerment work.

8.   See Sivanandan (1982), for a detailed review of this period and, in particular, the discussion of how the organisation developed.

6. Anti-racist youth work approaches in Germany

Bärbel Kampmann

The following examples of anti-racist youth work and the underlying principles were developed in the context of my work for the *Regionale Arbeitsstelle zur Förderung ausländischer Kinder und Jugendlicher* (RAA, Regional Resource Centre for Foreign Children and Youth), which the *Land Northrhine Westfalia* set up in 1980 together with several other such centres. The Activities of the RAA are guided by the idea that young people from different national backgrounds should not be put under pressure to integrate into German society. Rather, they should be given opportunities to develop their personal and cultural identities on a par with those of German youth: they have the right to be different. In the course of my work, and in reflecting upon my own situation as a member of the community of Black Germans, it became more and more obvious to me that the realisation of these principles required an explicit confrontation with racism in both a political and pedagogical sense. Young people mirror the world of adults in broad and sometimes distorted outlines. Their situation and our educational methods are, therefore, intricately linked to prevailing social and political concerns.

An encounter with racism is for young people not merely a matter that raises questions concerning their socialisation, but has to be part of a wider confrontation with racism in German society. Particularly after the fall of the Berlin Wall, violence motivated by racism became an unavoidable issue for youth work. All pedagogical intervention has to first ask: what are the functions that racism fulfills in a given society? (Holzkamp 1994). I regard young people as searching for orientation, and for reliable cognitive and emotional reference points in a world that is, ultimately, frightening for them (Held et al. 1995). The confrontation with racism is part of this search, and I try to facilitate their encounter with this phenomenon in such a way that they learn to understand it as an issue for society as a whole and to develop their own position in relation to it.

The fact that the overwhelming majority of the groups of youth and young adults that I work with are of a multi-cultural nature, (except for those representing specific sub-cultures), gives me the opportunity to relate the conflicts that arise amongst them to their position in the wider society. For the young adults, the connection is even more immediate because they have to deal with issues such as finding accommodation and jobs, dealing with bureaucracy, etc. This gives constant rise to conflicts, to exclusion, and to discrimination on the grounds of ideology. Whilst my work with the younger and the older age groups is based on the same principles, the second part of the programme has a different emphasis for each age group: I find conflict resolution strategies a priority for the younger group, whilst for the young adults of between 20 and 30 years, the programme is a kind of supervision in relation to work and training.

Anti-racist youth work for me has four main objectives:

- recognising the social and political structures within which racism fulfills specific functions;

- recognising one's own position within these structures and learning to exercise informed choices;

- working out appropriate strategies of conflict resolution;

- recognising one's own racist tendencies and to try to integrate them in a different way.

My understanding of racism is closely related to the factors identified by Memmi (1992) as constitutive of a racist ideology:

(a)   that racial differences have a biological basis which allows for the objective distinction of 'pure races';

(b)   that pure races are biologically superior to others and that this superiority also manifests itself in psychological, social and cultural terms;

(c)   these differences combine to legitimate the power and the privileges of the 'more advanced' groups.

Despite the utter rejection of the scientific basis of the logic of racism (for instance in the conclusions of the 1950 UNESCO meeting of experts), racist ideology is once more gaining prominence in all parts of Europe in various guises. In Germany, the term *'Ausländerfeindlichkeit'* (literally 'hostility against foreigners': xenophobia), dominated the public debates with, in my opinion, clear ideological intentions. Firstly, the term suggests that hostility is directed against all foreigners, whereas discriminatory and excluding practices affect different groups of foreigners in different ways, i.e. according to 'racially' informed classifications. Secondly, the term carefully avoids any connection with the discredited racism of Hitler Fascism. This plays down references to the specific German implications of racism in the light of German history.

Anti-racist youth work therefore has to deal with racism at two levels; firstly, at the level of the structural, cultural, and psychological factors that give rise to racism and, secondly at the political, social and individual level in terms of the functions it serves. I illustrate this with the following diagram:

Functions of racism

political level	social level	personal level
legitimates and reinforces power	creates scapegoats	fosters sense of superiority
conceals contradictions	reference point for collective identity	defence against anxiety
diverts attention away from political misjudgements		externalises negative traits
promotes exploitation		'ethnifies' problems

Anchoring of racism

structural/institutional level	cultural level	individual level
discriminatory legislation	stereotypical images	racialised socialisation
discriminatory official practices (housing, employment etc.)	undifferentiated media reporting	selective perception of 'the other'
'unintended' discriminatory practices (schooling, health etc.)	language (jokes, racist phrases etc.)	generalisation of of single cases
	advertising	cognitive distortion and ignorance

Racism is particularly attractive to some young people today because it seems to offer stability in terms of values and hierarchies, in a rapidly changing world where the need to make independent judgements and choices appears to become too burdensome. This simplified stability feeds on the personal fears, stereotypical images, and political and legal barriers, designed to ward off what is foreign and threatening. The coming together of these various factors is not the result of a conspiracy, but of a complex play of forces and interests that mutually reinforce each other unless they encounter resistance at the various levels simultaneously. My approach to anti-racist youth work attempts to take account of this complexity.

The tasks of the RAA in our part of Germany include the following:

- Offering community based support to young people of foreign origin through individual counselling and advice services, support for self-help initiatives, employment and training support schemes, cultural events etc.

- Liaison with educational institutions, parents, training agencies, and leisure centres, over issues of ethnic and cultural diversity.

- Networking of initiatives of similar inter-cultural orientation within the district and throughout schools.

- Opening out the school and the curriculum to questions and issues that directly affect pupils from different ethnic backgrounds in their social life.

- Development of a better understanding between different ethnic communities through an 'inter-cultural' educational approach.

- Assisting in the setting up of autonomous information and action centres that work against discrimination.

This means that our work has to be seen in the context of a range of responses to the racism and discrimination prevalent in Germany today to which we take a critical position, as outlined below.

1. Scientific analyses and research

Research projects in Germany in recent years, have tended to concentrate upon violence against migrants and asylum seekers, and on the apparent rise of Neo-Nazi groups amongst young people (Heitmeyer 1987). These studies usually concentrate on specific historical or social aspects of the phenomenon, such as racism in the media (Held et al. 1991; Gerhard 1992); the links between racism and migration (Castles 1987); and research on racism and ethnocentrism amongst young people in employment (Leiprecht 1992). Whilst such research is providing valuable data, it is often difficult to establish its relevance for direct work with young people.

2. Public appeals and campaigns

There have been several public campaigns in Germany in recent years, directed at specific aspects of xenophobia. A popularised slogan was "All people are aliens, almost everywhere", which aimed to reduce the gap between public perceptions of migrants and asylum seekers on the one hand, and 'people like us' on the other. However, the slogan contains serious misconceptions because discrimination is focused, not on people's status as foreigners, but on racialised characteristics, appearance, and social behaviour. It is easy for such campaigns to trivialise the underlying conflicts and to serve to ease the conscience of the population rather than to identify the areas in which change needs to be implemented.

3. Self-awareness projects and workshops

These initiatives have snowballed in Germany in recent years. They are run on the lines of 'race awareness training' and deal with the latent racist tendencies of the participants. They are mainly directed at staff in statutory and voluntary social services and at youth workers. Without wishing to deny that the recognition of internalised strategies of asserting power and the tendencies to oppress are an important aspect of anti-racist work, I am of the opinion that many of these projects become bogged down in producing feelings of guilt and self-blame within the left-leaning milieu to which they largely appeal, without placing these psychological components within an overall context of a political strategy.

4. Youth work with young people of a neo-nazi subculture

Research on the lifestyle and activities of gangs of young people with right-wing and racist political views and who are often responsible for violence against ethnic minority groups in Germany (Heitmeyer et al. 1992), has spawned a host of new youth work initiatives that are designed to 'reach' these young people. The extensive research findings indicate that they may be regarded as the 'victims of a risk society', who turn against the threat to their identity and self-worth that is posed by modernity, with the images and 'certainties' of nationalist, fascist, and racist ideologies (Butterwegge 1994). Their behaviour normally excludes them from using general youth clubs and centres, and so most of the new projects apply a street-work approach in order to gradually engage these groups of young people in a process of reflection on their own situation (Heim et al. 1991; Krafeld et al. 1993). The method applied has been termed 'accepting youth work' because it does not set any pre-conditions and at times operates with thrilling, adventurous activities set in direct 'competition' against the excitement generated by the gangs' troublesome behaviour ('sky-diving instead of football hooliganism'). The aim is to offer alternatives to their constant provocations of conflict that are born out of frustration. However, this is where my personal reservations set in. Such projects can amount to an attempt at 'pathologising' extremist and racist behaviour and are in danger of losing sight of the context of racism. Some of this work seems to play right into the hands of a macho culture because it attempts to 'meet the young people on their own territory' without questioning the political foundations of this culture. Nevertheless, this area of research has at least revealed the link between major social and political changes and the behaviour of these youngsters, particularly in terms of their vulnerability to racist ideology (Farin and Seidel-Pielen 1993).

5. 'Inclusive' youth work

Many youth projects in Germany now aim to provide opportunities for youth from different ethnic backgrounds to meet and become engaged in joint activities. These so-called 'join-in' projects, offer participants the opportunity to acquire skills for circus activities, playing theatre together (often on topics related to inter-cultural issues), and for producing films and videos. International youth exchange programmes with work-camps, and activities such as those described in the last chapter of this volume, also contribute to provide young people with the opportunity to see their localised experiences in a wider, and sometimes, global context. They are guided by the educational assumption that an encounter with young people from different ethnic and cultural communities at an early age, will make it harder for racist ideologies to have an effect upon them. However, in my experience, they can only deal with the issue of racism at a personal level if personal experiences are brought into focus, and if young people are given opportunities to broaden their positive experiences within a multi-ethnic group into wider social contexts. This becomes pedagogically difficult without 'moralising' and trivialising the issue of anti-racism as if it was just a matter of 'people getting on with each other'.

6. Direct support and civil rights campaigns

Lastly, and in this context, mention must be made of the numerous activities of voluntary groups, both inside and outside political organisations, that explicitly address the political issue of discrimination. In recent years, campaigns have been organised on issues demanding: the right for migrants resident in Germany to participate in elections; the right to dual nationality; a law against discrimination; compensation following racially motivated attacks; and for the banning of extreme right wing parties. In addition, there are direct support groups for refugees and asylum seekers in almost all German towns where refuges and camps exist. A considerable proportion of the local population become involved in acts of solidarity, ranging from offering protection on 'dangerous anniversaries' when the danger of racist attacks is greater, to voluntary work on language courses, help with school work, collections of clothing, etc. Not all of these activities have a broad and explicit political dimension but many of the volunteers become conscious of the wider connections with racism in the course of their work.

Through a review of these intitiatives, and reflecting upon my own work as a teacher, a psychologist, and a youth leader, I have become even more convinced that racism is not primarily a 'personal issue' and that activities focusing on a particular aspect must maintain a link that recognises the complexity of racism. It is not a matter of getting German nationals to recognise their latent racist leanings, nor is it a matter of conveying facts and relying upon the effects of reason and insight. Learning must simultaneously engage young people at both the affective and the cognitive level, and my approach reaffirms the traditional values of 'good education' that are 'holistic', and 'learning with head, heart and hand'.

Examples of my work in schools on the issue of anti-racism

RAA responds to requests from teachers who wish to deal with the issue of racism more explicitly within the classroom. These requests are usually occasioned by:

- a racist incident in the school (discovery of racist leaflets, open racism by pupils);
- conflict between groups of students belonging to different ethnic groups;
- curriculum items that have a topical relevance and which give rise to projects relating to refugees, migration, or other contexts in which racism plays a part;
- anniversaries and commemorations of events such as the Nazi pogroms against the Jews, the liberation of Auschwitz, or the defeat of Fascism.

Our programmes take account of the time allocated for the workshops, of the age of the pupils, and of the degree of their experience in this area. Each course differs greatly, but basically the work proceeds in four learning stages:

First phase: Warm-up and familiarisation

The games and exercises in this phase are designed to facilitate a more personalised way of working and learning from each other. Expectations, fears and anxieties need to be articulated so that we can approach the actual topic in a more open way.

One exercise is the designing of a personalised 'code of arms' where each participant chooses heraldic symbols, headed by a family motto, to represent a favourite hobby, a favourite meal, a religious affiliation, a preferred feast day.

Another exercise invites the class to divide according to agreement or disagreement with statements I propose, such as: 'I drink coffee for breakfast'; 'I live with my parents'; 'I have

brothers and sisters'; 'I was born in Germany'; 'I feel
comfortable in this group'; 'I would like to have a friend'; 'I
would like to have a different nationality'; 'I was afraid once of
a person who had a different nationality'. Invariably, the result
of this exercise is that the 'divisions' do not occur in the 'most
obvious' form: not all 'Turkish' pupils are born in Turkey, it is
not only foreign students who at times wish they had a different
nationality. In fact, it is usual that none of the German
participants, in contrast to the Turkish ones, are proud of their
nationality. These 'surprises' can then be discussed and
evaluated in their significance for the group.

In one case, I worked with a class of fourteen year olds at a
comprehensive school for six months, one double session per
fortnight, and we did not get beyond the stage of getting to
know each other and developing trust. The members of the
class knew so little about each other, despite having been
together for a whole year. It was appropriate to give that much
time to the building of trust, to practising respectful ways of
dealing with each other, and to forming some initial strategies
of conflict resolution.

In the process, the personal and specific family background of
the pupils gradually became accessible, and it emerged that
some of them were having to cope with very demanding
circumstances. There was: a boy whose family had to flee
Bosnia and who carried with him the trauma of his war
experiences; a girl whose parents had separated; a boy from a
Turkish background who was frightened of war breaking out in
Turkey; a youngster whose mother was German and the father
Greek; a boy who had been orphaned and who lived in a
home. These are just some of the biographical glimpses of one
class. In these circumstances, and at this stage of early teenage
anti-racist education, confidence in oneself, learning to respect
others, and the building up of communal social skills, become
of paramount importance.

Second phase: What is racism?

This phase is an experiential introduction to the effects of
racism. We normally start by allowing each other to freely
voice the stereotypes associated with different nationalities
which I call out. It can be a great relief to be able to come out
with stereotypes and prejudices that are all around us, despite
the 'censorship' normally experienced in public in the presence

of adults and particularly at school.

This is followed up with a key exercise in which I select a physical characteristic shared by some members of the group. I then refer to (fictitious) scientific evidence that correlates this characteristic with a negative personality trait, e.g. small height with a tendency to show off, blue eyes with intelligence, etc. The exercise is first carried out in silence, with the group singled out by the given category standing in a corner and the rest remaining seated. I then proceed to select another characteristic until each member of the group has had the experience of 'being singled out'. This exercise requires very careful de-briefing because most students are inclined to 'find a grain of truth' in the associations. We talk at length about the anxieties and interests on which such associations feed and their stability within a group context that supports such belief systems for the purposes of exclusion or as signs of superiority.

One class of 18 year olds at a grammar school showed strong resistance against this exercise. 'We are not putting up with this nonsense' was one of the spontaneous reactions, arising probably from their self-image as an 'elite' who were not used to experiencing negative labels. When I confronted them with some of their negative remarks about Turks which they had previously made, it made some of them think. Some changed their reactions very quickly – perhaps too quickly – yielding to the pressure of having to conform with the teacher rather than demonstrating a real change in attitude.

Third phase: Functions of racism

In the third phase I proceed to more cognitive processes. Through particular sets of games I try to convey how racism is connected with other processes, ideas, and interests in society. We explore phrases, popular songs, advertising slogans, statements by politicians, newspaper articles, etc., not with the intention of unmasking them as racist, but as a pool of images from which racism may be constructed. As there are bound to be simplifications, it is important to emphasise that racism is more than the sum of racist attitudes and behaviours of individuals. The aim is to allow the participants to make the connections for themselves. One group, for instance, quoted as functions of racism the atrocities of 'ethnic cleansing' in former Yugoslavia and the genocide of the Kurds in Turkey; these were situations to which many members of the group had painful direct connections. A discussion ensued on the issue of whether racism automatically and inevitably leads to genocide.

This group also pieced together by themselves the various 'groundings' of racism, using their experience and understanding of current political affairs. The work during this phase is particularly challenging for me as a moralising approach would undermine the autonomy and the initiative of the learners. I have to constantly remind myself to take the conflicts and experiences of the participants seriously within contexts that are very different from my own, but without letting go of my own views and understanding of racism.

Fourth phase: History of racism

The contents of this phase vary greatly with the age and the prior knowledge of the participants. With those who are totally unfamiliar with the history of colonialism I work through the medium of a game 'Conquest of a Continent'. This is an abstract and hypothetical exercise, in which the desire to acquire the wealth of a continent has to be reconciled with three moral-religious principles: all people are equal before God; love your neighbour as you love yourself; darkness is evil and of the devil, and must be opposed. The participants act out the roles of explorers entering a strange country with strange-looking people and whose enormous wealth and resources beckon. How can the 'conquerors' reconcile gaining access to that wealth with their moral principles?

The conflicts arising from the application of these references to Christian morality and its role in colonialism are the nub of the game, and not the reconstruction of actual historical events. Nevertheless, this often combines with details of historical knowledge and can lead to engaging debates about power and resentment, about nationalism and international competition, and to the realisation that the experience of oppression does not give immunity from becoming an oppressor of others. In this game, it is important that the recourse to racist principles does not become 'inevitable' and automatic, but that the function of racism in support of particular interests becomes evident.

With a group of older female students I raised the issue of the role of women in the colonisation of Africa and, following on from this historical start, the issue of 'women and racism'.

Some women found this most uncomfortable since they had seen themselves primarily as victims of male aggression, and had equated racism with sexism. This was, therefore, a problem that was external to themselves (Mamozai 1989, 1990). Our discussions and role plays developed this theme and we drew on situations such as a German mother demanding to gain a place for her child at a school 'where there are no foreign children', or a white woman addressing a black domestic worker in the familiar German form of greeting.

Detailed feedback from the participants throughout the programme and especially at the end, is essential. Often the students ask my opinion directly on whether I think their understanding and their work on feelings and beliefs has developed. It can be taken as a measure of the trust that has grown that I give very differentiated answers; this is not a matter of passing an exam, but of engaging in a continuous learning process that recognises social and cultural pressures and the responsibility of each individual in responding to them.

Further work

After a group has experienced these four learning stages, it is up to them to determine the further direction of their work. If there is time allocated, the process can turn to their own experiences and issues in greater detail, and the learning elements of the four stages deepened. For instance, an older class of 30 pupils contained 19 of Turkish background and, at all four stages, this group had touched on the Kurdish-Turkish conflict. As an understanding of the nature of racism grew amongst the Turkish members of the group and they could validate it from their own experiences at the receiving end of racist discrimination, they recognised also the racist nature of their attitudes towards the ethnic group of Kurds, but were unable to resolve the 'dissonance'. They learned that these very deep and emotive convictions cannot be cancelled out by factual information and by the persuasive force of other convictions. School, and other educational activities cannot by themselves transform the material in which racist beliefs are cast. Young people can share in this understanding of the limitations of educational work and thereby recognise the importance of anti-racist work at simultaneously different levels.

I have come to recognise that in all pedagogical work, but

particularly in work in relation to racism, there needs to be a correspondence between format and contents, between the dynamics that a group develops, and the cognitive material they work through, whilst still maintaining the importance of both levels. Racism is not a topic that can be packaged within the curriculum structure, and I have always refused to 'fit' my programmes into a given context. The approach needs to give room to the personal doubts, anxieties and conflicts with which the topic resonates, rather than censoring them from the moral high ground pupils expect educational institutions and their representatives to take. The curriculum does not allow enough space to address all those issues of personal humiliation, exclusion, and insecure personal identity that I witness. I remind myself of the depressing observation that oppression and exclusion can turn victims into oppressors (Bauriedl 1992), and that racism is not an exclusively German issue. Working in multi-cultural and multi-ethnic situations offers an opportunity to go beyond such simplifications and to recognise that anti-racism is indeed a common task.

Bibliography

Bauriedl, T. (1992), *Wege aus der Gewalt*, Freiburg: *Herder*

Castles, S. (1987), *Migration und Rassismus in Westeuropa*, Berlin: *Express Edition*

Butterwege, C. (1994), *"Ausländer" müssen zu Inländern gemacht werden*, in: *Sozial Extra*, May: 38-55

Ciompi, L. (1992), *Affektlogik*, Stuttgart: *Klett-Cotta*

Creighton, A. and Kivel, P. (1993), *Die Gewalt stoppen*, Mühlheim an der Ruhr: *Verlag an der Ruhr*

Dittrich, J. E. (1991), *Das Weltbild des Rassismus*, Frankfurt: *Cooperative Verlag*

Farin, K. and Seidel-Pielen, E. (1993), Skinheads, München: *Beck*

Gerhard, U. (1992), *Rassismus in den Medien*, in: *Diakonisches Werk der evangelischen Kirche in Westfalen, Dokumentation der Jugend- und Sozialhilfekonferenz* vom 5.2.1992

Heim, G. et al. (1991), *'Jugendarbeit mit rechten Jugendcliquen – Handlungsansätze aus der Praxis'*, Deutsche Jugend 11: 471-481

Heitmeyer, W. (1987), *Rchtsextremistische Orientierungen bei Jugendlichen. Empirische Ergebnisse und Erklärungsmuster einer Untersuchung zur politischen Sozialisation*, München: Juventa

Heitmeyer, W. et al. (1992), *Die Bielefelder Rechtsextremismus-Studie. Erste Langzeituntersuchung zur politischen Sozialisation männlicher Jugendlicher*, München: Juventa

Held, J. et al. (1991), *'Du musst so handeln, dass Du Gewinn machst', Empirische Untersuchungen zu politisch rechten Orientierungen jugendlicher Arbeitnehmer*, Duisburg: DISS

Held, J. et al. (1995), *Politische Orientierungen Jugendlicher im Vereinigten Deutschland*, in I. Leiprecht (ed.), *In Grenzen verstrickt. Jugendliche und Rassismus in Europa*, Duisburg: DISS

Holzkamp, K. (1994), *Antirassistische Erziehung als Änderung rassistischer Einstellungen?* in S. Jäger (ed.), *Aus der Werkstatt: Anti-rassistische Praxen; Konzepte – Erfahrungen – Forschung*, Duisburg: DISS

Krafeld, F., Lutzebäck, E., Schaar, G., Strom, C. and Welp, W. (1993), *Akzeptierende Jugendarbeit mit rechtsextremen Jugendlichen?* in H. Heil, M. Perik and P.-U. Wendt (eds.), *Jugend und Gewalt*, , Marburg: Schüren

Leiprecht, R. (1992), *Unter Anderen. Rassismus und Jugendarbeit*, Duisburg: DISS

Mamozai, M. (1989), *Schwarze Frau, Weisse Herrin*, Reinbeck: Rowohlt

Mamozai, M. (1990), *Komplizinnen*, Reinbeck: Rowohlt

Memmi, A. (1992), The Colonizer and the Colonized. Boston: Beacon

7. 'Article One' – an inter-cultural youth work project in the Netherlands

Edwin Hoffman and Rubén Maduro

Our approach to youthwork with young people from ethnic minorities is guided by what we consider to be a 'realistic' outlook on racism as the structural and cultural subordination on the basis of skin colour and/or of ethnic origin. To oppose and prevent racism demands a combination of structural-political as well as cultural actions. Structural action for us means taking action through which housing, work, and educational circumstances, as well as the political rights of the discriminated groups, are being improved. Cultural action is as concerned with the processes of awareness and changes in attitude of the privileged, as it is with those of discriminated groups in our society.

Whilst youth work can make a useful contribution to both processes a sense of realism is required. Racism and discrimination have been with us for a long time and both have their roots in the cultural patterns of Dutch society. Youth work scarcely touches the structural and social factors that are responsible for racism. Nevertheless, we feel that youth work can, within its limitations, make a contribution to the fight against racism.

In September 1994, we started a youth project on the theme of "promoting equal human and civil rights and combating racism" in Helmond, a city near Eindhoven in the Netherlands, with approximately 70,000 inhabitants. The project was initiated by a combination of educational and youth institutions in the area and the youth and community work college in Eindhoven.

Our guiding ideas were derived from the proposals for anti-racist youth work which form the final chapter of this volume. Originally, we gave the programme the title "Inter-cultural partnership in Helmond: for civil and human rights, against racism", but the participants soon changed it to "Project Article One – Helmond". They found the reference to 'anti-racism' too negative and chose instead Article One of the Dutch constitution as project title. This states: "All inhabitants of the Netherlands will be treated equally in equal situations. There shall be no discrimination on the grounds of religion, philosophy of life, political orientation, race, gender or any other grounds". A commitment to these principles seemed a good basis for positive action.

The organization of the project

The project has a steering group consisting of Jeanne van Beers of the *Brabants Steunpunt Jongerenwerk (BSJ)*, Ine van de Rijt of the *Stichting Welzijnsbevordering Helmond (SWH)*, Rubén Maduro of the *Stichting Progreso*, and Edwin Hoffman of the *Hogeschool Eindhoven*. The steering group manages the project with regard to finances and personnel, monitors and evaluates the progress of the project, and gives its activities a consistent theoretical framework based upon the concept of inter-cultural learning. The youth workers from the project liaise closely with other youth services and projects in the area, but particularly with organizations and institutions such as secondary schools, youth projects, and the city council, all of which are involved or interested in anti-racism.

The theoretical framework

In our vision of working with young people towards equal civil and human rights, and against racism, the development of identity plays an essential role. Young people between the ages 12 to 25 form and consolidate their own views, values, norms, and their own lifestyle, and search for their own positions within different groups and society in general. This development of identity may be seen as a continuous process of enclosure and exclusion: the differentiation of oneself from others in terms of gender, behaviour, ways of dressing, opinions, musical preference, type of education, sexual preference, ethnic identity, etc. We call the process of becoming associated with others who are alike 'enclosure'. It is accompanied by an emotional and cognitive distancing from other groups that are 'different', and this we call 'exclusion'. Exclusion may imply a personal distance from others or merely an inability to imagine what it would be like to be the other person in certain respects.

Enclosure and exclusion are necessary to create one's own identity. The problem of racism arises when the differences become fixed, when it becomes 'natural', self-evident, and common sense, that your own group is more sophisticated and intelligent and has achieved more than certain other groups. Preventative anti-racism must therefore engage in the process of identity formation and free itself from a notion of fixed identities.

The multicultural society

People are only gradually coming to terms with the fact that the Netherlands is a multi-cultural society. The diversity of lifestyles and cultural norms challenges all notions of 'normality', and highlights the chance nature of one's own identity and the relativity of all previous certainties. Autochtonous [1] people express this by saying that they feel like a stranger in their own neighbourhood. The questions of one's cultural identity has become unavoidable even though many people have never had to confront it.

Experiencing a multicultural society does not automatically lead to a positive or tolerant attitude towards other cultures. On the contrary, today's gulf of racism shows that the encounter with other cultures is often associated with fear. That is why, within the framework of inter-cultural education, it seems useful to start from the premise that the multicultural reality is one of conflict.

Identity as a dynamic and social process

Identity is not something that we are conscious of or talk about in everyday life. It becomes an issue when it is challenged, for example, when a group of Antillian students who had just arrived in the Netherlands overheard a remark on the bus: "In a while these Blacks will take over the bus if we are not careful".

The constant challenges of a multi-cultural reality make it clear that identity is not a fixed, objective, homogeneous, monolithic entity, but rather a dynamic intersubjective, and heterogeneous process. The notion of a definitive genuine 'self', stable and immutable, is a fiction. Of course, there is something like an inner consistency – a unique combination of personality and physical traits – but these have different meanings in different social contexts. We perceive them in the context of other people: with friends, with our own ethnic group, our own neighbourhood, with fellow-students, and with our own religious group. This sometimes temporary association with, and dissociation from, others (enclosure and exclusion) forms identity. The associations with others, which might have come about by chance, offer people existential and emotional support. According to Wildemeersch (1993), discovering and accepting the 'accidental' aspect of our identity can make us more receptive to the 'strangeness' of others. Inter-cultural education works with the tension between certainties (confidence, enclosure), and the realisation of their relativity. It moves between reassuring and challenging identity.

The contents of identity

According to De Wit and Van der Veer (quoted in Baert 1991), there are four important elements of identity:

1. A feeling of 'sameness' and inner consistency.
2. An awareness that one's personal lifestyle can be shared with or have meaning to others.
3. A sense of personal freedom in the face of a realisation of the lack of freedom in every human society.
4. A design for living with goals expressing essential values.

Young people ask questions such as 'Who am I? What do I mean to others? Where do I belong? With whom do I want to identify myself?" Identity is expressed, therefore, in the intricate connection between self-image, and the presentation of oneself to others. When young people in a predominantly autochthonous group are asked to describe themselves, it is likely that the allochthonous youngsters will describe themselves as allochthon and mention their ethnic identity, whilst autochtonous youngsters will probably not mention their ethnic background when they are in the majority. They will mention instead that they are male or female when, for example, they are in a mixed gender group. Identity is, therefore, socially constructed.

Social reality is, however,, characterised by a struggle over the representation of reality, by the contrast between dominant and subordinate social relations, and an imbalance of power. Those who exert power define reality for others, even retrospectively (Wildemeersch 1992). The dominant groups – in the Netherlands, autochthonous, 'White', middle-class, male groups – succeed regularly in asserting their versions of reality and represent them as being objective, universal, rules. Those definitions that do not fit into this ideology are rejected as being private and prejudiced.

The meaning of communication within identity-formation

Identity as a social process is formed through communication. In everyday conversations and within narratives, identity, self-images, and images of the other are constructed and affirmed. Sometimes they may also (perhaps unintentionally) be denied. For instance, a young woman in an ethnicly-mixed youth group was asked during a conversation about religion: "And how do they think about that in your culture...?" The young woman suddenly felt spoken to and identified as an allochthonous, Moroccan, Islamic woman. To her, the ('neutral') question felt like an exclusion and an affirmation of the divide between 'them' and 'us'. Or the (well-intended) remark of an autochthonous Dutch youth worker to an allochthonous youth: "You speak Dutch quite well already" may be perceived as a negative statement that implies "You have adjusted quite well to the Dutch society; you are already one of us". As with all communication, intended meanings, and the effects they have in their wider social context, may differ considerably. In references to identity we want to feel accepted, not excluded.

Identities, by their social nature, are always multi-dimensional. A member of a youth group may describe herself all at the same time as a: young woman, daughter, sister, aunt, Brabantine, Hindustani, Muslim, student, 'Black', neighbour, athlete, Salsa lover, etc. This is also reflected in the different names that the Dutch (and other countries) have given to foreigners: guest workers, Mediterraneans, foreigners, allochthones, fellow inhabitants, illegals, asylum seekers, migrants, ethnic minorities, etc. Each of these terms allocates a different position and set of social relations. The elements of identity are usually organised in hierarchies and are associated with feelings of inferiority or superiority, and imply a pressure to adjust to dominant norms.

Because hierarchies of identity are socially defined, there may be a discrepancy between how somebody gives a personal meaning to a certain identity aspect, and the meaning that the social environment gives to that same identity aspect. A pupil from Somalia may be seen by classmates primarily as an asylum seeker, a Muslim, or a Somali. However, he has no control over this and this can add to the conflicts experienced. Such conflicts affect identity formation adversely since there needs to be a minimum of correspondence between self-image and ascribed identity. This is particularly acute for allochtonous young people who receive conflicting messages about the value of their ethnic identity from within their own ethnic group as well as from the dominant group of autochthonous people, who often regard being allochtonous as identical with having social problems (such as drugtaking, delinquency, low school achievement, etc.).

Ethnic identity

An ethnic group is one that describes itself and is described by others on the basis of cultural characteristics such as, language, central values, ways of dressing, lifestyle, religion, and physical characteristics, for instance, a dark skin colour or type of hair (Vermeulen 1984). Solidarity within an ethnic group provides people with a feeling of security and of belonging. People experience this basic need more when they are in a minority position or when they feel under threat. Examples of such ethnic minority groups in the Netherlands are Hollanders, Frisians, Limburgers, Brabantines, Surinams, Indians, Hindustanis, Creoles, and Javanese. An Aruban woman who grows up, goes to school, and obtains a social position in Oranjestad on Aruba, will experience different cultural influences than an autochthonous Dutch woman of similar class, education, and professional background. It is also worth remembering that an ethnic group, like any other social system, is basically open, heterogeneous, and constantly changing.

The ethnic position of allochthones in the Netherlands

The importance we attribute to ethnicity does not mean that we see ethnic identity as the most important group characteristic. We believe that in every society, citizenship should prevail over ethnic identity. However, people will only attach a greater value to their citizenship of a nation state than to their ethnic identity and membership of an ethnic group, when the state ensures their human and civil rights and fulfills basic needs such as housing, education, and employment. In general, in the Netherlands, the sense of Dutch nationality amongst naturalised foreigners is less strong than ethnic identity. For instance, many Turkish people have Dutch nationality because it offers them practical advantages such as travelling without a visa. In the same way, older Moluccans see their Dutch passport as a work-document or as a travel document and not as a symbol of their Dutch nationality. However, in certain circumstances, nationality may become 'ethnicised', for instance, when the Moroccan Dutch support the Dutch national soccer team – provided that the game is not against Morocco. This transfers to return visits to Morocco, when the Moroccan-Dutch may also at times feel very Dutch and, therefore, distanced from their ethnic identity.

On the whole, allochthonous people living in the Netherlands are constantly reminded of their not being autochthonous. People in the street, politicians, and the media, emphasise ethnic differences and make an issue of the presence of allochthones in the Netherlands. Because of these differences, and the social significance attached to them, allochthonous people feel constantly watched. Members of our project group, for instance, report how, on entering a supermarket, they are watched more carefully. This watchfulness can easily turn into discrimination.

It is also worth noting that in the Netherlands, and despite the widely accepted use of terms such as 'allochthones' and 'foreigners' which are assumed to carry 'neutral' connotations, such terms usually refer only to specific groups, namely those that appear physically and culturally very different from autochthones. One does not usually refer to English, French or Germans as allochthonous, but one may, for example, to Surinamese, Turks, Moroccans and Antilleans. These groups who are visibly different are then also made responsible for social problems such as criminality, unemployment, and housing. This contributes to teachers having lower expectations of allochthoneous children. Differences also become more pronounced as a result of global political events. For example, during the Gulf war in 1991, the Islamic allochthones in the Netherlands were treated with greater suspicion and hostility. The racist attacks on foreigners in several European countries, including Holland, increased the feeling of a lack of safety in many allochthones – even in the Netherlands.

Members of ethnic minorities in turn seek a sense of security and safety in their religious communities. Some Islamic youths see their religious community and the status they have within that community as the only possibility of a positive identity. The Dutch newspaper the *Volkskrant* reported an increasing interest amongst young people in Islam, even outside the established Islamic institutions (6 June 1994).

There are also people who refuse to see themselves as part of an ethnic group and prefer to regard themselves simply as citizens of society or of the world. For instance a Moroccan boy in the project remarked that he did not feel Moroccan but European. His strategy to become accepted by his peer groups was to call himself Marco – after the famous Dutch soccer player Marco van Basten – but to no avail. He found himself constantly reminded of being Moroccan by the people around him.

With our illustrations above, we wish to stress the flexibility contained in the notion of ethnic identity, and the importance of political processes that activate aspects of it. This flexibility, and the confusion it sometimes causes, makes the formation of identity a pedagogical task and, at the same time, gives projects like ours their political significance.

Racism

A racist attitude is an extreme form of stereotyping and the acceptance of uncritical opinions. Racism sets up symbolic boundaries usually within a binary system that reduces social differences to assumed biological criteria. People tend to bow to these fixations whenever a threat to their identity overwhelms them. This is particularly so when economic, social-cultural and psychological uncertainties, are intense. A confrontation with an uncertain reality makes people shrink back from unexpected challenges, (for instance, the arrival of foreign neighbours), and to seek unambiguous explanations and 'simple solutions'.

Young people are extra-sensitive to these uncertainties. That is why we believe it is important to pay attention to their identity development in a programme that combats racism. This needs to balance basic trust with an openness towards new experiences, and an ability to accept the relativity of positions. The current multi-cultural environment, with its rich variety of lifestyles, central values, 'new' religions, etc, offers young people a large number of models of identity. Inter-cultural approaches can assist them in coping with both the need to choose and the discrimination differences entail.

Inter-cultural education

Our programme broadly follows the concept of 'inter-cultural education' proposed by Wildemeersch, and we wish to present it briefly here. Wildemeersch distinguishes between two basic educational directions: education 'in alliance' with others, and education towards self-reliance and autonomy.

'Education in alliance' with others places identity within a broad social context. Education then becomes concerned with strengthening those social bonds that are considered to be a positive extension of personal identity. An example of this would be the so-called empowerment approach of 'Black' youths in which they discover their own 'Black' history, 'Black' traditions, values, and examples, as new reference points.

'Education towards autonomy' concentrates upon the emancipatory unfolding of young people's potential. This must occur on their own terms and conditions and under their own control. Central to this approach is the encouragement of problem-solving abilities and independence from externally available certainties.

Both educational concepts carry risks, and particularly so within a multi-cultural society: 'Education in alliance' may over-emphasise the solidarity within one's own tradition and cultural group. In the extreme, this may lead to intolerance and a lack of respect toward other points of view and cultures as one's own viewpoint becomes dominant and absolute. 'Education towards autonomy' and self-actualisation leads, in the extreme, to total self-sufficiency, selfishness, loss of solidarity with others, consumerism and narcissism.

Wildemeersch's pedagogy seeks to avoid these pitfalls by combining the positive aspects of both with the motto 'education as taking responsibility'.

This concept of inter-cultural 'education as taking responsibility', was our starting-point for the project. We regard the multi-cultural diversity of Dutch society as an educational opportunity which forces us constantly to question our own views and positions and not to take given certainties for granted. At the same time, people need common sense certainties and fixed orientation points to gain a sense of direction. An over-zealous questioning may cause chronic insecurity and loss of confidence. That is why inter-cultural education for us must strive for a balance between 'opening' (the questioning of all 'given realities') and 'closing' (offering certainties, basic trust, and security).

Criteria for inter-cultural 'education as taking responsibility'

Following suggestions by Procee (1991), we formulated two general principles for effective inter-cultural education:

1. The principle of 'inclusive thinking', or 'non-exclusion'. This means that all participants in the learning process have equal access to learning opportunities and should not be obstructed by categories constructed by others on the grounds of race, sex, culture or class. This is obviously an ideal-typical anticipation of a state of society not yet achieved, but it marks an important ethical goal.
2. The principle that all interaction has to respect the uniqueness of each individual. This means that all educational methods, as well as all social policies and other organisational arrangements, need to be measured against this criteria.

Inter-cultural education can only function when both principles are considered and made operational. The outcome and contents of the inter-cultural education process cannot be fixed in advance because neither human identity, nor moral standards, nor criteria of true knowledge are fixed, immutable, and unchangeable. The direction of the process is determined by the diversity of positions and viewpoints that arise in continuous discussion with the participants. The process leads from the identification of differences to the creation of common concerns and back to the differentiation of individual goals in a continuous cycle.

The aim of the project

This comprehensive theoretical framework guided us in defining the objectives and nature of the project. Our main aim, derived from the above principles, is that the participating young people should become motivated and competent in interacting with people of different ethnic-cultural backgrounds on the basis of respect for themselves and for others.

We then formulated a catalogue of secondary aims which put these principles into pedagogical practice.

In relation to **attitudes**, young people should:

1. get to know themselves through an encounter with 'the other' or 'the stranger'; learn something about their own abilities and limitations, desires and expectations, and their own position in society;

2. become aware of how much their own situation is influenced by 'accidental' factors within a wider social context, and how culture separates them from others by virtue of culturally defined attributes, traditions, conceptions, emotions, and lifestyles;

3. develop their inner strength (empowerment) and a stronger sense of self-respect;

4. be motivated to defend the Dutch civil and human right of equality and anti-discrimination;

5. have the motivation to meet and interact with people who are 'different'.

With regard to **cognitive skills**, they should develop insight into:

6. stereotyping;

7. the basic effects of racism and discrimination;

8. social exclusion mechanisms that affect them and others;

9. power relations and their effects.

In terms of **skills**, they should acquire:

10. inter-cultural communication skills;

11. skills in dealing with differences and similarities;

12. skills in forming and expressing their own opinions and concepts;

13. anti-racist strategies and skills that help to counter-act the mechanisms of social exclusion.

The target group

Racism is part of the experience of most youth groups in the area. Some youths have experienced racism and discrimination directly, others fear that the violent racist attacks that have occurred in Germany will also occur in the Netherlands. Others find it difficult to accept that young asylum seekers and refugees live in their neighbourhood and that there are inter-ethnic tensions and conflicts.

Our contacts gave us the idea that a number of young people attending youth clubs wanted to work on the theme of racism and discrimination, and so we brought together a group of interested and motivated young people between the ages of 15 and 21 for the purposes of our project. Originally we wanted to form two groups that were ethnically heterogeneous. However, only Moroccan youngsters came forward for the boys' group, whereas the girls' group consisted of Turkish, Dutch and Moroccans. The gender separation accorded with the cultural preferences of the Moroccan community, although there were some joint activities. We saw the participating youngsters as 'multipliers' who would feed back some of their experiences to their own youth groups. For an initial period they could decide whether to continue with the group, but after that we expected a full commitment.

The boys' group had 20 members between the ages of 15 and 19 and was facilitated by 2 project youth workers, whilst the other group, consisting of 21 girls aged between 15 and 21, was facilitated by 3 workers. Two of the project workers were qualified and autochtonous Dutch but who had a special interest in this type of work. Two other project workers were still in training and from a Moroccan background. The local project coordinator was the fifth project youth worker.

All project workers received training in inter-cultural youth work together with other regular youth workers. This aimed at familiarising them with the objectives of the project and to provide them with awareness, insight, knowledge and the skills needed to work effectively with multi-ethnic youth groups against racism.

The contents of the training programme included:

- reflections upon the effect of personal and social stereotyped images on groups with a different cultural background;
- insight into the power structures and mechanisms of exclusion and racism in the areas of work, education, housing, law, civil and human rights;
- reflections on the workers' own experience as 'perpetrators' and 'victims' of discrimination and racism;
- intervention skills for working with youth against racism and for empowerment;
- strategies of organisational cooperation against institutional racism.

Our pedagogical and methodical principles for the training courses were derived from Wildemeersch (1992 and 1993) and Daman (1993), in line with the principles that informed the work and direction of the project.

1. The everyday situation of young people offers plenty of pedagogical opportunities; the stranger is within every group and within myself.

2. The questioning of taken-for-granted certainties needs to be balanced with reassurance and a basic trust in certainties.

3. Inter-cultural education is not primarily about tolerance. Tolerance has its limitations when opinions or behaviour violate basic rights and are, for instance, discriminatory.

4. Education is a modest instrument towards the realisation

of a tolerant society and is by no means a panacea. Economic, socio-cultural, psychological, and historical factors also play an important role and are largely beyond the control of youth workers.

5. Inter-cultural education takes risks. It cannot remain neutral in terms of moral values, but requires commitment and taking responsibility.

6. Inter-cultural youth work is concerned with creating a space within which multicultural experiences can take place. These need to be carefully introduced, made thematic, and be evaluated.

7. Young people need to gain distance from their experiences so that they can interpret them in a new light. On the other hand, they also need to have unexpected experiences.

8. The programme must contain cognitive, affective, and behavioural components. In particular, space needs to be given to expressing emotions in a safe manner.

9. Information must be relevant to the immediate context of the young people and should not encourage 'exoticism'.

10. Changes in attitudes do not necessarily lead to changes in behaviour. It is more useful to focus instead on the forming of opinions, feelings and motives that directly affect interaction with others.

11. Young people are able to educate themselves through making connections between their own knowledge and experiences, and new sources of information offered to them.

12. Investigation is a basic pedagogical principle. Young people should be enabled to investigate their reality with reliable concepts and to find their place and direction within it.

13. Inter-cultural education requires comprehensive and continuous supervision.

14. Inter-cultural education deals with cultural differences in their many manifestations; ethnic origin is only one element besides class, gender, sexual preference, ages etc. All these differences can be used as mechanisms of exclusion.

15. When comparing personal experiences, no story is superior to another; in this sense the youth worker is essentially on the same level as the youths. However, whilst youth workers may have more knowledge and abilities, these should not be used as ultimate standards.

Activities

The participants were given a choice of activities they wanted to focus on during the project. They favoured activities around sport, music, (local) radio, and television, as well as the more usual youth work activities.

The work within the area chosen by the participants was planned around three dimensions which we called the 'enclosure process', the 'opening process', and the 'interaction process'. Each of these processes, (or a combination of them), has a special significance at various stages of the project. 'Enclosure' looks inwards towards the group, establishes the identity and confidence of its members, and forms the basis from which 'openings' towards more conscious encounters with 'the other' may be launched. 'Interaction' then focuses on the development of particular skills and strategies within that encounter. To illustrate the practice implications we provide below an example of activities around the theme of racism in sport.

In the introductory phase the participants get to know each other and their facilitators. The project is introduced and house, cooperation and communication rules are settled. The participants and the facilitators explore and evaluate their feelings, thoughts, and experiences concerning racism, the exclusion of others and of themselves. This will become part of the ongoing evaluation of the project. Paramount in this first enclosure process is the reinforcement of self-confidence and self-respect: the first elements of empowerment.

Possible activities at this stage are:

1. Expressing feelings and experiences through discussion, acting, pictures, sounds, or writing, on interests, preferences, and experiences in sport, including ideals and dreams, and famous allochtonous sports heroes. This gives a first indication of the group's understanding of racism in sport.

2. Exploring how others (friends, parents, the ethnic community), see and think about sport, sports clubs, heroes, etc.

3. Inviting successful allochtonous sports personalities to the project, discuss with them their experiences and how they deal with discrimination and racism in the sport.

4. Interviewing allochtonous supporters and board members of sports clubs about how they deal with discrimination and racism in their particular sport.

5. Exploring, on the basis of these discussions, the choices members of the group have themselves. For example, "To which values and traditions of my (ethnic) group do I attach great inportance in relation to sport?"

6. Reflecting upon a more general understanding of the power structures and processes of exclusion and racism in the area of sport, and in related areas such as education and employment.

7. Inviting or interviewing 'white' autochtonous heroes, clubs, referees, and sport reporters who have a positive attitude towards allochtonous sports people, and who are active in initiatives against racism and discrimination.

The second phase is characterized by an opening process where the focus is on meeting 'the other' and 'the unknown'. Possible activities are:

1. Researching prevalent images of allochtonous youth and allochtonous sports people in the media, etc. How do these images work, what is their effect (supporting or discriminating), and how do we deal with them?

2. Interviewing autochtonous sports people,
   supporters/fans, and journalists, to obtain their images.
   At this stage their reactions are not discussed but are
   simply noted.

3. Making an inventory of existing activities against racism
   in sport that exist in the Netherlands at a regional,
   provincial, and national level.

The third phase combines 'enclosure' and 'opening'. The
purpose of this phase is to explore ways in which
empowerment and confidence in one's own identity do not
depend upon the exclusion of others. In other words, the
allochtonous youngsters also become aware of their role as
'perpetrators' of discrimination and 'racism' against others and
so search for alternatives. Being aware of differences does not
automatically mean exclusion of others who are different.

Possible activities appropriate to this phase are:

1. Identifying groups to whom the members of the project
   find it difficult to relate and exploring their positive and
   negative images, feelings and ideas, of these groups.

2. Listing and exploring the images and ideas these groups
   may have in relation to the members of the project.

3. Exploring their interests in sports and how these
   interests are perceived by the media and by people in
   sport.

4. Considering and becoming aware of the influence and
   effects of exclusion that these images and ideas may have
   on such groups.

The fourth phase leads from opening to interaction, and to
encounters with other groups at a level which allows a distance
to emerge from one's own values and opinions. By challenging
others and letting themselves be challenged, young people
learn to value differences without experiencing them as a
negative comment upon their own values and ideas, and
without experiencing differences as a fixed insurmountable
barrier.

Possible activities include:

1. Talking to youth of different ethnic and cultural backgrounds about their history, habits, ceremonies, feelings, heroes, interests in sports, experiences of discrimination.

2. Inviting their 'heroes' and talking with them about sport and racism.

3. Playing sports together in joint teams, rather than ethnic groups against each other.

The fifth phase is again an enclosure process. It allows the young people an opportunity to reflect upon actions and strategies to combat racism in the area of sport, and to enhance the participation of allochtonous youth in sports activities.

Possible activities include:

1. Joining activities of allochtonous and autochtonous people who promote anti-racism in sport.

2. Learning specific interactive skills such as debating, argumentation, handling conflict, negotiating differences of opinion, etc.

The sixth phase is an interaction process aimed at joint activities with other groups to combat racism in sport, and to enhance the participation of allochtonous youth and other 'discriminated' groups in sport.

Possible activities include:

1. Designing a poster campaign against the racist behaviour of football fans.

2. Formulating policy statements and suggestions for boards of football clubs along the lines of the British campaign "Let's Kick Racism out of Football".

3. Cooperating with committed supporter clubs.

4. Campaigning in local and provincial newspapers, on radio and television.

Evaluation

After 18 months, the first phase of the project is complete, and it is now possible to look back on some of the achievements and lessons of 'Article One'.

One harsh realisation was that the design of the project had been too ambitious in relation to the resources that we had been able to mobilise. We ran into all kinds of difficulties over funding. For instance, we found that some money would be available if we recruited participants from the most deprived socio-economic background. However, this would have required even greater resources in terms of the attention and support that such a group would have needed to become motivated, to realise their full potential for participation and shared decision-making, and to acquire the basic skills for working in a task-oriented group.

We also realised that the initial phases of the project required more time than we had originally allocated. Forming a group of motivated young people from the allochthonous communities requires careful and lengthy negotiations over the aims and objectives of such a venture. Equally, training the workers, setting up the programme contents and activities, forging links with other youth organisations, sports clubs, etc., took far longer than we had envisaged. The steering group and the management of the project themselves also needed more time to reflect upon the implications of the project both for themselves personally and their overall work.

Where we were able to spend sufficient time on preparation and received adequate resources, (such as the training of workers), we had considerable success. The training programme we devised was eagerly taken up by social workers and youth workers from outside the project. This reflected the general lack of training opportunities in anti-racist work in the Helmond area, and it was only in the course of their training that most of them became aware of the relevance of anti-racism in their work. As a result, we decided to produce a training manual for use by social workers, and youth and community workers, on how to deal with issues of racism and discrimination. This manual will form the basis of further training initiatives.

Despite the success of the training programme, the skills it identified for the workers, the motivation it gave them, and the personal enthusiasm it generated, most project workers found it difficult to put the principles and concepts they had learned into practice with a youth group of diverse ethnic backgrounds. Although they were familiar with the lifestyle and cultural characteristics of some of them, there were still considerable gaps in knowledge and understanding. Covering these areas took time and it required more supervision and reflection than we had allowed. In addition, the issues concerning racism and discrimination that the training raised, for the project workers themselves, were so immediate that they found it difficult to transfer their learning to the young people. This is not a reflection of their inadequacies but is, rather, a measure of the way in which they approached these issues and were prepared to work on their own experiences. They would have needed more support from the organisations sponsoring the project than the resources allowed to be able to fully follow through the implications of their learning.

We also encountered an interesting 'culture clash' between the methodological principles youth workers are used to working with (The ability to work with 'open programmes', where the activities are largely determined by the youngsters themselves and which can be changed at any stage) and the educational objectives we tried to introduce, which required a coherent and progressive (though by no means rigid) programme, and for which the workers took responsibility. We realised that both our planning and the preparatory training of the youth workers should have taken account of the specific educational nature of the project. We should have given more time to developing a coherent vision and piloting our methodology with the workers, paid more attention to the translation of the methodology into activities and structured interventions within those activities, and trained the workers more explicitly in working within a coherent methodology.

Despite these limitations, the project groups worked very successfully and developed a wider range of activities than had originally been envisaged. On the whole, the method outlined above, and the three steps of 'enclosure', 'opening', and 'interaction', proved, judging from the group's self-evaluation, appropriate. Interestingly, the participants stated they had learned most from each other. The sharing of experiences in which they encountered racism led to an awareness of the structural nature of racism and laid the foundations for a more positive self-image. This in turn led to the shared learning of new ways of addressing racism. For instance, at the beginning, most boys coped only by 'retaliating', by calling names or fighting back, when they were being abused. Gradually, they included other strategies, such as discussing issues with verbal 'attackers', asking them questions about the origins of their opinions, and confronting 'opinion makers' in the wider community with their prejudices. The transition from finding out about the extent of racism and discrimination to identifying positive allochtonous role models and making contact with people at the forefront of Black identity and anti-discrimination movements, was also successful. There were plenty of opportunities for confronting the discrimination and prejudice within the project groups themselves, expressed, for instance, in jokes about the Berbers, an ethnic minority in Morocco.

The young people became more aware of the coping strategies they had unwittingly adopted at school and in public, such as putting a brave face on jokes and remarks, laughing them off, bluffing, and avoiding issues. They acquired a wider choice of reactions and learned to talk about their choices. As one boy stated "I reflect more on what I am doing. At times I myself am discriminating! I understand much better now how, for instance, a Turk feels when he is being discriminated against. I don't make jokes so easily any more". Another said that he had learned not to start a fight immediately when somebody insulted or offended him. Now he will ask the other why he hates him. Above all, they developed a strong sense of being a team and of supporting each other at several levels.

The activities undertaken have vastly increased their self-respect and confidence. The boys with a Moroccan background in particular started off with highly negative views of themselves that mirrored the public image of their ethnic group. From having made successful contacts with sports personalities, with people in the media, with the police and local politicians, they gained a feeling of power, not only in an emotional sense, but also over their environment. They experienced, often for the first time, a feeling of being taken seriously in public, of having a contribution to make to the community, of being needed and, therefore, of having a worthwhile place in society. They also realised that such achievements do not come easily: they had to work hard for them – sometimes very hard and tenaciously.

The activities also gave them a wider choice of priorities. They realised how much of their life had been spent on the streets of the city simply for lack of alternatives, and the project, and the ideas it generated, were able to provide these. The range of activities was indeed far wider than originally envisaged and centred on the following main themes:

- Sports and racism (as described in our plans). In the course of this activity, and through encounters with sports commentators and reporters, of whom some were allochthonous, the project participants became interested in the media, started to do interviews themselves, and began to take the media more seriously. From this the next theme developed:
- Radio programmes on anti-discrimination and anti-racism. With the help of local, and some national, broadcasters the groups explained how issues of racism and discrimination could be presented through a local radio programme. In some twenty sessions they designed four initial radio programmes with which they approached the local radio station. The project, in which they can relate their experiences and interests and share their understanding of ethnic identity and their suggestions, will now be given a regular slot in their schedule. These activities in turn inspired the following:
- An edition of a local newspaper on racism and anti-discrimination.
- An information project for schools and other youth groups on how to recognise and stand up to discrimination and racism.

Encouraged by these experiences, the two groups now plan a series of more self-contained projects, if possible, by forming distinct workgroups on each task with members from both the boys' and the girls' groups. These projects will evolve in a series of steps from the orientation phase to basic social skills training, skills training in the particular tasks, finalising the programme, strategic plans to include other institutions, and finally, implementation.

The intended programmes are:

- The continuation of the radio project with a regular monthly slot featuring ethnic music, discussions and interviews that

deal with responses to racism and discrimination, news, and an ethnic cultural agenda.
- The development of an anti-racism and anti-discrimination newspaper. This will appear once every three months in schools and youth centres and will contain features along the lines of the radio programmes.
- An expansion of the information initiative for schools and other youth clubs, targeted to deal with specific situations of racism and discrimination.
- The formation of 'heterogeneous', ethnically-mixed, sports groups and clubs for the promotion of anti-racism in sports, but particularly among supporters.
- A music project leading up to the production of a musical and a cultural festival in the local city of Helmond. This will promote the music of different ethnic groups, particularly youth bands, and offer ethnic diversity to discos through disc jockeys skilled in widening the ethno-pop repertoire.
- Setting up a telephone information and advice line for local young people on issues of racism and discrimination. This will be run by the project members under the supervision of professionals from an existing advice bureau.

In addition to these activities, the project plans exchanges with similar youth groups in another European country. This had been the intention from the very start but they had failed to materialise originally because of a lack of resources.

Apart from these distinct activities, the young people also managed to network very successfully with local and regional institutions and organisations, such as schools, social services, youth projects and youth organisations, the police, etc. Through these contacts, both the project and its aims have become well-known, and they are being discussed in several contexts. This will have the 'multiplier effect' that we discussed earlier. The public events organised by the members reached between 200 and 300 other young people. Other youth clubs are becoming interested in our activities and are drawing on the project members' 'expertise' to develop their own initiatives. The local and county authorities are monitoring our developments with a view to adopting them in other projects.

At the present time, this project is one of the few initiatives in the Netherlands that have succeeded, in such an intensive and focused way, to combine social, cultural, recreational, and educational aspects in their activities, but without losing the commitment of participants. The majority of anti-racist projects remain at the recreational level and they have not as yet developed a broader vision. A systematic evaluation of the project, and of the suitability of our methodology, will be undertaken shortly, and it is hoped that it will form the basis for the development of a module to be included in the curriculum of youth work courses in polytechnics in the Netherlands.

Bibliography

Baert, D. (1987), *De persoon in een systeemtheoretisch ontwerp*, In Mattheeuws, A. and Baert, D. *Psychotherapie, Psychologische Theorieën, Systeemtheorie*, Antwerp: *V.St.P.*

Baert, D. (1991), Identiteit en identiteitsontwikkeling: een poging tot systeemtheoretische benadering. I: theoretisch zoekwerk, Systeemtheoretisch Bulletin 9, 1990-1991/2

Baert, D. (1993), *Identiteit en identiteitsontwikkeling: een poging tot systeemtheoretische benadering. II: de ontwikkeling van identiteit, Systeemtheoretisch Bulletin* 11, 1992-1993/4

Daman, K. (1993), *Intercultureel werken met jongern beeldvorming als methodiek, Vorming* 8:4 (April)

Hoffman, E. and Arts, W. (1994), *Interculturele gespreksvoering*, Bohn Stafleu Van Loghum: *Houten*

Procee, H. (1991), *Over de grenzen van culturen*, Boom: *Meppel*

Vermeulen, H. (1984), *Etnische groepen en grenzen*, Het Wereldvenster: *Weesp*

Wildemeersch, D. (1992), *Vorming in de multiculturele samenleving. Antwoorden op de oproep van de vreemdeling; Vorming* 7:2 (February)

Wildemeersch, D. (1993), *Multiculturele vorming tussen betrokkenheid en distantie, Vorming* 8:3 (March)

Notes

1.   We decided in this chapter to maintain the terminology of 'allochtones' and 'autochtones' which is used in the Netherlands to refer to people belonging to different cultural and ethnic groups.

'Allochthonous' is a term that was used originally in geology and which means "existing or formed from material coming from somewhere else; not formed on the spot where it is found". 'Allos' is Greek for 'other', 'auto' refers to 'one's own', and 'chtoon' means 'land, soil, country'. 'Allochtones', in a general sense, refers to people from abroad. The Dutch government has declared the following groups as being allochtones: Greeks, Italians, those from the former Yugoslavia, Cape Verdians, Moroccans, Portugese, Spanish, Tunesians, Turks, Arubans, Antilleans and Surinams, Moluccans, refugees, travellers, gypsies. In everyday conversations in the Netherlands however, this term is only applied to people with a darker skin colour, a different religion such as Islam, and/or coming from countries in Africa, Asia, and Latin America, such as Surinam, Antilleans, Aruba, Indonesia, Vietnam, Iran, Somaly, Morocco and Turkey. 'Autochthones' are people who have their roots (until what generation?) in the country in which they live.

8. Pedagogical principles for anti-racist strategies*

Walter Lorenz

In this chapter we would like to present a selected range of pedagogical instruments which were developed within the context of a project on anti-racism in European youth exchange programmes, in which many of the authors of this volume participated. The proposals integrate, illustrate, and apply many of the concepts presented in previous chapters, and reflect the practice experiences of the project participants. Our intention is not to develop a comprehensive pedagogical programme on how to deal with racism in schools and among young people; this is an important task which has to be addressed in its own way. Rather, our proposals start with the premise that there are groups of young people, and not just among minority populations, who through their daily encounter with the manifestations of racism and discrimination are aware of the issues. However, they have perhaps not had sufficient opportunity to develop effective personal and collective responses to such situations and to understand their direct experiences within a broader social and political context.

An intercultural/anti-racism programme of the kind we envisage needs to be sustained over a considerable period of time. Our suggestions focus on aspects of identity development and, whilst a particular skills programme might be organised for a short period of perhaps two to four weeks, it is important to plan events very carefully with the participants, and to offer supervision and support for a long time afterwards. The credibility of any programme rests on its ability to follow through the changes that it may have triggered, particularly where those changes lead to inevitable conflicts and frictions.

* The proposals contained in this chapter are based on a handbook developed by a European working party of youth workers and youth work educators sponsored by the PETRA Youth for Europe Programme, whose financial assistance we gratefully acknowledge.

Ethnic identity

The proposed activities assume that participating young people have a basic understanding of the social significance of ethnicity in general, and of their own position towards such criteria. Even in groups that appear to be homogeneous (and homogeneously White), ethnicity as a social construct, will be present. At the same time and as the previous chapters have indicated, the category of ethnicity is intrinsically problematic, and should serve only as a transitory instrument for the clarification of the 'reality' of those forces in society that categorise and create stereotypes (Jenkins 1994). The specific features and contents of ethnic identity are therefore less important than the process of moving from externally imposed definitions to self-determination. In this process, any notion of homogeneity will quickly be challenged as differences of gender, age, social status, and class, etc., become apparent. Nevertheless, the concept of ethnic or cultural identity can refer back to the collective component of identities and can remind members of a group that, in taking responsibility for their own 'belonging' (albeit in multiple groupings), they also share a responsibility for the sense of belonging of their group.

One commonly accepted definition of ethnic identity is that formulated by Tajfel (1981), where ethnic identity is "that part of an individual's self-concept which derives from his/her knowledge of his/her membership of a social group (or groups) together with the value and emotional significance attached to that membership".

Despite the existence of universal patterns of identity formation in childhood and adolescence, it is recognised that young people from Black and White communities follow different pathways in becoming aware of, and giving significance to, their ethnic identity and hence, to anti-racism. Each route is characterised by different stages (see below). In drawing attention to this observation, we want to emphasise that there is a basic asymmetry between the two types of identity development. This asymmetry exists for purely social and political reasons, and may be summarised: "In the context of a racist society, feeling proud of being Black is not analogous to feeling proud of being White" (Tizard and Phoenix 1993:35). However, we suggest here that the movement of ethnic identity development through each stage may be enhanced, and that anti-racism learning can develop a wider range of skills when young people from different ethnic groups consciously encounter each other at critical stages of their identity formation. This is particularly so when the encounter has been pedagogically well-prepared.

We do not pre-suppose that these stages are automatic psychological developments or that they are in any way biologically inherent. On the contrary, they are social processes whose patterns are determined by the 'learning situation' that the social environment provides. This means that the differences between pathways are relative to this social environment, and that pedagogues will learn to recognise which pathway a group of young people choose to explore. Once these patterns have been recognised, the contrasts between 'Black' and 'White' identity formation may again be relativised. The encounters that we propose as a way of enhancing this process can, therefore, take place within the same group. It is by no means necessary to look for obvious group characteristics, such as between a group of 'native' and 'immigrant' youngsters. Every group, regardless of how homogeneous it at first appears, will be able to discover multiple group identities among its group members, even though it may be important to ascribe to themselves one common ethnic identity.

What is clear from a review of the available literature, is that it is more appropriate to conceive of ethnic identity formation as a continuous process rather than as something leading to a definite and fixed end-product. This has to be borne in mind when reading and applying the proposals: young people have to be facilitated in **forming and expressing** their ethnic identity, not in **adopting** given identities. This is of particular relevance to the growing number of young people with 'mixed backgrounds' who might otherwise be entirely left out from this approach. Indeed, some of the particular difficulties encountered by children whose parents belong to different ethnic groups, have been created by the insistence of some anti-racist activists that ethnicity and ethnic identity must be regained in a 'pure' form (Tizard and Phoenix 1993).

The proposals outlined below should not therefore be used as a means of 'fitting young people into a pattern which experts decide is good for them'. On the contrary, it should be recognised that participants in any programme will have different levels of understanding the significance of ethnicity as an element in their individual and collective identity. In addition, each group will also have a different profile in terms of gender, age, class and, other socially significant categories, that closely interact with the factor of ethnicity. Therefore, no single programme can cover their different learning needs and we wish only to make suggestions as to how the concept of ethnic identity may be used in a pedagogically imaginative way so as to prepare young people more adequately for life in a multi-ethnic society.

The proposals share two inseparable objectives in relation to the participants' clarification of their ethnic identity: a) to enhance a positive expression of their own ethnic identity; and b) to lead to a positive acceptance of the ethnic diversity in their respective societies. It is vital for an understanding of the programme's anti-racism component that these two goals are intrinsically linked. Young people should realise and experience that there is no fundamental conflict of interest between these objectives, that they are not involved in a 'zero-sum game' where gaining one objective is at the expense of the other. Accordingly, we attempt to develop skills and competences in anti-racism that expose, and effectively oppose, those ideologies and social practices (including their embodiment in laws and regulations) that do not allow for both objectives to be simultaneously achieved. We maintain that only with the use of power can the incompatibility between both be asserted and maintained [1].

Inclusion and diversity

In understanding and utilising the psychological dynamics of identity and diversity it is important to distinguish between inter-group and inter-personal relationships. The way groups relate to one another may be quite different from the way individual members of those groups relate. These discrepancies can act as mutual correctives: participants will experience how powerful groups can be in both a negative and a positive way. Equal attention must, therefore, be paid to the importance of a group in developing a strong sense of belonging, and to the needs of individuals to 'remain

[1]   These two combined objectives were shared by all members of our international working group even when their own methodology differed in emphasis between 'multi-cultural education', 'anti-discrimination', 'empowerment and resourcefulness', 'accepting youth work', 'inter-cultural pedagogy' or 'anti-racist youth work'.

themselves' whilst retaining some control over the direction in which the group wants to go. Only then can they learn to build on positive experiences of collective action, identify with the goals of a group, and recognise the social structure of relationships: "What are likely to affect inter-group behaviour are not inter-*personal* relations, but inter-*group* relations of status, power, material interdependence and so on" (Hewstone and Brown 1986: 15). When groups with very different identities meet there is not only a danger that they may reject each other; they can also come to 'like' each other in an uncritical way. When this happens, often against all previous expectations, they may learn to regard each other as 'exceptions to the rule' – that this group (of 'Whites', 'Blacks', 'immigrants', 'gypsies', etc.) are not like all the others. In these 'enthusiastic' encounters, cognitive dissonance is reduced whilst negative stereotypes remain intact: young people fail to receive an opportunity to understand differences in a fuller sense, and beyond the level of prejudices. The pedagogical process must, therefore, seek to differentiate diversity from friendship, not make mutual understanding and sympathy dependent upon 'likeness', nor give friends a reason to feel guilty because they identify with very different groups. Trew observed in relation to Northern Ireland: "It would seem that when groups are in contact, but divided from each other by mutually exclusive political goals, specific strategies have to be adopted in order to enable interpersonal co-operation and friendships to develop between individuals, without threatening group allegiance" (Trew 1986: 105).

In formulating our pedagogical instruments it helped us to think of the overall task as a triangular field whose outer boundaries are marked by three principles:

- Personal uniqueness (the right of each group member to be different from others, to place herself outside collective characterisations and stereotypes).

- Group diversity (which consists of two dimensions; a unifying dimension that gives members of an 'in-group' a sense of belonging, and a diversifying one that makes each group realise that their own identity contrasts with those of other groups).

- Inclusive thinking (the principle of equality of access and of opportunities which is the opposite of selectivity on the grounds of fixed criteria).

Any of these three positions and principles, if taken in isolation or developed as an absolute goal, will inhibit or distort inter-cultural encounters and learning and may therefore have racist implications. For instance, if personal uniqueness alone is emphasised, it may deprive young people from experiencing support from a group, or they may fail to learn how to take responsibility for the effects of their actions and behaviour on the whole group. Equally, a one-sided emphasis on group diversity, which is based on the fact that values adopted by different groups have equal validity and that diversity has a value in itself, may leave young people totally disoriented in a sea of relativity. If the principle of inclusive thinking which insists that 'there is one rule for everybody' in all circumstances, is rendered as absolute, this may lead to injustices against those individuals whose special needs should be safeguarded against group interests.

Organisers of intercultural pedagogical initiatives should monitor the development of programmes against these three criteria so that each one forms a corrective for the other two.

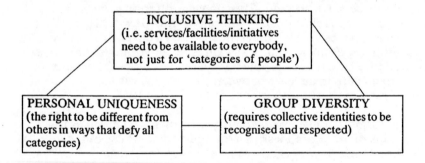

Starting with and validating personal experiences

An intercultural programme will only be relevant if it deals with the actual experiences of the participants at every stage. This assumes that racism, discrimination and exclusion are widespread phenomena in society, and which manifest themselves, not only in the ideologies and actions of extremists, but above all in everyday social practices. Participants will have witnessed, suffered from, become aware of, and denied, the existence of racist behaviour around them. At the same time, they will themselves have behaved in a racist manner, but it is also possible that they will have resisted and combated racism. It is important to realise that these practices exist around us and that we are all part of them. The programme seeks to connect those varied and probably conflicting experiences. This will ensure that it has 'relevance' for the participants and that it will inspire action.

Working on those experiences and emphasising personal involvement in their maintenance can easily generate guilt. It is a characteristic of present day societies that racism is generally deemed unacceptable and that even racist ideologies seek to camouflage their appearance. It should not be the intention of any programme to make young people discover how 'bad' they have been and to reform such inappropriate attitudes through the pressure of guilt. Generating guilt is a poor pedagogical principle and is likely to block, rather than promote, change. When guilt does arise, as it can – despite all intentions to the contrary – pedagogues need to provide the young people with opportunities to develop positive action, rather than dwelling on feelings of guilt.

An approach that avoids moralising over the issue of racism and discrimination and, that seeks instead to promote a sharing of experiences which makes visible the social forces and structures which produce racism, encourages action and participation in change. It initiates a self-directed learning process through which experiences may be accepted and validated as being relevant and authentic to the participants themselves. In giving meaning to their experiences they may also decide on their priorities and methods for change.

It is therefore appropriate that each programme should be the shared responsibility of organisers and participants from the very beginning. The young people not only need to know what to expect, they should also be given the opportunity to influence the programme according to their views and interests, to examine its assumptions critically, and to stop when they feel it is taking them to where they do not want to go. This is an important step towards addressing and overcoming the feelings of powerlessness which many of the young people may experience, particularly in relation to racism. Young people will only feel motivated to develop positive strategies if they feel they are in control, rather than being 'put through a programme'. Whilst there is a clear need for overall goals, organisers should be aware that there can be no fixed and preconceived outcomes which must be achieved. Rather, each group has to decide on its own goals and its own pace of change.

Action, not attitudes

Before we go into the details of our suggestions it would, perhaps, be useful to summarise what our pedagogy does *not* want to aim at:

Racism, for us, is not a product of personal resentment and deficient moral attitudes. Where the programme deals with prejudices, it sees them as instruments used in the pursuit of power and oppression, and as 'available material' which may be utilised for the aims of racism. A critical examination and, the consequent reduction, of prejudices in the participants is a useful by-product of a programme, but it is no more than that. This is not to say that we do not focus on awareness, as many of the exercises are designed to stimulate and direct awareness of experiences and stereotypes in relation to race and ethnicity. But we always aim at going beyond awareness towards action rather than viewing awareness as an end in itself.

Nor is it the primary aim of our programme proposals to create more 'tolerance' among the participating young people, although this has often been suggested as the key to any pedagogy of anti-racism. To start with tolerance before having examined the structural factors that lead to intolerance, will reduce the learning to moral categories, which in themselves will not convey the skills and means for social change. Tolerance, the prohibition of all critical assessments of other cultures, may lead to refraining from direct, open, committed interaction with other cultural groups, and becomes, instead, a gesture of condescendence. We aim to stimulate 'cultural interaction' in the sense of enabling participants to engage in critical, non-oppressive encounters with others who do not share their own cultural and ethnic background (Castoriadis 1987). Engaging meaningfully with other cultures and belief systems means being able to formulate opinions, which may at times be critical, rather than treating them as 'untouchable' and absolute.

We also propose that learning will not automatically take place when groups from different ethnic backgrounds come into contact with each other, and that this alone will not reduce negative stereotyping. On the contrary, studies have shown that such 'unstructured' encounters can confirm and increase stereotypical beliefs (e.g. Troyna and Hatcher 1992). The differences, including ethnic dimensions, to which personal contacts between different groups draw attention, should be established as socially constructed attributes mediated by socialisation processes, rather than as intrinsic qualities (Jenkins 1994). The likes and dislikes, friendships and aversions, which may result from personal contacts have a value in their own right. It is only through engaging in explicit exchanges over the social significance of group differences that common concerns and common ground can be established.

Finally, racism cannot be fought with reason (Taguieff 1990). A rationalist pedagogy not only rests on an inadequate theory of racism; it fails to grasp the fact that racism is indifferent to its inherent irrationality. This is because it utilises both rational and irrational arguments without scruples in its pursuit of power. This does not mean that information and data pointing out the nature and extent of discrimination and racism are useless. Indeed, we suggest they are tools for the participants. These 'facts', when researched and brought together by the young people themselves, are a step for their own understanding of the nature of the society in which they live, its history and institutions, rather than 'weapons' for refuting false racist beliefs. "We agree with Foucault's broad argument that one way to undermine a 'truth' is not to counterpose it with another 'truth' but to examine the discursive process by which true and false statements become distinguished" (Wetherell and Potter 1992).

Organisational reference points

Those operating a programme within the proposed framework should be thoroughly familiar with its basic principles and have received training and experience in inter-cultural/anti-racist approaches before they introduce it to youth groups. Whilst there is room to incorporate many other ideas into the programme, these must be carefully examined to ensure that they support the central principles of this approach. If they do not, there is a danger that young people will receive conflicting messages that may damage their confidence and self-image.

In addition, organisers should be able to broadly assess the stage at which a group of young people is in terms of their awareness of their ethnic identity and the significance that it has for them. Organisers should also be aware of the stage that they themselves have reached, the doubts that they may have, and the value they attribute to ethnic identity in principle.

Although the proposals are oriented mainly towards stimulating cognitive processes and practical skills, they should be developed in a playful, recreational atmosphere that takes into account the affective needs of participants. Playfulness regulates the immediacy and impact that these very serious issues may have on participants. In turn they must be able to say when they want to relax, make jokes, and generally vent their feelings.

Whilst these proposals provide some guidelines for evaluation, each programme should devise its own instruments for evaluation according to the composition of the group and the scope of its programme.

Target groups

The proposed programme aims at those young people who are 'potential disseminators' of the ideas and initiatives of an anti-racist pedagogy. This means, in effect, that it presupposes that participants are already positively motivated to come to terms with the multi-cultural nature of their society and that they have a basic awareness of racism. In wishing to participate they have demonstrated an interest in 'doing somethng about the situation'. This may mean, however, that they feel angry and defensive, or that they may be seeking the security of their own ethnic group. Young people who already adhere to an explicitly racist ideology will probably require a separate pedagogical approach before they may once again experience their identity as a fluid process. What should be avoided at all costs, however, is an invitation to participate under false pretenses, for instance under the pretext of purely recreational activities. If the young people are to trust in the aims of the programme, then the principle of 'no hidden agendas' must prevail. Honesty at all stages must be maintained.

Organisers will have to use their experience in assessing what activities are suitable for any particular age group. The majority of proposals are designed for young people in their teens. However, selected exercises may also be used with other age groups as 'triggers' that lead to other activities or discussions.

The ideas have been developed in the context of international youth exchanges in which the inter-cultural component is highly visible. As we stated above we presuppose that there is sufficient heterogeneity in every group to make the encounter with 'differences' pedagogically possible. However, it may be easier to plan the activities as an encounter between two youth groups, with each representing a visibly different cultural or ethnic identity. Alternatively, organisers may put together a balanced group of young people from different backgrounds, whilst carefully ensuring that the status differences of sub-groups are not too pronounced. In this case, participants should be assured of basic peer-group support through the selection of at least two group members who share the same ethnic background and who know each other very well. This helps to ensure that the programme is geared towards group processes and group identities. For the size of the overall group we suggest 20 to 30 participants.

Stages of racial identity development

"It is assumed that in a society where racial-group membership is emphasized, the development of a racial identity will occur in some form in everyone" (Tatum 1992:9). This is not to say that we regard belonging to a racial group as a biological fact, but that ethnic differences have become a visible and much talked-about social reality in every European society today. It is this social 'fact' that requires all young people to consider ethnicity as a factor in the formation of their identity. As they take a position on the challenges created for them, their reactions are likely to follow distinct patterns. Our pedagogical approach aims to relate them to these stages.

We also adopt, in a political sense, the polarisation of related but separate stages of Black and White identity formation. The difference is not caused by the colour of skin, but by the dominance and inferiority attributed to the White and Black groups respectively. It is as yet unclear from the research literature to what extent all dominant and oppressed groups conform to the same patterns, but there seems sufficient evidence to warrant a look at such stages as an organisational and pedagogical tool (Phinney 1990). The stages models of identity development introduced here act as a broad guide to programme planners. They may help them to select appropriately matched groups of participants and to identify the specific learning needs according to these stages. The movement between stages should not be understood as an automatic linear process where each stage inevitably leads to the next one. Rather, movement may occur in cycles or spirals, and earlier stages may be repeated several times. There appears to be three broad stages through which people of all ethnic backgrounds pass as the issue of ethnicity becomes a relevant and unavoidable question (Phinney 1989):

1. *Unexamined ethnic identity* At this stage ethnicity is not important; the dominant culture is accepted as providing the main reference points (even for minority groups striving to 'assimilate'); or one's own ethnicity is accepted without critical reflection on its social relativity.

2. *Ethnic identity search (moratorium)* At this stage the exploration of one's own ethnicity sets in (often triggered by an 'event' that poses an unresolved question).

3. *Identity achievement* This stage takes different forms for different groups but involves coming to terms with both status differentials and diversity.

Black racial identity development is assumed to include the following five stages (Cross 1991):

Pre-encounter At this stage beliefs and values of the dominant White culture have been absorbed: 'White is right'. The person may seek to be accepted by Whites and not regard race as a relevant factor: 'people are people' and succeed in life on the strengths of their personal merits.

Encounter This is typically precipitated by an incident (such as rejection, discrimination, a racially motivated attack, a campaign or public event that focuses on issues of race). At this stage race and racism emerge as meaningful concepts as they start to correspond, in a minimal way, to a 'reality'. The 'encounter' stage is often associated with spontaneous anger against Whites.

Immersion/Emersion   Typical at this stage is the desire to surround oneself with visible symbols of one's racial identity and a reversal of the prevailing or dominant values: glorifying Blacks, denigrating Whites. Here, aspects of one's own ethnic history become very important. White-focused anger tends to dissipate as the focus shifts to one's own characteristics as defined by one's own ethnic group, rather than by the dominant group.

Internalisation   At this stage, the person becomes less defensive and a greater security in one's own racial identity begins. Coalitions with other oppressed groups become very important and racial attributes lose their defining power.

Internalisation-Commitment   The security gained at this stage translates into strategies and specific activities against oppression that go beyond the goal of racial identity: "Blackness becomes the point of departure for discovering the universe of ideas, cultures and experiences beyond Blackness in place of mistaking Blackness as the universe itself" (Cross quoted in Tatum 1992: 12).

White racial identity development can usefully be categorised in six similar stages (Helms 1990):

Contact   Individuals have a vague awareness of different ethnic groupings in society but remain firmly rooted in their own values and stereotypes. They may demonstrate a naïve curiosity towards Blacks mixed with a fear that feeds on common stereotypes of inferiority.

Disintegration   This is often brought about by an event, an encounter, or personally mediated information about racism. It marks the beginning of a new understanding of cultural and institutional racism, whose effects may be feelings of discomfort, guilt, shame, anger. This may lead to attempts to reduce this discomfort through denial, or blaming victims of racism for having brought this upon themselves. These experiences, and the 'cognitive dissonance' created by new race-related information, may precipitate a defence reaction known as 're-integration'.

Reintegration   This is prompted by a desire for acceptance by the White group. It confirms an underlying racist orientation and a belief in White superiority. Identity is treated as a biological fact that does not require justification for the advantages it brings.

Alternatively, a deeper questioning of the nature of the 'threat' in the context of other discriminating forces in society, may move the person on to the stage of Pseudo-Independence. This marks a gradual abandoning of a belief in White superiority. However, it is associated with a risk of isolation, and of becoming an 'outsider'. Emotional and practical support and role models (for example, White anti-racists) are crucial at this stage as people respond to this discomfort with a continued search for new identities.

Immersion/emersion   At this stage individuals are able to sustain a degree of discomfort with their own Whiteness but are unable to fully come to terms with it. The stage is characterised by a search for a more comfortable 'way' of being White. This may imply a distancing from racist assumptions about White superiority and a realisation that being White does not automatically mean being racist.

Autonomy   This expresses a newly-defined and differentiated sense of oneself as White, but not, however, in opposition to being Black. The mechanisms of discrimination and exclusion are understood as being not dependent upon skin colour but as an exploitation of physical differences. This brings with it a confidence and energy to confront oppression in everyday situations.

Summary of stages models

STAGES OF BLACK IDENTITY FORMATION	STAGES OF WHITE IDENTITY FORMATION
pre-encounter	contact
	disintegration
encounter	reintegration
immersion emersion	pseudo-independence
internalisation	immersion/ emersion
commitment	autonomy

A possible use of the stages models is to identify the potential within a particular youth group for moving on to the next stage. This involves targeting the needs of young people at various stages more specifically, and providing them with the means and opportunities for reaching the next stage. In addition to this, consideration should be given to encounters and exchanges between youth groups whose ethnic compositions are different, and whose members are engaged in the exploration of their respective ethnic identities (and to which we shall refer in an abbreviated form, with due reference to the multiplicity of identities, as Black and White 'identity stages'). We suggest that encounters at the following stages contain a high pedagogical potential for the development of anti-racist competences.

1. Joint activities are planned at a stage when both Black and White groups take the 'White world' in which they live for granted. Such encounters will highlight the existence of stereotypes, be a first step in challenging them, and enquiring into their social significance (for example, why are Black footballers 'accepted' and on what terms?). It is important in this stage to refrain from 'pushing' the young people beyond the limitations of this phase. Rather, the effects of the ideas generated by contacts should be allowed to take their own course and without allowing them to be influenced by a concern with achievements typical of the final stages. The enforcement of stereotypes should also be avoided.

BLACK IDENTITY STAGE	WHITE IDENTITY STAGE	OBJECTIVE OF ENCOUNTER
(i)		broadening the experience; challenging stereotypes

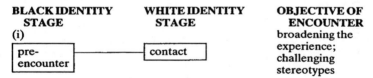

2. By placing an encounter from a preliminary stage into the context of the following stages, the Black group could prepare specific questions and exercises that are deliberately designed to challenge the 'taken-for-granted' world and culture of the White group. In this way, the 'reality' of racism may be explored, not only as an experience for Black people or as something for which the White group are directly responsible, but rather as an accumulation of daily practices, legal and societal rules, and structures. The aim is not to make the White group feel guilty or to force solutions on them, but rather to explore dilemmas at both an intellectual and an emotional level.

exploring
stereotypes;
Whites accepting
the reality of
racism,
questioning their
role in it,
exploring empathy

3. Alternatively, the contacts could be structured so that
    the relativity of ethnic differences between groups may
    be explained. It is in this way that the Black group may
    realise that White is also an ethnic category, rather than
    being something outside of and above ethnicity. This
    could lead to a questioning of the ambivalence of
    accepting White standards, and of racism as a 'reality'.
    Racism becomes not just something that is being done to
    them, but also as something that affects their own
    behaviour and perception of themselves.

experiencing
Whites as
an ethnic group;
Blacks acknowledge
impact of racism
on their lives;
intercultural
learning

4. In a similar way, but particularly when the majority of
    young people have reached the stage of internalisation,
    (i.e. where the importance of their separate Black
    identity has been established, but no longer in
    opposition to White groups), a Black group may
    challenge a White group who, already critical of their
    supposed superiority, to differentiate their 'Whiteness'
    from their 'superiority'. This could mean sharing the
    skills acquired by the Black youngsters in their particular
    context and learning together that the gain of one group
    (being proud to be Black), need not be built on the loss
    of the other. Groups can share in activities from which
    they both benefit, and from which they understand the
    effect of societal power on the lives of members of both
    groups.

5. A particularly attractive combination (in the pedagogical sense) appears to be that of Black and White groups being aware of their respective strengths and skills, where each furthers their own learning whilst identifying those tasks where direct cooperation is appropriate. This signifies an important step towards 'second level learning', with the young people examining how their personal experiences and their understanding of how society works, to improve together the control they have over their lives. They may learn, not only how differences between them have been socially constructed, but also how they might be re-constructed (within clearly defined limits). For example, friendships between Black and White youngsters become not just a matter of personal liking and interest, but something that should be 'defended' against prohibitive cultural conventions. In this way, expressions and styles in different activities (celebrations, leisure, sports etc.), which are acceptable to both communities, may be created.

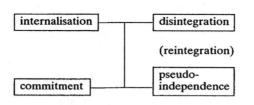

6. The significance of ethnicity begins to disappear in joint work between groups during these last stages. Indeed, the encounters should contribute to this disappearance. One of the main purposes of pedagogical work between and across groups of-distinct ethnic identity is to underline the relativity and limited relevance of the concept of ethnicity. Having a better understanding of

the mechanisms of discrimination, segregation, and racism in society allows young people to shift the focus in such collaboration away from preoccupations with their own identity and towards other affected groups. They may, for example, explain: how disadvantage is constructed for young people with handicaps in the school system and the urban environment; how young women are discriminated against in the job market; how role conflicts in inter-generational relationships arise, etc.

build alliances

plan networks, link local and global issues

It is possible for exchanges between Black ethnic groups to take place at the stages model level. This will facilitate progression for groups to a higher stage. In general, contacts between groups that have reached the same stage are fruitful. However, an exception of this would be contacts at the pre-encounter and immersion/emersion stages because here the dynamics of the groups are turned inwards. Alternatively, groups at one stage ahead may trigger a move forward for a group that has not yet made a transition from, for example, pre-encounter to encounter, from immersion/emersion to internalisation, or from internalisation to commitment. With regard to the transition between encounter and immersion/emersion, we are concerned that this should come from 'within' the particular group. In this way, it will 'own' its achievements rather than attributing them to the influence of another group. This would have an effect on the overall confidence of the group.

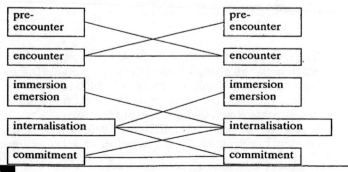

Literature and references

Castoriadis, C. (1987), Notations sur le racisme, in: Connexions: Psychosociologie, sciences humaines, 48: 107-118

Cross, W. E. Jr. (1991), Shades of Black: Diversity in African-American identity, Philadelphia: Temple University Press

Helms, J. E. (1990), Black and White Racial Identity: Theory, research and practice, Westport, C. T.: Greenwood Press

Hewstone, M. and Brown, R. (eds.) (1986), Contact and conflict in intergroup encounters, Oxford: Blackwell

Jenkins, R. (1994), Rethinking ethnicity: identity, categorization and power, Ethnic and Racial Studies 17;2: 197-223

Memmi, A. (1982), Le racisme, Paris: Edition Gallimard

Phinney, J. (1989), Stages of ethnic identity in minority group adolescents, Journal of Early Adolescence 9: 34-39

Phinney F. (1990), Ethnic identity in adolescents and adults: Review of research, Psychological Bulletin 108, 3: 499-514

Taguieff, P.-A. (1990), Réflexions sur la question antiraciste; Lignes, 12: 15-52

Tajfel, H. (1981), Human groups and social categories, Cambridge: Cambridge University Press

Tatum, B. D. (1992) Talking about race, learning about racism: the application of racial identity development theory in the classroom, Harvard Educational Review 62, 1: 1-24

Tizard, B. and Phoenix, A. (1993), Children of interracial marriage, London: Routledge

Trew, K. (1986) Catholic-Protestant Contact in Northern Ireland, in Hewstone, M. and Brown, R. (eds.), Contact and conflict in intergroup encounters, Oxford: Blackwell

Troyna, B. and Hatcher, B. (1992), Racism in children's lives: a study of mainly-white primary schools, London: Routledge

Wetherell, M. and Potter, J. (1992), Mapping the Language of Racism, London: Harvester Wheatsheaf

9. Practical activities for anti-racist work

Walter Lorenz

The following outline of activities and exercises is designed to serve as a starting point for the development of full, individual programmes. The choice of activities will depend upon factors such as: the age of the participants; the degree of their interest in working on personal and group identity; local facilities, etc. The majority of exercises have been designed for use when two groups with different ethnic backgrounds meet, or for when cultural differences within a group and within a local community are explored. Whilst there is no strict sequence in these components, their numbering suggests a 'flow' from group-centred exercises towards those dealing with racism as a feature of society.

We do not deal explicitly with what we consider to be fundamental aspects of good youth work and group work practice, such as: participation by the group in the planning of meetings and events; the provision of emotional support to group members; the setting of safe limits to all activities; and giving young people a commitment to staying with the kind of changes they may wish to bring about. Their relevance for all youth work and educational activities is taken for granted. However, we strongly recommend that these principles and skills should feature in any training programme for facilitators before such activities are undertaken.

The 'suggested activities' illustrate key activities around particular topics. In designing these exercises we had no specific age group in mind and youth workers should use their own judgement on this and make their modifications as they see fit.

1. Introduction

This phase, vital to the success of all future activities, is concerned with getting to know one another, the establishing of fundamental ground-rules, and the development of trust in the group. Our emphasis is not so much on exploring facts and acquiring information, which will feature later, but on process, which enables participants time and space to move towards each other at their own pace.

First impressions

A first round of introductions is appropriate even when group members seem to know each other quite well. The importance of everybody's name, for both personal and cultural identity, is highlighted by using big badges for names. Participants could then give each other brief explanations of what their different names might mean, how usual they are in a particular community, and perhaps why a name was given. In this way, individuals in the group begin to own a particular history that is linked to their family, their culture, and some other members of the group. Names are at one and the same time both personal and general, and the group may pay attention to patterns in name-giving which act as a first reference to social structures.

ACTIVITY 1: MASK MAKING

SUMMARY   This game, which can form part of the introductions, allows the group to decide, at this stage, on how close or how distant they want to be with each other, how much of themselves they want others to know directly or indirectly. It sets the scene for 'play-acting', which is a feature of this approach, and demonstrates the safety of being 'in a role'.

DURATION   One to two hours, including the part 'moving with masks', depending upon the enthusiasm of the group.

MATERIAL   Floor space, piles of old newspapers, sticky tape, staplers, glue and string. No colours or paint required.

PROCEDURE   The group members scatter around the room. They are told to each make a mask for themselves, using only the materials provided. The mask should not represent anything or anybody in particular, but should

---

'grow' from spontaneous ideas. Looking at other people's ideas should be encouraged.

When the masks are completed everybody is asked to put theirs on and to move around the room in a manner that fits the mask, Participants should get a feel for the movements as they develop and react to other masks and movements so that little improvised games commence.

EVALUATION   When the activity has run its course, participants talk about what went through their minds as they were moving and acting. Refrain from 'making interpretations' but seek statements which describe the emotional qualities attached to masks and movements.

Ground-rules

Every group needs to give itself rules. However, in the inter-cultural context of these activities, it is vital that rules are openly discussed and agreed upon, such as: what to do when one feels uncomfortable with the direction the activities are taking, whether such matters are to be decided by majority vote or whether a minority or individual can have a right of veto. By spending time on these 'preliminary details', and dealing with them in an imaginative and interesting way, it is possible to create an atmosphere of openness, an acceptance of the legitimacy of differences, a working style that builds on positive skills, and the avoidance of blame. Participants need to directly experience control over this process.

2.   Expectations

Whilst the programme will have been planned jointly with the participants, it is still valid to ascertain and clarify expectations when the activities begin. One instrument to facilitate this is the:

Wall of Expectations

We propose the use of a big display area on which all participants, including the facilitators, may either write or pin a word, a brief statement, or a symbol, that expresses their expectation of the event or programme after the theme has been introduced. The group then contemplates the statements, seeks clarification, and looks for 'patterns' by grouping them, and relating them perhaps to the wider social situation in which participants live. This 'wall' will act as a reference point throughout the programme allowing always for amendments, clarifications, major modifications, etc. It should be discussed at each session and provide the basis for planning the actual activities. It also serves as an instrument of ongoing evaluation. A separate 'wall' may serve as a place where spontaneous reactions can be expressed in the form of 'graffiti'. This gives a measure of the 'emotional temperature' of the group.

3. Co-operation

A series of joint tasks and activities should be set to initiate and enhance the interaction between different groups or sub-groups who do not yet know each other well. These activities should strike a good balance between co-operation and competitiveness (which will almost inevitably develop). For this purpose, they should be designed so that they lead, whenever possible, to success for the whole group. They should also be fun. Such activities include: preparing a joint meal, having a party to which everybody contributes, or:

ACTIVITY 2: EGGS DO FLY

SUMMARY   Whilst chickens fly and eggs may fly – but rarely land safely – this exercise attempts the impossible. The aim is to find a way of making raw eggs fly and land safely. The exercise may generate a degree of competition between the small groups who try to find their own solutions, but this should be fun and the cohesion among the groups normally grows.

DURATION   1 hour.

MATERIAL   Raw eggs (one for each group), paper, cardboard, string, glue, staplers, sticky tape, plastic drinking straws, thin wire, scissors.

PROCEDURE   The group is divided into small groups of about three or four each, and should mix friendship groups. The rules are that each group should invent a method that allows a raw egg to glide to the ground from an upstairs window (or travel the longest distance across a field) without breaking. Sucking out the egg is not permitted. There will be only one joint 'trial' display.

Each group has to deal with its own failures (by cleaning up the mess).

EVALUATION   Brief discussion or de-briefing on the process: how did solutions emerge? how did the groups react to different ideas? how important was it to succeed? what unusual solutions were considered and then dismissed?, etc.

It might be useful to get groups to explore the local environment with which not all members might be equally familiar. The relationship between the group and the social environment is a crucial pedagogical instrument:

ACTIVITY 3:   TREASURE HUNT

SUMMARY   Having to find one's way around an unknown locality mobilises a variety of communicative skills, and sharpens observation skills. The site for this treasure hunt should be a part of the town with which most of the participants are unfamiliar or do not visit often. The shared task gives participants a chance to get to know each other more closely and to take responsibility for one another. Personal experiences lead to structural observations.

DURATION   Half day.

MATERIAL   Maps/townplans, prepared clues, tokens on location, clipboards for each team, sets of instructions including 'emergency procedures', such as what to do on getting lost, or 'when a situation feels dangerous'.

PROCEDURE   As with every treasure hunt careful preparation pays off. The group is divided into sub-groups, their numbers depending upon their degree of confidence. The clues should lead to landmarks which will have a significance in future discussions (memorials, historical places, places of worship, shopping areas, markets, housing areas of different 'quality', etc.). Tokens, to be found as 'treasures', should be redeemable for refreshments at local snack-bars and shops, thus enhancing the interaction of the group with local people.

Organisers must ensure that participants will not encounter any hostility during their exploration of unfamiliar areas.

EVALUATION   Evaluation should concentrate upon the significance that the various localities held to those members with different social and ethnic backgrounds. The reactions the groups received from local people, which may include expressions of racism should be discussed. How did they respond to the challenges that this exercise posed?

4. *Building up trust*

This section allows participants to get to know each other more closely and focuses on the relationship between individuals and groups. In the development of trust all participants are learning resources for each other with their various backgrounds, experiences, skills and interests. These resources can only become available, however, if differences in power and status among members of the group are carefully addressed.

EXERCISE 4:   THE 'PEOPLE MAP'

Start by introducing the activity: "Imagine this room or this field is a map of your town/country/of the world; locate yourself on the place which you think marks the spot where you were born".

After these directions, encourage participants to make several attempts to gauge the proportions of the map and to settle everybody in a position which corresponds to their perception of their own location. Participants can comment on the map, determine the relative distance of various locations, clarify the position of the various regions, countries or cities until everybody 'has the overall picture'. The exercise can then be repeated for different 'age-steps' and life events with the direction: "place yourself where you first started school, where you found yourself at age 12, age 16, age 20 etc.". It could also be expanded to the birth locations of parents and grandparents.

This exercise could also form part of the introductions.

Relaxation

Relaxation exercises are a good preparation for the more intensive 'person to person' work later on. It might generally be a good idea to start activities with brief relaxation games, 'warm-ups' or 'ice-breakers', for instance:

ACTIVITY 5:   MIRROR IMAGES

SUMMARY   This is a relaxation exercise which, though simple enough, will train perception and bring participants physically close in a non-demanding way.

DURATION   Five to ten minutes.

MATERIAL   Empty room.

PROCEDURE   Participants (who do not yet know each other particularly well) stand in pairs facing each other. 'A' begins to make slow, deliberate, and continuous movements as if standing in front of a mirror. These begin with hands and arms but will eventually involve all parts of the body. 'B' copies this 'mirror image' as closely as possible, but without touching 'A'. After a while 'B' takes the lead, and 'A' mirrors. Gradually the change overs will become more frequent and 'fluent' until it becomes uncertain as to who is leading and who is mirroring.

(A variation of this is to walk around the room in pairs, with 'B' closely studying the characteristics of 'A's walk. 'B' then tries to copy. Roles are then reversed so that the pair really get to 'know each other's manners' without having to caricature).

EVALUATION   No evaluation is normally required.

Trust games

Activities in this section should never be introduced as 'tests' of the level of trust already achieved by the group or else they create distrust; exerting 'moral pressure' is always counter-productive.

EXERCISE 6:   'BLINDFOLD WALK'

This is a simple activity with a lot of potential. In pairs, one partner is blindfolded and is facilitated by the other in exploring the vicinity of the room or the environment a short distance away. The emphasis should be on making the walk interesting, enjoyable and safe rather than on making it frightening and surprising. After each walk the roles are reversed and partners learn to perceive each other's level of anxiety and relaxation. The experiences can be talked about in the whole group.

Related is an exercise which can also be a means of relaxing:

ACTIVITY 7:   FLOATING

SUMMARY   Relaxation and trust combine doing this activity. Some participants may be apprehensive and this should be respected.

DURATION   Half an hour, but possibly longer if the group wishes it to go further.

MATERIAL   A room free of all obstacles.

PROCEDURE   The activity is carefully explained. The group, by forming a tight circle of between 10 and 15 people, helps to let one person experience 'weightlessness'. In the centre stands an volunteer, eyes closed, who has been given assurances by the group that they will take care of her or him. As many of the group as possible touch the volunteer's shoulder, (who retains a fairly rigid but relaxed upright position), and begin to gently sway the person. The movement gradually widens out, involving the whole group in giving 'support', and until the movements get so wide that the person in the centre is gently lowered to the ground.

After a couple of rounds, and with different volunteers, the group may feel confident enough to carry on lifting the person from the ground, eyes still closed, on as many arms and hands as can reach. They continue conveying this sense of 'weightlessness' by avoiding all jerky movements or tossing in the air. Ideally, the volunteer will experience a sensation of floating around the room.

EVALUATION   It is important to provide the volunteers with the opportunity to describe their sensations and feelings during the various stages of this exercise, and for the 'supporters' to hear the extent of the anxiety and reassurance that they experienced.

EXERCISE 8:   THREE THINGS ABOUT MYSELF

The point of this exercise is not just to make group members more fully acquainted with each other, but also to assess the boundary between details which must remain personal, and those that can safely be shared with the whole group. Ideally, members who do not know each other well should 'interview' each other in pairs with the aim of establishing three things which each of them would like the whole group to know about themselves. After the pairs have clarified the items and checked that it is alright for the big group to learn about them, each partner presents the three items about the other person to the group.

Alternatively, drawings and symbols could be used whereby every person draws an object or symbol on a big badge which characterises something about his or her person. In this case the 'explanation' of the symbol is given by the owner of the badge.

This exercise could be widened out to, **telling a story / episode from my family** (something funny or unusual that happened in our family); again with details first checked out in pairs and then told to the whole group.

5. What the group should know about our country / our culture / our people

The emphasis in this section is on group identities and on inter-group relations. It gives participants the opportunity to meet each other not just as individuals, but also as representatives of different national, cultural and ethnic groups. Being aware of the stage in the development of ethnic identity (see above) is particularly relevant to this and subsequent sections.

EXERCISE 9: IMAGES OF OUR COUNTRY

Where the young people were born in different countries (or parts of the country) they could collect images and information on that country or region to be put on display during the whole programme or event. The aim is not to give one definitive version or one's personal image, but to present *different versions* of one's country or region. For instance, the version presented by the tourist boards and travel agencies in posters and brochures, by embassies and other government institutions, by industry, by different campaign groups, by the media etc. The guiding questions are, "what images are commonly 'available' and used to describe my country/region", and "what do I think others need to know about my country/region in order to understand me better". The exercise is best done in small groups and each 'national' group should avoid giving one agreed image, but should allow differences to become visible while learning to take responsibility for their 'statement'.

In this activity it is vital that both the members perceived as 'strangers' and the 'indigenous' members do their own work on these images and that each group present several different versions of the same country or part of the country.

The images should not be left to merely 'speak for themselves'. Brief introductions, reactions from others and discussions of the displays could be spaced throughout the programme. Ideally the displays would form a permanent 'background' which participants can

---

explore informally, ask further questions about and react
to. These exchanges can generate their own themes and
dynamics.

ACTIVITY 10:   WHAT AM I, WHAT ARE WE, WHO AM I?

SUMMARY   Individuals and groups have unique
features, but define them in very different ways. Here,
everybody is being given the chance to reflect upon their
own uniqueness within the context of other people's
definitions of ethnic and social groupings. (The 'internal'
and 'external' images which influence identity).

DURATION   One hour.

MATERIAL   Index cards (eight for each participant),
sheets of writing paper, A1 paper or display boards for
each ethnic or social group, markers, glue or sticky tape.

PROCEDURE   This exercise has three stages:

'What am I?' In mixed groups with approximately six
participants, each person writes (on index cards) four
responses (one on each card) to the question, 'What
makes me and all other human beings different from
other living creatures?' The group, having discussed the
significance of different ideas, arranges the answers in
clusters and presents them to the whole group.

'What are we?' The same procedure is applied, but with
'homogeneous' groups (according to the young people's
own definition): Individual responses to the question:
'What distinguishes an Irish, Scottish, Pakistani, English,
or West Indian person, from a person of a different
background?' are evaluated and arranged by the group.

'Who am I?' Each participant lists the personal
characterists that distinguish her/him as an individual
from all other individuals. These observations remain
'private' to each person. Participants are then invited to
comment on the process, how it felt, and whether there

are general points they would like the whole group to know, particularly on the agreement and the tensions between individual and group characteristics.

(adapted from G. Pike, D. Selby (1988), Human Rights Activity File, London: Mary Glasgow Publications, Activity 17)

ACTIVITY 11:   PICTURES OF 'THEM' AND 'US'

SUMMARY   Stereotypes exist not just in the minds of those people who use them against others, they also enter the minds of the people to whom they refer. Making these two sides of stereotyping visible can be a step towards achieving a more critical or comfortable distance. It challenges the negative aspects of stereotyping identities in discrimination and oppression. It also allows participants to develop their own personal identities.

DURATION   One hour.

MATERIALS   Felt pens and markers, small rolls of newsprint or old wallpaper, scissors.

PROCEDURE: The outlines of two persons are drawn onto the rolls of paper, and then cut in half from top to bottom. The group is divided into two sub-groups to represent the 'majority' and the 'minority' group in social or ethnic terms. Each sub-group receives either two left or two right sides. The task of each group is to: (i) write some characteristics about one's own group on one half of the figure as the group defines these for themselves; (ii) write those characteristics that one commonly presumes distinguish the other group on the other half figure.

The two half figures are then put together again and the match/discrepancies between characteristics from one's own and from other people's perspectives are established. Careful attention to linguistic nuances is required ('overtones' in descriptions, terms, nick-names etc.), as well as to the distinction between common stereotypes and those the group members would not use themselves.

EVALUATION   The emphasis is on the process of how difficult or easy it is to stereotype. Is there anything useful in stereotypes, are they all inappropriate, false, dangerous? and, what turns them into expressions of prejudice and racism?

6.   Personal experiences of racism

Before moving to this phase, it is paramount that a good level of trust has been established in the group overall. Participants should feel safe and supported and have had opportunities of exercising control over the programme, of setting limits, and of voicing divergent views without fear of recrimination.

The theme of this section is **'racism affects all of us, but in very different ways'**. This means that it is not only Black young people who experience racism, although they might be most directly affected. Where prejudices do arise, the aim is not to make participants feel guilty for having them, but to help them understand where they originate and what their social and political function is. At the start of this work, the 'ground rules' of the programme need to be re-affirmed: no personal attacks or abuse, no emotional pressure, the right to veto or to halt proceedings. The connection between this section and the following one is also very important in 'locating' the experiences in a wider context.

ACTIVITY 12:   DIFFERENT WAYS OF CUTTING THE CAKE

SUMMARY   This exercise develops the same theme as the previous ones, namely, categorisation and stereotypes. Again, the emphasis is on process and the group will, by now, have developed a good degree of trust from having learned to control categories and limits.

DURATION   20–30 minutes.

MATERIAL   Empty space.

PROCEDURE   The activity evolves in two main stages. The first is triggered by the question: "In how many different ways can we divide our large group into small groups, using one distinguishing characteristic each time?" The process will normally move from the 'obvious' physical signs (boys/girls, tall/small, dark/light skin) to attributes with immediate social implications. It is important to let the group make suggestions they feel safe and confident with, asking for approval before each division. If the activity stagnates, facilitators can try out their own ideas. The group will soon touch on personal issues (for example, smoking, eating habits, school achievements, income). When limits have been reached, the facilitators could carry on the exercise 'hypothetically': "What would it feel like to split on grounds of..." (body weight, shape of nose, religious observance, sexual orientation, etc.).

At the second stage, the leading question is: "How would outsiders divide up our group?" (such as teachers: according to ability groups; sports trainers: to put together a good 'olympic team'; immigration officials: according to type of passport held; going back in time: divisions before national immigration legislation, during colonial times, during fascism, during feudalism, etc.).

EVALUATION   Discussion and evaluation should take place during the activities to bring out the emotional quality of each categorisation process. At the same time, the link with everyday reality can be underlined: how do our daily routines place us in different categories and 'tell others' something about us?

It is important to gauge the emotional 'temperature' generated by the different criteria suggested and used in this activity: for some characteristics it is easy to identify with a sub-group, for others it feels uncomfortable. This discomfort is an important indicator but organisers must respond sensitively to objections against certain criteria for divisions.

Audit of personal and group experiences

These exercises build up a public and private 'language' in which experiences can be articulated and examined critically. They will probably range from 'being made to feel different' to 'being the victim of racism'. The idea is to get a measure of the pervasiveness of racial stereotypes, as confirmed by childhood memories, daily observations and in the media.

ACTIVITY 13: MEMORIES OF BEING DIFFERENT

SUMMARY   This activity is not a game, but a straightforward attempt to recall personal history and to construct the outlines of a collective history for both Black and White people in relation to racism.

DURATION   One to two hours.

MATERIALS   None, but as this is very much an oral activity a comfortable atmosphere that encourages remembering and story telling should be created.

PROCEDURE   Depending on the stage of ethnic identity formation in the group, participants should either work in small groups that reflect their own ethnic identity, or start in mixed groups of about six members. Each small group summarises their memories for a plenary session, but without adopting a formal format of taking notes etc. The memories should flow and spark further memories.

"Try to remember the following kinds of situations you might have experienced, and describe the feelings you associate with them:

How did your family talk about people of different skin colour/people who were not born in the local area?

When did you become aware of racist comments being made about yourself (in your street or town, at school, on a journey etc.)? or, people around you making racist comments about others?

How did it feel to be a member of a group that was in any way treated as superior to another group (in sports, other competitions, getting 'service' in shops and restaurants, etc.)?".

> EVALUATION   Different participants will use different criteria for what constitutes 'racism'. The discussion should allow such differences to stand rather than aiming to arrive at one common definition.

Similar themes are raised in:

ACTIVITY 14:   HEROES AND VILLAINS

SUMMARY   Figures in books, films, and public life are often embodiments of stereotypes that carry racist implications. Looking at these roles closely can reveal the 'sub-text' of the messages transmitted through these images.

DURATION   Two to three hours, or several sessions, depending upon the material available.

MATERIAL   Magazines, cartoons, posters, newspapers, well-known books, a variety of old and current films on video, video play-back facilities.

PROCEDURE   The groups prepare for this activity by collecting a selection of magazines, posters, videos, etc. In the first round, mixed groups browse through magazines and well-known cartoons, and pick out 'heroes and villains'. They should ask themselves how their qualities are portrayed and whether there are any hints to their ethnic identity. The group then watch clips from feature films, and ask: "could the ethnic characteristics of certain figures be changed and how would that affect the story?" "Have there been changes in recent years in the way black people are portrayed in films?", etc.

EVALUATION   Evaluation is part of the process. Divergent opinions are important and a dogmatic approach should be avoided. The 'disguises' of political correctness can create divisions among participants.

7. Migration, cultural identity and politics

This section is designed to raise awareness of the political context of personal experiences with racism and oppression. At the same time it draws attention to points in the political processes which the participants, even as young people, might be able to influence. The key to being able to take action is information and the knowledge about how to obtain information. While the actual information that any group can bring together might be very limited, the group can identify what kind of information would be important to their situation and what skills would be required to obtaining more information.

Although cognitive processes are more to the fore in this section, this should not be at the expense of affective qualities which need to be fostered throughout.

Multi-cultural societies

What is the evidence for the ethnic and cultural diversity of the societies in which we live? How did this diversity come about? This information will have to have been prepared beforehand. The sharing of the information can take various forms like presentations, displays or an activity such as:

ACTIVITY 15:   ROUND TABLE QUIZ

SUMMARY   This is a playful way of making factual information on immigration and ethnic diversity available to the group. Organisers, probably with the help of group members, will have prepared questions and solutions beforehand, selecting items that seem most relevant for the participants.

DURATION   One hour.

MATERIAL   Sheets of questions – one for each table, big display sheets for the solutions, tokens or prizes for the winners.

PROCEDURE   Participants form mixed groups of four. Questions are organised in sections and may give multiple choice or true/false categories for answers. Each table receives the same set of questions and discusses the answer they wish to put forward. The questions include: information concerning migrant populations; first dates for milestones in human rights and equality legislation (for example, abolition of slavery, voting rights for women, etc.); evidence of discrimination as reflected in unemployment, housing or school attainment statistics; details on languages spoken in parts of the country or in Europe; cultural traditions; the history of anti-racism movements; data on key figures in anti-racism campaigns, etc. The questions should be age-appropriate and reflect the interests of the group. The quiz is organised in small sections and answers are given after each section.

EVALUATION   The discussion after the answers have been revealed should draw out 'surprises' for the participants. These may include: facts they find hard to believe or with which they disagree and solutions which were a matter of heated debate in the small groups. Lack of knowledge should not be received as an individual attribute but should be evaluated in the light of the public being given selective information.

Inequality and legislation

In this section the group will assemble basic information on equality and anti-discrimination legislation in their country, perhaps by comparing it with other countries and with European rights. The group might want to invite a legal expert in the field of human rights to advise them. Together they can examine different typical situations they might have experienced and ask what protection the law would provide.

The purpose is to give a sense of the changes that have happened in recent years and a practical understanding of how these changes came about and what they amount to. What has been achieved and what are still vulnerable areas? How have declarations by the UN and the Council of Europe been implemented?

Resistance and emanicpation

Human rights and equality legislation are not merely granted by benign enlightened governments but have to be struggled and fought for. What were the driving forces behind anti-racism? Again, groups can prepare some illustrations of human rights movements, anti-racism campaigns, songs, posters, biographies of people in resistance from all over the world (USA, South Africa, India etc.). In addition, it might be possible to jointly watch and discuss video versions of well-known feature films, such as 'Gandhi', 'Cry Freedom', 'Malcolm X', 'Dances with Wolves', 'Mississippi Burning', 'Into the West', 'Schindler's List' etc.

ACTIVITY 16:   SNAKES AND LADDERS

SUMMARY   This activity presupposes the group's familiarity with the state of anti-discrimination legislation and practices. It uses this knowledge, and makes it available to others, by charting the pitfalls of discrimination and the counter-strategies available in the law and through campaigning.

DURATION   Half day or longer.

MATERIAL   Information and campaign leaflets, reference guides, big sheets of cartridge paper, writing paper, pencils, erasers, felt-tip pens, markers, old magazines for pictures, glue, playing dice.

PROCEDURE   Two mixed groups are formed and each chooses a theme relating to events in the lives of immigrants or of people with minority status. Using their personal experiences, as well as legal and practical knowledge of how discrimination works and how it may be countered, they first 'brain-storm' on a variety of 'obstacles' (when players have to go back to earlier points), and opportunities (when players can advance more quickly), arising in the chosen situation. These are then entered as symbols or pictures on a sheet of cartridge paper that has been divided into 100 fields. This forms a continuous story from 'birth' or 'arrival' to 'gaining full citizenship' (or whatever the group decides as goal). The rules, 'penalties', and 'opportunities' may be written up on separate paper or in the margins of the cartridge paper.

Examples of possible situations:

1. **Asylum seekers starting life in Britain**

    Ladders: having 'recognised political refugee status'; having money; knowing the language of the host country; having access to support networks; using a parliamentary deputy to support application; getting favourable news coverage of case; supportive local community; being allowed to work/having job opportunities/having skills that are in demand; finding permanent accommodation with relatives, etc.

    Snakes: host country wants to make a trade agreement with country of origin; asylum legislation being changed; unemployment crisis worsens; racial attack on hostel; passport and documents lost in bureaucracy; work found with criminal employer; critical statement in press about police investigations, etc.

2. **The situation of gypsies/travellers**

    Ladders: groups form an effective organisation; legal recognition as ethnic group; local business community interested in products; discovery that a local festival existed in Middle Ages; financial support from educational foundation, etc.

    Snakes: participants form rival factions; local protesters discover ancient bye-law against 'casual traders'; landowner withdraws permission to lease land; local council refuses to provide sanitary services, etc.

The groups swap the games they designed and try them out on each other.

EVALUATION A brief discussion might touch on how 'real' or 'unreal' the game has been; what kinds of groups might enjoy the game; what the participants gained from the exercise.

8. Moving between different cultures

In this section the focus moves again to personal and inter-group experiences of inclusion and exclusion, but reference has to be made on every occasion to the structural framework established in the previous section.

Exclusion and inclusion

The following activities again require re-assurance about safe limits and about the 'unreality' of games. As a warm-up we suggest the use of relaxation games and a simple fun task.

ACTIVITY 17   OPEN SESAME

SUMMARY   This is a simple warm-up game for the following batch of activities.

DURATION   10 minutes.

MATERIAL   Empty space.

PROCEDURE   The group is divided into two; one, much larger group, remains in the room whilst the other group goes out of hearing range. The remaining group forms a tight circle, single file. They agree upon which action or gesture would open the circle (for example, tickling under the arm, touching an ear, making someone laugh, etc.). The other group are brought in and asked to find, by trial and error, the 'magic' gesture' that opens the circle.

EVALUATION   A short de-briefing may be needed if the game became very involved.

The next activity dwells on the strong feelings created by exclusion and uncertainty. Participants will expect that everybody but themselves have been 'selected' and will develop their own 'theories' about why they themselves have been left behind. It is meant to underline the fact that no matter how arbitrary or fictitious the reasons for exclusion are, their effects are nevertheless very real.

ACTIVITY 18: LEFT BEHIND

SUMMARY   Although one part of the group is being 'tricked' in this game, the only 'damage' that they suffer will, in a sense, be inflicted by their own expectations.

DURATION   10 minutes.

MATERIAL   Open space, blindfolds for about three quarters of the group.

PROCEDURE   A quarter of the group is selected and briefed out of hearing range from the others. The remaining group is blindfolded and sit on the ground away from each other. They are told that members of the other group will go round and 'tick' or 'tag' them by holding both their hands. After this they may remove their blindfold, and speak and join the others. The selected group are briefed outside. They should move among the sitting participants and pretend to 'tick' the blindfolded group. The increasing noise and generating excitement should create the impression that more and more participants are getting to their feet and moving about – whereas, in fact, nobody joins their ranks.

Blindfolds are removed after five minutes and the 'trick' is revealed.

EVALUATION   Both groups are asked to describe the feelings of power and powerlessness they experienced; and the feeling of 'why did nobody turn to me…'. Debriefing is essential because this game may generate strong feelings. It is essential that roles are left behind and the group re-establishes trust, for example, by forming lines, placing arms over shoulders, Greek dancing, or similar joint activities.

Source: N. Schniedewind, E. Davidson (1983), Open Minds to Equality. A sourcebook of learning activities to promote race, sex, class and age equity, New Jersey: Prentice Hall.

ACTIVITY 19: IN-GROUP / OUT-GROUP

SUMMARY   Unlike the previous game, this activity deals overtly with exclusion and is concerned with collective, rather than individual, behaviour. It is a form of improvisation, but organised within strict 'safety limits'.

DURATION   10 minutes.

MATERIAL   Clear space in a room.

PROCEDURE   Six volunteers leave the room, out of hearing range, to be called in later one by one. Two of the remaining group members act as observers, whilst the rest are asked to 'form a cohesive group' by learning a chant, practising coordinated actions or movements, or simply by becoming absorbed in one activity.

Alternatively, they could form a tight circle by placing arms around each others' shoulders.

As soon as the group are absorbed in their joint activity, the volunteers are called in, one by one, after one minute intervals. No instructions or explanations are given to the group about the 'conditions' under which newcomers are allowed to 'become accepted' and to join in. Actions are left to develop their own dynamics, but facilitators should ensure that violence does not develop. If this occurs the game should stop immediately.

EVALUATION   With the help of the observers the phases of the interaction are reconstructed. What were the feelings of both sides?; what strategies did the 'outsiders' adopt to become 'accepted'?; what were the reactions of the 'in-group'?; what difference did the increase in numbers make? Debriefing for this exercise is essential. Facilitators must ensure that roles are left behind and that the group re-establishes trust by including everybody in, for example, an activity, song, dance, game, etc.

Source: Centre for Global Education, in G. Pike, D. Delby (1988), Human Rights Activity File, London: Mary Glasgow Publications, Activity 21.

9. Developing anti-racism strategies and skills

Empowerment of young people has been an objective throughout this chapter of the book. This final section tries to bring the various dimensions of empowerment together and to move more explicitly from analyzing experiences to learning how to effect change. The central message is that social and political change *can* be achieved, that young people are not passive victims of circumstances and that they can exercise some choice over the type of society they want to live in.

The activities in this section should relate to tasks which have immediate relevance for the participants in their specific circumstances.

The language of power

The use of power both at a personal and at an institutional level is central to the manifestation of racism. The following activities are designed to make this power visible and accessible and to recognise that developing an understanding of the 'language of power' is a first step towards dealing with it more effectively.

ACTIVITY 20: THE GREAT GAME OF POWER

SUMMARY   This activity, developed by Augusto Boal in the context of his 'Theatre of the Oppressed', traces the non-verbal language of power in a situation reduced to bare essentials.

DURATION   One to two hours.

MATERIAL   Table, six chairs, a bottle.

PROCEDURE   Part 1: The group sits on the floor in a circle with the objects placed randomly in the centre. The task is 'how to arrange these objects so that one chair becomes the most powerful object in relation to the table, the bottle, and the other chairs'. Participants come forward one by one to try out their suggestions, building

---

and revising the suggestions, but maintaining a continuous flow throughout. Any arrangement is allowed except removing an object from the circle. Discussion and comments should be kept to a minimum.

Part 2: When an arrangement has been designed which the group considers the most powerful, a group member is asked to take up a position of power in relation to it, but without moving anything. The others are then subsequently invited to place themselves in even more powerful positions, thereby taking away power from the first person.

EVALUATION   A review of the development of the various arrangements, and their connections with everyday situations can be made. For example, where did we 'learn' about the language of power 'positions' and postures? How is it maintained? What are the 'games' associated with it in different contexts and culture? Where are its limits? What kind of challenges to power are considered 'outrageous'? How can rules be subverted effectively?, etc.

Source: Augusto Boal (1992), Games for actors and non-actors London: Routledge.

Although this is intended more as a warm-up exercise, its non-verbal nature can convey very strong impressions and emotions which need to be followed up in the discussion and evaluation before moving to the next part.

ACTIVITY 21:   POWER FIGURES

SUMMARY   This activity develops the theme of the previous one, but relates it more closely to the participants' own experience. The aim is not primarily to recall memories, but 'how to get a handle on power'.

DURATION   Three hours, or up to one day (with breaks).

MATERIAL   Empty space.

PROCEDURE   The activity develops in three stages.

Part 1: "Creating power figures as 'posters' (sculpting)". In small mixed groups (3-5), participants recall memories of 'typical posturing' that carried with it an element of oppression, with, for example, police, landlords/ladies, newspaper reporters, government officials, social workers, etc. The group brainstorms upon possible themes, clarifying the context for each other, as these experiences may relate to different cultural traditions and social structures. The group then decides on which figure to work. One person 'moulds' the sculpture using the other group members as 'material'. These group members may contribute to suggestions on how to make the message of the sculpture more effective.

Part 2: 'dynamising' the picture. The power-figure at the centre of the sculpture is asked to produce one 'typical' gesture that expresses power and to repeat it 'mechanically' (pointing a finger, holding a camera in someone's face, etc.). The group can then experiment with what attributes and gestures make the figures appear more and less powerful. To what extent and in what ways are the gestures culture-specific?

Part 3: 'animating' the figures. The plenary group, having inspected the 'moving sculptures', decides to develop one of them further. They create a 'scene' around a particular power figure, using trigger statements such as:

"You can't do that around here";

"We can't allow this to happen";

"Go back to where you came from", or similar.

The ensuing role-plays involve more and more people who 'take sides' and who either escalate or reduce the differences initially created.

EVALUATION   Power attributes may be summarised, and a discussion held on which ones are context-specific, and which apply across social systems. The discussion should explore the switch between personal prohibitions ('because I decide') and impersonal 'rules' ('it's nothing to do with me, but...').

This exercise develops situations out of gestures and postures which express power. It allows participants to 'experiment' with them in a kind of 'laboratory situation', for instance, which movements lead to an increase in power?; how can it be decreased, made safe?; when is power legitimate? what distinguishes power from authority?

Strategies of change

The following activity involves the group designing a game. It is especially useful for a younger age group, and deals with a variety of challenging and threatening situations where racism is involved. Role-plays of actual situations which different participants have experienced themselves might help to give the activity more 'immediacy'. However, the 'solutions' should be kept deliberately at a 'playful' level to stimulate creativity and imagination.

ACTIVITY 22: STRATEGIES FOR CHANGE

SUMMARY   Devising a game for others that stimulates their thinking on anti-racism can be a playful way of validating one's experience. This activity can also provide a lighthearted look at some very serious issues and give participants a means of distancing themselves from 'problematic situations' without giving up on them. Because this game is non-competitive, it also underlines the importance of solidarity and cooperation.

DURATION   Half day or more.

MATERIAL   10 × A3 sheet of cardboard, 50-80 A7 index cards, white paper, old magazines, paints and brushes, crayons, scissors, glue, 25 red tokens, 25 yellow tokens.

PROCEDURE   1.   Small groups of between three and four brainstorm experiences of where conflicts over issues of race and 'difference' may arise. Participants sift their ideas and design one or two pictures, on the large pieces of cardboard, that represent these situations. These may

---

be either drawings or collages. The pictures need only give a general idea of the type of situation envisaged (such as: intimidation in the playground, remarks on a bus, ridicule by a teacher, etc.).

Each of the pictures should invite the telling of a story that contains a dilemma or a confrontation. Examples are set out below:

'The party invitation'. I get invited to a party at which it is likely that alcohol will be served and of which my tradition disapproves. How do I respond?

Racist threats. Outside the entrance to our youth club a group of hostile youngsters congregate, and rumours circulate that they will harass or attack us on the way home. How do we respond?

Working with friends in a small café. A customer refuses to pay for the service by threatening to report one of your friends whom he suspects to be an illegal immigrant. How do you respond?

2. In the next round, all groups design a set of 'solutions' on the index cards, using symbols and general visual references which do not relate specifically to the situations they were responsible for composing. These solution cards might depict:

telephone, police, news reporters, elderly relative, group of friends, money, knife, book, ladder, ghettoblaster, whispering secret. They may also include fantasy solutions, such as a magic potion, flying carpet, Superman; and symbols representing 'abstract' qualities such as patience, assertiveness, information, secrecy, deceit, flirtation, etc.

3. The game is tried out in turns by small mixed groups of between four and five. All the large cards are mixed and reversed. Each player receives two red tokens (for 'best solutions') and two yellow ones (for 'will-do' ideas). She or he then chooses one situation and three 'solution cards'. All remaining solution cards lie in a pile face down. The players turn over their 'solution cards', with the first player turning over the situation card and, using

her or his imagination, tells the others the story in the picture. She or he then examines the solution cards and tries to find a 'remedy', again by turning the card or symbol into an imaginative 'story'. If she or he feels the remedy fits well, the card is placed to the side of the situation, together with a red token. For solutions which are 'just alright' a yellow token is placed next to it. The other players are then asked to contribute 'remedies' from their own set of 'solution cards'. The first player decides whether to give these suggestions one of the remaining tokens depending upon how helpful the ideas are.

The first player should end up having placed all tokens on the solution cards. If this is not possible because some of the ideas have been unconvincing, the remaining tokens pass to the next player. Every player receives new 'solution cards' for each new situation, and replaces the ones previously used.

EVALUATION   The game is non-competitive. Its aim is to widen the range of responses available beyond the initial 'solutions'. An ideal solution is not being sought. All players are entitled to their subjective rating of remedies, but will experience the support of the group as a medium towards new perspectives.

For fun, the game can be played with 'crazy solutions'. This may help to bring out fantasies and fears in a more detached manner ('change all the laws in the country', 'get rid of all foreigners'). De-briefing for this way of playing will be essential!

The essence of the following activity is that sub-groups set themselves tasks that contain an element of challenge, both to themselves and to the people they meet (officials, people in power, reporters etc.) and that they plan and jointly carry out these tasks.

ACTIVITY 23: CHALLENGES

SUMMARY In preparation for a major initiative, and as confirmation of the confidence gained, the group can set itself a number of challenging tasks.

DURATION One day or more.

MATERIAL Dependent upon the choice of task. For example, access to a telephone, transport, directories, maps, etc.

PROCEDURE Three types of activities could be attempted, depending upon local facilities and resources. Each requires careful planning and preparation. Facilitators must be responsible for making the tasks 'safe', but should avoid being over-protective.

1. How to obtain information? Particularly information that might be treated as 'sensitive' by officials, such as statistics on unemployment, homelessness, or delinquency, and which indicate how ethnic groups are affected in different ways.

2. Feeling out of place. Doing something with confidence that one would not normally be expected to do. For example, going to an exclusive picture gallery, classical concert, or 'classy' hotel or restaurant; busking or dancing in the street, etc.

3. Addressing a wider public. Giving a message to the media about the activities of the group and controlling the way this message is transmitted can be a very involved task. Alternatives may be: doing a piece of street theatre, inviting the public to an open day or information event; publishing a local newsheet.

EVALUATION These activities need to be evaluated thoroughly since participants will each have experienced their roles differently. Negative experiences may also activate strong feelings, possibly with racist overtones. These will have to be dealt with by the facilitator.

10. Evaluation

Each programme may be evaluated in a number of different ways. The following suggestions are only broad indicators for the type of evaluation instruments facilitators should design for their particular purposes.

The Wall of Expectations provides an evaluation instrument throughout the programme. On it, participants can express their expectations, contribute suggestions to the programme, review and revise the progress of the exchange, and identify tasks to be tackled in the follow-up period.

Structured assessment of the programme

This part of the evaluation aims at obtaining a picture of how participants feel about organisational matters (meeting place, facilities, facilitation, group composition, value of different parts of the programme, learning and other benefits, mix of learning and recreation etc.). The following instruments can be used:

- Simple prepared questionnaires with a combination of satisfaction rating items and open-ended questions.

- Open discussions, inviting individual or group feed-back on different aspects of the exchange programme; group statements could also take the form of a collage or poster, or of a role-play or short sketch.

- 'Dartboard' (or 'Spiderweb') graphs which allow participants a more visual representation of their satisfaction ratings on different aspects of the exercises and interactions.

Self-evaluation

Participants could be encouraged to write personal diaries or keep scrap-books with drawings, magazine cuttings, pictures and other significant items over the period of the programme. They would remain confidential but might serve as a personal yardstick for any changes that might have occurred and their significance.

Gothic Horror

A Reader's Guide from Poe to King and Beyond

Edited by

Clive Bloom

First published 1998 by

MACMILLAN PRESS LTD
Houndmills, Basingstoke, Hampshire RG21 6XS
and London
Companies and representatives throughout the world

ISBN 0–333–68397–8 hardcover
ISBN 0–333–68398–6 paperback

A catalogue record for this book is available from the British Library.

This book is printed on paper suitable for recycling and made from fully managed and sustained forest sources.

10 9 8 7 6 5 4 3 2 1
07 06 05 04 03 02 01 00 99 98

Printed in Hong Kong

 Published in the United States of America 1998 by
ST. MARTIN'S PRESS, INC.,
Scholarly and Reference Division,
175 Fifth Avenue, New York, N.Y. 10010

ISBN 0–312–21238–0 cloth
ISBN 0–312–21239–9 paperback

For Natasha and Kirsty

Contents

Contents

ix

Acknowledgements

Thanks go to Margaret Bartley for her support and encouragement, Peter Vitale and Margee Husemann for research, Lesley Bloom for all her efforts, and Matthew Finn who provided the title for the Introduction.

The editor and publishers wish to thank the following for permission to use copyright material:

Manuel Aguirre, for the extract from *The Closed Space: Horror Fiction and Western Symbolism* (Manchester University Press, 1990), pp. 115–46; reproduced by permission of the author.

Julia Briggs, for the extract from *Night Visitors* (Faber and Faber, 1977), pp. 124–41; reproduced by permission of Faber and Faber Ltd.

Anny Cranny Francis, for the extract on *The Vampire Tapestry* from *American Horror Fiction*, edited by Brian Docherty (Macmillan, 1990); copyright © Brian Docherty, reproduced by permission of Macmillan Press Ltd and St Martin's Press, Inc.

Robert F. Geary, for the extract from *The Supernatural in Gothic Fiction* (Edwin Mellen Press, 1992), pp. 121–38; reproduced by permission of the Edwin Mellen Press.

Victor Gollancz Ltd, for the extract from H. P. Lovecraft, 'Supernatural Horror in Literature', in *Dagon and Other Macabre Tales*, vol. 2 (1985), pp. 141–5; reproduced by permission of Victor Gollancz.

Rosemary Jackson, for the extract from 'Afterword' in *Fantasy* (Methuen, 1981); reproduced by permission of Routledge.

J. Gerald Kennedy, for the extract from *Poe, Death and the Life of Writing* (Yale University Press, 1987), pp. 145–76; reproduced by permission of Yale University Press.

Playboy magazine, for the extract from 'Stephen King: An Interview with Eric Norden', *Playboy*, June 1983; reproduced by permission of *Playboy* magazine.

Judie Newman, for the extract from 'Shirley Jackson and the Reproduction of Mothering: *The Haunting of Hill House*' in *American Horror Fiction*, edited by Brian Docherty (1990); copyright © Brian Docherty, by permission of Macmillan Ltd and St Martin's Press.

John Nicholson, for the extract from 'Scared Shitless: the Sex of Horror', in *Creepers*, edited by Clive Bloom (Pluto Press, 1993); reproduced by permission of Pluto Press.

David Punter, for the extract from *The Literature of Terror* (Longman, 1980), pp. 314–16, 329, 334–40; reproduced by permission of Addison Wesley Longman Ltd.

Montague Summers, for the extract from 'Introduction' to *The Vampire in Literature*, from *The Vampire* (1995); reproduced by permission of Studio Editions.

Gina Wisker, for the extract from 'At Home All Was Blood and Feathers: the Werewolf in the Kitchen – Angela Carter and Horror' in *Creepers*, edited by Clive Bloom (Pluto Press, 1993); reproduced by permission of Pluto Press.

Every effort has been made to trace the copyright holders but if any have been inadvertently overlooked, the publishers will be pleased to make the necessary arrangement at the first opportunity.

Chronology of Significant Horror and Ghost Tales

including collections and related non-fictional works

1840	Edgar Allan Poe, *Tales of the Grotesque and Arabesque*
1845–7	J. M. Rymer, *Varney the Vampire*
1848	Disturbances at the Fox Household, Hydesville, New York State: origins of spiritualism
1849	Edgar Allan Poe dies
1850	Edgar Allan Poe, *Collected Works*, ed. R. W. Griswold (3 vols)
1851	Nathaniel Hawthorne, *The House of the Seven Gables*
1865	S. Baring-Gould, *The Book of Were Wolves*
1869	Sheridan Le Fanu, 'Green Tea'
1872	Sheridan Le Fanu, *In a Glass Darkly* (3 vols)
1875	Founding of Theosophical Society
1876	Madame Blavatsky, *Isis Unveiled* (non-fiction)
1879	Mary Baker Eddy founds Church of Christ, Scientist
1882	Society for Psychical Research founded (Great Britain)
1883	Villiers de L'Isle Adam, *Contes Cruels*
1886	Vernon Lee, *A Phantom Lover*; Robert Louis Stevenson, *The Strange Case of Dr Jekyll and Mr Hyde*
1887	Fitz-James O'Brien, *The Diamond Lens*
1888	Robert Louis Stevenson, *The Phantom Rickshaw and other Eerie Tales*; Madame Blavatsky, *The Secret Doctrine* (non-fiction)
1890	Vernon Lee, *Hauntings*
1891	J.-K. Huysmans, *Là Bas*; Ambrose Bierce, *Tales of Soldiers and Civilians*

1892   Charlotte Perkins Gilman, 'The Yellow Wallpaper'
1893   Edith Nesbit, *Grim Tales*; Ambrose Bierce, *Can Such Things Be?*
1894   Arthur Machen, *The Great God Pan*
1895   R. W. Chambers, *The King in Yellow*; Arthur Machen, *The Three Imposters*; John Meade Falkner, *The Lost Stradivarius*
1896   Mary Molesworth, *Uncanny Tales*
1897   Bram Stoker, *Dracula*; Arthur Machen, *The Hill of Dreams*; Richard Marsh, *The Beetle*
1898   Henry James, *The Turn of the Screw*
1899   Bernard Capes, *At a Winter's Fire*
1900   Robert Hichens, 'How Love Came to Professor Gildea'; Lafcadio Hearn, *Shadowings*
1902   W. W. Jacobs, 'The Monkey's Paw'
1903   A. C. Benson, *The Hill of Trouble*; Bram Stoker, *The Jewel of Seven Stars*
1904   M. R. James, *Ghost Stories of an Antiquary*; Frank Frankfort Moore, *The Other World*; S. Baring-Gould, *A Book of Ghosts*; Lafcadio Hearn, *Kwaidan*
1906   Algernon Blackwood, *The Empty House and other Ghost Stories*; Arthur Machen, *The House of Souls*
1907   R. H. Benson, *A Mirror of Shalott*
1908   Morley Roberts, 'The Fog'; William Hope Hodgson, *The House on the Borderland*; Perceval Landon, 'Thurnley Abbey' (*Raw Edges*); Algernon Blackwood, *John Silence: Physician Extraordinary*; G. K. Chesterton, *The Man Who Was Thursday*
1910   W. F. Harvey, *Midnight House*
1911   Bram Stoker, *The Lair of the White Worm*; M. R. James, *More Ghost Stories*: [George] Oliver Onions, *Widdershins*; Gaston Leroux, *The Phantom of the Opera*; F. Marion Crawford, *Wandering Ghosts*
1912   E. G. Swain, *The Stoneground Ghost Tales*; William Hope Hodgson, *The Night Land*; Bram Stoker dies
1913   Mrs Belloc Lowndes, *The Lodger*
1914   Bram Stoker, 'Dracula's Guest' [posthumous]; Ambrose Bierce 'disappears' in Mexico
1915   Gustav Meyrink, *The Golem*
1919   Sigmund Freud, 'The Uncanny' (non-fiction)
1920   Maurice Level, *Crises*

1921   Marjory Bowen, *The Haunted Village*

1922   Jessie Douglas Kerruish, *The Undying Monster*

1923   H. P. Lovecraft, 'The Rates in the Walls'; first issue of *Wierd Tales*; E. F. Benson, *Visible and Invisible*

1925   H. P. Lovecraft, 'The Horror at Red Hook'; M. R. James, 'A Warning to the Curious'

1926   H. P. Lovecraft, 'The Call of Cthulhu'; Cynthia Asquith, *The Ghost Book*

1927   H. P. Lovecraft, *The Case of Charles Dexter Ward*; Edward Lucas White, 'Lukundoo'

1928   H. P. Lovecraft, 'The Dunwich Horror'; H. Russell Wakefield, *They Walk at Night*; A. J. Alan, *Good Evening Everyone*; W. F. Harvey, 'The Beast with Five Fingers'

1930   Walter de la Mare, 'Crewe' (*On the Edge*)

1931   F. Tennyson Jesse, 'The Railway Carriage'; Charles Williams, *The Place of the Lion*; M. R. James, *Collected Ghost Stories*

1933   W. F. Harvey, 'The Ankardyne Pew' (*Moods and Tenses*); Guy Endore, *Werewolf of Paris*; Marjory Bowen, *The Last Bouquet*; Aleister Crowley, *The Book of the Law* (non-fiction)

1934   Elizabeth Bowen, 'The Cat Jumps'; E. F. Benson, *More Spook Stories*

1935   Charles G. Finney, *The Curse of Dr Lao*; Oliver Onions, *Collected Ghost Stories*; Dennis Wheatley, *The Devil Rides Out*

1936   R. E. Howard dies; M. R. James dies; White Eagle Lodge founded (Great Britain); Arthur Machen, *The Children of the Pool and other Stories*

1937   H. P. Lovecraft dies

1938   'Nicholas Blake', 'The Beast Must Die'

1939   H. P. Lovecraft, *The Outsider and Others*, ed. August Derleth (first publication of Arkham House Press)

1940   Harry Price, *The Most Haunted House in England* (non-fiction)

1943   Fritz Lieber, *Conjure Wife*

1944   Harry Price, *The End of Borley Rectory* (non-fiction)

1945   Evangeline Walton, *Witch House*; Charles Williams, *All Hallows' Eve*

1947   French legislation regarding children's 'horror' comics; Aleister Crowley dies; Arthur Machen dies

1949   Horror comics banned in Canada
1950   William M. Gaines (pub.), *Tales from the Crypt*, etc.
1954   Richard Matheson, *I am Legend*; *Weird Tales* magazine closes
1955   Children and Young Persons (Harmful Publications) Act (Great Britain); Jack Finney, *The Body Snatchers*; Gerald Kersh, *Men without Bones*
1959   Robert Bloch, *Psycho*; Obscene Publications Act (Great Britain); Shirley Jackson, *The Haunting of Hill House*; Herbert Van Thal, *Pan Book of Horror Stories*
1962   Robert Bloch, *Yours Truly, Jack the Ripper*
1967   Ira Levin, *Rosemary's Baby*
1969   Kingsley Amis, *The Green Man*; Angela Carter, *Heroes and Villains*
1971   William Peter Blatty, *The Exorcist*
1972   Angela Carter, *The Infernal Desire Machine of Doctor Hoffman*
1973   Robert Marasco, *Burnt Offerings*
1974   Stephen King, *Carrie*; James Herbert, *The Rats*
1975   Stephen King, *Salem's Lot*; Harlan Ellison, *Deathbird Stories*
1976   Anne Rice, *Interview with the Vampire*
1977   Joyce Carol Oates, *Night-Side*; Hugh B. Cave, *Murgunstrumm and others*; Bernard Taylor, *Sweetheart, Sweetheart*; Stephen King, *The Shining*; Julia Briggs, *Night Visitors* (non-fiction)
1978   Whitley Streiber, *The Wolfen*; George Hay (ed.), *The Necronomicon*
1979   Angela Carter, *The Bloody Chamber*; Virginia Andrews, *Flowers in the Attic*; David Morrell, *The Totem*; Ramsey Campbell, *The Face that Must Die*; Peter Straub, *Ghost Story*
1980   Julia Kristeva, *Pouvoirs de L'Horreur* (non-fiction); Suzy Mckee Charnas, *The Vampire Tapestry*; David Punter, *The Literature of Terror* (non-fiction)
1981   Rosemary Jackson, *Fantasy* (non-fiction); Stephen King, *Danse Macabre* (non-fiction)
1982   Shaun Hutson, *Slugs*
1983   Susan Hill, *The Woman in Black*
1984   Clive Barker, *The Books of Blood*, vols 1–3; Robert Holdstock, *Mythago Wood*

1985   Clive Leatherdale, *Dracula* (non-fiction); Anne Rice, *The Vampire Lestat*

1986   Lisa Tuttle, *A Nest of Nightmares*

1987   Whitley Strieber, *Communion* (non-fiction); Clive Barker, *Weaveworld*; Stephen King, *The Tommyknockers*, *Misery*; Ramsey Campbell, *Dark Feasts*; J. Gerald Kennedy, *Poe, Death and the Life of Writing* (non-fiction); James Herbert, *The Magic Cottage*

1990   Lisa Tuttle (ed.), *New Horror Stories by Women*; Richard Dalby (ed.), *The Virago Book of Ghost Stories*; Manuel Aguirre, *The Closed Space* (non-fiction); Brian Stableford, *The Werewolves of London*

1991   Peter James, *Sweet Heart*; Brian Docherty (ed.), *American Horror Fiction* (non-fiction)

1992   David Morris, *The Masks of Lucifer* (non-fiction)

1993   Clive Bloom (ed.), *Creepers* (non-fiction)

1994   Kenneth Grant, *Outer Gateways* (non-fiction)

1996   Clive Bloom, *Cult Fiction* (non-fiction)

Introduction: Death's Own Backyard

The Nature of Modern Gothic and Horror Fiction

CLIVE BLOOM

Bram Stoker's *Dracula* celebrated its centenary in 1997. One of the greatest horror tales ever told and, more importantly, one of the most significant pieces of literature ever written, the book has never been out of print since its first publication and it initiated a 'vampire' industry that spans film, radio, television, books, comics and merchandise – no fancy dress party would be complete without its 'Dracula'.

The genre within which Stoker wrote was already one hundred years old in 1897 and Stoker's literary style as well as much of his book's content represent a revisiting of the old gothic that had given way to a more contemporary attitude toward the fiction of the weird and supernatural by the middle nineteenth century. *Dracula* is both a synthesis and a nostalgic revival of gothic themes.

When this is considered it becomes clear that the term 'gothic' covers formal problems of style, and content, as well as a history of popular reading, all of which have evolved across two centuries. Horace Walpole's *Castle of Otranto* (the first gothic novel) bears as little or as much relationship to Edgar Allan Poe's tales as they do to Clive Barker's *Books of Blood*. Although the term 'gothic genre' may be singular its incarnations are diverse and often retain only the slightest genuflection toward an original 'core' or formal set of generic properties. Furthermore the nature of the gothic is so disparate that it can include (because of formal similarities) works of fiction that contain neither supernatural nor horror elements but which do contain similar attitudes to setting, atmosphere or style. Meanwhile, horror stories have moved away from the trappings of gothicism, and settings, atmosphere and style are dictated by contemporary events, psychology and social realism. Gothicism is, moreover, so versatile that it can be superadded to otherwise oppositional characteristics, hence, since the 1980s, Batman comics and films have invented a neo- or retro-gothic amongst the art deco of New York's skyscrapers, making these the equivalent of the crumbling castles and monastic ruins of old.

Other genres owe much to gothic concerns and neither detective fiction nor science fiction can be separated in their origins from such an association. Originating as one of the novel's major forms in the late eighteenth century and marking out much of popular fiction's imaginative territory, the gothic is *the* genre against which critics attempted to separate serious fiction from such popular entertainment and escapism. Gothicism may be viewed (without much exaggeration) as one pole of the fictional imagination the other of which (seen as its opposite, but actually on a continuum of effects) is the domestic or contemporary fiction of (often middle-class) sensibility. The continuum that links the gothic to the 'domestic novel' is marked by the fact that however arcane or historic the gothic setting it is always linked to the *desire* of contemporary readers. At once escapist and conformist, the gothic speaks to the dark side of domestic fiction: erotic, violent, perverse, bizarre and obsessionally connected with contemporary fears. It could hardly be otherwise and the debate over gothic's power to be subversive or conservative by turns is testimony to its immediacy as well as to its archaic (or 'eternal') elements.

Horror is the usual but not necessarily the main ingredient of gothic fiction and most popular gothic fiction is determined in its plotting by the need for horror and sensation. It was gothicism, with its formality, codification, ritualistic elements and artifice (its very origins as an aesthetic outlook and *literary* condition first and fore-most), that transformed the old folk tale of terror into the modern horror story. This link between horror and gothic was neither a necessary nor a permanent condition and by the time of Edgar Allan Poe the two were capable of separate existence. It is with Poe that the old 'German' gothic is finally brought into a contemporary setting and it is with his work that this anthology begins. Poe's 'The Fall of the House of Usher' first appeared in *Burton's Gentleman's*

Magazine in September 1839 and subsequently in 1840 and 1845. It marks a decisive break between the gothic of *Otranto* and the later psychological horror of the late nineteenth century but it also marks the appearance of a self-conscious aestheticism allied to, but different from, the popular tale of horror. For Poe it is *perversity* that marks horror just as *peculiarity* is the mark of *art* and both confront common sense, decency and normal moral codes. No longer does the external world threaten as much as the internal, and within that the ineffable demands of the will.

'The Fall of the House of Usher' is probably the most interpreted short story ever written, its ambiguities endlessly fascinating. Whatever might be said about the tale's significance it is clear that Poe combined physical horror (entombment and reincarnation; a collapsing house surrounded by a moat) with horror more closely associated with the mind (Usher's hypochondria and hysteria and Madeline's catatonia): horror has as its sources both traditional gothic *and* medical conditions garnered from a contemporary popular encyclopaedia. Moreover, the dual focus sustains an aesthetic battle between the old- and new style 'gothic'. If Usher's delight is in the old gothic of lost religion and the dénouement is brought about through the echoing of the 'German' tale 'The Mad Trist', nowhere does either impinge on the *reasons* for the horror – both supply mere atmosphere. Indeed, it is clear that the events that parallel the reading of 'The Mad Trist' are correlated physically to its recitation – a mere coincidence or irony on Usher's part. As Madeline returns from the tomb, it is also clear she is not dead, nor the dragon told of in the old tale. The medieval and modern coalesce leaving the old-style gothic behind as mere pastiche. The new gothic is the horror of the mind isolated with itself.

> Oppressed, as I certainly was, upon the occurrence of this second and most extraordinary coincidence, by a thousand conflicting sensations, in which wonder and extreme terror were predominant, I still retained sufficient presence of mind to avoid exciting, by any observation, the sensitive nervousness of my companion. I was by no means certain that he had noticed the sounds in question; although, assuredly, a strange alteration had, during the last few minutes, taken place in his demeanour. From a position fronting my own, he had gradually brought round his chair, so as to sit with his face to the door of the chamber; and this I could but partially perceive his features, although I saw that his lips trembled as if he were murmering inaudibly. His head had

dropped upon his breast – yet I knew that he was not asleep, from the wide and rigid opening of the eye as I caught a glance of it in profile. The motion of his body, too, was at variance with this idea – for he rocked from side to side with a gentle yet constant and uniform sway. Having rapidly taken notice of all this, I resumed the narrative of Sir Launcelot, which thus proceeded:

'And now, the champion, having escaped from the terrible fury of the dragon, bethinking himself of the brazen shield, and of the breaking up of the enchantment which was upon it, removed the carcass from out of the way before him, and approached valorously over the silver pavement of the castle to where the shield was upon the wall; which in sooth tarried not for his full coming, but fell down at his feet upon the silver floor, with a mighty great and terrible ringing sound.'

No sooner had these syllables passed my lips, than – as if a shield of brass had indeed, at the moment, fallen heavily upon a floor of silver – I became aware of a distinct, hollow, metallic, and clangorous, yet apparently muffled, reverberation. Completely unnerved, I leaped to my feet; but the measured rocking movement of Usher was undisturbed. I rushed to the chair in which he sat. His eyes were bent fixedly before him, and throughout his whole countenance there reigned a stony rigidity. But, as I placed my hand upon his shoulder, there came a strong shudder over his whole person; a sickly smile quivered about his lips; and I saw that he spoke in a low, hurried, and gibbering murmur, as if unconscious of my presence. Bending closely over him, I at length drank in the hideous import of his words.

'Not hear it? – yes, I hear it, and *have* heard it. Long – long – long – many minutes, many hours, many days, have I heard it – yet I dared not – oh, pity me, miserable wretch that I am! – I dared not – I *dared* not speak! *We have put her living in the tomb!* Said I not that my senses were acute? I *now* tell you that I heard her first feeble movements in the hollow coffin. I heard them – many, many days ago – yet I dared not – I *dared not speak!* And now – to-night – Ethelred – ha! ha! – the breaking of the hermit's door, and the death-cry of the dragon, and the clangour of the shield! – say, rather, the rending of her coffin, and the grating of the iron hinges of her prison, and her struggles within the coppered archway of the vault! Oh whither shall I fly? Will she not be here anon? Is she not hurrying to upbraid me for my haste? Have I not heard her footstep on the stair? Do I not distinguish that heavy and horrible beating of her heart? MADMAN!' – here he sprang furiously to his feet, and shrieked out his syllables, as if in the effort he were giving up his soul – 'MADMAN! I TELL YOU THAT SHE NOW STANDS WITHOUT THE DOOR!' ('The Fall of the House of Usher')

Whilst Poe's tales *invoke* the supernatural they never exploit it, rather Poe's tales are those of the irrational, concerned with perversity, monomonia and obsessions related to an ego-directed mysticism in which knowledge of the unknown coincides with knowledge of the self. In this sense all Poe's tales can be rationally explained and can indeed be seen in that romantic tradition from which both Freud and Nietzsche later emerge.

Poe attempted to bridge the gap between popular sentiment (he was a journalist by profession) and the new sublime. At one end of his writing, the parlour poem 'The Raven', at the other a mystical meditation, *Eureka*. If, for Baudelaire, Poe represented the *poète maudit*, the true aristocrat of literature his chosen genre, horror, then Poe also ironically offered insight into a new form of horror reared in democracy in the clear light of contemporary America.

In Poe, horror fiction aspired to an art form but that did not preclude it being a perfect vehicle for entertainment whether in the novel or in the more popular form of the 'tale' (a term later superseded by 'short story'), printed in annuals, magazines, newspapers, chapbooks and anthologies. At the same time cerebral horror did not supersede old-fashioned physical presence, although the frights were now more and more to do with a supernatural other world, demonically attached to our own and often with its own old-fashioned sense of sin and retribution.

From the middle of the nineteenth century a stream of writers developed and perfected the horror/ghost genre, placing it now in contemporary fashion and setting. Encouraged by the emergence of new mass reading and the immense increase in print and publishing, such writers (very often women) found an insatiable public demand for supernaturalism. The ghost story (a term used loosely to describe everything from demons to paranormal phenomena) was a 'genre' related to both horror and gothic but not wholly in either camp. It is this style of tale (itself both various and yet predictable) that encompasses the moral tale of Charles Dickens, the Christmas entertainments of M. R. James, the mystical pan-Celticism of Arthur Machen and the bizarrerie of William Hope Hodgson.

When Henry James came to write 'The Turn of the Screw' the ghost story was such an established form that almost all writers had attempted to produce at least one. Caught between serious art (to which he aspired) and commercial fiction (which he was 'forced' to write), James's story reveals his own ambivalence about the form of the tale and the value of art. Assigned to the oblivion of 'potboiler' by James, 'The Turn of the Screw' nevertheless remains not only his most popular work but also a moment in the formal evolution of horror combining the supernaturalism of writers such as Bernard Capes with the new horror realism of Robert Louis Stevenson.

If Henry James's tale looked toward art and the domestic novel it could not stifle the vitality of those popular horrors determined by the twin needs both to thrill and to mystify which used the inexplicable and the supernatural as their vehicles. M. R. James and H. P. Lovecraft were left unaffected by the literary avant garde, and assumed an almost antiquarian style, whilst *Dracula* looks back beyond the new horror of Stevenson's *Dr Jekyll and Mr Hyde* with its moral and psychological implications, with a nostalgia that embraces content, character and style from an earlier age (not only of gothic demons but of the novel form itself). Both forms reached the acme of popularity in parallel with the newly emerging interest in supernaturalism, 'spiritism', mysticism and theology that marked the latter nineteenth century and the early years of the twentieth. By the turn of the century gothicism was a byword for decadent 'Yellow Book' writers as well as popular 'yellow press' writers, as much the property of J. K. Huysmans (*Là Bas*) as of Conan Doyle (*The Hound of the Baskervilles*) and as much to do with horror writing per se (M. R. James, Ambrose Bierce) as with mystical meditation (Arthur Machen, Algernon Blackwood) – as much art as pulp.

By the 1930s, the formal ghost tale as exemplified by Algernon Blackwood or M. R. James could be said (and it is hotly debated) to have gone into a decline, with readers favouring detective fiction, science fantasy, the western, crime fiction etc. Nevertheless, the 1920s did see a resurgence of ghost tales and by the latter half of that decade new hybrid horrors had begun to emerge. In Britain, Dennis Wheatley harnessed the notoriety of Aleister Crowley ('The Beast 666') to the pace of the thriller to produce a horror adventure, *The Devil Rides Out* (1934), whilst preceding him, and unknown to most British readers, the emergence of the new pulp magazine in the United States (replacing the older dime novel) provided a new creative space for the fantastic. *Weird Tales* appeared in 1920 but this would be of little significance if it was not for the importance of one of its contributors and its most illustrious editor, H. P. Lovecraft. Lovecraft combined the mystical tale of Arthur Machen with an emergent American-style science fantasy to create tales at once supernatural (reincarnations abound) and cosmological (the space creatures from whose abode the horror comes). Like Stoker and his 'Transylvania' Lovecraft created a whole 'horror lifestyle' and culture around 'Arkham' and the mythos of Cthulhu. Never aspiring to the status of art, Lovecraft's work has achieved the status of a cult with its own book of magic – the dreaded 'Necronomicon'.

Lovecraft also encouraged other writers, one of whom, the seventeen-year-old Robert Bloch, later wrote one of horror's most enduring scenarios (I say scenario for it is Alfred Hitchcock's film that is remembered) the tale of Norman Bates and the Bates Motel: *Psycho*. Hitchcock's film recruited Freudian theory on behalf of horror effect and by so doing redirected the gothic imagination firmly toward the human-made-monstrous, its hero the marginalized, *sexually* deviant psychopath. At the same time in Britain, Hammer Films looked back for their subject matter to the classic horror film adaptations of *Frankenstein* and *Dracula*, nostalgic less for the original books than for their RKO revivals. But horror fiction did not merely reflect these two directions for a third opened up in the radiation-storm mixture of 1930s pulp science fiction, H. Bomb hysteria, B Movie radioactive mutation and UFO delirium.

With the emergence of weird science as an element both horrific and gothic by turns the genre took on another dimension, now with one eye on the world of B movies as well as influenced by the possibilities of the grotesque in the violent new adolescent-directed horror comics which were soon to be censored in both America and Britain. This pungent mixture influenced the 'revival' of horror in the 1970s and can be found in the early work of James Herbert (*The Rats*), Stephen King (*Carrie*), Guy N. Smith (*Crabs* series) and Richard Lewis (*Spider* series) and includes tales of psychokillers such as Ramsey Campbell's *The Face that Must Die* and of demonic possession such as Peter Blatty's *The Exorcist*.

By the 1980s the extraordinary increase in horror fiction sales embraced everything from revivals (Susan Hill's *The Woman in Black*) to supernatural thrillers such as Graham Masterton's *The Djinn* (1977) or James Herbert's *The Magic Cottage*, Stephen King's prolific output, Clive Barker's tales of violent dissection and 'factional' works such as Whitley Strieber's *Communion* or Jay Anson's *Amityville Horror*. H. P. Lovecraft became a cult figure and even British pulp writer R. L. Fanthorpe suddenly found renewed fame. Feminists too discovered a wealth of talented Victorian and Edwardian women writers and Angela Carter emerged as Britain's most important woman writer with her tales of perversity and dark desire. Indeed, on a wave of psycho-sexual debate the gothic itself seemed to lend itself to feminism as an ideal vehicle for the notations of gender. And the vampire too made a conspicuous reappearance in both films and novels. Equally from the 1970s reputable novelists fell over each other to co-opt horror for their purposes, ironically courting the horror form as assiduously as Henry James had attempted to escape it.

For current readers Stephen King and Clive Barker are probably the two most significant horror genre exponents but to a large extent their works represent opposite currents in popular taste. King is not only one of America's most prolific writers, he is also *the* bestselling American author of all time. His tales are often prolific explorations of small-town sensibilities into which horror is integrated as a plot device. As such, one can see King attached not only to the horror tradition (but outside the type initiated by Poe) but also to the grander *literary* tradition of American letters (in which Poe must be included). King is concerned with American values and (ironically) provincial security, his work is based in social relations and family ties and is both democratic and yet nostalgic and conservative. Despite his interest in film, King is himself nostalgic for print culture and the nature of authorship fascinates him, attitudes explored in both *The Dark Half* and *Misery*.

Clive Barker, on the other hand, is less universally read but has, through film, been able to create a very popular schlock horror universe based around the monstrous presence of 'Pinhead'. If Barker's early work looked back toward the type of horror anthology edited by Herbert Van Thal it also anticipated a newer visceral dimension that only film could properly provide. Although King invented the term 'splatterpunk' to describe the appearance of his book *Carrie* and James Herbert's *The Rats*, it is Clive Barker's *Books of Blood* that represent the sustained exploration of dissection and mutilation and his film *Hellraiser* explicitly dwells on the flayed body and the soft machinery of bodily functions. Although not averse to scenes that might disgust as well as horrify, King does not attach the same metaphysical and subversive significance to these as does Barker, who finds in fascistic and sadistic pleasures the borderline of taboo.

For Stephen King, horror fiction upholds the status quo, whilst for Clive Barker, such fiction transcends and demolishes the very nature of its limitations and the status quo that might be preserved in the first place.

＊　　＊　　＊

As I have already argued, gothic fiction need not be horrific and horror fiction need not be gothic. The two do share, however, parallel concerns and often interchangeable plots and settings – an affinity is, therefore, clear. Here, for instance, is part of the famous opening sequence of Daphne Du Maurier's book *Rebecca*, which invokes both the wild wood and labyrinthine versions of the gothic and emphasizes monstrosity without once being other than a disguised novel of domestic relations itself without interest in the supernatural except for atmosphere.

> Last night I dreamt I went to Manderley again.
> . . .
> No smoke came from the chimney, and the little lattice windows gaped forlorn. Then, like all dreamers, I was possessed of a sudden with supernatural powers and passed like a spirit through the barrier before me. The drive wound away in front of me, twisting and turning as it had always done, but as I advanced I was aware that a change had come upon it; it was narrow and unkept, not the drive that we had known. At first I was puzzled and did not understand, and it was only when I bent my head to avoid the low swinging branch of a tree that I realised what had happened. Nature had come into her own again and, little by little, in her stealthy, insidious way had encroached upon the drive with long, tenacious fingers. The woods, always a menace even in the past, had triumphed in the end. They crowded, dark and uncontrolled, to the borders of the drive. The beeches with white, naked limbs leant close to one another, their branches intermingled in a strange embrace, making a vault above my head like the archway of a church. And there were other trees as well, trees that I did not recognise, squat oaks and tortured elms that straggled cheek by jowl with the beeches, and had thrust

themselves out of the quiet earth, along with monster shrubs and plants, none of which I remembered.

The drive was a ribbon now, a thread of its former self, with gravel surface gone, and choked with grass and moss. The trees had thrown out low branches, making an impediment to progress; the gnarled roots looked like skeleton claws. Scattered here and again amongst this jungle growth I would recognise shrub that had been land-marks in our time, things of culture and of grace, hydrangeas whose blue heads had been famous. No hand had checked their progress, and they had gone native now, rearing to monster height without a bloom, black and ugly as the nameless parasites that grew beside them.   (*Rebecca*, Chapter 1)

Here, on the other hand, is Elizabeth Bowen's 'The Cat Jumps', in which horror is central to an otherwise modern domestic drama and in which the horrific is used to point beyond the material concerns of realism.

The Wrights had the floral wallpapers all stripped off and the walls cream-washed; they removed some disagreeably thick pink shades from the electricity, and had the paint renewed inside and out. (The front of the house was bracketed over with balconies, like an overmantel.) Their bedroom mantelpiece, stained by the late Mrs Bentley's cosmetics, had to be scrubbed with chemicals. Also, they had removed from the rock-garden Mrs Bentley's little dog's memorial tablet, with a quotation on it from 'Indian Love Lyrics'. Jocelyn Wright, looking into the unfortunate bath, *the* bath, so square and opulent with its surround of nacreous tiles, said, laughing lightly, she supposed anyone *else* would have had that bath changed. 'Not that that would be possible,' she added, 'the bath's built in . . . I've always wanted a built-in bath.'

('The Cat Jumps')

This need to integrate realist fiction and gothic fiction goes back to the origins of both, and caution over the use of supernatural elements per se has led to a 'supernaturalizing' of realist elements and attempts to put numinal qualities into the very heart of realism. Nowhere is this ambiguity better realized than in Emily Brontë's *Wuthering Heights*. By the early years of the nineteenth century, gothic fiction was rapidly becoming a sub-genre of proper fiction and still later the ghost story was a useful publisher's category in popular fiction (as opposed to serious literature) and therefore a diminished form of art.

The early gothic writers with their fascination for a mixture of Jacobean, medieval, graveyard and mock renaissance settings also placed emphasis on the sentimental and sublime – a move towards capturing in print a cultural disorientation that was as much political as it was aesthetic. The sentimental emphasized subjective experience and the imagination as transcendent features whilst the idea of the sublime linked individual consciousness to the supernatural and the ineffable. This new axis was the perfect vehicle for explorations of interiority, alienation, madness, isolation, perversity, obsession and erotic sadistic desire. Here was a landscape in which a demonized nature and a malevolent human nature could be plotted within the artifice of a new aesthetic outlook and a new literary genre.

Such landscapes could embrace a residual Christianity concerned with sin and redemption but they could equally be non-didactic, without any real hierarchy of values, without, indeed, a moral core. In Poe's tales, for instance, the 'will' overrules all moral desiderata in its overwhelming quest for self-awareness – for going beyond into the unspeakable and ineluctable sublime condition.

If the gothic is concerned with the manipulation and exploration of feeling (human nature) then horror is more closely concerned with the manipulation of effect. After all, the 'main aim of the ghost story is to scare its readers' and its interests are limited but more immediate than gothicism per se, and whilst the horror tale may approach the length of a novel it will rarely be willing or able to explore the traditional depths of the realist form. Significance beyond effect seems a *product* of horror literature rather than a precondition. Indeed, horror fiction need have no interest in 'proper' or rational explanations for the events described, making 'no attempt to explain away terrors' or naturalize violence or fear. In one sense, different from the gothic, horror fiction deals in the inexplicable whether from the realms of the supernatural or of the scientific; horror is the product of *a demonization* in either the material or non-material realms. Indeed, horror fiction based on scientific progress (radiation and mutation) is almost always apocalyptic in tone and plotting, its rationale the *unforeseen* disturbance caused by scientific interference in natural processes bringing about changes which cannot themselves be rationally explained.

Just as horror fiction can exploit the supernatural or the scientific, so too it need not be confined to the trappings of ancient castles and crumbling abbeys. The gothic taste for medievalism gives way by the middle of the nineteenth century to modern settings, often middle-class homes or hotels: bedrooms, libraries or gardens, where the weird is now given full rein. Of course this does not preclude the use of gothic trappings either as a contrast to modernity (*Dracula* or H. P. Lovecraft's tales) or in combination with modernity (the horror/thriller *Silence of the Lambs*) or as a reconstitution of modernity (Clive Barker's 'The Forbidden'), nor indeed need it be confined to this planet (*Alien* for instance), or to a 'gothic' past (as in the vogue for occasional Egyptian mummery).

The classic ghost story thrives on the necessary banality of its setting to gain its effects made more weird by the inexplicably demonic aspect of the ghostly visitant. Furthermore such tales are usually couched in the conversational tone of anecdotes told by middle-class witnesses who return to their own life baffled by their experiences. They are often recounted by 'editors' who stumble across manuscripts left by posthumous authors, from which information the narrative is then constructed.

At the same time ghost fiction and horror writing have been quick to seize on other genres in order to revitalize an otherwise limited stock of possible plots and effects which when not merely plagiaristic do suggest a necessary collusion between reader and author as to expectation: the repertoire of horror is relatively limited and conservative and many authors will combine or develop elements already known to their readership.

Nowhere is this more obvious than in a work like James Herbert's *The Magic Cottage*, which is an essentially nostalgic and sentimental tale which exploits elements of Dennis Wheatley's *The Devil Rides Out* with Stokeresque vampire tales, and consciously alludes to films such as *Psycho*, television series such as *The Twilight Zone*, actors such as Boris Karloff and producers such as Steven Spielberg. Even a friendly squirrel is called Rambo in honour of an even more famous character. Not to be outdone, the villain has the tongue-in-cheek name of Eldrich P. Mycroft. A self-conscious reworking of modern horror's main elements is behind the authorial motivation of the plot itself.

You've seen the film, you've read the book. You know the one – there've been so many: The young couple find the home of their dreams, the wife's ecstatic, the husband's happy but more controlled; they move in, the kids (usually one of each) tear around the empty rooms. But *we* know there's something sinister about the place, because we've read the blurb and paid our money. Slowly, THINGS start to happen. There's something nasty in the locked room at the top of the old creaky stairs; or something lurks in the cellar below, which is possibly itself the Gateway to Hell. You know the story. At first, Dad's oblivious to his family going nuts around him – *he* doesn't believe in the supernatural, or things that go *splodge* in the night; to him, there really is No Such Thing as a Vampire. Until something happens to him, that is. Then all hell breaks loose. You know it like you wrote the story yourself. (*The Magic Cottage*, Chapter 3)

Here is an exercise in horror as witty as it is thrilling. Here also is the contemporary dilemma of the horror writer where the horror film and its special effects now overshadow the written imagination. Invoked in order to be exorcised, film asserts its ghostly presence in the very space of writing itself: Freddy Kruger has the last laugh.

THEORIES OF GOTHIC HORROR

Theories of gothic and horror literature tend to be of two philosophical types. The first sees such fiction as disturbing but conservative, restoring things to the status quo and dedicated to the ultimate return to normalcy. The second sees such fiction in the opposite light as disturbing in order to change, not recuperative and conservative but radical and subversive, dedicated to excess and marginality.

> Gothic signifies a writing of excess. It appears in the awful obscurity that haunted eighteenth-century rationality and morality. It shadows the despairing ecstasies of Romantic idealism and individualism and the uncanny dualities of Victorian realism and decadence. Gothic atmospheres – gloomy and mysterious – have repeatedly signalled the disturbing return of pasts upon presents and evoked emotions of terror and laughter. In the twentieth century, in diverse and ambiguous ways, Gothic figures have continued to shadow the progress of modernity with counter-narratives displaying the underside of enlightenment and humanist values.[1]

The notion that 'gothic signifies a writing of excess' is often tied to theories of the excessive body, here usually identified with feminist approaches to the analysis of bodily functions and to boundary and identity transgression.

> [The grotesque], as almost every writer on the topic feels obliged to mention sooner or later, evokes the cave – the grotto-esque. Low, hidden, earthly, dark, material, immanent, visceral. As bodily metaphor, the grotesque cave tends to look like (and in the most gross metaphorical sense be identified with) the cavernous anatomical female body. These associations of the female with the earthly, material, and the archaic grotesque have suggested a positive and powerful figuration of culture and womanhood to many male and female writers and artists.
>
> . . .
>
> Blood, tears, vomit, excrement – all the detritus of the body that is separated out and placed with terror and revulsion (predominantly, though not exclusively) on the side of the feminine – are down there in that cave of abjection.[2]

A final aim of gothic writing may also be seen to be social disturbance, thereby questioning technological, scientific and social norms as well as class relations in a way unavailable to realist fiction.

Such theories are extremely pervasive, yet, like their conservative opposites they are all limited in their ability to provide universal explanations. The desire to find radical attitudes can sometimes create forced or simplistic (despite the theory) explanations of texts. Whilst gothic and horror writing may exemplify certain positions, different books will do so for different reasons at different times. There is no more particular proof that gothic and/or horror are oppositional styles disturbing normalcy, the rational or the flow of 'bourgeois' history than that they support the above. Whilst M. R. James, H. P. Lovecraft or Stephen King may have contradictory messages in their texts which disturb their innate conservatism the same argument (this time about recuperatism) may be applied to the subversive nature of Clive Barker or Angela Carter. Both positions are complicated by critical confusions which sometimes separate and sometimes conflate the terms 'gothic' and 'horror' and by immense difficulties in the definition of historical, cultural, sociological or psychological movements to which literary terms are often (too easily) attached.

As opposed to theories of gothic there are fewer theories about horror despite its popularity. Edgar Allan Poe has no theory per se about horror and indeed does not seem to have seen himself as a horror writer in the modern sense at all. Other exponents of the genre equally ignored theoretical issues or saw them as integral parts of imaginative works rather than separate intellectual issues. Typical of this mixed mode of story telling is 'Nightmare-Touch' by Lafcadio Hearn (in this volume) who considers fear to be both a primitive impulse of the 'species' as well as a basic response of the individual. Hence, 'fear of the touch of the dead', itself on the edge of deeply taboo-ed subject matter, has both a philogenic and an ontogenic basis. At its core such a theory is an extrapolation into the field of emotion from Darwinian theory.

Such an evolutionist base was the core of Freud's highly influential essay 'The Uncanny' (excerpts in this volume), which used an E. T. A. Hoffmann tale, 'The Sandman', to demonstrate the basis of uncanny feelings. For Freud, the 'uncanny' covers situations in which there is an inexplicable level of *affect*. He explains this as the result of repression (both paranormal and species), in which that which is known but should have remained hidden is suddenly exposed to view. This moment of taboo he relates to the structure of psycho-analytic theory, and especially the castration complex and the memory of the child's relationship to the pre-Oedipal mother's body or even to inter-uterine existence. Julia Kristeva, amongst others, has developed Freud's thesis of the 'hidden' body around the concept of 'abjection'. Kristeva's highly complex (and often obscure) musings concentrate on the fear of the 'archaic' mother and the nature of defilement (excremental and 'menstrual'), the mechanisms of symbolic rejection and the borderlines of taboo. Such abjection has religious and sacred undertones but its symbolism is still tied to evolutionist and biologist presuppositions.

Such theories (in all their sophistication and complexity) are essentially narcissistic (that which brings horror is that which we love, i.e. ourselves!) and are opposed by notions that horror is the result of a confrontation with the absolutely unknown, something much closer to demonic and folk explanations. That many modern critics see only the possible erotic (and therefore psycho-sexual) elements in *Dracula* is a reduction which diminishes the story's other elements. Before the appearance of Dracula's

'Brides' Harker witnesses an event that (uterine and gynaecological explanations apart) is a pure example of a confrontation with *that which cannot be* (against nature) and *not* something familiar but repressed.

> But my very feelings changed to repulsion and terror when I saw the whole man slowly emerge from the window and begin to crawl down the castle wall over that dreadful abyss, *face down* with his cloak spreading out around him like great wings. (*Dracula*, Chapter 3)

What is witnessed here is pure evil: something *without* human values – a movement into the 'abyss'. It is this side of horror that H. P. Lovecraft considers in his essay 'Supernatural Horror in Literature', and it is this that haunts Whitley Strieber's encounter with the 'grey' aliens whose *absolute* difference (they are not just 'other') is the most shocking element in their appearance, opening up a type of cosmic distance in which the soul is the bargaining counter.

THE RISE OF SPIRITUALISM

Any discussion of the topic of gothic horror fiction would be incomplete without a consideration of current social attitudes to the supernatural. These attitudes often parallel but only occasionally cross those presented in imaginative (as opposed to factual) literature on the supernatural and inexplicable, whose writers, for the most part, are rationalists or sceptics, interested in the genre for other than mystical reasons.

Whilst Bulwer-Lytton, Sheridan Le Fanu, Arthur Machen and Montague Summers actively participated in mystical attitudes, Edgar Allan Poe, M. R. James and H. P. Lovecraft remained rationalists and Stephen King retains a healthy scepticism.

The term 'the supernatural' embraces all those areas above or beyond the material realm and is the usual designation for the hierarchic planes, fantastic creatures and daemonic forces which exist in cosmic and parallel dimensions and which rule and direct our physical existence. To this end supernatural forces may take physical or visible form under exceptional or fortuitous circumstances or they may even take on permanent yet ambiguous physical properties whose amorphous nature is a bridge between the spiritual and material universes.

Belief in the supernatural realm appears to be a feature of all societies and although the meaning and significance may differ from one community to another there appears to be a certain consensus in the view that creatures and forces of the supernatural have specific abilities to transcend both time and space, cross the divide between life and death, move between the invisible and the visible and travel freely within both the spiritual and the material. Supernatural forces and beings are therefore understood to be of immense power and able to manifest themselves to human beings either at their own will or through invocation. Although (usually) immaterial, the supernatural planes are deemed to be superior to the visible and material and are feared and held in awe accordingly. This is so in all the major religions, in occult practice, in folk belief as well as (at a much more banal level) in modern newspaper horoscopes.

All supernatural systems include more or less complex cosmographies or mappings and often offer themselves as suitable subjects for increasingly arcane and involved investigations (cosmologies). The relationship these investigations have had with religious belief and practice has an extremely long, complex and confused history which is beyond the scope of this introduction. In the West, Judaism, Christianity and Islam all have elaborate belief systems which nevertheless deny or seek to exclude certain areas of belief, which are relegated to the realm of the irrelevant or, at worst, heretical.

These excluded areas, which often retain a strong peripheral or inverted relationship with orthodox religion (such as Kabbalistic numerology), embrace the practices usually termed the occult. In such systems there is a much more direct relationship with the invisible realms and an overt attempt to harness the power of daemonic forces or to interact with other (astral) planes of experience in order to bring about trans-substantiations, metamorphoses, or other acts of direct control over the material and invisible environment. To achieve this, one must combine belief with technique and a mastery over process.

Western religions see all such activities as suspect or evil whilst occult practice itself has developed its own morality and its own versions of good and evil, which may not necessarily be related to more commonplace orthodoxies. In this respect, religion would see occultism as trafficking with the forces of chaos, which occultists would view as forces of cosmic order in a cosmos whose explication is only dimly or perversely grasped by the religious establishment. Occultism, therefore, is not merely the mirror image of religion but rather, analogous to it.

Before looking at the progress of supernatural belief in recent times we can conclude that the term will always refer to superior invisible forces which can intervene in human affairs either for reasons of their own or because they have been invoked through prayer, ritual or some form of sorcery. These forces break into the human plane and the world of the everyday in the form either of the miraculous or of the horrific. Such forces range from the benevolence of angels and spirit guides to terrifying satanic (but not necessarily evil) entities called up from planes of existence sometimes higher and sometimes lower than the human. These entities exist in a spectrum that can embrace Celtic gods as well as extraterrestrials.

Occultists and spiritualists believe that the supernatural exists both as a physical reality and as a subjective truth but that unlike rationalist science there can be no enlightenment within the supernatural without inner or subjective illumination. This alone would serve to distance any system of occultism (spiritualism included) from any materialist enquiry proper, including that of science. For occultists, nature (including human nature but, rather problematically, excluding free will) contains and is also directed by hierarchic sources of energy as real as (indeed in control of) physical existence itself; time and distance are annulled. The visible and tangible (including what is known of the solar system etc.) serves as confirmation of a higher cosmic order which is essentially static, 'planned' and determined by the properties of a pantheistic force which consists of the energy of 'mind'. Spiritual and yet able to manifest itself through matter, 'mind' is the original diffused godhead, which is nevertheless detached from the common notion of a directing intelligence or god. The concept retains its sense of purpose however.

Although concerned with the properties of the eternal, supernaturalism has a long history. A decisive break came in that history in 1848 when the Fox family of Hydesville in New York State became the centre of a series of strange tappings associated with John Fox's daughters, Margaret and Kate. It might be expected that these events would have been forgotten but this was not the case, for their own brand of mysticism was steeped in the peculiarism and apocalyptic imagination of America at the time, which included such visionaries as Andrew Davies Jackson, 'The Seer of Poughkeepsie'.

By the 1850s, mediums had sprung up across the United States and Great Britain including Emma Britten, the Bang Sisters of Lily Dale near Buffalo and Daniel Dunglas Home, whose feats of levitation etc. helped inspire Henry Sidgwick and Frederic Myers amongst others to found the Society for Psychical Research in 1882. From a quite different starting point, Mary Baker Eddy had, in 1879, founded the first 'Church of Christ, Scientist' and by the twentieth century, Lily Dale had become spiritualism's largest summer camp with its focal point the re-erected Fox cottage. It was, however, with the advent of Theosophy that spiritism (later called 'spiritualism') and the occult gained a fully comprehensible and internally logical basis.

Helen Petrovna Blavatsky, usually referred to as Madame Blavatsky, began her rise to fame in the mid-1870s. With some psychic ability and much personal charm, she joined up with Colonel Olcott and together they formed a 'Miracle Club' followed by 'The Theosophical Society' in 1875. Claiming inspiration from mysterious entities first from Egypt and then from Tibet, Blavatsky went on to complete two highly influential works, *Isis Unveiled* (1877) and *The Secret Doctrine* (1888), and to create a spiritual centre in India. In keeping with spiritualism's origins Blavatsky later became an American citizen.

All forms of occultism and spiritualism grew rapidly after the First World War, encouraged by the formation of a variety of lodges and fraternities, and the opening of bookshops, the most famous of which was owned by Sir Arthur Conan Doyle who was also Britain's leading advocate of spiritualistic doctrine. Aleister Crowley, self-styled 'Great Beast 666', remains the best-known practitioner of the occult and (disputably) responsible for the revival of magical practice.

The term 'the supernatural' now embraces a bewildering variety of sub-branches which includes orthodox mediumship, the study of earth energies and lines of power, magical and pagan practices, eco- and feminist occultism, extraterrestrialism and ufology and much else besides, although common threads give continuity between branches.

In recent years the line between supernatural fiction and an actual belief in the supernatural has become blurred in the work of some authors. This is not a new phenomenon and it can certainly be detected in the stories of Arthur Machen during the First World War and the ghost hunting of Harry Price between the 1930s and 1940s. However, neither Machen nor Price presented their work in this hybrid form – a form both of millennial and ecological yearnings, in the case of Whitley Strieber's abduction tale *Communion*, and of post-religious satanic musings, in the case of Jay Anson's *Amityville Horror*. Both stories amalgamate literary and non-literary elements, both pose as fact, and both suggest the eruption of demonic (satanic or alien) forces into the terrestrial and mundane. Equally, neither produces any evidence in support of highly entertaining and equally disturbing plots.

✳   ✳   ✳

This anthology is divided into four chapters. Chapter 1 offers a range of accounts of the gothic and horror from the time of Edgar Allan Poe until the turn of the century. Poe wrote no account of his views of the gothic or of horror but he did interpose his stories with long discussions of states of mind and ideas about the cosmos, which his narratives often illustrated. Here we have chosen to include his comments from 'The Imp of the Perverse' and 'The Man of the Crowd', both concerned with the significance of compulsion and the 'need to know' even if that means annihilation. Poe's most famous essay is 'The Philosophy of Composition', concerned with the writing of 'The Raven' and the importance of singular effect – comments that have had great influence not in the writing of poetry but rather in the short story and especially the ghost tale. Mystical and other related musings are represented by extracts from *Eureka* and from his marginalia.

Next comes Nathaniel Hawthorne's Preface to *The House of the Seven Gables*, in which he sets out the distinctions between a *Romance* and a novel and in so doing offers an apology and a justification for the gothic imagination as one uniquely tied to the very nature of artistic imagination itself. He is followed in turn by Walter Pater's celebrated sado-erotic portrait of La Gioconda (*The Mona Lisa*) now turned into a vampiric temptress.

Finally in this opening chapter, we have the work of Lafcadio Hearn, a writer little known nowadays. These thoughts from one of his short stories (although more like a psychological meditation) have already been discussed but they do take us to the brink of the modern imagination and modern explanations of the nature of horror.

Chapter 2 not only includes comments by M. R. James as well as Dennis Wheatley's infamous 'disclaimer' placed at the beginning of all his supernatural tales, but it also provides excerpts from H. P. Lovecraft's essay 'Supernatural Horror in Literature' and Montague Summers's Introduction to *The Vampire in Literature*.

Summers's essay shows clearly his wide and esoteric knowledge and it provides a comprehensive overview of vampire literature and the cult of the vampire in both popular and educated taste. It is also noteworthy for his criticism of *Dracula* as a novel (with which this editor concurs) and his amusing misspelling of Bela Lugosi, then better known as a stage actor.

Chapter 3, 'Later Modern Accounts', begins with a short comment by Robert Bloch and takes us to the critical concerns and creative impulses behind Stephen King. Here too are both Whitley Strieber and Clive Barker with their thoughts on the nature of their chosen genre – and, in Streiber's case, the significance of Stephen King's work. Included in this section is also an important discussion, annotated by August Derleth between Robert Bloch, Fritz Leiber, Sam Russell, Arthur Dean Cox and Leland Sapiro on the work of H. P. Lovecraft, held in the early 1960s at the Los Angeles Science Fiction Society. This unique and illuminating pamphlet is extremely rare and will almost certainly be unknown to most, if not all, readers and therefore, both because of its subject and because of its participants, especially interesting.

The Collection's largest section (Chapter 4) is dedicated to selected contemporary scholarly accounts of modern gothic and horror. Included here are extracts from three classic studies of the genre. Julia Briggs offers thoughts on M. R. James from her book *Night Visitors*, and David Punter's comprehensive account of horror fiction *The Literature of Terror* provides information on turn-of-the-century horror tales, whilst Rosemary Jackson's book *Fantasy* provides a subversive account of the subject from the perspective of contemporary structuralism (see Tzvetan Todorov in this volume) and feminism. Anne Cranny Francis and Judie Newman continue the debate over feminism and the nature of horror (in the wake of the fashion for Lacanian psychoanalytic theory in the 1980s) when they concentrate on *The Vampire Tapestry* by S. M. Charnos, and *The Haunting of Hill House* by Shirley Jackson respectively. Gina

Wisker offers further thought on the sado-eroticism of Angela Carter's gothic fables.

Whilst John Nicholson offers an amusing (if often sickly) retrospective on the taste for 'schlock' horror of the 1970s, Steve Holland shows how the authorities censored and ultimately destroyed the 1950s horror comics of which later work (including work by Stephen King) was to act as both *homage* and echo.

J. Gerald Kennedy, Manuel Aguirre and Robert Geary return the reader to matters of theory. Kennedy's study of Poe and the nature of textuality shows the influence of Jacques Derrida's deconstructionist technique, Aguirre's study concentrates on the formal properties of the gothic genre in the hands of the Victorians, and Geary's work reminds us of the longevity of this mixed form and of its social and *religious* ambiguities.

The volume is completed with a select bibliography and also includes a chronology of significant authors and titles.

Notes

1. Fred Botting, *Gothic* (London: Routledge, 1995) p. 1.
2. Mary Russo, *The Female Grotesque* (London: Routledge, 1995) p. 1.

1 Early Accounts

EDGAR ALLAN POE

Extract from 'The Man of the Crowd'[1]

It was well said of a certain German book that '*es lässt sich nicht lesen*' – it does not permit itself to be read. There are some secrets which do not permit themselves to be told. Men die nightly in their beds, wringing the hands of ghostly confessors, and looking them piteously in the eyes – die with despair of heart and convulsion of throat, on account of the hideousness of mysteries which will not *suffer themselves* to be revealed. Now and then, alas, the conscience of man takes up a burden so heavy in horror that it can be thrown down only into the grave. And thus the essence of all crime is undivulged.

Extract from 'The Imp of the Perverse'[2]

In the consideration of the faculties and impulses – of the *prima mobilia* of the human soul, the phrenologists have failed to make room for a propensity which, although obviously existing as a radical, primitive, irreducible sentiment, has been equally overlooked by all the moralists who have preceded them. In the pure arrogance of the reason, we have all overlooked it. We have suffered its existence to escape our senses, solely through want of belief – of faith; – whether it be faith in Revelation, or faith in the Kabbala. The idea of it has never occurred to us, simply because of its supererogation. We saw no *need* of the impulse – for the propensity. We could not perceive its necessity. We could not understand, that is to say, we could not have understood, had the notion of this *primum mobile* ever obtruded itself; – we could not have understood in what manner it might be made to further the objects of humanity, either temporal or eternal. It cannot be denied that phrenology, and in great measure, all metaphysicianism have been concocted *à priori*. The intellectual or logical man, rather than the understanding or observant man, set himself to imagine designs – to dictate purposes to God. Having thus fathomed to his satisfaction the intensions of Jehovah, out of these intentions he built his innumerable systems of mind. In the matter of phrenology, for example, we first determined, naturally enough, that it was the design of the Deity that man should eat. We then assigned to man an organ of alimentiveness, and this organ is the scourge with which the Deity compels man, will-I nill-I, into eating. Secondly, having settled it to be God's will that man should continue his species, we discovered an organ of amativeness, forthwith. And so with combativeness, with ideality, with causality, with constructiveness, – so, in short, with every organ, whether representing a propensity, a moral sentiment, or a faculty of the pure intellect. And in these arrangements of the *principia* of human action, the Spurzheimites, whether right or wrong, in part, or upon the whole, have but followed, in principle, the footsteps of their predecessors; deducing and establishing every thing from the preconceived destiny of man, and upon the ground of the objects of his Creator.

It would have been wiser, it would have been safer to classify (if classify we must) upon the basis of what man usually or occasionally did, and was always occasionally doing, rather than upon the basis of what we took it for granted the Deity intended him to do. If we cannot comprehend God in his visible works, how then in his inconceivable thoughts, that call the works into being! If we cannot understand him in his objective creatures, how then in his substantive moods and phases of creation?

Induction, *à posteriori*, would have brought phrenology to admit, as an innate and primitive principle of human action, a paradoxical something, which we may call *perverseness*, for want of a more characteristic term. In the sense I intend, it is, in fact, a *mobile* without motive, a motive not *motivirt*. Through its promptings we act without comprehensible object; or, if this shall be understood as a contradiction in terms, we may so far modify the proposition as to say, that through its promptings we act, for the reason that we should *not*. In theory, no reason can be more unreasonable; but, in fact, there is none more strong. With certain minds, under certain conditions, it becomes absolutely irresistible. I am not more certain that I breathe, than that the assurance of the wrong or error of any action is often the one unconquerable *force* which impels us, and alone impels us to its prosecution. Nor will this overwhelming tendency to do wrong for the wrong's sake, admit of analysis, or resolution into ulterior elements. It is a radical, a primitive impulse – elementary. It will be said, I am aware, that when we persist in acts because we feel we should *not* persist in them, our conduct is but a modification of that which ordinarily springs from the *combativeness* of phrenology. But a glance will show the fallacy of this idea. The phrenological combativeness has for its essence, the necessity of self-defence. It is our safeguard against injury. Its principle regards our well-being; and thus the desire to be well, is excited simultaneously with its development. It follows, that the desire to be well must be excited simultaneously with any principle which shall be merely a modification of combativeness, but in the case of that something which I term *perverseness*, the desire to be well is not only not aroused, but a strongly antagonistical sentiment exists.

An appeal to one's own heart is, after all, the best reply to the sophistry just noticed. No one who trustingly consults and thoroughly questions his own soul, will be disposed to deny the entire radicalness of the propensity in question. It is not more incomprehensible than distinctive. There lives no man who are some period has not been tormented, for example, by an earnest desire to tantalize a listener by circumlocution. The speaker is aware that he displeases; he has every intention to please; he is usually curt, precise, and clear; the most laconic and luminous language is struggling for utterance upon his tongue; it is only with difficulty that he restrains himself from giving it flow; he dreads and deprecates the anger of him whom he addresses; yet, the thought strikes him, that by certain involutions and parentheses, this anger may be engendered. That single thought is enough. The impulse increases to a wish, the wish to a desire, the desire to an uncontrollable longing, and the longing (to the deep regret and mortification of the speaker, and in defiance of all consequences) is indulged.

We have a task before us which must be speedily performed. We know that it will be ruinous to make delay. The most important crisis of our life calls, trumpet-tongued, for immediate energy and action. We glow, we are consumed with eagerness to commence the work, with the anticipation of whose glorious result our whole souls are on fire. It must, it shall be undertaken to-day, and yet we put it off until to-morrow; and why? There is no answer, except that we feel *perverse*, using the word with no comprehension of the principle. To-morrow arrives, and with it a more impatient anxiety to do our duty, but with this very increase of anxiety arrives, also, a nameless, a positively fearful, because unfathomable, craving for delay. This craving gathers strength as the moments fly. The last hour for action is at hand. We tremble with the violence of the conflict within us – of the definite with the indefinite – of the substance with he shadow. But, if the contest have proceeded thus far, it is the shadow which prevails, – we struggle in vain. The clock strikes, and is the knell of our welfare. At the same time, it is the chanticleer-note to the ghost that has so long overawed us. It flies – it disappears – we are free. The old energy returns. We will labor *now*. Alas, it is *too late!*

We stand upon the brink of a precipice. We peer into the abyss – we grow sick and dizzy. Our first impulse is to shrink from the danger. Unaccountably we remain. By slow degrees our sickness, and dizziness, and horror, become merged in a cloud of unnameable feeling. By gradations, still more imperceptible, this cloud assumed shape, as did the vapour from the bottle out of which arose the genius in the Arabian Nights. But out of this *our* cloud upon the precipice's edge, there grows into palpability, a shape, far more terrible than any genius, or any demon of a tale, and yet it is but a thought, although a fearful one, and one which chills the very marrow of our bones with the fierceness of the delight of its horror. It is merely the idea of what would be our sensations during the sweeping precipitancy of a fall from such a height. And this fall – this rushing annihilation – for the very reason that it involves that one most ghastly and loathsome of all the most ghastly and loathesome images of death and suffering which have ever presented themselves to our imagination – for this very cause do we now the most vividly desire it. And because our reason violently deters us from the brink, *therefore*, do we the most impetuously approach it. There is no passion in nature so demoniacally impatient as that of him who, shuddering upon the edge of a precipice, thus meditates a plunge. To indulge, for a moment, in any attempt at *thought*, is to be inevitably lost; for reflection but urges us to forbear, and *therefore* it is, I say, that we *cannot*. If there be no friendly arm to check us, or if we fail in a sudden effort to prostrate ourselves backward from the abyss, we plunge, and are destroyed.

Examine these and similar actions as we will, we shall find them resulting solely from the spirit of the *Perverse*. We perpetrate them merely because we feel that we should *not*. Beyond or behind this there is no intelligible principle; and we might, indeed, deem this perverseness a direct instigation of the arch-fiend, were it not occasionally known to operate in furtherance of good.

'The Philosophy of Composition'[3] (on 'The Raven')

Let us dismiss, as irrelevant to the poem, *per se*, the circumstance – or say the necessity – which, in the first place, gave rise to the intention of composing *a* poem that should suit at once the popular and critical taste.

We commence, then, with this intention.

The initial consideration was that of extent. If any literary work is too long to be read at one sitting, we must be content to dispense with the immensely important effect derivable from unity of impression – for, if two sittings be required, the affairs of the world interfere, and every thing like totality is at once destroyed. But since, *ceteris paribus*, no poet can afford to dispense with *any* thing that may advance his design, it but remains to be seen whether there is, in extent, any advantage to counterbalance the loss of unity which attends it. Here I say no, at once. What we term a long poem, is, in fact, merely a succession of brief ones – that is to say, of brief poetical effects. It is needless to demonstrate that a poem is such, only inasmuch as it intensely excites, by elevating, the soul; and all intense excitements are, through a psychal necessity, brief. For this reason, at least one half of the 'Paradise Lost' is essentially prose – a succession of poetical excitement interspersed, *inevitably*, with corresponding depressions – the whole being deprived, through the extremeness of its length, of the vastly important artistic element, totality, or unity, of effect.

It appears evident, then, that there is a distinct limit, as regards length, to all works of literary art – the limit of a single sitting – and that, although in certain classes of prose composition, such as 'Robinson Crusoe' (demanding no unity), this limit may be advantageously overpassed, it can never properly be overpassed in a poem. Within this limit, the extent of a poem may be made to bear mathematical relation to its merit – in other words, to the excitement or elevation – again, in other words, to the degree of the true poetical effect which it is capable of inducing; for it is clear that the brevity must be in direct ratio of the intensity of the intended effect: – this, with one proviso – that a certain degree of duration is absolutely requisite for the production of any effect at all.

Holding in view these considerations, as well as that degree of excitement which I deemed not above the popular, while not below the critical, taste, I reached at once what I conceived the proper *length* for my intended poem – a length of about one hundred lines. It is, in fact, a hundred and eight.

My next thought concerned the choice of an impression, or effect, to be conveyed: and here I may as well observe that, throughout the construction, I kept steadily in view the design of rendering the work *universally* appreciable. I should be carried too far out of my immediate topic were I to demonstrate a point upon which I have repeatedly insisted, and which, with the poetical, stands not in the slightest need of demonstration – the point, I mean, that Beauty is the sole legitimate province of the poem. A few words, however, in elucidation of my real meaning, which some of my friends have evinced a disposition to misrepresent. That pleasure which is at once the most intense, the most elevating, and the most pure, is, I believe, found in the contemplation of the beautiful. When, indeed, men speak of Beauty, they mean, precisely, not a quality, as is supposed, but an effect – they refer, in short, just to that intense and pure elevation of *soul* – *not* of intellect, or of heart – upon which I have commented, and which is experienced in consequence of contemplating 'the beautiful'. Now I designate Beauty as the province of the poem, merely because it is an obvious rule of Art that effects should be made to spring from direct causes – that objects should be attained through means best adapted for their attainment – no one as yet having been weak enough to deny that the peculiar elevation alluded to is *most readily* attained in the poem. Now the object, Truth, or the satisfaction of the intellect, and the object Passion, or the excitement of the heart, are, although attainable to a certain extent in poetry, far more readily attainable in prose. Truth, in fact, demands a precision, and Passion a *homeliness* (the truly passionate will comprehend me) which are absolutely antagonistic to that Beauty which, I maintain, is the excitement, or pleasurable elevation, of the soul. It by no means follows from any thing here said, that passion, or even truth, may not be introduced, and even profitably introduced, into a poem – for they may serve in elucidation, or aid the general effect, as do discords in music, by contrast – but the true artist will always contrive, first, to tone them into proper subservience to the predominant aim, and, secondly, to enveil them, as far as possible, in that Beauty which is the atmosphere and the essence of the poem.

Regarding, then, Beauty as my province, my next question referred to the *tone* of its highest manifestation – and all experience has shown that this tone is one of *sadness*. Beauty of whatever kind, in its supreme development, invariably excites the sensitive soul to tears. Melancholy is thus the most legitimate of all the poetical tones.

The length, the province, and the tone, being thus determined, I betook myself to ordinary induction, with the view of obtaining some artistic piquancy which might serve me as a keynote in the construction of the poem – some pivot upon which the whole structure might turn. In carefully thinking over all the usual artistic effects – or more properly *points*, in the theatrical sense – I did not fail to perceive immediately that no one had been so universally employed as that of the *refrain*. The universality of its employment sufficed to assure me of its intrinsic value, and spared me the necessity of submitting it to analysis. I considered it, however, with regard to its susceptibility of improvements, and soon saw it to be in a primitive condition. As commonly used, the *refrain*, or burden, not only is limited to lyric verse, but depends for its impression upon the force of monotone – both in sound and thought. The pleasure is deduced solely from the sense of identity – of repetition. I resolved to diversify, and so heighten, the effect, by adhering, in general, to the monotone of sound, while I continually varied that of thought: that is to say, I determined to produce continuously novel effects, by the variation of *the application* of the *refrain* – the *refrain* itself remaining, for the most part, unvaried.

These points being settled, I next bethought me of the *nature* of my *refrain*. Since its application was to be repeatedly varied, it was clear that the *refrain* itself must be brief, for there would have been an insurmountable difficulty in frequent variations of application in any sentence of length. In proportion to the brevity of the sentence, would, of course, be the facility of the variation. This led me at once to a single word as the best *refrain*.

The question now arose as to the *character* of the word. Having made up my mind to a *refrain*, the division of the poem into stanzas was, of course, a corollary: the *refrain* forming the close of each stanza. That such a close, to have force, must be sonorous and susceptible of protracted emphasis, admitted no doubt: and these considerations inevitably led me to the long *o* as the most sonorous vowel, in connection with *r* as the most producible consonant.

The sound of the *refrain* being thus determined, it became necessary to select a word embodying this sound, and at the same time in the fullest possible keeping with that melancholy which I had pre-determined as the tone of the poem. In such a search it would have been absolutely impossible to overlook the word 'Nevermore'. In fact, it was the very first which presented itself.

The next *desideratum* was a pretext for the continuous use of the one word 'nevermore'. In observing the difficulty which I at once found in inventing a sufficiently plausible reason for its continuous repetition, I did not fail to perceive that this difficulty arose solely from the pre-assumption that the word was to be so continuously or monotonously spoken by a *human* being – I did not fail to perceive, in short, that the difficulty lay in the reconciliation of this monotony with the exercise of reason on the part of the creature repeating the word. Here, then, immediately arose the idea of a *non*-reasoning creature capable of speech; and, very naturally, a parrot, in the first instance, suggested itself, but was superseded forthwith by a Raven, as equally capable of speech, and infinitely more in keeping with the intended *tone*.

I had now gone so far as the conception of a Raven – the bird of ill omen – monotonously repeating the one word, 'Nevermore', at the conclusion of each stanza, in a poem of melancholy tone, and in length about one hundred lines. Now, never losing sight of the object *supremeness*, or perfection, at all points, I asked myself – 'Of all melancholy topics, what, according to the *universal* understanding of mankind, is the *most* melancholy?' Death – was the obvious reply. 'And when', I said, 'is this most melancholy of topics most poetical?' From what I have already explained at some length, the answer, here also, is obvious – 'When it most closely allies itself to *Beauty*: the death, then, of a beautiful woman is, unquestionably, the most poetical topic in the world – and equally is it beyond doubt that the lips best suited for such topic are those of a bereaved lover.'

I had now to combine the two ideas, of a lover lamenting his deceased mistress and a Raven continuously repeating the word 'Nevermore'. – I had to combine these, bearing in mind my design of varying, at every turn, the *application* of the word repeated; but the only intelligible mode of such combination is that of imagining the Raven employing the word in answer to the queries of the lover. And here it was that I saw at once the opportunity afforded for the effect on which I had been depending – that is to say, the effect of the *variation of application*. I saw that I could make the first query propounded by the lover – the first query to which the Raven should reply 'Nevermore' – that I could make this first query a commonplace one – the second less so – the third still less, and so on – until at length the lover, startled from his original *nonchalance* by the melancholy character of the word itself – by its frequent repetition – and by a consideration of the ominous reputation of the fowl that uttered it – is at length excited to superstition, and wildly propounds queries of a far different character – queries whose solution he has passionately at heart – propounds them half in superstition and half in that species of despair which delights in self-torture – propounds them not altogether because he believes in the prophetic or demoniac character of the bird (which, reason assures him, is merely repeating a lesson learned by rote) but because he experiences a frenzied pleasure in so modelling his questions as to receive from the *expected* 'Nevermore' the most delicious because the most intolerable of sorrow. Perceiving the opportunity thus afforded me – or, more strictly, thus forced upon me in the process of the construction – I first established in mind the climax, or concluding query – that query to which 'Nevermore' should be in the last place an answer – that query in reply to which this word 'Nevermore' should involve the uttermost conceivable amount of sorrow and despair.

Here then the poem may be said to have its beginning – at the end, where all works of art should begin – for it was here, at this point of my preconsiderations, that I first put pen to paper in the composition of the stanza:

'Prophet,' said I, 'thing of evil! prophet still if bird or devil!
By that heaven that bends above us – by that God we both adore
Tell this soul with sorrow laden, if within the distant Aidenn,
It shall clasp a sainted maiden whom the angels name Lenore –
Clasp a rare and radiant maiden whom the angels name Lenore.'
  Quoth the raven 'Nevermore.'

I composed this stanza, at this point, first that, by establishing the climax, I might the better vary and graduate, as regards seriousness and importance, the preceding queries of the lover – and, secondly, that I might definitely settle the rhythm, the metre, and the length and general arrangement of the stanza – as well as graduate the stanzas which were to precede, so that none of them might surpass this in rhythmical effect. Had I been able, in the subsequent composition, to construct more vigorous stanzas, I should, without scruple, have purposely enfeebled them, so as not to interfere with the climacteric effect.

And here I may as well say a few words of the versification. My first object (as usual) was originality. The extent to which this has been neglected, in versification, is one of the most unaccountable things in the world. Admitting that there is little possibility of variety in mere *rhythm*, it is still clear that the possible varieties of metre and stanza are absolutely infinite – and yet, *for centuries, no man, in verse, has ever done, or ever seemed to think of doing, an original thing*. The fact is, that originality (unless in minds of very unusual force) is by no means a matter, as some suppose, of impulse or intuition. In general, to be found, it must be elaborately sought, and although a positive merit of the highest class, demands in its attainment less of invention than negation.

Of course, I pretend to no originality in either the rhythm or metre of the 'Raven'. The former is trochaic – the latter is octameter acatalectic, alternating with heptameter catalectic repeated in the *refrain* of the fifth verse, and termininating with tetrameter catalectic. Less pedantically – the feet employed throughout (trochees) consist of a long syllable followed by a short: the first line of the stanza consists of eight of these feet – the second or seven and a half (in effect two-thirds) – the third of eight – the fourth of seven and a half – the fifth the same – the sixth three and a half. Now, each of these lines, taken individually, has been employed before, and what originality the 'Raven' has, is in their *combination into stanza*; nothing even remotely approaching this combination has ever been attempted. The effect of this originality of combination is aided by other unusual, and some altogether novel effects, arising from an extension of the application of the principles of rhyme and alliteration.

The next point to be considered was the mode of bringing together the lover and the Raven – and the first branch of this consideration was the *locale*. For this the most natural suggestion might seem to be a forest, or the fields – but it has always appeared to me that a close *circumscription of space* is absolutely necessary to the effect of insulated incident: – it has the force of a frame to a picture. It has an indisputable moral power in keeping concentrated the attention, and, of course, must not be confounded with mere unity of place.

I determined, then, to place the lover in his chamber – in a chamber rendered sacred to him by memories of her who had frequented it. The room is represented as richly furnished – this in mere pursuance of the ideas I have already explained on the subject of Beauty, as the sole true poetical thesis.

The *locale* being thus determined, I had now to introduce the bird – and the thought of introducing him through the window, was inevitable. The idea of making the lover suppose, in the first instance, that the flapping of the wings of the bird against the shutter, is a 'tapping' at the door, originated in a wish to increase, by prolonging, the reader's curiosity, and in a desire to admit the incidental effect arising from the lover's throwing open the door, finding all dark, and thence adopting the half-fancy that it was the spirit of his mistress that knocked.

I made the night tempestuous, first, to account for the Raven's seeking admission, and secondly, for the effect of contrast with the (physical) serenity within the chamber.

I made the bird alight on the bust of Pallas, also for the effect of contrast between the marble and the plumage – it being understood that the bust was absolutely *suggested* by the bird – the bust of *Pallas* being chosen, first, as most in keeping with the scholarship of the lover, and, secondly, for the sonorousness of the word, Pallas, itself.

About the middle of the poem, also, I have availed myself of the force of contrast, with a view of deepening the ultimate impression. For example, an air of the fantastic – approaching as nearly to the ludicrous as was admissible – is given to the Raven's entrance. He comes in 'with many a flirt and flutter'.

Not the *least obeisance made he* – not a moment stopped or
    stayed he,
But with mien of lord or lady, perched above my chamber
    door.

In the two stanzas which follow, the design is more obviously carried out: –

Then this ebony bird beguiling my sad fancy into smiling
By the *grave and stern decorum of the countenance it wore*,
'Though thy *crest be shorn and shaven* thou,' I said, 'art sure no
    craven,

Ghastly grim and ancient Raven wandering from the nightly
　　shore –
Tell me what thy lordly name is on the Night's Plutonian shore?'
　　Quote the Raven 'Nevermore.'

Much I marvelled *this ungainly fowl* to hear discourse so plainly
Thought its answer little meaning – little relevancy bore;
For we cannot help agreeing that no living human being
Ever yet was blessed with seeing bird above his chamber door –
Bird or beast upon the sculptured bust above his chamber door,
　　With such name as 'Nevermore.'

The effect of the *dénouement* being thus provided for, I
immediately drop the fantastic for a tone of the most profound
seriousness: – this tone commencing in the stanza directly following
the one last quoted, with the line,

But the Raven, sitting lonely on that placid bust, spoke only, etc.

From this epoch the lover no longer jests – no longer sees any
thing even of the fantastic in the Raven's demeanour. He speaks of
him as a 'grim, ungainly, ghastly, gaunt, and ominous bird of yore',
and feels the 'fiery eyes' burning into his 'bosom's core'. This
revolution of thought, or fancy, on the lover's part, is intended to
induce a similar one on the part of the reader – to bring the mind
into a proper frame for the *dénouement* – which is now brought
about as rapidly and as *directly* as possible.

With the *dénouement* proper – with the Raven's reply,
'Nevermore,' to the lover's final demand if he shall meet his mistress
in another world – the poem, in its obvious phase, that of a simple
narrative, may be said to have its completion. So far, everything is
within the limits of the accountable – of the real. A raven, having
learned by rote the single word 'Nevermore', and having escaped
from the custody of its owner, is driven at midnight, through the
violence of a storm, to seek admission at a window from which a
light still gleams – the chamber-window of a student, occupied half
in poring over a volume, half in dreaming of a beloved mistress
deceased. The casement being thrown open at the fluttering of the
bird's wings, the bird itself perches on the most convenient seat out
of the immediate reach of the student, who, amused by the incident
and the oddity of the visitor's demeanour, demands of it, in jest and

without looking for a reply, its name. The raven addressed, answers with its customary word, 'Nevermore' – a word which finds immediate echo in the melancholy heart of the student, who, giving utterance aloud to certain thoughts suggested by the occasion, is again startled by the fowl's repetition of 'Nevermore.' The student now guesses the state of the case, but is impelled, as I have before explained, by the human thirst for self-torture, and in part by superstition, to propound such queries to the bird as will bring him, the lover, the most of the luxury of sorrow, through the anticipated answer 'Nevermore.' With the indulgence, to the extreme, of this self-torture, the narration, in what I have termed its first or obvious phase, has a natural termination, and so far there has been no overstepping of the limits of the real.

But in subjects so handled, however skilfully, or with however vivid an array of incident, there is always a certain hardness or nakedness, which repels the artistical eye. Two things are invariably required – first, some amount of complexity, or more properly, adaptation; and, secondly, some amount of suggestiveness – some under-current, however indefinite, of meaning. It is this latter, in especial, which imparts to a work of art so much of that *richness* (to borrow from colloquy a forcible term) which we are too fond of confounding with *the ideal*. It is the *excess* of the suggested meaning – it is the rendering this the upper instead of the under current of the theme – which turns into prose (and that of the very flattest kind) the so-called poetry of the so-called transcendentalists.

Holding these opinions, I added the two concluding stanzas of the poem – their suggestiveness being thus made to pervade all the narrative which has preceded them. The under-current of meaning is rendered first apparent in the lines –

'Take thy beak from out *my heart*, and take thy form from off my door!'
    Quoth the Raven 'Nevermore!'

It will be observed that the words, 'from out my heart', involve the first metaphorical expression in the poem. They, with the answer, 'Nevermore,' dispose the mind to seek a moral in all that has been previously narrated. The reader begins now to regard the Raven as emblematical – but it is not until the very last line of the very last stanza, that the intention of making him emblematical of *Mournful and Never-ending Remembrance* is permitted distinctly to be seen:

And the Raven, never flitting, still is sitting, still is sitting,
On the pallid bust of Pallas just above my chamber door;
And his eyes have all the seeming of a demon's that is dreaming,
And the lamplight o'er him streaming throws his shadow on the floor;
And my soul *from out that shadow*, that lies floating on the floor
  Shall be lifted – nevermore.

Extract from *Eureka*[4]

. . . Let me declare, only, that, as an individual, I myself feel impelled to *fancy* – without daring to call it more – that there *does* exist a *limitless* succession of Universes, more or less similar to that of which we have cognizance – to that of which *alone* we shall ever have cognizance – at the very least until the return of our own particular Universe into Unity. *If* such clusters of clusters exist, however – *and they do* – it is abundantly clear that, having had no part in our origin, they have no portion in our laws. They neither attract us, nor we them. Their material – their spirit is not ours – is not that which obtains in any part of our Universe. They could not impress our senses or our souls. Among them and us – considering all, for the moment, collectively – there are no influences in common. Each exists, apart and independently, *in the bosom of its proper and particular God.*

Extract from Marginalia[5]

There are moments when, even to the sober eye of Reason, the world of our sad humanity must assume the aspect of Hell; but the Imagination of Man is no Carathis, to explore with impunity its every cavern. Alas ! the grim legion of sepulchral terrors can*not* be regarded as altogether fanciful; but like the Demons in whose company Afrasiab made his voyage down the Oxus, they must sleep, or they will devour us – they must be suffered to slumber, or we perish. . . . That individuals *have* so soared above the plane of their race, is scarcely to be questioned; but, in looking back through history for traces of their existence, we should pass over all biographies of 'the good and the great', while we search carefully the slight records of wretches who died in prison, in Bedlam, or upon the gallows.

Notes

1. First published in *Burton's Gentleman's Magazine* (1840).
2. First published in *Graham's Magazine* (1845).
3. First published in *Graham's Magazine* (1846).
4. First published in 1848.
5. First published in *Democratic Review* (1844).

NATHANIEL HAWTHORNE

Preface to *The House of the Seven Gables*

When a writer calls his work a Romance, it need hardly be observed that he wishes to claim a certain latitude, both as to its fashion and material, which he would not have felt himself entitled to assume, had he professed to be writing a Novel. The latter form of composition is presumed to aim at a very minute fidelity, not merely to the possible, but to the probable and ordinary course of man's experience. The former – while, as a work of art, it must rigidly subject itself to laws, and while it sins unpardonably, so far as it may swerve aside from the truth of the human heart – has fairly a right to present that truth under circumstances, to a great extent, of the writer's own choosing or creation. If he think fit, also, he may so manage his atmospherical medium as to bring out or mellow the lights and deepen and enrich the shadows of the picture. He will be wise, no doubt, to make a very moderate use of the privileges here stated, and, especially, to mingle the Marvellous rather as a slight, delicate, and evanescent flavour, than as any portion of the actual substance of the dish offered to the Public. He can hardly be said, however, to commit a literary crime, even if he disregard this caution.

In the present work, the Author has proposed to himself (but with what success, fortunately, it is not for him to judge) to keep undeviatingly within his immunities. The point of view in which this Tale comes under the Romantic definition, lies in the attempt to connect a by-gone time with the very Present that is flitting away from us. It is a Legend, prolonging itself, from an epoch now gray in the distance, down into our own broad daylight, and bringing along with it some of its legendary mist, which the Reader, according to his pleasure, may either disregard, or allow it to float almost imperceptibly about the characters and events, for the sake of a picturesque effect. The narrative, it may be, is woven of so humble a texture as to require this advantage, and, at the same time, to render it the more difficult of attainment.

Many writers lay very great stress upon some definite moral purpose, at which they profess to aim their works. Not to be deficient, in this particular, the Author has provided himself with a moral; – the truth, namely, that the wrong-doing of one generation lives into the successive ones, and, divesting itself of every temporary advantage, becomes a pure and uncontrollable mischief; – and he would feel it a singular gratification, if this Romance might effectually convince mankind (or, indeed, any one man) of the folly of tumbling down an avalanche of ill-gotten gold, or real estate, on the heads of an unfortunate posterity, thereby to maim and crush them, until the accumulated mass shall be scattered abroad in its original atoms. In good faith, however, he is not sufficiently imaginative to flatter himself with the slightest hope of this kind. When romances do really teach anything, or produce any effective operation, it is usually through a far more subtle process than the ostensible one. The Author has considered it hardly worth his while, therefore, relentlessly to impale the story with its moral, as with an iron rod – or rather, as by sticking a pin through a butterfly – thus at once depriving it of life, and causing it to stiffen in an ungainly and unnatural attitude. A high truth, indeed, fairly, finely, and skilfully wrought out, brightening at every step, and crowning the final development of a work of fiction, may add an artistic glory, but is never any truer, and seldom any more evident, at the last page than at the first.

The Reader may perhaps choose to assign an actual locality to the imaginary events of this narrative. If permitted by the historical connection (which, though slight, was essential to his plan), the Author would very willingly have avoided anything of this nature. Not to speak of other objections, it exposes the Romance to an inflexible and exceedingly dangerous species of criticism, by bringing his fancy-pictures almost into positive contact with the realities of the moment. It has been no part of his object, however, to describe local manners, nor in any way to meddle with the characteristics of a community for whom he cherishes a proper respect and a natural regard. He trusts not to be considered as unpardonably offending, by laying out a street that infringes upon nobody's private rights, and appropriating a lot of land which had no visible owner, and building a house, of materials long in use for constructing castles in the air. The personages of the Tale – though they give themselves out to be of ancient stability and considerable prominence – are really of the Author's own making, or, at all events, of his own mixing; their virtues can shed no lustre, nor their defects redound, in the remotest degree, to the discredit of the venerable town of which they profess to be inhabitants. He would be glad, therefore, if – especially in the quarter to which he alludes – the book may be read strictly as a Romance, having a great deal more to do with the clouds overhead, than with any portion of the actual soil of the County of Essex.

Note

First published in 1851.

WALTER PATER

Extract from *The Renaissance*

Leonardo da Vinci learned . . . the art of going deep, of tracking the sources of expression to their subtlest retreats, the power of an intimate presence in the things he handled. He did not at once or entirely desert his art; only he was no longer the cheerful, objective painter, through whose soul, as through clear glass, the bright figures of Florentine life, only made a little mellower and more pensive by the transit, passed on to the white wall. He wasted many days in curious tricks of design, seeming to lose himself in the spinning of intricate devices of line and colour. He was smitten with a love of the impossible – the perforation of mountains, changing the course of rivers, raising great buildings, such as the church of *San Giovanni*, in the air; all those feats for the performance of which natural magic professed to have the key. Later writers, indeed, see in these efforts an anticipation of modern mechanics; in him they were rather dreams, thrown off by the overwrought and labouring brain. Two ideas were especially confirmed in him, as reflexes of things that had touched his brain in childhood beyond the depth of other impressions – the smiling of women and the motion of great waters.

And in such studies some interfusion of the extremes of beauty and terror shaped itself, as an image that might be seen and touched, in the mind of this gracious youth, so fixed that for the rest of his life it never left him. As if catching glimpses of it in the strange eyes or hair of chance people, he would follow such about the streets of Florence till the sun went down, of whom many sketches of his remain. Some of these are full of a curious beauty, that remote beauty which may be apprehended only by those who have sought it carefully; who, starting with acknowledged types of beauty, have refined as far upon these, as these refine upon the world of common forms. But mingled inextricably with this there is an element of mockery also; so that, whether in sorrow or scorn, he caricatures Dante even. Legions of grotesques sweep under his hand; for has not nature too her grotesques – the rent rock, the distorting lights of even on lonely roads, the unveiled structure of man in the embryo, or the skeleton?

All these swarming fancies unite in the *Medusa* of the *Uffizii*. Vasari's story of an earlier Medusa, painted on a wooden shield, is perhaps an invention; and yet, properly told, has more of the air of truth about it than anything else in the whole legend. For its real subject is not the serious work of a man, but the experiment of a child. The lizards and glow-worms and other strange small creatures which haunt an Italian vineyard bring before one the whole picture of a child's life in a Tuscan dwelling – half castle, half farm – and are as true to nature as the pretended astonishment of the father for whom the boy has prepared a surprise. It was not in play that he painted that other Medusa, the one great picture which he left behind him in Florence. The subject has been treated in various ways; Leonardo alone cuts to its centre; he alone realises it as the head of a corpse, exercising its powers through all the circumstances of death. What may be called the fascination of corruption penetrates in every touch its exquisitely finished beauty. About the dainty lines of the cheek the bat flits unheeded. The delicate snakes seem literally strangling each other in terrified struggle to escape from the Medusa brain. The hue which violent death always brings with it is in the features; features singularly massive and grand, as we catch them inverted, in a dexterous foreshortening, crown foremost, like a great calm stone against which the wave of serpents breaks.

The science of that age was all divination, clairvoyance, unsubjected to our exact modern formulas, seeking in an instant of vision to concentrate a thousand experiences. Later writers, thinking only of the well-ordered treatise on painting which a Frenchman, Raffaelle du Fresne, a hundred years afterwards, compiled from Leonardo's bewildered manuscripts, written strangely, as his manner was, from right to left, have imagined a rigid order in his inquiries. But this rigid order would have been little in accordance with the restlessness of his character; and if we think of him as the mere reasoner who subjects design to anatomy and composition to mathematical rules, we shall hardly have that impression which those around Leonardo received from him. Poring over his crucibles, making experiments with colour, trying, by a strange variation of the alchemist's dream, to discover the secret, not of an elixir to make man's natural life immortal, but of giving immortality to the subtlest and most delicate effects of painting, he seemed to them rather the sorcerer or the magician, possessed of curious secrets and a hidden knowledge, living in a world of which he alone possessed the key. What his philosophy seems to have been most like is that of Paracelsus or Cardan; and much of the spirit of the older alchemy still hangs about it, with its confidence in short cuts and odd byways to knowledge.

. . .

Curiosity and the desire of beauty – these are the two elementary forces in Leonardo's genius; curiosity often in conflict with the desire of beauty, but generating, in union with it, a type of subtle and curious grace.

. . .

In him first appears the taste for what is *bizarre* or *recherché* in landscape; hollow places full of the green shadow of bituminous rocks, ridged reefs of trap-rock which cut the water into quaint sheets of light, – their exact antitype is in our own western seas; all the solemn effects of moving water. You may follow it springing from its distant source among the rocks on the heath of the *Madonna of the Balances*, passing, as a little fall, into the treacherous calm of the *Madonna of the Lake*, as a goodly river next, below the cliffs of the *Madonna of the Rocks*, washing the

white walls of its distant villages, stealing out in a network of
divided streams in *La Gioconda*.

. . .

Sometimes this curiosity came in conflict with the desire of beauty;
it tended to make him go too far below that outside of things in
which art really begins and ends.

. . .

La Gioconda is, in the truest sense, Leonardo's masterpiece, the
revealing instance of his mode of thought and work. Its
suggestiveness, only the *Melancholia* of Dürer is comparable to it;
and no crude symbolism disturbs the effect of its subdued and
graceful mystery. We all know the face and hands of the figure, set in
its marble chair, in that circle of fantastic rocks, as in some faint
light under sea. Perhaps of all ancient pictures time has chilled it
least.[1] As often happens with works in which invention seems to
reach its limit, there is an element in it given to, not invented by, the
master. In that inestimable folio of drawings, once in the possession
of Vasari, were certain designs by Verrocchio, faces of such
impressive beauty that Leonardo in his boyhood copied them many
times. It is hard not to connect with these designs of the elder, by-
past master, as with its germinal principle, the unfathomable smile,
always with a touch of something sinister in it, which plays all over
Leonardo's work. Besides, the picture is a portrait. From childhood
we see this image defining itself on the fabric of his dreams; and but
for express historical testimony, we might fancy that this was but his
ideal lady, embodied and beheld at last. What was the relationship
of a living Florentine to this creature of his thought? By what strange
affinities had the dream and the person grown up thus apart, and yet
so closely together? Present from the first incorporeally in
Leonardo's brain, dimly traced in the designs of Verrocchio, she is
found present at last in *Il Giocondo's* house. That there is much of
mere portraiture in the picture is attested by the legend that by
artificial means, the presence of mimes and flute-players, that subtle
expression was protracted on the face. Again, was it in four years
and by renewed labour never really completed, or in four months
and as by stroke of magic, that the image was projected?

The presence that rose thus so strangely beside the waters, is
expressive of what in the ways of a thousand years men had come to
desire. Hers is the head upon which all 'the ends of the world are

come', and the eyelids are a little weary. It is a beauty wrought out from within upon the flesh, the deposit, little cell by cell, of strange thoughts and fantastic reveries and exquisite passions. Set it for a moment beside one of those white Greek goddesses or beautiful women of antiquity, and how would they be troubled by this beauty, into which the soul with all its maladies has passed! All the thoughts and experience of the world have etched and moulded there, in that which they have of power to refine and make expressive the outward form, the animalism of Greece, the lust of Rome, the mysticism of the middle age with its spiritual ambition and imaginative loves, the return of the Pagan world, the sins of the Borgias. She is older than the rocks among which she sits; like the vampire, she has been dead many times, and learned the secrets of the grave; and has been a diver in deep seas, and keeps their fallen day about her; and trafficked for strange webs with Eastern merchants: and, as Leda, was the mother of Helen of Troy, and, as Saint Anne, the mother of Mary; and all this has been to her but as the sound of lyres and flutes, and lives only in the delicacy with which it has moulded the changing lineaments, and tinged the eyelids and the hands. The fancy of a perpetual life, sweeping together ten thousand experiences, is an old one; and modern philosophy has conceived the idea of humanity as wrought upon by, and summing up in itself, all modes of thought and life. Certainly Lady Lisa might stand as the embodiment of the old fancy, the symbol of the modern idea.

Notes

First published in 1878.

1. Yet for Vasari there was some further magic of crimson in the lips and cheeks, lost for us.

LAFCADIO HEARN

Extract from 'Nightmare-Touch'

What *is* the fear of ghosts among those who believe in ghosts?

All fear is the result of experience – experience of the individual or of the race – experience either of the present life or of lives forgotten. Even the fear of the unknown can have no other origin. And the fear of ghosts must be a product of past pain.

Probably the fear of ghosts, as well as the belief in them, had its beginning in dreams. It is a peculiar fear. No other fear is so intense; yet none is so vague. Feelings thus voluminous and dim are super-individual mostly – feelings inherited – feelings made within us by the experience of the dead.

What experience?

Nowhere do I remember reading a plain statement of the reason why ghosts are feared. Ask any ten intelligent persons of your acquaintance, who remember having once been afraid of ghosts, to tell you exactly why they were afraid – to define the fancy behind the fear – and I doubt whether even one will be able to answer the question. The literature of folklore – oral and written – throws no clear light upon the subject. We find, indeed, various legends of men torn asunder by phantoms; but such gross imaginings could not explain the peculiar quality of ghostly fear. It is not a fear of bodily violence. It is not even a reasoning fear – not a fear that can readily explain itself – which would not be the case if it were founded upon definite ideas of physical danger. Furthermore, although primitive ghosts may have been imagined as capable of tearing and devouring, the common idea of a ghost is certainly that of a being intangible and imponderable.[1]

Now I venture to state boldly that the common fear of ghosts is *the fear of being touched by ghosts* – or, in other words, that the imagined Supernatural is dreaded mainly because of its imagined power to touch. Only to *touch*, remember! – not to wound or to kill.

But this dread of the touch would itself be the result of experience – chiefly, I think, of prenatal experience stored up in the individual by inheritance, like the child's fear of darkness. And who can ever have had the sensation of being touched by ghosts? The answer is simple: – *Everybody who has been seized by phantoms in a dream.*

Elements of primeval fears – fears older than humanity – doubtless enter into the child-terror of darkness. But the more definite fears of ghosts may very possibly be composed with inherited results of dream-pain – ancestral experience of nightmare. And the intuitive terror of supernatural touch can thus be evolutionally explained.

＊　　＊　　＊

Let me now try to illustrate my theory by relating some typical experiences.

II

When about five years old I was condemned to sleep by myself in a certain isolated room, thereafter always called the Child's Room. (At that time I was scarcely ever mentioned by name, but only referred to as 'the Child'.) The room was narrow, but very high, and, in spite of one tall window, very gloomy. It contained a fire-place wherein no fire was ever kindled; and the Child suspected that the chimney was haunted.

A law was made that no light should be left in the Child's Room at night – simply because the Child was afraid of the dark. His fear of the dark was judged to be a mental disorder requiring severe treatment. But the treatment aggravated the disorder. Previously I had been accustomed to sleep in a well-lighted room, with a nurse to take care of me. I thought that I should die of fright when sentenced to lie alone in the dark, and – what seemed to me then abominably cruel – actually *locked* into my room, the most dismal room of the house. Night after night when I had been warmly tucked into bed, the lamp was removed; the key clicked in the lock; the protecting light and the footsteps of my guardian receded together. Then an agony of fear would come upon me. Something in the black air would seem to gather and grow – (I thought that I could even *hear* it grow) – till I had to scream. Screaming regularly brought punishment; but it also brought back the light, which more than consoled for the punishment. This fact being at last found out, orders were given to pay no further heed to the screams of the Child.

Why was I thus insanely afraid? Partly because the dark had always been peopled for me with shapes of terror. So far back as memory extended, I had suffered from ugly dreams; and when aroused from them I could always *see* the forms dreamed of, lurking in the shadows of the room. They would soon fade out; but for several moments they would appear like tangible realities. And they were always the same figures. . . . Sometimes, without any preface of dreams, I used to see them at twilight-time – following me about from room to room, or reaching long dim hands after me, from storey to storey, up through the interspaces of the deep stairways.

I had complained of these haunters only to be told that I must never speak of them, and that they did not exist. I had complained to everybody in the house; and everybody in the house had told me the very same thing. But there was the evidence of my eyes! The denial of that evidence I could explain only in two ways: Either the shapes were afraid of big people, and showed themselves to me alone, because I was little and weak; or else the entire household had agreed, for some ghastly reason, to say what was not true. This latter theory seemed to me the more probable one, because I had several times perceived the shapes when I was not unattended; – and the consequent appearance of secrecy frightened me scarcely less than the visions did. Why was I forbidden to talk about what I saw, and even heard – on creaking stairways – behind waving curtains?

'Nothing will hurt you,' – this was the merciless answer to all my pleadings not to be left alone at night. But the haunters *did* hurt me. Only – they would wait until after I had fallen asleep, and so into their power – for they possessed occult means of preventing me from rising or moving or crying out.

Needless to comment upon the policy of locking me up alone with these fears in a black room. Unutterably was I tormented in that room – for years! Therefore I felt relatively happy when sent away at last to a children's boarding-school, where the haunters very seldom ventured to show themselves.

* * *

They were not like any people that I had ever known. They were shadowy dark-robed figures, capable of atrocious self-distortion – capable, for instance, of growing up to the ceiling, and then across it, and then lengthening themselves, head-downwards, along the opposite wall. Only their faces were distinct; and I tried not to look at their faces. I tried also in my dreams – or thought that I tried – to awaken myself from the sight of them by pulling at my eyelids with my fingers; but the eyelids would remain closed, as if sealed. . . . Many years afterwards, the frightful plates in Orfila's *Traité des*

Exhumés, beheld for the first time, recalled to me with a sickening start the dream-terrors of childhood. But to understand the Child's experience, you must imagine Orfila's drawings intensely alive, and continually elongating or distorting, as in some monstrous anamorphosis.

Nevertheless the mere sight of those nightmare-faces was not the worst of the experiences in the Child's Room. The dreams always began with a suspicion, or sensation of something heavy in the air – slowly quenching will – slowly numbing my power to move. At such times I usually found myself alone in a large unlighted apartment; and, almost simultaneously with the first sensation of fear, the atmosphere of the room would become suffused, half-way to the ceiling, with a sombre-yellowish glow, making objects dimly visible – though the ceiling itself remained pitch-black. This was not a true appearance of light: rather it seemed as if the black air were changing colour from beneath. . . . Certain terrible aspects of sunset, on the eve of storm, offer like effects of sinister colour. . . . Forthwith I would try to escape – (feeling at every step a sensation *as of wading*) – and would sometimes succeed in struggling half-way across the room; – but there I would always find myself brought to a standstill – paralyzed by some innominable opposition. Happy voices I could hear in the next room – I could see light through the transom over the door that I had vainly endeavoured to reach – I knew that one loud cry would save me. But not even by the most frantic effort could I raise my voice above a whisper. . . . And all this signified only that the Nameless was coming – was nearing – was mounting the stairs. I could hear the step – booming like the sound of a muffled drum – and I wondered why nobody else heard it. A long, long time the haunter would take to come – malevolently pausing after each ghastly footfall. Then, without a creak, the bolted door would open – slowly, slowly – and the thing would enter, gibbering soundlessly – and put out hands – and clutch me – and toss me to the black ceiling – and catch me descending to toss me up again, and again, and again. . . . In those moments the feeling was not fear: fear itself had been torpified by the first seizure. It was a sensation that has no name in the language of the living. For every touch brought a shock of something infinitely worse than pain – something that thrilled into the innermost secret being of me – a sort of abominable electricity, discovering unimagined capacities of suffering in totally unfamiliar regions of sentiency. . . . This was commonly the work of a single tormentor; but I can also remember

having been caught by a group, and tossed from one to another –
seemingly for a time of many minutes.

III

Whence the fancy of those shapes? I do not know. Possibly from
some impression of fear in earliest infancy; possibly from some
experience of fear in other lives than mine. That mystery is forever
insoluble. But the mystery of the shock of the touch admits of a
definite hypothesis.

First, allow me to observe that the experience of the sensation
itself cannot be dismissed as 'mere imagination'. Imagination means
cerebral activity: its pains and its pleasures are alike inseparable
from nervous operation, and their physical importance is sufficiently
proved by their physiological effects. Dream-fear may kill as well as
other fear; and no emotion thus powerful can be reasonably deemed
undeserving of study.

One remarkable fact in the problem to be considered is that the
sensation of seizure in dreams differs totally from all sensations
familiar to ordinary waking life. Why this differentiation? How
interpret the extraordinary massiveness and depth of the thrill?

I have already suggested that the dreamer's fear is most probably
not a reflection of relative experience, but represents the incalculable
total of ancestral experience of dream-fear. If the sum of the
experience of active life be transmitted by inheritance, so must
likewise be transmitted the summed experience of the life of sleep.
And in normal heredity either class of transmissions would probably
remain distinct.

Now, granting this hypothesis, the sensation of dream-seizure
would have had its beginnings in the earliest phases of dream-
consciousness – long prior to the apparition of man. The first
creatures capable of thought and fear must often have dreamed of
being caught by their natural enemies. There could not have been
much imagining of pain in these primal dreams. But higher nervous
development in later forms of being would have been accompanied
with larger susceptibility to dream-pain. Still later, with the growth
of reasoning-power, ideas of the supernatural would have changed
and intensified the character of dream-fear. Furthermore, through
all the course of evolution, heredity would have been accumulating
the experience of such feeling. Under those forms of imaginative

pain evolved through reactions of religious beliefs, there would persist some dim survival of savage primitive fears, and again, under this, a dimmer but incomparably deeper substratum of ancient animal-terrors. In the dreams of the modern child all these latencies might quicken – one below another – unfathomably – with the coming and the growing of nightmare.

It may be doubted whether the phantasms of any particular nightmare have a history older than the brain in which they move. But the shock of the touch would seem to indicate *some point of dream-contact with the total race-experience of shadowy seizure.* It may be that profundities of Self – abysses never reached by any ray from the life of sun – are strangely stirred in slumber, and that out of their blackness immediately responds a shuddering of memory, measureless even by millions of years.

Notes

First published in *Shadowings* (1900).

1. I may remark there that in many old Japanese legends and ballads, ghosts are represented as having power to *pull off* people's heads. But so far as the origin of the fear of ghosts is concerned, such stories explain nothing – since the experiences that evolved the fear must have been real, not imaginary, experiences.

2 Early Modern Accounts

SIGMUND FREUD

Extract from 'The Uncanny'

One is curious to know what this peculiar quality is which allows us to distinguish as 'uncanny' certain things within the boundaries of what is 'fearful'. . . .

This is the place now to put forward two considerations which, I think, contain the gist of this short study. In the first place, if psycho-analytic theory is correct in maintaining that every emotional affect, whatever its quality, is transformed by repression into morbid anxiety, then among such cases of anxiety there must be a class in which the anxiety can be shown to come from something repressed which *recurs*. This class of morbid anxiety would then be no other than what is uncanny, irrespective of whether it originally aroused dread or some other affect.

. . . for this uncanny is in reality nothing new or foreign, but something familiar and old-established in the mind that has been estranged only by the process of repression. This reference to the factor of repression enables us, furthermore, to understand Schelling's definition of the uncanny as something which ought to have been kept concealed but which has nevertheless come to light. . . .

To many people the idea of being buried alive while appearing to be dead is the most uncanny thing of all. And yet psycho-analysis has taught us that this terrifying phantasy is only a transformation of another phantasy which had originally nothing terrifying about it at all, but was filled with a certain lustful pleasure – the phantasy, I mean, of intra-uterine existence.

Note

First published in 1919. This translation is by Joan Riviere (1925).

HILAIRE BELLOC

On Algernon Blackwood

It is the penalty of true literary success that a man who has achieved it shall be seriously criticized. Mr Blackwood's book *The Empty House*, a book of ghost stories, was reviewed in these columns with a praise due to a work of the greatest merit. It was much more worthy of the term 'genius' than are nineteen out of twenty of the books to which this term is applied in a decade of reviewing. It has the quality, inseparable from genius, of conviction; it had the second quality, inseparable from genius, of creation; it had the third quality, inseparable from genius, of art. It was remarked in that former review that if the English people possess one quality more than another remarkable in European letters that quality is the quality of the romantic and the mysterious; and certainly Mr Blackwood presented the English ghost story to his readers in a way that reminded them of the triumphs of the past in this region of literature and which was yet startlingly modern in its methods and in the scientific basis upon which that method reposed. So excellent was the work that some were tempted to see in it the disguise of an older and better known hand. The present writer has heard it suggested (he discarded the suggestion) that Ambrose Bierce, the master of Bret Harte and of all the Californians, was the true author of the work. Indeed, *The Empty House* was so widely and justly discussed that the mere discussion was a true compliment to its powers.

Mr Blackwood has followed that book up by his volume called *John Silence*. It must first be described in what way *John Silence* differs from *The Empty House*.

John Silence is a collection of stories dealing with the supernatural. *The Empty House* was a considerable series of short stories, quite a number of them. In *John Silence* the most important stories are lengthy; no story of this description appears in *The Empty House*. In *The Empty House*, therefore, Mr Blackwood was attempting the easier task; the task easier to anyone who desires to be poignant, and especially to be poignant in the sphere of awe. In *John Silence* there is more of the underlying philosophy which has produced this marvellous talent; for, when one says that Mr Blackwood's work approaches genius the phrase is used in no light connection, and when one says that genius connotes conviction one is asserting something which the breakdown of modern dilettante writing amply proves. There is no doubt that the writer of these arresting and seizing fictions most profoundly believes the dogmas upon which they repose; in all there is the supposition (universal before the advent of Christian philosophy) that Evil can capture the soul of a man whether that soul be deserving or undeserving, and in all there is the presupposition that (in the words of St Thomas) 'All things save God have extension,' that spiritual essences can take on, or rather must take on, corporeal form.

What has hitherto been said of this very remarkable book tells the reader little of its intimate character or of its subjects. Its subjects are a case of Possession, a case of Transmutation into another and more evil World, a case of Devil Worship, a case of an old Fire-Curse that went down the ages from Egypt and ended in an English country house, and a case of Lycanthropy. Through all of these runs the personality of a man who has given ample means and leisure to the study of occult things and who has graduated in medicine for the purpose of healing psychic disorders. But this personality, which is that of John Silence, connects rather than dominates the book; what dominates the book is its method. And that method consists in presenting human life (and animal life too, for that matter) as being a close part of one whole, and but a small part of that whole, in which vast Intelligences and vaster Wills stand towards the boundary and control everything within. It is the scheme of the Mystic, but of the Mystic absolute. It is not a mysticism in which the dual solution of Right and Wrong is afforded: it is a sort of Monist Mysticism in which, while Evil and Good are recognized, each is regarded as but one out of two poles attaching to a common substance.

All this would mean very little but for the art in which all of it is involved. Mr Blackwood's writing is of that kind which takes the reader precisely as music takes the listener. It creates a different mood. A man in the middle of one of these stories does not leave it.

If he is interrupted he takes it up again where he put it down. It dominates his thought while he is concerned with it; it remains in his mind after he has completed it. In a word, the whole work is a work of successful literary achievement in the most difficult of literary provinces. It is, as its writer must by this time know, a considerable and lasting addition to the literature of our time and let it be remembered that, tedious and paltry as the literature of our time may be, excellent writing stands in exactly the same place whether it appear among a few, and an elect few, under conditions of high taste, or in a time like ours, when everyone writes, and when most of the best of those who write are less than the worst of other and more worthy generations.

Note

Article attributed to Hilaire Belloc. First published in 1908, and reprinted in Stephen Jones and Kim Newman (eds), *Horror: 100 Best Books* (London: Hodder and Stoughton, [1988] 1992).

M. R. JAMES

from the Preface to *The Collected Ghost Stories*

In accordance with a fashion which has recently become common, I am issuing my four volumes of ghost stories under one cover, and appending to them some matter of the same kind.

I am told they have given pleasure of a certain sort to my readers: if so, my whole object in writing them has been attained, and there does not seem to be much reason for prefacing them by a disquisition upon how I came to write them. Still, a preface is demanded by my publishers, and it may as well be devoted to answering questions which I have been asked.

First, whether the stories are based on my own experience? To this the answer is No: except in one case, specified in the text, where a dream furnished a suggestion. Or again, whether they are versions of other people's experiences? No. Or suggested by books? This is more difficult to answer concisely. Other people have written of dreadful spiders – for instance, Erckmann-Chatrian in an admirable story called *L'Araignée Crabe* – and of pictures which came alive: the State Trials give the language of Judge Jeffreys and the courts at the end of the seventeenth century: and so on. Places have been more prolific in suggestion: if anyone is curious about my local settings, let it be recorded that St Bertrand de Comminges and Viborg are real places: that in *Oh, Whistle, and I'll Come to You*, I had Felixstowe in mind; in *A School Story*, Temple Grove, East Sheen; in *The Tractate Middoth*, Cambridge University Library; in *Martin's Close*, Sampford Courtenay in Devon; that the cathedrals of Barchester and Southminster were blends of Canterbury, Salisbury, and Hereford; that Herefordshire was the imagined scene of *A View from a Hill*, and Seaburgh in *A Warning to the Curious* is Aldeburgh in Suffolk.

I am not conscious of other obligations to literature or local legend, written or oral, except in so far as I have tried to make my ghosts act in ways not inconsistent with the rules of folklore. As for the fragments of ostensible erudition which are scattered about my pages, hardly anything in them is not pure invention; there never was, naturally, any such book as that which I quote in *The Treasure of Abbot Thomas*.

Other questioners ask if I have any theories as to the writing of ghost stories. None that are worthy of the name or need to be repeated here: some thoughts on the subject are in a preface to *Ghosts and Marvels* [*The World's Classics*, Oxford, 1924]. There is no receipt for success in this form of fiction more than in any other. The public, as Dr Johnson said, are the ultimate judges: if they are pleased, it is well; if not, it is no use to tell them why they ought to have been pleased.

Supplementary questions are: Do I believe in ghosts? To which I answer that I am prepared to consider evidence and accept it if it satisfies me. And lastly, Am I going to write any more ghost stories? To which I fear I must answer, Probably not.

Note

First published in 1931 by Edward Arnold.

H. P. LOVECRAFT

Extract from 'Supernatural Horror in Literature'

The oldest and strongest emotion of mankind is fear, and the oldest and strongest kind of fear is fear of the unknown. These facts few psychologists will dispute, and their admitted truth must establish for all time the genuineness and dignity of the weirdly horrible tale as a literary form. Against it are discharged all the shafts of a materialistic sophistication which clings to frequently felt emotions and external events, and of a naively insipid idealism which deprecates the aesthetic motive and calls for a didactic literature to 'uplift' the reader toward a suitable degree of smirking optimism. But in spite of all this opposition the weird tale has survived, developed, and attained remarkable heights of perfection; founded as it is on a profound and elementary principle whose appeal, if not always universal, must necessarily be poignant and permanent to minds of the requisite sensitiveness.

The appeal of the spectrally macabre is generally narrow because it demands from the reader a certain degree of imagination and a capacity for detachment from everyday life. Relatively few are free enough from the spell of the daily routine to respond to rappings from outside, and tales of ordinary feelings and events, or of common sentimental distortions of such feelings and events, will always take first place in the taste of the majority; rightly, perhaps, since of course these ordinary matters make up the greater part of human experience. But the sensitive are always with us, and sometimes a curious streak of fancy invades an obscure corner of the very hardest head; so that no amount of rationalisation, reform, or Freudian analysis can quite annul the thrill of the chimney-corner whisper or the lonely wood. There is here involved a psychological pattern or tradition as real and as deeply grounded in mental experience as any other pattern or tradition of mankind; coeval with the religions feeling and closely related to many aspects of it, and too much a part of our innermost biological heritage to lose keen potency over a very important, though not numerically great, minority of our species.

Man's first instincts and emotions formed his response to the environment in which he found himself. Definite feelings based on pleasure and pain grew up around the phenomena whose causes and effects he understood, whilst around those which he did not understand – and the universe teemed with them in the early days – were naturally woven such personifications, marvellous interpretations, and sensations of awe and fear as would be hit upon by a race having few and simple ideas and limited experience. The unknown, being likewise the unpredictable, became for our primitive forefathers a terrible and omnipotent source of boons and calamities visited upon mankind for cryptic and wholly extra-terrestrial reasons, and thus clearly belonging to spheres of existence whereof we know nothing and wherein we have no part. The phenomenon of dreaming likewise helped to build up the notion of an unreal or spiritual world; and in general, all the conditions of savage dawn-life so strongly conduced toward a feeling of the supernatural, that we need not wonder at the thoroughness with which man's very hereditary essence has become saturated with religion and superstition. That saturation must, as a matter of plain scientific fact, be regarded as virtually permanent so far as the subconscious mind and inner instincts are concerned; for though the area of the unknown has been steadily contracting for thousands of years, an infinite reservoir of mystery still engulfs most of the outer cosmos, whilst a vast residuum of powerful inherited associations clings round all the objects and processes that were once mysterious; however well they may now be explained. And more than this, there is an actual physiological fixation of the old instincts in our nervous tissue, which would make them obscurely operative even were the conscious mind to be purged of all sources of wonder.

Because we remember pain and the menace of death more vividly than pleasure, and because our feelings toward the beneficent aspects of the unknown have from the first been captured and formalised by conventional religious rituals, it has fallen to the lot of the darker and more maleficent side of cosmic mystery to figure chiefly in our popular supernatural folklore. This tendency, too, is naturally enhanced by the fact that uncertainty and danger are always closely allied; thus making any kind of an unknown world a world of peril and evil possibilities. When to this sense of fear and evil the inevitable fascination of wonder and curiosity is superadded, there is born a composite body of keen emotion and imaginative provocation whose vitality must of necessity endure as long as the human race itself. Children will always be afraid of the dark, and men with minds sensitive to hereditary impulse will always tremble at the thought of the hidden and fathomless worlds of strange life which may pulsate in the gulfs beyond the stars, or press hideously upon our own globe in unholy dimensions which only the dead and the moonstruck can glimpse.

With this foundation, no one need wonder at the existence of a literature of cosmic fear. It has always existed, and always will exist; and no better evidence of its tenacious vigour can be cited than the impulse which now and then drives writers of totally opposite leanings to try their hands at it in isolated tales, as if to discharge from their minds certain phantasmal shapes which would otherwise haunt them. Thus Dickens wrote several eerie narratives; Browning, the hideous poem *Childe Roland*; Henry James, *The Turn of the Screw*; Dr Holmes, the subtle novel *Elsie Venner*; F. Marion Crawford, *The Upper Berth* and a number of other examples; Mrs Charlotte Perkins Gilman, social worker, *The Yellow Wall Paper*; whilst the humorist W. W. Jacobs produced that able melodramatic bit called *The Monkey's Paw*.

This type of fear-literature must not be confounded with a type externally similar but psychologically widely different; the literature of mere physical fear and the mundanely gruesome. Such writing, to be sure, has its place, as has the conventional or even whimsical or humorous ghost story where formalism or the author's knowing wink removes the true sense of the morbidly unnatural; but these things are not the literature of cosmic fear in its purest sense. The true weird tale has something more than secret murder, bloody bones, or a sheeted form clanking chains according to rule. A certain atmosphere of breathless and unexplainable dread of outer, unknown forces must be present; and there must be a hint, expressed with a seriousness and portentousness becoming its subject, of that most terrible conception of the human brain – a malign and particular suspension or defeat of those fixed laws of Nature which are our only safeguard against the assaults of chaos and the daemons of unplumbed space.

Naturally we cannot expect all weird tales to conform absolutely to any theoretical model. Creative minds are uneven, and the best of fabrics have their dull spots. Moreover, much of the choicest weird work is unconscious; appearing in memorable fragments scattered through material whose massed effect may be of a very different cast. Atmosphere is the all-important thing, for the final criterion of authenticity is not the dovetailing of a plot but the creation of a given sensation. We may say, as a general thing, that a weird story whose intent is to teach or produce a social effect, or one in which the horrors are finally explained away by natural means, is not a genuine tale of cosmic fear; but it remains a fact that such narratives often possess, in isolated sections, atmospheric touches which fulfil every condition of true supernatural horror-literature. Therefore we must judge a weird tale not by the author's intent, or by the mere mechanics of the plot; but by the emotional level which it attains at its least mundane point. If the proper sensations are excited, such a 'high spot' must be admitted on its own merits as weird literature, no matter how prosaically it is later dragged down. The one test of the really weird is simply this – whether or not there be excited in the reader a profound sense of dread, and of contact with unknown spheres and powers; a subtle attitude of awed listening, as if for the beating of black wings or the scratching of outside shapes and entities on the known universe's utmost rim. And of course, the more completely and unifiedly a story conveys this atmosphere, the better it is as a work of art in the given medium.

Note

This extract is from 'Supernatural Horror in Literature' in H. P. Lovecraft, *Dagon and other Macabre Tales* (London: Victor Gollancz, 1967).

MONTAGUE SUMMERS

Extract from *The Vampire in Literature*

A consideration of the Vampire theme in literature must of necessity be somewhat eclectic, if not even arbitrary in the selection of works which it reviews and with which it sets out to deal. Any exhaustive inquiry is well-nigh impossible, and this not so much, perhaps, on account of the wealth of the material, although indeed there is a far vaster field than might generally be supposed, as owing to the very vague definition and indeterminate interpretation one is able to give to vampirism from a purely literary point of view. It is the craft of an artist in the telling of ghost-stories to see that his colours should not be too vivid and too clear, and no mean skill is required to suggest without explanation, to mass the shadows without derangement, to be occult yet not to be obscure. Accordingly it would be a matter of extreme difficulty to differentiate the malignant and death-dealing spectre or it may be even corpse who returns to wreak his foul revenge from the Vampire, – using this latter word in its widest sense, as one must employ it when speaking of literature, a caution which here given as regards this Chapter will serve once for all. In such a story, for example, as Dr M. R. James' *Count Magnus* is the horrible revenant a ghost or a vampire? The writer has left the point ambiguous. It is of the very essence of his happy invention that he should do so, and the deftly veiled incertitude adds to the loathly terror of the thing.

. . .

This story may, I think, certainly be considered as Vampire lore, and although it must, of course, be perfectly familiar to all who delight in tales of the supernatural I have related it at some little length here, partly because it is told so excellently well, and partly because it so admirably fulfils and exemplifies the qualities that this kind of literature should possess. It is brief and succinct, although there are many details, but every touch tells. No ghost story should be of any length. The horror and the awe evaporate with prolixity. The ghost is malevolent and odious. In fiction a helpful apparition is a notable weakness, and the whole narrative becomes flabby to a degree. The authentic note of horror is struck in the eerie suggestion which, as we have noticed, is of intent left ill-defined. Nothing could be more crude than an explanation, and it is this banality that often ruins a story which otherwise might be of the very first order.

. . .

Since some point must be chosen at which to consider vampirism in literature we may most fairly recall to mind the many academic and philosophical treatises upon the Vampire which were rehearsed and discussed in German Universities during the earlier part of the eighteenth century, and these startling themes soon began to attract the attention of poets.

. . .

In the Gothic romance we have horror heaped upon horror's head; mouldering abbeys, haunted castles, banditti, illuminati, sorcerers, conspirators, murderous monks and phantom friars, apparitions without number until the despairing reviewers cried aloud: 'Surely the *misses* themselves must be tired of so many stories of ghosts and murders.' We have such titles as the famous *Horrid Mysteries*; *The Midnight Groan*; *The Abbot of Montserrat, or, The Pool of Blood*; *The Demon of Venice*; *The Convent Spectre*; *The Hag of the Mountains*; and a hundred such lurid nomenclatures, but until we come to Polidori's novel [*The Vampyre*], nowhere, so far as I am aware, do we meet with the Vampire in the realm of Gothic fancy. So vast, however, is this fascinating library and so difficult to procure are these novels of a century and a quarter ago that I hesitate sweepingly to assert that this theme was entirely unexploited. There may be some romance which I have not had the good fortune to find where a hideous vampire swoops down upon his victims, but if such be the case I am at least prepared to say that the Vampire was not generally known to Gothic lore, and had his presence made itself felt in the sombre chapters of one votary of this school I think he would have re-appeared on many occasions, for the writers were as accustomed to convey from one another with an easy assurance, as they were wont deftly to plunder the foreign mines. Inevitably one of the band, T. J. Horseley Curties, Francis Lathom, William Herbert, Edward Montague, Mrs Roche, Eliza Parsons, Miss M. Hamilton, Mrs Helme, Mrs Meeke, Isabella Kelley, and many another beside insatiably agog for horrid phantasmagoria, would have utilized the Vampire in some funereal episode.

. . .

The first separate edition of *The Vampyre* appeared in 1819, and was published by Sherwood. The first issue of this, which is now very rare, contains a certain amount of preliminary matter concerning the Shelleys, Byron and Godwin. This was omitted in later issues, and accordingly one often finds that copies of *The Vampyre* are described as First Edition, which is strictly quite correct, although they are the Second Issue, and naturally of far less value in a bibliographer's eyes. A large number of reprints increased with amazing rapidity and in the same year the novel was translated into French by Henri Faber, *Le Vampire, nouvelle traduite de l'anglais de Lord Byron*, Paris, 1819. In February 1820, there followed under the aegis of Charles Nodier a very obvious imitation, or rather continuation by Cyprien Bérard, *Lord Ruthwen, ou les Vampires*. 'Roman de C. B. Publié par l'auteur de *Jean Sbogar* et de *Thérèse Aubert*. Paris, 1820.' In 1825, a new translation of Polidori's story was given by Eusèbe de Salles. Nor was Germany behind hand, for *The Vampyre* was first translated in

1819: *Der Vampyr. Eine Erzahlung aus dem Englischen des Lord Byron. Nebst einer Schilderung seines Aufenthaltes in Mytilene*, Leipzig, 1819. In the following year there appeared at Frankfort a version by J. V. Adrian of Byron's poems and prose, wherein was included *Der Blutsuger*. In a collection of Byron's work the first volume of which was published at Zwickau in 1821, *The Vampyre* again found a place in volume V (1821), translated by Christian Karl Meifsner as *Der Vampyr*. The tale has also been included in various other continental collections and translations of Byron's work even until a recent date.

. . .

As might have been expected it was not long before the Vampire appeared upon the stage, and the first play of this kind would seem to be the famous melodrama by Charles Nodier (with Achille Jouffroy and Carmouche) which, with music by Alexandre Piccini and scenery by Ciceri, was produced in Paris on 13 June 1820.

. . .

Immediately upon the furore created by Nodier's *Le Vampire* at the Porte-Saint-Martin in 1819 vampire plays of every kind from the most luridly sensational to the most farcically ridiculous pressed on to the boards. A contemporary critic cries: 'There is not a theatre in Paris without its Vampire! At the Porte-Saint-Martin we have *le Vampire*; at the Vaudeville *Le Vampire* again; at the Variétés *les trois Vampires ou le clair de la lune*.'

Jean Larat further mentions a play by Paul Féval, *Le fils Vampire*. The version by John Wilson Ross of *The Loves of Paris*, a romance, published by G. Vickers, 3, Catherine Street, Strand, 1846, is said to be 'Translated from the French of Paul Féval, author of "The Vampire", "The Loves of the Palais-Royal", "The Receipt at Midnight", "Stella", "The Son of the Devil", etc., etc.', but it does not appear whether 'The Vampire' mentioned here is a play or a romance. Probably it is the latter but no such translation is known.

. . .

Les Trois Vampires, ou le clair de la lune, which was being played at the Variétés, is a thoroughly amusing farce in one act by Brazier, Gabriel, and Armand.

. . .

Another farce, *Encore un Vampire*, which when produced in 1820 at Paris, met with considerable success, was published as by Emile B. L., and yet another vampire burlesque was contributed by A. Rousseau. *Les Etrennes d'un Vampire* at a minor theatre was billed as from a manuscript 'trouvé au cimitière de Père-Lachaise'.

More amusing is the work of Désaugiers who, in August 1820, gave *Cadet Buteux, vampire, avec relation véridique du prologue et des trois actes de cet épouvantable mélodrame écrit sous la dictée de ce passeaux du Gros Caillou, par son secrétaire, Désaugiers*. When published by Rosa, 1820, this libretto bore the motto: '*Vivent les morts!*'

. . .

There was even a *Polichinel Vampire*, which when performed at the Circus Maurice in 1822 attracted all who had a mind for a hearty laugh, and a contemporary visitor to Paris merrily wrote that 'Polichinel is the very jolliest fellow in the world.'

A comic operetta in one act, *Le Vampire* by Martin Joseph Mengals, which was produced at Ghent, 1 March 1826, deserves no more than passing mention.

James Robinson Planché speedily adapted Nodier's *Le Vampire* as *The Vampire, or, The Bride of the Isles*, and his version with music by Joseph Binns Hart was brought out at the English Opera House, 9 August 1820.

. . .

On 28 March 1828, at Leipzig, was produced an opera, 'Grosse romantische Oper', *Der Vampyr*, founded on the original French melodrama, the scene being changed from Scotland to Hungary. The libretto is by Wilhelm August Wohlbrück and the music by his yet more famous brother-in-law Heinrich August Marschner. *Der Vampyr* was an enormous success.

. . .

In England Dion Boucicault's *The Vampire*, in three acts, was produced at the Princess's Theatre, London, 19 June 1852.

. . .

In Germany sensational fiction was long largely influenced by Polidori, and we have such romances as Zschokke's *Der tote Gast*, Spindler's *Der Vampyr und seine Braut*, Theodor Hildebrand's

Der Vampyr, oder die Totenbraut. Edwin Bauer's *roman à clef* the clever *Der Baron Vampyr*, which was published at Leipzig in 1846, hardly concerns as here, whilst Ewald August König's sensational *Ein moderner Vampyr*, which appeared in 1883, or Franz Hirsch's *Moderne Vampyr*, 1873, productions which only use in their titles the word 'Vampire' to attract, – one might say, to ensnare attention, are in this connexion no more deserving of consideration than mere chap-books and pedlar's penny-ware such as Fiorelli's *Der Vampyr*, and Dr Seltzam's pornographic *Die Vampyre der Residenz*.

Undoubtedly the vampire tradition has never been treated with such consummate skill as by Théophile Gautier in his exquisite prose poem *La Morte Amoureuse*, which first appeared in the *Chronique de Paris* on 23 and 26 June 1836, when the young author was not quite twenty-five. Although the theme is not original yet perhaps nowhere beside has it been so ingeniously moulded with such delicacy of style, with such rich and vivid colouring, with such emotion and such repression.

, , ,

There are in English not a few stories which deal with the vampire tradition, and many of these are well imagined and cleverly contrived; the morbid horror of the thing has often been conveyed with considerable power, but yet it will, I think, be universally allowed that no author has written pages comparable to this story of Gautier. It is hardly to be disputed that the best of the English vampire stories is Sheridan Le Fanu's *Carmilla*, which the authorities upon the bibliography of this author have not traced further back than its appearance in the collection entitled *In A Glass Darkly*, 1872. *Carmilla*, which is a story of some length, containing sixteen chapters, is exceedingly well told and it certainly exhibits that note of haunting dread which is peculiar to Le Fanu's work. The castle in Styria and the family who inhabit it are excellently done, nor will the arrival of Carmilla and the mysterious coach wherein sat 'a hideous black woman, with a sort of coloured turban on her head, who was gazing all the time from the carriage window, nodding and grinning derisively towards the ladies, with gleaming eyes and large white eyeballs, and her teeth set as if in fury', easily be forgotten.

It must suffice to mention very briefly but a few short stories in English where the vampire element is present. E. F. Benson has evoked real horror in his *The Room in the Tower* and the horrible creature tangled in her rotting shroud all foul with mould and damp who returns from her accursed grave is loathly to the last degree.

The Flowering of the Strange Orchid, by H. G. Wells, introduces a botanical vampire. An orchid collector is found dead in a jungle in the Andaman Islands, with a strange bulb lying near him. This is brought to England and carefully tended by a botanist until it comes to flower. But when at last the blossoms burst open great tendrils suddenly reach out to grasp the man, sucking his blood with hideous gusto. The unfortunate wretch has to be violently torn away from the plant, which drips with blood, scarce in time to save his life.

This idea closely resembles Fred M. White's story, *The Purple Terror*, which appeared in the *Strand Magazine*, September 1899, Vol. xviii, No. 105. Here Lieutenant Will Scarlett, an American officer and a number of his men have to make their way across a certain tract of Cuban Territory. Spending the night in a country posada they are attracted by a pretty dancing girl who is wearing twined round her shoulders a garland of purple orchids larger than any known variety. The blossoms, which have a blood-red centre, exhale a strange exotic perfume. Scarlett is fired with the enthusiasm of giving a new orchid to the horticultural world, and on the following morning a native, named Tito, undertakes to guide him to the spot. He learns that the natives call them 'the devil's poppies' and that the flowers grow in the high trees where their blossoms cling to long green tendrils. As night falls the little company arrives at a plateau ringed by tall trees whose branches are crowned with great wreaths of the purple flower nestling amid coils of long green ropery. To their alarm they note that the ground is covered with bleaching bones, the skeletons of men, animals, and birds alike. Yet perforce they must camp there rather than risk the miasma of the lower valley. Scarlett keeps watch. In the darkness there is a rustling round and suddenly a long green tendril furnished at the end with a sucker armed with sharp spines like teeth descends and snatches one of the men from the ground. As it is about to withdraw, Scarlett with inconceivable swiftness slashes it through with his knife. But the man's clothing has even in that moment been cut through by the razor spines and his body is marked by a number of punctures where his blood is oozing in great drops. Immediately half-a-dozen and more lithe living cords with fanged mouths fall groping for their prey. The men are hurriedly awakened and with difficulty they extricate themselves by sending their whingers ripping and tearing in every direction. It appears that the vampire poppies at night send down these tendrils to gather moisture. Anything which the fearful suckers can catch they drain dry, be it man or beast or bird. Lieutenant Scarlett and his men have been deliberately led into this trap by Tito, who is madly jealous of their compliments to Zara, the dancing-girl. They hold him prisoner and threaten him with condign punishment at headquarters.

Algernon Blackwood brings together two types of vampires in his story *The Transfer*. One is a human being, the psychic sponge, who absorbs and seems to live upon the vitality of others. He is thus described by the governess: 'I watched his hard, bleak face; I noticed how thin he was, and the curious oily brightness of his steady eyes. And everything he said or did announced what I may dare to call the *suction* of his presence.' There is also a yet more horrible monster, if one may term it so, the Forbidden Corner, an arid barren spot in the midst of the rose garden, naked and bald amid luxuriant growth. A child who knows its evil secret says: 'It's bad. It's hungry. It's drying because it can't get the food it wants. But I know what would make it feel right.' When the human vampire ventures near this spot it exerts its secret strength and draws him to itself. He falls into the middle of the patch and it drinks his energy. He lives on, but he seems to be nothing more than a physical husk or shell without vitality. As for the Forbidden Corner 'it lay untouched, full of great, luscious, driving weeds and creepers, very strong, full fed and bursting thick with life'.

Sir Arthur Conan Doyle, in his little story *The Parasite*, has depicted a human vampire or psychic sponge in the person of Miss Penelosa, who is described as being a small frail creature, 'with a pale peaky face, an insignificant presence and retiring manner'. Nevertheless she is able to obsess Professor Gilroy who says: 'She has a parasite soul, yes, she is a parasite; a monster parasite. She creeps into my form as the hermit crab creeps into the whelk's shell.' To his horror he realizes that under her influence his will becomes weaker and weaker and he is bound to seek her presence. He resists for a while, but the force becomes so overmastering that he is compelled to yield, loathing himself as he does so. When he visits her, with a terrific effort he breaks the spell and denounces her unhallowed fascination in burning words. However, his victory is short indeed. She persecutes him most bitterly, and when he unburdens his troubles to his college professor the only result is a prescription of chloral and bromide, which promptly goes into the gutter. With devilish craft the vampire destroys his reputation as a scholar, and brings about ill-natured gossip and comment. She is able to confuse his brain during his lectures, so that he talks unintelligible nonsense and his classes become the laughing-stock of the university, until at length the authorities are obliged to suspend him from his position. Almost in despair he cries: 'And the most dreadful part of it all is my loneliness. Here I sit in a common-place English bow-window looking out upon a common-place English street, with its garish buses and its lounging policemen, and behind me there hangs a shadow which is out of all keeping with the age and place. In the home of knowledge I am weighed down and tortured by a power of which science knows nothing. No magistrate would listen to me. No paper would discuss my case. No doctor would believe my symptoms. My own most intimate friends would only look upon it as a sign of brain derangement. I am out of all touch with my kind.'

The unfortunate victim is driven even deeper still by his unhallowed influence, which causes him to rob a bank, violently assault a friend, and finally to come within an ace of mutilating the features of his betrothed. At length the persecution ceases with the sudden death of the vampire, Miss Penelosa.

The True Story of a Vampire is a pathetic little story, very exquisitely told, in *Studies of Death*, by Stanislaus Eric, Count Stenbock, who wrote some verses of extraordinary charm in *Love, Sleep, and Dreams*; *Myrtle, Rue, and Cypress*; *The Shadow of Death*; and who at least once in *The Other Side* told a macabre legend with most powerful and haunting effect. A mysterious Count Vardaleh visits the remote styrian castle of old Baron Wronski, and before long attains an occult influence over the boy heir, Gabriel. The lad wastes away, and Count Vardaleh is heard to murmur: 'My darling, I fain would spare thee; but thy life is my life, and I must live, I who would rather die. Will God not have *any* mercy on me? Oh, oh! life; oh, the torture of life! . . . O Gabriel, my beloved! My life, yes, *life* – oh, my life? I am sure this is but a little I demand of thee. Surely the superabundance of life can spare a little to one who is already dead.' As the boy lies wan and ill, the Count enters the room and presses a long feverish kiss upon his lips. Vardaleh rushes forth, and can never be traced again. Gabriel has expired in the agony of that embrace.

In a novel, *The Vampire*, by Reginald Hodder, a woman who is the leader of an occult society is forced to exercise her powers as a vampire to prevent the ebbing of her vitality. Here her ravages are pyschic rather than physical, albeit in fact the two so closely commingled that they are not to be separated. A curious feature in the tale is that this woman is represented as putting forth her energies through the medium of a metallic talisman, and various struggles to gain possession of the object form the theme of the story. It falls into the hands of persons who would employ it for evil purposes, when it constitutes a very formidable menace, but at the last after a number of extraordinary happenings it is happily recovered.

The traditional, but yet more horrible vampire is presented to us by F. Marion Crawford in *For the Blood is the Life*. Here a young man, who has been loved by a girl whose affection he was unable to return, is after her death vampirized by her, and when his friends suspect the truth they determine to rescue him. They find him upon her grave, a thin stream of blood trickling from his throat. 'And the flickering light of the lantern played upon another face that looked up from the feast, – upon two deep, dead eyes that saw in spite of death – upon parted lips redder than life itself – upon gleaming teeth on which glistened a rosy drop.' The situation is effectively dealt with according to the good old tradition. A hawthorn stake is driven through the heart of the vampire who emits a quantity of blood and with a despairing shriek dies the last death.

Almost equally vivid in its details must be accounted the tale *Four Wooden Stakes*, by Victor Roman. The ghastly events in the lonely old house with its little grey crypt, some ten miles from the small town of Charing, a place of not more than fifteen hundred souls, are most vividly described. There lived the Holroyds, the grandfather, the father, and three brothers. Whilst in South America the grandfather 'was attacked while asleep by one of those huge bats. Next morning he was so weak he couldn't walk. That awful thing had sucked his life blood away. He arrived here, but was sickly until his death, a few weeks later.' So says Remson Holroyd, who is left the sole survivor of the family, and who has summoned his old college friend to help him solve the secret of the hideous doom which is taking toll one by one. The grandfather was not buried in the usual way; but, as his will directed, his remains were interred in the vault built near the house. Remson Holroyd continues: 'Then my dad began failing and just pined away until he died. What puzzled the doctors was the fact that right up until the end he consumed enough food to sustain three men, yet he was so weak he lacked the strength to drag his legs over the floor. He was buried, or rather interred with grand-dad. The same symptoms were in evidence in the cases of George and Fred. They are both lying in the vault. And now, Jack, I'm going, too, for of late my appetite has increased to alarming proportions, yet I am as weak as a kitten.' The next morning the visitor finds himself so weak that he is hardly able to rise and he feels a slight pain in the neck. 'I rushed to examine it in the mirror. Two tiny dots rimmed with blood – my blood – and on my neck! No longer did I chuckle at Remson's fears, for *it*, the thing, had attacked me as I slept.' The host himself is in a state of utter exhaustion. That night watch is kept by the friend, and as from his concealment he is gazing into Remson's rooms he notices 'a faint reddish glow outside one of the windows. It apparently emanated from nowhere. Hundreds of little specks danced and whirled in the spot of light, and as I watched them fascinated, they seemed to take on the form of a human face. The features were masculine, as was also the arrangement of the hair. Then the mysterious glow disappeared.' After a few moments there appears a vague form of which the watcher is able to distinguish the head, and to his horror he sees that the features are the same as those of a portrait of the grandfather which is hanging in the gallery of the house. 'But oh, the difference in expression! The lips were drawn back in a snarl, disclosing two sets of pearly white teeth, the canines over developed and remarkably sharp. The eyes, an emerald green in colour, stared in a look of consuming hate.' The horror is revealed. The house is infested by a vampire. In the morning the two friends visit the vault. 'As if by mutual understanding, we both turned toward the coffin on our left. It belonged to the grandfather. We unplaced the lid, and there lay the old Holroyd. He appeared to be sleeping; his face was full of colour, and he had none of the stiffness of death. The hair was matted, the moustache untrimmed, and on the beard were matted stains of a dull brownish hue. But it was his eyes that attracted me. They were greenish, and they glowed with an expression of fiendish malevolence such as I had never seen before. The look of baffled rage on the face might well have adorned the features of the devil in hell.' They drive a stake through the living corpse, which shrieks and writhes, whilst the gushing blood drenches coffins and floor spurting out in great jets over the very walls. The head is severed from the body, and 'as the final stroke of the knife cut the connexion a scream issued from the mouth; and the whole corpse fell away into dust, leaving nothing but a wooden stake lying in a bed of bones'. The remaining three bodies are treated in the same way, and thus the thrall of the curse is lifted from the old house, ten miles from the little town of Charing.

. . .

In 1845 there was published at the Columbian Press, Weston-super-mare, a little book entitled *The Last of the Vampires*, by Smyth Upton. The chief, some critics might say the only, merit of this tale is its excessive rarity. The narrative is somewhat curiously divided into Epochs, the first of which takes place in 1769, the second in 1777, the third and last in 1780. Chapter I opens in an English village named Frampton, but in Chapter II 'we find ourselves upon the borders of Bohemia' in the Castle Von Oberfels. Four chapters of no great length and somewhat disconnected in their sequence comprise the First Epoch. A little later we meet with the mysterious Lord de Montfort, and apparently he has just committed a murder, since he is one of the two men who stand in a dreary outhouse adjoining Montfort Abbey. 'Red blood, yet warm, stains their murderous hands, and is seen also in pools upon the floor; the same marks are observable, also, on their clothes.' 'The scene is a fearful one; it is one of those of which the mere recital makes the blood run cold,' and the writer wisely does not attempt the task. In the penultimate chapter of this extraordinary production we are introduced to 'a certain young German, the Baron Von Oberfels,' who weds Mary Learmont, the elder daughter of 'Sir James Learmont, who being a Baronet, was, moreover, a Knight of the Bath and M.P.' Unfortunately the Baron 'was one of that horrible class, the Vampires! He had sold his soul to the evil one, for the enjoyment of perpetual youth; being bound, besides, to what are understood to be the penalties of that wretched and accursed race. Every tenth year a female was sacrificed to his infernal master. Mary Learmont was to be the next victim; may she escape the threatened doom.' But apparently, so far as I can gather, she is not so lucky for we are vaguely told: 'The Baron and his bride departed on his wedding tour. Her father and mother never hear of her more.' A page or two later there is 'a midnight wedding' at the Castle Von Oberfels. Of the bride we are told nothing save that she had a 'fair presence'. 'The Baron Von Oberfels was there, once more arrayed in the garments of a bridegroom.' The ceremony proceeds. The grand organ peals; the heavenly voices of white-robed choristers added greatly to the beauty of the scene. 'But hark! another noise is heard; sulphureous smoke half fills the sacred building; the floor opens for an instant; and mocking shrieks are audible as the spirit of the Last of the Vampires descended into perdition.'

I am bound to acknowledge that after a somewhat careful reading of this curious and most disjointed little piece of seventy-six pages the only impression with which I am met is that Mr Smyth Upton knew nothing whatsoever of what the word vampire connotes. The idea of the victims who are sacrificed for the sake of eternal youth is, of course fairly common and was very effectively utilized by G. W. M. Reynolds in his romance *The Necromancer*, which ran in *Reynolds's Miscellany* from Saturday, 27 December 1851, to Saturday, 31 July 1852. Incidentally it may be remarked as a somewhat curious fact that this prolific novelist never availed himself of the vampire tradition in his melodramatic chapters.

The Vampyre, 'By the Wife of a Medical Man,' 1858, is a violent teetotal tract, of twenty-seven short chapters presented in the guise of fiction. The villain of the piece is 'The Vampyre Inn', and the dipsomaniac hero – if it be allowable to use the term in such a context – is given to ravings such as these: 'They fly – they bite – they suck my blood – I die. That hideous "Vampyre!" Its eyes pierce me thro' – they are red – they are bloodshot. Tear it from my pillow. I dare not lie down. It bites – I die! Give me brandy – brandy – more brandy.'

A Vampire of Souls, by H. M. P., published in 1904, is a book of little value. The hero, George Ventnor, when aged twenty, is killed in a railway accident, and the narrative consists of his after experiences, which are singularly material and crude. There is, perhaps, a good touch here and there, but the thing certainly does not deserve to be rescued from oblivion.

It will have been noticed that beyond the titles these two last works have really little or nothing to do with vampires at all, but we may now consider a romance which may at least be ranked as a very serious rival to – in my opinion it is far ghostlier than – its famous successor *Dracula*. *Varney the Vampire, or, The Feast of Blood*, is undoubtedly the best novel of Thomas Preskett [Peckett] Prest;[1] a prolific writer of the fourth and fifth decades of the nineteenth century. It is true that his productions published by the well-known Edward Lloyd, of 231, Shoreditch, may be classed as simple 'shockers', but none the less he has considerable power in this kind, and he had at any rate the craft of telling his story with skill and address. There is a certain quality in his work, which appeared during the years from 1839 to the earlier fifties, that is entirely lacking in the productions of his fellows. To him have been ascribed, doubtless with some exaggeration, well nigh two hundred titles, but the following list comprises, I believe, his principal romances: *Ela, the Outcast, or, the Gipsy of Rosemary Dell*; *Angelina, or, the Mystery of S. Mark's Abbey*, 'a Tale of Other Days'; *The Death Grasp, or, A Father's Curse*; *Ernnestine De Lacy, or, The Robbers' Foundling*; *Gallant Tom, or, The Perils of a Sailor Ashore and Afloat*, 'an original nautical romance of deep and pathetic interest'; *Sweeney Todd, the Demon Barber of Fleet Street* (the most famous of Prest's novels); *Newgate* (which has some capital episodes); *Emily Fitzormond*; *Mary Clifford*; *The Maniac Father, or, The Victim of Seduction*; *Gertrude of the Rock*; *Rosalie, or, The Vagrant's Daughter*; *The Miller's Maid*; *Jane Brightwell*; *Blanche, or, The Mystery of the Doomed House*; *The Blighted Heart, or, The Priory Ruins*; *Sawney Bean, the Man-eater of Midlothian*; *The Skeleton Clutch, or, The Goblet of Gore*; *The Black Monk, or, The Secret of the Grey Turret*; *The Miller and His Men, or, The Secret Robbers of Bohemia*. To Prest also has been attributed, but I conceive without foundation, *Susan Hoply*, an audacious piracy upon the famous novel by Mrs Crowe, *Susan Hopley*.

Varney the Vampire, or, The Feast of Blood was first published in 1847. It contains no less than 220 chapters and runs to 868 pages. The many incidents succeed each other with such breathless rapidity that it were well-nigh impossible to attempt any conspectus of the whole romance. The very length would make this analysis a work of extreme difficulty, and incidentally we may note the amazing copiousness of Prest,[2] which must ever remain a matter for wonderment. Such a romance, for example, as *Newgate* runs to no less than one hundred and forty-nine chapters comprising 772 pages. *The Maniac Father* has fifty-four chapters, each of considerable length, which total 604 pages, and I have not selected these on account of their exceptional volume.

Varney the Vampire was among the most popular of Prest's productions, and on account of its 'unprecedented success' it was reprinted in 1853 in penny parts. To-day the book is unprocurable and considerable sums have been for many years in vain offered to secure a copy. Indeed, it may be noted that all Prest's work is excessively scarce.

It is hardly an exaggeration to affirm that of recent years there have been few books which have been more popular than Bram Stoker's *Dracula, A tale*, and certainly there is no sensational romance which in modern days has achieved so universal a reputation. Since it was first published in 1897, that is to say one and twenty years ago, it has run into a great number of editions, and the name has veritably become a household word. It will prove interesting to inquire into the immediate causes which have brought this book such wide and enduring fame. It has already been remarked that it is well-nigh impossible for a story which deals with the supernatural or the horrible to be sustained to any great length. Elements which at first are almost unendurable will lose their effect if they are continued, for the reader's mind insensibly becomes inured to fresh emotions of awe and horror, and *Dracula* is by no means briefly told. In the ordinary reprints (Tenth Edition, 1913) it extends to more than four hundred pages, nor does it escape the penalty of its prolixity. The first part, 'Jonathan Harker's Journal', which consists of four chapters, is most admirably done, and could the whole story have been sustained at so high a level we should have had a complete masterpiece. But that were scarcely possible. The description of the journey through Transylvania is interesting to a degree, and even has passages which attain to something like charm. 'All day long we seemed to dawdle through a country which was full of beauty of every kind. Sometimes we saw little towns or castles on the top of steep hills such as we see in old missals; sometimes we ran by rivers and streams which seemed from the wide stony margin on each side of them to be subject to great floods. It takes a lot of water, and running strong, to sweep the outside edge of a river clear.' Very effective is the arrival of the English traveller at the 'vast ruined castle, from whose tall black windows came no ray of light, and whose broken battlements showed a jagged line against the moonlit sky'. Very adroitly are the various incidents managed in their quick succession, those mysterious happenings which at last convince the matter-of-fact commonplace young solicitor of Exeter that he is a helpless prisoner in the power of a relentless and fearful being. The continual contrasts between business conversations, the most ordinary events of the dull listless days, and all the while the mantling of dark shadows in the background and the onrushing of some monstrous doom are in these opening chapters most excellently managed.

So tense a strain could not be preserved, and consequently when we are abruptly transported to Whitby and the rather tedious courtships of Lucy Westenra, who is a lay figure at best, we feel that a good deal of the interest has already begun to evaporate. I would hasten to add that before long it is again picked up, but it is never sustained in the same degree; and good sound sensational fare as we have set before us, fare which I have myself more than once thoroughly enjoyed, yet it is difficult not to feel that one's palate has been a little spoiled by the nonpareil of an antipast. This is not to say that the various complications are not sufficiently thrilling, but because of their very bounty now and again they most palpably fail of effect, and it can hardly escape notice that the author begins to avail himself of those more extravagant details of vampirism which frankly have no place outside the stories told round a winter's hearth. It would have been better had he confined himself to those particulars which are known and accepted, which indeed have been officially certified and definitely proved. But to have limited himself thus would have meant the shortening of his narrative, and here we return to the point which was made above.

If we review *Dracula* from a purely literary point of approach it must be acknowledge that there is much careless writing and many pages could have been compressed and something revised with considerable profit. It is hardly possible to feel any great interest in the characters, they are labels rather than individuals. As I have said, there are passages of graphic beauty, passages of graphic horror, but these again almost entirely occur within the first sixty pages. There are some capital incidents, for example the method by which Lord Godalming and his friend obtain admittance to No. 347 Piccadilly. Nor does this by any means stand alone.

However, when we have – quite fairly, I hope – thus criticized *Dracula*, the fact remains that it is a book of unwonted interest and fascination. Accordingly we are bound to acknowledge that the reason for the immense popularity of this romance, – the reason why, in spite of obvious faults it is read and re-read – lies in the choice of subject and for this the author deserves all praise.

It might not have seemed that *Dracula* would have been a very promising subject for the stage, but nevertheless it was dramatized by Hamilton Deans and produced at the Wimbledon Theatre on 9 March 1925. This version was performed in London at the Little Theatre, 14 February 1927. On the preceding Thursday the *Daily Mirror* published a photograph of the late Mr Bram Stoker accompanied by the following paragraphs. 'Herewith, one of the very few photographs of the late Bram Stoker, who, besides being Sir Henry Irving's manager for years, was an industrious novelist. As I have already said, a dramatic version of his most famous book,

"Dracula," is to be done at the Little on Monday, and the scene of the Grand Guignol plays is appropriate, for the new piece, I hear, is so full of gruesome thrills that, in the provinces women have been carried fainting from the auditorium. Truly we take our pleasures sadly.

'The dramatic adaptation is by Hamilton Deans, whose grandfather, Colonel Deans and the Rev. Abraham Stoker, Bram's father, lived on adjoining estates in County Dublin. Young Bram and Hamilton Deane's mother, then a young girl, were great friends. Stoker had the book "Dracula" in his mind, and the young people used to discuss its possibilities. Strange that it should be young Hamilton Deane who has dramatized the book and brought the play to London.'

. . .

By no stretch could it be called a good play, whilst the presentation, at the best, can hardly be described as more than reasonably adequate. In one or two instances the effects, upon which so much depends and which obviously demanded the most scrupulous care, were so clumsily contrived as to excite an involuntary smile. 'It was only a step from the devilish to the ridiculous on Monday night,' said the *Era*, 16 February 1927. Very remarkable was a lady, dressed in the uniform of a hospital nurse who sat in the vestibule of the theatre, and it was bruited that her services were required by members of the audience who were overcome owing to the horrors of the drama. I can only say that I find this canard impossible to believe, *quodcumque ostendis mihi sic, incredulus odi.*[3] As an advertisement, and it can surely have been nothing else, the attendance of a nurse was in deplorable taste. I am informed that after the first few weeks a kind of epilogue was spoken when all the characters were assembled upon the stage, and it was explained that the audience must not be distressed at what they had seen, that it was comically intended for their entertainment. So gross a lapse of good manners, not to speak of the artistic indecorum, is hardly credible.

Confessedly the play was extremely weak, and yet such is the fascination of this subject that it had an exceptional success, and triumphantly made its way from theatre to theatre. On 25 July 1927, *Dracula* was transferred to the Duke of York's; on 29 August, following to the Prince of Wales; on 10 October to the Garrick; and all the while it was given to thronging houses. It has also toured, and at the present moment is still touring the provincial theatres with the most marked success, the drama being given with more spirit and vigour than originally was the case at the Little, and Wilfrid Fletcher in particular playing the lunatic Renfield with a real touch of wistful pathos and uncanny horror. This is extremely instructive, and it is curious that the vogue of the 'vampire play' in London should be repeated almost exactly after the interval of a century. On 5 November 1927, a new version of *Dracula* by Charles Morrel was presented at the Court Theatre, Warrington.

In America the dramatization of *Dracula* was produced at the Shubert, New Haven, 19 September 1927. This was given at the Fulton, New York, upon the following 5th October. Jonathan Harker was acted by Terence Neil; Abraham Van Helsing by Edward Van Sloan; Renfield by Bernard Jukes; and Count Dracula by Bela Lugosa [misspelt as *Lugoni* in original].

Notes

First published in 1928.
1. Actually J. M. Rymer – Ed.
2. Summers confuses the work of Prest and Rymer.
3. 'Whatever you show me thus, I dislike with disbelief.'

DENNIS WHEATLEY

Author's Note from *The Devil Rides Out*

I desire to state that I, personally, have never assisted at, or participated in, any ceremony connected with Magic – Black or White.

The literature of occultism is so immense that any conscientious writer can obtain from it abundant material for the background of a romance such as this.

In the present case I have spared no pains to secure accuracy of detail from existing accounts when describing magical rites or formulas for protection against evil, and these have been verified in conversation with certain persons, sought out for that purpose who are actual practitioners of the Art.

All the characters and situations in this book are entirely imaginary but, in the inquiry necessary to the writing of it, I found ample evidence that Black Magic is still practised in London, and other cities, at the present day.

Should any of my readers incline to a serious study of the subject, and thus come into contact with a man or woman of Power, I feel that it is only right to urge them, most strongly, to refrain from being drawn into the practice of the Secret Art in any way. My own observations have led me to an absolute conviction that to do so would bring them into dangers of a very real and concrete nature.

Note

First published by Hutchinson (1935).

3 Later Modern Accounts

ROBERT BLOCH

On Horror Writers

I'm neither a philosopher nor a psychiatrist, and I must opt for the easy explanation. On the basis of personal belief and observation, I'd say that those of us who direct our storytelling into darker channels do so because we were perhaps a bit more mindful than most regarding our childhood confusions of identity, our conflicts with unpleasant realities and our traumatic encounters with imaginative terrors. Although there are significant exceptions, it would appear that the majority of writers who deal with the supernatural have repudiated the tenets of organised religion. In so doing they may have lost the fear of hellfire but they've also sacrificed any hope of heaven. What remains is an all-too-vivid fear of pain and death and a final, total, eternal oblivion.

Note

First published in 1986 in Tim Underwood and Chuck Miller (eds), *Kingdom of Fear: The World of Stephen King* (London: Hodder and Stoughton, 1986).

LOS ANGELES SCIENCE FICTION SOCIETY

Symposium on H. P. Lovecraft

Panelists:

> Fritz Leiber
> Robert Bloch
> Sam Russell
> Arthur Jean Cox
> Leland Sapiro

Annotations

> August Derleth

SAPIRO: To start, I'll summarize a couple of Lovecraft's stories on a common theme, which we can call psychic displacement or demoniac displacement. First, *The Colour Out of Space*. In this story, members of a New England family are controlled by a sentient gas liberated from a fallen meteor, and this sentient gas eventually drains their vitality, and causes insanity and death. Then, *The Haunter of the Dark*. In this story, the consciousness of a writer, Robert Bloch, or Robert Blake, if you want to call him that – is forced to merge with that of an alien presence which inhabits an abandoned church. In 'The Whisperer in Darkness,' there is a scholar whose brain is removed from his body and imprisoned in a cylinder. This story is an example of what August Derleth refers to as Lovecraft's mask motif, where the face of an acquaintance or relative serves merely as a mask for the alien personality underneath. Then, of course, there's *The Shadow out of Time*; and let me mention one more, 'The Thing on the Doorstep'. In this story, the detached soul of the murdered Asenath Waite seizes the body of her husband, whose own consciousness, in turn, is translated to her body, which is buried in the cellar.

Psychic displacement, of course, is not original with Lovecraft; It has an old and honorable lineage in the weird tale. But Lovecraft seems to have had a special affinity for this theme, so I might open with the question: Why was he drawn to this particular theme? Mr Bloch, since one of these stories was written about you, you should have some personal knowledge of this.

BLOCH: I think Lovecraft was particularly attracted to this theme because he realized that there is nothing more horrible than to find the unfamiliar when you expect the familiar, Lovecraft was always seeking the ultimate in horror. To personalize it, he thought that the displacement of identity of someone familiar to you would be the most shocking and terrifying possibility. Lovecraft was very analytical: He didn't write without a great deal of premeditation, and I believe that he was inclined to delve to the full in search of elements which would trigger the emotions of fear and revulsion.

LEIBER: I think that in this question of displaced identity – or exchanges of souls, as it would have been called by most writers of that time – we come very close to the deepest sort of metaphysical problem: how our consciousness, how this vivid picture of reality in my mind that seems to extend out into space – and into time, by way of memory – how this picture of reality can exist in the material world, the world we know about through bumps and knocks, the world that has been described by science as the bumps and knocks that a number of people have agreed upon. What consciousness is and how it exists in the world is eternally a puzzle, and I think that Lovecraft tended to go to these ultimate points for basing his stories and tying them down.

And the very fact that he avoided the Christian cosmology made his points even more acute, because he didn't take the easy way out, used by so many writers of ghost stories and supernatural fiction, of setting the story against an all-religious background that provides an easy explanation at the end.

COX: I might remark about what Mr Bloch says. Lovecraft does not use the theme of ego displacement purely as a subject of horror. For instance, in *The Shadow Out of Time* the effect is one of fascination rather than horror. Here he uses the scheme of putting his narrator in the body of a creature of an alien race, and therefore provides a method of giving a picture of this alien society and world.

BLOCH: There is one other possibility: that with Lovecraft, as with me, fascination and horror are synonymous.

LEIBER: In some of his stories, particularly the later stories, the so-called monsters, actually highly intelligent members of other species, become – to me, at least – the sympathetic characters. The Old Ones at *The Mountains of Madness* – who, after having been in suspended animation for millions of years, awake in a howling blizzard [to be] attacked by savage dogs, with one of them being vivisected by a human scientist – the way they face this situation and fight their way out – Lovecraft himself in that story has one of the scientists say, 'By God, whatever they were, they were men!'

So without making the old suggestion that the author feels himself to be the monster, I would suggest that there is the possibility, at least, that Lovecraft's sympathy went out to them. The monsters at the end turn out to be scholars above everything else, who spend their lives doing things like carrying the brains of other scholars around the universe with them in metal canisters in order that these brains could see and talk about and hear the explanations of everything there was in the universe.

SAPIRO: Mr Bloch said that for Lovecraft, fascination and horror were synonymous. I think you almost might say that this is the key to all his writings. Lovecraft was an antiquarian; for example, he liked to date his letters two hundred years back, and expressed preference for living in the 18th century. His antiquarianism was a special instance of his desire to escape from 'the galling tyranny of time, space, and natural laws.'

But, on the other hand, you have his deep *aversion* to such a liberation, his conception of 'the stark, outrageous monstrousness of any departure from nature.' You remember Lewis Padgett's *The Fairy Chessmen*, in which a fellow grasps a doorknob, and the doorknob winks at him. This is the sort of thing, I imagine, that Lovecraft would envisage as uniquely horrible – the perversion of natural laws. It seems to me that Lovecraft's attitude was strictly ambiguous; this desire for escape and at the same time his aversion to it.

LEIBER: Well, this ties in to what we were talking about before. I can't help but feel that the brains in the cylinders in *The Whisperer in Darkness* represent to some extent a scholar's utopia, and yet the brain of the one Earthly scholar, Henry Akeley, that does speak from one of these cylinders speaks in a frightened and horrified way. There *is* a conflict there, and it runs through the story.

SAPIRO: Let me open another topic: [Lovecraft's] actual beliefs, which were in the stories, versus those things which were only literary conventions. In 'The Thing on the Doorstep' he says: 'A soul like hers is half detached, and keeps right on after death as long as the body lasts.' Now, Lovecraft did not believe in a soul and he did not believe in any kind of post-mortem survival, so this is one case where his actual beliefs do not coincide with the beliefs one might infer from the story.

Not only this, he used phrases like, 'if heaven ever wishes to grant me a boon,' or 'if there be a hell,' or 'what it is, only God knows.' Lovecraft called himself 'an atheist of Protestant ancestry'; he believed in neither heaven nor hell nor God. So I'd like to ask: Is it possible to separate in Lovecraft's writings the things that he believed from the things which were merely fictional conventions?

COX: Obviously, some of the phrases he used are purely literary conventions; his repetition of certain phrases, which he's been much blamed for, are primarily, I think, an indication to the reader of the way in which the story is to be taken. That is, the story is not supposed to be taken with a great deal of seriousness. He repeats words like 'eldritch' and 'unhallowed' and 'blasphemous' to tell the reader that the tone of his story is not meant to be serious.

LEIBER: He wrote many of his stories in a vivid first person: generally the narrator was explaining himself or writing a document explaining what had happened to him or making one of those pleas that a certain area not be investigated for fear of what would be discovered. With this sort of first person I don't think we can take the remarks and interjections as belonging to the author. In any case, an atheist scholar or scientist will still use expressions like 'great god' and so on, and 'gad' that runs through *Pickman's Model*. He'll use them as emotional expressions without meaning any belief by them.

In my short correspondence with him one of the first things that came up, I remember, was that I made some rather complimentary remarks about Charles Fort's books, saying something to the effect that these books showed that scientists didn't know everything and that there was lots of information that scientists were deliberately disregarding because they couldn't figure out any good explanation. He came back with a rather hot defense of the scientist: he pointed out that he was a materialist himself and that the scientist had to demand that recorded events be confirmed in the most detailed way, that if a thing be seen, that you describe how an experiment could be set up to produce the same effect again. He assured me that although Fort's books, his collections of newspaper and magazine clippings, were very interesting and great background material for the writer, they weren't to be taken seriously in the way of a refutation of scientific theory. I just cite that as an example of his thoroughgoing scientific approach to life outside of his stories.

SAPIRO: Let me quote Sam Moskowitz: 'Lovecraft was so knowledgeable and interested in the sciences, it became increasingly difficult for him to write a weird tale that was not plausibly and in most cases scientifically explained.' So certainly science influenced him more and more. In view of this I'd like to read a quotation from him which to me has always been rather puzzling:

> Modern science has in the end proved an enemy to art and pleasure; for by revealing to us the whole sordid and prosaic basis of our thoughts, motives, and acts, it has stripped the world of glamour, wonder, and all those illusions of heroism, nobility, and sacrifice which used to sound so impressive when romantically treated.
>
> ('Lord Dunsany and His Work', *Marginalia*

So it seems here that Lovecraft's attitude would be that science was a detriment (*sic*) to fiction.

LEIBER: A detriment to fiction? I understand him to say it's a detriment to art and pleasure simply by taking away illusions, revealing that the universe is a machine, and that the actions that we feel are noble or idealistic are, after all, the actions of a machine that is run by physics and chemistry, I mean physiological chemistry of the human body. Illusions like the idea of indwelling spirits, the sort of thing that would add charm to mythology and the earlier religions, that there were beings, some perhaps frightening and some benign in the objects around us, in sticks and stones and trees – well, science takes this away – and it says that any idealistic impulse is still based on chemical reactions in the nerves, in the glands; and this is a difficult thing to face up to.

BLOCH: I believe that Lovecraft indicated in that statement and in his work that he was a very practical realist. He faced what he thought was his objective view of reality and at the same time realized that in order to write a story he would have to present his own picture of the cosmos in a fashion to produce terror in his audience, and he did so.

I don't think it is always accurate to say that a man's work is necessarily a prefiguration of his own personal attitudes and beliefs. There's a great tendency today to feel that any reader by virtue of having purchased, borrowed, or stolen a book, can use it to indulge in a parlor psychoanalysis of the author. So many people who have discussed Lovecraft think of him as an eccentric who more or less believed in the strange cosmos he created, and this is not the case.

LEIBER: I would second that. In the majority of his stories, especially his later and longer stories involving what has come to be called the Cthulhu Mythos, he invented an alternate world superficially like our world but different in that there was evidence, available to certain scholars, that there were other forces, other beings, operating in the world by various secret methods, that this proved that witchcraft had a real material background, and so on. I don't think that any one but a seriously realistic writer would have made such a point of inventing this alternate (*sic*) world.

RUSSELL: Must the realistic writer always describe the physical world around him? Isn't a fantastic writer – a science-fiction writer or any writer of fantasy – trying to be as realistic as possible in trying to create by his scribblings in the minds of his readers a vision of reality that will be as real to them while they're reading his scribblings as their world will be when they open their eyes to what is beyond that page?

SAPIRO: Mr Bloch has remarked on the attempts of critics to give a parlor psychoanalysis of Lovecraft, and this leads into another topic: Lovecraft's obsession with heredity and racial degeneracy. In *The Lurking Fear* the inhabitants are a 'degenerate squatter population'; then *The Call of Cthulhu* where the prisoners conducting these secret rites 'all proved to be men of a very low, mixed-blooded, and mentally aberrant type.' In *The Dunwich Horror* the natives are 'repellently decadent, having gone far along that path of retrogression so common in many New

England backwaters,' and then, of course, you have that famous 'Innsmouth look,' which is the most well-known manifestation.

In his article 'Shadows over Lovecraft' [*Fantasy Commentator*, II (1948), pp. 237–46] Dr Keller says: 'Heredity is an important factor in many Lovecraft stories, and is always of a degenerative type. . . . In such descriptions Lovecraft gives many excellent case histories . . . duplicated in actual life . . . studies of patients bearing the stigma of hereditary syphilis.' Dr Keller points out the significance of the demise of Lovecraft's father being attributed to an advanced stage of paresis, Keller's thesis being that this obsession with his own heredity from his father was more or less evident in all of Lovecraft's stories. He says: 'There was a constant repetition of this theme song – the terror of heredity, the mental and physical degeneration . . . the ultimate, unavoidable end. Lovecraft not only wrote this song again and again but he lived it, under a shadow from which he could not escape.'[1]

BLOCH: I would say that Lovecraft again was investigating the sources of fear. Some of these, of course, a writer will find within himself, and he will attempt to prefigure them and see whether or not these are common sources. And I think fear of decay – physical decay and decadence ascribable to hereditary traits – is a very common one. Undoubtedly it was brought forcibly to his attention by the case of his own father, but I don't believe it was by any means an obsession. I think he merely used a very common theme. It's a theme which you'll find in the writings of many men whose fathers were not victims of paresis. *That*, I think, is the point: It is so easy to take almost any statement of a writer and find some personal problem which it may exemplify, without realizing that the same problem is basic and endemic to the entire population.

COX: I'm afraid that I will probably expose myself as a parlor psychoanalyst. It seems to me that something along the line of Dr Keller's article must be true. Dr Kenneth Sterling had a letter in the *Fantasy Commentator* [III (1952), 153–4] some time after the Keller article in which he pointed out various errors which Dr Keller had made. He said that Keller's ideas of syphilis and so forth were taken over from the 19th century, that he was not up on modern research and study. However, the point, of course, is not what the actual mechanics of the transmission of syphilis is, but simply what Lovecraft believed. It seems to me that his stories express this theme so predominantly that it must have had some personal relevance to him.

LEIBER: It had a relevance, yes, but the theme – the theme of decay – is the theme of death, and it is universal. Although Lovecraft used that particular theme often – the theme of a degenerate population, in *The Shadow over Innsmouth*, *The Lurking Fear*, *He*, and to a lesser extent, in *The Dunwich Horror* – I don't feel that Lovecraft was obsessed in the sense that his judgment as a realist and as a creative artist was impaired.

After all, we could make the same statement about Arthur Machen. Machen wrote *The Novel of the Black Seal* about degenerate Pictish cave-dwelling beings in the Welsh hills, *The Great God Pan* about a woman who was the child of Pan and a mad mother, and who brought to the people she came in contact with an influence that caused them to reverse their evolution. In *The Novel of the White Powder* a powder is developed that is the basis of the wine of the Sabbat; and this does the same thing to the people who drink it: it degenerates them in a matter of weeks; they literally go back through various savage stages to the primal ooze. Now I don't recall hearing about any particular influences of a parallel sort in Machen's family life.

RUSSELL: We might have if fantasy fiction had been as important in his time as it is in ours, but anyway I agree with everything you said. This does not, however, dispose of the question of whether Lovecraft was a totally conscious artist in everything he wrote. Now, I think he was very largely a conscious artist, as Mr Bloch said, but I think that in his choice of subjects he was not. This is a question we really ought to take up, but I don't know if we can because there isn't enough evidence.

It doesn't seem to me that Lovecraft would be the sort of person who would be terribly influenced by the appearance on the stands of a given type of magazine. He made his living by revising other people's stuff. Am I right, Bob?

BLOCH: To a great degree. Also, Lovecraft had a very low opinion of his work. When Farnsworth Wright rejected a story he would generally circulate it throughout the Lovecraft circle and say: What's wrong with it? – what can I do to improve it? He was modest to the point of insecurity about the value of his writings.

RUSSELL: Did this continue to the end of his life?

BLOCH: Yes. He was constantly striving to improve his style and to study market needs – he really did – within his field.

RUSSELL: Did he say anything about the changes in his style that occurred toward the end of his life, that is during the 1930s?

BLOCH: He said that he was trying to write with a greater scientific objectivity. He was drawing away from his earlier work, which had been largely of a more poetic cast. You know, of course, that he wrote *The White Ship*, which was a Dunsanian tale, before he ever read any Dunsany.

RUSSELL: Did he explicitly renounce that type of story?

BLOCH: He didn't write anything similar to it, I believe –

RUSSELL: After the early 20s?

BLOCH: – That's right. I'd say that *Through the Gates of the Silver Key*, which he wrote in collaboration with E. Hoffman Price, probably was the last story which contained any elements of this sort of thing.

RUSSELL: [Were they contained in] *The Dream Quest of Unknown Kaddath* – which was never published [in his lifetime] – which apparently he never submitted?

BLOCH: Yes, and I would say he was right [not to submit it] because he realized it was an inferior product.

SAPIRO: About Lovecraft and Farnsworth Wright – Lovecraft mentions Wright's 'incurable dislike of any subtlety in a story, He wants everything spoiled by a diagram,' and then Lovecraft continues, 'No, I certainly wouldn't give in to his demand for a flat, explained ending. I'd rather not place a story than twist it to his mold.' [Letter quoted in *The Acolyte*, I (Fall 1942), 4–5.]

So could it be that Lovecraft did have some appreciation of the worth of his own stories – that he realized that Farnsworth Wright had limitations himself?

LEIBER: I would say that although he was very doubtful about the worth of his own particular stories – easily shaken by editorial disapproval – he wasn't at all weak as far as what he considered aesthetic judgments in general. A contrived ending on a horror tale, the idea of building up an atmosphere of supernatural horror and then explaining it was just a dream or a mechanism that waves the white sheet, offended his artistic sense.

RUSSELL: In his essay on the writing or weird fiction Lovecraft objects to the bald description of simple facts in a weird story, the flat description of what exactly happens, what the man does, what he sees, and so on. In other words, he objected to the naturalistic approach toward the writing of a weird story. This was what he hated because it did not create in the reader's mind that aura, that atmosphere, that buzzing inside the subconscious which he felt was necessary to create fear.

Lovecraft had read [M. R.] James, and knew that in a weird tale you have to start with very slight adumbrations of something spooky and then build with larger ones and slightly larger ones . . .

SAPIRO: I'd like to ask very bluntly: Does Lovecraft really scare anybody? I read his stories [because] I enjoy the way he uses the English language, but he doesn't scare me one bit. In line with this I'd like to read a criticism from Anthony Boucher:

> I will maintain to the death that the only true horror is that of understatement (I am basically an M. R. James man); and it annoys me, as a theorist, that both Poe and HPL managed to attain horror by explicit overstatement. For even HPL's cryptic, allusive manner is not true understatement. He simply makes *nameless* and *indescribable* and *unmentionable* into very definite connotative namings and descriptions . . .'
> (*The Acolyte*, II (Summer 1944), p. 29)

Mr Cox, would you say that Lovecraft scares you at all?

COX: No, I wouldn't. In my case anyway, there is not a word of horror in Lovecraft. He is fascinating, one of my favourite writers – but for actual fear, no. In fact, I don't know very many people who ever said they were frightened by Lovecraft. Mathew H. Onderdonk once had an article in *Fantasy Commentator* in which he spoke of the horror that Lovecraft inspired in him; but in writing about it, he uses these same words, 'blasphemous,' 'unholy,' and so on, so I gather he's just playing at being frightened.

LEIBER: I guess I must be a bit out of the ordinary, because Lovecraft did frighten men when I first read him. The first story I ever read by Lovecraft was *The Colour Out of Space* in *Amazing* – and that story really spooked me. It affected me and frightened me at the same time, as a boy of around seventeen.

About the business of using words like 'eldritch,' 'nameless,' it has to be remembered that these words were used along with very explicit detailed descriptions; they were an added mist of color that he put on his story. It's like a painter doing some kind of final spread on top of everything else, sort of filling up the empty spaces in the mosaic. He did get these very general words like 'strange' and 'weird' and 'horrible,' but they didn't stand alone: there was always explicit description with them, and I think he used them for a kind of musical quality.

Lovecraft did use overstatement, admittedly. Writers, even quite versatile writers, get wedded to certain ways of telling stories, and it's rarely that they break completely free. It's rare that a man who writes by way of extremes, almost a kind of overstatement, will decide to change and go in for understatement. It would have been extremely strange if someone like Lovecraft had been able to tone down his stories to the point where he was writing things that were only meant half or a quarter seriously, say like John Collier's stories, which had a persistent humorous element. I don't think that writers, even the hard-working writers, make changes to that degree. Lovecraft gambled his creativity from the start on the Edgar Allan Poe sort of story and that is why he stuck to it.

COX: There is a lot of humor in Lovecraft, in a story like *Pickman's Model*, for instance. It's submerged, a little bit below the surface.

RUSSELL: This is just irony underneath the surface.

LEIBER: You mean, in the sense of –

COX: Grim humor.

LEIBER: It has a little such. You get characterization a bit like Marquand's pictures of some Bostonians.

COX: In his description of Pickman's paintings there was humor.

DAVID FOX (*from the floor*):   In a story like *The Shadow Out of Time* the thing that makes it horrible – if it is – is Lovecraft's persistent effort to make it seem that way. The protagonist is taken back to a rather fascinating civilization, and his main reaction is to keep harping on the gloomy horror of the place, where I'm sure that an intelligent anthropologist (say) would be delighted for this opportunity to study an alien civilization. But you either had to be horrified or you weren't a Lovecraft character.

JACK HARNESS (*from the floor*):   Lovecraft can frighten. The first I read was the [very effective] *Dunwich Horror*. But after I read more Lovecraft and more of the Lovecraft school I reached the saturation point.

RUSSELL: This must be especially true when you read stories of the Lovecraft school, as well as a Lovecraft story. Then you're getting into the branches going out from Lovecraft.

BLOCH: I think that Mr Leiber answered the question best by citing his own personal example and putting his statement in the past tense: this story *did* frighten me. And I think this is important. This is where Mr Leiber and myself have a certain small advantage. We were actually around at the time the stories were being written, at the time they actually were appearing.

I think it might help to consider what that world was really like, that world of the middle and late 20s and early 30s, in terms of the reader of the date, teenage or adult. Anyone interested in fantasy fiction in those days could read Edgar Allan Poe; he could read M. R. James, Machen, and one or two other writers. But as of that time there were not in print in this country half a dozen contemporary anthologies of horror stories.

There were no magazines containing such stories as a steady diet except for *Weird Tales*; the radio program *Lights Out* didn't get under stride until the mid 1930s. There were a few motion pictures, a few stage plays, but by and large the average citizen would find exposure to that type of material almost exclusively in *Weird Tales*. Also, science-fiction had not yet come into its own. There were not very many stories of lost races, of alternate (*sic*) universes, of other worlds developed in anything except the pseudo-Gernsbackian–Ray Cummings style, with A. Hyatt Verrill's ant-worlds of the late 1920s.

So many of the themes have become commonplace to all of you: you've read hundreds, even thousands, of such stories; you've read dozens or hundreds of pocket books which didn't even exist in those days; you've read hard cover anthologies; you've been exposed to radio, television, and motion pictures embodying these concepts time and again. You live in a different world.

You live also in a world of much greater sophistication. At that time the average adolescent or post-adolescent had not traveled more than several hundred miles in any direction from his or her home; only one family in six owned an automobile; and there was a much lesser degree of knowledgeability (*sic*). Anthropology *per se* was a much more mysterious subject, as were the Antarctic and Arctic regions. There were still strange places on the Earth which the white man had never explored and still many avenues of scientific investigation which had not reached the general public, [of which] less than three percent had attended college or university.

Now, against this background, with *Weird Tales*, as perhaps the only exemplar of this type of fiction, Lovecraft's work exerted a very strong influence. The things he talked about were strange, were novel, were mysterious. The whole concept of a cosmology in which evil forces controlled the universe was very fresh, and some of his characters and characterizations were quite shocking. Today, when one reads Lovecraft, one reads him with echoes of countless science-fiction, television, and motion picture images in his or her mind. But at the time, I can assure you, most of the people I knew that had met the work of Lovecraft for the first time were quite frightened by it.

AL LEWIS (*from the floor*): The very first time I read *The Shadow Out of Time* it scared the pants off me. I was fourteen or fifteen at the time. To me [what] created the atmosphere of horror were the very basic things, the certainty of death and the insignifiance of the human race. Humanity was just an incident, not the master of creation, not the pinnacle of evolution. The great climax, of course, is the final scene down in the catacombs of the Australian desert – this is one of the few real horror stories I ever read.

BLOCH: My point is that Lovecraft's stories were written long before John W. Campbell explained the mysteries of life in his editorials.

LEIBER: That particular story, *The Shadow Out of Time,* was the most extended and systematic imaginative effort that Lovecraft made to give body and substance to the idea of mankind being only an incident. He had several stages of recollection there, where the narrator remembers talking with Nug-Soth, magician of the dark conquerors who were to come in 500 AD, and then jumps back to the great-headed brown people who ruled Africa in 50,000 BC. He gives you a feeling of the mutability of the human race – and then goes on with detailed explanations of how, after mankind, a race of beetles, a coleopteroid race, develops on Earth; then there is a migration, I think, to Venus and finally to Mercury of different races sort of joined together because the Great Race had taken their minds over – and he slips in, just is one sentence, something that is extremely terrifying, and one example of understatement in Lovecraft: He says, 'The fate of the human race affected me so much that I won't set it down here.'

SAPIRO: Let me come back to this list of people with whom the scholar discourses (I'm reading a passage out of *The Shadow Out of Time*): 'I talked with the mind of Yiang-Li, a philosopher from the cruel empire of Tsan-Shen, which is to come in 5,000 AD; with that of a general of the great-headed brown people who held South Africa in 50,000 BC – and then he goes on: 'I talked with the mind of Nug-Soth, a magician of the dark conquerors of 16,000 AD –'

LEIBER: Sixteen thousand?

SAPIRO: – yes. The point is that none of these entities belong to the Cthulhu mythology, [and] I think that the story could have gotten along just as well without it. Did he bring it in [elsewhere in the story] because he felt he was obliged to all the other people who had used it?

LEIBER: I don't know. I don't think that he felt bound by that particular mythology. How about that, Bob?

BLOCH: I don't at all, because there were many times that he departed from it, as in some of the stories written almost contemporaneously, like *In the Vault* and *Cool Air*. He used it when it seemed *a propos*.

ANON *(from the floor)*: Mr Bloch, how much influence did Lovecraft's writing have on your own work?

BLOCH: A tremendous influence. I consciously imitated him for several years, as did Henry Kuttner and a number of other, then-neophyte, writers. He criticized my writing and helped direct it through correspondence in a four-year period.

I have many times gone on record as saying Lovecraft was my literary mentor, as he was for so many others. It's interesting to see just how much of the works of Donald Wandrei and Frank Belknap Long was not only derivative of Lovecraft but in some cases written by Lovecraft. In *The Horror from the Hills* the whole Roman dream sequence was Lovecraft's. It was very common in the group to circulate stories before they were submitted, and you get a sort of congruity of references to the mythos in terms of general styling.

ANON: Do you still feel yourself strongly influenced by Lovecraft?

BLOCH: No, I do not. I haven't written a Lovecraftian story since about 1945, with one exception. That was a story called *The Shadow in the Steeple*, in which I disposed of Mr Leiber.

DAVID FOX *(from the floor)*:   Wasn't this sort of a handy thing to have? When you people had the mythos built up, you've conceived a language [the readers] have been trained to understand. All you do is mention Cthulhu or Azathoth or one of the other horrors, and there is no explanation needed.

BLOCH: Yes, that terminology could almost be considered as a sort of professional fancyclopedia.

SAPIRO: However, to an outsider this gives a very unfavorable impression. Some of you have read Edmund Wilson's article. He mentions the Lovecraft circle, and says, Well, they're just a bunch of cultists. I think one of the criticisms Edmund Wilson had in mind [was that] this is sort of an incestuous relationship, not entirely healthy.

BLOCH: Regarding this incestuous in-group publishing, which Wilson probably was not aware of, we – I use the term loosely for members of the Lovecraft circle – were writing supernatural fiction for only one market, *Weird Tales*. There *were* no other markets. At that time there was not the remotest possibility that anybody would reprint any of these stories, except, perhaps, for the *Not at Night* series, published in England.

We were writing to audiences that were pre-conditioned. We were writing for this specific audience and this specific market. I don't think there was a conscious affectation: It was a delight in furthering a vehicle which already had an audience and for which there was a definite demand at the time. If these stories were created for a larger audience, then I think complications would have come in.

The way to set Mr Wilson straight is to reorientate his frame of reference. Many of the so-called Lovecraft circle were not writers exclusively for *Weird Tales*. Frank Belknap Long, Donald Wandrei, August Derleth were writing widely in many markets, and in none of their non-*Weird Tales* stories did they utilize the

Mythos or the Lovecraftian technique; and this was true of Henry Kittner when he got into the group. So it was not a self-conscious cult. As a matter of fact, it wasn't really called the Lovecraft circle by any of the people who corresponded with Lovecraft.[2]

LEIBER: We were moved by his simple generosity. My later memories are of the large amounts of really good advice he gave me. I'd say something in a letter about thinking of writing a novel set in Roman times. Back would come four or five pages of good advice on how to prepare a novel set in the times of Republican Rome, a longer and shorter bibliography of books that I should read for background. Lovecraft was a writer in the old sense of the word, of a man who wrote a great deal and who had taken some sort of oath of Aesculapius suitable for writers rather than doctors, who felt called upon to teach a pupil that came to him. It was something I'm still very grateful for.

BLOCH: I think, strangely enough, that in their peculiarly different ways both Avram Davidson and Edmund Wilson would have found a good deal of affinity with Lovecraft, had they known him personally. You see in him many of Avram's attributes and eccentricities and his widespread general knowledge. He had much of Edmund Wilson's objectivity, and I think he knew probably as much about Marcel Proust and a few other contemporary writers as Wilson did – although he didn't reveal it in his weird fiction.

LEIBER: I would like to say that I think Lovecraft posthumously became a symbol of something that he wasn't in reality – for science-fiction writers rebelling against the *Weird Tales* influence, and it's an indication of how strong that influence was that there was such a passionate rebellion. To some of the very young science-fiction writers of the time it was convenient to make Lovecraft stand for the superstitious interpretation of reality, as opposed to the straight-forward, scientific sort of sociologically bedded approach. As a result they would point at Lovecraft and criticize or merely shout Nyeh! – or satirize, as Phil Strong did. He sort of set the note of using Lovecraft as symbolizing the superstitious old-fashioned horror and science-fiction story.

BLOCH: I think there's another link in that chain. That's August Derleth. August Derleth became the spearhead of the forces that set out to perpetuate Lovecraft's works in definitive form, and I think that when August Derleth took off on science-fiction and said it was very definitely a branch of fantasy, this was what enraged the science-fiction writers and readers *per se*.

BOB LICHTMAN (*from the floor*): Don't you think Derleth did Lovecraft a disservice by bringing out all the old unfinished things of his?

BLOCH: I would say Lovecraft's work must stand or fall by virtue of those stories he completed himself, presented for publication, and had accepted for publication. This is true of almost any writer.

There are some pretty ridiculous things in print regarding writers, their laundry lists and their menus and their carping letters to their publishers, which don't do any of them any particular service. I agree in part that perhaps a greater share of the material would not have been approved by Lovecraft himself.[3]

LEIBER: But I think it's testimony to the interest in the man. When a writer becomes of sufficient interest, why then all his stuff does get looked up and published.

SAPIRO: I'd like to ask one more question before they kick us out. It's a question I'd like to ask Mr Bloch to satisfy my own curiosity about Lovecraft's ideas on the unification of time. Lovecraft says that:

> The commonest form of my imaginative aspiration . . . is a motion backward in time, or a discovery that time is merely an illusion and that the past is simply a lost mode of vision which I have a chance of recovering . . .

Now, Mr Bloch mentions Lovecraft and Proust. Of course, this was Proust's greatest obsession also – the conquest of time – which he did by his theory of essences, as in that famous incident of the madeleine dipped in tea. I should like to ask how Lovecraft regarded Proust.

BLOCH: He thought that Proust was a very fine stylist. He mentioned him to me because I happened to be reading Proust at the time, and any writer that I was interested in he was likely to comment upon. But he didn't bring him up in regard to his own theory of time. He just had a great sense of tradition and a great affinity for the past: He was an antiquarian; he loved New England; he loved to journey to the still remaining relics of a previous age when life was gentler and kinder.

Notes

First published in 1962.

1. We have no evidence to show that Lovecraft was ever aware of the real cause of his father's death. We learned of this only by consultation of the record. We do not know, through any written or spoken word of Lovecraft's, that he knew. He was but eight when his father died, and his references to Winfield Scott Lovecraft's death in letters extant do not include any awareness of his father's syphilis and/or paresis. He has written that his father 'was seized with a complete nervous breakdown.' But there is nowhere, to my knowledge, any reference to his father's syphilis and paresis, and his reference to his father is always in a hazy context – 'my image of him is but vague.' The point, however, is moot; it can be argued that he knew but never publicly admitted it, and that the profit of that knowledge lies in his rather strict moral code and his abhorrence of anything at all abnormal in sex.

2. No one seriously accepts Edmund Wilson's 'Lovecraft circle' because he made reference to a mythical sycophantic cult group similar to the Baker Street Irregulars. The only real Lovecraft circle – in the sense that Lovecraft was actively a part of any circle of friends – was very probably the old Kalem Klub, and there was nothing sycophantic about that. The term 'Lovecraft circle' came to be used to describe both the writers who furthered the Cthulhu Mythos, and also those people who corresponded regularly with Lovecraft. Thus, today, when reference is made here at Arkham House to 'The Lovecraft circle,' such reference is always to those people who remain from the small group of Lovecraft's regular correspondents – among them Bob Bloch, Frank Long, Fritz Leiber, Don Wandrei, Duane Rimel, and myself.

3. Here at Arkham House we would be the first to admit that Lovecraft would certainly not have wanted a good deal of what he wrote put into print – and this includes not only his juvenilia, but also some of the stories prized by his readers, and his correspondence. Of his earliest stories he saved only *The Beast in the Cave, The Transition of Juan Romero*, and *The Alchemist* as of more merit than those pieces he destroyed. Such earlier pieces as were reprinted were found in the possession of a collector, in manuscript form. Their printing by Arkham House was in limited edition only, with no reprint in any form, specifically for collectors.

STEPHEN KING

Extract from an interview in *Playboy*[1]

PLAYBOY: Along with your difficulty in describing sexual scenes, you apparently also have a problem with women in your books. Critic Chelsea Quinn Yarbro wrote, 'It is disheartening when a writer with so much talent and strength and vision is not able to develop a believable woman character between the ages of 17 and 60.' Is that a fair criticism?

KING: Yes, unfortunately, I think it is probably the most justifiable of all those leveled at me. In fact, I'd extend her criticism to include my handling of black characters. Both Hallorann, the cook in *The Shining,* and Mother Abigail in *The Stand* are cardboard caricatures of superblack heroes, viewed through rose-tinted glasses of white-liberal guilt. And when I think I'm free of the charge that most male American writers depict women as either nebbishes or bitch-goddess destroyers, I create someone like Carrie – who starts out as a nebbish victim and then *becomes* a bitch goddess, destroying an entire town in an explosion of hormonal rage. I recognize the problems but can't yet rectify them.

. . .

What I try to do – and on occasion, I hope, I succeed – is to pour new wine from old bottles. I'd never deny, though, that most of my books have been derivative to some extent, though a few of the short stories are fairly *sui generis*, and *Cujo* and *The Dead Zone* are both basically original conceptions. But *Carrie*, for example, derived to a considerable extent from a terrible grade-B movie called *The Brain From Planet Arous*; *The Shining* was influenced by Shirley Jackson's marvelous novel *The Haunting of Hill House*; *The Stand* owes a considerable debt to both George R. Stewart's *Earth Abides* and M. P. Shiel's *The Purple Cloud*; and *Firestarter* has numerous science fiction antecedents. *'Salem's Lot*, of course, was inspired by and bears a fully intentional similarity to the great classic of the field, Bram Stoker's *Dracula*. I've never made any secret of that.

. . .

In fact, the only books of mine that I consider pure unadulterated horror are *'Salem's Lot*, *The Shining*, and now *Christine*, because they all offer no rational explanation at all for the supernatural events that occur. *Carrie*, *The Dead Zone*, and *Firestarter*, on the other hand, are much more within the science fiction tradition.

Extract from 'An Evening at Billerica Public Library'[2]

But horror fiction is really as Republican as a banker in a three-piece suit. The story is always the same in terms of its development. There's an incursion into taboo lands, there's a place where you shouldn't go, but you do, the same way that your mother would tell you that the freak tent is a place you shouldn't go, but you do. And the same thing happens inside: you look at the guy with three eyes, or you look at the fat lady, or you look at the skeleton man or Mr Electrical or whoever it happens to be. And when you come out, well, you say, 'Hey, I'm not so bad. I'm all right. A lot better than I thought.' It has that effect of reconfirming values, of reconfirming self-image and our good feelings about ourselves. . . .

I said that horror fiction was conservative and that it appeals to teenagers – the two things go together because teenagers are the most conservative people in American society.

. . .

I also think that some of horror's current popularity has to do with the failure of religion. My wife is a fallen-away Catholic and I'm a fallen-away Methodist. As a result, while we both keep in our hearts a sort of realization of God, the idea that God must be part of a rational world, I must say that our children are much more familiar with Ronald McDonald than they are with, let's say, Jesus or Peter or Paul or any of those people. They can tell you about the Burger King or the Easter Bunny but some of this other stuff they're not too cool on. Horror fiction, supernatural horror fiction, suggests that we go on.

. . .

Last reason for reading horror: it's a rehearsal for death. . . . everybody's alone.

Notes

1. First published in June 1983. Reproduced in Tim Underwood and Chuck Miller (eds), *Bare Bones: Conversations on Terror with Stephen King* (London: New English Library, 1990).
2. First published in 1983. Reproduced in Tim Underwood and Chuck Miller (eds), *Bare Bones: Conversations on Terror with Stephen King* (London: New English Library, 1990).

WHITLEY STRIEBER

On Stephen King

My copy of the August issue of *The Crypt of Terror* flutters down to the lawn. It has been torn to pieces by my outraged and uncomprehending father.

My enjoyment of horror became permanent on that night. I realised that it was forbidden and despised; by reading it I declared myself to the world as a rebel, a member of a secret cabal of screwed-up kids who were cheerful at funerals, who giggled when ordered to say a prayer at the sound of an ambulance siren, who weren't above putting a dead rattlesnake in bed with their sister to see if the EEEYAAAHHHs scattered across EC Comics were accurate renderings of the sound of horror.

Watching the beginning of *Creepshow* I detected parallel experience. Somewhere back there Stephen King must have gone through something similar, at least in spirit. He's written that he was a fan of EC Comics, so we have to thank the Crypt-Keeper – and the Old Witch and the others, for that matter – for a great deal.

Horror fiction is the essential fiction of rebellion in modern times. In Stephen King's work it is the rebellion of the middle against all extremes. On one level his books are about supernatural – or at least, inexplicable – horrors. On another, they are about injustice. When I was a young man Norman Thomas told me that 'the republic stops where the secrets start,' and said that the greatest political problem of my generation would be the tendency of bureaucracy to hide behind classification laws. *Firestarter* is a book of rage against the cancerous spread of secrecy in our government. Its message is that governmental secrets diminish the life of the ordinary man. In its fury and its driving narrative power it stands far above the more conventional novels on the subject, with their vapid warnings and constructed prose.

. . . But his work is also important both as literature and as cultural matter. He writes from the heart of the American experience. There is something in his voice that fits our American ear very well. We feel comfortable with a guy like this telling us a good story, and we know that he comes to us with truth. We like justice, and to see it done fulfils one of our deepest longings. King talks American and even though he might now be as rich as he can be, he was once down at the bottom and he knows what it is to be an ordinary member of our society.

His language, his situations, reflect this strange and glittering culture accurately. If by some odd chance the people of the future read, and they want to learn about America in our time – not the history, but the smell and taste and feel of it – they will certainly turn to Stephen King for guidance.

Note

First published in Tim Underwood and Chuck Miller (eds), *Kingdom of Fear: The World of Stephen King* (London: New English Library, 1986).

CLIVE BARKER

On Horror and Subversion

Why, you may ask, do I put such a high value upon subversion?

There are many reasons. The most pertinent here is my belief that fantastic fiction offers the writer exceptional possibilities in that direction, and I strongly believe a piece of work (be it play, book, poem) should be judged according to how enthusiastically it seizes the opportunity to do what it can do *uniquely*. The literature of the fantastic – and the movies, and the paintings – can reproduce, at its best, the texture of experience more closely than any 'naturalistic' work, because it can embrace the complexity of the world we live in.

Which is to say: our minds. That's where we live, after all. And our minds are extraordinary melting pots, in which sensory information, and the memory of same, and intellectual ruminations, and nightmares, and dreams, simmer in an ever-richer stew. Where else but in works called (often pejoratively) *fantasies* can such a mixture of elements be placed side by side?

And if we once embrace the vision offered in such works, if we once allow the metaphors a home in our psyches, the subversion is under way. We may for the first time see ourselves as a *totality* – valuing our appetite for the forbidden rather than suppressing it, comprehending that our taste for the strange, or the morbid, or the paradoxical, is contrary to what we're brought up to believe, a sign of our good health. So I say – *subvert*. And never apologise.

Note

First published in Tim Underwood and Chuck Miller (eds), *Kingdom of Fear: The World of Stephen King* (London: New English Library, 1986).

4 Contemporary Critical Accounts

JULIA BRIGGS

Extract from *Night Visitors*

Montague Rhodes James set out his rules for the ghost story, such as they were, in the various brief prefaces to his collections of tales. Unlike Vernon Lee, he believed it important to establish a setting that was

> fairly familiar and the majority of the characters and their talk such as you may meet or hear any day. A ghost story of which the scene is laid in the twelfth or thirteenth century may succeed in being romantic or poetical: it will never put the reader into the position of saying to himself, 'If I'm not very careful, something of this kind may happen to me!' (Preface to *More Ghost Stories of an Antiquary*, 1911).

He also attempted to answer some of the more obvious questions his readers put to him, explaining why he wrote his tales: '[if] they have given pleasure . . . my whole object in writing them has been attainted'; when he wrote them – they were 'read to patient friends, usually at the season of Christmas'; and whether he believed in ghosts, to which he replied that he was 'prepared to consider the evidence and accept it if it satisfies me'.

As an author, James maintained an attitude of critical detachment which seems to have been the exception rather than the rule. He did not share the concern shown by other writers (Blackwood or Le Fanu, for instance) with the significance of spirits, the state of mind in which ghosts are seen, or the condition of a universe that permits the maleficent returning dead. His stories assert a total acceptance of the supernatural that his scepticism apparently denies. It is as if the implications of what he wrote never disturbed him, and he enjoyed writing them primarily as a literary exercise, governed only by certain rules he had evolved. A classicist both by temperament and profession, James had read a great many ghost stories and worked out from them his own methods, employing traditional themes in highly original settings.

His scepticism about ghosts did not derive from a general agnosticism. The son of a clergyman, M. R. James was a committed Christian and theologian who spent many years collating the Apocryphal Gospels, perhaps in the hope that they might provide some independent evidence of Jesus's supernatural powers with which to refute the 'Higher Criticism'. His ghost stories seem almost to parody his scholarly investigations into Holy Writ, for they frequently adduce biblical or literary references to prove the existence of spiritual forces, yet these appear to be introduced in the spirit of an academic joke, to show that anything can be proved by the citation of learned texts. Such allusions also function as an effective device for convincing the reader, by giving a spurious air of academic authenticity.

That suspension of the laws of nature which makes many of these stories so irrationally alarming results partly from his detached attitude and partly from the minor rôle that his fiction played in his life. It was simply a bagatelle for an idle hour, the construction of a delicate edifice of suspense with which to entertain the young people whose company he so much enjoyed. He saw his main career as one of dedicated scholarship, as a theologian, bibliographer and iconographer, a Fellow of King's College, Cambridge, and subsequently Provost of Eton. It is one of time's ironies that he is now remembered for his ghost stories long after his contributions to scholarship have been bypassed or superseded. A story by James is almost *de rigueur* in any ghostly anthology, and he is the only writer whose *Collected Ghost Stories* have remained continuously in print.

Like Henry James and Vernon Lee, M. R. James admitted to finding places 'prolific in suggestion', and his earliest stories were inspired by visits to France ('Canon Alberic's Scrapbook' is set in St Bertrand de Comminges, near Toulouse) and Scandinavia (Viborg, in Denmark, is the scene of 'Number 13', and 'Count Magnus' takes place in Sweden). 'Lost Hearts', apparently the second story he wrote, is set at

Aswarby Hall, a tall, red-brick house, built in the reign of Queen Anne. Similar houses are Wilsthorpe, Mr Humphreys' inheritance, and Castringham, of 'The Ash-Tree', although the latter has a stuccoed façade, and a pillared portico added later in the eighteenth century. Commonly these country houses are set in East Anglia, his home for nearly fifty years. His father was Rector of Livermere, near Bury St Edmunds, until his death in 1909, and, being based here and at Cambridge, James had explored a great deal of the area on foot or bicycle. The east-coast resorts of Felixstowe and Aldeburgh are lightly disguised as Burnstow and Seaburgh, in '"Oh, Whistle, and I'll come to you, My Lad"' and 'A Warning to the Curious'.

James describes scenery and domestic architecture with knowledge and affection, but when he comes to ecclesiastical architecture, he is in his element. Barchester and Southminster ('blends of Canterbury, Salisbury and Hereford', he explains) are described in detail, and with the warmest enthusiasm for their baroque interiors, before Sir Gilbert Scott and the Gothic Revival destroyed them forever. 'The Stalls of Barchester Cathedral' set in 1810, takes a paragraph to depict the classical pediments and gilt cherubs then in evidence. The events of 'An Episode of Cathedral History' actually occur during the Gothic renovations, and the old verger, Worby, laments the beautiful carvings being wantonly destroyed. The chapel at Brockstone Court, in 'The Uncommon Prayer-Book', is, however, a perfect example of seventeenth-century decoration, and after Mr Davidson has gloated over 'the completeness and richness of the interior', the author pulls himself up with the remark that 'this is not an archaeological review'. Detailed accounts of screens, organs and stalls may not always have an essential bearing on the story but scholarly enthusiasm of this kind lends an air of conviction to the narrative.

Accurate and vivid description becomes of primary importance when particular objects play key rôles in the story, as they so often do: 'Canon Alberic's Scrapbook', 'The Mezzotint', the Anglo-Saxon whistle in '"Oh, Whistle"', the stained glass window with its odd juxtaposition of Job, John and Zechariah in 'The Treasure of Abbot Thomas', 'The Tractate Middoth', 'The Stalls of Barchester Cathedral', and 'The Uncommon Prayer-Book'. In each case, the style and period of the object is carefully established. The contents of the renaissance scrapbook are described in great detail, and James informs us that, minus the satanic illustration, it is now 'in the Wentworth Collection in Cambridge'. It is somehow fitting that the 'unprincipled Canon . . . who had doubtless plundered the Chapter library' of its manuscript treasures, should have entered into further negotiations with the powers of darkness for more conventional wealth. In describing objects such as the scrapbook, James not only conveys their physical appearance, he also provides them with inscriptions, often in Latin, in the correct style for the period. In fact there is a great deal of literary pastiche throughout his work. Nineteenth-century diaries and letters are imitated in 'The Stalls of Barchester Cathedral', 'The Residence at Whitminster' and 'The Story of a Disappearance and an Appearance'. 'Mr Humphreys and his Inheritance' includes an ornate passage from an imaginary seventeenth-century sermon, and 'The Diary of Mr Poynter' itself also dates, supposedly, from the same period. 'Martin's Close' is the most sustained of his inventions for it takes the form of a verbatim account of a trial before Judge Jeffreys. His peculiar ability to imitate the different styles and tricks of different periods, in both English and Latin, was probably linked with his powers of mimicry, which he first demonstrated at prep. school. S. G. Lubbock has described how Monty and his brother Herbert used to adopt the personae of two quarrelsome Suffolk tradesmen, Barker and Johnson. 'Barker' continued to be a favourite impersonation of James's all his life, and may be the original of some of his humorous minor characters. Gwendolyn McBryde referred to James as 'a born actor', adding that he 'would sometimes personate some countryman or cockney'.

Yet despite his ability to re-create the past in lucid pictorial detail, James gives several of his most fearful spirits, quite ordinary, even prosaic locations. He understood the importance of a 'fairly familiar' setting, and some of his worst moments take place in modern hotel bedrooms, or even in one case, on an electric tram. Recent inventions are utilized: a special pair of field-glasses which make the past visible ('looking through dead men's eyes') is the subject of 'A View from a Hill', and a magic lantern show is used to create panic at a children's party by the maleficent Karswell, in 'Casting the Runes'. This story is an exercise in what the other James termed 'the strange and sinister embroidered on the very type of the normal and easy'. The fatal runes are planted on the victim in the British Museum Reading Room, and returned in a railway carriage. An advertisement in a tram window becomes a portent of death, and the victim, putting his hand under his pillow to find a match, discovers – well, something very unpleasant. The idea of an invasion of one's bed, of a horror lurking beneath the pillow (the very place where one expects to feel secure) is deeply disturbing. If we are not safe in our beds, then the last sanctuary has gone. The peculiar sense of violation that arises at the thought of one's bedroom being invaded is effectively exploited in '"Oh, Whistle"', where the bedclothes on an empty bed are possessed by an evil spirit. Many sensitive readers have subsequently experienced a certain reluctance to sleep in a room containing an unoccupied bed. And if hiding under the bedclothes is one traditional resort better avoided, so is pulling the curtains to shut out the dark, for the curtains themselves may be harbouring a restless ghost, as they do in 'The Diary of Mr Poynter'. James has shown us fear in a handful of dust, in a Punch and Judy show, and a fragment of wet cloth sticking out of a cupboard.

Fear of the supernatural is essentially circular, for what we fear most is the sensation of being afraid, which endows the most familiar objects with frightful possibilities. The source of terror in a ghost story may be totally irrational, and even incapable of inflicting anything but the experience of fear itself, as in '"Oh, Whistle"', perhaps the most terrifying of all. Here the 'intensely horrible face *of crumpled linen*' seems to possess this power alone: 'The Colonel . . . was of the opinion that if Parkins had closed with it, it could really have done very little, and that its one power was that of frightening.' Yet this is a far more effective piece than the otherwise similar story, 'A Warning to the Curious', where the phantom actually murders the victim. By placing too great a strain on the reader's credulity, the effect of terror is here diminished, rather than increased.

When it comes to describing the source of fear, the ghost story writer must tread delicately. A certain vagueness, an element of mystery is essential. Too much power over the material world, such as the ability to commit a murder, can reduce the creature's potential effect. Henry James laid down that the writer must make his reader '*think* the evil . . . and you are released from weak specifications'. M. R. James had none of Henry James's subtle powers of suggestion, but he too recognized that a vague description might be far more disturbing than a precise one. Often the witness is, in any case, too distraught to describe what he has seen with any accuracy, so that he only provides hints on which the reader's imagination may build:

'I was conscious of a most horrible smell of mould, and of a cold kind of face pressed against my own, and moving slowly over it, and of several – I don't know how many – legs or arms or tentacles or something clinging to my body.' ('The Treasure of Abbot Thomas')

'I don't know,' he said, 'but I can tell you one thing – he was beastly thin: and he looked as if he was wet all over: and . . . I'm not at all sure that he was alive.'   ('A School Story')

What he chiefly remembers about it is a horrible, an intensely horrible, face *of crumpled linen.*   ('Oh, Whistle, and I'll come to you, My Lad')

Sometimes there are allusions to incidents that are never actually related, for example, at the end of 'Casting the Runes', 'Harrington repeated to Dunning something of what he had heard his brother say in his sleep: but it was not long before Dunning stopped him.' Such vague allusions help to prod the imagination into action. They are also part of a more general use of understatement that characterizes James's style. Implicit in the restrained, gentlemanly, even scholarly tone is the suggestion that it would be distasteful to dwell on unpleasant details, and this consistent 'meiosis' serves to increase our apprehension. Recognition that the story-teller is deliberately understating his case serves to increase its effectiveness. James may have learnt the use of a deadpan narrative technique from such French exponents of *Grand Guignol* as Mérimée, Maupassant and the Erckmann–Chatrian collaborators, but it was quite evidently a tone that came perfectly naturally to him, perhaps because it is also a characteristically English one.

Although James relies largely on the traditional character of his spirits to make them fearful, he often likes to touch up the standard shapes with a few details of his own. The sheeted ghost becomes 'a horrible hopping creature in white' which makes away with a child in Karswell's sinister magic lantern show, or the summoned spirit in the bedclothes in '"Oh, Whistle"' which, having no eyes, 'seemed to feel about it with its muffled arms in a groping and random fashion'. It does not finally discover Parkins until he lets out an uncontrollable cry of disgust. Since skeletons have become the familiar property of art and medical students, James resorts instead to the resuscitated corpse, an unclean thing of decaying flesh whose appearance is hinted at in 'Lost Hearts': '. . . what he saw reminds me of what I once beheld myself in the famous vaults of St Michan's Church in Dublin, which possess the horrid property of preserving corpses from decay for centuries'.

Sensations of normal physical repulsion are also used to reinforce supernatural terrors. Flies (by association with the Lord of them) haunt the sites of satanic pacts in 'An Evening's Entertainment' and 'The Residence at Whitminster'. The guardian of 'The Treasure of Abbot Thomas' which slips its horrid arms round Somerton's neck was 'perhaps more like a toad than anything else', and there is a truly nightmarish sequence in 'Mr Humphreys and his Inheritance' where the effect derives from an unpleasantly familiar analogy: 'It took shape as a face – a human face – a *burnt* human face: and with the odious writhings of a wasp creeping out of a rotten apple there clambered out the appearance of a form.'

Perhaps the commonest of James's domestic terrors is the spider, used either to provide a point of comparison, as the spinner of gloomy cobwebs, or, in 'The Ash-Tree', as the agent of evil itself. The hairy and horribly emaciated demon of 'Canon Alberic's Scrapbook', the prototype of a number of such creatures in James's work, may well have been inspired by a similar figure crouching in Brueghel's painting of the Archangel Michael. When first encountered in the scrapbook illustration, it resembles 'one of the awful bird-catching spiders of South America translated into human form'. At the climax Dennistoun, alone in his room, first notices 'A penwiper? No, no such thing in the house. A rat? No, too black. A large spider? I trust to goodness not – no. Good God! a hand like the hand in that picture!'

Draped cobwebs are a source of horror in 'The Tractate Middoth'. The form that the unfortunate librarian, Garrett, encounters in the Cambridge University Library has its face covered from eyebrows to cheekbones with them. At the end of the story, the only living things present at the scene of Eldred's death are large spiders, running in and out of a mass of cobwebs. Both the apparition in the library, and the apparently harmless spiders of the ending seem to be connected with the unpleasant old man who left his will in the Tractate, and demanded to be buried in the bricked-up room beneath the spot where Eldred died so mysteriously. In 'The Ash-Tree' spiders act at the agents of the witch's maleficence, apparently springing from her buried bones, and feeding, like vampires, on the blood of her enemies. 'The Ash-Tree' is a most carefully constructed piece, each episode building towards a final climax where the familiar is brought into a grotesque juxtaposition with the surreal in the account of Sir Richard's death. The reader does not yet know the exact form that the inhabitants of the ash-tree take:

> . . . it seems as if Sir Richard were moving his head rapidly to and fro. . . . And now you would guess, so deceptive is the half-

darkness, that he had several heads, round and brownish, which move back and forwards, even as low as his chest. It is a horrible illusion. Is it nothing more? There! something drops off the bed with a soft plump, like a kitten, and is out of the window in a flash.

The sense of discomfort here results from the different interpretations offered. They alternate alarmingly from normality (a man moving his head) to total abnormality (a man with several heads, sharply realized by the adjectives 'round and brownish'). The final comparison to a kitten, an animal connected primarily with the pleasures of touch, appals, particularly on a second reading, when the reader will mentally contrast the attractive feel of the kitten with the repulsion of the spider. All through the passage runs the suggestion of the spider's characteristic movement, rapid, silent (except when it falls to the floor) and intimately linked with the fear it arouses.

The spiders of 'The Ash-Tree' will work on our sense of physical repulsion if we share with its author 'a horror of spiders, especially large ones and of the lone spider which will turn up unaccountably in the bath'. The theme of the story, witchcraft, relies on more intellectual responses. Most readers know something of the seventeenth-century witch hunts, and have some idea of the supposed practices of witches, if only from *Macbeth*. The 'slips of yew' there presented as a standard cauldron ingredient can be paralleled by the sprigs of ash collected by the malevolent Mrs Mothersole, particularly when it is remembered that the ash is often associated with black magic, the witch's besom being traditionally made of ash. In case some of this esoteric lore is unfamiliar, the Bishop of Kilmore reminds Sir Richard in the course of the story that his Irish peasants consider 'it brings the worst of luck to sleep near an ash-tree'. The spiders, then, provide a fresh elaboration on the traditional theme of the witch's *maleficium*. The familiar characteristics of her behaviour help to authenticate the tale.

M. R. James adapted a variety of time-hallowed themes from folklore and legend, myth and ballad, and his stories are largely constructed from such traditional elements. Recognizing this process, he wrote: 'I have tried to make my ghosts act in a way not inconsistent with the rules of folklore.' His ability to manipulate familiar material is everywhere in evidence; so too is his scholarly interest in it. In 1914 he edited that strange hotchpotch of legend and learning, Walter Map's *De Nugis Curialium*, which contains several stories of the returning dead, and he published a group of medieval ghost stories he had unearthed in the *English Historical Review* in 1922. He had also read many nineteenth-century ghost stories, both fictional and veridical, his favourite author being Joseph Sheridan Le Fanu, whose imaginative treatment of Irish folklore he greatly admired. He found in the ballad a useful source of supernatural episodes, and was particularly interested in the Danish and Breton versions. It is worthwhile, in the light of his interest in the ballad, to consider how far his own narrative technique was influenced by it. The prosaic, matter-of-fact tone with which natural and supernatural events alike are presented, the build-up of suspense by steps, the overall importance of the action and the subordination of characterization to it, the stiff and conventional nature of the character-drawing, and perhaps above all, the sense of a background of shared traditional beliefs conveying further implications to the audience – all these qualities are present in James's work. We need to know something of the hats o' the birk and the red cock to understand the events of 'The Wife of Usher's Well', just as we need to know something of the associations of witches and ash-trees for 'The Ash-Tree' to work on us as its author intends. It may be that the self-effacing story-teller, the impersonal narrative technique and the extensive use of understatement were characteristics that James took over from the ballad, the supreme form for a tale of terror, as the Romantic poets had realized.

Much of the effect of his stories depends on our recognizing certain archetypal patterns of temptation and vengeance as typifying the workings of the supernatural world. The different allusions in a single study do not derive from any one origin, however, but from a compound in sources both in literature and in folklore. It is often difficult to distinguish these elements completely, since ancient beliefs survive in a variety of contexts. In '"Oh, Whistle, and I'll come to you, My Lad"' the malevolent spirit that appears in response to Parkins' blowing the whistle may be connected with the sailors' superstition about whistling on deck, the prototype of which is at least as old as Homer, and Odysseus' *contretemps* with the bag of winds. Witches, too, traditionally had power over the winds, as Shakespeare showed in *Macbeth*. As late as 1814 wise women sold winds to sailors, for in that year Walter Scott recorded buying one from a certain Bessie Miller of Stromness, Orkney. In the course of the story, the Colonel points out that Northern Europeans still believe that a sudden wind has been whistled for, adding 'there's generally something at the bottom of what these country-folk hold to'. Thus the very antiquity of a superstition is put forward as some sort of evidence of its validity. The horrible thing that responds to the summons is bodiless, as traditionally spirits often were, so it has to assume the body of bedlinen.

It first appears on the beach as Parkins returns from the Templars' Church, having found, but not yet blown, the whistle: 'an indistinct personage who seemed to be making great efforts to catch up with him, but made little, if any progress'. The sight of this figure throws up a completely new and quite different literary allusion, this time to Bunyan's Apollyon, which Parkins involuntarily associates with the distant pursuer, wondering what he would do

> . . . if I looked back and caught sight of a black figure sharply defined against the yellow sky, and saw that it had horns and wings? I wonder whether I should stand or run for it. Luckily that gentleman behind is not of that kind, and seems to be about as far off now as when I saw him first.

The spirit's identity becomes clearer in Parkins' subsequent dream of flight along the beach. Its failure to catch up with him on that first afternoon had been due to the fact that he had not yet actually blown the whistle, thus placing himself, both literally and metaphorically, within its reach. Another significant literary reference lies in the title, taken from a song of Burns, the refrain of which has a distinctly sinister ring:

> Though father and mother and brother go mad,
> Oh, whistle and I'll come to ye, my lad.

This elaborate network of allusion helps to provide a focus for our fears, which are themselves the more alarming for being vaguely familiar. The superstitions and quotations exploited here seem to lend an air of almost historical verification to the evil spirit that comes, just as the Sortes Biblicae in 'The Ash-Tree', or the quotations from Ecclesiasticus and Isaiah at the end of 'Canon Alberic's Scrapbook' convince by apparently supplying evidence from the Book of Truth itself.

Because the ghosts and demons in these tales act in accordance with certain traditional rules, they acquire an alarming predictability, which James exploited to increase his reader's anticipation.

When whisperings are first heard in the cellar or the rose garden, a man feels that he is being followed or has a vivid and curious dream, the reader's attention is alerted, and certain vague apprehensions take shape, based on our existing knowledge of similar manifestations – witches, ghouls, demons or whatever. The protagonist of the story, however, frequently does not share this response, and fails to impute significance to the events, so that the reader is in the position of the child at the pantomime, wanting to warn the actor of what stands behind him. This gives an extra degree of involvement, which is part of the secret of James's success. He stated his own rules for this gradual opening, which so often puts the reader one step ahead of the protagonist, in his introduction to *Ghosts and Marvels*. The majority of his tales adhere to them rigorously:

> Let us, then, be introduced to the actors in a placid way; let us see them going about their ordinary business, undisturbed by forebodings, pleased with their surroundings; and into this calm environment let the ominous thing put out its head, unobtrusively at first, and then more insistently, until it holds the stage.

The hero's insensitivity to forebodings, his cheerful frame of mind, which may even cause him to dismiss the first 'unobtrusive' appearances of the thing, whatever it is, are among the means by which we are involved in his situation.

For James, the plot was of paramount importance, and characterization is accordingly reduced to a minimum. In this respect his practice contrasts strikingly with that of Henry James, who felt 'the thickness in the human consciousness' to be essentially to the ghost story since it is 'the only thickness we do get'. M. R. James keeps his characters thin to the point of transparency. They are quite deliberately washed free of all subtlety or complexity which might cloud or impede the all-important progress of the plot. In the delineation of character James employed no tricks; there were no new developments, no sudden revelations to catch the audience unprepared, for all the devices of surprise are limited to that element of the story which concerned him most, the plot. Psychology is totally and defiantly excluded from his writings.

James's characters are types or what E. M. Forster calls 'flats', and he often uses the same device for creating 'flats' as, Forster points out, Dickens does (perhaps not surprisingly for he admired Dickens intensely and knew extensive passages by heart): this device is the reiterated phrase or speech trick. So Catell, in 'The Diary of Mr Poynter', has a Shakespearian quotation, delivered in broad cockney, to meet every situation. 'The last,' James adds, with a wry admission of the inevitable, 'began with the words "There are more things".' Dialect, either country or cockney, usually denotes simplicity and honesty, often a reliable witness, for example Mrs Bunch, the kind housekeeper of 'Lost Hearts', or Patten, the old retainer in 'A Neighbour's Landmark'. Many similar characters remain unnamed and unidentified, except in so far as their speech shows them to be 'locals'. They often play important rôles in the build-up of suspense. The frightened lad in '"Oh, Whistle"', who wails 'Ow, I seen it wive at me out of the winder . . . and I don't like it', is one example; the old man who starts Paxton on his disastrous quest, in 'A Warning to the Curious', is another.

Apart from the use of dialect and speech tricks to 'place' them, James's characters qualify as flats because of their total predictability. A single line usually suffices to describe them, and they never deviate from this first account of them, whether pleasant – 'Professor Parkins, one of whose principal characteristics was pluck . . .', or 'Mr Garrett was a cheerful and pleasant-looking young man . . .' – or sinister, in which case they are usually identified by an *absence* of information: 'Very little was known of Mr Abney's pursuits or temper . . .', or '. . . just at present Mr Karswell is a very angry man. But I don't know much about him otherwise . . .'. Secrecy is itself suspicious and these early intimations are confirmed when Abney and Karswell turn out to be dabblers in the black arts, and even murderers.

What has been said of James's minor characters also applies to the central figure, the hero who dominates the situation and acts as the focus of the supernatural events. These characters have a transparent simplicity, transparent, because we are required to look *through* them at the unfolding plot, where the emphasis is placed. The reader sees not merely what *is* happening, but also what is going to happen, anticipating, if only vaguely, the disaster that is on the point of overtaking the hero, and is filled with a corresponding sympathy and alarm on his behalf. These transparent, anonymous heroes, often distinctively twentieth-century in their practical, sceptical approach to life, are frequently academics of some kind, if their professions are referred to at all. They have a selfless enthusiasm for knowledge (or perhaps a fatal curiosity) which ironically leads them on 'where angels fear to tread', as old Cooper warns Mr Humphreys. From one angle the hero is thus a reflection of his sceptical and detached creator; from another he is the clear window through which the reader perceives the plot unfolding, unfolding far faster than the hero himself realizes. For this hero unknowingly inhabits an animistic world where anything might happen, a world into which only the minor characters are given intuitive glimpses so that they may warn the protagonist of what impends. But the hero's materialism, his doubt, prevents him from giving due weight to the warnings he receives.

Such a warning is usually provided in the early stages of the tale, partly in order to increase the sense of suspense and imminent danger, but also to provide an element of dramatic justice. In everyday terms, the hero is mildly culpable in that he wilfully rejects, because of his scepticism perhaps, the advice of wiser or older men. In metaphysical terms, his refusal to be warned is symptomatic of a wider rejection of unproven forces and inexplicable powers, and hence is duly revenged by these powers, whether they are conceived as emerging from an outer darkness or an inner id. Nearly all of the stories provide this warning element in some form or another: in 'Canon Alberic's Scrapbook', there is not only the excessive anxiety of the sacristan and his daughter, but even the sight of the fearful drawing itself; in 'The Ash-Tree', the Bishop of Kilmore warns Sir Richard with his allusion to Irish peasant beliefs. The Colonel fulfils this function in '"Oh Whistle"'. 'The Treasure of Abbot Thomas' provides a caveat at the end of the coded message, 'Gare à qui la touche'. Thus the hero has to some extent wilfully placed himself 'on the edge'. In the rare cases where visitations fall on the totally innocent, as in 'Casting the Runes', the victim is provided with helpful friends, as Dunning is with Henry Harrington, whose advice he is only too eager to adopt.

The warnings constitute dramatic justice only, however, and there is inevitably a degree of disproportion in their working. Yet there is nearly always a distinct moment when the hero commits some error, perhaps a form of hubris, by taking a wrong decision, or by choosing against advice to prosecute some scheme or investigation on hand. What impels him to press on at this juncture in the plot may be one of a variety of emotions; it may involve avarice or covetousness, but equally it may be simply a desire to carry through a projected plan perfectly innocent in itself, such as having curtains made up in an eighteenth-century design, opening up an old maze, or building a rose garden. There is no apparent folly in such undertakings and the act of hubris then lies in not heeding warnings or signs. But perhaps the emotion that most frequently lures the unwitting hero on is curiosity, sometimes quite justifiable, and at other times, strange, even perverse. Curiosity is always marginally present, often accompanying avarice, or the desire to complete a projected plan, but in several tales it provides the primary motivation, as in the purest example of this motif, the tale of Bluebeard. Sometimes an investigation is carried out in the spirit of scientific enquiry, as when Parkins blows the whistle, or Anderson investigates room 13. Sometimes there is a motive of historical discovery, as there is for Dennistoun with the scrapbook, or for Paxton with the Anglo-Saxon crown, but behind every rationalization lies the dreadful itch of pure curiosity, morbid, perverse and inexplicable. It drives the wretched Wraxall, to his own apparent astonishment, to repeat three times, 'Ah . . . Count Magnus, there you are. I should dearly like to see you.' Each time he utters this, one of the three padlocks falls from the Count's massive tomb.

The story that resembles the prototype, Bluebeard, most closely is a short piece called 'Rats', in which one Thomson, 'in a mood of quite indefensible curiosity' unlocks the door of a room in his lodgings and discovers a horribly animated corpse. Before finally leaving the house, he feels compelled to visit it again, and this time his intrusion arouses it. The tale is inconclusive: Thomson has received a lasting fright, and the landlord is left to observe grimly 'what he may do now there ain't no sayin' . . .'. Curiosity has its academic and obsessive aspects; perhaps James's experience of the former gave him some insight into the latter. Both are dramatized in the large group of stories that conform to this pattern, in which the central character, whether deliberately or accidentally, fails to heed a vital warning. To a certain extent, all authors who write of the supernatural are expressing their feelings of curiosity about it, however publicly they may declare their scepticism and lack of interest in psychic research. Yet for the majority such curiosity stops short of direct investigation, and their ghost stories embody a form of speculation which may be safely indulged from the sidelines.

A more sinister and reprehensible curiosity is the subject of James's stories of black magic, and its disastrous consequences for those who practise it. Here the model is no longer the innocent curiosity of Bluebeard's wife, but the legend of Faust's hunger for forbidden knowledge, which ultimately proved fatal. In the tales based on this theme, a necromancer ventures too far in his dark enquiries, loses control of the spirits he has summoned up, or perhaps tries to evade the final reckoning, and is destroyed by the spirits he has attempted to exploit, or otherwise carried off. James first used this motif in an early tale, 'Lost Hearts', but it occurs more frequently in his later work, for example in 'The Residence at Whitminster', 'An Evening's Entertainment' and 'A View from a Hill'. These three pieces are elaborately and amusingly presented, but their dénouements are marred by the excessive violence which often weakens his handling of this theme. Two of the tales described in a later essay, 'Stories I Have Tried to Write', deal with the same subject: in the first, an evil Roman priest is destroyed by the familiar he has called up to destroy another, while the second tells of a sixteenth-century Cambridge witch, carried off by a mysterious company. Both these stories would have employed a historical setting which, for James, frequently accompanied this plot.

The last group of James's stories, considered thematically, is perhaps the most classical and traditional: these are stories of revenge spirits, familiar from Shakespeare and his contemporaries, as well as from the great Victorians such as Dickens, Wilkie Collins and Le Fanu. As in *Richard III* or *Macbeth* the ghosts of the murdered appear to haunt the murderer and hasten his final downfall. These spirits seem to derive their power from the guilt caused by a forbidden action, such as murder, particularly of the helpless or weak. This classic pattern is used in 'Martin's Close', 'The Stalls of Barchester' (where further spirits come to effect the punishment of the guilty) and 'A Disappearance and an Appearance', each time with ingenious elaborations on the basic pattern of murder revenged.

All James's ghost stories resolve themselves into one of these three basic patterns, 'Bluebeard', 'Faust' or the spirits of revenge – even those stories which he did not finally complete, and this is hardly surprising in view of his enormous respect and feeling for classical structures. Nevertheless, one cannot help noting that many of his most successful stories occur in the first two collections, and that the two later volumes are largely made up of variations on earlier designs: 'The Haunted Dolls' House' is, quite openly, a replay of the dazzlingly simple idea of 'The Mezzotint', while 'A Warning to the Curious' recombines many of the elements of '"Oh, Whistle"', less successfully. Probably this sort of repetition is inevitable. It is certainly common to a number of other ghost story writers, including the admired Le Fanu, and may well be a measure of the form's limited possibilities, as James himself once suggested. His avowed motive in writing was to tell a good story, and having discovered from his wide reading certain well-established structural patterns, he adopted them and made them the bases on to which he grafted a variety of settings, incidents and characters. Throughout his work, he was strictly regulated by his particular notions as to how the suspense and climax should be achieved, and his practice reveals a close adherence to a limited number of techniques that he had evolved for himself, through his acquaintance with so many examples of the genre. He was perhaps the only writer who deliberately studied the ghost story in order to write it himself, and the resulting pieces exhibit a unique degree of critical control and an exceptional grasp of the force of traditional elements. Without being in any sense experimental or exploratory, his stories demonstrate the power that the classically well-made tale may still exert over a modern reader.

The apparent simplicity of M. R. James's technique and his immediate and lasting success naturally attracted a number of imitations, the best of these being written in the spirit of affectionate emulation that characterizes modern sequels to the Sherlock Holmes adventures. W. F. Harvey, a doctor who composed ghost stories in various different styles, produced a notable example in 'The Ankardyne pew' (*Moods and Tenses*, 1933). A gloomy eighteenth-century house has, a special architectural feature, a passage leading from the main bedroom straight to the chapel. Here in the family pew a rakehell squire once staged a cockfight, and afterwards tortured his defeated bird to death. The haunting is described in passages from a diary and letters dating from the late nineteenth century, but the full explanation is only discovered later from an entry in the *Gentleman's Magazine* for 1789. Other writers who adapted the formula to good effect were H. Russell Wakefield, notably in *They Walk at Night* (1928), and the scholar A. N. L. Munby, whose collection *The Alabaster Hand* (1949) was written in a prisoner-of-war camp, and is gracefully dedicated in Latin to James's own shade. William Croft Dickinson, a professor of Scottish history at Edinburgh University, has recorded a series of *Dark Encounters* (1963) which unfold in the authentic manner, straightforwardly and sequentially, often related by academics. All three of these authors display a mastery of technique which has made them popular with connoisseurs of the genre.

The most sustained tribute to the antiquary must surely be

Kingsley Amis's novel *The Green Man* (1969). Although it goes far beyond its original, both in terms of length and of licence (James would have been profoundly shocked by some of the scenes and language), it shows an imaginative grasp of his effects which is more telling than any commentary could be. A seventeenth-century magician, Doctor Thomas Underhill, haunts a smart pub called 'The Green Man'. Its name may derive from his familiar, a wood demon whose presence is indicated by a peculiar sound as of rustling twigs, a detail that is both precise, yet unpleasantly suggestive. Aided by a reference in an early collection of folklore, the narrator, Maurice, tracks down Underhill's diary to a Cambridge college library. Passages quoted from it provide an opportunity for an amusing double pastiche – it is a document not unlike 'The Diary of Mr Poynter'. James, however, declared that he had omitted from his diary quotation any reference to 'unpleasant habits and reputed delinquencies'. His disciple goes into these in some detail. Maurice recovers from Underhill's grave a silver talisman representing the fearful familiar, which alarmingly materializes to create a climax as relentlessly violent as any by James himself. The story is built up through a series of insubstantial hints and warnings: Underhill is first seen by Maurice's father, incoherent in the grip of a fatal heart-attack; the green man is initially glimpsed in a hypnagogic vision.

Amis has made one significant concession to modern taste: he casts doubt on Maurice as a reliable witness by making him an alcoholic. James had in fact sanctioned such a device (though he never used it himself) when he wrote 'it is not amiss sometimes to leave a loophole for a natural explanation; but . . . let the loophole be so narrow as not to be quite practicable'. His prescription is exactly followed, and the explanation of DTs is never really plausible' despite the introduction of the extra psychological levels that a modern audience expects from a novel, Kingsley Amis has remained remarkably faithful to the spirits of his original.

Note

First published by Faber & Faber (1977).

DAVID PUNTER

Extract from *The Literature of Terror*

In *Turn of the Screw* and the stories of de la Mare, we can see Gothic fiction taking on a new psychological sophistication and deploying for this purpose a masterly range of literary ambiguity. Also, earlier on, [we looked at] a group of works from the late nineteenth century – *Dr Jekyll and Mr Hyde*, *The Island of Doctor Moreau*, *The Picture of Dorian Gray* and *Dracula* – in which various elements of the Gothic tradition proved still capable of acting as conductors for a range of new anxieties and attitudes, both historical and scientific. Yet the two more recent figures to whom we have so far given any attention, Lovecraft and Machen, both in different ways demonstrate a falling-away in originality, a kind of hardening of stylistic and thematic arteries, and in this they are not alone. In moving now more fully into the twentieth century, I want to depict what seems to me an important bifurcation. On the one hand, some of the more important constituents of Gothic – the exploration of paranoia, the fear of the intrusion of the barbaric, the alienation accompanying divisions between social groups and between areas of knowledge and feeling – appear to me to have recently received very considerable attention, and to have generated a range of very important fictions, some of them recognisable as Gothic in the traditional sense, some not. Most of these works belong to the last three or four decades . . . I intend to follow a different tradition, the highly mannered phase of Gothic which is represented in the ghost story of the early twentieth century, a mode which has been, and in some ways still is, immensely popular despite lack of originality and a constant repetition of themes and images which we have come across before.

I want to start with some comments on the horror stories of two of the most popular writers of the early century . . ., Algernon Blackwood and M. R. James; finally, I want to talk about one of the very few twentieth-century ghost stories which seems to me to have something of the power of the older Gothic, the power, that is, to use the supernatural as an image for real and carefully depicted social fears: David Lindsay's *The Haunted Woman*, which was written in 1922 and which, in many respects, brings us round again to a recollection of the purposes and themes of Radcliffe and her contemporaries while not sacrificing an intense and accurate perception of the historical dimension of terror. The principal interest of this whole development is concentrated on a single dialectic, which culminates in the shockingly bland tones of M. R. James, the dialectic between disturbance and comfort. [Julia] Briggs writes that 'the combination of modern scepticism with a nostalgia for an older, more supernatural system of beliefs provides the foundation of the ghost story, and this nostalgia can be seen as inherently romantic', and this is true as far as it goes; but it is also worth pointing out a further twist in this situation, whereby the tendency of the ghost story to reside in the trappings of the historical past has itself become reduced to a formula, a formula no doubt still capable of interesting variation, but nonetheless altering our reactions to the fiction from fear towards a more reassured awareness of the self-conscious fictionality of the works. Part of the terror to be derived from Conan Doyle or M. R. James arises not from ways in which the stories overturn our predictions, but precisely from the way in which they conform to them, the way in which, from the very first sentence, from the first act of settling into an armchair, or from the first intrusion of the surprise visitor, we know in advance the intention and approximate structure of what we are reading. If, of course, the writer can in fact exploit precisely this sense of security to any effect, then the achievement may be considerable, and all five of these writers seem to me at times able to do so; but for every one of them there are ten other writers of ghost stories for whom Gothic accessories have become a trap, and in whose works they merely conjure up for us a secure atmosphere of suspended disbelief.

. . .

The stories of Algernon Blackwood are very different, in that they are generally informed by, and contribute to the formation and validation of, a single world-view. In Blackwood, the realm of the supernatural is accepted as existent, his stories are full of 'explanations' – particularly those which feature the 'ghost-hunter', John Silence – but they are explanations which presuppose belief. And the peculiar terror which he often exploits is at an opposite pole to the moralistic tenor of tales like Conan Doyle's 'The New Catacomb' or Wells's 'The Moth', in that his chief characters (here Grimwood in 'The Valley of the Beasts' (1921) is a notable exception) rarely bring upon themselves a deserved doom. The supernatural forces which he posits are fundamentally *indifferent* to man: the wendigo, the elemental forces in 'The Willows' (1907), the forests in 'The Man whom the Trees Loved' are not hostile entities, but if disturbed, for one reason or another, they are able to act in powerful and terrifying ways.

. . .

The insistence on the importance of the sexual elements in terror in Blackwood's work is part of a larger and more general concern with the psychology of fear. In this area he is in strong contrast with the other major figure of the later ghost story, M. R. James. Briggs speaks of James's total lack of interest in the workings of the mind, saying that 'psychology is totally and defiantly excluded from his writings', but this is perhaps not quite true: what James *is* uninterested in is the psychology of his *characters*. Blackwood displays to us the operation of fear within and upon particular minds: James, on the other hand, constructs minute and intricate working models which have as their end product fear in the mind of the *reader*. If his characters are not very interesting, complex or even concrete, this is precisely because he does not want them to form a veil between us and the terror. Other writers have tried to achieve the same end by making their characters so 'like us' that we locate our own feelings within them: James, instead, makes his characters totally cardboard and concentrates on the direct flash of terror between the event on the printed page and the reader. His characters are rarely provided with interesting motivations for the dangerous activities in which they indulge: in 'The Treasure of Abbot Thomas', for instance, although the structure of the plot looks conventional in that a search for treasure produces dreadful effects, the protagonist is moved not by greed or ambition but merely by intellectual curiosity; the fact that he ends up face to tentacle with the treasure's obnoxious guardian is in no way organic to him, and thus the breach in the natural order is all the more horrifying. Then again, there is perhaps a general connexion, but it is very long-range: if the only motivation of most of James's characters is curiosity, then behind all curiosity, according to Freud, lies the displaced sexual urge, and James's characters do move in an entirely bachelor world.

. . .

Almost all of the stories are structurally identical in what they proceed steadily through a series of prefigurations towards a single moment of revelation or encounter. Sometimes the prefigurations are at a distance, as with the appearance of the mutilated children in 'Lost Hearts', or the fate of Anders Bjornsen in 'Count Magnus', who 'was once a beautiful man, but now his face was not there, because the flesh of it was sucked away off the bones'. But some prefigurations and the final encounters are generally marked by an intensely rendered proximity, as in the well-known nightmarish sequence in 'Casting the Runes', when Dunning puts his hand under the pillow to find his watch, 'only, it did not get so far. What he touched was, according to his account, a mouth, with teeth, and with hair about it, and, he declares, not the mouth of a human being'; or in the subtler form of 'The Stalls of Barchester Cathedral': 'I was pursued by the very vivid impression that wet lips were whispering into my ear with great rapidity and emphasis for some time together.' In most of these cases, it is the very indefiniteness and incompleteness of the images that accounts for a large part of their effect: they are momentary glimpses, imprinted on the brain, as it were, by flashlight.

But thus far, one might say that there is nothing very unusual in James's presentations of terror; and in fact it is curiously difficult to find within his texts the exact grounds of his effectiveness. Partly, it has to do with another aspect of proximity, with the fact that James is constantly affirming that he is presenting his tales just as they were told to him. In this way he seeks to assert a continuity between the events and the reader, with himself as mediator: in 'Number Thirteen', he passes between high points of the action with the offhand comment that the protagonist 'had nothing to tell me (I am giving the story as I heard it from him) about what passed at supper'. In 'The Treasure of Abbot Thomas', he languidly discusses the possibility of himself making a visit to the scene of the story:

> It has not seemed to me worth while to lavish money on a visit to the place, for though it is probably far more attractive than either Mr Somerton or Mr Gregory thought it, there is evidently little, if anything, of first-rate interest to be seen – except, perhaps, one thing, which I should not care to see.

But more importantly it has to do again with predictability, with the fact that from the very first moment of the story a physical literary background is established which promises precisely the mixture of the comforting and the disturbing on which this kind of ghost story thrives.

. . .

The approach is reminiscent of the fairy story, with its self-conscious anecdotalism, its terseness of description and the halo of suspense surrounding apparently mundane detail. And James, of course, also builds up his own norms: to read basically the same opening to four or five different stories is to learn the markers by which he invests the everyday with a sense of anticipation. Already in these brief sentences one can feel the haste to get the story moving, the almost impatient brushing aside of setting and even character so that the events themselves can take the forefront of the stage.

James is an intensely mannered writer, both in the local matter of his scholarly style – 'An Episode of Cathedral History' ends, and makes its point, with the untranslated phrase *Ibi cubavit lamia* – and also in his insistence on self-conscious fictionality. 'The Tractate Middoth', '"Oh, Whistle, and I'll Come to you, my Lad"', 'The Ash-Tree', 'Mr Humphreys and his Inheritance' all hinge on ludicrous coincidences which are left happily unexplained even in terms of the supernatural. The coherence of the stories is not a matter of 'real' probability, but of literary probability: the probability, which he partly inherits and partly establishes within his own range of texts, that stories to do with ancient cathedrals, decaying towns, old manuscripts will 'naturally' move in a world of terror. Unlike Blackwood, he makes no attempt whatever to explain why this should be so: it is simply assumed as a convention. James is often regarded as a master of understatement, and this is true, but the understatements only work because of their context, because he establishes a dialectic of the predictable.

. . .

But fundamentally, James's stories work through irony, and it is an irony of a particular kind in that it depends entirely on a prior acquaintance – not necessarily conscious – with the assumptions of the Gothic. There is the constant use of the device whereby, early on in the stories, the character becomes aware of the presence of something which *he* assumes to be perfectly natural, but which we already know not to be.

. . .

In his stories the Gothic has become a habit, and displays the repetitive power which habits possess. The kinds of basic fear which he exploits – fear of the archaic, the irruption of chaos into an ordered world – are precisely those of the Gothic writers, but his stories are perfected forms drained of content. They *work* well, but they *mean* almost nothing, because they are not independent: they are extended footnotes, further examples of a kind which, it is assumed, we already know. In this sense, James represents a final decay of the Gothic into formalism.

Essentially, in James the Gothic is not longer a mode for dramatising problems: there are no points of hiatus or contradiction in his ghost stories. In David Lindsay's *The Haunted Woman*, however, one can still sense the pressure exerted on the form by the material with which it is trying to cope – issues about the relations between the sexes, about the power of social convention, about the possible balefulness of the past. Lindsay is best known, perhaps, as the writer of *A Voyage to Arcturus* (1920), an uneven but powerful fantasy which has recently re-emerged as an object of cult attention, and the style of the two books is in some ways similar: Lindsay was not a good writer, and it is often obvious how hard he has had to struggle to achieve a reasonably flowing narrative. But despite this, *The Haunted Woman* commands attention, rather as *Frankenstein* does, because the issues raised spread far beyond the author's conscious attempt to control them.

. . .

The Haunted Woman is one of the clearest statements of the importance of sexual roles as a motif in Gothic fiction; Lindsay comes out with comments that would not be out of place sixty years later. 'History', says Isbel [the 'heroine'], 'has been written by men, and men aren't the most enlightened critics where women are concerned. All that will have to be re-written by qualified feminine experts some day'. The book uses the form of the ghost story to suggest the sexual revolution which Isbel herself fails to achieve on a personal level: 'henceforward', she claims, 'men are going to exist for us, not we for them'; but that, clearly, is a long way in the future. In the meantime, there is only the distorted glimpse of liberation, a life haunted by dreams of possibility.

This is, of course, not the only modern work of the supernatural in which Gothic is made over again into the service of real social commentary, but it is one of the most whole-hearted; the remarkable thing, perhaps, is that the apparatus of haunted houses, mysterious staircases and distant music can still be made to say anything at all. During the last sixty years, although Gothic has continued to exert an influence – and indeed in many ways an increasing one – it has usually been only a partial one, with particular elements of the tradition being adapted to new purposes, as we shall see later; what is rare about *The Haunted Woman* is that, despite the draining of content which we have seen particularly in [Conan Doyle and] M. R. James, the entire ageing skeleton can still be made to dance.

Notes

First published by Longman (1980).

1. Julia Briggs, *Night Visitors: The Rise and Fall of the English Ghost Story* (London: Faber, 1977). All quotes are from this Volume.

TZVETAN TODOROV

Extract from *The Fantastic*

We are now in a position to focus and complete our definition of the fantastic. The fantastic requires the fulfillment of three conditions. First, the text must oblige the reader to consider the world of the characters as a world of living persons and to hesitate between a natural and a supernatural explanation of the events described. Second, this hesitation may also be experienced by a character; thus the reader's role is so to speak entrusted to a character, and at the same time the hesitation is represented, it becomes one of the themes of the work – in the case of naive reading, the actual reader identifies himself with the character. Third, the reader must adopt a certain attitude with regard to the text: he will reject allegorical as well as 'poetic' interpretations. These three requirements do not have an equal value. The first and the third actually constitute the genre; the second may not be fulfilled. Nonetheless, most examples satisfy all three conditions.

. . .

The fantastic, we have seen, lasts only as long as a certain hesitation: a hesitation common to reader and character, who must decide whether or not what they perceive derives from 'reality' as it exists in the common opinion. At the story's end, the reader makes a decision even if the character does not; he opts for one solution or the other, and thereby emerges from the fantastic. If he decides that the laws of reality remain intact and permit an explanation of the phenomena described, we say that the work belongs to another genre: the uncanny. If, on the contrary, he decides that new laws of nature must be entertained to account for the phenomena, we enter the genre of the marvelous.

Note

Reproduced from *The Fantastic: A Structural Approach to a Literary Genre*, translated by Richard Howard (London, 1973).

ROSEMARY JACKSON

Extract from *Fantasy*

I look elsewhere and differently, there where there is no spectacle.

Hélène Cixous[1]

The crucial thing is not what is behind the images, but what is visible in them as a speck of white. The beyond . . . is the repressed, censored portion of the 'this-side' of things . . . the raising of the dead, that is in fact the real triumph of disorder. An event beyond all interpretability, outside any context. A zero point, another white speck, a gap in the chain of causality. When Freud began to describe the Unconscious and to comprehend it in a theoretical manner he could only establish that he was in an area where the conceptual apparatus of the existing sciences broke down. That it was the great Other on which we all depend, and which, at first, could only be conceptualized by means of negative categories.

Frieda Grafe[2]

Throughout its 'history', fantasy has been obscured and locked away, buried as something inadmissible and darkly shameful. Spenser's long allegorical poem, *The Faerie Queene*, locks away the giant Phantastes, spinner of endless fantasies, in a dark chamber concealed within the centre of the House of Temperance. Phantastes is significantly hidden within the mansion of order and propriety, left to spin

> Infinite shapes of thinges dispersed thin;
> Some such as in the world were never yit,
> Ne can devized be of mortall wit.

The fantastic has constantly been dismissed by critics as being an embrace of madness, irrationality, or narcissism and it has been opposed to the humane and more civilized practices of 'realistic' literature. Belinsky, for example, condemned Dostoevsky's *The Double* for its 'fantastic colouring', declaring that 'The fantastic in our time can have a place only in an insane asylum, and not in our literature'.[3] Walter Scott similarly dismissed E. T. A. Hoffmann's tales for hovering on the edge of insanity and for not being 'reconciled to taste'.

An implicit association of the fantastic with the barbaric and non-human has exiled it to the edges of literary culture. Novelists redeploying some fantastic elements, such as Dickens, Gogol, or Dostoevsky, have been placed differently from Jane Austen, George Eliot, or Henry James, in the establishment of a canon of 'great' literature, whilst Gothic novelists, Sade, M. G. Lewis, Mary Shelley, James Hogg, R. L. Stevenson, Calvino, have been relatively neglected. Only recently has the influence of French theory begun to encourage a less hostile reading of and response to these fantastic texts and begun to formulate some of the critical problems which they articulate – problems which need much more extensive discussion than has been possible, problems to do with the relation between language and *eros*, to do with the 'unconscious' formation of the subject, the interplay of imaginary, symbolic and real, and the violent intersection of 'fantastic' narratives in the midst of this interplay. Precisely because it is situated in this crucial area, the fantastic demands much more theoretical attention, in relation to literary and film texts, and much more analysis of its linguistic and psychoanalytical features.

Not surprisingly, fantastic art has been muted by a tradition of literary criticism concerned with supporting establishment ideals rather than with subverting them. In so far as it is possible to reconstruct a 'history/ of literary fantasy, it is one of repeated neutralization of its images of impossibility and of desire – both in the trajectories of the literary texts themselves and in the criticism which has mediated them to an intellectual audience.

The dismissal of the fantastic to the margins of literary culture is in itself an ideologically significant gesture, one which is not dissimilar to culture's silencing of unreason. As an 'art' of unreason, and of desire, fantasy has persistently been silenced, or re-written, in transcendental rather than transgressive terms. Its threatened un-doing, or dissolution, of dominant structures, has been re-made, re-covered into moral allegory and magical romance. As Foucault writes of unreason, 'Any transgression in life becomes a social crime, condemned and punished . . . imprisoned in a moral world [for offending] bourgeois society.'[4] From a rational, [monological' world, otherness cannot be known or represented except as foreign, irrational, 'mad', 'bad'. It is either rejected altogether, or polemically refuted, or assimilated into a 'meaningful' narrative structure, re-written or written out as romance or as fable. Otherness is transmuted into idealism by romance writers and is muted, made silent and invisible by 'realistic' works, only to return in strange, expressive forms in many texts. The 'other' expressed through fantasy has been categorized as a negative black area – as evil, demonic, barbaric – until its recognition in the modern fantastic as culture's 'unseen'.

Fantasies moving towards the realm of the 'marvellous' are the ones which have been tolerated and widely disseminated socially. A creation of secondary worlds through religious myth, faery, science fiction, uses 'legalized' methods – religion, magic, science – to establish other worlds, worlds which are *compensatory*, which fill up a lack, making up for an apprehension of actuality as disordered and insufficient. These fantasies *transcend* that actuality. Their romance base suggests that the universe is, ultimately, a self-regulating mechanism in which goodness, stability, order will eventually prevail.

They serve to stabilize social order by minimizing the need for human intervention in this benevolently organized cosmic mechanism.

Critics of fantasy have tended to defend it in terms of this *transcendent* function. One of the first apologists was Charles Nodier, whose essay 'The Fantastic in Literature' was published by the *Revue de Paris* in 1830. Nodier detected a line of continuity between religious and secular fantasies: the second were a later development of the first and had a similar cultural function, to tell tales of escaping, or of transcending, the human condition.[5] As late as 1973, Jean-Baptiste Baronian echoes this sentiment in an article defining 'the property of the fantastic' as being 'to transcend reality, even beyond the most elementary sounds and voices'.[5] French critics such as Caillois, Lévy and Vax, English critics including John Batchelor, C. N. Manlove and Stephen Prickett, have all passed on this notion of the fantastic as an escapist literature and have made this the centre of their apologies. The works of the last three are situated within an academic tradition of liberal humanist criticism, to which transcendentalism is no stranger, but it leaves their ideas cut off from those vital theoretical areas essential to an understanding of the fantastic.

In many ways these traditional defendants of fantasy are repeating one of Freud's ideas as to the cultural function of art itself. The creation of artistic products, according to Freud, is a 'phantasizing' activity which provides man with compensation for having renounced instinctive gratification. 'Men have always found it hard to renounce pleasure', writes Freud. 'They cannot bring themselves to do it without some kind of compensation' (*Introductory Lectures on Psychoanalysis*). When fantasy has been allowed to surface within culture, it has been in a manner close to Freud's notion of art as compensation, as an activity which *sustains* cultural order by making up for a society's lacks.[6] Gothic fiction, for example, tended to buttress a dominant, bourgeois, ideology, by vicarious wish fulfilment through fantasies of incest, rape, murder, parricide, social disorder. Like pornography, it functioned to supply an object of desire, to imagine social and sexual transgression.

Merely on a thematic level, then, fantastic literature is not necessarily subversive. To attempt to defend fantasy as inherently transgressive would be a vast, over-simplifying and mistaken gesture. Those elements which have been designated 'fantastic' – effecting a movement towards undifferentiation and a condition of entropy – have been constantly re-worked, re-written and re-covered to *serve* rather than to *subvert* the dominant ideology. As Jonathan Culler writes, 'For the most part, fantasy in literature testifies to the power of the reality principle to transform its enemies into its own mirror image. In the face of this power, it is all the more important that we assert fantasy's responsibility to resist before we accept Yeats's formula: "In dreams begins responsibility".'[7]

An understanding of the subversive function of fantastic literature emerges from *structuralist* rather than from merely *thematic* readings of texts. It has been seen that many fantasies from the late eighteenth century onwards attempt to undermine dominant philosophical and epistemological orders. They subvert and interrogate nominal unities of time, space and character, as well as questioning the possibility, or honesty, of fictional re-presentation of those unities. Like the grotesque, with which it overlaps, the fantastic can be seen as an art of estrangement, resisting closure, opening structures which categorize experience in the name of a 'human reality'. By drawing attention to the relative nature of these categories the fantastic moves towards a dismantling of the 'real', most particularly of the concept of 'character' and its ideological assumptions, mocking and parodying a blind faith in psychological coherence and in the value of sublimation as a 'civilizing' activity.

A unified, stable 'ego' lies at the heart of this systematic coherence and the fantastic explodes this by seeking to make that heart's darkness visible. From Hoffmann and German Romanticism, to the modern fantastic in horror films, fantasy has tried to erode the pillars of society by un-doing categorical structures. As Hélène Cixous writes, 'The machine of repression has always had the same accomplices; homogenizing, reductive, unifying reason has always allied itself to the Master, to the single, stable, socializable subject, represented by its types or characters.' In fantastic works where the 'I' is more than one, there is a resistance to such reduction. 'These texts baffle every attempt to summarization of meaning and limiting, repressive interpretation. The subject flounders here in the exploded multiplicity of its states . . . spreading out in every possible direction . . . transegoistically.' They erode the supports of 'logocentrism, idealism, theologism, the scaffolding of political and subjective economy'.[8]

Far from construing this attempt at erosion as a mere embrace of barbarism or of chaos, it is possible to discern it as a desire for something excluded from cultural order – more specifically, for all that is in opposition to the capitalist and patriarchal order which has been dominant in Western society over the last two centuries. As a literature of desire, the fantastic can be seen as providing a point of departure, in Bersani's words, 'for an authentically civilizing scepticism about the nature of our desires and the nature of our being'.[9]

Irène Bessière's study of fantasy indicated its position as one of *relationality*, as a narrative situated in a relation of opposition to dominant orders. Bessière connects this function to Sartre's distinction between the *non-thetic* as opposed to the *thetic*.[10] The fantastic, in its movement towards non-signification, pulls towards the non-thetic, to all that is opposed to dominant signifying practice. The theoretical work of Julia Kristeva suggests that the non-thetic can be linked to all those forces which threaten to disrupt a tradition of rationalism. Such forces have been apprehended as inimical to cultural order from at least as far back as Plato's *Republic*. Plato expelled from his ideal Republic all transgressive energies, all those energies which have been seen to be expressed through the fantastic: eroticism, violence, madness, laughter, nightmares, dreams, blasphemy, lamentation, uncertainty, female energy, excess. Art which represented such energies was to be exiled from Plato's ideal state. Literature mentioning 'the Rivers of Wailing and Gloom, and the ghosts of corpses, and all other things whose very names are enough to make everyone who hears them shudder' was to have *no place* in the Republic. The working life of slaves, the oppression of women, or any intimation of their suffering, any reference to sexuality or childbirth, were similarly banned from fictional representation. Socrates and his audience agree that 'We must forbid this sort of thing entirely'. The fantastic, then, is *made invisible* in Plato's Republic and in the tradition of high rationalism which it fostered: alongside all subversive social forces, fantasy is expelled and is registered only as absence. 'Plato feels his rational and unified Republic threatened from within by forces, desires and activities which must be censored or ostracized if the rational state is to be maintained.'[11]

Through the introduction of some of the theories of Freud and of Lacan, it has been possible to claim for the fantastic a subversive function in attempting to depict a *reversal* of the subject's cultural formation. If the symbolic is seen as 'that unity of semantic and syntactic competence which allows communication and rationality to appear', the imaginary area which is intimated in fantastic literature suggests all that is other, all that is absent from the symbolic, outside rational discourse.[12] Fantasies of deconstructed, demolished or divided identities and of disintegrated bodies, oppose traditional categories of unitary selves. They attempt to give graphic depictions of subjects *in process*, suggesting possibilities of innumerable other selves, of different histories, different bodies. They denounce the theses and categories of the thetic, attempting to dissolve the symbolic order at its very base, where it is established in and through the subject, where the dominant signifying system is re-produced. This does not imply that subjects can exist outside of ideology and of the social formation, but that fantasies image the possibility of radical cultural transformation through attempting to dissolve or shatter the boundary lines between the imaginary and the symbolic. They refuse the latter's categories of the 'real' and its unities.

The modern fantastic, as exemplified for instance in the tales of Kafka, does not simply embrace chaos, nor does a theoretical approach to these texts simply urge a lapse into the pre-linguistic or pre-cultural. As Kafka's *Metamorphosis* makes clear, it is not a matter of seeking a dissolution of 'civilizing' forms as such, nor of advocating a 'new barbarism'. Rather it is a matter of apprehending the symbolic as repressive and crippling to the subject, and of attempting to transform the relations between the symbolic and the imaginary. Kafka's Gregor Samsa has no simple desire for death: the tale incorporates as part of its internal structure a tension between the symbolic and the imaginary, expressing a reluctance to give in to a desire for something other, yet apprehending this other as the only alternative to a hostile, patriarchal order. Kafka is well aware of the de-humanizing implications of fantastic transformation, and the dilemma articulated here is central to modern fantasy.

> But what if all the quiet, the comfort, the contentment were now to end in horror? . . . Did he really want his warm room, so comfortably fitted with old family furniture, to be turned into a naked den in which he would certainly be able to crawl unhampered in all directions but at the price of shedding simultaneously all recollection of his human background?

To introduce the fantastic is to replace familiarity, comfort, *das Heimlich*, with estrangement, unease, the uncanny. It is to introduce dark areas, of something completely other and unseen, the spaces outside the limiting frame of the 'human' and 'real', outside the control of the 'word' and of the 'look'. Hence the association of the modern fantastic with the horrific, from Gothic tales of terror to contemporary horror films. The emergence of such literature in periods of relative 'stability' (the mid-eighteenth century, late nineteenth century, mid-twentieth century) points to a direct relation between cultural repression and its generation of oppositional energies which are *expressed* through various forms of fantasy in art.

Fantasy has always articulated a longing for imaginary unity, for unity in the realm of the imaginary. In this sense, it is inherently idealistic. It expresses a desire for an absolute, for an absolute signified, an absolute meaning. It is no accident that the Faust motif is so central, recurring explicitly or implicitly in post-Romantic fantasies and fictions from *Vathek*, *Frankenstein*, *Melmoth the Wanderer* and *Confessions of a Justified Sinner*, through Balzac's *Louis Lambert* and *Le Recherche de L'Absolu*, to Alfred Jarry's *Dr Faustroll*, Mann's *Doctor Faustus* and Pynchon's *V*, for Faust signifies precisely this desire, within a secularized culture. Whereas fantasies produced from within a religious or magical thought mode depict the possibility of union of self and other, fantasies without those systems of belief cannot realize absolute 'truth' or 'unity'. Their longings for otherness are apprehended as impossible, except in parodic, travestied, horrific or tragic form.

Like its mythical and magical predecessors, then, the fantastic desires transformation and difference. Unlike its transcendental counterparts (found in recent 'faery' literature), the fantastic refuses to accept supernatural fictions: it remains non-nostalgic, without illusions of superhuman intervention to effect difference. 'The great realizations of the modern fantastic – the last unrecognizable avatars of romance as a mode – draw their magical power from their *unsentimental* loyalty to those henceforth abandoned clearings across which higher and lower worlds once passed'.[13] As Todorov pointed out, fantasy is located uneasily between 'reality' and 'literature', unable to accept either, with the result that a fantastic mode is situated between the 'realistic' and the 'marvellous', stranded between this world and the next. Its subversive function derives from this uneasy positioning. The negative versions (inversions) of unity, found in the modern fantastic, from Gothic novels – Mary Shelley, Elizabeth Gaskell, Dickens, Poe, Dostoevsky, Stevenson, Wilde – to Kafka, Cortazar, Calvino, Lovecraft, Peake and Pynchon, represent dissatisfaction and frustration with a cultural order which deflects or defeats desire, yet refuse to have recourse to compensatory, transcendental other-worlds.

The modern fantastic, the form of literary fantasy within the secularized culture produced by capitalism, is a subversive literature. It exists alongside the 'real', on either side of the dominant cultural axis, as a muted presence, a silenced imaginary other. Structurally and semantically, the fantastic aims at dissolution of an order experienced as oppressive and insufficient. Its paraxial placing, eroding and scrutinizing the 'real', constitutes, in Hélène Cixous's phrase, 'a subtle invitation to transgression'. By attempting to transform the relations between the imaginary and the symbolic, fantasy hollows out the 'real', revealing its absence, its 'great Other', its unspoken and its unseen. As Todorov writes, 'The fantastic permits us to cross certain frontiers that are inaccessible so long as we have no recourse to it.'[14]

Notes

First published by Methuen (1981).

1. Hélène Cixous 'The Character of Character', *Revue des Sciences Humaines* (December 1977) p. 487.
2. Frieda Grafe and E. Patalas, *Suddeutsche Zeitung*, 9/10 (February 1974); tr. R. Mann, from Mark Nash, *Dreyer*, p. 80.
3. Cited in Edward Wasiolek, *Dostoevsky: The Major Fiction* (Cambridge, MA: Harvard University Press, 1964) p. 5.
4. Michel Foucault, *Madness and Civilization*, tr. Richard Howard (London, 1967) p. 288.
5. Charles Nodier, 'The Fantastic in Literature', in Jean Baptiste Baronian (ed.), *La France Fantastique de Balzac à Louÿs* (Verviers, 1973) pp. 17–31.
6. Sigmund Freud, *Introductory Lectures on Psychoanalysis*, tr. James Strachey (London, 1953) p. 119.
7. Jonathan Culler, 'Literary Fantasy', *Cambridge Review*, 93 (1973) p. 33.
8. Cixous, op. cit., p. 389.
9. Leo Bersani, *A Future for Asyanax: Character and Desire in Literature* (Toronto, 1976) p. 313.
10. Irène Bessière, *Le Récit fantastique* (Paris, 1974) p. 75.
11. Allon H. White, *L'éclatement du Sujet: The Theoretical Work of Julia Kristeva* (Birmingham, 1977) p. 3.
12. Ibid., p. 8.
13. Fredric Jameson, 'Magical Narratives: Romance as Genre', *New Literary History*, 7 (Autumn 1975) p. 146.
14. Tzvetan Todorov, *The Fantastic: A Structuralist Approach to a Literary Genre*, tr. Richard Howard (London, 1973).

ANNE CRANNY FRANCIS

On *The Vampire Tapestry*

The Vampire Tapestry[1] is an innovative exploration of the horror genre by Suzy McKee Charnas, American author of the feminist dystopia *Walk to the End of the World* and its disturbing and ambiguous sequel, *Motherlines*. Horror literature, like all fantasy,[2] has the potential to be either a radical exploration of contemporary definitions of the 'real' or a conservative affirmation of that 'real', via the political ideologies (of gender, race, class) operative in the text. In this essay I analyse Charnas's textual inflections of these ideologies, principally through her characterisation of the vampire. This characterisation is remarkable for Charnas's sophisticated manipulation of textual polyphony, characteristically foregrounded in the fantasy text. Accordingly, her characterisation of the vampire is subject to neither humanist reductionism nor generic stereotyping. Instead Charnas constructs him as a fragmented consciousness, the decentred subject, characteristic of the fantastic in its most radically interrogative mode. By tracing Charnas's textual strategies and their ideological consequences, I present a case for *The Vampire Tapestry* as an example of the use of generic fiction by a politically committed writer to raise fundamental debate about social and political ideologies within a popular and accessible fictional format.

The Vampire Tapestry describes a period in the life of a vampire, currently masquerading as eminent anthropologist and academic Dr Edward Weyland. Charnas's story is not a chronologically direct narrative, but is told as five separate narratives; hence the 'tapestry' of the title. In each narrative Charnas describes a crucial episode in the life of Dr Weyland. In the first, 'The Ancient Mind at Work', Weyland's identity as a vampire is detected and he is shot and seriously wounded by his discoverer, Katje de Groot. In part II, 'The Land of Lost Content', the injured Weyland has been found by a group of petty criminals who, in collusion with a pathetic satanist character, put him on display. Part III, 'Unicorn Tapestry', sees Weyland free again, bargaining for the restoration of his academic position by agreeing to psychoanalysis for his delusion that he is a vampire. His analyst is Floria Landauer, and through her Weyland begins to discover some empathy with humans, who, until then, he had regarded merely as a food source. In part IV, 'A Musical Interlude', Weyland has moved to a university in New Mexico, significantly without killing Floria Landauer, who knows his true nature. Here Weyland attends a performance of Puccini's opera *Tosca* and is aroused by it to blood lust. He kills needlessly and indiscriminately. In the final episode, 'The Last of Dr Weyland', the vampire is threatened with possible exposure and decides to end his masquerade as Dr Weyland.

I   'The Ancient Mind at Work'

Charnas's novel works very well as an example of the vampire sub-genre of horror. She employs a number of the conventions associated with vampire novels since *Dracula*. And she employs them sensitively and intelligently; this is not a splatter text. The first of these conventions is the interrogation of the possibility of the vampire – the absurd notion that such a creature can have a real existence. This convention does not have its origins in *Dracula*, where Jonathan Harker's discovery of the vampire nature of his host, Count Dracula, is preceded by very little knowledge of the topic. Certainly Harker experiences the fear of Transylvanian peasants, but this is not the learned scepticism of twentieth-century Americans. The reason for this modification of the convention is audience familiarity with the story of *Dracula* and other vampires, in literature and film. For modern audiences horror that such a creature can exist is replaced by a kind of second-order scepticism. No longer does such a creature seem so extraordinary. His feeding-practice is relatively fastidious and his motivation is rational and almost acceptable compared with the butchery most contemporary audiences witness night after night on their television screens. The vampire is no longer horrific because of his nature; in fact, his nature renders him understandable, explicable, in human terms. He sucks blood in order to live, not as a sexual thrill. He is not a psychopath; he is a human mutation, and a relatively civilised one.

For modern audiences, then, the vampire is a curiosity – a dangerous curiosity – but not quite the monster he once was. Modern audiences are not learning vampire lore; they know that already – garlic, crucifixes, wooden stakes, and so forth. The fun for contemporary audiences is in discovering how many of these elements of lore the urbane, modern vampire will reject. Movie audiences especially are familiar with the scene of a modern vampire laughing scornfully at the crucifix- and garlic-wielding human combatant, accusing her/him of belief in superstitious nonsense.

And, of course, fundamental to this play with the fictional

vampire knowledge is the question of the *reality* of the vampire. This is an investigation which operates simultaneously on a number of levels. In the modern story, the world of the narrative, contemporary characters are assumed to be familiar with the notion of the vampire. The major difficulty they face is accepting that such a creature, so familiar from late night TV reruns, is not purely fictional. The biggest obstacle they face in their battle with the vampire is not her/his monstrous nature, but their own scepticism. Only when they can accept that the vampire is *real* can they begin to fight her/him on informed ground.

Then comes the process of discovering how much of that information is superstition, and how much of it is effective against the creature – how much of the fiction is fiction and how much of it is real. The reader of contemporary vampire novels is thus caught up in a debate about the relationship between fiction and reality at the level of narrative. The 'hesitation' which Todorov described as the distinguishing characteristic of the fantastic has a structuring function in the narrative itself.

This narrative hesitation has a reflexive function, positioning us as readers to question our relationship to the text we are reading. What about *this* text is real and what is fictional? How is the 'real' signified/represented/discursively formulated in a fictional text? Does the 'reality' have to do with the responses of people just like ourselves to a creature so utterly different from ourselves? These questions are fundamental to the narrative of part I, 'The Ancient Mind at Work'. They are fundamental also to the sexual politics of the text, to Charnas's investigation of the ideology of gender which is implicit in this text, just as an affirmation of conservative gender relationships is implicit in most other vampire texts.

In part I Katje de Groot, expatriate South African Boer and widow of a university professor, discovers that the distinguished academic Dr Edward Weyland is a vampire. De Groot discovers this because she is at the university at a time when most other people have left, and that is because she works there as a domestic. With Katje de Groot Charnas constructs an unusual vampire-hunter. Politically conservative in the best traditions of vampire literature, de Groot is, however, a woman and she has no respect for the politics of either class or race. De Groot learns much from her interaction with the vampire and the mechanism of her education is crucial to Charnas's investigation of gender politics.

In choosing to work as a domestic Mrs de Groot shows her

contempt for the class politics of the university, a point Charnas drives home by linking her work ironically with that of a black maid. Charnas has the black handyman Jackson make this connection: "'Yeah. Well, you sure have moved around more than most while you been here; from lady of leisure to, well, maid work." She saw the flash of his grin. "Like my aunt that used to clean for white women up the hill. Don't you mind?"' (p. 33).

Mrs de Groot also declares herself immune to race politics. Unlike her husband, she did not take part in the Black Majority Movement as an exile. She wants to return to South Africa, to buy her own house, and ignore the politics:

> Her savings from her salary as housekeeper at the Cayslin Club would eventually finance her return home. She needed enough to buy not a farm, but a house with a garden patch somewhere high and cool – she frowned, trying the picture the ideal site. Nothing clear came into her mind. She had been away a long time. (p. 17)

Eventually, however, she realises that it is not possible to ignore the politics of South Africa, and it is because of her interaction with Weyland that she comes to this realisation:

> Reluctantly she admitted that one of her feelings while listening to Dr Weyland talk had been an unwilling empathy: if he was a one-way time traveller, so was she. She saw herself cut off from the old life of raw vigour, the rivers of game, the smoky village air, all viewed from the heights of white privilege. To lose one's world these days one did not have to sleep for half a century; one had only to grow older. (p. 44)

Mrs de Groot recognises the identity of difference, of alienation, between herself and Weyland; each feels like 'a stranger in a strange land'. This identity between female protagonist and vampire is a crucial element in Charnas's analysis and is pursued throughout the novel.

Gender politics are also discussed overtly in this section of the book. Students have been raped on campus and Mrs de Groot's co-workers worry about her vulnerability. Her response to the rapist is characteristically conservative, as is shown in her scornful rejection of the concern expressed by female academics: 'Katje wasn't interested. A woman who used her sense and carried herself with self-respect didn't get raped, but saying so to these intellectual women wasted breath. They didn't understand real life' (pp. 27–8).

Again de Groot has to change her ideas. In the final showdown with the vampire, symbolically the attempted rape, she only survives because she protects herself, abandoning her dignity to do so. Only when she identifies wholly with the vampire is she able to fight on familiar ground:

> In her lassitude she was sure that he had attacked that girl, drunk her blood, and then killed her. He was using the rapist's activities as cover. When subjects did not come to him at the sleep lab, hunger drove him out to hunt.
> She thought, *But I am myself a hunter!* (p. 50)

The identification between the woman and the vampire is also an identification of power, of strength. Having made that recognition de Groot is able to defend herself:

> She jerked out the automatic, readying it to fire as she brought it swiftly up to eye level in both hands, while her mind told her calmly that a head shot would be best but that a hit was surer if she aimed for the torso.
> She shot him twice, two slugs in quick succession, one in the chest and one in the abdomen. He did not fall but bent to clutch at his torn body, and he screamed and screamed so that she was too shaken to steady her hands for the head shot afterwards. (p. 51)

This identification is interesting in that de Groot is not only a Boer and a trained hunter, but also a woman. The race politics of the Boer, of white supremacism and of exploitation, can be read as having close parallels with the predatory behaviour of the vampire – but women in our society are conventionally disempowered. Which leaves the reader to ponder the significance of this dual identification – as Boer, as woman.

The ending of this first narrative is unconventional on a number of grounds. First, the vampire is shown to be vulnerable to bullets. Even if they do not kill him, they stop him in his tracks. Fictional vampire lore maintains that the vampire, being an undead, a vivified corpse, cannot be bodily injured by normal human means. Secondly, the vampire is shown to be a natural, rather than supernatural, being. He is a great predator, a great hunter – in Weyland's own terms, 'living . . . off the top of the food chain' (p. 37). Charnas develops this theme in some detail by means of the public lecture that Weyland gives during this narrative. The 'ancient mind' of the title (of the lecture and of part I) refers in the first place to the unconscious mind which Weyland explores in his sleep research. As question time continues, however, the topic turns to vampires and, with the conventional hubris of the vampire, Weyland describes his true nature to his unsuspecting audience. The ancient mind becomes the mind of the vampire, the mind of Weyland himself. And, of course, this episode is part of the fiction–reality debate in which Katje de Groot (and the reader, in a different way) is involved. Thirdly, the vampire is vanquished by a woman, not a man – and by a woman who, via the identification process described above, refuses her conventional role as victim. Instead this woman acts as a hunter:

> Then Scotty's patient voice said, 'Do it again,' and she was tearing down the rifle once more by lamplight at the worn wooden table, while her mother sewed with angry stabs of the needle and spoke words Katje didn't bother to listen to. She knew the gist by heart: 'If only Jan had children of his own! Sons, to take out hunting with Scotty. Because he has no sons, he takes Katje shooting instead so he can show how tough Boer youngsters are, even the girls. . . . And to train a *girl* to go stalking and killing animals like scarcely more than an animal herself!' (pp. 22–3)

The gender politics of this narrative had started conventionally enough, with the vampire identified as a sexually attractive man. De Groot's co-worker Nettie describes her encounter with Weyland at the sleep lab:

> He leaned over me to plug something into the wall, and I said, 'Go ahead, you can bite my neck any time.' You know, he was sort of hanging over me, and his lab coat was sort of spread, like a cape, all menacing and batlike – except white instead of black, of course – and anyway I couldn't resist a wisecrack. (p. 31)

The irony of this wisecrack is not lost on de Groot, of course. Weyland also becomes the subject of a T-shirt popular among the students: 'SLEEP WITH WEYLAND HE'S A DREAM' (p. 23). One of Weyland's academic colleagues notes, 'This T-shirt thing will start a whole new round of back-biting among his colleagues, you watch'

(p. 24). Charnas here evokes the jealousy which male characters have traditionally displayed towards the vampire. This is how *Dracula*, for example, has often been read, with the male characters' pursuit of the vampire an attempt to destroy his great sexual potency, an oedipal hunt after the *Ur*-father. Yet Weyland is vanquished not by his male colleagues, but by a female housekeeper. He is ousted by a woman who realises her strength through her identification with him, the 'other', the biologically different, the victim/hunter.

II *'The Land of Lost Content'*

This identification between woman and vampire is implicit in part II, 'The Land of Lost Content'. Again Charnas exploits a familiar vampire convention – that the bloodsucking of the vampire is erotic. In vampire novels the bloodsucking conventionally signifies sexual intercourse, and so the vampire's attack on (usually) women signifies rape. This rape fantasy is a continuing preoccupation of (politically conservative/ reactionary) horror fiction. Subsequently the female victim is often either made to feel guilty for putting herself in the vampire's power, no matter what struggle he has to go through to get to her (an example is Mina Harker in *Dracula*), or transformed by her own rape into something disgusting and repulsive, an undead – in other terms, reading the semiosis of the novel, a sexually assertive woman (Lucy Westenra in *Dracula*). The disgusting potency of the latter type of victim has to be destroyed by a group of marauding males, sometimes by the kind of symbolic pack rape to which Lucy is subjected.

In 'The Land of Lost Content' Charnas shows the vampire stripped of his power, a victim to the greed and voyeurism of others. In this section the identification process is reversed: what is revealed is not the monster, the biologically different, the 'other', in the woman, but the woman in the monster. Bereft of power, Weyland is placed in the traditional female role. Restrained in a cell-like room, he is put on display, an object of gaze, his subjectivity denied. Weyland points out to the boy, Mark, who has helped him, 'Have you noticed, Roger never refers to or addresses me by name? He is preparing himself to be indifferent to my death' (p. 105). And Roger himself confirms this when he tells Mark, 'Reese said absolutely not to feed the animal . . .' (p. 109).

Reese is the pathetic satanist who intends to use Weyland to consolidate his own power, a kind of ultimate macho man. When introduced to the weakened and helpless Weyland, Reese immediately manhandles the vampire:

There was nothing silly in the scene anymore. Dr Weyland's fear touched Mark like a cold breath.

Reese bent and clamped the vampire's head hard against his thick thigh with one arm. Seizing him by the jaw, he wrenched his mouth open.   (p. 77)

Reese goes on to examine the vampire's mouth:

'It's true there are no fangs, but here – see that? A sort of sting on the underside of the tongue. It probably erects itself at the prospect of dinner, makes the puncture through which he sucks blood, and then folds back out of sight again.

'Sexy', Roger said with new interest.   (pp. 77–8)

The language used in the description confirms the association between sexuality and bloodsucking. Accordingly, the vampire's mouth is synonymous with his genitals. Reese's brutal exposure of Weyland's mouth, together with the identification established between woman and vampire, can thus be read as a displaced representation of the exposure of female genitals to male gaze which characterises, signifies and defines the gender power relationships in our society.

The helpless vampire is humiliated by Reese and Roger, to the disgust of the boy Mark: 'Reese gripped and twisted the passive body of the vampire brutally, like a guy wrestling an alligator in a movie about the Everglades'; 'Roger looked high, as if exhilarated by the defeat of someone who had scared him' (p. 78). After this episode Weyland is forced to feed in public, for the voyeuristic pleasure of Reese's followers. The connection between sexuality and bloodsucking is a constant theme. When Bobbie, a female follower, allows Weyland to suck her blood, she responds sexually to him: 'She put out her hand as if to push the vampire's head away, but instead she began to stroke his hair . . . "oh, this is so far out, this is real supernova, you know?" Until he finished she sat enthralled, whispering, "Oh, wow", at dreamy intervals' (p. 71). Later, when another woman becomes distressed, yet another remarks, 'If she'd just relaxed and rolled with it, I bet she could have got off on that' (p. 92). Mark is not entirely sure of the significance of what he is seeing and questions Weyland about it. When Weyland responds that eating in public is common, Mark responds, 'It isn't just eating to the ones who come here. They make it dirty' (p. 98). Towards the end of the episode Mark feeds the vampire to save him from further exploitation by Reese, a situation which enables Charnas to present a naïve and innocent view of patriarchal sexual relationships: 'To have someone spring on you like a tiger and suck your blood with savage and single-minded intensity – how could anybody imagine that was sexy? He would never forget that moment's blinding fear. If sex was like that, they could keep it' (pp. 116–17).

When powerless, the vampire is a victim motivated by fear. His only weapon is the exhibition of that fear, that vulnerability, to someone young and innocent enough to be affected by it. Through that innocent character the vampire regains his strength and power. That scenario can be followed through in the vampire–woman identification, though not so simply. Children are often the only source of power, of strength, of identity, that women have in a patriarchal society. But that power is never so immediate, so focused, so controllable, as the vampire's power, centred as it is in his own body, his difference, which is also superficially a male body. Perhaps Charnas is suggesting that women do have an enviable power inherent in their difference – that of reproduction – but that that power is controlled by men who humiliate and degrade women by defining them purely in terms of that biology (a cunt) and/or terms of difference: from them, from men, from humanity. This is the chain of significations in which normality, humanity, is defined in terms of masculinity; the feminine is, therefore, both abnormal and inhuman ('cattle'). Women are denied subjectivity because of their otherness and because of the frightening (to men) power it engenders. Interestingly, fictional vampires are often also assigned that power, of reproducing by transforming their victims into undeads like themselves.

'The Land of Lost Content' is an exploration of the subject–object relationship which defines the gender politics of our (contemporary Western) society. In a land of lost content, only form remains. Charnas reveals the formal or structural characteristics of gender relations isolated from particularising detail. The dominant gender ideology of our society, sexism, is described in this narrative as essentially a power relationship in which masculinity is identified with dominance and control, femininity with passivity and submission.

Just as Reese uses the paraphernalia of satanism to control his followers, so men in the past have used charges of witchcraft to control women. Who are the peasants with torches – the mob hunting the vampire, or witchburners?

III   'Unicorn Tapestry'

In part III Weyland encounters what he considers a modern form of the 'screaming peasants with torches', the psychological examination. Where the peasants would dismember him physically, the psychologist dismembers him emotionally: the result in both cases may be the same. If the psychologist destroys his distance from his victims, his food, his cattle, he will be unable to hunt. His identity, his subjectivity, will be destroyed.

The interest in this section for Charnas's analysis of gender relationships is that here the *difference* between women and vampire is explored. This difference is a function of power. At the end of part II it became clear that the identification woman–vampire only holds fully when the vampire is powerless. In 'Unicorn Tapestry' Charnas explores the other side, the vampire in control, the predator hunting his victims. This is the more conventional representation of the vampire, exploiting his erotic power to hypnotise his victims. Again, however, Charnas uses the convention innovatively, to deconstruct the gender ideology of Western society. Weyland's victims are identified as those without power in our society – women and gay men. While sexual attraction is an element in both cases, the power relationships involved simply confirm the powerlessness of both groups in patriarchal society. Weyland explains,

> Yet no doubt you see me as one who victimizes the already victimized. This is the world's way. A wolf brings down the stragglers at the edge of the herd. Gay men are denied the full protection of the human herd and are at the same time emboldened to make themselves known and available.
>
> On the other hand, unlike the wolf I can feed without killing, and these particular victims pose no threat to me that would cause me to kill. Outcasts themselves, even if they comprehend my true purpose among them they cannot effectively accuse me.   (p. 144)

Women too are accessible to him because of the social conventions governing gender relations, because he fits a particular social role which permits him to approach them, in that identity, in suitable places – 'galleries or evening museum shows or department stores' (p. 136). Weyland prefers men mainly because the encounter is likely to be brief and inexpensive.

So, in identifying the vampire's victims, Charnas exposes what traditional texts hide: the collusion of patriarchal ideology in the violent repression of large sections of the population – women and gay men. Both groups are denied the right to fulfil their sexual desires openly and honestly, and so are prey to a being who seems to embody patriarchal respectability. Women are attracted by the image of that lonely, handsome, ageing scholar; gays by the gentle closet gay who picks them up on a beat. Weyland uses the gender ideology of patriarchy to facilitate his bloodsucking/fucking, and that ruthless bloodsucking/fucking characterises the gender ideology of patriarchy. Charnas uses his story to expose that ideology.

Problems arise for Weyland when his psychoanalyst, Floria Landauer, begins to disrupt that relationship. Landauer asks Weyland to picture his relationship with the victim from the victim's viewpoint. Weyland responds, 'I will not. Though I do have enough empathy with my quarry to enable me to hunt efficiently. I must draw the line at erasing the necessary distance that keeps prey and predator distinct' (p. 146). When Landauer questions him about his sexuality, Weyland responds with the arrogance of Dracula: 'Would you mate with your livestock?' (p. 150). Weyland used this identification of human beings with cattle early in the book: 'Stop staring, cattle' (p. 51). It is used throughout Bram Stoker's novel, and is explored further by Charnas in this section.

As I noted earlier, in vampire texts bloodsucking signifies sexual intercourse so consistently that genital intercourse comes to seem an appalling aberration. Hence the reader's incredulousness at Mina Harker's conception of a child in *Dracula*. If the vampire was to have genital intercourse voluntarily (other than as a hunting-strategy), it would be a betrayal of his identity as a vampire. And in his role as an archetypal representative of patriarchal gender relations – an exploiter/oppressor of women and gays – it would signify his rejection of patriarchy.

So far Weyland's only encounter with a less unequal sexuality has been through watching ballet. Landauer records his response in her session notes:

> But when a man and a woman dance together, something else happens. Sometimes one is hunter, one is prey, or they shift these roles between them. Yet some other level of significance exists – I suppose to do with sex – and I feel it – a tugging sensation, here – touched his solar plexis – 'but I do not understand it'. . . . W. isn't man, isn't woman, yet the drama connects. His hands hovering as he spoke, fingers spread towards each other . . . 'We are similar,

we want the comfort of like closing to like.' How could that be for him, to find – likeness, another of his kind? 'Female?' Starts impatiently explaining how unlikely this is – No, forget sex and pas de deux for now; just to find your like, another vampire.

He springs up, agitated now. There are none, he insists; adds at once, 'But what would it be like? What would happen? I fear it!' Sits again, hands clenched. 'I long for it.' (p. 165)

Weyland expresses the longing of many in our society for an equal sexual relationship, a longing abrogated by the patriarchal ideology which dominates so many interactions.

Later Weyland states, according to Landauer's notes, 'Your straightforwardness with me – and the straightforwardness you require in return – this is healthy in a life so dependent on deception as mine; (p. 165). So Weyland begins the process which will be his undoing. If Weyland is able to meet his victim face to face, without the mask, he will begin to empathise. If he empathises, as he explained earlier, he will no longer be able to hunt. In the same way, if those who conduct their sexual relationships in traditional patriarchal terms begin to empathise with their partners, they will no longer be able to operate. Once emotional engagement occurs, rather than emotional manipulation, equality results. But patriarchy is not based on equality; it is based on dominance–submission, hunter–victim relationships. Under patriarchy women are barely recognised as human (vampire–woman); they are the not-men, the 'other', 'cattle', 'livestock' (woman–victim). Landauer's examination of Weyland becomes an examination by Charnas of the function of patriarchal gender relationships. When Landauer and Weyland make love, a fundamental change in Weyland occurs. Once again he fails to eliminate someone who knows his true identity. Emotional engagement has taken place. Weyland is no longer a vampire; Landauer is safe.

The peasants with their torches are banished – but not for very long. Patriarchy is a powerful ideology.

IV 'A Musical Interlude'
Weyland leaves Landauer and heads for New Mexico. He cannot cope any longer with the challenge she poses to his identity. However, the disintegration continues, and again it is bound up with Weyland's new-found empathy – and also with a woman named Floria. Here the Floria is a character in Puccini's opera *Tosca*.

Weyland attends the opera at the request of colleagues at his new workplace. At the interval Weyland feels disturbed by the effect on him of the music:

> the music had been powerful; even he had felt his hackles stir.
> Why? Art should not matter. Yet he responded – first to the ballet back in New York, and now to this. He was disturbed by a sense of something new in himself, as if recent events had exposed an unexpected weakness.

As the opera continues, Weyland's empathetic response continues and increases:

> Now the pattern of the hunt stood vividly forth in terms that spoke to Weyland. How often had Weyland himself approached a victim in just such a manner, speaking soothingly, his impatience to feed disguised in social pleasantry . . . a woman stalked in the quiet of a bookstore or a gallery . . . a man picked up in a park. . . . Hunting was the central experience of Weyland's life. Here was that experience, from the outside.   (p. 213)

Now Weyland has to face his nature from the role of the spectator, the victim, the role he refused to adopt for Floria Landauer. The opera reminds Weyland of his past and his whole identity starts to press in on him – not just Weyland the academic, the hunter, the vampire, but also the outcast, the stranger, the 'other':

> More than once in such an office he had stood turning in his hands his tradesman's cap, or rubbing his palms nervously on the slick front of his leatherwork apron, while he answered official questions. When questions were to be asked, Weyland, always and everywhere a stranger, was asked them.   (pp. 214–15)

Finally Weyland recognises himself in Scarpia:

> Resonances from the monster's unleashed appetite swept Weyland, overriding thought, distance, judgement.
> The lady in the snakeskin-patterned dress glanced at the professorial type sitting next to her in the aisle seat. Heavens, what was wrong with the man? Sweat gleamed on his forehead, his jaw bunched with muscle, his eyes glittered above feverishly

flushed cheeks. What was that expression her son used – yes: this man looked as if he were *freaking out.*   (p. 216)

Weyland's empathy is now so intense that his knowledge of artistic form, of genre, is eradicated. Weyland empathises with the dynamics of the narrative, but without the 'civilised' control which allows him to see it as a performance rather than a reality. Now it is the vampire who confuses the status of fiction and reality. And yet maybe also the naïve response of the vampire tells us some fundamental truth about our acceptance of fictions imbued with ideologies which we might rationally reject, just as Mark's response to bloodsucking as eroticism constitutes a fundamental interrogation by Charnas of patriarchal sexual relationships.

When Weyland experiences a former, murderous identity under the stimulus of the opera, perhaps Charnas is suggesting that we as readers/viewers are insufficiently critical of similarly murderous (physically, emotionally, intellectually, spiritually) ideologies which structure the fictions of our society – from 'high' culture such as opera to 'popular' forms such as the horror novel.

Weyland is appalled to find that he has killed 'without need, without hunger' (p. 220). So the ideologies which structure our fictions are operative in our lives. We consume them uncritically and they structure our actions, our beliefs, our values. We act out desires 'without need, without hunger'. Charnas follows this questioning of the ideological function of art with an interpretation of the opera which ties it to the preceding narrative section, through the character of Floria Tosca/Landauer.

When the art-dealer McGrath rejects the opera as rubbish, a character, identified only as an art-collector, responds negatively:

> 'Other people do, too; they honestly feel that *Tosca*'s just a vulgar thriller', she observed. 'I think what shocks them is seeing a woman kill a man to keep him from raping her [shades of Katje de Groot]. If a man kills somebody over politics or love, that's high drama, but if a woman offs a rapist, that's sordid.'
>
> McGrath hated smart-talking women, but he wanted her to buy another bronze; they were abstract pieces, not easy to sell. So he smiled.   (pp. 226–7)

Effectively Floria Landauer has done the same thing, destroyed Weyland the vampire, the rapist. Charnas seems to be working hard to ensure that we, the audience, make this connection: she has already had Weyland call attention to the name Floria – 'I knew someone in the East who was named after Floria Tosca' (p. 197). Floria Landauer's assault on the vampire/rapist is not physical, but psychological and ideological. By inducing in him an empathetic response to her, engaging him emotionally, Landauer began the deconstruction of the ideology and subjectivity that sustains Weyland. Now he feels an empathetic response to the opera and he resents its ability to touch him, to make him one with his prey:

> He feared and resented that these kine on whom he fed could stir him so deeply, all unaware of what they did; that their art could strike depths in him untouched in them. . . . But was he growing more like them, that their works had begun to reach him and shake him? Had he somehow irrevocably opened to the power of their art? (pp. 235–6)

In the first sentence Weyland also expresses his dismay that this art should touch him as it does not touch humans, though we know that the young artist Elmo has also been severely affected by his first night at the opera. Charnas seems to be making a number of points here, summarising the analysis presented in this narrative and again attempting to position the reader reflexively in relation to this and any other text. Weyland's literal empathy with the opera, set in a time he has experienced in a past life, calls into question our 'sophisticated' tendency to ignore textual politics for the sake of some aesthetic norm. Weyland's anger that he has been more affected emotionally than those around him corroborates this point, questioning the distancing-effect of artistic convention. How are we, as audience, affected by an artwork? How is empathy constructed in/by a text? The second part of the quote follows up this point. Weyland feels that his response to the artwork is an indication of humanness. Exactly how does response to art or culture of any kind define our humanness, our subjectivity? What are the crucial aspects of the spectator–artwork interaction which assist in or produce the effect of individual subjectivity? And is Charnas also making a case for the subversive potential of the artwork? Is the art-collector's interpretation of *Tosca* part of a strategy of rereading which will open up textual politics to intense scrutiny – as *The Vampire Tapestry* scrutinises vampire literature? Is Weyland's fear of the subversive effect of the artwork the cry of a patriarchal ideology under attack, from subversive writers of popular fiction as well as rereaders of traditional texts?

Perhaps one element of Weyland has met the peasants with torches and recognised himself among their number.

V 'The Last of Dr Weyland'

Once the defining practices of an ideology are exposed, it is difficult for a practitioner to operate unself-consciously. And, once the practitioner empathises with the situation of those victimised by those ideological practices, it is unlikely that she or he will be able to persist in that victimisation. The hunter can no longer hunt. The hunt looks less like a heroic struggle than like a witch-hunt.

In the final narrative Dr Weyland is laid to rest, again by the agency of a woman. Charnas is concerned here not so much with the woman–monster identification as with the more traditional characterisation of the vampire as patriarch *par excellence*. As his latest lover tells him as she ends their relationship, 'this would be a lot easier if you weren't – you have the face of everybody's dream-father, you know that?' (p. 245). But this patriarch has begun to feel. Formerly a brilliant rationalist, a hunter, a manipulator, an exploiter, the patriarch is beginning to be troubled by his own identity, by the practices which make him what he is. The memories which begin to plague Weyland are fragments of his consciousness, his subjectivity. As I noted earlier, in characterising Weyland in this way Charnas avoids the simplistic humanist model of consistent subjectivity, representing instead a fragmented consciousness, the decentred subject, which is characteristic of the fantastic. It is this fragmentation of the subject, this process of continual formation and renegotiation, that produces the possibility for change. But Weyland does not change – at least, not in this life.

Once again his difference, his otherness, is recognised, this time by a female artist, Dorothea. As both artist and woman Dorothea recognises the insubstantiality of Weyland, his disguise which masks no substance: 'In the lecture hall in January I tried to draw you with my eye, but I saw that you do not draw. You have a stylized, streamlined quality, as if you were already a drawing rather than a man' (p. 270). Dorothea confirms Weyland's loss of contrived cohesiveness, contrived identity.

In this section, too, Weyland has his last encounter with Reese, the victimiser – the torch-bearing peasant – and he defeats him; he kills him. The narrative dynamics of this final encounter are fascinating to tease out. Weyland is by this time in a highly unstable state and calls on his former selves to help him:

> If he could release his grip on his human surface and sink back into the deeper, darker being at his core, his root-self . . . this was not so simple as in simpler times. He suffered a frightful moment of imbalance and disorientation. Then something hot and raw began coiling in his body.
>
> I am strong, I am already bent on departure, and I am hungry; why should I not hunt the hunter in my own house tonight? (p. 287)

As a capitulation to that 'hunter' identity, Weyland's transformation can be read as a rejection of the empathy which had undermined the (patriarchal) ideology by which he operated – and which formed him as a subject. He hunts Reese on grounds they both understand, as representative of a violent patriarchy. Like Harker, Godalming and Van Helsing of *Dracula*, Reese has come to subdue the vampire to his will (the former by death, Reese by imprisonment). The Oedipal conflict is once more enacted, but in this text the vampire wins. Charnas here rejects one of the most prominent conventions of the vampire text, the ritual and savage killing of the vampire at the end of the narrative – the triumph of the peasants with torches. The peasants are vanquished, but so, in a sense, is Weyland: he wins, but also loses. His killing of Reese is his last feeding as Weyland. The disintegration of that character is now complete.

But how does the killing of Reese interact with that other level of signification whereby there is an identification between woman and monster? As I noted above, Weyland does summon up his former selves, reject his empathetic responses, in order to confront Reese as an equally ruthless member of a patriarchal order. In this guise the woman–monster identification perhaps does not operate. However, there is a kind of pleasure, a sense of justice, in his confrontation with Reese which seems to be related to more than the reassertion of patriarchy and/or Charnas's modification of vampire convention. And, in fact, this non-destruction of the vampire is now becoming a convention of the genre, particularly in film, in which the final scene often shows one of the heroes or heroines lunging at the other's jugular. Rather, it seems that, on some level, the woman–monster identification continues to work and that Weyland's destruction of

Reese is an assertion of female opposition to patriarchy. And perhaps that is supported by Weyland's final conjectures, as he prepares for hibernation:

> He had cared enough to preserve when it was no longer secure his Weyland identity and all its ties and memories. Tonight, in deadly jeopardy because of that recklessness, he had owed his fury only to past pain or the promise of future suffering at Reese's hands. He had burned also at the thought of Floria Landauer caught unknowing in Reese's net; of young Mark flying into a fugitive's perils from the net flung after him; of Reese obscenely alive. . . .
>
> Now he knew with bitter clarity why in each long sleep he forgot the life preceding that sleep. He forgot because he could not survive the details of an enormous past heavy with those he cared for. . . . I am not the monster who falls in love and is destroyed by his human feelings. I am the monster who stays true.
>
> (pp. 300–1)

Weyland deliberately destroys a representative of oppressive patriarchy, and in so doing destroys a part of himself, the part that enables him to survive. As Weyland drifts into sleep, his personality as Weyland, that subjectivity, is secured in terms of his empathetic responses:

> Then for a time came an unexpected gift. The voices of people returned vividly to him, their faces, gestures, laughter, the swirling brightness of the opera crowd, the jingle of coins in Irv's pocket, Mark's warm, bony shoulder under his hand as they walked towards the river, the scent of Floria's skin. Intense pleasure filled him as he yielded himself to the mingled ache and joy of memory, as he gathered in his Weyland life. (p. 302)

The ending of *The Vampire Tapestry* is unconventional in that the vampire is neither destroyed nor left active (though in a different body); instead he is rendered harmless, his identity destroyed. The patriarchal order as represented by Reese is shown defeated by an even more ruthless member of that order, Weyland acting out his former self, as hunter. But that Weyland also contains the empathetic monster, the woman-identified subjectivity, who rejects that patriarchy and the victim role it offers him and woman. In this sense Reese is destroyed by the deconstruction of the ideology which engenders him. This ending is not simply a victory for patriarchy: it is also, simultaneously, a victory for those who reject that ideology. On the most subversive level, it is a victory achieved by the enemies of patriarchy, using the strategies of patriarchy. And that perhaps is a fitting description of Suzy McKee Charnas's achievement in *The Vampire Tapestry*.

I noted at the beginning of this essay that horror, like other forms of the fantastic, has the potential for either criticism and subversion or conservatism. *Dracula*, the text which is the most obvious literary antecedent of *The Vampire Tapestry*, is an extremely conservative text. The gender ideology of that text is extremely repressive, with active female sexuality singled out for particularly brutal punishment. *Dracula* is, among other things, a patriarchal response to the strong and vocal Women's Movement of the 1890s.[3] The rape fantasy fundamental to the text is the correction rod applied to the psyche of assertive women of that time. *The Vampire Tapestry* can also be read as a response to the Women's Movement of the 1970s and 1980s. However, this text demonstrates that other potential of the fantastic, for criticism and subversion.

   Charnas uses generic conventions established in *Dracula*, such as the sexual attractiveness of the vampire, the vampire's pride, his classification of humanity as cattle. She also uses more recent modifications of the conventions, such as the scepticism of contemporary character towards the existence of such a creature. And in each case her use of generic convention is extremely self-conscious. As my analysis of the text shows, Charnas is always acutely aware of the ideological consequences of those conventions. Accordingly she modifies her text so that her use of the conventions focuses reader attention on their ideological function. *The Vampire Tapestry* is not only a text about the gender relationships of contemporary society; it is also a text about the way that contemporary texts, including horror novels, position readers as patriarchal subjects, reinforcing the repressive gender ideology of patriarchy.

   Charnas's characterisation of the vampire is a crucial strategy in her textual politics. Instead of presenting him as a unified subject or melodramatic villain, she gives him the complexity and contradiction of the decentred subject, a strategy facilitated by the discontinuous narrative in which he operates. The vampire is thus able simultaneously to function conventionally as *Ur*-patriarch and unconventionally as woman-identified subject. Through the negotiation of this contradiction Charnas focuses on the gender politics of contemporary society, along with their textual representation and reinforcement. The text thus operates not only as an exploration of gender relations, but also reflexively as an interrogation of textual politics.

The subversive power of *The Vampire Tapestry* resides in these two textual functions. Charnas subverts the conventional vampire novel by using its own generic conventions to reveal its textual politics. In so doing she challenges the continuing operation of those texts, positioning readers to perform radical rereadings of the more traditional texts. She also, nevertheless, produces an entertaining vampire novel, effectively transforming the conventional political function of those texts, changing the genre from within in a classical subversive move.

* * *

The peasants with torches suddenly feel rather foolish. Who has put them in such an embarrassing position, chasing over the countryside after some poor damned creature/woman/victim? After all, what kind of thugs do they think we are! As torches are lowered and put out, dawn appears over the horizon.

Notes

First published in Brian Docherty (ed.), *American Horror Fiction* (Basingstoke: Macmillan, 1990).

1. Suzy McKee Charnas, *The Vampire Tapestry* (London: Granada, 1983). Page references are given in the text.
2. For valuable discussions of fantasy literature and the horror genre, and their conventions, see Rosemary Jackson, *Fantasy: The Literature of Subversion* (London: Methuen, 1981); David Punter, *The Literature of Terror: A History of Gothic Fiction from 1765 to the Present Day* (London: Longman, 1980); and M. M. Bakhtin, *The Dialogic Imagination*, ed. M. Holquist and C. Emerson (Austin: University of Texas Press, 1981).

3. See 'Sexual Politics and Political Repression in Bram Stoker's *Dracula*',
   in Clive Bloom, Brian Docherty, Jane Gibb and Keith Shand (eds),
   Nineteenth-Century Suspense: From Poe to Conan Doyle (London:
   Macmillan, 1988).

JUDIE NEWMAN

On *The Haunting of Hill House*

One of the most enduring mysteries of horror fiction consists in its
exploitation of the attractions of fear. Why, one may ask, should a
reader seek out the experience of being terrified, particularly by
horror fiction, which adds abhorrence, loathing and physical
repulsion to the purer emotions of terror evoked by the supernatural
tale? For H. P. Lovecraft[1] the answer lay in the human fear of the
unknown. Freud,[2] however, developed a different hypothesis,
describing the experience of the 'uncanny' (*unheimlich*) as that class
of the frightening which leads back to what is known of old and
long-familiar. Observing that *heimlich* (familiar, homely) is the
opposite of *unheimlich*, Freud recognises the temptation to equate
the uncanny with fear of the unknown. Yet he noted that *heimlich*
also means 'concealed', 'private', 'secret', as the home is an area
withdrawn from the eyes of strangers. In Freud's argument,
therefore, the experience of the uncanny arises either when primitive
animistic beliefs, previously surmounted, seem once more to be
confirmed (Shirley Jackson's 'The Lottery' is a case in point) or when
infantile complexes, formerly repressed, are revived (a theory which
brings *The Haunting of Hill House* into sharp focus). For Freud,
various forms of ego disturbance involve regression to a period
when the ego had not marked itself off sharply from the external
world and from other people. In the context of a discussion of ghosts
and doubles, Freud cites Otto Rank's description of the double as
originally an insurance against the destruction of the ego, an
energetic denial of the power of death. (In this sense the 'immortal
soul' may be considered as the first double of the body.) The idea of
doubling as preservation against extinction therefore springs from

the unbounded self-love of the child. When this stage of primitive narcissism is surmounted, however, the double reverses its aspect, and, from being an assurance of immortality, becomes the uncanny harbinger of death and a thing of terror. Since Freud considered art as an organised activity of sublimation, providing the reader with pleasures 'under wraps', it is tempting to argue that the horror tale actively eliminates and exorcises our fears by allowing them to be relegated to the imaginary realm of fiction.[3] Rosemary Jackson, however, has indicated the case for the fantastic as a potentially subversive reversal of cultural formation, disruptive of conventional distinctions between the real and the unreal.[4] Arguably, although Shirley Jackson builds her horrors on the basis of the *heimlich* and of repressed infantile complexes, in the process she subverts the Freudian paradigm, both of art as sublimation, and in broader psychoanalytic terms. In this connection, new developments in psychoanalytic theory offer fresh insights into Jackson's work.

Recent feminist psychoanalytic theorists[5] have set out to revise the Freudian account of psychosexual differences, which bases gender, anatomically, on possession or lack of the phallus. In the Freudian paradigm, the male achieves adulthood by passing through the Oedipus complex, which fear of castration by the father induces him to overcome. Fear facilitates acceptance of the incest prohibition, promoting the formation of the superego, which thereafter polices desire in accordance with adult social norms. In a parallel development, the female discovers the lack of the phallus, sees herself as castrated, recognises her mother as similarly inferior, and therefore abandons her attachment to the mother to form the Oedipal relation with the father, which is the necessary precursor of adult heterosexual relationships – always the Freudian goal.

Feminist analysts, however, have shifted the focus from the Oedipal to the pre-Oedipal stage, tracing the influence of gender on identity to the dynamics of the mother–infant bond. Nancy Chodorow in *The Reproduction of Mothering* offers a persuasive analysis of early infant development in these terms. Because children first experience the social and cognitive world as continuous with themselves, the mother is not seen as a separate person with separate interests. In this brief period of immunity from individuality, the experience of fusion with the mother, of mother as world, is both seductive and terrifying. Unity is bliss; yet it entails total dependence and loss of self. In contrast the father does not pose the original threat to basic ego integrity, and is perceived from the beginning as

separate. Thus, the male fear of women may originate as terror of
maternal omnipotence in consequence of the early dependence on
the mother, and may be generalised to all women (in images such as
the witch, the vampire and the Terrible Mother[6]) since it is tied up
with the assertion of gender. Boys define themselves as masculine by
difference from, not by relation to, their mothers. Girls, however, in
defining themselves as female, experience themselves as resembling
their mothers, so that the experience of attachment fuses with the
process of identity formation. Girls therefore learn to see themselves
as partially continuous with their mothers, whereas boys learn very
early about difference and separateness. Male development
therefore entails more emphatic individuation, and more defensive
firming of experienced ego boundaries, whereas women persist in
defining themselves relationally, creating fluid, permeable ego
boundaries, and locating their sense of self in the ability to make and
maintain affiliations. Female gender identity is therefore threatened
by separation, and shaped throughout life by the fluctuations of
symbiosis and detachment from the mother. Girls may also fear
maternal omnipotence and struggle to free themselves, idealising the
father as their most available ally. Daughterly individuation may be
inhibited by paternal absence and by over-closeness to mothers, who
tend to view their daughters as extensions of themselves.
Conversely, coldness on the mother's part may prevent the loosening
of the emotional bond because of the unappeased nature of the
child's love. In maturity women may form close personal relationships with other women to recapture some aspects of the fractured
mother–daughter bond. Alternatively they may reproduce the
primary attachment, by themselves bearing children, thus initiating
the cycle once more, as the exclusive symbiotic relation of the
mother's own infancy is re-created.

Mothering therefore involves a double identification for women in
which they take both parts of the pre-Oedipal relation, as mother
and as child. Fictions of development reflect this psychological
structure. Recent reformulations of the female *Bildungsroman*[7] have
drawn attention to the frequency with which such fictions end in
deaths (Maggie Tulliver, Rachel Vinrace, Edna Pontellier) understandable less as developmental failures than as refusals to accept an
adulthood which denies female desires and values. In addition, a
persistent, if recessive, narrative concern with the story of mothers
and daughters often exists in the background of a dominant
romance or courtship plot.

An exploration of *The Haunting of Hill House* in the light of feminist psychoanalytic theory reveals that the source of both the pleasures and the terrors of the text springs from the dynamics of the mother–daughter relation with its attendant motifs of psychic annihilation, reabsorption by the mother, vexed individuation, dissolution of individual ego boundaries, terror or separation and the attempted reproduction of the symbiotic bond through close female friendship. Eleanor Vance, the central protagonist, is mother-dominated. On her father's death the adolescent Eleanor was associated with an outbreak of poltergeist activity, in which her family home was repeatedly showered with stones. The event invites comparison with another tale, 'The Lottery', in which the victim of the stoning, Tessie Hutchinson, is not only a mother, but a mother who sees her daughter as an extension of herself. Eleanor also clearly resented her recently dead mother, whom she nursed for eleven years: 'the only person in the world she genuinely hated, now that her mother was dead, was her sister' (p. 90).[8] Initially her excursion to Hill House to participate in Dr Montague's study of psychic phenomena appears as an opportunity for psychological liberation, the first steps towards autonomy. The trip begins with a small act of assertion against the mother-image. When Eleanor's sister refuses to allow her to use their shared car ('I am sure Mother would have agreed with me, Eleanor' – p. 14), Eleanor reacts by simply stealing it, in the process knocking over an angry old woman who is clearly associated with the 'cross old lady' (p. 10) whom she had nursed for so long. Once *en route*, Eleanor is haunted by the refrain 'Journeys end in lovers meeting', suggesting (as the *carpe diem* theme of the song confirms) that Eleanor's goal is the realisation of heterosexual desires.

Eleanor's fantasies on the journey, however, imply that her primary emotional relation remains with her mother. In imagination she dreams up several 'homes', based on houses on her route. In the first, 'a little dainty old lady took care of me' (p. 19), bringing trays of tea and wine 'for my health's sake'. The fantasy reveals just how much Eleanor herself wishes to be mothered. In the preceding period, as nurse to a sick mother, Eleanor may be said to have 'mothered' her own mother, losing her youth in the process. A second fantasy centres upon a hollow square of poisonous oleanders, which seem to Eleanor to be 'guarding something' (p. 20). Since the oleanders enclose only an empty centre, Eleanor promptly supplies a mother to occupy it, constructing an enthralling fairy world in which 'the queen

waits, weeping, for the princess to return' (p. 21). Though she swiftly
revises this daydream of mother–daughter reunion, into a more
conventional fantasy of courtship by a handsome prince, she remains
much preoccupied with images of protected spaces and magic
enclosures, of a home in which *she* could be mothered and greeted as
a long-lost child. A subsequent incident reinforces this impression.
Pausing for lunch, Eleanor observes a little girl who refuses to drink
her milk because it is not in the familiar cup, patterned with stars,
which she uses at home. Despite maternal persuasion, the child
resists, forcing her mother to yield. The small tableau emphasises
both the child's potential independence and resistance to the mother,
and the attractions of the familiar home world, here associated with
mother's milk and starry containment. Eleanor empathises with the
little girl's narcissistic desires: 'insist on your cup of stars; once they
have trapped you into being like everyone else you will never see your
cup of stars again' (p. 22). Eleanor's final fantasy home, a cottage
hidden behind oleanders, 'buried in a garden' (p. 23), is entirely
secluded from the world. Taken together, her fantasies suggest her
ambivalent individuation and the lure of a magic mother-world.
They form a striking contrast to the reality of Hillsdale, a tangled
mess of dirty houses and crooked streets. For all its ugliness,
however, Eleanor deliberately delays there over coffee. Despite her
reiterated refrain 'In delay there lies no plenty', Eleanor is not quite
so eager to reach her goal and realise her desires as she thinks.
Another scene of enforced delay, negotiating with a surly caretaker at
the gates of Hill House, further retards her progress. The emphasis
here on locked gates, guards against entry, a tortuous access road,
and the general difficulty in locating the house reinforces the
impression of its desirability as *heimlich*, secret, a home kept away
from the eyes of others.

Entry to this protected enclave provokes, however, a response
which underlines the consonance of the familiar and the uncanny:
childish terror. Afraid that she will cry 'like a child sobbing and
wailing' (p. 34), tiptoeing around apprehensively, Eleanor feels like
'a small creature swallowed whole by a monster' which 'feels my
tiny little movements inside' (p. 38). The intra-uterine fantasy
immediately associates Hill House with an engulfing mother.
Eleanor's fellow guest, Theo, reacts in opposite terms, characterising
the two women as Babes in the Woods (abandoned by parents) and
comparing the experience to the first day at boarding-school or
camp. The vulnerable continuity between fear of engulfment and

fear of separation is indicated in the women's response to the threat. Reminiscing about their childhoods, they eagerly associate themselves through fancied family resemblances, until Theo announces that theirs is an indissoluble relationship: 'Would you let them separate us now? Now that we've found out we're cousins?' (p. 49). Yet on the arrival of the remaining guests, Luke and Dr Montague, Theo's assertion of female strength through attachment is swiftly replaced as the four establish their identities, in playfully exaggerated form, through separation and differentiation: 'You are Theodora because *I* am Eleanor'; 'I have no beard so *he* must be Dr Montague' (pp. 53–4). Fantasy selves are then elaborated. Luke introduces himself as a bullfighter; Eleanor poses as an artist's model, living an 'abandoned' life while moving from garret to garret; Theo describes herself as a lord's daughter, masquerading as an ordinary mortal in the clothes of her maid, in order to escape a parental plot of forced marriage. Interestingly, though both women characterise themselves as homeless, Eleanor converts homelessness into an image of abandonment, Theo into active escape from an oppressive parent by asserting a different identity. For Eleanor, however, identity remains elusive. In envisaging herself as an artist's model she acquiesces in a self-image created by a controlling other.

Introductions over, the foursome make a preliminary exploration of Hill House which confirms its character as an ambivalent maternal enclave. Comfortable, its menu excellent, the house has 'a reputation for insistent hospitality' (p. 59), and is distinguished by inwardness and enclosure. Labyrinthine in layout, its concentric circles of rooms, some entirely internal and windowless, make access to the outside world problematic. Doors close automatically on its occupants, who are further confused by its architectural peculiarities. In Hill House every apparent right-angle is a fraction off, all these tiny aberrations of measurement adding up to a large overall distortion, which upsets the inhabitants' sense of balance. An encircling verandah obscures awareness of the distortion. While this structure mirrors the conventional twisted line of Gothic (in plot as in architecture), baffling the reader's sense of direction and threatening to lead at any point out of one world and into another, it also emphasises an internalised entrapment which threatens reason and balance. Luke is in no doubt as to the house's identity: 'It's all so motherly. Everything so soft. Everything so padded. Great embracing chairs and sofas which turn out to be hard and unwelcoming when you sit down, and reject you at once –' (p. 174). The ambivalent suggestions here of maternal comfort and maternal rejection invite comparison with *The Sundial*, in which the labyrinthine connection between mother as security and mother as trap is foregrounded in a physical maze, to which only Aunt Fanny knows the key. The pattern of the maze is built upon her mother's name, Anna, so that, by turning right, left, left, right, then left, right, right, left, the centre is reached. As long as the mother's name is remembered, Fanny is secure in 'the maze I grew up in',[9] despite the activities of the matriarch, Orianna, the murderess of her own child.

Paradoxically, the doctor's history reveals that Hill House is actually notable for an absence of mothers. The first Mrs Crain died in a carriage accident in the drive, the second in a fall, the third in Europe of consumption. Since Hugh Crain's two daughters were therefore brought up without a mother, the house is simultaneously associated with mothering and with motherlessness. Later the older of the two daughters took possession of the house, dying there amidst accusations that her young companion had neglected her. The latter, persecuted by the younger sister's attempts to regain the house, eventually hanged herself. The history of the house therefore provides a psychic configuration not unlike Eleanor's own, which also involves a dead mother, two warring sisters, and a neglected old lady. Eleanor later accuses herself: 'It was my fault my mother died. She knocked on the wall and called me and called me and I never woke up' (p. 177). On learning the history of the house, however, Eleanor empathises with the unmothered girls and the companion. Eleanor has been both mother and child. On the one hand she detests the mother's dominance, resenting the loss of her own youth in the forced assumption of the 'mothering' role. On the other, she feels guilt at not having mothered adequately. Both images are internalised so that Eleanor is haunted by guilt as a mother over the neglected child within herself.

As a result two rooms in Hill House are of special significance to her – the library and the nursery, the one associated with the mother, the other with the unmothered child. Eleanor is quite incapable of entering the library: '"I can't go in there." . . . She backed away, overwhelmed with the cold air of mould and earth which rushed at her. "My mother –"' (p. 88). Eleanor's mother had forced her to read love stories aloud to her each afternoon, hence the library's sepulchral associations. The library is also the point of access to the tower, where the companion hanged herself. Theo jokes, 'I suppose she had some sentimental attachment to the tower; what a nice word "attachment" is in that context' (p. 88). If attachments can be linked with annihilation and wilful surrender of the self, their absence can be equally damaging. The nursery of the unmothered girls is marked by a cold spot at its entrance 'like the doorway of a tomb' (p. 101). On its wall is painted a frieze of animals which appear as if trapped or dying. Ironically Dr Montague describes this area of cold nurturance as 'the heart of the house' (p. 101).

The stage is now set for the first appearance of the 'ghost', which occurs at the heart of Jackson's novel, almost exactly at its centre. Eleanor's internalisation of both the 'unmothered child' and the 'neglected mother' images is reflected in the double mother–child nature of the haunting. Awakening, Eleanor at first thinks that her mother is calling and knocking on the wall. In fact a tremendous pounding noise, beginning close to the nursery door, accompanied by a wave of cold, has disturbed her. The violence of the phenomenon suggests a force strong enough to threaten the boundaries of the ego; amidst deafening crashes it very nearly smashes in the door. Nevertheless, Eleanor's first reaction is relief that it is *not* her mother, but 'only a noise' (p. 108). Indeed, she sees it as 'like something children do, not mothers knocking against the wall for help' (p. 108). The ghost now undergoes a metamorphosis, its vehement demands yielding to an insidious seductive appeal. The doorknob is 'fondled', amidst 'little pattings' 'small seeking sounds', 'little sticky sounds' (p. 111). The relentless emphasis on smallness and the affectionate pattings suggest a child. Eleanor and Theo, huddled together in fear, have also been reduced to 'a couple of lost children' (p. 111). Importantly, the haunting is limited to the women. (The men, outside chasing a mysterious dog, hear nothing.) Alarmed, Dr Montague draws the conclusion that 'the intention is, somehow, to separate us' (p. 114). Eleanor, however, argues that 'it wanted to consume us, take us into itself, make us a part of the house' (p. 117). The threat which the men perceive in terms of separation is understood by both women in terms of fusion and engulfment. In the light of this identification of the haunting with the reassertion of the ambivalent mother–daughter bond, it is unsurprising that Eleanor awakens next day with a renewed feeling of happiness, a fresh appetite and the urge to sing and dance. When Dr Montague argues for the reality of the haunting, given the presence of independent witnesses, Eleanor cheerfully suggests the possibility that 'all three of you are in my imagination' (p. 118). The doctor's warning that this way madness lies – a state which would welcome Hill House in a 'sisterly embrace' (p. 118) – points to an incipient narcissism in Eleanor which would make self and world conterminous once more, assimilating all to the subjective imagination.

Initially Eleanor responds to the threat of ego dissolution by a strategic attachment to Theo, quickly forming a close friendship in which more than one reader has detected lesbian content (as the film version also implied). A similar uncertainty besets the reader of *Hangsaman*: is Natalie's mysterious friend Tony real, imaginary, supernatural, a double or a lesbian lover? Since Natalie is always terrified of being alone with *her* mother, the attachment may be read as the result of the projection of the symbiotic bond onto an alter ago. Similarly Eleanor fosters autonomy by division, creating in Theo a double as insurance against the destruction of her own self, and as simultaneous confirmation of relational identity. Several incidents in the novel make sense only in these terms. On her first evening at Hill House, Eleanor revels in her own individuality, contemplating her feet in new red shoes: 'What a complete and separate thing I am . . . individually am I, possessed of attributes belonging only to me' (p. 72). In contrast she regards her hands as ugly and dirty, misshapen by years of laundering her mother's soiled linen. Theo, telling Eleanor teasingly that she disliked 'women of no colour' (p. 99), paints Eleanor's toenails red in celebration of her emergent independence. Unlike the highly individuated Theo, Eleanor is drab, mousy, with a tendency to merge into her surroundings. Theo's subsequent casual comment that Eleanor's feet are dirty provokes a violent emotional reaction, for Eleanor cannot cope with the clash between colour and grime, between individuation and association with the mother. The sight of her feet now fills her with an immediate sense of helpless dependence: 'I don't like to feel helpless. My mother –' (p. 99). In what follows Eleanor fluctuates ambivalently between an antagonistic and an associative relation to Theo.

When a second apparent manifestation occurs (the message 'HELP ELEANOR COME HOME' chalked in the hall) Eleanor both revels and recoils. On the one hand the message expresses her own desire for home. On the other, she is anxious at being identified by name. *Her* identity is targeted; she has been 'singled out' (p. 124) and separated from the group. Indeed, the message also effectively divides Eleanor and Theo, sparking a quarrel when each accuses the other of writing it. Eleanor's outburst reveals both her own suppressed need for attention, and her projection of the childish identity onto Theo: 'You think *I* like the idea that I'm the centre of attention? *I'm* not the spoiled baby after all' (p. 124). Separate identity is thus both desired and rejected. When the message is reinscribed on Theo's walls, and her clothes smeared with a substance which may be paint or blood, Theo immediately accuses Eleanor, who views the 'bloody chamber' with smiling satisfaction, admitting that it reminds her of Theo applying red polish (p. 131). The reader puzzles as to whether the hauntings are supernatural or caused by Eleanor, thus drawing attention to the central question of the novel – the degree of Eleanor's independent agency. Eleanor's apparent hostility is double-edged. Scrubbing the colour off Theo, she feels uncontrollable loathing for her polluted alter ego, who is 'filthy with the stuff', 'beastly and soiled and dirty' (p. 132). Watching her, Eleanor thinks, 'I would like to batter her with rocks' (p. 133). The conjunction of the two images of enforced laundering and of stoning indicates Eleanor's hostility to the mother, and to the mother within herself. The destruction of Theo's clothes, however, suggests an attempt to destroy an independent identity (the reader recalls Theo's previous fantasy of disguise), rendering Theo colourless and bringing the women into close association. Theo now has to share Eleanor's clothes and bedroom. As she comments, 'We're going to be practically twins' (p. 133). The entire sequence culminates in an admission from Eleanor of her own fear of disintegration. Contemplating Theo, dressed in Eleanor's sweater and therefore presenting an alternative self-image in which narcissism and self-hate are almost equally involved, Eleanor expresses her desire to return to a state of primal unity:

> There's only one of me, and it's all I've got. I hate seeing myself dissolve and slip and separate so that I'm living in one half, my mind, and I see the other half of me helpless . . . and I could stand any of it if I could only surrender.   (p. 134)

Forming a close relation with Theo, constituting Theo as 'other half', are strategies which culminate disastrously in the replication rather than the repudiation of the symbiotic bond, and a desire to surrender autonomy altogether.

In consequence, the subsequent 'haunting' is quite different in character, and limited to Eleanor. In the night Eleanor appears to hear a voice in Theo's empty room: 'It is a child', 'I won't let anyone hurt a child' (p. 136). While the voice babbles, Eleanor tries but fails to speak; only when it pauses is she able to cry out. It thus appears to emanate from her. Indeed, Eleanor recognises its screams from her own nightmares. Throughout the scene Eleanor has been holding Theo's hand for reassurance, clutching it so hard that she can feel the 'fine bones' (p. 137) of the fingers. On coming to consciousness (it has all been a dream) she discovers Theo sitting apart in her own bed, and shrieks, 'Whose hand was I holding?' (p. 137). The juxtaposition of a skeletal dead hand, first as reassurance then as terror, with a child's voice screaming is consonant with Eleanor's deepening neurosis. Although she adopts a mothering role ('I won't let anyone hurt a child') the penalty is to be associated with a form of security which is also a horror, with the mother as death to the self.

In desperation Eleanor makes a last attempt to establish identity with the mother–daughter bond. But when she solicits a confidence from Luke, in a bid for a special token of affection, his response horrifies her: '"I never had a mother." The shock was enormous. Is *that* all he thinks of me' (p. 139). Luke's subsequent comment, that he had always wanted a mother to make him grow up, prompts Eleanor's acid reply, 'Why don't you grow up by yourself?' (p. 140), indicating her impatience with a courtship model which provides no escape from the dynamics of the original relationship. That night, when Theo teases Eleanor about Luke, the women are the victims of another haunting while they are following a path through the grounds. Ostensibly squabbling over Luke, they are described in terms which suggest the persistence of a more primary bond. Each is 'achingly aware of the other' (p. 145) as they skirt around an 'open question'. The language suggests that they are trembling on the brink, *not* of an open quarrel, but of mutual seduction; 'walking side by side in the most extreme intimacy of expectation; their feinting and hesitation done with, they could only wait passively for resolution. Each knew, almost within a breath, what the other was thinking' (p. 146).

As they draw closer, arm in arm again, the path unrolls before them through a suddenly 'colourless' (p. 147) landscape, in an 'annihilation of whiteness'. Ahead there appears a ghostly tableau of a family picnic, in a garden full of rich colour, 'thickly green' grass (p. 148), red, orange and yellow flowers, beneath a bright blue sky. Theo's immediate response is to run ahead, screaming, 'Don't look back', placing colourlessness behind her, along with the risk of annihilation in a symbiotic relationship. Eleanor, however, her development definitively arrested, collapses, feeling 'time, as she had always known time, stop' (p. 149). The haunting foreshadows the outcome of their relationship.When Eleanor announces her intention of accompanying Theo to her home, Theo rejects her once and for all, impatient with what she perceives as a schoolgirl crush, 'as though I were the games mistress' (p. 177). As Eleanor's identity founders, Theo's is secured: her clothes are now restored to their original condition.

The image of the two women trampling the 'happy family' vignette under foot also foregrounds the insufficiencies of the Oedipal model, a point which is generalised by Luke's discovery of a book, composed by Hugh Crain for his daughter. Ostensibly a series of moral lessons, with illustrations of Heaven, Hell, the seven deadly sins, the book purports to guide the child in the paths of righteousness, threatening her with various terrible fates, and offering the reward of reunion in her Father's arms in Heaven 'joined together hereafter in unending bliss' (p. 143). The erotic content of the offer is fully revealed in the obscenity of Crain's accompanying illustration to 'Lust'. The pretence of guiding the child's moral development is actually an excuse to indulge in sensation, transgressing in the guise of moral admonition. Jackson thus explodes both the Freudian view of the father as former of the superego, and of art as an activity of sublimation, replacing instinctual gratifications. Here, far from being the basis of psychic ascension, the Oedipal model is an alibi for male self-indulgence, and a legitimation of patriarchal tyranny. Importantly, Crain has cut up several other books to form his own, so that his individual text draws upon all the resources available in the cultural formation of the female subject.

The arrival of Dr Montague's wife, a conventional spiritualist, measures the disease between fashionable psychic explanations and more radical theories of the psyche. The parodic Mrs Montague is primarily notable for the bookishness of her images of psychic phenomena, most of which are drawn from obvious sources.[10] Thus, receiving a spirit message via 'planchette' from a mysterious nun, she promptly conjures up a monk and extrapolates to a heterosexual courtship model, broken vows and the nun walled up alive. (Nuns remain the most common of reported apparitions,[11] their popularity possibly the result of the recognition that the repression of female desires is a source of psychic disturbance [as in *Villette*].) 'Planchette' also produces the words 'Elena', 'Mother', 'Child', 'Lost', 'Home', endlessly repeated. As a result of botched introductions Mrs Montague takes Theo for Eleanor, and passes the message to the former. The suggestion lingers that Eleanor's bid for independent identity has failed, and that she is locked into psychic repetition.

It is therefore appropriate that the next haunting repeats the features of the others (Theo remarks on the ghost's exhausted repertoire – p. 166). Noisy knockings are followed by a 'caressing touch' (p. 168) 'feeling intimately and softly', 'fondling' and 'wheedling' at the door, and by a babbling both inside and outside Eleanor's head. For Eleanor, the distinction between self and world is collapsing: 'I am disappearing inch by inch into this house, I am going apart a little bit at a time' (p. 168). As Eleanor resists dissolution, so the house shakes and threatens to fall, until she surrenders: 'I will relinquish my possession of this self of mine, abdicate. . . . "I'll come," she said' (p. 170). Instantly all is quiet, and the chapter ends with Theo's joke 'Come along, baby. Theo will wash your face for you and make you all neat for breakfast' (p. 171). Eleanor has thus given up all hope of mature individuation, welcoming the role of child.

From this point on, only Eleanor is haunted, by ghostly footsteps and a welcoming embrace (p. 178), and by a child's voice at the empty centre of the parlour singing 'Go in and out the windows' (p. 189) – a singing-game which replaces the earlier refrain. In surrendering to the child within, Eleanor finally becomes herself the haunter, assuming the attenuated identity of the ghost. Rising by night, she thinks 'Mother', and when a voice replies 'Come along' (p. 190) she runs to the nursery, to find the cold spot gone, darts in and out of the encircling verandah, and continues the childish game by pounding on the others' doors. Around her the house is 'protected and warm' (p. 193), its layout entirely familiar. Ego dissolution has become primal bliss. Hearing Luke's voice, she recognises that of all those present she would least like *him* to catch her, and flees from male pursuit into the library, now 'deliciously fondly warm' (p. 193), its rotten spiral staircase perceived not as a danger but as a means of escape. Though in fact Eleanor is caught in a spiral of fatal repetition, moving towards complete annihilation, she is exultant: 'I have broken the spell of Hill House and somehow come inside. I am home' (p. 194). Eleanor has transferred her 'crush' to the house, described by Luke as 'a mother house, a housemother, a headmistress, a housemistress' (p. 176), and now becomes entirely conterminous with her chosen world, alive to sounds and movements in all its many rooms. Unsurprisingly, when Dr Montague excludes her from his experiment, Eleanor finds separation unthinkable and accelerates her car into a tree in the driveway. Her last thoughts reveal a fatal connection between female self-assertion and annihilation: 'I am really doing it, I am doing this all by myself, now, at last; this is me, I am really really really doing it by myself' (p. 205). In the second before collision her last lucid thought is '*Why* am I doing this?' Feminist psychoanalytics offers an answer which is oddly confirmed in the conclusion. The novel closes with a repetition, almost without alteration, of its own original paragraph, as the cycle of creation closes only to begin once more.

If, by repressing desire, human beings condemn themselves to repeat it, the appeal of Jackson's work to both male and female readers is secure. Just as each individual 'haunting' derives its horrors from the fear of regression to infantile complexes, specifically of fusion with the mother, so the general features of Jackson's fiction are comprehensible in terms of the reproduction of mothering. The anticipation of revisionist psychoanalytics in the reformulation of the sources of horror may also be traced in *The Bird's Nest*, which attributes Elizabeth Richmond's breakdown to her motherlessness; in the murdered child of *The Road through the Wall*; in the murderous and eventually murdered mother of *The Sundial*, and in Jackson's own fascination with the Lizzie Borden case, which looms behind the acquitted murderess, Harriet Stuart, of *The Sundial* and the unconvicted Merricat (*We Have Always Lived in the Castle*), who poisons the rest of her family in order to establish the symbiotic bond with her sister. It would be impertinent, not to say impossible, to speculate on the influence of Jackson's own experience of mothering on her fiction. She was herself a devoted mother of four children, as her two humorous chronicles of family life reveal. Interestingly, the titles of these celebrations of maternal experience, *Raising Demons* and *Life among the Savages*, immediately suggest works of horror fiction.

Notes

First published in Brian Docherty (ed.), *American Horror Fiction* (Basingstoke: Macmillan, 1990).

1. H. P. Lovecraft, *Supernatural Horror in Literature* (New York: Dover, 1973).
2. 'The Uncanny', in *The Standard Edition of the Complete Psychological Works of Sigmund Freud*, ed. James Strachey, vol. XVII (London: Hogarth Press, 1955).

168 *Contemporary Critical Accounts*

3. See Peter Penzoldt, *The Supernatural in Fiction* (London: Peter Nevill, 1952).
4. Rosemary Jackson, *Fantasy: The Literature of Subversion* (London: Methuen, 1981).
5. See Nancy Chodorow, *The Reproduction of Mothering* (Berkeley, CA: University of California Press, 1978); Carol Gilligan, *In a Different Voice: Psychological Theory and Women's Development* (Cambridge, MA: Harvard University Press, 1982); Jean Baker Miller, *Towards a New Psychology of Women* (London: Allen Lane, 1978).
6. A motif traced, in Jungian terms, in Jackson's work by Steven K. Hoffman, in 'Individuation and Character Development in the Fiction of Shirley Jackson', *Hartford Studies in Literature*, 8 (1976) 190–208.
7. Elizabeth Abel, Marianne Hirsch and Elizabeth Langland (eds), *The Voyage In: Fictions of Female Development* (Hanover, NH: University Press of New England, 1983).
8. Page references in parentheses relate to Shirley Jackson, *The Haunting of Hill House* (London: Michael Joseph, 1960).
9. Shirley Jackson, *The Sundial* (New York: Penguin, 1986) p. 109.
10. Mrs Montague's discoveries recall the worst excesses of the ghost hunter, at Borley Rectory in Essex. See Harry Price, *The Most Haunted House in England: Ten Years' Investigation of Borley Rectory* (London: Longmans, Green, 1940) and *The End of Borley Rectory* (London: George G. Harrap, 1946). Jackson refers to Borley in the text (p. 101). Though an examination of Jackson's sources would run to another essay, it is worth noting that almost all the psychic phenomena are drawn from the above work, including a haunted Blue Room, a cold spot, the girl in the tower, the nun and monk, immurement, the digging-up of an old well (proposed by Mrs Montague), messages on walls and from planchette, nightly crashings and patterings at doors, and investigation by a team of psychic researchers. Jackson described her book as originating in an account of nineteenth-century psychic researchers, almost certainly those of Ballechin House, also referred to in the text (p. 8). See A. Goodrich Freer and John, Marquess of Bute, *The Alleged Haunting of Ballechin House* (London: George Redway, 1899).
11. See Peter Underwood, *Dictionary of the Occult and Supernatural* (London: George G. Harrap, 1978) p. 147.

J. GERALD KENNEDY

On Edgar Allan Poe

Longer and more troubling than any other work in the Poe corpus, *The Narrative of Arthur Gordon Pym* has become the pivotal text in current discussions of the author. The notable discontinuities which thwart conventional explication have engendered several recent studies concerned with the novel's self-referential aspects. In important ways, *Pym* calls into question key theoretical relationships: between writer and reader; between text and meaning; between language and truth. We have come to understand the narrator's voyage as a series of interpretive crises which collectively suggest the unreadability of the signs constituted by nature and culture. And when we recall that Von Jung, in 'Mystification,' referred his adversary to a book 'ingeniously framed so as to present to the ear all the outward signs of intelligibility, and even of profundity, while in fact not a shadow of meaning existed,' it is hard to resist the notion that Poe was slyly alluding to his strategy in *Pym*.[1] [Here] I want to explore the implications of illegibility, focusing first on the nature of the hermeneutic dilemma which the reader shares with Pym, and then shifting attention to the metaphysical crux of this impasse. The narrator's abortive quest for meaning seems ultimately related to his progressive immersion in the phenomenology of death; Pym's rehearsals for death and his confrontations with the body of death epitomize the unreadability of lived experience as they disclose the origins of radical uncertainty.

Like 'MS. Found in a Bottle,' *Pym* stages the progressive disorientation of a narrator who disappears within a fold of the text he is said to inscribe. But far more explicitly than the short story, the novel challenges its own textual status by flaunting its problematic 'authenticity'; the narrator successively discovers the unstable or illusory nature of sensory perception, rational thought, social order, and divine providence. He finds the world pervaded by a violence that discloses only the precariousness of life and the imminence of death. Amid horror and despair, only writing seems to provide a source of coherency; Pym sustains identity by registering the ordeal of self-preservation. But finally writing too reveals its provisionality: Pym vanishes in the white vortex, the victim of textual necessity or authorial whim. His fate reminds us (like Borges's 'The Circular

Ruins') that one never knows whether he is the creator of a dream or the effect of someone else's dream.

If the novel refuses to yield a consistent, unifying meaning, contemporary criticism has nevertheless noted suggestive repetitions within the text. The present effort to deconstruct uncertainty in *Pym* builds upon two principal insights into its recurrent figurality. The first derives from the early work of Patrick Quinn, who has characterized *Pym* as a 'profoundly oneiric drama' dominated by 'the pattern of recurrent revolt' and by 'the theme of deception.' Quinn maintains that rebellion and duplicity parallel an ongoing conflict between appearance and reality: '*Pym* is caught up in a life in which nothing is stable, in which nothing is ever really known.'[2] Edward Davidson has subsequently reinforced the idea that deception in Poe's novel is inherent in 'the very construction of the world itself,' forcing upon Pym the realization that 'everything, even the most logically substantial, is an illusion.'[3] The perception of Pym's voyage as a metaphor for intellectual or imaginative discovery has clarified the epistemological matrix of the novel and shifted attention to the philosophical crisis figured by the narrator's perplexity. But both Quinn and Davidson assumed that their respective readings bracketed an intelligible thematic consistency. Neither considered the text itself as an extension of the radical confusion represented within its pages. Consequently neither had much to say about internal, narratorial contradictions or about the framing notes which – as we shall discuss later – render the entire narrative problematic.

The second metaphorical implication has been located in the last decade as a result of poststructuralist inquiries into the self-sustaining and self-referential nature of writing, particularly the *écriture* characteristic of modernism. *Pym* has become focal for theoretical critics because it calls attention to its own insufficiency as a written text, raises the question of how writing can – under any circumstances – represent truth, and demonstrates through narrative action the slippery relationship between inscription and meaning, sign and referent. Jean Ricardou initiated his reconsideration of *Pym* with his observation that the narrator's adventure allegorizes a voyage 'au bout de la page,' which in its black–white oppositions forms 'une dramatisation de l'antagonisme encre-feuille.' Ricardou concludes that in symbolizing the movement toward the end of the written page, the very gesture by which it has been constituted, *Pym* illustrates the way in which modernist writing evokes a material

world only to mirror its own textual strategies. A subsequent essay
by John Carlos Rowe has probed the 'metaliterary' aspect of the
novel: 'This text enacts the deconstruction of representation as the
illusion of the truth and prefigures the contemporary conception of
writing as the endless production of differences.' Rowe sees Pym's
voyage as the journey toward a 'metaphysical' center which is
endlessly 'displaced, disrupted, deferred' by 'the very effort of writing
such a story.' Likewise, John Irwin projects the narrator's voyage as a
search for the origins of language in the mythic emergence of human
self-consciousness. But by placing in doubt the credibility of the
narrator, the novel – in Irwin's view – forces us to contemplate the
inability of language to deliver primary truths: 'Since in a narrative
the certainty of our knowledge seems to rest upon the credibility of
the narrator, putting the latter in question puts the former in
question, thereby directing our attention to the coincidence between
the limits of knowledge and the limits of the written discourse.'[4]

Irwin's remark suggests the point at which earlier discussions of
revolt and deception begin to intersect with more recent
commentaries on the self-referential nature of *Pym*. It now seems
clear that the narrative itself partakes of the metaphysical crisis which
it represents; whatever confusions of purpose inhere in its chaotic plot
and brutal images, *Pym* in some sense reflects upon the life of writing
and the profound indeterminacy of texts. As the narrator struggles to
record the 'truth' of his adventures by translating remembered scenes
into verbal signs, he inadvertently betrays both his own inability to
'read' the text of phenomenal experience and the incapacity of
language to register its overwhelming nature. And beyond the
anxieties of writing consciously noted by Pym, Poe permits us to
apprehend problems and inconsistencies of which the narrator is
unaware; by casting doubt (in the concluding note) on 'the entire
truth of the latter portions of the narration,' the author forces us to
regard the narrator and the narrative as elements of a colossal
deception, a plot against the reader.

Poe initiates his covert reflections on the hazards of reading and
writing in the introductory note. Here, the putative narrator
identifies two obstacles which have supposedly delayed the
composition of the text: Pym says he doubted his ability 'to write,
from mere memory, a statement so minute and connected as to have
the *appearance* of that truth it would really possess'; and he feared
that the incidents to be related were 'of a nature so positively
marvellous' that the public would regard his account as 'merely an

impudent and ingenious fiction.' These remarks express a surface concern for the relationship between language and truth and assume the possibility of a verifiable correspondence between words and facts which can be distinguished from the spurious referentiality of fiction. But both comments also undercut the notion of a distinction between truth and fiction. In suggesting the difficulty of affecting the *appearance* of the truth inherent in his statement, Pym acknowledges a potential slippage between remembered experience and its verbal reconstruction. Here Poe subtly insinuates that appearance and reality may not coincide, and that if fact can have the look of fiction, fiction can surely masquerade as fact. The truth of a memory (itself an indeterminate criterion) cannot insure the impression of truthfulness. Ironically, Pym implies that his task is to create through 'minute and connected' detail that illusion of truth which the writer of fiction would call verisimilitude. His remark contains a further irony insofar as Poe covertly signals the controlling strategy of the hoax: to contrive the appearance of truth in a statement which possesses no grounding in fact. Pym's ostensible concern that his narrative will be perceived as 'an impudent and ingenious fiction' likewise adverts to its actual nature. Through the mask of 'A. G. Pym,' Poe alludes to an underlying objective – to produce an ingenious deception – while evincing a high-minded concern for its reception as truth.

Poe confuses the issue of truth further when Pym recalls the counsel of 'Mr Poe,' formerly of the *Southern Literary Messenger*: 'He strongly advised me, among others, to prepare at once a full account of what I had seen and undergone, and trust to the shrewdness and common sense of the public – insisting, with great plausibility, that however roughly, as regards mere authorship, my book should be got up, its very uncouthness, if there were any, would give it all the better chance of being received as truth'. Here the true author fictionalizes himself to enforce the impression that his narrator is an actual, living personage. Behind the pretense of complimenting the public on its collective 'shrewdness and common sense,' Poe manifests scorn for readers disposed to regard 'uncouthness' as a sign of truth. And once again he insinuates his underlying tactic – to produce the sense of authenticity through an affected crudeness – with the impunity of one who knows that his irony will not be discerned by those at whom it is directed. The author's implied mockery bears out the accuracy of Daniel Hoffman's remark that 'for Poe, satire serves to display the follies of mankind – and the personal superiority of the Artist-Genius to the generality of fools.'[5] In the guise of Pym, who later proves to be a caricature of the American fool, Poe intimates that the reading public cannot possibly distinguish between fact and fable.

As if to give the problem of truth one last twist, the preface refers finally to the two installments of the narrative published earlier in the *Messenger* as the work of Poe. Obviously the author had to manufacture some explanation for the prior association of his own name with the story of Pym's adventures. Accordingly, Pym explains how 'Mr Poe' induced him to supply 'facts' which were then published *'under the garb of fiction.'* Poe's name was attached to the pretended fiction, he adds, so that it would be received as an invention by readers of the magazine. But the ruse backfired: despite the 'air of fable' introduced by Mr Poe, 'the public were still not at all disposed to receive it as fable.' Here real fiction is characterized as pretended fiction to bolster the illusion of its factuality; but in retrospect we see that the only pretense is Poe's attempt to pass off the magazine installments as a deceit. Indeed, Pym's explanation of how 'fact' was palmed off as fiction by the use of Poe's name merely reverse the strategy of the longer narrative.

In accounting for the decision to compose his statement, Pym reports that many clever readers saw through the *Messenger* ploy because the 'facts' of his narrative carried with them 'sufficient evidence of their own authenticity.' He implies that truth is inherent in the notation of detail and circumstance, an exactness of observation couched in verbal signs and yet somehow independent of style – for the 'air of fable' evoked by 'Mr Poe' has not changed 'a single fact.' With this declaration the author arrives at the philosophical crux of the preface, the relation of the written text to the truth (or truths) which it purports to record. By equating truth with fact, Pym implies that the presence of verifiable data establishes the truth of a text quite apart from stylistic eccentricities or fabricated details. Yet this argument obscures the fact that writing always involves the representation of appearances. Even the simplest declarative sentence ('the sun is shining') refers not to a pure, immanent fact but to what the speaker or writer wishes his audience to construe as a fact. For example, the semblance of precision and objectivity in Pym's later notation, 'At noon of this day we were in latitude 78° 30′, longitude 40° 15′ W,' hides the reality that these verbal and numerical signs contain no inherent validity and manifest instead only the desire of a writer to represent himself in such a situation. Writing may convey facts – truths confirmable by both writer and reader – but the actual marks upon the page constitute neither truth nor fiction. They merely point to phenomena which might be empirically true. But the truth of which Pym speaks lies forever outside the text, beyond the field of writing. In effect, Poe evokes the concept of the fact to sustain the illusion of legitimacy and authority which facts produce in a culture that prizes rational, scientific discourse – such as travelogues of the kind emulated by *Pym*. As the novel itself demonstrates, however, any textual distinction between truth and fiction must remain intractably problematic.

The interpretive questions raised in the preface rapidly assume concrete form. As the narrative opens, Poe establishes a paradoxical persona: a young man who is simultaneously innocent and devious, a perpetual victim of misleading appearances and a participant in countless deceptions. His ingenuous recitation of family history (a standard feature of the imaginary voyage) leads to a preliminary episode in which Pym fails to perceive the intoxication of his friend Augustus and so nearly loses his life in the night-time caper aboard the *Ariel*. But Pym is 'resuscitated from a state bordering very nearly upon death,' and he manages to hide from his family the effects of a ghastly neck wound, blithely remarking that 'school-boys . . . can accomplish wonders in the way of deception.' This back-and-forth movement between blindness and dissimulation in the *Ariel* sequence typifies the contradictory nature of Pym, who freely admits his predisposition to trickery even as he solicits the confidence of the reader. Alternately deceiving others and being deceived by his own impercipience, the narrator fails to recognize a connection between his duplicity and the treachery inherent in phenomenal experience. Yet this failure of insight makes possible the more comprehensive deception perpetrated by Poe. For Pym's inability to discern analogies between his contrivances and the plots of others (like the natives of Tsalal) or the more incomprehensible scheme of nature itself conceals the analogical relationship between those deceptions which occur as events in the narrative and those 'quizzes' encountered by its reader. This theoretical distinction becomes clearer when we examine Pym's relationship to the fraudulent letter by which he covers his departure from home.

Written and possibly delivered by Pym's counterpart, Augustus, the note, supposedly from a Mr Ross in New Bedford, invites Pym to spend a fortnight with his sons, Robert and Emmet. The stratagem succeeds, and shortly after the letter's arrival, Pym departs to begin his long adventure. Everything about the missive hints at its double nature: the invitation to spend two weeks with two boys actually enables two other boys to go to sea together. Three chapters later – after Pym experiences living burial as a stowaway – we find that the letter is itself the duplicate of an earlier forgery duplicating the hand-writing of Mr Ross. This fact comes to light when Augustus accounts for the note warning Pym of the mutiny above decks:

> Having concluded to write, the difficulty was now to procure the materials for so doing. An old toothpick was soon made into a pen; and this by means of feeling altogether, for the between-decks were as dark as pitch. Paper enough was obtained from the back of a letter – a duplicate of the forged letter from Mr Ross. This had been the original draught; but the handwriting not being sufficiently well imitated, Augustus had written another, thrusting the first, by good fortune, into his coat-pocket, where it was now most opportunely discovered. Ink alone was thus wanting, and a substitute was immediately found for this by means of a slight incision with the penknife on the back of a finger just above the nail – a copious flow of blood ensuing, as usual from wounds in that vicinity.The note was now written, as well as it could be in the dark and under the circumstances. It briefly explained that a mutiny had taken place; that Captain Barnard was set adrift; and that I might expect immediate relief as far as provisions were concerned, but must not venture upon making any disturbance. It concluded with these words: '*I have scrawled this with blood – your life depends upon lying close.*'

This paragraph recreates a primal scene: writing emerges from darkness and blood, bearing a message of dire importance. Augustus must wound himself to inscribe the words which stand between Pym and death. Inscription entails the sacrifice of life's blood to produce the enduring, written word which sustains life and breaches the gap of silence (always potentially the void of death) between writer and reader.

Ironically, Augustus uses the reverse side of the duplicitous letter to indite his warning of treachery and danger; thus an instrument of betrayal becomes a means of salvation. Such at least is the writer's intent, but meaning is invariably hostage to the vagaries of reading, a problem already illustrated through the tortuous process by which Pym discovers the note and glimpses a portion of its fateful message.

The first five paragraphs of chapter 3 in effect create a paradigm of unreadability, staging the crisis of interpretation recurrently encountered in *Pym*. In considerable detail Poe depicts first the finding of the note (which has been attached to Pym's dog, Tiger) and then his effort to discover an inscription by rubbing phosphorus on the paper:

> I placed the slip of paper on the back of a book, and, collecting the fragments of the phosphorus matches which I had brought from the barrel, laid them together upon the paper. I then, with the palm of my hand, rubbed the whole over quickly, yet steadily. A clear light diffused itself immediately throughout the whole surface; and had there been any writing upon it, I should not have experienced the least difficulty, I am sure, in reading it. Not a syllable was there, however – nothing but a dreary and unsatisfactory blank; the illumination died away in a few seconds, and my heart died away within me as it went.

Failing to perceive a message, Pym tears up the note but later recovers the scraps to check the unexamined side. There he sees 'several lines of MS in a large hand,' but ironically, in his desire to 'read all at once,' he can discern only the last seven words: '*blood – your life depends upon lying close.*' Pym observes that the entire message could not have aroused as much 'indefinable horror' as this 'fragmentary warning,' for it is precisely the ambiguity of the communication which evokes panic. The disjointed reference to 'mystery, and suffering, and terror' creates a 'paroxysm of despair,' as the narrator succumbs to interpretive anxiety. Without invoking the name of death, the cryptic message activates Pym's sense of dread; indeed, its uncertainty becomes a figure of the indecipera-bility of death. In this crucial scene, reading proves itself a risky business, literally an exercise in obscurity. Try as he might, Pym cannot grasp the entire message; writing and reading prove to be ineluctably separate activities, each the function of a subjectivity operating under different pressures at different times, struggling with an arbitrary and imperfect system of signs.

Even as he deconstructs the act of reading, Poe transposes the scene into an interpretive dilemma for the reader of *Pym*. For between the narrator's account of finding 'a dreary and unsatisfactory blank' on one side of the paper and Augustus' explanation that he penned his message on the back of the original letter to Mr Ross, Poe constructs an unresolvable contradiction. Instinctively, one dismisses the problem as an instance of authorial carelessness, for (as the recent edition by Burton Pollin has shown) the narrative is full of inaccuracies. Yet the puzzle bears the mark of intentionality: Poe incorporates a hint of his doubleness by locating a vital message on the reverse side of a duplicate of a forged letter. As I have contended [in an earlier essay], the letter from Augustus actually bears two messages, one visible and one invisible.[6] The seven words, '*blood – your life depends upon lying close*,' offer a fragmentary warning of revolt and deception, of the cruelty and illusoriness of the world. The blank side carries an equally unsettling message, which reveals to the alert observer (if not to Pym) our inescapable limitations as readers of texts. John Carlos Rowe has more recently commented on this supposed textual error: 'The note demonstrates the difficulty of transcending the differential system of language to deliver a unified truth. The note is a palimpsest – *the* palimpsest of language itself, whose messages are always intertexts. Writing appears to defer the presence it desires by constituting a divided present that prefigures its own erasure. Meaning may be situated only within the functions produced by this play of differences.'[7] Rowe implies that the unreadability of the invisible message is symptomatic of the 'erasure' produced by the delay between writing and reading. But in another sense, the 'dreary and unsatisfactory blank' constitutes the only possible representation of that silence which constitutes the obverse of language. What lies on the other side of the fragmentary warning – the reality of death as opposed to its verbal representation – must remain unreadable, for it is precisely the never-to-be-imparted secret, the inscrutable blankness toward which Pym is moving from the beginning of his voyage.

A later scene in *Pym*, overlooked by both Rowe and Irwin, grimly illustrates the way that Poe projects nature and phenomenal experience as an unintelligible text in which death figures as the ultimate cipher. Here Pym's encounter with a complex emblem of fatality brings the writer to the margins of discourse and the limits of intelligibility. The beginning of chapter 10 finds the narrator and Augustus – along with the half-breed Dirk Peters and a man named Parker – shipwrecked and clinging to the hulk of the *Grampus*. Hungry and exhausted by their ordeal, the men have unsuccessfully tried to recover some provisions from a submerged cabin. Suddenly Augustus spies a ship on the horizon; he turns pale, his lips begin to quiver 'in the most singular and unaccountable manner,' and he loses the power of speech. The appearance of the ship has the same effect on Pym: 'I sprang to my feet as if a musket bullet had suddenly struck me to the heart; and, stretching out my arms in the direction of the vessel, stood in this manner, motionless, and unable to articulate a syllable'. Curiously, this image of apparent deliverance suppresses language and produces the sensation of sudden death.

Such a reversal appropriately introduces an episode defined by paradox and suffused by ironic inversions so overwhelming that language cannot represent their nature. For Pym and his companions encounter a ship littered with corpses – not the benign 'ghosts of buried centuries' figured in 'MS. Found in a Bottle' but rotting, stinking cadavers. As the vessel approaches, the castaways attribute its erratic movement to a helmsman 'in liquor.' And they fancy that a tall sailor on the bow is reassuring them: 'He seemed by his manner to be encouraging us to have patience, nodding to us in a cheerful although rather odd way, and smiling constantly so as to display a set of the most brilliantly white teeth'. Here Poe depicts interpretation as flagrant self-delusion, for the reading posited by Pym turns out to be not only incorrect but also foolish in its assumption that phenomenal reality can be reduced to rational coherence. Significantly, the narrator's recognition of his misperception occurs within the context of a celebration of divine benevolence:

> The brig came on slowly, and now more steadily than before, and – I cannot speak calmly of this event – our hearts leaped up wildly within us, and we poured out our whole souls in shouts and thanksgiving to God for the complete, unexpected, and glorious deliverance that was so palpably at hand. Of a sudden, and all at once, there came wafted over the ocean from the strange vessel (which was now close upon us) a smell, a stench, such as the whole world has no name for – no conception of – hellish – utterly suffocating – insufferable, inconceivable.

In this passage as elsewhere in *Pym*, Poe inscribes the idea of providential order only to erase it with an instance of deception, violence, or death. The ship which seems to promise the castaways a 'glorious deliverance,' thereby furnishing a sign of God's mercy, reveals itself as a ghastly emblem of their corporeal fate. And the stench which turns Pym's attention from providence to putrefaction surpasses verbal expression: its nature is 'inconceivable' and therefore unspeakable.

As the black ship sails past, Pym and the other discover the horrific reality signified by the stench. Here again Poe projects the desire of language to break the silence of death, even to establish a dialogue with the dead:

> Shall I ever forget the triple horror of that spectacle? Twenty-five or thirty human bodies, among whom were several females, lay scattered about between the counter and the galley, in the last and most loathsome state of putrefaction! We plainly saw that not a soul lived in that fated vessel! Yet we could not help shouting to the dead for help! Yes, long and loudly did we beg, in the agony of the moment, that those silent and disgusting images would stay for us, would not abandon us to become like them, would receive us among their godly company!

As if unable to surrender their original, mistaken expectation of imminent rescue by the Dutch ship, the survivors of the *Grampus* paradoxically clamor to join the dead crew in order to preserve their own lives. They are simultaneously repulsed by these 'silent and disgusting images' and long to enter into their 'goodly company.' At this moment of extremity, death and life become confused; the living victims confront a vision of what they will become and beg for deliverance as if death alone offers the possibility of life.

And within the economy of symbolic exchange in *Pym*, such proves to be the case. The cry of the castaways finds an answer in the scream of a gull, which is 'gorging itself with the horrible flesh' of the tall sailor on the bow. Life feeds upon death in an act of predation which anticipates – and in some sense inspires – the cannibalism episode two chapters later. But the image of the dead sailor also discloses to Pym his own vacuous misreading; this figure which earlier seemed to be 'encouraging' the four survivors has been animated only by 'the exertions of the carnivorous bird.' Indeed, when the body swings round to reveal the face, Pym grasps the sickening irony of his previous assumptions: 'The eyes were gone, and the whole flesh around the mouth, leaving the teeth utterly naked. This, then, was the smile which had cheered us on to hope! this the – but I forbear'. Unable to contemplate further the difference between death and life, Pym suspends his rereading of the text as if dimly conscious of the pitfalls of interpretation. While the narrator elsewhere seems bereft of memory or intelligence (or both), he nevertheless confronts in this scene the limits of his own knowing.

As he gazes at the decomposing back and face of the tall sailor, he senses that the disconfirmation of his initial reading does not amount to the 'truth' about the man or the vessel. Rather, it reveals the more profound enigma embodied by the ship, about which he admits: 'I have, since this period, vainly endeavored to obtain some clew to the hideous uncertainty which enveloped the fate of the stranger.' His ruminations upon its fate are in fact speculations on the origin and meaning of death itself and the 'hideous uncertainty' of its phenomenal manifestations. However, the text of death cannot be read, for as Pym finally realizes: 'It is utterly useless to form conjectures where all is involved, and will, no doubt, remain for ever involved, in the most appalling and unfathomable mystery'.

Between these two sites of hermeneutic perplexity – the note from Augustus and the ship of death – Poe brackets the problem of unreadability in *Pym*, positing an analogy between two texts: the world of signs encountered by Pym and the devious narrative attributed to him. And while both texts have been in the most literal sense inscribed by Poe, the unreadability of the novel simply transcribes an unreadability already implicit in the textuality of being. Freud claimed that all anxiety was rooted in the fear of death, and in *Pym*, Poe alludes to the radical source of uncertainty through the narrator's repeated encounters with and rehearsals for his own annihilation. In virtually every instance, Pym's immersion in the phenomenology of death yields a more disturbing awareness of its unintelligibility and its threat to the myth of personal immortality. More broadly, the resistance of death to interpretation and naturalization finally jeopardizes the illusion that knowledge itself rests upon a bedrock of coherent experience. Death is not simply an isolated, unsolved problem in an essentially intelligible world; it is the defining reality which enables one to see the provisionality, even the unreality of our usual ways of conceptualizing self and existence.

In a sequence of scenes related to those already discussed, Poe illustrates the power of death to disrupt or invalidate the act of interpretation. The first of these occurs when Pym as a stowaway on the *Grampus* submits to temporary burial in an 'iron-bound box.' With characteristic naïveté, the narrator tells us: 'I proceeded immediately to take possession of my little apartment, and this with feelings of higher satisfaction, I am sure, than any monarch ever experienced upon entering a new palace'. Perceiving the box as an 'apartment' rather than a coffin, Pym fails to recognize that he has entered what Michel Ragon calls 'the space of death.'[8] In mythic readings of *Pym*, this symbolic burial at the beginning of the voyage is said to portend a rebirth into a more enlightened selfhood. Yet the discernible effect of Pym's misreading is disorientation and terror; he falls into a long sleep, awakens 'strangely confused,' loses all sense of time, and – prefiguring the dilemma of the Norwegian fisherman in 'A Descent into the Maelström' – finds that his watch has stopped altogether. Now out of time literally and symbolically, he discovers that a piece of cold mutton has turned to 'a stage of absolute putrefaction,' imaging the fate which he risks in his little apartment. His consequent fear of sleep transparently displays an anxiety about the sleep which never ends.

During his slumber, Pym also experiences dreams 'of the most terrific description' in which he is smothered by 'demons,' throttled by 'immense serpents,' and surrounded by leafless trees waving their 'skeleton arms.' These oneiric projections reveal the psychic itinerary of Pym's voyage. But far from indicating an incipient rebirth, they point toward a dread till now masked by a conscious fantasy of adventure. Before boarding the ship, the innocent youth declares, 'My visions were of shipwreck and famine; of death or captivity among barbarian hordes; of a lifetime dragged out in sorrow and tears, upon some gray and desolate rock, in an ocean unapproachable and unknown'. This daydream, which forms the ostensible basis of the burial nightmare, derives from the same works of romance which would later inspire Tom Sawyer's scheme to liberate Jim in *Huckleberry Finn*. But Pym's dream of annihilation later in the same chapter marks a transformation of the fantasy and suggests the intrusion of death as a semiconscious fear. In the darkness of the hold, which simulates the black confines of the grave, Pym experiences a recurrence of his 'gloomy imaginings,' which include 'the dreadful deaths of thirst, famine, suffocation, and premature interment.' Now these images of extinction bring him close to madness and imply an antithetical relationship between reason and the thought of death.

In a subsequent episode, Poe deconstructs the visual horror of death to reveal its phantasmic, undecidable nature. Significantly, he couches this experience of 'reading' death within a double strategy of deception – one aimed at fictional characters within the text and one directed at the reader of the text. The passage in question depicts the process by which Pym becomes a 'corpse,' impersonating a dead sailor named Hartman Rogers. Until this scene, the narrator has remained hidden beneath the deck of the *Grampus*; when the mutineers divide into two factions, Augustus, who sides with Dirk

Peters, decides to enlist Pym's help in defeating the mate's gang. Augustus brings Peters down to Pym's hiding place, where the three plot to overthrow the other faction. Poe frames the ensuing deception of the rival gang with a piece of narrative trompe-l'oeil, for Pym suggests that a surprise attack will have greater success if he disguises himself to resemble Rogers, who was evidently poisoned by the mate. He observes:

> Rogers had died about eleven in the forenoon, in violent convulsions; and the corpse presented in a few minutes after death one of the most horrid and loathsome spectacles I ever remember to have seen. The stomach was swollen immensely, like that of a man who has been drowned and lain under water for many weeks. The hands were in the same condition, while the face was shrunken, shrivelled, and of a chalky whiteness, except where relieved by two or three glaring red splotches, like those occasioned by the erysipelas: one of these splotches extended diagonally across the face, completely covering up an eye as if with a band of red velvet.

The gruesome details obscure the fact that Pym could have observed neither the 'violent convulsions' of Rogers nor the 'horrid and loathsome' appearance of his body a few minutes after death. While it is true that Pym, several hours later, helps to remove Rogers' shirt and to drop the body overboard, his eyewitness report of the man's death throes amounts to a 'quiz' of the reader; Pym was hiding below decks when Rogers died.

Yet this misrepresentation conveys a psychic truth. For the visual spectacle of death is irresistible; the sight of the corpse exerts a disquieting hold, in this case prompting the narrator to imagine a scene he could not have observed. We find ourselves engrossed by Pym's depiction of the dead sailor, perhaps for the same reason that the child never forgets his first sight of a corpse. Because we know death only through the signs of its presence, which are themselves signs of an absence, signifiers of mortality have a tantalizing opacity. The strange aspect of the corpse – the 'look of distance on the face of death,' as Emily Dickinson phrased it – raises the question of the dead body's relationship to the departed being. Resemblance and difference cancel each other; the corpse both is and is not the self that was. Morin remarks that the most violent *perturbations funéraires* arise from the conflict between the idea of personal immortality and the signs of decay: 'La terreur de la décomposition n'est autre que la terreur de la perte de l'individualité.'[9] At bottom the phenomenon of decomposition evokes the fear that individual essence disappears forever at death. The transformation of Rogers into a repulsive object poses precisely this threat, exciting a gesture of psychic denial. The narrator notes that the mate, getting a glimpse of the 'disgusting condition' of the body, order the remains sewn up in a hammock and accorded the rites of sea burial. 'Having given these directions he went below, as if to avoid any further sight of his victim,' Pym reports, limning a scene which anticipates the isolation and concealment of death in the twentieth century.

If the mate suffers from guilt, he also fears the physical signs of death. Thus, when Pym disguises himself to imitate the 'horrible deformity of the swollen corpse,' his masquerade produces a fatal shock. Indeed, the narrator can barely endure his *own* reflected image: 'As I viewed myself in a fragment of looking-glass which hung up in the cabin, and by the dim light of a kind of battle-lantern, I was so impressed with a sense of vague awe at my appearance, and at the recollection of the terrific reality which I was thus representing, that I was seized with a violent tremour, and could scarcely summon resolution to go on with my part'. Pym accounts for his 'violent tremour' as an effect of recognition, a sudden 'recollection' of the dead man's appearance. Yet the reaction is more complex than that, for the disguise itself – a shirt stuffed with bedclothes, white woollen mittens filled with rags, a face rubbed with chalk and streaked with blood – consists of ludicrous makeshift effects. These contrivances arouse fear not through mimetic efficiency but because their blatantly semiotic function (as signs of the signs of death) points to the dead end of the signifying chain, to signs which themselves have no proper intelligibility. For the signifiers of death refer solely to a lack, to the absence of life, rather than to an immanent signified. If death constitutes an actual presence, its signification is forever deferred within the life world of human signs. And so the clinical symptoms of dissolution mark a semiotic disruption, an impasse to meaning which thus insures both their unreadability and their irresistible fascination.

When Pym appears before the sailors in the guise of Rogers, the scene in effect deconstructs the experience of terror. Poe notes that while an apparition of doubtful authenticity can evoke only a partial 'anticipative horror,' the phantasm simulated by Pym has an absolute effect: 'The mate sprang up from the mattress on which he was lying, and, without uttering a syllable, fell back, stone dead . . .

[while] four others sat for some time rooted apparently to the floor, the most pitiable objects of horror and utter despair my eyes ever encountered'. Pym explains that the sailors had no doubt 'that the apparition of Rogers was indeed a revivification of his disgusting corpse, or at least its spiritual image.' For them, the intrusion of Rogers amounts to a return of the repressed, a scandalous encounter with an image already forgotten, consigned to the deep (or so the mate believes) and thus figuratively hidden in the unconscious. Morin points out that the enclosure of the dead body in a shroud, coffin, vault, or mausoleum has always had the double function of protecting the living as well as the dead: 'Les pierres funéraires sont-elles là pour protéger le mort des animaux, ou pour l'empêcher de revenir parmi les vivants?'[10] His question uncovers the anxiety of the return exploited by Pym and his companions. The mate expires precisely because reason cannot accommodate the threat embodied by the 'disgusting corpse.' The dead must stay buried, else we go mad with the anxieties they bring to full consciousness.

Pym's impersonation of a corpse places him in the singular position of being both a living subject and a dead object; for a moment (when seized by the 'violent tremour') he experiences the alienation of the self from itself which – as Kafka figuratively suggests in 'The Metamorphosis' – belongs to the phenomenology of dying. While the masquerade facilitates a violent revolt which leaves Pym physically unharmed, on the psychic level he has been unnerved by the glimpse of what he will himself become. Ineluctably he has begun to conceive of his own physical transformation, and subsequent encounters with putrefaction (as in the 'Flying Dutchman' episode) activate the primal anxiety. Thus in a subsequent scene, Pym participates in a grisly attempt to forestall death through a paradoxical consuming of death's body.

This scene of cannibalism has been inspired (as noted earlier) by the gull gorging itself on the back of the dead sailor aboard the phantom ship. The unspeakable idea is broached just after Providence has again seemingly taunted the victims (at the end of chapter 11) with false hopes of deliverance. When Parker proposes a lottery to determine which man should die to preserve the lives of the others, he articulates a solution that is at once sane and mad, evincing a dispassionate logic about human sacrifice. Poe presents the scene as a crisis of civilized values; the survivors have reached a 'horrible extremity' in which instinct has eclipsed reason, belief, and duty. Proximity to death has brought them face to face with their own craving for physical survival; yet while Pym remonstrates with Parker 'in the name of everything which he [Parker] held sacred,' the episode principally exhibits collective despair. Poe underscores this faithlessness through the ironic imagery of communion ritual; as Irwin has pointed out, the slaughter of Parker stands in telling contrast to the sacrificial death of Christ: 'Unlike Parker's sacrifice in which the body that is eaten becomes part of the person who eats it, in Christ's sacrifice the person who eats the body becomes part of what is eaten: he is incorporated into the mystical body of Christ. By eating the dismembered parts of Christ's body, the disciples become members of that body; and after their own deaths when their physical bodies have decayed, that membership will be the means by which they are remembered by Christ and saved from everlasting destruction.'[11] In Christian ritual, the devouring of the sacramental body serves precisely to insure the survival of the soul against the corruptibility of the flesh. The consuming of Parker, however, affords no spiritual nourishment; it parodies the Christian communion only to reveal the absence of faith and a concomitant anxiety about survival.

In various nature religions, the sacrifice of the scapegoat king secures a temporary postponement of death (often figured as a blight or curse) for participants willing to mark themselves with the victim's blood or to ingest a portion of the body. According to the logic of ritual, only through a metaphorical embracing of death can death be deferred. By virtue of his capacity to incarnate that which the community dreads, the scapegoat king inspires fear as a demigod; he is set apart, marked as different, despite his representative function. In some ways the killing of Parker replicates this archetypal practice: marked by fate and thus transformed into a living dead man, Parker takes upon himself the fear of death shared by the group; the eating of his body displays the desire to protect oneself from corporeal dissolution. But in actuality, Parker's death carries no talismanic or sacrificial force; the 'fearful repast' mainly illustrates the condition of modern culture which René Girard calls 'the sacrificial crisis,' a symptom of social disorder in which the distinction between the pure and impure (or sacred and profane) has been effaced, precluding any purgation through sacrificial violence and thereby unleashing the contagion of reciprocal violence.[12] Girard's theory of 'sacrificial crisis' elucidates the general problem of violence in Poe as well as the particular butchery heralded on the original title page of *Pym*. For Poe projects a world devoid of redemptive sacrifice and therefore helplessly exposed to the ultimate violence of death. Faced with the threat of mortality, his characters project their own sense of victimization as a violence toward others, as if blindly seeking a surrogate, a double whose death will have the effect of sacrificial ritual: to relive one's own fear of death. The killing of Parker, which occurs between the violence of the mutiny and the massacre on Tsalal, manifests the insistence of reciprocal violence in a secular, death-haunted world.

Once again, Pym's encounter with death (he nearly loses the lottery himself) results form an inattentiveness which for Parker has fatal consequences. Two days after the last of the body has been consumed, Pym remembers leaving an axe in one of the larboard berths. With no awareness of his unfortunate timing, he remarks: 'I now thought it possible that, by getting at this axe, we might cut through the deck over the storeroom, and thus readily supply ourselves with provisions.' The recovery of the axe soon yields provisions and later enables the castaways to cut up and preserve a sea turtle. Although Pym fails to register the irony of his belated recollection, its proximity to the 'fearful repast' enables the reader to grasp the monstrous implication. Pym's forgetfulness reveals the importance of surface-depth relationships in *Pym*: the immediate, tangible 'facts' of a situation mask an unseen and often contradictory set of conditions discoverable only through violence. As an instance of repression (which is less a misreading than a denial of the text), Pym's inability to remember the axe until after the bloodshed also discloses a more complicated meaning. On the one hand it seems to betray an unconscious longing for the kind of renewing, sacrificial violence described above – a motive contrary to Pym's conscious disgust with the idea of human sacrifice. The narrator's lapse insures the unfolding of the plan proposed by Parker. On the other hand, his forgetting also appears to signal Pym's own unconscious desire for the lasting forgetfulness of death. His psychic denial of the lifesaving tool manifests not an instinct for survival but an inchoate desire for oblivion, which (as we shall see) becomes more insistent as the narrator approaches the polar sea.

Like the killing of Parker, the subsequent death of Augustus seems charged with contradictory meanings. The sudden, ghastly manner of his demise calls attention to both the literal and metaphorical significance of decomposition. Pym writes that

his death filled us with the most gloomy forebodings, and had so great an effect upon our spirits that we sat motionless by the corpse during the whole day, and never addressed each other except in a whisper. It was not until some time after dark that we took courage to get up and throw the body overboard. It was then loathsome beyond expression, and so far decayed that, as Peters attempted to lift it, an entire leg came off in his grasp. As the mass of putrefaction slipped over the vessel's side into the water, the glare of phosphoric light with which it was surrounded plainly discovered to us seven or eight large sharks, the clashing of whose horrible teeth, as their prey was torn to pieces among them, might have been heard at the distance of a mile.

Within a few hours, Augustus is transformed from a living being to a putrid corpse, his fate anticipating the instantaneous decomposition of Monsieur Valdemar. For Pym, the spectacle represents another image of his own death, insofar as Augustus has been from the outset identified as Pym's alter ego. The narrator at one point affirms that the 'intimate communion' between the two has 'resulted in a partial interchange of character'. In the putrefaction of his friend's body, Pym sees the corruptibility of his own flesh; more importantly, he discovers the precarious and problematic nature of that which constitutes being. Augustus dies 'without having spoken for several hours'; he leaves no verbal trace of essence as last words. There is no spiritualized scene of departure, and the physical falling apart of his body suggests that self is simply an effect of corporeal presence. This deconstruction of the human repeats an idea enacted in the cannibalism episode: prior to the 'fearful repast,' Parker's head, hands, and feet were removed, as if to efface his human identity. Reading the death of Augustus in this way, we perceive that decomposition implies the erasure of self.

In another sense, the decaying of Pym's friend occurs as a self-conscious irony and a portent of the narrator's own subsequent erasure by Poe. Augustus is written out of the novel in chapter 13 despite an explicit reference in chapter 5 to a conversation between Pym and his companion 'many years' after their adventure. Though this discrepancy may be attributed to authorial carelessness – Pollin dismisses it as a 'relic of the first rough plan' for the novel – the sudden disintegration of Augustus bears the mark of an intentional 'quiz.' For Poe dispatches the youth on the first of August, calling attention by this heavy-handed coincidence and the rapidity of his decay (itself a kind of visual pun) to the arbitrariness of his existence as a textual

construct. Augustus is merely a product of writing; he can be de-
composed as readily as he has been verbally embodied. As the author
of a forged letter, the writer of the notes scrawled in blood, and the
copyist of business documents prior to the mutiny, the youth has
already been identified with the act of inscription; hence the mortification of his right arm, said at the last to be 'completely black from the
wrist to the shoulder,' serves to confirm his further uselessness in any
project of writing. When Peters throws the corpse overboard, his
gesture anticipates the maneuver by which Poe finally jettisons a
narrator whose death is figured by a suspension of the text itself.

Like his encounter with the phantom ship, Pym's several rehearsals
for death – his premature burial, his masquerade as a corpse, his
consuming of death's body, and his witnessing the decomposition of
Augustus – are all framed by delusions or deceptions which shift
attention from the narrative to its problematic textuality. The
narrator's misreading of the tall sailor on the bow of the Dutch brig
becomes a model of the reader's relationship to the body of the novel.
Pym's inability to see the 'text' as a corpse corresponds to the modern
inclination to read death in Poe as the sign of something else. More
specifically, it exemplifies the way in which death disrupts the process
of reading as it disrupts the semiotics of daily experience, imposing
its blankness and silence upon the signs by which its presence-as-
absence is known. Whenever Pym approaches death, he verges upon
the limit of signification itself, thus repeating the dilemma in 'MS.
Found in Bottle.' The discontinuities of *Pym*, whether inscribed as
narratorial misperceptions or authorial games of credibility, point to
the radical uncertainty of reading itself within the zone of mortality.
Death can only be misread; its signs produce a cognitive disturbance
which not only thwarts our efforts to construe the text of mortality
but which exposes the provisionality of all signs by which we read the
terms of existence.

Having reached a narrative dead end in chapter 13, with Pym and
Dirk Peters stranded in midocean on the floating hulk of the
Grampus, Poe opens another adventure in misprision: 'by the mercy
of God' the *Jane Guy* arrives to rescue the survivors. Subsequent
events cast doubt on this providential reading, however, as the ship's
crew falls victim to a massacre; Pym and Peters escape the slaughter
only to disappear into a milky vortex at the South Pole. In some
respects, *Pym* becomes a different novel once the narrator has
boarded the *Jane Guy*: geographical observations, cribbed from
contemporary sources, mark a temporary escape from dread. But

once the ship reaches Tsalal, an island inhabited by dark-skinned natives, Pym reenters the sphere of treachery and annihilation. This return to violence coincides with an increasing attention to cultural practice, speech, and hieroglyphs, as these phenomena pose problems of interpretation for Pym and his comrades. Juxtaposing death and hermeneutic crisis, Poe restates the problem of uncertainty as an effect of writing. For the ubiquitous opposition of black and white, which on one level issues in genocide, also stages (as Ricardou has remarked) 'a dramatization of the ink–paper opposition,' placing the concluding action of *Pym* within the metaphoricity of inscription. Pym's final voyage toward the vortex is in some sense a movement toward figurality itself, toward a trope of writing and textual closure.

Unlike his seemingly innocent rendering of adventures aboard the *Grampus*, Pym records his experiences on Tsalal with a reflective self-consciousness. A sudden passion for scientific discovery leads him to analyse details and to contemplate the meaning of observations. From the behavior of the black natives he surmises: 'It was quite evident that they had never before seen any of the white race – from whose complexion, indeed, they appeared to recoil'. But Pym professes his inability to understand the natives' fear of 'several very harmless objects – such as the schooner's sails, an egg, an open book, or a pan of flour.' His mistake in classifying the objects as 'harmless' rather than white has far-reaching consequences, for he thereby fails to perceive the principle of taboo which impels the natives to destroy their white visitors. This blatant misreading betrays the ethnocentricity of the narrator, who cannot conceive of whiteness as evil or deadly and thus cannot imagine himself as a mortal threat, an embodiment of death.

While alerting readers more attentive than Pym to the eventual massacre, Poe's insistence upon black–white oppositions also prefigures the end of the novel, in which Pym vanishes into the perfect whiteness of the polar region. Even those skeptical of Ricardou's theory that the text represents the 'voyage to the end of the page' must grant that the description of Tsalal suggests an analogy between the physical terrain and inscription, between the site of death and the space of writing. As Pym and Peters explore the chasms amid the hills, they encounter hieroglyphs upon the walls and – as the concluding note explains – in the very configuration of the abyss. Rowe points out that 'the relation between the irreducibly figurative landscape and the graphic nature of the narrative is made explicit in Pym's drawings of the shapes of the chasms themselves.'[13] If we trust Poe's appended translations of the hieroglyphic writing, the markings on the walls – a human figure beside the phrases 'to be white' and 'the region of the south' – are inscribed within an abyss which spells out the 'Ethiopian verbal root . . . "to be shady."' That is, 'the inflections of shadow or darkness' contain and physically subsume 'inflections of brilliancy and whiteness,' thus forging a pre-scription of the recent massacre. But more broadly, the representation of a human form within the abyss of shadow or darkness refers to the universal fate of mortals. Pym and Peters find themselves literally within the valley of the shadow of death, in which the only vestige of human essence is the problematic inscription which portends their obliteration.

Curiously, Pym finds the graven text unreadable; indeed, he fails to perceive the markings as writing and convinces Peters that they are 'the work of nature' rather than 'alphabetical characters.' As Irwin remarks, this refusal to see the inscriptions as man-made amounts to 'a denial of human presence that is symbolic of that death of the self to itself in opposition to which self-conscious life is differentiated, a death that is not simply the external limit of self-consciousness but its internal limit as well, a death lying at the core of self-consciousness and inhabiting the objective otherness of the inscribed image.'[14] Pym represses the reality embodied by the hieroglyphic markings, unable to accept consciously the fate already determined as a narrative inevitability. The human figure on the wall, said to be 'standing erect' (there is indeed the suggestion of a tumescent phallus), incarnates in its cold fixity the principle of death as it stimulates a priapic lust for life. Pym refuses to contemplate the mark as a pictographic representation of the fate of desire and so continues to resist the thought of his own perishability.

Yet in a subsequent scene, Poe implies that his narrator unconsciously yearns to complete his textual destiny – to become an inscribed figure, purely the 'I' of writing and no longer the self who writes 'I.' When Pym and Peters attempt to escape the hill scored with chasms (Ethiopian letters), they discover that the promontory is ringed by cliffs; the 'text' is itself defined by the abyss which encircles it. By dint of strength and agility Peters manages to descend the cliff, but Pym finds himself at the brink of the gulf overwhelmed by an 'irrepressible desire,' an irrational urge to fall:

> The more earnestly I struggled *not to think*, the more intensely vivid became my conceptions, and the more horribly distinct. At length arrived that crisis of fancy, so fearful in all similar cases, the

crisis in which we begin to anticipate the feelings with which we *shall* fall – to picture to ourselves the sickness, and dizziness, and the last struggle, and the half swoon, and the final bitterness of the rushing and headlong descent. And now I found these fancies creating their own realities, and all imagined horrors crowding upon me in fact. I felt my knees strike violently together, while my fingers were gradually yet certainly relaxing their grasp. There was a ringing in my ears, and I said, 'This is my knell of death!' And now I was consumed with the irrepressible desire of looking below. I could not, I would not, confine my glances to the cliff; and, with a wild, indefinable emotion half of horror, half of a relieved oppression, I threw my vision far down into the abyss. For one moment my fingers clutched convulsively upon their hold, while, with the movement, the faintest possible idea of ultimate escape wandered, like a shadow, through my mind – in the next my whole soul was pervaded with *a longing to fall*; a desire, a yearning, a passion utterly uncontrollable.

Pym momentarily surrenders to this urge and plunges into the void – directly into the arms of Dirk Peters.

This lengthy passage demands attention for it brings into the open Pym's fear of death, now experienced as that 'oppression' which death alone can relieve. The desire to cast oneself into the abyss, which Poe later attributed to 'perverseness,' manifests here the burden of psychic experience in *Pym*. Irwin notes that Pym's swoon on the brow of the cliff marks his third fainting episode; these 'symbolic deaths' all signal 'the imaginative anticipation of death.'[15] A witness to countless deaths and a survivor of two separate massacres, the narrator now feels for the first time a previously unconscious desire to die. Lifton's analysis of 'survivor guilt' seems particularly apposite to the nature of Pym's ordeal:

The survivor of disaster, and especially holocaust, faces several formidable problems concerning guilt. He has been witness not to death in appropriate sequence but random, absurd, grotesque, and in many cases man-made death; which, in turn, threatens his most basic commitments and images concerning life's reliability and significance; that is, radically threatens his centering and grounding. He is susceptible to the sense that it could or even should have been he, instead of the other, who died. . . . His debt to the dead can become permanent and unpayable.[16]

As Lifton suggests, the recurrence of gratuitous, violent death destabilizes the individual psyche by exposing the radical unreliability of suppositions about life's meaning. The horror of Pym's experience culminates in this suicidal impulse, which expresses at once the yearning to fall into oblivion or forgetfulness and the compulsion to pay his debt to the dead.

But this reading of the precipice scene takes into account only one of the metaphorical associations of the abyss. As we have seen, the landscape of Tsalal also defines a textual space, in which the chasms themselves are configured as archaic writing. When Pym tells us that 'with a wild, indefinable emotion half of horror, half of a relieved oppression,' he gazes 'far down into the abyss,' he also expresses the unconscious desire to fall into writing, to surrender his mortal being to the timelessness of the inscribed text. If we could imagine a rewriting of 'The Oval Portrait' in which the painter destroyed himself in producing a self-portrait, the analogy would be exact. Pym's contemplated fall into writing entails the literal death of the writer while promising his symbolic survival as an inscribed presence. Poe thereby projects the notion that the deepest appeal of writing lies in its inherent fatality: it extracts life to perpetuate it; it emulates death to deny it. George Steiner remarks that 'all great writing springs from *le dur désir de durer*, the hard contrivance of spirit against death, the hope to overreach time by the force of creation.'[17] There is another sense, however, in which Pym's fascination with death in the abyss betrays the yearning not for immortality but for that confrontation with oblivion which makes writing possible. Blanchot quotes from the journal of Kafka ('*Write to be able to die – Die to be able to write*') to elucidate the sense in which 'art is a relation with death,' a problem of mastery and self-possession which originates in the threat of annihilation. Not until one establishes an equality with death can writing occur: 'If you lose face before death, if death is the limit of your self-possession, then it slips the words out from under the pen, it cuts in and interrupts. The writer no longer writes, he cries out – an awkward, confused cry which no one understands and which touches no one.'[18] In this sense Pym's fall may be said to dramatize the beginning of writing: perhaps not until he has thrown himself into the abyss, plunged into the experience of his own death, can be inscribe the first word of his narrative.

To be sure, the scene on the cliff displays more abandon than self-possession. Not until the novel's final scene, in fact, does Pym appear to accept his mortal condition. As his canoe drifts further toward the brilliant whiteness of the pole, Pym, Peters, and their hostage Nu-Nu become increasingly listless. The approach of the polar winter inspires no terror; Pym writes, 'I felt a *numbness* of body and mind – a dreaminess of sensation – but this was all'. The strange apathy of the voyagers increases with the velocity of their approach to the luminous but silent void. Like the narrator of 'MS. Found in a Bottle,' Pym finds himself approaching 'a region of novelty and wonder'; on the verge of the abyss – a 'limitless cataract' – he evinces no fear of annihilation: 'And now we rushed into the embraces of the cataract, where a chasm threw itself open to receive us. But there arose in our pathway a shrouded human figure, very far larger in its proportions than any dweller among men. And the hue of the skin of the figure was of the perfect whiteness of the snow'. Drawing a connection between the chasms on Tsalal and the milky cataract, Irwin points out that 'Pym's confrontation with the hieroglyphic human figure in the cavern *foreshadows* his final confrontation with the apotheosized human figure in the mist,' and he speculates that the latter form is either an optical illusion, a projection of Pym's own shadow upon the white curtain, or an imagined 'spectral illusion' – both symptomatic of a 'veiled narcissism' associated with the psychic origins of language.[19]

One can discern a parallel between the two chasmic scenes, however, which leads to quite a different view of the 'shrouded human figure.' The fact that Pym's narrative breaks off dramatically as he approaches 'the embraces of the cataract' reminds us again of the metaphoricity which associates the abyss with writing. Disappearing into the whiteness, he exchanges his putative historical existence for that of a purely textual entity. The 'shrouded' form in Pym's pathway may be understood simply as an objectification of death, a defined representation of the indefinable and unknowable. But if we recall his prior misreading of the figure on the wall of the chasm, another possibility presents itself. Whereas he earlier mistook the written figure for a natural form, the narrator here conversely mistakes for a human presence the palpable body of the narrative rising before him to deliver him from silence. He is about to be gathered into the artifice of the text, to become an enduring subject caught in language like a fly in amber. The vortex scene enacts the process through which Pym is delivered from anxiety by the possibility of writing; he loses his fear by gazing upon the 'perfect whiteness' of the textual space in which the life of writing unfolds. Only in this brilliance does the unreadable side of the letter from Augustus at last reveal its paradoxical signification: death's 'dreary and unsatisfying blank,' the source of terror and uncertainty, is also the necessary ground of inscription. The shrouded form speaks wordlessly, its blankness revealing that the space of death and the space of writing are one.

Beyond its difficult imagery, the ending raises an additional question: when did Pym compose the work attributed to him? The appended editorial note speaks of 'the late sudden and distressing death of Mr Pym,' which has ostensibly prevented completion of the manuscript; reference is made to 'the loss of the two or three final chapters' under revision at the time of Pym's fatal 'accident.' But this information seems more incredible than the novel's ending, insofar as it implies Pym's survival of the polar vortex. Through this strategy, the narrative projects three contradictory propositions: Pym surely died at the South Pole in the vastness of the cataract; he was delivered from certain death and ten years later wrote his marvelous narrative; he died during the writing of that story at the very juncture which narrates his own death. Each proposition entails an impossibility: if Pym died, his narrative could not exist; if he plunged into the cataract, he could not have survived; if he survived, his putative textual death could not coincide with his physical death. Late in the narrative Pym admits that he 'kept no regular journal' during the early portion of his adventure, thus implying that the logbook content of chapters 13 through 25 coincides with material inscribed at the time of the voyage. In portraying the configuration of the chasms on Tsalal, he comments: 'I had luckily with me a pocket-book and pencil, which I preserved with great care through a long series of subsequent adventure, and to which I am indebted for memoranda of many subjects which would otherwise have been crowded from my remembrance'. He mentions this 'pencil memoranda' again in confessing the approximate nature of the dates assigned to his last recorded episode, the voyage into the cataract. But these touches of verisimilitude expose the very problem they seek to conceal, for, like the narrative of premature burial, Pym's account seems to arrive from beyond the grave. The reader questions the survival not of the 'pencil memoranda' but of its writer. The report of the author's recent 'distressing' death places the whole story in yet another context: the writer of these words, manifestly alive in the representation of his adventure, is already dead. A living presence in the preface and a corpse in the postscript, Pym in effect dies during the time of reading. His literal fate thereby appears to corroborate his figurative itinerary. Indeed, it suggests again that the really hazardous adventure was not the excursion to the South Pole but the ordeal of writing. His reported decease renders entirely problematic both the site of death and the scene of writing. Like the inconceivable painting in 'The Fall of the House of Usher,' said to represent an underground vault without any visible source of light and yet suffused by a 'flood of intense rays' producing a 'ghastly and inappropriate splendor', Poe produces in *Pym* a narrative which could not have been written.

It is likewise a book that does not permit itself to be read, if we understand reading to be the reconstruction of a coherence lodged in the text. Despite the patterning suggested by Pym's rehearsals for death, his encounters with living burial, putrefaction, murder, cannibalism, and suicidal fantasy only underscore the point that mortality cannot be naturalized, denied, comprehended, or indefinitely deferred. It disrupts the system of signs as it destabilizes contemporary metaphysics, posing the question of individual survival in the spectacle of decay. The unreadability of death deprives the natural order of a final intelligibility; unlike Emerson's vision of nature – that plenitude of transparent symbols affirming the connectedness of being – Poe imagines in *Pym* a world of deceptive and opaque surfaces which determine the isolation of the perceiving self. In the hermeneutic failures of the narrator, who learns nothing from his continuing bafflement and instead 'enacts over and over again the same scenario without every becoming aware of it,' Poe represents the condition of uncertainty enforced by the modern crisis of death.[20]

As if to seal the narrative in an enveloping contradiction which would insure the book's unreadability, Poe, in the editorial appendix, not only disposes of his narrator but undermines his credibility through a series of tactics which lead back finally to the enigmatic complicity between death and writing. He first indicates that 'the gentleman whose name is mentioned in the preface' ('Mr Poe') has refused to complete the writing of Pym's tale, on account of the 'general inaccuracy of the details afforded him' and – more tellingly – because of his 'disbelief in the entire truth of the latter portions of the narration'. With this stratagem, 'Mr Poe' challenges the veracity of the work he has already endorsed in the preface, leaving the reader to puzzle out the contradiction as well as the issue of reliability which it raises. Poe thereby presents himself as a shrewder judge of narrative than the implied reader who has succumbed to Pym's blandishments about 'fact' and 'truth.' But the supposed editor (Poe in another guise) imagines himself to be even more astute than 'Mr Poe.' In glossing the hieroglyphs on Tsalal, he contradicts Pym's theory that the figures were the work of nature and then, as if to dismiss the skepticism of 'Mr Poe,' exposes the latter's failure to construe the chasms themselves as writing: 'The facts in question have, beyond doubt, escaped the attention of Mr Poe.' Through these supplemental disclosures, the editor leaves the whole matter of authority unclear, even as his exercise in 'philological scrutiny' invites speculation on writing and the problem of meaning.

The riddle of Tsalal, the cry 'Tekeli-li,' and the polar oppositions of black and white may be traced, he implies, to the chasms or the figures 'so mysteriously written in their windings.' But whether the inscriptions portend racial massacre or refer more broadly to the yearning for escape from the shadow of death (the arm of the human form is 'outstretched toward the south,' toward 'brilliancy and whiteness'), this commentary on writing within the abyss – or writing *as* abyss – calls attention to engravings which bear witness to the dilemma of mortality. In some primal scene, perhaps coeval with the formation of the chasms themselves, an unknown writer conscious of the ephemerality of speech and his own perishability as a speaking subject carved upon the wall those 'alphabetical characters' by which he might continue to speak after is own decease.

Whatever their topical content, the ancient inscriptions on Tsalal thus refer to the genesis of writing, to an originary defiance of silence, which is of course the paradigm of all writing. In its most elemental form, inscription manifests a revolt against death, and this seems to be the implication of the unattributed final sentence in *Pym*: *'I have graven it within the hills, and my vengeance upon the dust within the rock'*. The postscript is cryptic because of its unknown provenance and because it posits an esoteric relationship between writing and vengeance. It is also cryptic in its allusion to the tomblike abyss on Tsalal and to the dust within the chasm. This dust may be understood both as a metaphor for mortality and as the detritus of writing; as it produces dust, inscription constitutes (in Irwin's words) man's 'revenge against death, the revenge that man attempts to take, through art, against time, change, and mortality, against the things that threaten to obliterate all trace of his individual existence.'[21] Interestingly, the 'alphabetical characters' endure because they are 'graven,' scored deeply in stone, given over to the sepulchre. Though etymologically distinguishable, *grave* and *engrave* fuse in the word which implies the survival of writing. By assuming the conditions of death, language embarks upon a life of its own.

In this model of the relationship between writing and mortality, the fall into the abyss (the chasm or the cataract) suggests metaphorically that in a world claimed by death and divested of efficacious belief in salvation, inscription opens an alternative to oblivion, insuring the remembrance of the one who writes. Through writing, the word ostensibly preserves what the Word no longer redeems. At least such is the theoretical notion graven within the hills, written into the figurality of Pym's encounter with the catastrophe of death. As he approaches his own vanishing point, the narrator sees Nu-Nu stirring in the bottom of the boat, 'but, upon touching him, we found his spirit departed.' Death-in-life, Poe's recurrent image of existence without soul, epitomizes the prison house of materiality in which the denizen of the modern world must contend with his own fear and trembling. Pym's epistemological confusion is symptomatic of our metaphysical anxiety; the ubiquity and purposelessness of death throw in doubt the Providential design in which the narrator strives vainly to believe. Through the spectacle of violence and putrefaction and through the willed incoherence of the text itself, Poe achieves in *Pym* his most disturbing treatment of the new death.

Notes

From J. Gerald Kennedy, *Poe, Death and the Life of Writing* (New Haven, CT: Yale University Press, 1987).

1. For a helpful survey of critical responses to *Pym* see Douglas Robinson, 'Reading Poe's Novel: A Speculative Review of *Pym* Criticism, 1950–1980,' *Poe Studies*, 15 (December 1982), 47–54. For an earlier discussion of Poe's covert strategy see J. Gerald Kennedy, 'The Preface as a Key to the Satire in *Pym*,' *Studies in the Novel*, 5 (Summer 1973), 191–6.
2. Patrick H. Quinn, *The French Face of Edgar Poe* (Carbondale, IL: Southern Illinois Press, 1957) pp. 176–7, 181, 188.
3. Edward H. Davidson, *Poe: A Critical Study* (Cambridge, MA: Harvard University Press, 1957) pp. 168, 169.
4. Jean Ricardou, 'Le Caractère singulier de cette eau,' *Critique*, 243–4

(August–September 1967) pp. 729–30; John Carlos Rowe, *Through the Custom-House: Nineteenth-Century American Fiction and Modern Theory* (Baltimore, MD: The Johns Hopkins University Press, 1982) pp. 95, 99; John T. Irwin, *American Hieroglyphics: The Symbol of the Egyptian Hieroglyphics in the American Renaissance* (New Haven: Yale University Press, 1980) p. 117.

5. David Hoffman, *Poe Poe Poe Poe Poe Poe Poe* (New York: Doubleday, 1972) p. 192.

6. J. Gerald Kennedy, 'The "Infernal Twoness" of *Arthur Gordon Pym*,' *Topic*, 30 (Fall 1976) p. 53.

7. *Through the Custom-House*, 102. Rowe's chapter on *Pym* is a revision of his essay in *Glyph*, 2 (1977) pp. 102–21.

8. Michel Ragon, *The Space of Death: A Study of Funerary Architecture, Decoration, and Urbanism*, tr. Alan Sheridan (Charlottesville: University of Virginia, 1983).

9. Edgar Morin, *L'homme et la mort* (Paris: Éditions de Seuil, 1970) p. 41.

10. Ibid., 33.

11. *American Hieroglyphics*, p. 139.

12. René Girard, *Violence and the Sacred*, tr. Patrick Gregory (Baltimore, MD: The Johns Hopkins University Press, 1977) p. 49.

13. *Through the Custom-House*, p. 105.

14. *American Hieroglyphics*, p. 170.

15. Ibid., p. 186.

16. Robert J. Lifton, *The Broken Connection* (New York: Simon & Schuster, 1980) p. 145.

17. George Steiner, *Language and Silence: Essays on Language, Literature, and the Inhuman* (New York: Atheneum, 1976) p. 3.

18. Maurice Blanchot, *The Space of Literature*, tr. Ann Smock (Lincoln: University of Nebraska Press, 1982) pp. 91, 94.

19. *American Hieroglyphics*, p. 213. Douglas Robinson has recently argued that the white figure may be 'an iconic dream-body that will permit a visionary habitation of the gap' between presence and absence. This icon compels interpretation, he claims, precisely to reveal the 'uncertainty of interpretation' which is the novel's 'rhetorical focus'. See *American Apocalypses* (Baltimore, MD: The Johns Hopkins University Press, 1985) pp. 119, 121.

20. Ibid., p. 183.

21. Ibid., p. 230

MANUEL AGUIRRE

On Victorian Horror

> If in many of my productions terror has been the thesis, I maintain that terror is not of Germany but of the soul.
>
> Edgar Allan Poe

> One need not be a Chamber – to be Haunted –
> One need not be a House –
> The Brain has corridors – surpassing
> Material Place –
>
> Emily Dickinson

The Labyrinth

The Gothic labyrinth grows. In the Victorian age it spreads into Nature, into the city, into the mental environments of the characters; and through these puzzling landscapes the individual moves 'as one who pursued with yell and blow / Still treads the shadow of his foe' (*The Ancient Mariner*). The Victorian age does not forsake the Gothic findings. Dracula's castle is a true heir of Otranto and Udolpho. The list of Victorian haunted houses is long; however, Victorian horror introduces several modifications and additions to the field. It shows a trend towards adapting the fantastic to the bourgeois and replacing the castle by mansions, houses, apartments. Curiously, as the symbol is democratised, the world is more and more defined as if the daily reality were but a surface which we need only pierce to disclose depths of symbolic significance behind it. The two trends are complementary, aiming at unifying the Here and the There; while Carlyle raises the worker, that victim of history, to hero-status, at the level of the history-maker, Karl Marx will try to bring history-making down onto the shoulders of the working classes. Matching these socio-philosophical developments, Victorian horror will, on the one hand, pry beyond reality into a higher world of meaning in the work of Hawthorne; and, on the other, have a humble real-estate clerk solve the sordid haunting of a house-for-rent (Charlotte Riddell, *The Uninhabited House*, 1875).

By the side of the Haunted House, however, and soon over-shadowing this older symbol, a figure which had been peripheral in the Gothic stage now comes to the fore: the haunted individual. In James Hogg's *Private Memoirs and Confessions of a Justified Sinner*

(1824), a morally ruined Robert Wringhim on the run from his demon associate Gil-Martin takes refuge in a farm reputed to be haunted by a ghost. As terrifying noises are heard outside by night, Wringhim tells us that

> the consternation of the menials has been extreme. They ascribe all to the ghost, and tell frightful stories of murders having been committed long ago. Of late, however, they are beginning to suspect that it is I that am haunted.   (*Private Memoirs*)

Here, in a nutshell, is the shift from the old to the new haunting. The domain within which the haunter has power over his victim is no longer limited to the four walls of a house but expands, until it becomes a maze encompassing all of the victim's possible space, the very world he lives in:

> I was particularly prone to lying . . . so that I found myself constantly involved in a labyrinth of deceit, from which it was impossible to extricate myself.

Though the word 'labyrinth' does not occur significantly in Charles Maturin's *Melmoth the Wanderer* (1820), we feel its presence throughout the book, a shadow, as it were, cast by Melmoth's appellation. It is, furthermore, compounded with the familiar prison-symbol, the dream-existence, the death-in-life: 'all Spain is but one great monastery, – I must be a prisoner every step that I take'. 'Wherever I may be, there I am a prisoner', said Faustus. 'Denmark's a prison, the whole world's one', said Hamlet. Like them, the nameless parricide is in the hands of the Church; so is Stanton in those of his keepers in the madhouse; so is Immalee in those of her family. And in their prison-world, they wander: Stanton, for whom catching up with Melmoth has become 'the necessary condition of my existence'; Moncada, pursued by monks and Inquisitors and, in turn, indefatigable pursuer of Melmoth; and Immalee, an exile in her own native Spain where 'her mansion was a prison'. When Moncada rejects monastic life but begins 'to doubt if this very repugnance was not itself a sin'; when Immalee's tragic love for Melmoth causes her, the innocent child of nature, to 'begin to love the storm better than the calm'; or when Walberg, mad with hunger, tries to massacre his family, we are apprised of the extent to which their minds have lost their moorings, of how easily their mental and moral world loses its familiar landmarks until they can but roam in it, sometimes hoping for a 'conversion' such as Caleb Williams experienced:

> In some circumstances, where the whole world is against us, we begin to take its part against ourselves, to avoid the withering sensation of being alone on our own side. (*Melmoth*)

Maturin seems to have taken over from Dante a gallery of crimes and retributions, gratuitous misery and sordid poetic justice; while betrayal, for which Dante reserved his ninth and last circle, lies at the heart of his novel. Stanton is betrayed by his family and locked up in the madhouse. Moncada, betrayed by family and confessor, ends up imprisoned by the monks, then by the Inquisition. Walberg, in the inserted 'Tale of Guzman's Family', is cheated out of his inheritance by the Church, and as the gradual starvation of his family drives him mad he turns against his loved ones and attempts multiple murder – an echo of Wieland's and Caleb Williams' fate: an act of human treason against the self. And Melmoth, the ultimate betrayer of others and of himself, roams the world trying – the contract allows this – to exchange destinies with some other individual willing to obtain the Wanderer's powers at the cost of his or her soul.

A satanic tempter, Melmoth exists 'amid fire and darkness', in the Darkness Visible of Milton's Hell. Every punishment in Hell is a twisted image of earthly action which cannot find in itself its own justification because its meaning lies 'offstage'; in itself, the 'text' of Hell is meaningless, requiring for its understanding a context from which it is severed. This context is, in theological terms, God: and the greatest suffering of the damned is that derived from the absence of God. In ontological terms, the validating context for human action is this world on which alone certain events or actions are given meaning by their own occurrence, or by their own purposes or results. On earth, there is a point in rolling a boulder uphill; on earth wheels do not turn for ever, fruit does not systematically elude us. In the Tartarus of Sisyphus, Ixion, Tantalus things go on in an unending, meaningless round.

For Saxo Grammaticus, woman's cyclicness had lost its justification and come to be seen as perverse fickleness. The phenomenon belongs in a process whereby the cycle gradually yields to the line and a Christian myth takes over from a pagan one. But the older cyclic time does not disappear; just as Christianity demoted pagan deities to the rank of demons, so it preserved the older conception of time in a de-ranked way as that time-structure which befitted devils. So that, whereas in former mythologies circular time had a measure of renewal, fulfilment, and endless creation, now it became the epitome of sterility, vacuous repetition, senseless eternity. The earlier cyclic ontology gave a self-fulfilling, self-validating character to human existence; the infernal cyclicness turns existence into a self-cancelling, meaningless experience. This, however, is the very concept of time which now begins to reassert itself, 'from below', in Victorian horror. The world of Melmoth is one where action has lost much of its meaning, and compulsive behaviour replaces it. The endless, and pointless, repetition of words or gestures long forgotten in their meaning is the worst torment Stanton has to undergo from his fellow-prisoners in the asylum. In the convent, Moncada exhorts the dying monk:

> 'But, my brother, you were always punctual . . .' 'That was mechanism – . . .' 'But your regularity in religious exercises –' '*Did you never hear a bell toll?*' 'But your voice was always the loudest and most distinct in the choir'. '*Did you never hear an organ played?*' (the emphasis is Maturin's)

Shelley's *Ode to the West Wind* ends with a statement of longing for cyclicness: 'If Winter comes, can Spring be far behind?', and this is a major concern of Romanticism. On the other hand, the nineteenth century fears, as much as it craves, cyclicness, and its expression in Victorian horror is systematically tainted by this dread. The regular but unmeaning behaviour of the denizens of Hell will haunt readers all through the Victorian period. In Margaret Oliphant's 'The Open Door' (1885), the ghost can only repeat its original moans mechanically, unable to vary or exceed one single syllable or tone. In Edith Nesbit's 'John Charrington's Wedding' (1893) John dies on the eve of his wedding, but his ghost doggedly shows up for the ceremony in a kinds of reflex-action after death. Reynolds' *Wagner the Wehr-Wolf* (1846–7) must submit to the cycle of his curse on the last day of every month. Once a year, Amelia Edwards' 'Phantom Coach' (1864) and its ghostly passengers must re-enact the accident that cost them their lives. And we are all familiar with sunset and dawn, the midnight bell, the full moon, All Hallows's Eve, New Years' Eve – time-points that mark the turning of some sterile, meaningless cycle. Nature is reasserting herself as a numinous domain, multiplying the Other's points of entry into the world of man. But the Numen which thus emerges is the dark one: the world of Melmoth is a ubiquitous version of the man-made hell Vivaldi beheld in the dungeons of the Inquisition.

Described as 'one who had traversed life from Dan to Beersheba, and found all barren, or – made it so', Melmoth, like Hamlet or Midas, creates his own Waste Land as he advances; but much of it he finds already desolate. Not only the Wanderer, but man, too, is now active in the role of corruptor. 'What enemy has man so deadly as himself?'. In the Gothic age, Evil was mostly static, a haunting which was laid to rest when injustice had been repaired, or which played itself out in the destruction of a man, a family, or a house. In the age of Victorian horror, Evil seems to become a mobile force – it wanders – and it spreads like a plague. A corrupted Falkland manages to lay his curse on Caleb: evil deeds are repeated, and evil engenders more of itself. Clara and her brother Wieland undergo just this changes at the hands of the demonic Carwin. Stanton is warned of the time when his fear of madness shall become a hope, 'to escape the agony of consciousness' (*Melmoth*). The drama in Moncada's life arises from the unremitting efforts by the Church to convert rather than subdue him – exactly O'Brien's design on Smith in *Nineteen Eighty-Four*. Evil must become their Good. The dread of exactly this change is expressed by the villagers of Salem in Elizabeth Gaskell's *Lois the Witch* (1860):

> 'It is bad enough to feel that my body can be made to suffer through the power of some unknown evil-wisher to me, but what if Satan gives them still further power, and they can touch my soul, and inspire me with loathful thoughts leading me into crimes which at present I abhor?' and so on, till the very dread of what might happen, . . . really brought about the corruption of imagination at last, which at first they had shuddered at.   (*Lois the Witch*)

Transformations, conversions, the growth of an individual's or institution's power, the multiplication of haunted places, objects, persons in Victorian literature, all these are manifestations of one phenomenon, the spread of Evil.

> *Faustus*: What good will my soul do thy lord?
> *Mephist*: Enlarge his kingdom.
> *Faustus*: Is that the reason why he tempts us thus?
> *Mephist*: *Solamen miseris, socios habuisse doloris.*
> (Marlowe, *Doctor Faustus*)

'It is a comfort in wretchedness to have companions in woe'. In *Melmoth*, Mephistopheles' words are used almost to the letter by the dying monk: 'It is natural for the miserable to wish for companions in their misery'; Melmoth himself has 'no hope – but that of plunging others into his own condemnation'. The parricide vindicates himself in God:

> the exhaustion of my resentment on you, may diminish that of the deity towards me. If I persecute and torment the enemies of God, must I not be the friend of God?

His Moloch-like god is Blake's Urizen, Robert Wringhim's intolerant deity, Swinburne's 'supreme Evil, God'. The ontology of the Closed Space excludes a numinous God from its definition of the world of man, but only at the cost of becoming unable to justify the resulting chaos and lack of meaning. Yet the chaos and meaninglessness are themselves gateways to the dimension of Evil – they reflect Hell, and thus a new standard is formed, of which the human world tries to be a more and more precise image. In this endeavour, the Closed Space begins to open anew; there is again transcendence and hence, paradoxically, meaning: a new Numen emerges. And with this new ontology of a transcendental world arises a new theology:

> Mine is the best theology, – the theology of utter hostility to all beings whose sufferings may mitigate mine. . . . I need not repent, I need not believe; if you suffer, I am saved.

'I rejoiced', says Wringhim the fanatic, 'at being used as a source in the hand of the Lord' (*Private Memoirs*). Christian theology requires that suffering be contained within the individual, not propagated; and therein lies its sublimation: our sufferings transcend us and rise upwards as an offering to God. Now, this is the doctrine which Melmoth rejects:

> There is no error more absurd, and yet more rooted in the heart of man, than the belief that his sufferings will promote his spiritual safety. (*Melmoth*)

If this justification is, as Melmoth claims, false, all that is left for us is unredeemed misery, unless we learn to make our sufferings transcend us in some other way. In this light, the entire book is a study in dark devotion to the 'saving' force of Evil. To mankind's self-centred, closed nature, the Wanderer actually proposes a new gospel, offering redemption from the senseless egocentric system; Evil begins to appear as a new life-force, a *positive* principle. A new numinous order may lurk in its chaos, a new ritual may actually lie in its senseless repetitions, a new fertility in its barrenness. With endless variations, this is one theme Victorian horror will harp on: a seduction by the liberating Other, a transformation or conversion of the individual, a glimpse of a meaningful Hell:

> The whole story seemed to me now to resemble one of those puzzle pictures or maps which I have played with as a child, where each bit fits into some other until the outline is complete. It was as if I were finding the pieces one by one of a bygone history, and fitting them to one another until some terrible whole should be gradually built up and stand out in its complete deformity.
>
> (J. Meade Falkner, *The Lost Stradivarius*, 1895)

In other words, the solution of the puzzle no longer dissolves the dread; it is towards the formation of a new meaningful, if terrible, pattern that the puzzle-solver works.

The Haunted

The 'official' philosophy of the Enlightenment would have held that everything which is – including the Deity – belongs in the sphere of the rationally acceptable; the claim that there is an Other, non-rational domain is untenable. It follows that claims concerning experience of that Other must be based on deluded perception. As the Age of Sensibility moves on, the dark Other begins its ascent, insinuates itself into a building, haunts a castle, takes a first stronghold against the rational world. Walpole or Reeve handle this Other as if it were a discrete, objective, external entity intruding into the world of man; as if it could be contained within the limits of its 'proper' domain, the haunted castle; and as if it could be laid to rest by the appropriate operations of reason and a rational morality. But as the eighteenth century wears out, the dark Other initiates a second strategy: the haunted domain expands. Not just one particular locus, but the world itself of some specific individual is tainted, has a labyrinthic nature; whereby the Minotaur, bound indeed between four walls, is now restricted only by the four corners of a man's earth. The haunter is no longer contained by a mere castle, the ghost walks; and man cannot successfully escape it because his whole world is its labyrinth.

Corresponding to this change, another kind of development takes place: just as it is no longer quite possible to distinguish between the lair of the haunter and the world of man, so it begins to be hard to maintain the boundaries between the operations of an outside Other and those of the human mind. The numinous creature is no longer a ghost, or a villainous pursuer: rather, numinous elements are descried both in Nature and in the average individual, in the commonest protagonist, even in a first-person narrator. Wieland, Caleb Williams, Ambrosio are transformed; Clara Wieland is aware of how close the Evil has brushed past her; Moncada cannot help being painfully aware of his share in guilt. When the Other comes to be defined partly in terms of mind, a metaphysical relativity seems to set in whereby the Numinous – and by this is meant now, primarily, Evil – ceases to be a purely external affair: Evil has an inner, subjective human component. The subject of the experience of fear becomes as important as its object; and it could be argued that the horror novel is the first psychological novel.

The experience of the Numinous can no longer be comfortably ascribed to deluded perception. – Or can it? It is here that several sets of opposites become classic ingredients of the horror tale: the Cartesian distinctions inner–outer, matter–spirit, appearance–reality will obsess the Victorians, whose horror relates to the agony of boundaries which are too weak, to the frustration of all-too-solid walls. One concept to express this is *ambiguity*. From Charles Brockden Brown to Henry James, ambiguity is a favourite method of expressing the impossibility of maintaining separate the two domains of the objective and the subjective, the real and the imaginary:

> Old Cooper opened the door. There was no one near it, but at the angle of the gallery was a shadow. . . . He raised the candle a little, and it seemed to beckon with a long hand as the head drew back. . . . Candle in hand he walked to the corner . . . and as he moved the light, he saw precisely the same sort of shadow, and as he advanced the same withdrawal, and beckon.
>
> (Le Fanu, 'Squire Toby's Will', 1868)

The reality of the vision is dependent (or is it?) on the beholder's disposition and movement towards what he sees. Two kinds of explanation are offered us, and neither is foolproof: the shadow *may* be cast by the light of the candle, but it just seems a bit too purposeful, too consistent for a coincidence. Alternatively, it *may* truly be out there, but the evidence we have hardly admits of it, and our reason denies its independence. Le Fanu is at his best in this game of candle and shadow. Maupassant's 'Le Horla' (1887) leaves the question open whether madness or outside agency is the case, this time by resorting to a first-person narrator who tells us he is possessed. Something did kill Brayton in Bierce's 'The Man and the Snake' (1891), but was it his own fear as he looked into the eyes of the snake, or the vision of a reptile divinity? In this death Bierce, close to the end of the Victorian period, echoes Hoffmann, seventy-seven years earlier: 'If events are to be judged by their results, this is the most terrible supernatural story conceivable' ('Automata', 1814). Ultimately, the point goes back to Radcliffe and Brown: it matters little whether our enemy be supernatural or not, if the consequences of his actions are truly numinous.

In the case of Hoffmann, another concept seems appropriate: not ambiguity but *ambivalence*. His hero

> has apparently not separated the events of his inner life from those of the outside world; in fact, we cannot determine where one ends and the other begins. . . . You will be in a strange magical realm where figures of fantasy step right into your own life.
>
> ('Die Abenteuer der Silvester-Nacht',
> 'A New Year's Eve Adventure', 1816)

The way this story is written, its purpose seems to be actually to *blur* supposed boundaries. Le Fanu's 'frames' are designed to allow us the benefit of the doubt on the experience they bracket; Hoffmann's seem constructed rather to prove that it takes just one glass of wine too many to make the crossover into the Other domain: that there is actually no barrier. In another way this, too, is the point made by Théophile Gautier:

> Sometimes I thought I was a priest who dreamed every night that he was a nobleman, sometimes that I was a nobleman who dreamed that he was a priest. I could no longer distinguish dreams from real life; I did not know where reality began and illusion ended. ('La Morte amoureuse', 1836)

The dream may be used as a wall, a safety boundary; but it may also function as a door, through which we enter the Other reality – or, as Wilkie Collins' 'The Dream Woman' (1855) suggests, through which the Other manages to enter our world. Le Fanu's Dr Hesselius writes of Reverend Jennings' visions as caused by

> a poison which excites the reciprocal action of spirit and nerve, and paralyses the tissue that separates those cognate functions of the senses, the external and the interior. Thus we find strange bed-fellows, and the mortal and immortal prematurely make acquaintance. ('Green Tea', 1869)

The inner and the outer may thus touch, whether the frame be provided by a meeting-point or moment, by the operation of some drug, or by a state of mind. At times the suggestion is that the 'unreal' can be *intensified* into actuality: 'Glancing at the looking glass, we behold . . . a repetition of all the gleam and shadow of the picture, with one remove farther from the actual, and nearer to the imaginative' (Hawthorne, *The Scarlet Letter*, 1850). The difference is a matter of degree, the mirror provides the *next step* into the non-actual. And there is also the power of the will:

> 'Thought is real; and the man who can hold to his thought long enough endows it with objectivity. . . . What are dreams? Give them a little more intensity . . . and they are real.'
> (Beale, *The Ghost of Guir House*, 1895)

Here we detect the Berkeleyan view that makes reality dependent on the mind, but also the re-emergence of a notion that had lain dormant for seven centuries. For an x to be intensifiable into a y, both x and y must be part of the same continuum; exactly this view was held by Anselm of Canterbury, whose Ontological Argument hinged on a continuity between mind and reality whereby the mental could be intensified into actuality.

After ambiguity, ambivalence and intensification, we must look at a fourth term relating to the oppositions mind–matter, world–spirit, inner–outer. The late eighteenth century had a concept, 'sensibility', that expressed the individual's capacity to experience and respond to the Otherworldly in the world of man. Perhaps one of the main innovations of Victorian horror is the introduction of a concept which does not express merely a form of contact between the two domains. Notions of kinship, bond, nearness, similarity, a sense that not only the individual's faculties but his very identity are to some extent bound up with the Numinous, a relationship partaking of attraction and repulsion, empathy, correspondence as between mirror-images – all of these are contained in the concept of *affinity*.

'Elective affinities' (a Goethean notion) bind Hoffmann's hero in an uncanny love to the mechanical doll Olimpia ('The Sand-Man', 1817). Affinity between man and his numinous Other self is the concept behind Schlehmil's desperate search for his shadow in Chamisso's *Wonderful Adventure of Peter Schlehmil* (1814). The bond that the individual must establish freely between himself and the undead is a constant in vampire literature. Affinity between this world and the Other world underlies the Romantic and Transcendentalist view of Nature, the bond that ties Ahab to the numinous Whale, the theory of correspondences that inspires the Symbolist movement. Often it is a question of sympathies, as when a lover of history dreams of the coming of a woman dead all these three hundred years:

> Why should there not be ghosts to such as can see them? Why should she not return to the earth, if she knows that it contains a man who thinks of, desires, only her?
>
> (Vernon Lee, *Amour Dure*, 1890)

Of course the human need not be the one who initiates the active search for the Other:

> [Ghosts] certainly choose suitable persons, . . . that is, not credulous persons, but those whose senses are sufficiently keen to detect the presence of a spirit. (E. & H. Heron, 'The Story of Yand Manor House', 1898)

Affinity may also emerge in terms of meaning, the Otherworldy significance linking things in the here to the numinous world:

> All visible things, man, are but as pasteboard masks. But in each event . . . some unknown but still reasoning thing puts forth the mouldings of its features from behind the unreasoning mask.
>
> (Melville, *Moby-Dick*, 1851)

Affinity in this case is conveyed in the mask-and-face metaphor for the relationship between the two worlds: the dichotomy of Locke's philosophy between appearance and substance is mediated by the Berkeleyan notion that

> some certain significance lurks in all things, else all things are little worth, and the round world but an empty cypher.

In the concept of *cypher* we see the world as a symbol, as a writing; and its significance leads us to understand the affinity Here–There in terms of *language*:

> the word of God is the creation we behold; and it is in this word . . . that God speaketh universally to man.
>
> (Thomas Paine, *The Age of Reason*, 1794)

Now the world begins once more to be what it had been in the Middle Ages, a stupendous network of semantic elements crossing, multiplying, enriching each other as well as pointing to an Other world, or to each other's Otherness: a symbolic system.

The horror novel is the first psychological novel. Its characters may be cardboard ones except where fear is concerned, for there we have a wealth of analysis and detail. And what the psychological exploration of fear leads to is the insight that there is an affinity between the source of fear and its victim, between the Haunter and the Haunted. Perhaps the text which best condenses the principle of affinity is E. A. Poe's 'The Fall of the House of Usher' (1830). Everything resounds in this tale where, through a policy of consanguinity which has excluded the outside world, the House of Usher is the man is the building is the family is the title, all to itself. It generates its own atmosphere, 'an atmosphere which had no affinity with the air of heaven . . . – a pestilent and mystic vapour' ('Usher'); on the other hand, Roderick Usher's is a mind 'from which darkness, as if an inherent positive quality, poured forth upon all objects of the moral and physical universe in one unceasing radiation of gloom'. Positive darkness, radiating gloom – a Miltonian 'Darkness Visible', an entropic atmosphere generated by Usher. Among several other correspondences between house and occupant, we may mention that Usher's poem 'The Haunted Palace' conveys the tottering of the man's reason in house-metaphors; on the other hand, he claims that there is a *sentience* in the inanimate matter of the grey stones. If his mind is like a house, the house is like a living organism. Further, the house resembles Roderick's painting, the painting foreshadows

Madeline's tomb. Roderick and Madeline Usher are held together by 'sympathies of a scarcely intelligible nature'. Then again, the building may have a sentience, but it takes an Usher to sense this. A 'peculiar sensibility', a 'morbid acuteness of the senses' render him defenceless against the Numinous. His is the Gothic sensibility brought to its ultimate consequences, the power 'to see the world in a grain of sand', as Blake put it – and the inability to shut off the vision. Like the narrator of 'The Tell-Tale Heart', like Reverend Jennings in Le Fanu's 'Green Tea', Usher cannot help seeing that in things which it is deadly for man to hear or see.

In 'The Fall of the House of Usher' Poe asks what the fate would be of a House that cultivated the Gothic sensibility to its logical end. Hawthorne posed the same question in *The House of the Seven Gables* (1851) where Clifford and his sister Hepzibah lead a ghostly existence in a house, described animistically, which seems to have power over them. Melville's *Moby-Dick* addresses aspects of a parallel question. As Ahab the man seeks to cross the threshold of the physical reality, to 'reach outside . . . by thrusting through the wall' (*Moby-Dick*), so Clifford the ghost seeks to step over another threshold, out of the Pyncheon House and *into* the physical reality. As for Usher, he is an Ahab unwillingly sinking with the Whale, he is what Clifford might have become had he not been able to find the door back to the human world. Oneness seems to be a key concept. Ahab is united with the Whale – and sinks. *The Seven Gables* ends when a Pyncheon marries a Maule and the antagonistic Houses are reconciled at last. And Usher dies with Madeline, the two die with the mansion, the mansion dies with – upon – its reflection in the tarn: a world of growing and narrowing affinities has reached its centre. This inward collapse corresponds to the image of the whirlpool that grasps the ghost-ship in 'Ms. Found in a Bottle', to the similar image in 'A Descent Into the Maelström', to the ending of *The Narrative of Arthur Gordon Pym*, to the whirlwind that on the fatal night gathers around the House of Usher: achieving oneness with the Other means reaching the centre of the whirlpool, the ultimate vision, the final darkness.

The House of Usher has gone past the point of possible regeneration to the world and begun, like the house of Stevenson's 'Olalla', to establish or discover affinities with its own lower kingdoms – with the animal kingdom in Stevenson's story, with the 'kingdom of inorganisation' in Poe's. But the lower is also the 'higher': both the animal and the inanimate – the Albatross, the

Raven, the White Whale, the monster made of dead limbs, the mechanical creatures of Hoffmann's 'The Sand-Man' and 'Automata' – are favourite nineteenth-century carriers of the Numinous. The House reacts to itself, to its own Other kingdoms: a sign of reunification that begins with an awareness of the uncanny aspects of the self. Within the House of Usher there are, at the end of the story, no real doors: it has lost the power of self-differentiation; it has no centrifugal forces, hence cannot be escaped by those who are fully a part of its universe; it gradually collapses upon itself. At the end of the story, Roderick is no longer a discrete individual but a part of the House trying ineffectually to regain its autonomy.

'The Fall of the House of Usher' is a story about wholeness, about the ultimate unity of the universe – but a wholeness and unity which are dreaded and therefore presented in negative terms. The Victorian mind fears to accept the Other, and will lament the downfall of Reason at its hands; it fears wholeness, and will only see in it the pull of the whirlpool. And yet, it knows that this dreaded Other is more *real* than what the rational world offers; this much, the narrator himself had intuited, and refused to accept, on his approach to the mansion at the very beginning of the tale:

> I looked upon the scene before me . . . with an utter depression of soul which I can compare to no earthly sensation more properly than to the after-dream of the reveller upon opium – the bitter lapse into every-day life – the hideous dropping off of the veil.

The lifting of the Veil is one of our most fruitful symbols. Phoebe Pyncheon wonders, 'Had this veil been over [Clifford] from his birth – this veil under which far more of his spirit was hidden than revealed, and through which he is so imperfectly discerned the actual world –?' (*The Seven Gables*). Dr Hesselius reassures Reverend Jennings that 'we are all alike environed [by evil spirits]. It is only that in your case, the "paries", the veil of the flesh, the screen, is a little out of repair, and sights and sounds are transmitted' (Le Fanu, 'Green Tea'). To lift the veil is to see the face of the Dreadful, a presence of such power that it destroys the illusion of a rational, ordered reality; the Numinous does not appear only as an intrusion, but also as a revelation.

Medieval philosophers and theologians held that evil is in its essence so horrible that the human mind . . . must perish at its contemplation. Such realization was by mercy ordinarily withheld, but its possibility was hinted at in the legend of the *Visio Malefica*. . . . It was supposed that the Malefic Vision . . . had actually been purposely called up by some few great adepts, and used by them to blast their enemies. But to do so was considered equivalent to a conscious surrender to the powers of evil, as the vision once seen took away all hope of final salvation.

(J. Meade Falkner, *The Lost Stradivarius*, 1895)

As far as I can ascertain, the *Visio Malefica* is not a medieval legend but a remarkable invention of Falkner's, aptly expressing the double edge of *seeing*: through lifting the veil we gain power or knowledge; but such knowledge and such power will destroy us. Seeing = being seen, and we become the first victims of the power we wield against others. There is a Christian morality here, and a kind of poetic justice; but stronger by far than these is a pure notion of symmetry, the awareness of an ominous affinity between ourselves and our mirror-images.

'The ancients knew what lifting the veil means. They called it seeing the God Pan.' (Machen, *The Great God Pan*, 1894)

Dr Raymond performs a slight operation on the brain of his ward Mary, which 'will level utterly the solid wall of sense, and, probably for the first time since man was made, a spirit will gaze on a spirit world'. The result is predictable: Mary does see Pan lurking behind the fabric of things – but Pan sees her too, with awesome consequences, 'when the house of life is thus thrown open, there may enter in that for which we have no name'.

Latimer, the narrator of George Eliot's *The Lifted Veil* (1859), is gifted with the ability to hear the thoughts of others, and with the power to see the future: yet people's minds and time-to-come yield him only images of misery; he complains of not being loved; he despises the dull world; he loathes himself. Like Hamlet, he sees the rot in Denmark – but, like Hamlet, he himself is not able to live. And we realise that the veil has indeed been lifted and he can only look at himself: the misery lies in the eye of the beholder, the whole secret world is a mirror of his barren soul. The veil may disclose the awful truth behind an illusory world, or else the true countenance of our inmost soul. In either case, it reveals reality.

The Personal Haunter

The labyrinth imposes the condition of wanderers on its denizens. Man and Minotaur roam the maze, and there is between them an affinity whereby, if the haunter pursues its prey motivated by a form of hunger, so does the haunted seek his destroyer, even though he dreads the encounter, urged by a need for something he lacks and his haunter possesses. Caleb, Moncada, Frankenstein, Wringhim all fear their antagonist while simultaneously gravitating around him; and Falkland, Melmoth, Frankenstein's monster, Gil-Martin, whether they seek a worshipper, a soul, or a father, pursue their victims with an almost religious zeal.

In *The Wonderful Story of Peter Schlehmil* (1814), Chamisso, drawing on folk- and Faust-lore, creates a symbol for this haunting: the man who loses his shadow ceases to belong in the human world and must wander the earth fearing yet searching for the new owner of his shadow, who will offer to return it in exchange for Schlehmil's soul. It is a Faustian theme, but the new Mephistopheles has replaced an abstract contract with a very concrete, physical embodiment of the man's humanity. In substituting a shadow for a signature, a public deprivation for a secret contract, Chamisso comes close to turning the devil-owned shadow into a haunter, and one which is tailor-made to its prey, a specifically personal haunter. Schlehmil makes a guest-appearance in Hoffmann's 'Abenteuer der Silvester-Nacht' ('A New-Year's Eve Adventure') (1816), where he is joined by Erasmus Spikher, the man who sold his reflection to the devil. With the loss of shadow, reflection, soul, these characters cease to be human: theirs is not true life, but Death-in-Life. On the other hand, the detached human copy may be inspired with a semblance of animation, and appear as the Life-in-Death: Hoffmann's Talking Turk is a 'living puppet' ('Automata', 1814), an image of 'living death or inanimate life'. In Hoffmann's 'The Sand-Man' (1817), Olimpia's ice-cold hand seems to warm up as 'she' is touched by her human lover, and if the latter sees life in her it is because she wears his own eyes, mysteriously 'stolen' from him by Coppelius. To the shadow and the reflection, we must therefore add the mechanical imitation of humanity: the automaton that becomes what we relinquish, the Life-in-Death that counterpoints our Death-in-Life.

In striving towards a non-transcendental interpretation of Nature, the mechanistic system succeeded instead in incorporating the transcendental into its description of the world. The emergence of evolutionary thinking almost repeats this paradox. Separate acts of creation for each natural kingdom had allowed medieval thinkers to accord man a unique place in the Chain of Being, positionally continuous, qualitatively discontinuous in regard to the rest of Creation. But the consequence of postulating one single, pervading, generative principle is a *continuity* among the different species, ultimately among the different kingdoms: and the sentience that Usher discerned in the 'kingdom of inorganization' is only the prelude to the claim

> that all matter is sentient, that every atom is a living, feeling, conscious being. . . . There is no such thing as dead, inert matter: it is all alive. (Bierce, 'Moxon's Master', 1894)

What Moxon is championing is no less than machine intelligence – that his automaton chess-player thinks, and feels: in effect, that it belongs in the Chain of Being, or in the evolutionary tree. From the traditional point of view, Moxon's automaton, if intelligent, is that which cannot be, an impossibility, the Life-in-Death' there is only one place for the machine to occupy in the traditional Chain of Being: the bottom end, the place of that which has no *ens* but masquerades as being. The automaton is an imitation of man – but it has that repetitiveness and regularity which characterise the appearance of the ghost, the transformation of the werewolf, the compulsiveness of the madman; and like these, it may easily be granted numinous powers:

> When I went up to the Turk, I asked, thinking of my beloved: 'Will there ever again be a time for me like that which was the happiest in my life?' . . . Then the figure said . . . 'Unhappy man! At the very moment when next you see her, you will be lost to her forever!' ('Automata')

The question concerning the lost beloved, asked of an 'imitation of human beings' believed to have oracular powers, is the same question Poe's narrator asks of the Raven – another imitator whose repetitive behaviour raises him to a numinous status – and the numinous bird and the numinous automaton give practically the same fatal answer. The machine opposes man, whether it be oracularly, or through the seductions of the clockwork doll Olimpia, or as the killing machine in Léroux's *La poupée sanglante*, or as a vindictive chess-player in 'Moxon's Master'. Inexorably, the individual will be haunted by something lost within his shadow, within his reflection, within his mechanical creation: from Hoffmann's automata to the modern computer, the machine is time and again presented as numinous, as evil, and as antagonistic to humanity's goals.

Up to now I have purposely avoided the term 'double', but almost every haunter mentioned in this chapter so far is a *Doppelgänger* of some sort. Victorian horror is concerned mostly (though not mainly, as will be shown later) with the Double-motif, and with a growing realisation that the Double cannot be severed from its original. The difference with the Gothic haunter is a simple one: then it was bonded to a house, a castle, a family; now, to an individual; then it was circumscribed to a specific locale, now it stalks the world; then it was purely a being from the Other side, now it is *also* part of a human individual: his shadow, his reflection, his mechanical parody. In Le Fanu's 'Mr Justice Harbottle' (1872) it is Chief-Justice Twofold, a 'dilated effigy' of Harbottle himself. In Hogg's *Private Memoirs* it is Robert's imitator Gil-Martin. In Gautier's 'La Morte amoureuse' (1839) it is the man's dream-self. In Wilde's *Picture of Dorian Gray* (1891), the portrait. In Braddon's 'Mystery at Fernwood' (undated), the idiot twin. In every case it exists solely on the principle of *affinity*, on the recognition that the Other is a part of ourselves and not a purely objective domain that can be simply contained, destroyed, or denied.

Next to individuals or institutions whose power stretches to encompass a character's world, next to the multiplication of haunted points or objects in the world of man, next to the theology of terror which requires of us that we do unto others as we would not be done by, and next to the conversions and transformations, the Plague of Evil manifests itself in 'doubling': that the dark side of man acquires an independent existence means that Evil has obtained generative powers. Schlehmil's shadow and Spikher's reflection 'reproduce' the form of their originals; in a different way, man 'reproduces' himself when he constructs mechanical imitations of himself. By the side of these, we may consider the *organic* imitations of humanity: the freak Quasimodo, the animal-men of Wells' Doctor Moreau, the monkey-like spirit that haunts Jennings in Le Fanu's 'Green Tea', Doctor Jekyll's alter ego, the werewolf, the all-brain, dwarf-bodied martians evolved from a human-like species in Wells' *War of the Worlds* (1898); more recently, the mutant, the android, the clone and the cyborg. Of all these, the first and best-known one is undoubtedly Mary Shelley's monster in *Frankenstein* (1818).

God, in pity, made man beautiful and alluring, after his own image; but my form is a filthy type of yours, more horrid even from the very resemblance. (*Frankenstein*)

Both creator and creature are exiles from the world of man. If Victor Frankenstein complains 'I was encompassed by a cloud which no beneficial influence could dissipate', the monster begs to 'feel the affections of a sensitive being and become linked to the chain of existence'. 'Sympathy' is one key word in the novel; in the absence of sympathy, the urge to belong in that 'chain of existence' gives way to the urge to leave a mark, even if an evil one, on the world: Victor creates his own demon, who in turn demands a mate. Dreading that 'the first results of those sympathies for which the daemon thirsted would be children', Victor destroys the unfinished body of the female creature – whereupon the monster in turn murders Victor's bride. They are bound to each other 'by ties only dissoluble by the annihilation of one of us'. If Victor sees his creation as 'my own spirit let loose from the grave and forced to destroy all that was dear to me', he himself 'walked about the isle like a restless spectre, separated from all it loved'. Both lead a ghostly existence, the one as the Death-in-Life, the other, literally put together from limbs and organs belonging to corpses, as the Life-in-Death. Both exist in hell: 'I, like the arch-fiend, bore a hell within me', says the monster, and 'Evil henceforth became my good'; and Victor: 'like the archangel who aspired to omnipotence, I am chained in an eternal hell'.

Like Faustus, Frankenstein had devoured the works of Agrippa, Albertus Magnus, and Paracelsus, and sought 'the raising of ghosts or devils'. But, with him, science becomes the modern magic, helping to raise, not devils or ghosts, but a man, the modern haunter. Victor does not fear ghosts; but he is all too susceptible to a new kind of terror, and when he returns to his rooms, fearing to find the monster still there.

I threw the door forcibly open, as children are accustomed to do when they expect a spectre to stand in waiting for them on the other side. (*Frankenstein*)

It is fitting that the man of science should find in science his own spectres, that the dream of reason should literally breed monsters. Frankenstein replaces Faustus as a representative of the outward quest for knowledge. But the bond that holds the scientist and his creation together is much tighter than it was in Marlowe's drama: the monster is not *only* an entity from beyond, he is *also* human flesh; not a being *summoned* but a being *made*; his existence is bound up with that of his creator, and when the one dies the other's *raison d'être* vanishes. The man of science does no longer try to invoke the Other: he is now extracting the Other from within his own world. And this difference is consonant with the fact that magic was for Faustus, at least initially, an instrument of liberation from an imprisoning world, while Frankenstein, in spite of his best intentions, wields science as an instrument of domination. The one violated God's law; the other, the laws of Nature.

> The most learned philosopher . . . had partially unveiled the face of Nature, but her immortal lineaments were still a wonder and a mystery. . . . I had gazed upon the fortifications and impediments that seemed to keep human beings from entering the citadel of nature, and rashly and ignorantly I had repined. (*Frankenstein*)

Veil, fortifications, the citadel of nature: familiar symbols that come back with a vengeance. Because it is now in Nature herself that 'immortal lineaments' are discerned, the quest for a numinous reality is now 'directed to the metaphysical, or in its highest sense, the physical secrets of the world'. Yet this endeavour is no quest but a conquest. It matters little whether the search be directed towards other lands, towards outer space, into the sources of life or the subatomic dimension: the purpose is to subdue a world that is turning against the ordering mind. Paradoxically, as its power over the *res extensa* seems to increase, the *res cogitans* shrinks more and more into itself: formerly it was cosmos opposing a localised chaos; now it is mind opposing a chaotic cosmos; soon it will be mind opposing itself.

Gil-Martin proposes to Robert Wringhim a fratricide 'at which common nature would revolt, but he who is dedicated to the sword of the Lord, must raise himself above common humanity' (*Private Memoirs*). Melmoth sought immortality, thereby becoming a Living Dead. Poe's 'Ligeia', 'Morella', 'Mr Valdemar' are examples of the same endeavour to oppose death. *Wagner*,[1] like Goethe's Faust, sells his humanity for youth and power. Ahab pursues the Whale in an attempt at overcoming the finiteness of mere humanity. Frankenstein harangues Walton's men with an eloquence worthy of Ahab:

> Be men, or be more than men. Be steady to your purposes and firm

as a rock. This ice is not made of such stuff as your hearts may be; it is mutable and cannot withstand you if you say that it shall not. (*Frankenstein*)

Rupert Orange sells his soul in exchange for five years' health and wealth: 'an astonishing violation of the order of the universe' (O'Sullivan, 'The Bargain of Rupert Orange', 1896). In Augustine's definition, Evil stems from nothingness, from a misapplication of the human will, and constitutes precisely this unnatural violation of the order of things.

When Nature acquires Otherworld features, journeys are apt to become Otherworld voyages once more. Coleridge's Mariner is driven towards 'the land of mist and snow', and there slays the 'bird of good omen'. This assault on numinous Nature will be punished by his ship's becoming 'as idle as a painted ship / upon a painted ocean': a condition of death-in-life, at the mercy of its opposite, 'the Night-Mare LIFE-IN-DEATH'. Walton, on his way to the North Pole, writes: 'I am going . . . to "the land of mist and snow", but I shall kill no albatross' (*Frankenstein*). But, like Coleridge's Wedding Guest, meet the Other he will, in the twin shape of Victor Frankenstein and the monster pursuing each other across the wastes of the polar Otherworld, the ultimate expression of the barren Hell in which alone they exist. The immortal wanderer of Bulwer-Lytton's 'The Haunters and the Haunted' (1859), a man who, through his own power, 'wills to live on', is described as 'an execrable image of life in death and death in life': his fate will be to be forever haunted by the spectre of Death in the desolation of the northern ice. The narrator's ship in Poe's 'Ms. Found in a Bottle' (1833) is swallowed by a polar whirlpool; in Poe's *Narrative of Arthur Gordon Pym* (1838), Pym and his companion are carried by a powerful current into a vortex at the South Pole. This polar theme is taken up again in the 20th century by Lovecraft, J. W. Campbell, and the cinema industry. The *modern* Prometheus is not at war with the deity but with Nature – ultimately, with his own nature. And the bird, whale, monster, the denizens of the numinous domain of Nature, retaliate against the human invasion: Nature's *sanctum* becomes the source of destruction for those who violate it.

Evolutionary thinking argues that the one 'intelligent' being on earth stems from beings traditionally seen as non-intelligent. Hence, if there is soul, spirit, mind, reason or sentience in man, some degree of the same must be found in brutes – this is Usher's premise just as it is

Ahab's. Conversely, if there is animality in Nature, there must equally be some in man. As distinct from fundamentalist views, an evolutionary theory implies a kind of *affinity* between man and the 'lower' kingdoms. It follows then that the very progress of scientific rationality has come to reveal the beast in man. And the beast must be extracted, and suppressed. Yet it will not yield: Moreau's animal-men turn against their creator; Frankenstein's monster, against his maker; Moxon's machine, against its builder. 'There is no such thing as dead, inert matter,' Moxon had said; as if to confirm this, the earth itself yells in pain when Professor Challenger bores into its core (Conan-Doyle, 'When the World Screamed', 1913). In Victorian horror, Nature begins to *confront* and *oppose* man; it will not be long before the *revolt* of the animal, of the monster, of the automaton, of Nature becomes one great theme in Cosmic and Modern terror.

The Vampire

One of the best symbolic representatives of human nature at war with itself is the vampire myth. In studying it we must, however, distinguish between the vampire and his kin; we confuse the issue if, like Montague Summers, we call 'vampire' anything and everything not-under-the-sun. As one representative of human fears, the vampire belongs in an illustrious *class* of universal myth; as a literary *species* with characteristic attributes and values, the vampire is a Victorian creation. Further, as a haunter of individuals, he belongs (to extend a biological image) in the *population* of nineteenth-century *Doppelgängers*. We may thus find that the vampire is related to classical figures: lamia, siren, empusa, striga, and to the malevolent tempters of folklore: the Germanic Lorelei and Elf-King, the Slavic Russalka, the Turkish Giaour; corpse-eating ghoul, ghost, revenant, Demon-Lover. Nor can we fully understand the vampire without taking into account Christian motifs: incubi, succubi, or the Faustian theme, since the vampire myth is a simplified version of the compact with the devil. The myth was formed out of a gradual conflation of many or most of these. Coleridge's *Christabel* (1798–1801) lacks only the name 'vampire' for its unearthly character Geraldine, and is the source for Le Fanu's 'Carmilla'. Byron gives us a very recognisable description, name and all, in *The Giaour* (1813). But the first definitive condensation – and still one of the best – of the myth in western fiction appears to be Tieck's 'Bride of the Grave' (*c.* 1815), which reads like a catalogue of every major motif touched upon in this and the previous chapter. In the extremity of his love, Walter obtains the means to revive his dead wife

Brunhilda, thus daring 'to tear aside the veil that separates the mortality that dreams, from that which dreameth not'. Like Frankenstein, he is haunted by this entity which he has raised from the dead; since 'the dead possess no sympathy with life', it follows that 'by uniting himself with the dead, he had cut himself off from the living'. Her 'desolating pestilence' inexorably turns the castle into a living tomb – a mirror-image of her Life-in-Death nature. Yet in all this she *must* love him:

> [her] body was not able of itself to . . . nourish the flame whence spring all the affections and passions. . . . It was nevertheless necessary that she should love [Walter], to whose passion alone she was indebted for her renewed existence.

To love she must drink blood; eventually, when only Walter is left alive, she will attempt to take his blood. This recalls the mechanical behaviour of the denizens of Hell, the meaningless round in which the means transcends the end and becomes its own end. As the Renaissance seeker lost himself in the prolegomena to the Quest, as Hamlet destroys the world he meant to improve, as Falkland commits base murder to safeguard his honour, as Moncada speaks of substituting 'the pleasure of the pursuit for that of the attainment', so Brunhilda must destroy her husband's world and life in order to be able to fulfil an infinitely protracted goal of love. And with the 'malignant, withering glance' of her numinous Eye, she lays waste the house and life of her paramour.

If Tieck's is the first vampire in western prose fiction, J. W. Polidori's 'The Vampyre' (1819) is the first in the Anglo-Saxon world. Ruthven has a 'dead grey eye' that sparkles only with the joyful malignity of the destroyer, and Aubrey finds it impossible to fathom.

> the character of a man entirely absorbed in himself, who gave few other signs of his observation of external objects, than the tacit assent to their existence, implied by the avoidance of their contact.
> ('The Vampyre')

The dead have indeed 'no sympathy with life' – except for young Aubrey, a dreamer estranged from life's realities. And because of this affinity, Ruthven attaches himself to him and destroys the world of his affections, first his lover Ianthe, then his sister. Like Brunhilda, Ruthven attaches himself to his own kin, then to that of his human companion and counterpart: as if in the grip of an iron law, the vampire must feed on his own – on his own world, or on those who place themselves under his power. No matter what stratagem he may use to extend the plague of his destruction, this basic law abides. Byron's *Giaour* is doomed to feed on 'daughter, sister, wife'. Gautier's 'La Morte amoureuse' attaches herself to one who has looked on her with desire. Le Fanu's 'Carmilla', to one who has welcomed her into her home. Stoker's *Dracula*, to those who willingly cross his threshold or invite him to cross their own. Indiscriminate attacks on unknown passers-by seem to be only a recent development, yet even there modern works such as A. Rice's *Interview with the Vampire* (1976) abide by a revision of the basic law, laid down in 'Carmilla': the vampire may *feed* on just about anyone, but those who are to become the offspring of his or her love must give themselves of their own free will, even if the snags on free will are without number. It is the basic principle of affinity already found in *Doctor Faustus*, where Mephistopheles comes to one who calls to him and is already in danger of losing his soul.

There is no question of offspring yet in 'The Vampyre': Ruthven's Plague of Evil consists in the moral corruption of his victims. All in all, the vampire is still, like Melmoth or Frankenstein's monster, basically laying waste his own world. But it may also occur that the influence of the vampire helps to *unfold* the nature of his or her victim. In Théophile Gautier's 'La Morte amoureuse' (1836) Clarimonde's love calls up Romuald's other self, and from the 'tomb', 'prison', 'nightmare' of religious life the young priest awakes of nights into a reality in which he is a handsome nobleman in love with a beautiful woman who takes his blood, like Brunhilda, in order to be able to love him; but, unlike perhaps any other vampire in literature, she does so with infinite care not to endanger his health. In truth, they seem happy together, and hardly evil – except for Romuald's priest-self, who hates the nobleman-self, as much as the latter hates the former. Indeed, Gautier's originality lies in his having shifted the tragedy, from the conflict with the vampire, to the existential conflict created within the man himself, the vampire being only the catalyst for a struggle of the self with his own inner double, a struggle which, in this context, can only lead to the destruction of one of the two selves. Worn out with this double life, Romuald decides to kill Clarimonde,

> wishing to learn, once and for all, whether the priest or the nobleman was the victim of an illusion.

The anonymous story 'The Mysterious Stranger' (1860) was imitated, almost plagiarised, by Stoker (Parry, 1977), and through *Dracula* the vampire myth has since adhered to a forgotten model. Most of the later clichés appear in this tale: a Carpathian location, the vampire's ruined castle, his nocturnal sallies and diurnal rest, his emergence out of a mist, the specific throat-wound he inflicts, his mastery over the beasts, etc. But it adheres to older models too. The ruined Castle Klatka is not far from the castle, which the knight of Fahnenberg has just inherited, and the former is part of the latter's domain: two houses, of which that of Klatka will prey on that of Fahnenberg although, or precisely because, they are related – shades of Lewis's *Mistrust*. The haunting itself, however, is no longer Gothic but Victorian. Azzo von Klatka, the wild predator, attaches himself to one member of the knight's household, Franziska, who, like him, longs for passion and adventure: 'even pain', says she, 'may become a pleasure if it saves one from the shallow monotony of everyday life' ('Mysterious Strangers', 39). An affinity grows between them which, together with a freely extended invitation 'to visit', allows Azzo to feed on her; and the fate to which she nearly succumbs may be gauged from the explanation that 'vampires were deceased persons, who had either once served as nourishment to Vampires, or who had died in deadly sin, or under excommunication'. This *physical* transformation into a vampire as a result of being bitten by one represents the final codification of the vampire's reproductive strategy. At this point, Evil begins to spread geometrically.

By their very existence, vampires violate Nature – Nature as conceived by the rational mind; and those who invite them or otherwise accept them similarly act against Nature. However, as a product of an animistically conceived universe, the vampire is a natural phenomenon. Let me illustrate this. An oath seals Aubrey's lips while Ruthven preys on his sister; a promise is extracted from Laura and her family not to inquire into Carmilla's parentage – thus preventing them from knowing who their guest really is, and from deducing where Laura's strange illness comes from. The oath and the formality of the invitation show that vampires exploit their prospective victims' chivalric code of honour in order to further their own dishonourable ends.

Many vampires represent cyclic nature representatives of the Eternal Return; so Carmilla, who arrives on a full-moon night, a time of 'special spiritual activity' (Le Fanu, 'Carmilla', 1872). When

Laura's father refers to the Creator as humanity's safeguard in the face of adversity, Carmilla replies vehemently:

> Creator! *Nature* . . . And this disease that invades the country is natural. Nature. All things proceed from Nature – don't they? All things in the heaven, in the earth, and under the earth, act and live as Nature ordains? I think so.   ('Carmilla')

The vampire displays 'an engrossing vehemence, resembling the passion of love'. But Carmilla's *is* love, though of an intensely physical, sensuous kind: everything from which the utterly ignorant Laura has been sheltered. Inevitably, hers is a cruel love: 'Love', says Carmilla, 'will have its sacrifices. No sacrifice without blood'. While Laura's dreams possess an orgasmic quality under Carmilla's kiss, the terms in which they are conveyed ('a sobbing', a 'sense of strangulation', 'a dreadful convulsion' clearly show an inversion of passion. Yet this, too, is Nature: numinous, if evil. And this love cannot be enforced: 'it seems to yearn for something like sympathy and consent'. If not love, this is an ominous imitation; it is much harder to tell genuine from counterfeit passion here than it was in the case of the mechanical doll. The Double is learning to walk closer and closer to its original, though with no purposes of reconciliation.

At this point in the evolution of the myth, vampire biology has reached a high degree of streamlining: one single act now serves the functions of nourishment, sexual satisfaction, and reproduction. At this point, too, *physical* reproduction begins to be a major aspect of the myth:

> A suicide, under certain circumstances, becomes a vampire. The spectre visits living people in their slumbers; *they* die, and almost invariably, in the grave, develop into vampires.

Frankenstein's monster was denied the possibility of perpetuating his species; but another haunter has gradually found the means.

Like Clarimonde or Carmilla, Bram Stoker's *Dracula* (1897) is the catalyst that *unfolds* the nature of his victims. This is recognised, and at the same time denied, by those who would only see sweetness and light in humanity; thus, of his first victim we read: 'Lucy – I call the thing that was before us Lucy because it bore her shape'. It is a comfort to the vampire-hunters to be able to convince themselves that their erstwhile friend is now 'something else' – a double, an imitation of her. And not only Lucy either:

> Just think what will be [Dracula's] joy when he, too, is destroyed in his worser [*sic*] part, that his better part may have spiritual immortality.

It is a pious thought. But the line that separates the haunter and the haunted is ever so thin here: in his irritating English, Van Helsing tells us that the vampire 'throws no shadow; he make in the mirror no reflect'. It is as if Schlehmil's shadow and Spikher's reflection had been given independent thought and motion, and turned against their owners. The haunter cannot cast a shadow because he *is* one. As Schlehmil is the Death-in-Life, so Dracula (like Schlehmil's shadow) is the Life-in-Death. But what is the difference between a man's shadow given over to the Evil one, and an evil Shadow coming to a man, between a man's reflection surrendered to the dark Numen, and the numinous imitation of man coming to him, between a man's eyes going out to a mechanical doll, and a human-eyed automaton seducing him? Something of us goes out to the Enemy, and something of the Enemy comes to us: there is little to choose, for in the end something dark always stands half-way between our world and the numinous one, and it is *both* ourselves *and* an Other. It is significant that a distinction should be made at all, that even the Enemy should be split up between the man-that-was and the thing-that-possesses-him-now; it is almost wishful thinking that makes the all-too-human being into two distinct entities – except that, as if in glorious vindication, an expression of Christian peace does transfigure the faces of Lucy and Dracula at the moment of their 'real' death.

And here, clearly, lies the crux of the novelty. *Dracula* is, like all vampire tales, a novel about love, and it contains very explicit sensuous and sexual scenes. But sexuality is actually downplayed in favour of religion: there is that definite Christian element to which we are used by now, but which is practically new in the history of the myth. Mina's drinking of Dracula's blood is called by Van Helsing 'the Vampire's baptism of blood', and it also looks like a communion; and to the nourishment–sex–reproduction qualities of the blood exchange we must add this religious function. Then there is that inexhaustible supply of consecrated hosts in Van Helsing's pocket and the many crosses they employ to ward off the Evil ones –

and the Evil ones do heed the sacred signs.Clarimonde was a non-Christian vampire, but Dracula is definitely anti-Christian. When he says to the mad, fly-eating Renfield,

> All these lives will I give you, ay, and many more and greater, through countless ages, if you will fall down and worship me!

we know this is not just a fiendish shadow, but the Tempter himself – who does not only try to survive and/or give his own kind of love, but to rule. 'All that die from the preying of the Un-Dead become themselves Un-Dead, and prey on their kind. And so the circle goes on ever widening'. The Plague of Evil is now fully launched: *all* victims become vampires. And there is more: from the outset, this haunter has a *plan*:

> Everything had been carefully thought out, and done systematically and with precision. He seemed to have been prepared for every obstacle which might be placed by accident in the way of his intentions being carried out.

This goes beyond reproductive efficiency: his plan is to become 'the father or furtherer of a new order of things, whose road must lead through Death, not life'. The Plague is a structured undertaking: the Double becomes a would-be conqueror.

Self-haunting

So far I have written as if the Double were the main theme in Victorian horror. In many ways it is; but though shadow or reflection or monster are undeniable *Doppelgängers*, is the vampire one? Is Brunhilda? How much logic and how much ingenuity do we bring in when we accept a female figure for a man's Double, and vice versa? The problem increases with other types: are ghosts *Doppelgänger* figures? If so, whom do they 'double'? Again, the witch, that important if infrequent type of nineteenth-century horror, qualifies as a haunter of the community but hardly as a Double figure. If 'Doubling' is not the common denominator of Victorian haunters, what is? For an answer, let us turn to a scene in Gaskell's *Lois the Witch* (1860) where Grace Hickson echoes the self-righteous indignation of the town of Salem against witches:

> she wished that the first-discovered witch had been a member of a

godly English household, that it might be seen of all men that
religious folk were willing to cut off the right hand, and pluck out
the right eye, if tainted with this devilish sin.   (*Lois the Witch*)

The image is biblical (Matthew 18: 8–9), its use here most telling:
the Salem community is haunted *by a member of itself*. If the literal
expression of this image gives us the haunting hands that crawl their
way through a number of 19th- and 20th-century texts (Le Fanu's
'Narrative of the Ghost of a Hand', 1861; Maupassant's 'La main',
1883; Harvey's 'The Beast With Five Fingers', 1928; Brandel's *The
Lizard's Tail*, 1979; Wiene's film *The Hands of Orlac*, 1925), its
metaphorical expressions shape the bulk of Victorian horror. The
man made of dead limbs antagonises man. The dead body comes to
vampirise the living. The man-made automaton imitates organic and
spiritual life. The idiot brother murders his twin. The disembodied
spirit threatens the living. The portrait, shadow and reflection
incorporate the soul of the individual. The member of a family turns
against his kin (Gaskell, 'The Crooked Branch', 1859: the *branch* of
the family that deviates from the upright tree). The members of a
community turn against their fellow human beings (as the witches
do in Ainsworth's *The Lancashire Witches*, 1848, or as the villagers
do in *Lois the Witch*, *The Scarlet Letter*, Meinhold's *The Amber
Witch*, 1825). And all of these resemble that part of Nature, man
himself, which haunts, and is haunted by, the Albatross, the Raven,
the Whale, Nature itself. In every case, the hauntings can be reduced
to one formula: the part that turns against the whole. The bulk of
Victorian horror enshrines Grace Hickson's assumption that a
member of the whole may be infected by Satan, Evil, the dark
Numen, and join the Other side independently of the rest of the
body, and her further assumption that, once thus infected, the
offending member can and must be isolated, cut off, plucked out
that the body may live. With infinite variations, of which the Double
is perhaps the most prominent, this is the great Victorian theme.
Man and Minotaur roam the maze – but the Minotaur is part man,
is a part of man and his world.
   A classic example is the metamorph. There are many entities from
the Other domain that can take on an animal shape to prey on the
living. These have to be distinguished from, and contrasted with,
human beings who turn into wolves or other beasts. The wolf-spirit
emerges for the first time in Victorian horror in Marryat's *The
Phantom Ship* (1839), a fragment of which, usually anthologised as

'The White Wolf of the Harz Mountains', tells of an evil spirit who may appear as a beautiful woman but whose natural physical shape is the wolf. The same goes for the woman-looking White Fell in C. Housman's 'The Were-Wolf' (1896). On the side of the wolf-man, that is to say, of the man who turns into a wolf, there are medieval instances, notably in Marie de France's 'Lai de Bisclavret', but as a horror type it has a first (and misleading) appearance in Sutherland-Menzies' 'Hughes, the Were-Wolf' (1838). The first wolf-man properly so called is Reynolds' *Wagner the Wehr-Wolf* (1847), forced to turn into a beast once a month. The kind of problem raised by these two types: the beast-spirit and the beast-man, is exemplified in Blackwood's 'Ancient Sorceries' (1908), where it is suggested that the *true* nature of certain individuals is the feline one, though they may pose as human in daytime. When timid Vezin finds out he is 'one of them', he has to make a momentous choice between giving in to the lure of a shapeshifting cat's existence (fiery love included) and leading an upright, human, fear-filled life. His dilemma reminds us strongly of Romuald's agonised decision to destroy the vampire Clarimonde and thus to deny his own existence as a loving and loved nobleman, and to accept instead a priest's fear-filled life. Which is Romuald's and Vezin's *true* nature? A parallel situation crops up in R. Marsh's 'The Mask' (1900):

> Our faces, in a sense, are nothing but masks. Why should not the imitation be as good as the reality?   ('The Mask')

On this premise, a mad Mary Brookes dons masks and disguises of an absolutely convincing character; her real face (which she only uncovers when she is about to kill her victim) turns out to be a hideous, half-burnt one; but this is her *true* persona. In her case, therefore, the human form is the imitation, the monstrous one the reality. If the monster may be the *real* person, then the difference between a man who turns into a wolf and a supernatural wolf-being who appears in human form may be a fictitious one.

Wieland, Ambrosio, Falkland had undergone a moral transformation into their dark selves. Frankenstein succeeded in projecting this dark self outwards, onto a thing physically distinct from himself, and thus a thing he could oppose, and perchance destroy. But even this step is eventually doomed to failure: the monstrous *Doppelgänger* will give us the slip by coming so close to its original as to be indistinguishable from it, hence indestructible. *Qua* physical entity, it begins as the shadow close to the man, it develops into the beast inside the man, it ends up as the man inside the man. *Homo homini lupus* yields to *homo homini homo*: enter Mr Hyde.

> [Jekyll] thought of Hyde, for all his energy of life, as of something not only hellish but inorganic. This was the shocking thing: that the slime of the pit seemed to utter cries and voices; that the amorphous dust gesticulated and sinned; that what was dead, and had no shape, should usurp the offices of life. And this again, that that insurgent horror was knit to him closer than a wife, closer than an eye.   (Stevenson, *Dr Jekyll and Mr Hyde*, 1886)

That the evil Nothing should seem so real, so human, and so personal: that that which is supposed to have no *ens* 'should usurp the offices of life': this is what Augustine's careful denial of the *being* of Evil has come to. Jekyll's evil is closer to him 'than an eye' and awakens in him a 'consciousness of the perennial war among my members'. Grace Hickson could believe that the offending eye and hand could be plucked out or cut off, that the Evil had a certain objective nature. Jekyll is still trying to believe that Hyde is no part of himself but a human-looking entity from Hell, and his despair comes from the realisation that the one cannot be cut off from the other, that they are one. The distance between Original and Double narrows down until it ceases to exist; affinity becomes identity, and Jekyll finds it harder and harder to remain Jekyll:

> I was slowly losing hold of my original and better self, and becoming slowly incorporated with my second and worse.

The Double is becoming the Original, the labyrinth is inside, the haunting is of the mind: of a mind at war with itself.

Victorian horror literature has little to do with a Manicheistic vision of the world; the struggle with the dark Other is not one between two opposing principles, Good and Evil, but between reason and non-reason, between a closed-up Here and an excluded There, between a society false of itself and an aspect of its denied Truth. The adversary is not such because it is evil, but because it is rejected; the man of reason does not oppose it because he is good, but because he fears it. Fearing it, Jekyll applies his 'active good will' to subvert Nature, for humanity's sake, through the modern magic of a drug. Others had sought to tame Nature in her farthest *sanctum*, the Pole: Jekyll tries it at her innermost centre, within himself. And one and the same beast confronts them all.

The Nature of the Mirror

A scene in Hooper's film *Poltergeist* (1982) shows a man looking at himself in the mirror. He sees a decomposing face. Terrified, he clutches at his own features and tries to tear off the rot from the flesh. His mirror shows that he is tearing his own face apart.

A mirror is a thing of mystery. It functions as a humble purveyor of replicas. But because it is only in such replicas that we can have an idea of ourselves, it also functions as a model on which we construe and to which we orientate our being. And in this sense we imitate our imitations.

In its multiple manifestations, the Victorian Double is the mirror of human darkness; but in choosing that particular mirror, the individual defines himself in accordance with a dark *speculum*. Erasmus Spikher's social standing and self-respect, his 'image', vanish with the loss of his reflection: he will do almost anything to receive a new, Satan-given image. In acquiring power over Falkland, Caleb Williams becomes the latter's victim and loses his own sense of existence: he will only be able to recover it through total submission to his pursuer.Robert Wringhim finds in Gil-Martin a servile alter-ego – who eventually becomes his master. Nathanael's eyes go literally out to a quiet automaton: 'she' will destroy him with his own passion. Walter gives his love to Brunhilda, and Lucy to Dracula, only to be destroyed by their vampires. Poe's narrator invests the Raven with the gift of prophecy, only to be unmade by the prophetic bird. Frankenstein creates the life that will ruin his life. Latimer's mind-reading gift becomes his curse when he can only define himself in terms of other people's thoughts. The town of Salem conjures up the sin of witchcraft: it will soon fall prey to the enemy it has summoned. Jekyll arouses his dormant double, and finds him turning into his original. Faustus summoned a servant, yet found a master. King Basilio prophesied Segismundo's wildness, and came to see a wild Segismundo haunt him. ''This the sport to have the enginer / hoist with his own petar', says Hamlet. The specifics of the myth is Victorian, its source Elizabethan. For centuries, man's new *speculum* has been becoming his exemplar, a centre to orientate himself by.

In the second half of the nineteenth century, a new vision of language flourishes: Positivism sees language as a reality-oriented construct, the statements of which can be verified or falsified by comparing them with the physical reality they are claimed to reflect. This anti-metaphysical vogue opposes the older, reality-transcending view of language. The Berkeleyan view of the world as a sign-system pointing to a supra-physical reality is dismissed by the Positivists: language and physical world are two distinct phenomena, of which the first points at the second. Language becomes a mirror of the world. Through the transcendental sign-world, man could reach the Other; now, on an opaque sign-system, man sees only his own world – or fails to see it, and then endeavours to make language conform to its reflective mission. In this respective, the scientific enterprise may be said to be groping for means to shun the *Visio Malefica*, the new exemplar, model, centre, *speculum*, in whose dark image the human world would seem to be recreating itself.

Positivism continues a Cartesian theme. Descartes codified a break between existents (the rational) and non-existents (the non-rational). As the second domain emerges *from within* the first, as the non-rational, seen as evil, appears to infect the rational, Positivism is driven further back into the *res cogitans*: the haunting is of the mind: *language begins to be used as the next buffer zone between the human world and the Other*. Through a careful 'clarification' of the meaning of linguistic statements, man may yet tame the world. The ultimate expression of this trend is Orwell's *Nineteen Eighty-Four*, where the best means of absolute control over man and nature is the reduction of language to an automatised behaviour incapable of more meaning than the Party wills it to have. As the scientist strives for domination of nature and of a nature-reflecting language, the horror-fiction character again and again seeks, even as he dreads, a nature-transcending image of himself. The Victorian theme is that of man's *confrontation* with his Double, with a part of himself, with the Minotaur in the world-labyrinth. Dracula or Hyde are obviously sources of terror in the specifics of several situations in which the human characters find themselves. As readers, however, we are forced time and again to *face* a concrete being who stands, be it ever so vicariously, for a part of ourselves.

In Victorian horror, a window is opened to the Other, and a shadow emerges into our universe. For the most part, it is one shadow at a time; it is generally a Christian (or anti-Christian) one; and for the most part, its mission fulfilled, it departs, or else it is destroyed, even if its destruction involves that of its original. But suppose that the shadow begins to come in numbers, so that we must lie ever wakeful in fearful expectation of the next one. Or suppose it does not leave after its ostensive mission is fulfilled but remains attached to its bearer who, though physically, mentally or morally broken, remains yet alive and conscious to see his shadow usurp command and use him to further some grander aim which involves a radical alteration of the man's world: that the man is now but a pawn in the larger game plotted by the – now organised – forces of Evil. Suppose the shadow becomes the Original while we, now its reflections, surrender to it the power to shape our own destinies, whereby the Other becomes the true maker of history. It is true that the transcendental windows into the Other are now discredited by the tamers of language, that the personal hunters are chased out of Nature, or destroyed, or ignored: but just when Nature seems bereft of numinous possibilities the Other re-emerges in force, as besieger and conqueror, from the past of antiquarians, from the future of the science-visionaries, from outer space, from the bowels of the Earth and the abysses of the ocean, as well as from the nooks and crannies of that startling new Nature adumbrated by modern physics. Now Evil, filth and desolation cease to be isolated, remediable incidents and become ingrained in the very fabric of things: the Thomistic vision of a universal decay comes to be codified by science as the Second law of Thermodynamics (Rudolph Clausius, in 1850), which states that the entropy of any *closed* system must be continuously increasing. This decay, the same closed, entropic universe that Positivism affirms, arises from that struggle of the part against the whole, the perennial war among the members, the effort at plucking out and cutting off the infected part of us, so that, in effect, King Varlan maims King Lambar, we maim ourselves, and our world acquires the lineaments of the Waste Land.

This, then, is the shape of things to come.

Note

First published in Manuel Aguirre, *The Closed Space: Horror Fiction and Western Symbolism* (Manchester: Manchester University Press, 1990).

1. See p. 228: *Wagner the Wehr-Wolf* (1847).

GINA WISKER

On Angela Carter

Angela Carter's sense of horror is based on the grotesque, the bizarre and excessive, a kind of baroquely overlaid nightmare which has uneasy echoes for us. She investigates the stuff of myth and dreams and in doing so unearths rather unpleasant, perverse sexual fantasies, digging further behind the suburban mind to identify the interest in the werewolf tale, the fairytales of Bluebeard and his wives, and Beauty and the Beast. In investigating our subconscious horrors, Carter brings a chill to the domestic and the everyday. Opening a kitchen drawer in the Carter kitchens of our minds, we are always, like Melanie in *The Magic Toyshop*, likely to meet something horrid:

> Melanie hummed to herself as she hung cups from their hooks and propped the plates. She opened the dresser drawer to put away the knives and spoons. In the dresser drawer was a freshly severed hand, all bloody at the roots.[1]

The details are domestic and realistic, the episode and object monstrous, inexplicable, though Uncle Philip is a sort of urban Bluebeard in his own way, and Melanie has been thinking of Poe. In Carter's horror, the mazes of the ordinary mind in the ordinary house are entered to reveal gothic torture chambers and spiral staircases leading down to dungeons.

In 'The Fall River Axe Murders' Carter looks at the catalysts, the events and moments which made murder inevitable in the claustro-phobic middle-class normality of the Fall River, Massachusetts Borden household. She does not linger on the blood. Threat permeates the descriptions: of ties which 'garotte' their virtuous wearers and the oppressive constricting clothes the women wear in this sweating, constrained household. Carter investigates. Her probing of details reveals gaps and silences, 'what the girls do on their own is unimaginable to me' and of Emma, Lizzie's sister, that 'she is a blank space' (*Black Venus*). The iron-backed, capital-accumulating father, the repressed, stifled sisters, the air of suppurating normality; these permeate Carter's descriptions of this fated family, our knowledge of whose violent fate lurks and drips over every restrained comment, calm as the clichéd 'still waters' of

Lizzie's nature as she drives hatpins into her hat or weighs the axe which slaughtered her pigeons to make a pie for her stepmother.

Horror in much of Angela Carter's writing captures a sense of a potion containing the monstrous and the everyday. Lizzie Borden is a figure for this, and we are reminded that given the right circumstances and the appropriate kind of suburban claustrophobia, we might all erupt and give our family 40 whacks with an axe.

Carter explores those locked rooms. The mazes and corridors and doors of conformity and normality which we use to confine and hide away our destructive drives, and our nightmares are replicated in the twists and turns of the fiction's realistic artifice, while networks of imagery hint, suggest and occasionally dramatically reveal the sources of the terror, the disgust and the horror. There are blood, feathers and much worse, in all of Angela Carter's kitchens. 'The structure of fantastic narratives is one founded upon contradictions.'[2] There are many recognisable realistic details, dates, times, typical clothing and furniture in the text. The places are familiar, and at the same time the surreal and the symbolic provide another layer of meaning. Metaphor combines with metonymy and the oxymoronic mixture is the fabric of her language.

Carter's fiction disinters and utilises the stuff of dreams. The fiction proves dreams palpably 'real', and so shows itself as psychologically based horror which owes much to Freud, Jung and to Melanie Klein. Her dream- and magic-based landscapes are rendered tangible because, she insists, dreams are part of our lives, and related to the myths we use to describe and direct our lives, 'There is certainly confusion about the nature of dreams, which are in fact perfectly real: they are real *as* dreams and they're full of *real* meaning as dreams.'[3]

Like Bruno Bettelheim, whose work influenced *The Bloody Chamber*, Carter uses dream and fantasy material to reflect inner experiences and processes, ways of rendering and coping with the palpable conscious world and the reactions of the unconscious.

The break with the notion of a straitjacket of the real releases energies leading to a fuller understanding of how meanings are created, values constructed and versions of worth and reality validated over other versions. Fantasy is a useful mode 'Because it is a narrative structured upon contraries, fantasy tells of limits, and it is particularly revealing in pointing to the edge of the "real".'[4] And as Rosemary Jackson says, 'breaking single, reductive "truths", the fantastic traces a space within a society's cognitive frame. It introduces multiple, contradictory "truths": it becomes polysemic.'[5]

Horror, gothic and the use of fantasy combine in Carter's work. The collapse of boundaries and divisions between the animate and the inanimate is a regular element of fantasy, while one chief tool of terror is the reduction of man to an object, a machine, a doll or an automaton. This is a frequent characteristic in an Angela Carter story or novel. In her examination of sexual politics, their psychological motivation and their social representations, she repeatedly presents scenarios where women are manipulated as marionettes (*The Magic Toyshop*), or preferred as tableaux vivants: disempowered objects of desire, as in the hideous living-sex museum of Madame Schreck in *Nights at the Circus*, or preferred dead and kept as mementoes in Bluebeard's castle. She allies her examination of the basis of terror and horror with an interest in sexual power and perversion, and so it is that the ones rendered immobile and automated are usually women in the hands of men, manipulated by power or for money; it is a logical enactment of the 'living doll' image.

The most consistently developed example of the recurring automaton, puppet or doll image in Carter's fiction can be found in the early 'The Loves of the Lady Purple' (*Fireworks*), where the doll who enacts the quiet circus professor's violent erotic fantasies, comes to life and finally repeats them in reality, draining him in an act of vampirism.

The Asiatic professor reminds us of Carter the author.

The puppet master is always dusted with a little darkness. In direct relation to his skill he propagates the most bewildering enigmas for, the more lifelike his marionettes, the more godlike his marionettes and the more radical the symbiosis between inarticulate doll and articulating fingers.

He acts as intermediary between the audience and the dolls, the 'undead', here deliberately described in the language used to describe vampires. The puppet master's dolls are a mixture of magic and realism; the stories they enact speak to the audience of a certain repressed and unspeakable reality and the more extreme, bizarre or perverse the incidents in which they are involved, the closer the recognition of those selves and secrets the readership keep behind their own locked doors.

The professor has no language which can be understood and his apprentice is deaf, his other foundling helper dumb, but the Lady Purple blazons her messages in her actions accompanied by the appropriately weird but untranslatable stories of the professor. As Queen of the Night, the Lady Purple, object of all the professor's sexual fantasies, is 'filled with necromantic vigour' with the vitality of the professor passing directly through into her, draining him while she embodies that traditional perverse twinning of sex and pain, the erotic and power. She is 'a distillation of those of a born woman . . . the quintessence of eroticism'. Nightly she acts out the story invented of her life, lusts and eventual reduction to a marionette. The stylised, symbolic puppet characters and sexual scenarios are equally figures 'in a rhetoric' where the abstract essence of erotic woman can be bought, used, manipulated and later shelved. The constant oscillation between the language of artifice and the language of the real, tells the story Lady Purple enacts, as if it were a true record.

Ironically her power is emphasised as one who encourages the acting out of fantasies, which then reduce her lovers to objects. 'She, the sole perpetrator of desire, proliferated malign fantasies all around her and used her lovers as the canvas on which she executed boudoir masterpieces of destruction. Skins melted in the electricity she generated.' For those watching the show she embodies the object of their desire as well as their fears, rendering them ultimately safe because of the awareness of artifice. This mimics the activity of horror fiction: embodiment, audience enjoyment, and a sense of release and security. The interest, the drive, the fears do not disappear. Indeed, Carter suggests they return nightly.

Modern horror tales emerged as a genre with the secularisation of society and the leaking away of religious explanations of the odd and inexplicable.[6] Science also could not explain all that was unusual and strange, so a space for these expressions was found in the genre of horror, which itself was enabled to ask questions about the power of religious controls as well as the dangers of science. Things 'out of control' and objects 'come to life' emerge as the main example of these expressions. As Martin Barker puts it looking at the lobby surrounding the horror comic censorship of the 1950s in *A Haunt of Fears*:

> It is the sense of helplessness in the face of unpredictable objects and processes that makes such narratives work as horror. In this . . . they come closest to film horror, where the classic motifs – dark nights, unknown threats, and ritual incantations to control the forces of evil – are just what leave us deliciously shuddering when they are well manipulated.[7]

Lady Purple is a thing come to life, and a thing out of control. She is more than that though, for she is the embodiment of the perverse and lustful thoughts and dreams of both her creator the professor and the audiences who enjoy watching a doll act out sado-masochistic fantasies. Her coming to life is ironically the downfall of those who have thus positioned her (the professor and future male victims in the brothel). She also embodies the frighteningly circular and inevitable re-enactment of myth. Lady Purple is a vengeful fetishistic object, sado-masochistic and horror fantasy combined.

Fetishism is the stuff on which pornography thrives and Carter takes further into social critique her manipulation of fantasy and horror's technique of confusing the boundaries between animate and inanimate, objects of desire and object to be controlled and destroyed. In *The Magic Toyshop* is a palimpsest of popular fictional forms, fairytales, myths, girls' own paper stories. Through examination of Melanie's adolescent construction of herself in the semi-pornographic art modes in which woman is represented by great painters and writers, Carter examines how the myths of our femininity, our sexual being comes to be fashioned upon us and come to be that part of us with which we willingly collude, blind to their reifying implications. These implications: rape, violation, pregnancy, are indicated in the positioning of Edward Bear, 'swollen stomach concealing striped pyjamas', and Lorna Doone, 'splayed out, face down in the dust under the bed' – remnants of childhood. Moreover, we are also presented with the sacrificial tone of the virginally white bridal pictures of Melanie's mother.

> Her mother exploded in a pyrotechnic display of satin and lace, dressed as for a medieval banquet. . . . A wreath of artificial roses was pressed low down on her forehead. . . . She carried a bunch of white roses in her arms, cradled like a baby.

She is a meal to be devoured, a firework display, and when Melanie tries on her mother's dress it acts as a malevolent object, drowning and capturing her.

Bunty, *Judy*, *Schoolfriend* and *Girl* [British girls' comics] stories often concentrate on the 'little mother' who stands as a surrogate for her siblings when their parents are, as are Melanie's, killed in a plane crash. Plucky tomboys also abound. Melanie pictures herself in all these roles, and rejects them, but still awaits the kiss of a Prince Charming to awaken her from herself into a role he designs. In the

working-class East London toyshop there is a wicked uncle, no
stepmother or wicked aunt, and it is his designs on Melanie which
cast her in the role of the traditional female victim, manipulated into
a rape victim through his control. Uncle Philip is a child's nightmare
figure, a character from a fairytale by the Brothers Grimm.

> Uncle Philip never talked to his wife except to bark brusque
> commands. He gave her a necklace that choked her. He beat her
> younger brother. He chilled the air through which he moved. His
> towering, blank-eyed presence at the head of the table drew the
> savour from the good food she cooked.

His menace is both physical and psychological and the spell he casts
over the household renders them mute and powerless.

The moment in which Melanie, reified by her role as Leda in Uncle
Philip's puppet version of that high art pornographic favourite, *Leda
and the Swan*, is overwhelmed by the monstrous wooden and
feathered swan, is both horror and pure farce. In her mixture of the
horrific and the humorous, Carter resembles Roald Dahl, whose short
stories have similar twists to hers, and who similarly re-writes 'Little
Red Riding Hood'. Dahl comments, 'What's horrible is basically
funny . . . in fiction I mean.'[8] Angela Carter's delicate mixture of
slapstick, irony and the machinations of Sadeian horror typifies her
stylistic strategies; an ornate overlay of Western myths and
representations, funny, fantastic and frightening. It is deeply
revelatory about the forms and intentions of Western art from the
National Gallery and Sadlers Wells to the toyshop. Melanie last
recalls 'Swan Lake' when her father took her to see it. The embrace of
the plywood and feathered swan is a mock up of the many languorous
godlike embraces between a loving Leda and an elegant swan found in
the world's great art galleries, celebrated in hauntingly beautiful tones
by Yeats in 'Leda and the Swan' where phrases such as 'terrified vague
fingers' and 'feathered glory' suggest that the aesthetic enjoyment
overcomes the sense of the strange and horrific; a version of a
grotesque, power rape myth many women readers find bizarre.
Carter's version emphasises the otherness, the disempowering and
the horror.

> All her laughter was snuffed out. She was hallucinated. She felt
> herself not herself, wrenched from her own personality, watching
> this whole fantasy from another place; and in this staged fantasy,

anything was possible. Even that the swan, mocked up swan, might assume reality itself and rape this girl in a blizzard of white feathers.

Horror here is a direct effect of the dramatic embodiment of despotic patriarchal power writ large and backed up by the collusion of that other patriarchal power base – high art. Carter's debunking of this high art, patriarchy's dubiously intellectually tarted up sadistic power games, empowers us all to reveal the unpleasant-nesses, the potential sick violence, underlying everyday mythic representations of sexual relations.

The dangers are no less real despite the slapstick rendering of events, but Carter's irony and slapstick humour provide themselves with a liberating vehicle to expose and defuse such powers. 'Like fate or the clock, on came the swan, its feet going splat, splat, splat.'

In *Nights at the Circus*, male fear, horror and fascination at female sexual parts are figured in the geography of Madame Schreck's brothel, where the girls work in the basement.

Madame Schreck organised her museum, thus: downstairs, in what had used to be the wine cellar, she'd had a sort of vault or crypt constructed, with wormy beams overhead and nasty damp flagstones underfoot, and this place was known as 'Down Below', or else, 'The Abyss'. The girls was all made to stand in stone niches cut out of the slimy walls, except for the Sleeping Beauty, who remained prone, since proneness was her speciality. And there were little curtains in front and, in front of the curtains, a little lamp burning. These were her 'profane altars' as she used to call them.

The offhand, everyday Cockney tones of the winged, iconic aerialiste Fevvers renders these traditionally gothic horrors almost domestic, but visions of a visiting judge who ejaculates when black hooded and when a noose is placed round his neck, and of clients who revel in the gothic nightmare of clanking chains, who are turned on only by recumbent, seemingly dead women, and all the trappings of a mixture of Poe and de Sade illuminate the dubious interrelationship between a love of horror and a perverse sexuality: a desire to brutalise women. Women, of course, collude in their own dehumanisation. Fevvers's avarice leads her into the clutches of the determinedly male, sadistic Duke, whose own brand of mastery consists of reducing his objects of desire to just that, a miniaturised, gilded *objet d'art*. The Grand Duke represents sterile power.

> His house was the realm of minerals, of metals of vitrification – of gold, marble and crystal; pale halls and endless mirrors and glittering chandeliers that clanged like wind-bells in the draught from the front door . . . and a sense of frigidity, of sterility, almost palpable.

It is a gothic horror threat of potential disempowerment and reification since all therein is artifice and glitter.

Murderous histories, sexual mutilations of women, and the *frisson* of total control of the human by rendering it entirely useless, pure art ornament and entertainment: the Duke's collection embodies his vile proclivities.

Fevvers's earlier encounter with Christian Rosencreutz, whose sexual perversity was related to his wish to gain new powers by sacrificing what he feared, is an echo of a familiar gothic encounter with Rosicrucianism. Carter replicates the seductive powers, the *frissons* of horror, and exposes a basis of horror in desires to dehumanise, to control, to fix, pin, collect and, perhaps, destroy the adored object. Humour, iron and slapstick undercut and disempower the perpetrators of torture, terror and death in her work and female victims soar above what could destroy them, using for their own ends the very images and forms which could otherwise represent them in a constrained sense.

Fevvers's own canny common sense enables her to turn the Duke's lust against him and she escapes into the Fabergé model of the trans-Siberian railway: a celebratory moment when magic and realism confusingly and amusingly unite. Fevvers escapes, a feathered *intacta*, icon of dreams, 'bird' woman and yet her own person. The last laugh is on the loving journalist Walser who wishes to pin her down with facts, and on the readers who want her metaphors explained, but who are left instead realising that the best thing to do with myths and metaphors is to reclaim them for our own variety of interpretations, rather than accepting any fobbed off on us by a patriarchal culture.

Reclamation is the key also for Rosaleen, the Red Riding Hood figure in *Company of Wolves*. The grotesque horror of being eaten alive by a lascivious wolf is replaced by the turning of the tables, as she celebrates her own sexual powers, burns her own clothing, becomes a werewolf herself and so tames the beast, thus proving her mother's comment, 'If there's a beast in man it meets its match in women too'. It might seem trite, or even dangerous as some have suggested that Carter merely repeats much of the sexist psychology of eroticism, but it is a way of suggesting reversal, using irony and the technique of 'the pulling of the plug' on a socially constructed version of horror based on a pornography which always renders the woman as victim.

Slow mental and physical torture, claustrophobia, a living death . . . this is the stuff of her horror and recalls Poe as it does the Jacobean. But her vision is more ironic and amused. Her aims are related to reversal, there is a consistent drive towards celebration and carnival. In the midst of being almost eaten by the big bad wolf, Red Riding Hood/Rosaleen is empowered by her awareness of the strength of her own virginity, as well as that of her emergent sexuality. This is a reclamation of the body as a site for woman's empowerment. Virginity in myth 'normally' renders a woman both magically safe and ideally fitted to be a sacrificial victim, in a system which sees virginity as a commodity. Here Rosaleen celebrates, her clothes burned by choice in her granny's fire, a werewolf herself?

Fires such as that in *The Magic Toyshop* are purgatorial: the evil die, the good are doubtless rescued. This is in the true tone of Shakespearian late Romance, which suggests tragedy and horror but ultimately avoids or overcomes it. There are hints of death by drowning, of tragedy entering our living rooms when Tiffany, the Ophelia-like spurned innocent stripper in *Wise Children*, disappears, but she escapes and lives again. Twins are produced from pockets, dead uncles reappear twice as large and filled with largesse. Reunions and unifications replace the open endings of some of the earlier works. Carnival, towards which all Carter's work has long leant, triumphs over horror in *Wise Children*.

Carter's best horror writing is more suited to the art of the short story than to longer fiction. Like Poe she goes for 'unity of effect', telling individual, perfectly controlled tales which retell and often revalue a myth or legend, which develop and embody a particular lurking perversity or nightmare, and which explore the horrific sources of real events. As in traditional gothic tales, we are terrified because the atmosphere threatens us, the familiar is our familiar nightmare. Beautifully, fatally, realistic, encyclopedic details combine with the immediate, mythic, nightmarish and surreal. In *The Company of Wolves*, we are told that, at night, the eyes of wolves shine like candle flames yellowish reddish, but that is because the pupils of their eyes fatten on darkness and catch the light from your lantern and flash it back to you – red for danger; if a wolf's eyes reflect only moonlight, then they gleam a cold and unnatural green, a mineral, a piercing colour.

The movement of nightmare is enacted with a rich mixture of visual and psychologically threatening imagery:

If the benighted traveller spies those luminous, terrible sequins stitched suddenly on the black thickets, then he knows he must run, if fear has not struck him stock still.

But those eyes are all you will be able to glimpse of the forest assassins as they cluster inevitably around your smell of meat.

And her language draws the reader in and implicates them as it reproduces a fascinating and compelling mixture of terror and the *frisson* of joy at such terror.

The title story of *The Bloody Chamber* is one such perfect gothic tale in which we are seduced and drawn in as slowly as the victim, the virginal wife of this art-collecting Bluebeard. The language of food consumption, aesthetic pleasure and avaricious cruelty dominates her descriptions of him, his wooing and her collusion. Threat drips slowly from every crevice. He is 'possessed of that strange, ominous calm of a sentient vegetable life, like one of those cobra-headed funereal lilies whose white sheaths are curled out of a flesh as thick and tensely yielding to the touch as vellum'. His desire she perceives but does not understand though the 'choker of rubies, two inches wide, like an extraordinarily slit throat' presages the total ownership he has in mind while his 'sheer carnal avarice' watching her in gilded mirrors positions her both as consumable meat, and art object. Mirrors, billowing gauze curtains, indecipherable imprecations from (traditional, gothic) menials, huge beds and lilies: those gothic familiars draw in and thrill the reader, who wants yet to cry out a warning.

Carter's intertextuality provides a smile of recognition, 'All the better to see you' says the lupine, leonine, vampirish, art/wife-collecting descendant of Browning's Duke who keeps pictures and relics of previously, mysteriously, dead wives. The ravishment is surreal, particularly as he removes all her clothes except the choker, and mirrors reflect every move:

Rapt, he intoned: 'Of her apparel she retains / Only her sonorous jewellery'.

A dozen husbands impaled a dozen brides while the mewing gulls swung on invisible trapezes in the empty air outside.

Carter investigates also the notion of the 'pleasures of the flesh' and here reveals a link between pornography and horror: man as flesh, skin covering meat, the source of the horror of cannibal tales and movies like *The Silence of the Lambs*. 'The strong abuse, exploit and meatify the weak, says Sade' (*The Sadeian Woman*). 'She knew she was nobody's meat' is a challenge Rosaleen holds up to the wolf, though necrophagy (exposition of the meatiness of human flesh) and cannibalism lurk behind Bluebeard's delights at his new wife. 'I saw him watching me in the gilded mirrors with the assessing eye of a connoisseur inspecting horseflesh, or even of a housewife in the market, inspecting cuts on the slab.' This terrifies but attracts her, as she recognises her own potential for corruption. His sexual 'appetite' and then his 'taste' for her she mistakenly feels will protect her when she investigates the locked rooms of his house in his absence. We know versions of the story, know she will find the remains of dead ex-wives. As with many gothic horror tales of castles, locked door, horrid secrets, threatening husbands and marital violence, walled-up wives, spiders, jeweled daggers and necklaces, the very familiarity produces a *frisson* for the reader, and the familiarity here of the old tale captures and captivates us. Languorousness, inevitability, these entrap the reader as they entrap the bride about to be turned into a 'meal' for her murderous husband who swings a cruel sword, and forces her to dress in white as the sacrificial victim, to his lustful power. The warrior mother rescues the bride with the aid of the new servant. The story becomes a romp, but its horror has a sexual and social basis we won't forget, and which returns in many another of her tales.

In *The Sadeian Woman* Carter notes, 'Sexuality, stripped of the idea of free exchange, is not in any way humane; it is nothing but pure cruelty. Carnal knowledge is the infernal knowledge of the flesh as meat.' The potential of devouring lurks behind Carters 'The Tiger's Bride' but the proud voyeuristic beast is tamed with the girl's love and her recognition of her own tigerishness. In 'The Lady of the House of Love', a female vampire strikes a familiar terror, her necessary plan involving the capture of male morsels. Her room is funerary, pungent with smoke and elaborate, and in true vampire fashion her seemingly virginal beauty is evidence of her desires as, 'In her white lace negligee stained a little with blood, the Countess climbs up on her catafalque at dawn each morning and lies down in an open coffin.' Metamorphosis takes place as she turns into a nocturnal creature sniffing out lesser prey. Change and the question of what it means to be human, that fearsome ingredient of Victorian horror of the *Dr Jekyll and Mr Hyde* type, but with its roots further back in the Jacobean horror of wolfish brothers carrying legs of corpses over their shoulders in *The Duchess of Malfi* – these crowd many of Carter's short stories. Here the rococo strangely juxtaposes images and descriptions which conjure up a night world of horror.

> the voracious margin of huntress's nights in the gloomy garden, crouch and pounce, surrounds her habitual tortured somnambulism, her life or imitation of life. The eyes of this nocturnal creature enlarge and glow. All claws and teeth, she strokes, she gorges; but nothing can console her for the ghastliness of her condition, nothing.

Employing what David Punter calls 'the dialectic of persecution', Carter's gothic investigates the extremes of terror, leading the audience gradually into realms which are nightmarish and horribly familiar.[9]

Influences on Carter's work include Isak Dinesen, who continued gothic interest in decayed aristocracy, and as a feminist writer, filtered society's problems 'through a pervading and ironic self-consciousness' much as does Fevvers, and the protagonist of *The Bloody Chamber*.[10] Another main influence is in the nightmarish, surrealist and psychologically fired night wanderings of transvestite characters in Djuna Barnes, particularly the highly Jacobean *Nightwood* (1937). *Nightwood* belongs to a tradition of lesbian gothic writing, which highlights the sexuality implicit in such horror figures as vampires, werewolves and zombies. Richard Dyer comments that,

> a number of . . . writers on the horror film have suggested, adapting Freudian ideas, that all 'monsters' in some measure represent the hideous and terrifying form that sexual energies take when they 'return' from being socially and culturally repressed.

Yet the vampire seems especially to represent sexuality . . . s/he bites them, with a bite that is just as often described as a kiss.[10]

Werewolves are favourites in *The Bloody Chamber* collection, their sexuality emphasised as handsome young men who leap in front of girls, men with eyebrows meeting suspiciously in the middle; men who want to eat you up and devour you sexually.The main vampire is a woman in 'The Lady of the House of Love' who lures in wandering men who, 'led by the hand to her bedroom . . . can scarcely believe their luck'.

Investigating her relationship to other postmodernist writers we find many parallels with the American gothic of Purdy, Pynchon and Coover. Recognition of this appears in her epigraph to *Heroes and Villains*, which comes from Leslie Fiedler's exploration of the American gothic, *Love and Death in the American Novel*.[12] The epigraph runs: 'The Gothic mode is essentially a form of parody, a way of assailing clichés by exaggerating them to the limit of grotesqueness.'[13]

One of Carter's main stated aims is demythologising, unpicking and unpacking the myths and legends (those fictions) which shape and control our lives, whether safely contained in a fairytale or shaped around us in newspaper articles, adverts or television stereotypes. The human mind forces experience into familiar shapes so that it can comprehend it, but in so doing it simplifies into stereotype and myth, which themselves seem then to us to have safely embodied the less pleasant of those experiences, mental or physical, by objectifying and fictionalising them in this way. Stereotypes, myths and fictions are shorthand, but they exercise a control on the expressions and forms of the everyday world. Carter particularly intends to demythologise the fictions related to sexuality, and horror is one of her means. She exposes the relationship between sex and power, the erotic, the perverse; she digs behind the ostensibly comfortable and safe surfaces and shows up oppressions, reification, torture and dehumanisation lurking in the everyday. One way she does this is by re-examining and re-writing fairytales and myths, and another is to explore incidents in which the everyday explodes, revealing the horrors which lurk behind it.

Violence against women has long been a characteristic of much horror writing, as well as pornography. The essential powerlessness of the virginal, entrapped, victimised girl is a stock feature of pornography as it is of gothic horror, which deals with taboos:

'Incest, rape, various kinds of transgressions of the boundaries between the natural and the human'.[14] Angela Carter is a clever manipulator of the techniques of horror, terror and the gothic. She takes the impetus and the structure of gothic-based romance tales for women and reappropriates them for a sexual politics which demythologises myths of the sexual powerlessness and victim role for women. She uses their structure to turn their usual dénouements on their heads. As Tania Modleski argues in *Loving with a Vengeance*, gothics are 'expressions of the "normal" feminine paranoid personality' which incorporates guilt and fear, 'the paranoid individual faces physical persecution (as in dreams of being attacked by murderous figures)'.[15]

Moral and more importantly physical persecution predominate, and the readers are encouraged to wallow in the guilt and fear, and to imagine themselves as victim, while in romantic developments of gothic fiction, persecution is 'experienced as half-pleasurable'. Romantic heroines turn their 'victimization into a triumph'. If we explore the novels which combine the gothic and romantic there is a (for a feminist reader) tremendous disempowering celebration of this victimisation as satisfying and ultimately productive of reward. Paulina Palmer, examining Margaret Atwood's *Bodily Harm*, makes comments as appropriate for Carter as for Atwood, about the reappropriation of a genre, the gothic romantic, designed very much for women,

> the Gothic genre, traditionally noted for its representation of woman as victim, becomes in Atwood's hands the perfect medium for depicting contemporary woman caught unaware in the 'rape culture' which pervades society. Motifs associated with the genre . . . include: the ingenuous heroine as the victim of male manipulation and attack; an intrigue plot in which the male protagonists compete for power; the collapsing of conventional boundaries between external/internal and animate/inanimate; and the reference to certain socially taboo topics – in this case cancer, and sado-masochistic sexual practice.[16]

The resurgence in interest in horror writing by women which has produced *The Virago Book of Ghost Stories*[17] and the fiercer, more radical *Skin of Our Soul*[18] enables us to ask questions about where Angela Carter relates to other women horror writers and what might be said to be any specifically female characteristics in the horror genre. The very latest of the popular fictional forms to be reclaimed by feminist critics, investigating the operation of popular fictional characteristics in the work of women writers within the genre, horror writing might very properly be said to have originated with women, with the work of Ann Radcliffe's *Mysteries of Udolpho* or with Mary Shelley's *Frankenstein*. Great women writers throughout the centuries have produced ghost stories and horror stories, but perhaps one of the problems of reclaiming horror as a genre for women is this very equation of the female victim, the edge of the pornographic, with horror.

Lisa Tuttle argues that men and women's perceptions of fear are to some extent similar, but in other ways different because of their social positioning:

> Territory which to a man is emotionally neutral may for a woman be mined with fear, and vice-versa, for example: the short walk home from the bus-stop of an evening. And how to understand the awesome depths of loathing some men feel for the ordinary (female) body? We all understand the language of fear, but men and women are raised speaking different dialects of that language.[19]

Women's contemporary horror fiction explores sexual licence, alternative sexual relationships, and the power in 'normal' relationships. There are many tales which feature fear of incest, of patriarchal rape, of a life-draining mother, hatred of devious, bitchy, beautiful women. There are hidden cruelties in what are 'normally' perceived as loving or nurturing relationships, and there are forbidden fantasies of lesbian partnerships or incestuous partnerships. Taboos are explored.

Angela Carter's gothic horror reappropriates women's powers. The thrills and spills of the romantic gothics are there, but the terroriser turned faithful lover is not. The main gains are self-respect, liberty and equal relationships. Red Riding Hood ends up happy with the wolf, Bluebeard's wife is liberated, Fevvers settles for Walser, and retains her secret, her magic. Glittering, contradictory, intertextually familiar and playful, Angela Carter's horror brings into the clear light of the semi-realistic domestic kitchen, the nasty thoughts, fears and nightmares lurking in the cellars of our minds. And she gives us something magical too. Hers is not the horror of the abyss: it is not ultimately a black vision, it's too Rabelaisian for that, too funny and celebratory.

Notes

First published in Clive Bloom (ed.), *Creepers* (London: Pluto, 1993).

1. Books by Angela Carter referred to in the text: *The Magic Toyshop* (London, 1967); *Heroes and Villains* (London, 1969); *Fireworks* (London, 1974); *The Bloody Chamber* (London, 1979); *The Sadeian Woman* (London, 1979); *Nights at the Circus* (London, 1984); *Black Venus* (London, 1985); *Wise Children* (1991).
2. Rosemary Jackson, *Fantasy: The Literature of Subversions* (London, 1981) p. 41.
3. Angela Carter in conversation with John Haffenden, *The Literary Review*, v (1984) p. 37.
4. Iris le Bessière, *Le Récit Fantastique: La Poétique de l'Incertain* (Paris, 1974) p. 62.
5. Jackson, op. cit., p. 23.
6. Lee Daniells, *Fear: A History of Horror in the Mass Media* (London, 1977).
7. Martin Barker, *A Haunt of Fears: The Strange History of the British Horror Comics Campaign* (London, 1984) p. 129.
8. Roald Dahl interviewed in *Twilight Zone* (Jan.–Feb. 1983).
9. David Punter, *The Literature of Terror: A History of Gothic Fictions from 1765 to the Present Day* (London, 1980) p. 130.
10. Ibid., p. 379.
11. Richard Dyer, 'Children of the Night: Vampirism as Homosexuality, Homosexuality as Vampirism', in Susanna Radstone (ed.), *Sweet Dreams: Sexuality, Gender and Popular Fiction* (London, 1988) p. 54.
12. Leslie Fiedler, *Love and Death in the American Novel* (New York, 1960).
13. Angela Carter, *Heroes and Villains* (London, 1969).
14. Punter, op. cit., p. 19.
15. Tania Modleski, *Loving with a Vengeance* (New York, 1984) pp. 81 and 83.
16. Paulina Palmer, *Contemporary Women's Fiction* (Brighton, 1989) p. 91.
17. Richard Dalby (ed.), *The Virago Book of Ghost Stories* (London, 1990).
18. Lisa Tuttle (ed.), *The Skin of Our Soul: New Horror Stories by Women* (London, 1990), Introduction.
19. Ibid., p. 5.

JOHN NICHOLSON

On Sex and Horror

> In the world of fantasy, in dreams and in tales of horror, things happened which were the work either of evil spirits or of perverted sexuality. Could it be that the lonely fantasies of masturbation . . . were taking over the collective fantasies of religion? . . . The horror story stood at the meeting of the ways, its ambiguous fascination explicable either in sexual terms as fear of parents or in religions terms as fear of the wrath of God and the works of the Devil.[1]

Horror has a special relationship with its audiences. Unlike science fiction, which rarely acknowledges feelings, let alone sex, horror relies on emotions. Horror is an emotion and it must arouse a reaction. Horror awakens hidden fears and desires. While science fiction uses the intellect as a tool, horror engulfs the reader. Science fiction explores the possibilities of technology and investigates the unknown to bring order. Horror neither explores nor investigates. It experiences – or rather its readers react.

In 1973, horrors were everywhere and unavoidable. Horror fiction also got a shock. The one film which transformed public consciousness had profound effects. *The Exorcist* created ripples still felt nearly 20 years later. In 1990 and 1991 the British courts were saturated by cases about children supposedly attacked sexually and satanically.

The second taboo transgressed irrevocably in 1973 was the public confession and insistence by women that they masturbated – and enjoyed it![2] Indeed the idea was so horrible that when *The Exorcist* showed a young girl on the verge of puberty exhibiting sexual proclivities the public accepted the explanation that she must be demonically possessed. Suddenly there were tangible proofs of the existence of the Devil, if not God.

The novel which began it all was quite explicit – more than the film – which is a point I will elaborate. The girl, Regan, was portrayed as suffering the stereotypical fate of masturbators: she became an addict. She masturbated so compulsively and with such relish that she had obviously lost her mind. She masturbated all the time, especially in front of others. When she was examined medically and psychiatrically 'she pulled up her nightgown, exposing her genitals. "Fuck me! Fuck me!" she screamed at the doctors, and with both her hands began masturbating frantically'.

She had begun to 'go wrong' when she urinated in front of her mother's guests. She defecated in front of authority figures. 'The priest heard the sound of diarrhetic voiding into plastic pants.' Her contempt for proper behaviour was inhuman. She forced her mother's face into her genitals. She used a crucifix as a dildo. She vomited on priests and spewed verbal filth at visitors.

At least this is how she behaved in the book. The film could show only some of this. It was a landmark because it showed *any* of it. Bad language in a major film in 1973 still evoked controversy – but from the mouth of an innocent young girl? We must remember that the battle for films to show female pubic hair was only won at the end of the 1960s while 30 years later male genitals have not become a regular feature of main-house films.

The image hit some nerve because a glut of films and books followed about young girls needing exorcism – in 'fact' as well as fiction.[3] All exhibited the same signs: sexual perversity in terms of abnormal ejaculations. Horror provided the perfect excuse for audiences to consume scenes of girls pissing, shitting, vomiting, and masturbating to orgasm. There was an obvious displacement by association since all these acts guarantee a person has lost control of their body. They were therefore possessed since no girl in her right mind would do any of these things.

Horror had long been a coded language. After *The Exorcist* a whole new area could be included. The element of domination had been a staple of horror but now it was linked to sexuality. Hollywood was inventing a new vocabulary for unacceptable behaviour.

The chief confusion of sexuality has received little comment though it is the basis of the horror. The novel claimed to be based on a true case but in real life the child was a boy. So it transpired that 'no girl in her right mind' had done these things. But then neither had the boy. Why the sex change for the book and film? Could it be that sexually outrageous acts by a boy would not need supernatural explanation? Faced with the publicly admitted horrific behaviour of women, Hollywood supplied an answer.

According to its publicity the film evoked a parallel response in its audiences. The stunt of having emergency staff to save the terrified move up a notch. Cinemas had to cope with patrons being physically overcome. Stories spread of vomiting, possession, even death in the auditorium.

Another effect of the impact of *The Exorcist* was the immediate obsolescence of the previously shocking. The languorous looks and heaving bosoms (even when bared) of Hammer films lost any claim to credibility. They looked silly. Suggestiveness that there might be something going on when vampires bit victims could only cause laughter in audiences rapidly used to on-screen acts of explicit sexual abnormality.

Besides, if the plot of films with lesbian vampires was stripped of period costume the situations were derisory. Victorian society might have been horrified by the possibility of predatory lesbians but it did not scare the West after the sexually liberated 1960s! Instead of drippy Victorian maidens in some Ruritania, the audiences could identify with the 'all-American girl next door'. Yet *The Exorcist* retained the religious framework of the Hammer films: a priest could still banish the Devil.

Three years after the success of *The Exorcist* another box office smash began with a pubertal heroine being disgraced when she wet herself publicly. *Carrie* revolved around a young girl who was so innocent – another pure all American girl next door – that she didn't know the blood trickling down her legs meant she had started to menstruate. Her schoolmates humiliated her again by drenching her in blood in front of the whole school. Nasty, explicit and never before shown and only possible in the context of horror. Again, the girl was just leaving her state of bodily innocence, which was regarded as the proper moment for her to awaken sexually. But Carrie, like Regan, was so aroused that she awoke other psychic powers. Regan was able to levitate, move objects without touching them and twist her head round on her neck. Carrie got her revenge by unleashing a psychic fury which destroyed much of her town. If there was any doubts that female sexuality in the context of horror was breaking taboos, in the same year as *Carrie* another main-house film, *The Man who Fell to Earth*, gave audiences a close-up of a girl urinating through her knickers. She had discovered she had been having sex with an alien, a monster. The depth of her horror was plain to see. However, there was no need for any supernatural explanation for her act. Her behaviour was entirely natural and understandable. (That also excused the watching audiences.) Everybody admitted the physical effect of being possessed by fear. This was a huge admission however – Mrs Radcliffe's heroines may have been frightened out of their wits but we had never needed the soggy pants.

If *The Exorcist, Carrie* and *The Man who Fell to Earth* were not strictly exploitative horror there could be no doubt about *The Last House on the Left*, which came out the year before *The Exorcist*. Certainly not a main-house release – indeed it was run out of the exploitation circuit in disgust – the film offered a familiar plot: a girl being victimised. Why the outrage? The teenager was forced to commit sexually degrading acts such as having sex with her friend, female. So what? She was instructed to piss her jeans while the tormentors – and audiences – watched the stain spreading. The revenge by her parents was a bloodbath, raising the question as to who were the monsters. The atmosphere was realistic, documentary, and lacked any suggestion of supernatural forces. The sexual degradation had only sexual motives: the tormentors wanted to see the girl wet herself. The context of sexual perversion was as unacceptable as satanic possession was acceptable.

The scale of the change in horror between 1973 and 1983 can be seen from a list of hits from the main houses and cult circuits.[4] Here were post-apocalyptic worlds full of inhuman monsters: suburban houses with white sticky stuff coating the walls, rape by tree trunk, a woman in the subway writhing as muck streamed from between her legs, a fat transvestite eating a fresh dog turd, a woman vomiting devotionally into a toilet and a musical starring a drag queen from outer space. After these what price Bela Lugosi?[5]

Or the horror novel? How could writing compete with images such as *Videodrome* where the hero inserted a video cassette into the gaping vagina-like slot in his chest?

Both special effects and the sheer daring of horror cinema left the horror novel bereft of imagery. American horror writers responded to the challenge by joining the cinema. After the success of *Carrie* all Stephen King's work was rushed onto the screen. Indeed the author himself was seen as an actor!

*   *   *

How did American horror and cinema horror affect British horror writing?

The English have a propensity for horrible thrills. For 30 years Hollywood horror was dominated by Hitchcock. The mixture of Daphne du Maurier and Laurence Olivier in *Rebecca* provided a yardstick for the psychological thriller – set in England. Hitchcock's last film, *Frenzy*, also revolved around a very English location: the capital's fruit and vegetable market, Covent Garden. There was irony in this vegetarian setting for dead human meat. A hint of cannibalism? One image of supreme nastiness remains: the killer in the back of a lorry getting a corpse out of a sack then snapping its rigor mortis finger to remove a ring. Maybe this gives us a clue as to why the English are so good at horror. Hitchcock represents a particular sort of horror, a nastiness rather than the sexual repression we have noted in the Americans. It is horror based on revulsion – like Shaun Hutson who can be relied on to provide a scene with slugs or some such clamminess. There is a nightmare sense of being at the mercy of something monstrous, a merciless relentless all-destroying power.

In a society which elevates secrecy and self-control is it surprising that the lure of the forbidden and unknown makes people obsessed with repression and abnormality? English society is so clearly at the mercy of invisible forces, if only the class system, that there is an endless supply of stimulants for conspiracy freaks and occult enthusiasts.

Both share a sort of perverse worship. They believe there is a vastly superior power which controls everything and everybody. Paranoia is the last refuge of the powerless.

Clairvoyance, remote viewing, precognition are early signs that the mind can manipulate, even destroy, physical and biological objects. Right now secret researches are being made in special laboratories by military and intelligence agencies because the psychic war will soon be on!

Thus Melanie in *Premonitions of an Inherited Mind* by Andrew Laurance. This is the first in a trilogy. It indicates how the action has moved on. From the 1960s British audiences had grown used to the idea of a secret war. James Bond, the secret agent with a licence to kill, had spawned not only films but nightly doses on television. Soon these agents became weirder: *The Avengers*, *Adam Adamant*, *The Man From Uncle* and a glut of lesser breeds, created a public acceptance. A topography of paranoia and kinkiness lurked under the surface. A cupboard in a drycleaners was the doorway to a world of bunkers and gadgets. Soon they were given a new generation of special powers, not just lasers disguised as cigarette lighters. They were trained to use psychic abilities as weapons, like the comic-book heroes X Men who could see through solids, burn with their glances and touch or fly without mechanical aid. These agents relied no on fists but on ESP.

Andrew Laurance's trilogy introduced an element which could not be shown, or even implied on screens. Melanie explains, 'The orgasm creates the energy which enables one to leave one's physical casing.' Hence she provokes her astral projection by 'masturbating feverishly' in a mirror. 'If you try to reproduce yourself a mirror helps.'

In *The Link*, volume two, the hero becomes aware of his psychic powers and of the powers competing to harness him. In a series of episodes he sees 'messengers', a pair of children about seven or eight years old, who materialised as they are coupling. They are not ghosts but the astral bodies projected by the real children. When he meets them in the flesh he asks the boy's mother, Melanie, if the children copulate to trigger their projection. 'Their bodies actually experience the pleasure of orgasm, otherwise they wouldn't do it.'

We have already met Melanie in the first book, where she deliberately gets pregnant then kills the father. Clearly we have moved beyond the satanic excuse for childish sexuality given in *The Exorcist*.

The Scar offers a female who revels in her sexuality and the power it gives her. First published in 1981, *The Scar* was one of eight novels by Gerald Suster. A beautiful teenager, Helen, moves into town. Soon everybody she befriends dies horribly. With the help of her sexual dupe, a resentful punk, Helen kills the élite of Thatcherland who hypocritically desire her. There are none of the social ironies of American horror as in the films of Romero, Craven or Spielberg. Helen is descended from a witch mutilated and murdered by her victims' ancestors. The revenge by seduction echoes *I Spit on your Grave*, a plot which reappeared regularly throughout the 1980s. Surprisingly nobody seems to have noticed that the traditional image of a serial killer is female. What is noteworthy is how *The Scar*'s twist, of making the villain a woman, enables a parade of female sexual powers. Helen is not only powerfully sexed – she chooses her partners and initiates sex – but is also the controlling partner.

He wanted her body to acknowledge him as master and to crown him king with screams of pleasure she couldn't suppress. Yet even as he thrust he was alert to the suspicion not that he was penetrating her but that she was enclosing him.

Helen enjoys her orgasms. She comes before, during and after fucking. She has orgasms without partners. Is she a masturbator driven mad by Satan? Hardly. Firstly she gets aroused by evil. Secondly she enjoys it. She dies unrepentant and satisfied.

Yet if Helen is a monster so is her killer. He, too, is a descendant of The Witch Finder General. He is killed by a policeman as he is about to kill Helen's little daughter who also bears the witch's scar.

Suster sets *The Offering* in another idyllic English village. The ancient curse is the power inside an artefact. It is the centrepiece for a secret cult (conspiracy) of female worshippers continuing practices which activate psychic powers. These are fed by the sacrifice of men's genitals. A sect of castrating women.

Striker is the name of the narrator, who discovers his psychic power while at an English boarding school when he causes the death of the headmaster. The story is remarkable for its description in passing of a non-mysterious horror: the way the English treat their children. In New York, Striker is taken up by a secret group researching 'mutants' (humans who have evolved). A detailed scientific explanation is given for the powers. It turns out the mutant monsters are really being manipulated by the government, by monster powers.

As usual it is hard to avoid thinking of film equivalents: *Scanners* by Cronenberg, *Firestarter* from Stephen King's novel and *The Fury* from a novel by John Farris, and indeed, Suster's early books read more like film scripts. His next titles, *The Block* and *The Force*, were longer (*The Force* is 367 pages) and more ambitious. Both are complicated and set in institutions: an apartment building and a large firm. They have large casts, which only draws attention to the lack of characterisation.

By contrast, *Necromancer* shows a novelist's skills. Robert Holdstock later moved from the horror genre to develop the fantastical themes touched on in *Necromancer* and appeal to a different audience with *Mythago Wood*. At the other extreme he showed he was capable of potboilers by writing a series under a pseudonym, *The Night Hunter* by Robert Faulcon. In five books, which were issued in two batches, he exploited some themes he had previously treated seriously. The plot was absolute stock: a struggle between goodies and baddies, chases and psychic powers. The blurbs capture the tone: 'One man against the monstrous evil of the occult'; 'Both the evil and the innocent were summoned to the hellborn gathering'; 'Beneath the earth a spider-web of ancient evil – soon to be awakened.' There was scope for set episodes (and perhaps a television spin-off?) dealing with specific local colour: the Ghost Dance Red Indians. The main figure was a sort of psychic private eye. The powers and the procedure were the usual: psychic and sex. The story raced along and provided readers with a cracking good yarn.

Necromancer's plot contains familiar elements but Holdstock is original in his ideas and treatment. He develops the secret research into dormant powers by relating it to Earth mysteries.

> He did not acknowledge that there might be some unknown forms of energy eluding detection except in the tentative relationships of stones, leys and underground streams. He did accept that, under certain circumstances, known energy forms could be elusive. And it was people like dowsers and sensitive . . . who might be the 'machines' of a new technology, a technology for reading more from standing stones than that which the eye could see and the mind could imagine.

There is a reference to *The Stone Tape*, a television play which had dramatically illustrated the notion of memories as ghosts trapped inside the stones of buildings.[6] The ancient surviving artefact is in a church. A megalith is embedded in the earth and its tip, projecting above the floor and converted into a font, is still active. At times people commit suicide to fill the font with their blood. A baptism goes wrong when a baby's head hits the font. The child lives, although pathologically withdrawn, and its mother believes its spirit is trapped inside the font. An American scientific researcher, whose open-minded attitude is quoted above, investigates. By contrast, the father is an Englishman whose proper behaviour, emotionally dead, extends to an inability to refer to his wife by her name. He habitually calls her 'my wife'. He regards her belief about their son being trapped inside the font as madness. He believes the boy is trapped inside himself. The daughter, almost 16, is on the verge of expulsion for aggressive behaviour. She is open about her sexuality but suffers from nightmares that make her wet herself in arousal and terror. The boy, who refuses to speak or walk, expresses himself by biting through his finger: a happy English family.

A psychic describing herself as a necromancer is enrolled to 'tap' the stone. She recounts how touching stones overwhelms her, 'a strange sort of orgasm. It was beautiful in a cruel sort of way.' There is a struggle between psychic forces. In this case the villain is a demon imprisoned in the stone. It is manipulating people and killing them or making them kill themselves. It possesses the boy, who behaves destructively and swears – just like Regan. Yet we get no compulsive masturbating, pissing or shitting. No filth, just normal vomit. The demon feeds on fear, a sort of psychic vampire, 'possessed by something we don't really understand, except in such words as Ancient God, Dark Power, and Supernatural Force'. This evil imprisoned by ritual use of a code or spell – a prayer – what would to Christianity be an exorcism. However, the key can turn the opposite way and unlock the prison, releasing the forces of havoc. The resulting devastation is total.

Soon ancient stones and sites became regular plot devices. In *The Worm Stone* the way the ancient evil re-enters the world is explicit. The heroine describes the start of her possession. She copulated during a picnic at a site.

> It sounds silly, but I had some sort of vision, hallucination, God, I don't know. I'd started to come. It was incredible, I've never come so strongly in my life. It was beautiful. I expect you could feel it. I was right in the middle of it and it felt as though it would go on for ages when it stopped and I had this awful feeling of emptiness and everything went blank. I thought, Oh God, this is stupid – I'm going to pass out in the middle of my climax. And then I saw this thing.

By the early 1980s English horror novels were again showing signs of becoming clichéd. They were again relying on a kind of antiquarianist escape clause. The Hammer vampire or Poe curse had been replaced by another sort of curse or psychic vampirism. The supernatural was being replaced by the unnatural, which reflected the paranoia that science had unleashed monsters.

Everybody in Britain knows Stephen King but few have heard of Guy N. Smith? Yet he is probably Britain's most prolific and biggest selling horror novelist, with more than 30 titles. These include many series on the theme of unnatural creatures. *Killer Crabs*, *Origin of the Crabs*, *Crabs on the Rampage*. The *Sabat* series is about witches and there is also a set of werewolf novels.

In 1981, Smith produced *Warhead* whose front cover showed a skull with a missile sticking into its mouth while the tip poked out of the top. The ultimate penetration by the ultimate weapon? The legend offered: 'The old gods were threatening mankind with the ultimate holocaust.' The blurb tells potential buyers, 'But there was another power that could destroy utterly. Created by man it lay dormant but always ready.' More ancient psychic demons? No. 'Underground, fuelled and targeted, it lurked in secret launch silos.'

The mixture now includes psychic forces, mad science and an equation between the nuclear armageddon and Earth mysteries. Had the End of the World happened before and were the ancient sites something to do with saving Earth? It is necessary to re-awaken powers through procedures, usually sexual, then certain places can help because of their potency. Setting aside the arcane mixture which sustained mystical and Fortean magazines for more than a quarter of a century, we have here much in the way of sites as ancient power points which can be re-activated by the correct combination.

Melanie and Helen, like Regan and Carrie, not only have special powers linked to sex but their abilities are inherited. Here the British and Americans diverge. The newcomers to the continent have no archaeology. Instead the original inhabitants are familiar with the land. People have an ancient genetic power which is still inside waiting to be revived.

During the hippie period interest in LSD was in terms of it being a new type of drug. It was a 'psychedelic' or consciousness expanding mechanism. Psychedelics would chemically trigger off latent powers. The leap was into biology. These abilities were supposed to be in the silent part of the mind (the silent majority) where they lay dormant. They were benevolent lurkers at the threshold. Mankind had once been as intelligent as aliens from outer space. It could communicate again if it restored its whole intelligence. In the meantime a secret few descendants had never lost those powers, witness Melanie and Helen.

In real life this genetic dream relates to another English obsession: genealogy. Such an obsession with origins and continuity was upheld and disturbed by the power of sex-induced Earth mysteries.

The paranoia of the nuclear age suggested that man was interfering in God's work. Proof was the fear of biological monsters. For every lost continent full of giant apes there were plagues of mutant creatures swarming over the planet: killer crabs and slugs were the latest in the genealogy which included freak plants like triffids. Nature could become monstrous just as supernature, the biological heaven, could produce angels with non-human powers. The chemically induced new human, the psychic mutant, was the other side of the same coin.

The new intelligence was not just evolutionary but could give birth to a new species. 'Our consciousnesses linked up, formed a new entity that was not human, and wasn't inhuman either.'[7] If this was what was going on in experiments conducted by Harvard personnel in 1963 what might not happen once the drug was used by anybody? The advocates preached it would spread like an infection, a virus. Was this the biological counterpart of the domino theory?

By the 1980s horror had become big business. Here was a viral infection spreading out of control! In the late 1960s it had been like belonging to a secret society to admit you read horror. Few publishers and fewer shops bothered. When Derek 'Bram' Stokes in his early twenties was working in one of the Popular Book centres (half price back when returned), he ran a side line: The Vault of Horror. Realising there was a market he spread his importing of American paperbacks to include science fiction. Within six years he had moved twice and expanded tenfold. By the 1980s horror was on every paperback list and in every town. Horror had its own section, even a livery: every cover was black. Was horror turning into a huge industry like science fiction?

The kinky and criminal – the refusal to obey nature's laws – were stock in horror. Likewise sexuality in children could be described in the guise of perversity. Odd and inexplicable behaviour was allowed with the excuse of horror. In reality, it was only odd and inexplicable because people refused to admit it was neither. Instead they preferred much more bizarre explanations.

Alan Garner's books for youngsters revolve around awakening special powers: supernaturally and sexually. His first books in the

1960s were creepy precisely because the sexuality was unstated. *The Owl Service* (1973) was as cryptic as *The Turn of the Screw*, being full of 'strange goings on' with sexual hints. By 1975 in *Red Shift*, his characters were more explicitly drawn and reflected the changed social climate.

A pair of young lovers slip back and forwards in time. They are lovers in the physical sense too. At the start of the book the girl betrays her pregnancy by being dramatically sick. However, hers is no demonic filth manifesting. Her behaviour is natural while the horror is the monstrous attitude of her parents who regard her as a monster for behaving naturally. In 1976, *The Story of the Weasel* was set in *Turn of the Screw* period dress. A brother and sister are an odd couple. She loves him and they consummate. She has their child. The reviewers enthused about 'sadism, madness and mutilation. . . . dark gothic doings . . . add . . . immeasurably to their erotic and mysterious power'. *Waterland* by Graham Swift (1983) had similar undertones, including incest and a baby.

By 1981, a young girl did not have to be demonically possessed to exercise sexual powers. The main character in *The Birthday Treat* is a 12-year-old girl. Admittedly she is an American who has to live in England. Nevertheless her adventures are a long way from Regan. She is secretly destroying the neighbourhood. She engineers assaults on the children in her group, often lethally. To help her she needs the help of a boy. He sets his price: she must show him her pants. As she does so she wonders how much more cruelty she can inflict. Looking at the agitated boy 'something like an enormous smile began in her stomach, rose up fluttering her chest, blossomed on her face'.

The prestigious Maugham Award for 1976 went to a collection of short stories which was 'rapturously received . . . dark and dangerous . . . gruesome . . . perverted lives'. Because the judges were literary people unaware of horror, they dutifully read a story about a 14-year-old boy's sexual awakening told in a dead-pan tone familiar to horror fans. He finally learns how to fuck and orgasms inside his younger sister. She corrects him after his ignorant attempts. 'I know where it goes. I know where the hole is.' The other stories contained elements which were as familiar to horror readers as they were exotic to followers of literature. The author was Ian McEwan.

McEwan's second collection provided more shocks for such readers. Perversions were the staple, presented in a matter-of-fact way which evoked horror. Literature lovers were introduced to a nurse who initiates a sleazoid into her 'wants' and his unacknowledged tastes. She sexually degrades him, pissing on him during sex. Literature now included females who openly played sexual games previously so horrific and perverted they needed the excuse of satanic possession! Women enjoyed behaviour regarded as perverse. They didn't have to be possessed by demons or terrified out of their wits – they pissed for erotic effect. McEwan's stories are full of such horrific behaviour.

The Cement Garden was McEwan's first full-length novel. It is a psychotically nasty place. A family has become isolated and when the last parent dies the children keep her by walling up her corpse in the cellar. They cement over everything – the physical repression reflecting their emotional state.

The eldest children, Julie, who is 17, and Jack the narrator, who is 14, play 'The Game' with Sue, who is 12. They all pretend Sue is a specimen from outer space. The Game 'climaxes' in them taking turns to masturbate Sue. As the boy gets older he prefers to withdraw to masturbate, thinking 'of Julie's pale brown fingers between Sue's legs'.

Jack and Julie have their own games. He terrifies her 'coming to get you'. Julie 'stares at the huge filthy gloves', which overpower her so much she loses control: 'One hand plucked at the coarse material of the glove. As I moved forward to be in a better position to hold her down, I felt hot liquid spreading over my knee.'

Julie performs a Regan-like exhibitionist act in front of the family. Though it is received as innocent and delightful, its effect on Jack is undeniably sexual. When Julie performs a cartwheel,

> Her skirt fell down over her head. Her knickers showed a brilliant white against the pale-brown skin of her legs and I could see how the material bunched in little pleats around the elastic that clung to her flat, muscular belly. A few black hairs curled out from the white crotch. Her legs, which were together at first, now moved slowly apart like giant arms.

Eventually matters reach a conclusion. Julie's frustrated man friend smashes the cement to expose the rotting corpse. His thuds coincide with the thrusts of Julie and Jack consummating to the delight of their siblings. As they finish they hear the police cars. The horror, the real world, is about to break in. In McEwan's world, as in *The Weasel* or *The Birthday Treat*, there are no external horrors.

No bug-eyed monsters, no supernatural forces, simply the unnatural. Nastiness and creepiness take place in the setting of real life. The unnatural creatures are children.

The sexual element of horror, and vice versa, was now in the open. The coded language of pubertal girls doing perverse sexual acts no longer automatically proved they were possessed by unearthly forces. Were they evil or just perverts?

Hollywood and American horror novels did offer a new twist. Heroines did not have sexual feelings so when they experienced orgasm without a partner they were being raped psychically. Involuntary climaxes were the stars of *The Entity* and *The Searing*. The climaxes of the victims in *The Institution* are so physical they gush out as their life-blood. The victims in *Whispers* are not responsible for their climaxes because they are controlled by behavioural code words. Even the mother in *Poltergeist* was assaulted when she lay on her bed wearing no skirt. Invisible forces lifted her sweater and opened her thighs so audiences focused on her heaving crotch.

Nancy Friday produced more documentary confessions during the next 20 years, culminating in *Women on Top*. This was the generation after Regan and Carrie with women who no longer felt guilt. Here was a parade of perverted women in real life. Their sexual imaginings were recounted in a matter-of-fact way. These scenarios, like horror stories, were useless unless they provoked an emotional and physical effect. Successful business women detailed how they regularly spent hours photographing themselves with dildoes in their anuses. And that was apart from the fantasy.

The narrator of Iain Banks's *The Wasp Factory* is a 16-year-old boy who is the sole human in a world of totemic animals, a monster among monstrosities. The story is set in one of those lost places, like *The Cement Garden* or *Waterland*, which are on the edge of the world. In this case, it is a desolate coast off Scotland. The few humans in the nearby village ignore the narrator and his solitary parent. He has the characteristics of the other flora and fauna: left-overs, social debris like the carcasses which litter the waste land. The narrator lays a mythology over the topography of despair. He maps it out with personal fetishes: skulls on posts on which he ceremonially urinates. We are inside a mind of madness, childish, cruel, nasty and perverse. As savage and barbaric as Kurtz in *Heart of Darkness* who goes native. It does not come as a surprise to learn the boy has already killed humans.

Two years after I killed Blyth I murdered my younger brother Paul for quite different and more fundamental reasons . . . a year after that I did for my young cousin Esmeralda. That's my score to date. Three. I haven't killed anybody for years and don't intend to ever again. It was just a phase I was going through.

The complicated mythology of tortured creatures relates to his attempt to make his own order or creation out of the perversity surrounding him. His own life is officially ignored, his parents did not register him, so he attends no school.[8]

He suffered a ghastly denial as a child when a dog bit off his genitals. Consequently he is reduced to urinating like a woman, squatting. This he does even when drunk in public, followed by copious vomiting. No satanic possession but too much beer! There are more loathsome twists to this story – the childhood mutilation is a lie. His father is the mad creature–torturer who made tiny marzipan genitals to deceive his daughter.

The Wasp Factory earned raves and disgust but Banks would move away from the horrific and perverse towards the fantastical or science fiction in his later novels.

*   *   *

By the mid 1980s a new British horror had emerged. If there is one element which can be isolated from Alan Garner, *The Birthday Treat*, *The Story of the Weasel*, *Waterland*, *The Cement Garden* and *The Wasp Factory*, it is perversion and murder in the world of children. Could this have any relation to the previous observations about the twisted way the English treat their children? Is there any relation between these horrors and another sort of horror which emerged next, noticeably among British writers? Can we see any social echoes in the cross-over of stock from horror to literature, years before they were claimed for *American Psycho*?

Many of the writers mentioned here are lesser-known even in the horror genre. Nick Sharman certainly merits that comment despite the brave puff, 'Stephen King and James Herbert . . . have a chilling challenger . . . Nick Sharman'. *The Switch* was a workmanlike horror about a girl and her parents being taken over, possessed, literally. 'Hauntings' are revealed as a conspiracy to inhabit their bodies. People who interfere are killed mysteriously. It turns out that the doctor is the villain. She is central to the conspiracy as are her son, daughter and husband. The son intends to 'switch' the spirits of his dead father and sister into living bodies. He chooses these victims because the heroine's father had caused their deaths in a car crash. The youth's mediumistic powers are related to his sexual feeling for his sister. They were lovers and are having a baby.

Apart from some twists on the idea of possession (as a type of forcible re-incarnation) this story is useful as an example of another sort of switch. The real world is fantasy while the person accused of imagining things knows the truth. People who realise there is a conspiracy are killed or dismissed as mad. Consequently when the switch occurs there is a moment of shock horror: the extent of the evil is revealed. Also the extent to which the ignorant dupes have been accomplices.

This is a staple device in horror. The misunderstood messenger is treated as mad, evil or alien. To the normal world the truth is mad, outlawed, criminal, perverse, monstrous, horrific – because the normal world is mad, illegal. Yet there is a further dimension familiar to every horror fan: the reader's relationship to this quandary. The reader is another powerless onlooker, part victim, part accomplice. The readers know but can't warn, therefore they are part of the perversion before the reversal. Not that the reversal is inevitable. Horror doesn't always end happily. The truth doesn't always triumph. The powerless onlookers are forced to watch the approach of the inevitable catastrophe. They share the plight of the solitary mad person or alien. The horror of being right but treated as wrong, of not being believed, will end if the warning is heeded and everybody wakes. Then they will see a monstrosity has been in control – of minds, bodies, towns, countries. . . . The reversal is total and revolutionary. The real villain is the authority figure, normality.

Normality is evil while the truth is a troublemaker. This situation provides plenty of opportunities for paradox and bitter irony. The fake control, the loss of contact with reality, the separation of the mind from feelings are clinical symptoms.

The glut of 'slasher' movies and books had a strange echo. In real life in the early 1980s a new phenomenon was identified: the serial killer. Suddenly everything transformed. Many of the plots described here are about figures who must now be re-categorised. The narrator of *The Wasp Factory* is a serial killer. So is Helen in *The Scar*.

In novels, killers were no longer used simply as plot devices.

Another shift took place – from the supernatural we had moved to the unnatural creatures, now the focus became sharper. Most remarkably the change came from England. We have seen how English novelists explored a previously taboo area: childish sexuality. The perversity they found now surfaced in another form. Between 1982 and 1984 a surprising number of novels appeared in England with a plot that was very different. The peculiarity was that these novels shared the same new plot! All were strangely horrible and concerned lethal perversity.

That so many writers attempted to portray the mind of a ghastly murderer at the same time may be dismissed as coincidence. It is certainly uncanny. The less sceptical may wonder if there was some malaise in Britain in the early 1980s. Again it may be coincidental that the second term of Thatcherism began in 1983 after a war fought for national pride. The characteristic shared by these fictional killers is their total split from the rest of the world coupled with their ferocious belief in their moral imperative. *Jacqui, The Banquet, The Sandman, The Wasp Factory, The Cement Garden, The Watcher* and McEwan's short stories all depict moral disorder of pathological proportions which must destroy all opposition or doubt. There is no alternative. Most of the accounts of atrocities are narrated in the first person to increase the sensation of being inside the mind of the killer. All are eager to make the readers appreciate them. They do not seek understanding but recognition. They deserve recognition. They regard themselves as normal, proper, even as benefactors.

They share the same tone of sweet reasonableness as they recount ghastliness. Yet one can sense how thin is this surface. Underneath swirls burning rage! They are motivated not by lust to murder but by moral indignation. They are driven by self-righteousness to a perverse degree. The Yorkshire Ripper, active between 1975 and 1981, claimed he was simply 'cleaning the streets' of immoral – and therefore worthless – women.

Come the Night was originally published in 1984 as *Chainsaw Terror*. A boy peeps on his parents as they row in their bedroom. The wife is leaving and the husband prevents her. He attacks her brutally, finishing by stabbing her to death with a shard of mirror. Then he cuts his own throat. 'He felt his bladder give out, the warm urine running down his leg and then, as blackness finally swept over him, his sphincter muscle failed.' Readers accept this as pathology. Of course everybody knows the ultimate loss of control is death. Except we have come a long way from the introduction of such matters as a sign of satanic possession. We have accepted such behaviour as natural when terrified. We have even acknowledged that some people find sexual pleasure in perversion. Now we see it as the proof of death. Soon such descriptions will be obligatory in horror.

The boy goes in to look at the charnel room. 'The stench which flooded over him was almost palpable and he recoiled momentarily, coughing as the pungent coppery odour of blood and the even more powerful stench of excrement assaulted his nostrils.'

He withdraws into himself. He is self-possessed. When his sister comes home to this scene she goes into a state near catatonia. Both victims separate themselves from the outside world in mutual support. After five years the sister begins to re-build a normal life with a boyfriend. The brother's focus however is on his sister. He becomes aroused just watching her preparing a meal. When she has a bath he watches her through a peephole. After she takes her sleeping drugs he creeps into her room to sniff her underwear. He knows she will not wake as he uncovers her to look at her naked body.

He cannot face the possibility of his sister leaving so he re-enacts the scene he saw performed by his parents. Again we get *schaden-freude*, both by the characters and by the voyeurs, the readers: 'her clothes drenched in blood, she noticed the puddle of urine between her legs'. Realising she is dying she deliberately focuses on her lover-brother, hacking away until he beheads her,

> [she] noticed that he had a strong erection. He looked at the blood splattered body of Maureen and found that the throbbing between his legs was even more powerful but he tried to force the thoughts to the back of his mind. He had other things to do.

He embarks on a programme of street cleaning. He brings prostitutes home to show them the rotting head of his sister. As they react he thrusts his tool into their bodies. The sexual confusion means the tool he uses is a chainsaw. Their bodies explode literally in a total body spasm.

Jacqui is presented in the form of a monologue, taking us inside the mind of a monster. As he talks to us he builds up layer on layer of horror. His version of normality is so far removed from that of the world – and presumably of the readers – that the suspense becomes unbearable. He keeps telling us that he had to kill his girlfriend and as he recounts their story he continually emphasises how right his behaviour was compared with hers. The readers listen powerless to warn the unsuspecting victim that she is living with a monster and her death is inevitable. The supreme irony is the madman's respectability. He never tires of emphasising how his behaviour is proper while the girl is disgusting.

> God knows how she was cramming a five-month pregnancy into skintight jeans, the poor baby must have been stifled. . . . When I laid her out in her tomb I bought beautiful things for her, a long black silk skirt and a beautiful honey coloured silk blouse.

What 'tombs'? Her corpse lies at the bottom of his kitchen's deep freeze for a year. Having investigated all ways of disposing of the body the madman picks 'the ancient Egyptian' method: embalming. He takes out the corpse, thaws it and cuts it open. The innards are thrown into a wine-fermenting plastic drum.

'If you put it in a horror movie and showed it to the Ancient Egyptians, they'd have wondered what you were going on about.' *The Sandman* delves even more deeply into horrors and irony.

> I have killed 18 men and women . . . I am an artist. My work has been shown on TV and acclaimed as a national scandal. The popular press has followed my career with feverish enthusiasm. My work has been reviewed in several languages. I am celebrated.

The killer is much more self-conscious and critical than in *Jacqui*. He knows he is doing evil and is philosophical, almost religious about his 'work', his mission. He sees himself as a manifestation which comes in many shapes and guises. He is an incarnation. Is he therefore possessed? He considers himself rational and fully aware. He chooses to kill. When he was rehearsing he saw himself as a conjurer who makes people disappear. He wandered the streets and, in his imagination, chose victims.

> My moment to reveal an imaginary revolver or knife. Blades sprang from the tips of my shoes. Acid spat from my buttonhole. My thumbs were loaded pistols. I slaughtered men and women at random. . . . It was a macabre game for a bright young man.

As the Sandman he brings sleep. He sets himself up to begin his work in earnest. He has a laugh at the expense of the stereotype of the habitual or serial killer.

Killers, I knew from my boyhood visits to the cinema, dwelt in basements ugly as caves, full of broken bottles and bundles of damp newspaper. They crouched at smeared windows and stared up at the feet of the people who passed on the street above. . . . The rooms I chose . . . were small and pretty. The chairs were sweet and plump . . . here I would sit and contemplate murder in comfort.

Soon he is massacring strangers in batches: 'In that moment I felt as huge as an angel watching over the slumbering world.' The Sandman's alienation grows from isolation in a seaside boarding-house with a mother who gets madder. His companion, a girl slightly older than him, sets her mark on his sexuality. She delights in being dominated and progresses to other perversions until she is killed by her husband, a butcher, who puts her carcass in his freezer.

The madmen in *Jacqui* and *The Sandman* live happily ever after. They could be your neighbour.

Though the author of *The Banquet* is a woman, the only voice to speak in the first person is a man. This is not because the woman is the victim – her thoughts are reported. There is an intense feeling between them which makes them consenting. 'Perhaps he will kill me, she thought, her eyes wide and strange, perhaps he will. And she was more exhilarated and terrified than at any time in her life.' As we have seen, horror fiction has no shortage of females who kill either or both sexes. Likewise for real-life murderers gender is not an issue. The thrill is dominance.

In *The Banquet* the pattern is classic. The predator, the lover, stalks a victim. The irony in this novel is that the processes are seen as so similar as to be interchangeable. The vocabulary is full of metaphors and similes for passion *as eating*. True love is all-devouring. Their love affair follows the traditional route: 'at first . . . a rapport . . . eager and fragile, then deepening to a consuming passion'. The girl also realises their desire to unite is literal. 'Our frenzy of possession could only be eased by a total consumption of one another – mind, flesh and soul.' They inhabit a world of sensual pleasures, joy, laughter, good living. There is no sexual oddness, no nastiness, no perversion. There is no agent of death, no crazy with a chainsaw or knives. Only appetite.

In fact he doesn't kill her. She falls down stairs and breaks her neck. Yet the logical climax follows. The lovers have their ultimate banquet, uniting in a love-feast. 'Set out beside him was a small covered dish.'

The Banquet is by the author of *The Story of the Weasel*. Both novels describe love in a world set apart. In *The Banquet* there is an echo of childish perversity. A 15-year-old girl suddenly appears at an adult party and, Regan-like, performs an act of perverse exhibitionism. It turns out it was in revenge for being sexually abused by her uncle.

These writers, Slaughter, Gibson, Rush, Swift, Banks, McEwan, Garner, are not regarded as horror writers. The horrors they describe are increased precisely because the context of horror is removed. Similar scenes may have been stock in horror but there was the escape clause of *condemnation*. These new writers offer a world *without* moral judgement. Regan and Carrie could not be further apart from little girls who help their brothers with 'I know where it goes'. But there is a further notch. These novels are presented as real life, unlike much horror. This is how people really behave. The use of the confessional–documentary device increases this impression. If these stories were not literature they would belong in the outer regions of exploitative pulp.

This point can be expanded by thinking of Dennis Wheatley who dominated the horror and satanism area from 1935, with *The Devil Rides Out*, until the 1970s when he edited the *Dennis Wheatley Library of the Occult*, containing more than 40 titles, for Sphere paperbacks. Wheatley left no doubt that the people and antics he described so often and luridly should be condemned. The same stern prurience dominated *The Exorcist*, which otherwise dealt in subject matter that could only be found in highly specialised perversion or pornography.

The most powerful of these madman novels is *The Watcher*. It stands between the psychic horrors and the interior horrors of killers. It was first published in America in 1982 and is set in the New York area. However, it was written by an Eton and Oxford Scotsman.

The trigger as always is simple, trivial and unremarkable. The hero becomes alienated by chance as he is outside his house. Looking up at a window he watches his wife undressing. He imagines how it would be for a voyeur, 'I was an alien pair of eyes. She was unknown, forbidden territory, inviting exploration. Like some Peeping Tom scarcely able to believe his luck I concentrated my whole gaze on that bathroom window, determined to miss nothing.' It turns out she knew he was watching and had deliberately exhibited herself. Both are sexual conspirators.

But he is in an alien world, a world where he is no longer himself. A world where his actions are horrendous. Next morning he leaves his sleeping wife, goes downstairs and butchers their dogs. He puts the bits in a box as a present for her and leaves.

He has a sort of breakdown or, in non-psychiatric terms, sees visions. He hears noises at night in his anonymous boarding-house room. It vibrates to the rhythm of a masturbating young woman behind a screen in the corner. '"Fuck me" she howls against the din, "under the tail, sweet Jesus!" Faster, faster, rocking violently, to and fro, in, out – slipping it to herself, she reaches her solitary climax in a long defiant snarl of ecstasy.' He goes to look and finds instead the maggot-squirming body of a ten-year-old girl with a vent in her abdomen, 'loose grayish knots of intestine spilled over into her hardly pubescent groin'.

Under hypnosis he 'releases' at least six personalities (he is possessed in the non-supernatural sense). The idea of multiple personality was becoming the new explanation for serial killers. They were not possessed by devils and not schizophrenics like Jekyll and Hyde, nor psychotics – they were inhabited by many personalities.

These six personalities span time. The most recent is a half-breed Cherokee. The hero tracks him down and discovers that he really existed. More extraordinary, the Indian vanished at exactly the same instant the hero was born. This re-incarnatory instant coincides with another death and birth: the dropping of the atomic bomb on Hiroshima. Are the personalities sequential and is there any other link? He realises the Indian believed he was a Watcher, a sort of cosmic guardian. The hero therefore inherits this role: of watching for signs that the world is ending, this time for certain. He learns that the first incarnation was tricked into parting with a talisman. This must be recovered to save Earth. There is knowledge of an act so monstrous it generates a need for atonement. This need takes on a life of its own. It is a psychic creature which ignores time and space. It can possess persons or places.

Of course this mystical interpretation is at odds with the psychiatric version. *The Watcher* operates on different levels of reality. Not only does it play off the contradictory views of events by letting the readers hear the hero's own voice and then the psychiatrist's notes, but it also puts readers in a new variation of suspense. They have to make their own choice about what is real. Gradually and subtly we notice the two accounts of the same events diverge until we are not sure who is telling the truth.We are courted by rival conspiracies. We become peepers as we see what is in the secret notes of the psychiatrist, who is manipulating the patient with the collusion of his wife and friendly doctor. This paranoia, of the reader, is increased by the hero's account of how he uncovers another secret side to the psychiatrist. He finds a hidden library containing works of deviance: sexual and religious. An illustration shows a nun committing fellatio while being penetrated by a girl with a dog's head. The Watcher's visions also involve mixtures of a half dog, half woman. Are the psychiatrist and his female assistant planting this deliberately or do they belong to some ancient sect of heretical perverts?

The young dog-woman is the key between the conflicting realities. Does she come to his seedy rooming house to betray the psychiatrist or is she part of the psychiatrist's conspiracy against The Watcher? Does she really come or is it all part of his fantasy about her? Their coupling synthesises many strands, real or imagined. She has doglike attributes: hair down her spine and she behaves like a bitch in heat. 'Moisture ran down the inside of her thighs, gushing out of her like a stream.' She emits 'grunts and cries' as she 'began to circle around . . . on all fours nosing and nipping and licking me all over'. He grabs her hair, bites her neck and mounts her 'doggie style'. They set up the room as a sex aid where they behave like animals. He watches her from behind the screen with 'one hand curled between her thighs and her livid tongue lolling out of the corner of her mouth, lips all frothy with white stuff' and howling.

To The Watcher her visit is real and 'exorcises' the confusion he had when he first used the room. His sense of mission reinforced, he attacks the psychiatrist. He knows the psychiatrist is the re-embodiment of the figure who, for centuries, has tried to thwart his mission to save Earth. But, he realises, 'who would believe me?' in preference to the authority figure? What he asserts is so unimaginable it will be regarded as the fantasy of a madman. The climax leaves the choice to the reader. The Watcher goes off to fulfil his messianic role.

The ultimate horror must be the extinction of all life: doomsday.

Horror often deals with this fear in metaphoric terms. In 1987, *The Power* took Armageddon as its literal starting point. The author, Ian Watson, was introduced to readers as being involved, in real life, with social and disarmament politics and *The Power* has a very recognisable English setting: a 'wimmins' peace camp outside an American nuclear base, hunt saboteurs, student activitists. Watson's next novel approached The End from an ecological angle.

The Power makes full use of horror effects, whereas *The Watcher* dealt in psychological 'subtleties' in terror and played with the reader. *The Power* is unequalled for its parade of sexual confusion as a metaphor for evil. Jenni, the 35-year-old heroine, is a sexual mess. This manifests itself in her confusion about her natural functions. On the toilet she feels a long sausage slide out of her. Moments later in the kitchen she has to squat urgently to pour out a mess on to newspapers quickly spread on the floor. There is no doubt this is shit so what was 'the toilet thing'? She realises it must have been 'born' from her vagina and finally she takes to stalking the countryside and murdering: a monster of perversity.

But there are other killers lurking in the hedgerows. If Jenni, the respectable primary school teacher, conceals horrors so does the picture-book English village.

> Behind almost every other herd of cows there seemed to lurk some item of the next world war. To city dwellers the extent of doomsday packaging was virtually invisible. Not in the green and pleasant land, once you looked beyond the scenery.

Behind the façade of essential England we find the now familiar association of the nuclear holocaust with some atavistic religious rite. The blurb's appeal has nothing to do with libertarian politics and everything to do with horror: 'An ancient Power awakes. . . . A modern evil mushrooms into apocalypse. . . . Cocooned in a nightmare world the village of Melfort waits, as The Power feeds on the death and destruction, fuelling its gross appetite.'

The monstrous happens. Jenni witnesses a bomb explode, the nuclear war is taking place. Jenni's response is natural, she pisses herself in terror like the woman faced with the unthinkable in *The Man who Fell to Earth*. In post-apocalyptic England perversion is the norm. A priest's decapitated head vomits, Regan-like. Except that in Jenni's functionally confused world vomit takes second place. The mouth vomits excrement.

Survivors, the undead, stagger zombie-like, keeping up a parody of normal life and even spending the evenings in the village pub. Their loss of human status is signified by their loss of control over their natural functions: they leak urine and excrete continually like incontinent babies or seniles. People turn to Jenni to save them. Didn't she have a miraculous birth, the Madonna of the Toilet? We get a scene that could never be filmed. Jenni has to copulate with a dead man. *It* insists Jenni makes its penis erect otherwise the act can't happen. To help herself she uses her secret masturbatory fantasy: being forcibly masturbated by her college friend, a nurse. The climax is a collector's item. A bucket full of shit whizzes up a well – or Jenni's throat. As it surfaces (shit? vomit?) it ejaculates out of Jenni's mouth over her partner.

Horrible certainly. Yet it is essential to stress that all this perversity is not simply for effect but is the result of a very complicated ideological plot. English political attitudes had become perverted by the late 1980s.

By the end of the book Jenni reaches a sort of peace. When she sees another nuclear flash she pisses herself again. However, this time she is not disturbed and lets nature take its course. The sun will dry her out. She wanders off with her dog happily nuzzling her unsavoury crotch. Though this is not the attitude of the book, Jenni's new behaviour is now not unnatural: she is reconciled to her perverse nature.

Is it possible to go further? If so what will we find – about horror or about the English? English horror writers had found material which certainly put their books beyond anything which could be shown on screens.

At the same time as the burst of killer novels already mentioned appeared, there was a publishing event more noted in retrospect. In 1984, three anthologies of short stories by Clive Barker were issued. Next year came three more. They had a catchy serial title, *Books of Blood*. A year and 30 short stories later Clive Barker was hailed as the new hope of British horror. His growth continued to be extraordinary. Within less than five years he had diversified with full-length novels which crossed genres. More significantly he broke out of books and into films, following the example of American horror writers.

By the age of 39 Clive Barker is already an industry. English horror is out! Here I have given indications of how this became possible. Instead of being a sudden monstrous growth, Clive

Barker's work inherits the legacy of a host of British writers inside and outside horror. In a review of Barker, *Private Eye* suggested Barker was offering a new twist on an old theme: hatred or fear of women. Perhaps there is more. Barker is exploring perversion under the guise of horror. This is not a horror of sex but the sex of horror. Barker's regular reports of fear causing loss of control, signalled by bladder and bowel, or the hint of ambiguous thrills in torture, are replacing satanism with sex.

Between 1975 and 1985, English horror found its own areas beyond cinema and American horror. It explored small enclosed worlds ruled by a perversity which was far too strong for screens. Though the presumed messiah of English horror, Clive Barker left England and moved into film. Nevertheless, experimental writing is now *indistinguishable* from horror. Small presses such as Creation/ Annihilation with their stables of writers chart even more ghastly regions.

Personalities and bodies merge and devour each other. Bowels, bladder, blood are everywhere. *Red Hedz* is typical of their work: 'Like some obscene practical joke: there was TOO much blood. . . . Innards. Faeces. The stench was horrendous. Sickening . . . a domestic . . . abattoir.' The police have trouble establishing an identity for the remains. Literally. They know it is human but 'there was only one body immediately visible; the other person we found sat huddled into a corner of the living-room, covered in the victim's blood. Staring. Seemingly hypnotised by the slaughter.' In Creation Press's anthology from its first year, *Cease to Exist*, the last contribution gives us a paedophile serial killer as the 'hero'. All the horrors rise up to form a creature, which advances devouring everybody. The two monsters face each other. The thrill killer faces his reflection. 'He felt as if he was on display, some prime side of beef up for raffle.' By now readers know what to expect. Does it still shock? 'His erection wilted, so much useless meat. His sphincter loosened as the shit in his bowels turned liquid. Diarrhoea seeped out and traced the line of his arse, warm as a finger.' The monster metamorphosises its 'meat' to produce a cunt out of which protrudes an erect penis. 'As it fucked him into unconsciousness, he speculated idly on the relationship between sex and death.' He names it: 'Passion'.

English horror moves from one century into another producing work of a uniquely English character.[9]

Notes

First published in Clive Bloom (ed.), *Creepers* (London: Pluto, 1993).

1. Derek Jarret, *The Sleep of Reason: Reality and Fantasy in the Victorian Imagination* (New York, 1989).
2. See, for example, Shere Hite, *The Hite Report* (New York, 1975), and Nancy Friday, *Our Bodies Ourselves* (Hardmondsworth, 1979).
3. See, for example, Malachi Martin, *Hostage to the Devil* (London, 1988).
4. See, for example, such films as *El Topo* (1972), *Wicker Man* (1973), *The Texas Chainsaw Massacre* (1974), *Shivers* (1975) and many others.
5. The career of David Cronenberg is indicative of the discussion here.
6. Nigel Kneale also created *Doomwatch*, which foreshadowed much ecological horror.
7. Jay Stevens, *Storming Heaven: LSD and the American Dream* (London, 1989).
8. England 1991: this essay was completed in December 1991 as the media told of a case in darkest Surrey, a place not associated with remoteness or bleakness. An eleven-year-old boy has never been to school or been registered as born. He and his mother lived surrounded by more than two dozen carcasses of pets and 'thousands of maggots'. They were surrounded by neighbours who gave interviews which showed no puzzlement at their own behaviour.

   Later the same evening television offered a documentary about Dennis Nilsen who chopped up at least 15 young men. He buried the remains in the back garden of his respectable suburban house. What of his bleak background? Or his neighbours who complained at the smell – he boiled human heads. The man who came to inspect the blocked drains found human flesh and bone – flushed down the toilet. The remains in the garden and drain are so muddled as to be impossible to identify let alone count.

   Next day a man in charge of homes for disturbed youngsters is found guilty of systematically raping and buggering boys and girls in his care. Then an even bigger scandal is uncovered. In another complex of homes the staff were acting as pimps for the top authorities including senior police.

   The child abuse paranoia has come full circle. Case after case is being thrown out and parents are being exonerated of sexually abusing their children for satanic purposes. Instead it is being revealed that there was a conspiracy against children. It was run by the authorities appointed to care and protect those children. Even Nilsen was an official in charge of helping young men.

   These three stories are from the same week. They are all true. Real-life horror in England at the end of the twentieth century.

9. Exploration of this theme was unique when I undertook it. In the subsequent 5 years the transformation is striking.

I was restricted to British horror fiction and predicted the way lay with small presses. Creation would veer off, concentrating on sex or horror with true crime and porn. Likewise, a study of British sex in cinema came from Sun Tavern Fields, also a study of Italian horror films. Sex in European horror films, 1950–1984, was covered masterfully by 'Immoral Tales' from Primitive (1991). Aquarian published an edition of small presser Clive Leatherdale's 1985 study of Dracula containing a chapter about the sex which decoded 'a kind of incestuous necrophilous, oral–anal–sadistic all-in-wrestling match'. Horror is about bodies – so how had it been possible to keep the secret for so long?

Sex had always underpinned horror but it 'came out' with Clive Barker. Or so runs the line which I questioned in my essay. I tried to show how most of 'Barker's' ingredients were in place before 1984. How has he affected the genre? Less than would show. He provided the introduction to the US Scream Press 1987 collection by his fellow Liverpudlian Ramsey Campbell, his predecessor prodigy. Yet *Scared Stiff: Tales of Sex and Death* did not appear in the UK as a paperback for another four years, when it rapidly needed reprinting. Meanwhile, British small press Xanadu issued the UK edition of *Splatterpunks* (1990). This attempted to identify a new wave. It dated the breakthrough to Clive Barker: 'Clive Barker interestingly arrived on the horror scene at the very moment that Maggie Thatcher was tightening her stranglehold on his country. As for why Barker was noticed . . . well, to put it crudely, it was sex and violence.' Unlike Bram Stoker, Barker left nowhere to hide. 'Barker's fascination with homosexuality, S&M, golden showers, and so on – indeed, with almost any form of sexual, "perversion' – reoccurs enough to suggest a hidden manifesto.' Sex had moved to the foreground. In all the new horror titles, sex would take priority on the cover.

Regardless of Barker, American women writers had been calmly building up a body of work which, although lacking dogma, made the case. By concentrating not on sexual politics but on sex the stories gained increasing acceptance. Subjects otherwise banished to pornography were openly explored with the excuse of literature. Nevertheless, the bottom line remained sexual arousal, the thrill. Lonnie Barbach edited a number of collections which eased the way for the efforts of Susi Bright who came from small presses. Both would start with erotica for women by women, in Bright's case a lesbian audience, then cross over by ignoring gender. Bright would progress not only to Penguin but also to a sort of national status with her annuals. This liberation gave opportunities for other forbidden genres to come out in the context of erotica.

The thrill of a collection of horror stories entirely by women cleared the way for major new talents. Since the early 1980s, Anne Rice had been producing mildly erotic novels under another name, a sort of Barbara Cartland with knobs in. This was hardly daring since regular historical romances had changed. Prolific authors such as Rebecca Brandywine offered plenty of sexually thrilling scenes, thinly veiled by a gushing vocabulary. Rice would find success with a series of vampire novels, fags with fangs. The vampire/sex theme attracted a host of other women writers from Nancy A. Collins through Elaine Bergstrom, Jeanne Kalogrides, etc.

More notable were the women writers 'discovered' by the Abyss series. Koja's novels were permeated by obsessive atmosphere. *Skin* dealt with fetishistic body mutilation in the context of a lesbian affair. Male gays from youth tribes provided the milieu for Poppy Z. Brite, with vampirism and the transfer of body fluids. Less literary were the novels of Valentina Cilescu which, while lacking vampire trimmings, remained in the lesbian series of Masquerade, the huge porn imprint. *Dracula: The Darker Passions*, by Aramantha Knight, another Masquerade title, described the porn side which Stoker had concealed. Knight revealed the hidden sexuality in *Frankenstein, Jekyll and Hyde* and *The House of Usher*, as well as editing anthologies of erotic horror: *Flesh Fantastic, Love Bites* and *Sex Macabre*. Masquerade experimented with another mixture, sex with crime, verging on horror, and a collection of erotic pieces which explored areas previously relegated to horror. All these titles came from a publishing house specialising in the erotic but there were many other cross-over anthologies including *Deathport, 100 Vicious Little Vampires, 100 Wicked Little Witches, 100 Creepy Little Creatures, Bizarre Sex and Other Crimes of Passion*: volumes 1 and 2, *SM Futures, By Her Subdued, Black Sheets*, and *City of Darkness*, etc.

STEVE HOLLAND

On Horror and Censorship

Tales from the Crypt: The British Horror Comics Campaign
The history of censorship of comics in Britain dates back to the 1950s and the introduction of the Children and Young Persons (Harmful Publications) Bill in 1955, the government's response to many years of increasing concern at what were originally called the

'American comics' that were flooding the country. The campaign later narrowed to focus on 'horror comics' which had come to the attention of the media,[1] with questions raised in the Church and in the House of Commons. The campaign was accompanied by spirited correspondence in newspapers and groups such as the Comics Campaign Council were formed with an aim to stop the publication of comics that were deemed unsuitable for children.

Fredric Wertham's *Seduction of the Innocent* has historically been seen as the culmination of the American campaign against what he and others saw as comics capable of corrupting the young. Violence, subliminal sexual messages, racism and outright obscenity were all to be found in comic books aimed at children, said Wertham. The results of Wertham's erratic and hysterical tirade against comics is well known, the destruction of crime and horror comics in the USA and the foundation of the Comics Code Authority in 1954.

In Britain, *Seduction of the Innocent* was published on 23 February 1955 by the Museum Press, only after the introduction of the Harmful Publications Bill to Parliament on 11 February. Wertham's work was known in the UK and cited by a number of campaigners during the years of campaigning, but the attacks on horror comics came about independently in the UK.

The roots of the British campaign date back to the immediate postwar years, but did not gather steam until 1952. Although not the first to voice unhappiness with 'American comics', George Pumphrey, a headmaster at a junior school near Horsham, Sussex, was an early campaigner, having found comics in the possession of children at his school; he published his first article against them in 1948 in the pages of *Teacher's World and Schoolmistress* under the title 'English or American?' Peter Mauger, a history teacher, was another outspoken critic of the American comics, having first discovered them on a train journey where he was astounded at the concentration – rarely seen in the classroom – of a young boy who was reading them.

Pumphrey and Mauger were only two of many teachers and clergymen waking up to the 'threat' of comics. Many local campaigns were launched and newspapers began to pick up the threads of a witch-hunt: in 1949 the Reverend Marcus Morris – later famous for his co-creation and editing of *The Eagle* – voiced his fears in an article entitled '"Comics" that Bring Horror to the Nursery', saying 'Morals of little girls in plaits and boys with marbles bulging in their pockets are being corrupted by a torrent of indecent coloured magazines that are flooding the bookstalls and newsagents.'[2] These papers were being read by 'sons and daughters from seven to seventeen', hardly nursery age.

Morris put into words the worries of many individuals and groups. The growing campaign against comics has been charted by Martin Barker in his remarkable study of the horror comics, *A Haunt of Fears*. Some of the results and conclusions of Barker's research are worth repeating here. His research, for instance, showed that amongst the first groups to point the finger at American comics was the British Communist Party, of which Peter Mauger and others involved were members. The Communist Party was running an anti-American campaign under the agenda that many aspects of British culture were being Americanised: the Communist Party condemned all American culture, and Mauger in particular condemned American comics, in his speech on children's reading habits at the 1951 Cultural Conference, and elsewhere.

The involvement of the Communist Party goes some way to explain why the thrust of the campaign was for many years against 'American comics'; as newspapers and other independent groups became more involved the whole campaign became more narrow in its attack, aimed almost solely at horror and crime comics, and the headlines switched from 'American' to 'horror'.

An American Comic in London
The campaign was actually aimed primarily at British black and white editions of American comic books, and British comics in the American format; import restrictions in the postwar years made bringing in the real thing almost impossible.

The trade for British reprint editions (BREs) had grown up soon after the beginning of the Second World War: the American comic-book was very popular in the UK and had been brought across, alongside pulp and film magazines, in bulk in the 1930s for sale at Woolworths and on market stalls. With imports restricted and the major companies cutting down on their output due to the paper shortage, numerous 'pirate' publishers sprang up to take advantage. Paper may have been in short supply, but children were not!

The BRE had come about because of the closing of a loophole during the Second World War: a Midlands publisher realised that the import ban did not extend to newspapers, and was importing Canadian Sunday papers, throwing away the paper and keeping the comic strip section. When the loophole was closed, the publisher imported the printing matrixes and printed his own editions. Thus a whole new industry arose, catering for the young fans of the American comic book and displaced GIs stationed in the UK. There were many publishers involved, producing countless titles, including a number of comics attacked by Wertham in *Seduction of the Innocent*; amongst the titles cited during the British horror campaign were BREs of *Black Magic* (Prize), *Crime SuspenStories* (EC), *Eerie* (Avon), *Ghostly Weird Tales* (Star), *Planet Comics* (Fiction House), *Startling Terror Tales* (Star), *Tales from the Crypt* (EC) and *Vault of Horror* (EC). Probably the two most prolific publishers were Streamline Publications, also known as United Anglo-American Book Co., who produced mostly war and western titles, some of which included their own self-censorship, with some panels removed and replaced with crudely drawn balloons; and L. Miller & Co., best known for reprints of Fawcett publications, including *Captain Marvel* which was later to become *Marvelman*. Leonard Miller's son, Arnold Miller, was head of Arnold Book Company, another prolific publisher of BREs which included the notorious *Haunt of Fear* of which more shortly.

At the end of the war, import restrictions were maintained to help the sterling/dollar balance of payment. The War Loan accepted by Britain in 1946 was not fully paid off until 1959, and all restrictions lifted; in November 1959, National (DC) began exporting their titles to the UK.

The Campaign

The attack on 'horror comics' came to a head in 1954, when a combination of circumstances finally forced the government into action.

It his always surprised me that the campaign took so long to produce results. Even France, where publishing has always been considered far less restrictive, had brought in legislation against comics and children's literature in 1947. Canada banned horror comics in 1949, and Australia and New Zealand bought in new rules in 1954. Was Britain slow moving? As early as 1951 the Public Morality Council had drawn attention to the 'problem' in England, but no action was taken by the Home Office.

Perhaps one reason why comics may not have seemed such a threat at the time was the appointment of Sir David Maxwell-Fyfe as Home Secretary in 1951. Maxwell-Fyfe led a three-pronged attack on vice which included the witch-hunting of homosexuals, the harrying of prostitutes and a crusade against pornography, primarily in books and magazines, the latter culminating in 1953 when 197 prosecution cases were brought against obscene literature. Some newspapers took up a stand against Maxwell-Fyfe, particularly *The Recorder*, in which editor Edward Martell attacked his campaign against obscenity, saying 'a book' that may have been selling regularly for 20 or 30 years without a word of objection from anybody may suddenly be seized and condemned'.

The campaign against books lasted until 1954 when a number of cases were dismissed by enlightened Judges who realised that the campaign against obscenity was running into problems: the law needed to be redefined. If murder and bloodshed were 'obscene', that meant Edgar Wallace novels were obscene – and Wallace was second only to the Bible in terms of sales. The voice of reason began to make itself heard. The Society of Authors set up a Committee presided over by Sir Alan Herbert to examine the existing laws, and a new Obscene Publication Bill was drafted to embody changes, the principal reforms being to shift the emphasis from 'a tendency to deprave and corrupt' to 'intention', and to take into account the artistic merit in a book. It should not be forgotten that the call for reform only came when five literary publishers were taken to court over hardcover novels – the countless cases against paperbacks and the mass-market publishers were welcomed by many who considered eroticism, under the guise of erotic art or literature, a rich man's right. The classic case, of course, was that of *Lady Chatterley's Lover* at which the prosecuting council asked whether it was a book the jury would wish their wives or servants to read? Randolph Churchill, in his introduction to the British edition of *Seduction of the Innocent* seemed to welcome public opinion on the subject of comics – but particularly 'enlightened public opinion as expressed in the correspondence columns of *The Times*'.

The campaign against books ground to a halt in 1954 as the number of convictions against publishers dropped. The defenders of books were asking for literary merit to be taken into account, and that the work as a whole had to be read and considered rather than a judgement be made on the titillating extracts read out in court. Books were bad news to prosecuting counsels.

Re-enter the comic. Where pornography and obscenity were subjective, as the difficulty in prosecuting books had proved, the 'Perversion of Our Children' may have seemed a far easier target. In May 1953 a meeting of the National Council for the Defence of

Children (later the Council for Children's Welfare) was called by Dr Simon Yudkin, a consultant paediatrician at the Whittington Hospital, London; Yudkin, who had seen horror comics being passed from bed to bed by children in hospital, felt that a more co-ordinated campaign by the numerous small groups would put greater pressure on the government. Out of the meeting came the Comics Campaign Council, chaired by Mr A. H. Holloway and with George Pumphrey as its chief publicist. Pumphrey's *Comics and Your Children* was published in 1954, selling over 3000 copies.

The campaign against comics was fuelled by numerous articles in the media: Kingsley Martin wrote a piece in the *New Statesman* (September 1954) entitled 'Sadism for Kids', and on 17 September a letter from Pumphrey was published in *The Times Educational Supplement* in which he attacked the Arnold Book Company for publishing a comic entitled *Haunt of Fear* (made up of American reprints from *Haunt of Fear 23* and *Shock SuspenStories 14*, both published by EC). Martin Barker, who interviewed Pumphrey in 1981, quotes him as saying: 'It is not too much to say that when I first saw it, I was delighted. I said to myself – this is it, they have gone too far, this is something the campaign can really use'.[3]

With the campaign against books behind them, other papers picked up Pumphrey's lead: *Picture Post*, *The Daily Worker* and *The Daily Dispatch* were just three of many papers to report on the publication of *Haunt of Fear*; the Ministry for Education (Special Services Branch) contacted Pumphrey to borrow the comic and the Institute for the Study and Treatment of Delinquency contacted many campaign bodies and MPs which led to a question in Parliament. All this, as Barker points out, over one comic.

The acceleration of the campaign after September 1954 was to lead directly to action by the government. In the autumn of 1954 the Comics Campaign Council had a Bill drafted by lawyers which was presented to the then new Home Secretary, Major Lloyd-George, who would later accept a deputation from the Church of England Education Council led by the Archbishop of Canterbury on 12 November.

Another pivotal group involved during this period was the National Union of Teachers (NUT). There had been 14 motions submitted for debate about comics raised at their annual conference in 1952, but there was no great activity until the NUT opened a display of horror comics in London on 11 November 1954 to create public awareness of them; it was widely attended by the public and the media, later moving to the House of Commons before touring the country.

The NUT had formed a committee, but a study of their records shows that they were fairly inactive until October 1954 when the exhibition of comics was mooted and put together very quickly. Barker implies that the sudden burst of activity was due to the fact that the NUT were just about to enter a wage negotiation, and needed to be seen as vital to the moral well-being of our nation's children.

The campaign had narrowed its outlook, moving from specific allegations against crime and horror comics until towards the end the media seemed full of emotive but essentially meaningless phrases: 'Drive Out the Horror Comics' and 'Now Ban this Filth that Poisons our Children' were just two of the headlines of the day, although there was little evidence outside of repetitive accusations to show exactly what was 'perverted', 'filthy' and 'degrading' about any particular title. However, 'public opinion' was outraged: the tabloids were full of anti-comic hysteria and the no doubt 'enlightened' Randolph Churchill was writing that the course of action was for the Director of Public Prosecution to initiate actions against publishers who 'enrich themselves at the expense of the minds of young children. If the magistrate or judge should prove to be so illiterate as to fail to punish the defendant, then that will be the time to consider an alteration in the law.'

There was good reason for him to write thus: to attack individual titles would have required specific charges being brought. Under the laws of the time they would have had to be bought under the Obscene Publications Act, then under review and which even the Home Secretary admitted had itself become perverted by judicial decisions: the word 'obscene' was almost wholly restricted to matters relating to sex, and it was unlikely that a successful prosecution could be brought on horror or crime comics which, whilst violent, could hardly be accused of being sexually porno-graphic (except to Wertham, who could see female genitalia in the shadow of a man's shoulder blade).

Since the horror comics were not unlawful, the campaign thrust became to change the law and *make* them unlawful. This meant government legislation, which the government was slow to take. Churchill's blinkered attitude (only an illiterate magistrate would fail to punish the defendant? – as the law stood, comics were innocent until judged guilty by a jury if a publisher cared to defend a destruction order) and formulaic brandishing of horror comics as obscene contained the same ingredients all pressure groups use to whip up support:

- generalise about their 'filthiness' (by late 1954 nobody dared deny that the horror comics were filthy, but nobody could pinpoint the exact nature of their filthiness other than to extract single frames or parts of frames which generally supported the idea that they were violent and unwholesome, as Wertham had);

- implying that their publication degraded the minds of children and turned them into monsters (the case most often cited during the British campaign was that of Alan Poole who shot a policeman and was himself shot resisting arrest in 1952; Poole was reported as having a library of comics that ranged from the generally reported 50 to a social worker's estimate of 300. The truth was revealed in a parliamentary debate – Poole possessed just *one* comic, a western);

- implying that they are published by shameless men who reap a vast profit from producing sordid material aimed at the defenceless minds of children and distributed by equally callous vendors (e.g., headlines such as 'Still Cashing in on Muck');

- implying that 'all those men and women who want their children to grow up kindly, decent human beings are joining in' (and by implication that parents who were indifferent would damn their children who would grow up unkindly, indecent, and inhuman);

- ignoring evidence to the contrary (a contemporary study by the Committee on Maladjusted Children, chaired by Lord Under-wood, did not mention comics as being a cause for maladjustment or disturbance in children);

- isolating the argument about comics from other contemporary issues (e.g., the witch-hunting of publishers of 'obscene' books or the rise of 'teddy boys');

- and, lastly, never let a redeeming feature sway you from your argument (in most of the crime and horror comics under consideration, the worst guys always came to the stickiest end, although this argument of a comic's essential morality is probably the most subjective used by pro-comics campaigners; it could – and was – argued that two wrongs don't make a right). If there is a redeeming feature ('The average American comic is skilfully and sometimes brilliantly drawn . . .'), turn it against itself: ('this manifest proficiency makes the frequently violent content even more dangerous').[4]

The Harmful Publications Bill

The situation in late 1954 made it impossible for action not to be taken: the Home Secretary, Major Lloyd-George, had received a draft proposal from the Comics Campaign Council and the NUT exhibition and calls for action had whipped up the House. The result was the publication of the Children and Young Persons (Harmful Publications) Bill on 11 February. The Bill was introduced on 22 February and consisted of two proposals:

1 This Act applies to any book, magazine or other like work which consists of stories told in pictures (with or without the addition of written matter), being stories portraying:
   (a) the commission of crimes; or
   (b) acts of violence and cruelty; or
   (c) incidents of a repulsive or horrible nature;
in such a way that the work as a whole would tend to corrupt a child or young person into whose hands it might fall (whether by inciting or encouraging him to commit crimes or acts of violence or cruelty or in any other way whatsoever.

2 A person who prints, publishes, sells or lets on hire a work to which this Act applies, or has any such work in his possession for the purpose of selling it or letting it on hire, shall be guilty of an offence and liable, on summary conviction, to imprisonment for a term not exceeding four months or to a fine not exceeding £100 or to both.

The Bill was met with a degree of opposition, although a great deal of the debate was more concerned with clarifying the position of newspapers such as the *News of the World* and the *Empire News* which (according to MP Michael Foot) were pornographic and made vast sums of money for their publishers. There was also the argument that the Bill's aims were not clear, that it retained the

Hicklin rule of 'tendency to corrupt' which at the same time was under attack from the Herbert Committee Bill which hoped to clarify the problems with obscene publications, and that it was vague. A picture-spread about war in *Picture Post* could well fall within the bounds of the Bill.

However, the Bill was given a second reading and referred to a Committee where there would be an opportunity to amend. The Committee opened its discussions on 24 March, ending on 29 March, and whilst numerous amendments were suggested, only two were accepted: that all proceedings under the Bill were to be undertaken with the consent of the Attorney-General, and that the Bill was limited to a ten-year duration. When the Bill reached the House of Lords there were further amendments which protected vendors who could prove that they had not read the contents of a work or had no reason to suspect that it was one which could be charged under the Act and that the new law limited its scope to publications 'of a kind likely to fall into the hands of children or young persons'. With these amendments it became the Children and Young Persons (Harmful Publications) Act (1955).

After the Act: A Postscript

How many cases have been bought under the 1955 Act? To my knowledge only one. The Horror Campaign had effectively destroyed the horror comics before the Act was passed. Speaking in February 1955, Sir Hugh Linstead, MP, said that the two main firms that had been printing and publishing horror comics (Thorpe & Porter of Leicester and Cartoon Art Publications of Glasgow) had stopped publications of this sort and it was now virtually impossible to buy any horror comics. They had been hounded out of existence already.

The end of the horror comics era meant that no test cases could be bought under the Act – no doubt the reason why the Act was renewed ten years later without discussion and is still in force. The one known case was against L. Miller & Co., responsible for producing so many BREs in the 1950s. Ironically, the new Miller comics were partly reprints from the 1950s horror and crime titles, and the firm was found guilty and fined £250. By then, the firm was run by Florrie Miller, the elderly wife of the late Len Miller, and in the wake of the trial she put the company into voluntary liquidation. Perhaps that day in 1970 the campaigners had their final revenge . . .

Notes

First published in this volume.

The primary source of information and quotes for this feature is Martin Barker's *A Haunt of Fears* (London: Pluto Press, 1984). Barker's extraordinary (and entertaining) study of the horror comics campaign contains a great many interviews with those directly involved, as well as a very good bibliography of material relating to both British and American anti-comics campaigns.

1. The media often insisted the titles campaigned against were 'so-called "comics"' without defining which particular aspect of these stories told through graphic narrative set them apart from plain and simple 'comics'.
2. Marcus Morris, '"Comics" that take Horror into the Nursery', *Sunday Dispatch*, 13 February 1949.
3. George Pumphrey, quoted by Martin Barker, *A Haunt of Fears*, p. 11.
4. R. P. Hewett, 'These Comics are Not Funny,' *The Schoolmaster*, 28 March 1952.

ROBERT F. GEARY

On Horror and Religion

From the crash of the gigantic helmet upon Manfred's hapless offspring at the opening of *The Castle of Otranto*, through the Victorian tales of haunted houses, fiendish imps, and vampires, and down to today's explosion of books and movies concerning the dreadfully demonic, surely one of the most obvious aspects of the Gothic stories and their successors has been the supernatural. Yet the supernatural element has, perplexingly, been the one critics have least probed. A reader suspecting that the appearance and trans-formations of supernatural horror tales bear some relationship, perhaps a complex one, to religious belief at various historical moments will discover little clarification of that connection in the considerable body of serious critical material devoted to the Gothic novel and the ghost story. At best one may occasionally find the

Gothic novel treated as a quest for the numinous. . . . But more often any discussion of the background of belief from which the Gothic emerged is unfortunately obscured by outdated concepts of the entire eighteenth century in England as an age of chilling rationalism. Moreover, the reader finds the same frigid rationalism hastily invoked to explain the popularity of nineteenth-century horror tales, leaving one to wonder if the cultural climates of 1764 and 1864 were equally arctic and, if so, why the Gothic novel failed while the Victorian tales of supernatural terror endured and thrived. Nor will one be better informed by many of the largely psychoanalytic discussions of contemporary supernatural shockers like *The Exorcist*. These can hardly explain the popularity of works which, given the assumptions behind many analyses, should scarcely be finding readers at all.

This paradoxical critical avoidance of the obvious becomes less mystifying when one considers the relation of the supernatural in Gothic and later fiction to dominant cultural attitudes and then explores the source of the inherited critical paradigms often used to interpret popular supernatural fiction. These critical presuppositions, in many cases, turn out to be based on the denial of what the supernatural tale asserts – the persistence of numinous reality in the modern world. Predictably, then, many critics have difficulty taking at all seriously the essence of much supernatural fiction, for doing so would call into question their assumptions not simply about such writing but about the nature of modern people and the status of belief, in the modern world.

To understand why so many explanations of supernatural horror are less than adequate we need briefly to summarize a rather detailed thesis concerning the role of the supernatural in the Gothic novel and its progeny. The Gothic novel was not so much a reaction against the rationalistic currents of the later eighteenth century, since their product in that religious latitudinarianism and Enlightenment scepticism weakened the older theological contest of providential belief, releasing the supernatural as numinous terror. But the supernaturalism of the Gothic novels was an uncertain, awkward affair, half in and half out of the providential context and vulnerable to charges of superstition alike from the orthodox and the fashionably sophisticated. Unable to achieve any coherent framework of belief or focus for its unearthly terrors, the Gothic soon faltered into overwhelming sensationalism. But the Victorian tale of supernatural terror found just such a coherent context and corresponding narrative strategies in its determined reaction against the rationalism, the scientism, and materialism which, now oppressively powerful, a minority found deeply threatening. The very cultural secularization which had first freed the Gothic's rather aimless numinous terrors became itself the focus of attack. In the classic nineteenth-century horror story, a smugly bigoted secular rationalism, the heritage of profane Enlightenment principles, is first disturbed, then assaulted, and finally shattered by what it had supposed not to exist. No longer bound by Christian orthodoxy, and disillusioned with the materialism of science, the writers of supernatural shockers could concentrate on building up to an explosion of terror devastating the prevailing rationalism.

This same culturally prestigious rationalism stands behind the considerable critical obtuseness to the supernatural horror fiction which enacts the conflict between lingering and unfashionable beliefs and modern scepticism. For literary criticism of the supernatural tale involves the intersection, more often the collision, of beliefs from antagonist cultural strata as the assumptions of an academic and generally secular class are brought to bear upon a popular form appealing to older and, to many intellectuals, primitive or childish sensibilities. Thus criticism of the ghost story is often based on premises formed from elements of the cultural configuration which for over a century fiction of the supernatural has doubted, undermined, and attacked. It is not, therefore, from lack of acumen that so few studies do justice to the supernatural; rather it is because the criticism and the fiction often imply counter paradigms, each of which denies what is central to the other.

Exemplifying and perhaps causing much of this misalignment of paradigms is the immediate source of many critical perceptions of supernatural fiction. Critics have often turned not to the history, sociology, or the psychology of religion – which have much to say concerning the numinous and its appeal – but to the ideas and the spirit of Sigmund Freud, who thought comparatively little was worth saying of phenomena he saw as relics of premodern ages. In his 1919 essay translated as 'The Uncanny' (still a *locus classicus* for much theorizing on supernatural fiction), Freud attributed the special sense of 'dread and creeping horror' evoked by these stories to a residue of the childhood of the race or the childhood of the individual. 'An uncanny experience occurs either when repressed infantile complexes [or repetition-compulsion] have been revived by some impression, or when the primitive beliefs we have surmounted seem one more to be confirmed.' In speaking of these primitive, animistic beliefs he sees as the core of the supernatural, Freud voices a confident rationalism of the sort pronounced by so many characters in ghost stories who learn too late its limitations:

> We – or our primitive forefathers – once believed in the possibility of these things and were convinced that they really happened. Nowadays we no longer believe in them; . . . but we do not feel quite sure of our new set of beliefs, and the old ones still exist within us ready to seize upon any confirmation.

The classic supernatural terror tales do indeed unsettle the 'new set of beliefs', and Freud's description of the fiction writer's creation of dread by insinuating the eerie into 'the world of common reality' is accurate. But the essay epitomizes the blind spots of the rationalism often attacked in the terror tales by assuming throughout that the modern person is, perhaps a bit imperfectly, fundamentally secular and clearly destined to become more so as reason progresses. 'All so-called educated people', we are told, 'have ceased to believe, officially at any rate' in such things as ghosts. The weird tale, then, is something of a vulgar trick, in which the writer 'takes advantage of our supposedly surmounted superstitiousness', and we, in turn, 'retain a feeling of dissatisfaction, a kind of grudge against the attempted deceit'. Supernatural horror stories, Freud implies, fortunately have little future as education solidifies the new order of profane belief and society comes of age in a disenchanted world.

The approach was enormously persuasive for a variety of reasons, even apart from Freud's unequalled stature in psychology. For one thing, it represented in its time the most recent and compelling articulation of the Enlightenment view that religion and the supernatural, products of humanity's infancy, would soon vanish before the power of reason. Furthermore, as [commentators have] noted, Freud's analyses here and elsewhere consoled and vindicated secularized intellectuals by implicitly portraying them as lonely, enlightened bearers of a disillusioned maturity all would someday come to possess.

Given the prestige of this view, one can well see why critical treatments of the specifically supernatural in the horror tales so frequently are ahistorical, perfunctory, embarrassed. In contrast, say, to the unashamed approach recently taken in serious analyses of science fiction (another popular form most specimens of which are not of distinguished aesthetic merit), critics of stories of ghostly terror primly avoid looking too closely at the spectres and demons. They prefer instead to focus on intricacies of narrative mechanics and, especially, on psychological overtones (in a form not usually noted for subtleties of symbolism and characterization). Two hundred years after Mrs Radcliffe, an odd reversal has taken place: while the new Gothic writers unabashedly pour forth chillingly realistic supernatural horrors as if the Enlightenment had been repealed, it is the critics who feel compelled to explain away the ghostly elements for fear of being seen as backward, superstitious, and undignified.

Thus in study after study of the Gothic and the ghost story, the Enlightenment premises behind Freud's essay generate strange contortions as critics seek to account for what, given their assumptions, readers should have outgrown. H. P. Lovecraft's often quoted *Supernatural Horror in Literature*, for example, grounds the appeal of the supernatural shockers in 'the oldest and strongest kind of fear', the 'fear of the unknown'. To avoid the historical and cultural questions concerning why horror tales have gained not lost appeal since the eighteenth century despite any 'amount of rationalization, reform or Freudian analysis', Lovecraft simply invents what he calls the 'plain scientific fact' that 'man's very hereditary essence has become saturated with religion and superstition', a condition to be 'regarded as virtually permanent as far as the subconscious mind and inner instincts are concerned'. The denigrating remark about the impotence of Freudian analysis and the generally appreciative tone of comments on supernatural horror fiction should not conceal that Lovecraft's analysis of the horror story, except for the assertions about 'an actual psychological fixation of the old instincts in our nervous tissue', is in its key points the same as Freud's. Like Freud, Lovecraft regards the supernatural as a residue of the childhood of the race, repeated in every person. Since history and culture can have little impact on such supposed universal constants as Lovecraft's 'heredity impulse' to fear the unknown or on Freud's 'repetition-compulsion' complex, there is no need to inquire very far into any relation between the climate of belief and the rise and changes in the literature of supernatural fear. [In 'Supernatural Horror in Literature'] it is enough for Lovecraft to intone that 'a literature of cosmic fear . . . has always existed and always will exist'.

If questions of cultural content prove easy to evade, much more difficult is the stigma of immaturity and vulgarity attendant upon a literature whose essential appeal is supposedly to inherited superstition. Freud's urbane condescension would seem more suited to such writing than, say, Lovecraft's approving tone. Somehow supernatural fiction must be made respectable, in a word, mature. Peter Penzoldt provides one of the earliest of the current efforts to reconcile the received Freudian paradigm with his fondness for horror fiction by means of the following novel explanation of the impact of such writing:

> The short story of the supernatural is one of the most effective devices for combating that secret and persistent faith in the unknown. As we close the book we can feel delightfully certain that the horrors . . . are nought but fiction. Thus the modern weird tale meets a deeply rooted psychological necessity. One could even say that it has a sociological importance and a high moral value, in so far as it actively contributes to the elimination of ancient and modern superstitions and does not preserve them as is usually supposed.[1]

Since most supernatural fiction of this and the last century explicitly or implicitly attacks this very sort of confident secular rationalism which dismisses the supernatural as a relic of the primitive past, it is no surprise that readers have not 'usually supposed' that these stories were undermining older beliefs.

A related but more subtle approach to vindicating the weird tale involves positing a teleological movement from the supernatural to the psychological. Thus the ghost story can be said to have come of age. Henry James, Walter De La Mare, and others, Penzoldt writes, 'usher in the modern psychological ghost story' in which the weird figures of demons, vampires, and spectres 'reappeared but this time in their true forms, as symbols of the subconscious'. With this development the form has reached its ultimate goal, having 'attained a degree of perfection which is unlikely to be surpassed in the near future'.[2] Julia Briggs is more genuinely sensitive to the relationship between secularization and such fiction, seeing the Victorian ghost story as, in part, a 'reassertion of older and more spiritual values' against modern scepticism. Nevertheless, opening her study with the 'childhood of the race' idea from Freud (whose account of the appeal of the ghost story she finds more than 'merely persuasive'), she is obliged to conclude that the form has now degenerated into a 'mode of nostalgia'. The legacy of psychoanalysis has freed us from 'superstitious dread' and legitimated 'irrational impulse, . . . spontaneous and uninhibited action', and 'the value of subjective vision' – all the things disguised by the symbolic spooks. Now, with the old psychological taboos about the inner life 'tidied away', the ghosts can depart in peace to be succeeded by the more contemporary fantasy figures of science fiction.[3]

Todorov's analysis of the supernatural arrives at the same conclusion, stated more bluntly. Since the supernatural was but a covert means of exploring once forbidden themes of the self and other, it no longer has a place in a post-Freudian world: 'psychoanalysis has replaced (and thereby made useless!) the literature of the fantastic. There is no need today to resort to the devil to speak of sexual desire'.[4] Lastly, we find a kindred psychological model governing Elizabeth MacAndrew's *The Gothic Tradition in Fiction*, which views the form as an almost entirely symbolic expression of the sentimental novel's dilemma of innocent ignorance confronting evil knowledge. With James's *The Turn of the Screw* comes the ghost story's 'arrival at consciousness' as the realization at last is brought 'to the surface' that 'the real danger' to innocence 'may be in twisting human nature into weird shapes of monsters that feed on superstition'.[5] Henceforth, it would seem, the elements of supernatural terror, if used at all, must be used only as self-conscious psychological symbols. The old supernatural chillers are dead.

At the least, this seems a case of premature burial. The non-psychological supernatural story has by no means vanished in the twentieth-century. The last two decades' surge of books and movies of unearthly terror, stimulated by the enormous success of *Rosemary's Baby* (1968) and *The Exorcist* (1971), would perhaps be less of a surprise to anyone familiar with the astonishing popularity in England of Dennis Wheatley's blend of occultism and adventure. Since *The Devil Rides Out* in 1935, Wheatley's books, including over a half dozen explicitly devoted to black magic, have sold over thirty million copies and been translated into more than twenty languages. For some years now American popular writers like Stephen King, Peter Straub, and a legion of others have found that there exists [in the United States] as well as in England a public highly receptive to supernatural shocks. And these works remain as anti-psychological as any in the [nineteenth] century. One may recall that in *The Exorcist* the younger priest, Fr. Karras, is a psychiatric counsellor who at first dismisses possession as something which 'doesn't happen anymore . . . Not since we learned about mental illness; about paranoia; split personality.' But 'all those things that they taught me at Harvard', he finds, have no force against what is in the child. It would seem that the official model of secular moderns who are beyond belief in the supernatural has problems.

Nor will it salvage the 'childhood of the race' paradigm to maintain, as does Julia Briggs, that the present horror tales are mere popular nostalgia, advancing secularization having deprived the form of attraction for serious writers. All along, the Gothic novel and the ghost story have been popular rather than high literature, occasionally luring writers distinguished in other areas. It would be, for instance, no easy matter to discern wherein might be the intrinsic artistic superiority of 'Monk' Lewis over, say, Stephen King or William Blatty. From the nineteenth century we may recall the ghost stories of Stevenson or Le Fanu but forget that Amelia Edwards, Rosa Mulholland, Rhoda Broughton, Elizabeth Gaskell and others actually dominated the form in the 1860s and 1870s. Although it has proved at least as attractive to major writers as have other popular forms such as science fiction, the western, or the detective story, the supernatural story has no more than these depended for survival on highly sophisticated writers. That nobody of the stature of Henry James seems to be writing supernatural horror stories at the moment does not, then, dissolve the fact that millions of modern people, at least as literate and probably more educated than their Victorian counterparts, are devouring novels of the supernatural, a mode which the major critical model has, at least until very recently, consigned to historical oblivion.

Obviously, we need something more subtle than the 'childhood of the race' notion if we are to understand the relation of the supernatural in the Gothic and its successors to secularization in the modern world. For in contrast to simplistic ideas of cultural evolution, modern secularization is an exceedingly complicated but surely partial phenomenon whose direction is anything but certain. The view of modern people are ineluctably outgrowing any sense of the supernatural or any need for religion simply does not correspond to reality. Over a century ago, for example, many shared the belief of Engels that religion would soon vanish from the English working class. Yet in our time religion holds about the same position it did in 1850. In America technological advances and mobility have not caused the withering away of religious beliefs; church attendance remains higher than in most industrialized nations. Anyone viewing the plethora of books on astrology, witchcraft, occult psychic powers, as well as assorted manifestations of the dark supernatural on sale in university bookstores to the nation's educated youth might come away sufficiently disabused of the idea that humanity has transcended the supernatural. The rootless, profane modern who has, or will soon have, outgrown any need for the sacred appears to exist chiefly in the minds of cultural interpreters whose understanding of the world is shaped less by the experience of most modern people than by inherited intellectual models defining modernity as inevitably secular. Alasdair MacIntyre has remarked on this 'misidentification . . . of the nature of modern secular man' by theologians who, sharing the Enlightenment paradigm, envision 'a technological Prometheus, . . . able to control his own destiny' and live happily self-sufficient in 'a world of intellectual vigour and scientific clarity'. Specimens of this new creature, the noblest creation of rationalism and technology, prove remarkably rare.

> Certainly, industrial growth and technological change can now be predicted in new ways, but the proportion of human beings who are in a position to participate in this kind of prediction and the consequent decision making is very small, and it is not clear that those who do participate feel themselves able to affect more than a very small area of their own lives.[6]

Modern technological society, in short, has not abolished the need for ultimate meaning or the desire for the sacred.

Of course, over the last two centuries there has indeed taken place a massive secularization in the sense of a decline in the power of traditional religious beliefs, attitudes, and institutions. Whether one looks at the figures on low active church membership abroad or the internal secularization, more common in the United States, which takes the form of rationalizing away older theological doctrines, in either case it would be foolhardy to contend that traditional religion provides a shared set of ultimate norms in the West, let alone a widely held, rich, coherent picture of the world containing an extensive supernatural dimension. Quite the contrary. . . .

Yet none of this – not the decline of the churches, not the theological levelling, not the withdrawal of certain spheres of activity from under the umbrella of religious ethics – none of this adds up to the picture of a general march into the Age of the Profane, an age from which the sacred and the supernatural have been forever banished. Serious studies simply do not support such an assumption, however tenaciously it is held by some literary intellectuals. Instead, the matter of secularization is a complicated phenomenon, whose causes, nature, extent, and direction permit no easy generalizations. In *The Invisible Religion* Thomas Luckmann argues persuasively that what has happened is not the replacement of a sacred by a profane ethos but something far more complex. In our world the religion of the churches becomes increasingly peripheral as the specialization of social institutions, with their norms of functional rationality, removes more areas of life from overarching religious values. The result, however, is not the triumph of a completely rationalist ethos; rather, religious norms, once 'total life values', shrink to 'part-time norms', while 'the functional rationality of segregated institutional norms' based on performance alone 'makes *them* seem trivial' to the person. Thus '*one* obligatory hierarchy' of religious values gives way to an 'assortment' of ultimate values from which individuals can construct, in consumer fashion, their own 'syncretistic and vague' systems of ultimate meaning. Nor is this situation marked by a movement toward total desacralization: no official model of ultimate norms – sacred or rational – is emerging. Uncertain fluctuation rather than clear direction characterizes the situation in which public norms of functional rationality are experienced as partial and unsatisfying while each individual sacred cosmos, being a private and somewhat eclectic construct, is inherently unstable.[7]

Far from expunging a sense of the numinous from modern consciousness, such partial secularization is actually conducive to the quest for the sacred and the supernatural in unlikely areas. Luckmann maintains, for instance, that for many people the private sphere has become quasi-sacred, as 'autonomy' and 'personal growth' acquire an ultimacy whose semi-religious character may be nearly invisible behind the veil of jargon from popular psychology. But this divinization of the self is only one aspect of the ever more private struggle to build a sacred cosmos. As the single, normative world of traditional religion fades, the results are extremely diverse, even contradictory. Roland Robertson's six-category typology indicates the complexity of modern 'arrested secularization'. A religious framework may be retained, but the beliefs are either rationalized or given a therapeutic, instrumental emphasis; the religious framework may be neutralized, leading either to stress on the quasi-sacred qualities of social life itself (as in radical theologies) or to rampant supernaturalism outside a moral or theological context. Lastly, the framework of religion may be abandoned for either positive intellectual atheism or practical amorality. Thus we find in the same partially secularized society such heavily rationalized religious groups as Unitarians existing alongside devotees of astrology, witchcraft, and demonology. Nor can one discern any clear movement toward classical atheism or the areligiosity which nineteenth-century positivists and pessimistic Christians saw engulfing the entire population. Instead, Robertson concludes, '[t]he prevalence of the arrested forms of secularization . . . seems to indicate that the mainly secular world is certainly not immediately at hand'.[8]

In this atmosphere of partial secularization, a bewildering variety of parareligious fads compete amiably for acceptance, however provisional. Self-help books promising psychic transformation, tracts extolling the marvels of holistic health, astrological forecasts in the daily papers – all these and countless other examples testify to the confusing and eclectic effort of millions to attain some shaky contact with an ultimate reality which will give them some measure of control over their destiny or, at least, connect that destiny with something more fascinating and awesome than the mundane flux of events. For the amusing and baffling parareligious mix of the psychological, the scientific, and the supernatural, one example still remains a favourite and can suffice for many. The March 1981 issue of *Science Digest*, amid articles purporting to reveal hitherto undiscovered powers of brain and body, contained a full-page colour advertisement for a deluxe leather-bound and silver-edged copy of *The Necronomicon*, supposedly an ancient handbook of sorcerer's magic. This 'talisman against the Forces of Darkness', readers were assured, 'reveals charms against demons who assail in the night, how to call spirits from the land of the lost dead, and even how to win the love of another'.[9] For fifty dollars the readers of *Science Digest* could acquire this small monument to the secularization of religion and the rise not of Profane Man but of the do-it-yourself sacred cosmos.

The complex of forces and changes we call secularization has not, then, abolished the sacred, the supernatural, or religion. Instead secularization has meant a plurality of more or less unofficial and provisional meaning systems – sacred and quasi-sacred – which individuals increasingly construct or choose to fit their personal preferences. Once this is realized, the continuing, indeed the flourishing, popularity of the occult (including the fiction of supernatural terror) ceases to be regarded as an unaccountable residue of 'the childhood of the race'. In the modern world, no single, coherent, 'official' set of beliefs has replaced the weakened power of religion to give people a sense that their values and actions are grounded in something ultimately real. Thus for many the occult offers a sense of control and of purpose in a world where people seem at the mercy of huge impersonal forces beyond their power, perhaps beyond anyone's power, to alter or direct. Analysing the 'occult explosion of the seventies', Mircea Eliade astutely discerned the 'parareligious dimension' such bizarre phenomena as witchcraft and astrology hold for the many people left unsatisfied by the vision of life's meaning (or meaninglessness) put forth by some scientists and existentialist philosophers. Astrology, for example, affords an intimacy with a cosmic order, something no longer done by many churches which have slighted the supernatural to be 'vigorously relevant on the social plane'. Yet it is often 'considered superior to the existing religions because it does not imply any of the difficult theological problems'.[10] Again, rationalized religion and the free-floating supernatural of the horror novels and films appear alike as products of a partial secularization. Both share what Luckmann describes as typical of the more psychologized forms of conventional religion – 'a weakly coherent and nonobligatory sacred cosmos and a low degree of "transcendence" . . .'.[11]

To be sure, popular novels and films of supernatural horror do not convey what the more extreme forms of the occult offer, the promise of a 'mystical restoration of man's original dignity and powers'.[12] Yet these tales of demons and dark forces persecuting nearly helpless individuals and even threatening humanity itself are not without their consolations. In a world beset by political, social, and economic convulsions beyond the comprehension let alone control of most people, the descendants of the Gothic novel personalize evil, making it, if no less terrible, at least specific. Shapeless dreads are given shapes, however horrid. And that can be an improvement.

More fundamentally, supernatural thrillers have no difficulty thriving in a secularized age which has weakened the old sacred cosmos without creating a replacement universally, or even generally, accepted. As the quest for the sacred takes ever more diverse and personal forms, the later day Gothic shockers give many the vicarious chill of the darkly numinous without binding them to institutional religion or its moral and theological framework. For those not satisfied by psychologized religion or salvific psychological fads, these works have an appeal in today's cultural marketplace. More vividly than parapsychology and much contemporary religion, these stories of terror do posit the reality of another dimension of existence:

> Any story which in any sense refers to the intervention of the supernatural in human affairs necessarily affirms that the supernatural exists. It holds out the reality of alternative modes and realms of existence beyond . . . our material life. In doing so, it responds directly to what is certainly man's most abiding concern, the prospect of his own personal annihilation and oblivious in death.[13]

Nor, it should be emphasized, is the appeal of horror fiction merely a temporary phenomenon, a symptom of the transitional period between older religious beliefs and the coming of complete secular rationalism. The paradigm of modern secular humanity as having outgrown belief, a view dear to so many since the eighteenth century, must be discarded utterly. There is no force inherent in the essential nature of modern society generating a Kingdom of Reason, however belated. Daniel Bell has pointed to a confusion at the core of this view of evolutionary secularization. Bell distinguishes sharply between *secularization*, involving the loss of religious influence over economic and political areas of public life, and *profanation*, the more general rejection of religious belief, of the sacred, and the supernatural. The impulse toward secularization, understood in this restricted sense, does indeed inhere in the specialization and functional rationality basic to the techno-economic order. But no such principle of inexorable change exists in the cultural sphere, the realm of ideas and values from which modern disbelief springs. Indeed, the modern rivals of religion – rationalism, aestheticism, existentialism, civil and political religions – seem less able than ever to provide compelling answers to the ultimate questions of human existence which religions have always addressed. Such timeless dilemmas and the need for codified, emotionally meaningful answers to them are relatively independent of modes of social organization. 'Culture,' Bell insists, 'by its nature confounds historicism': *Antigone*, for instance, is not part of the childhood of the race.[14]

Nor is the ghost story. Its long-predicted demise is but an indication of the power, among those most influenced by nontraditional ideas, of a thesis only now showing strong signs of collapse. Whether there will take place, as Bell predicts, a 'return of the sacred' or simply a continuation of the existing state of competing, unofficial, quasi-sacred systems of belief, the appetite and indeed the need for a dimension of the unknown, of the transempirical, will remain in literature. No historical dynamic will govern its popularity but only the commonplace fluctuations of literary taste related to market saturation, the relative talents of writers, competing cultural and political events, and so on. Whatever the changes, the literature of supernatural terror will find some lasting reception, continuing, as it has for two centuries, to feed some portion of that hunger for the numinous.

The curious progression of the supernatural in literature since the 1700s – from traditional providential *exemplum* to Gothic novel to ghost story to contemporary full-length novelistic chiller – reveals much concerning, for example, the nature of literary change as well as the relation between popular and high literature and of both to the culture as a whole. But like the characters in so many of the stories, if we are to understand the situation we must be willing to explain – not explain away – what we see before us in the literary supernatural. Only if we are willing to do so will we reach a fuller understanding of the meaning, significance, and lure of these darkly fascinating works.

Notes

First published in *The Supernatural in Gothic Fiction* (Lampeter: Edwin Mellen Press, 1992).

1. Peter Penzoldt, *The Supernatural in Fiction* (London, 1952) pp. 6–7.
2. Ibid., p. 57.
3. Ibid., pp. 7, 11, 16, 211–12.
4. Tzvetan Todorov, *The Fantastic: A Structural Approach to a Literary Genre*, tr. Richard Howard (London, 1973) pp. 159–60.
5. Ibid., pp. 223, 239, 160–1.
6. Alasdair MacIntyre, *Secularisation and Moral Change* (London, 1967).
7. Thomas Luckmann, *The Invisible Religion: The Problem of Religion in Modern Society* (New York, 1967), pp. 39, 96, 98–117.
8. Ibid., pp. 236–8.
9. *Science Digest*, March 1981, p. 109.

10. Mircea Eliade, *The Two and the One*, tr. J. M. Cohen (London, 1975) pp. 64, 59, 61
11. Ibid., p. 117.
12. Ibid., p. 52.
13. Glen St John Barclay, *Anatomy of Horror: The Masters of Occult Fiction* (London, 1978) p. 9.
14. Daniel Bell, *The Coming of Post-Industrial Society* (New York, 1973), p. 425.

Select Bibliography

Aguirre, Manuel, *The Closed Space: Horror Fiction and Western Symbolism* (Manchester: Manchester University Press, 1990).

Bloom, Clive, *Cult Fiction* (Basingstoke: Macmillam, 1996).

Bloom, Clive (ed.), *Creepers* (London: Pluto, 1993).

Docherty, Brian (ed.), *American Horror Fiction* (Basingstoke: Macmillan, 1990).

Hughes, William and Smith, Andrew (eds), *Bram Stoker: History, Psychoanalysis and the Gothic* (Basingstoke: Macmillan, 1998).

Jackson, Rosemary, *Fantasy* (London: Methuen, 1981).

Punter, David, *The Literature of Terror* (London: Longman, 1980; reissued as two volumes 1996).

Punter, David, *Gothic Pathologies: The Text, the Body and the Law* (Basingstoke: Macmillan, 1998).

Mulvey-Roberts, Marie (ed.), *A Handbook to Gothic Literature* (Basingstoke: Macmillan, 1998).